Recent Advances in Applying Identity and Society Awareness to Virtual Learning

Andrew G. Stricker
The Air University, USA

Cynthia Calongne
Colorado Technical University, USA

Barbara Truman
University of Central Florida, USA

Fil J. Arenas
The Air University, USA

A volume in the Advances in Educational Technologies and Instructional Design (AETID) Book Series

IGI Global
DISSEMINATOR OF KNOWLEDGE

Published in the United States of America by
IGI Global
Information Science Reference (an imprint of IGI Global)
701 E. Chocolate Avenue
Hershey PA, USA 17033
Tel: 717-533-8845
Fax: 717-533-8661
E-mail: cust@igi-global.com
Web site: http://www.igi-global.com

Library of Congress Cataloging-in-Publication Data

Names: Stricker, Andrew, editor. | Calongne, Cynthia, editor. | Truman, Barbara, editor. | Arenas, Fil J., editor.
Title: Recent advances in applying identity and society awareness to virtual learning / Andrew G. Stricker, Cynthia Calongne, Barbara Truman, and Fil J. Arenas, editors.
Description: Hershey, PA : Information Science Reference, an imprint of IGI Global, [2020] | Includes bibliographical references and index. | Summary: "This book addresses new ways of thinking in the use of 3D design thinking and cognitive apprenticeship in virtual learning spaces for team science, transdisciplinarity, idea development, and curation"-- Provided by publisher.
Identifiers: LCCN 2019006531 | ISBN 9781522596790 (hardcover) | ISBN 9781522596806 (softcover) | ISBN 9781522596813 (ebook)
Subjects: LCSH: Virtual reality in education.
Classification: LCC LB1044.87 .R44 2020 | DDC 371.33468--dc23
LC record available at https://lccn.loc.gov/2019006531

This book is published in the IGI Global book series Advances in Educational Technologies and Instructional Design (AE-TID) (ISSN: 2326-8905; eISSN: 2326-8913)

British Cataloguing in Publication Data
A Cataloguing in Publication record for this book is available from the British Library.

Advances in Educational Technologies and Instructional Design (AETID) Book Series

Lawrence A. Tomei
Robert Morris University, USA

ISSN:2326-8905
EISSN:2326-8913

Mission

Education has undergone, and continues to undergo, immense changes in the way it is enacted and distributed to both child and adult learners. In modern education, the traditional classroom learning experience has evolved to include technological resources and to provide online classroom opportunities to students of all ages regardless of their geographical locations. From distance education, Massive-Open-Online-Courses (MOOCs), and electronic tablets in the classroom, technology is now an integral part of learning and is also affecting the way educators communicate information to students.

The **Advances in Educational Technologies & Instructional Design (AETID) Book Series** explores new research and theories for facilitating learning and improving educational performance utilizing technological processes and resources. The series examines technologies that can be integrated into K-12 classrooms to improve skills and learning abilities in all subjects including STEM education and language learning. Additionally, it studies the emergence of fully online classrooms for young and adult learners alike, and the communication and accountability challenges that can arise. Trending topics that are covered include adaptive learning, game-based learning, virtual school environments, and social media effects. School administrators, educators, academicians, researchers, and students will find this series to be an excellent resource for the effective design and implementation of learning technologies in their classes.

Coverage

- Adaptive Learning
- Bring-Your-Own-Device
- Social Media Effects on Education
- E-Learning
- Instructional Design Models
- Online Media in Classrooms
- Collaboration Tools
- Digital Divide in Education
- Curriculum Development
- Higher Education Technologies

IGI Global is currently accepting manuscripts for publication within this series. To submit a proposal for a volume in this series, please contact our Acquisition Editors at Acquisitions@igi-global.com or visit: http://www.igi-global.com/publish/.

The Advances in Educational Technologies and Instructional Design (AETID) Book Series (ISSN 2326-8905) is published by IGI Global, 701 E. Chocolate Avenue, Hershey, PA 17033-1240, USA, www.igi-global.com. This series is composed of titles available for purchase individually; each title is edited to be contextually exclusive from any other title within the series. For pricing and ordering information please visit http://www.igi-global.com/book-series/advances-educational-technologies-instructional-design/73678. Postmaster: Send all address changes to above address.

Titles in this Series

For a list of additional titles in this series, please visit: www.igi-global.com/book-series

Handbook of Research on Ecosystem-Based Theoretical Models of Learning and Communication
Elena A. Railean (Siberian Federal University, Russia & Moscow State Pedagogical University, Russia & Free International University of Moldova, Moldova)
Information Science Reference • copyright 2019 • 401pp • H/C (ISBN: 9781522578536) • US $245.00 (our price)

Comparative Perspectives on Inquiry-Based Science Education
Stuart Bevins (Sheffield Hallam University, UK) Louise Lehane (St. Angela's College, Ireland) and Josephine Booth (Sheffield Hallam University, UK)
Information Science Reference • copyright 2019 • 298pp • H/C (ISBN: 9781522554394) • US $185.00 (our price)

Opening Up Education for Inclusivity Across Digital Economies and Societies
Patricia Ordóñez de Pablos (The University of Oviedo, Spain) Miltiadis D. Lytras (Effat University, Saudi Arabia) Xi Zhang (Tianjin University, China) and Kwok Tai Chui (City University of Hong Kong, China)
Information Science Reference • copyright 2019 • 352pp • H/C (ISBN: 9781522574736) • US $185.00 (our price)

Cultural and Social Implications of Artificial Intelligence in Education
Dennis Anderson (St. Francis College, USA) and Robert Niewiadomski (Hunter College, USA)
Information Science Reference • copyright 2019 • 305pp • H/C (ISBN: 9781522577935) • US $185.00 (our price)

Mobile Technologies in Educational Organizations
Alona Forkosh Baruch (Levinsky College of Education, Israel & Tel Aviv University, Israel) and Hagit Meishar Tal (Holon Institute of Technology, Israel)
Information Science Reference • copyright 2019 • 320pp • H/C (ISBN: 9781522581062) • US $195.00 (our price)

An Invariant-Based Approach to Second Language Acquisition Emerging Research and Opportunities
Elena Orlova (Lobachevsky State University of Nizhny Novgorod, Russia)
Information Science Reference • copyright 2019 • 164pp • H/C (ISBN: 9781522582205) • US $145.00 (our price)

Performance-Based Assessment in 21st Century Teacher Education
Kim K. Winter (Western Carolina University, USA) Holly H. Pinter (Western Carolina University, USA) and Myra K. Watson (Western Carolina University, USA)
Information Science Reference • copyright 2019 • 295pp • H/C (ISBN: 9781522583530) • US $175.00 (our price)

Modern Technologies for Teaching and Learning in Socio-Humanitarian Disciplines

IGI Global
DISSEMINATOR OF KNOWLEDGE

701 East Chocolate Avenue, Hershey, PA 17033, USA
Tel: 717-533-8845 x100 • Fax: 717-533-8661
E-Mail: cust@igi-global.com • www.igi-global.com

Editorial Advisory Board

Table of Contents

Detailed Table of Contents

Over the last few decades there has been a rise in the prevalence of overweight and obesity in American youth. This chapter describes the rationale for the virtual world features of an obesity prevention project that engaged middle-school-aged girls in a 3-week summer science enrichment program. The Get in the GROOVE! program was designed to promote self-efficacy for health behavior change, increase health knowledge, facilitate healthy behaviors related to physical activity and nutrition, encourage a healthy body image, and promote the development and consolidation of a health self-identity. The virtual world, which was explored by the girls via realistic and healthy avatars, supplemented experiences and reinforced curriculum and concepts learned in the physical world component of the program. Findings suggest that a virtual world is a promising platform to promote a health self-identity and healthy lifestyle in children.

Chapter 9
Who Am I as a Healthcare Provider? Identity and Transformative Learning in Virtual Environments 164
Rachel Umoren, University of Washington, USA
Natalia Rybas, Indiana University East, USA

The U.S. healthcare delivery system relies on the formation of ad hoc teams of experienced, highly trained providers of various specialties. The providers work in interprofessional teams that converge to address situations around acute patient care. Various models of virtual training provide structured opportunities for interprofessional education, whereby learners engage with roles and responsibilities essential for their professions and active collaboration with other team members. This learning is transformative as it influences the development of professional identity and teamwork skills needed for successful collaborative practice in interprofessional teams. This chapter explores the role of training healthcare professional students using virtual simulations and the emerging potential of virtual and augmented reality for health professional education.

Chapter 10
Cognitive Apprenticeship for Teaching Computer Science and Leadership in Virtual Worlds 180
Cynthia Calongne, Colorado Technical University, USA
Andrew G. Stricker, The Air University, USA
Barbara Truman, University of Central Florida, USA
Fil J. Arenas, The Air University, USA

Cognitive apprenticeship refers to the development of skills under the guidance and tutelage of a domain expert. This chapter covers the theory and highlights 10 years of virtual learning experiences and 52 classes using the cognitive apprenticeship model. It reflects on the impact of presence and explores how learning communities develop as students assume roles and learn by working next to skilled faculty. The examples reinforce the value of deep immersion and identity in situated learning. The software design activities illustrate the benefits experienced when students assume ownership and structure their activities. Through self-reflection, learners illustrated the power of design thinking through group and individual design studios. The chapter concludes with observations from 400 eighth graders and reflections on future work in the design of sustainable learning programs for computer science and leadership education.

This chapter will discuss educational projects for learning problem-solving strategies in virtual worlds that encourage people to respect human rights as a lifelong learning experience. The discussion includes philosophical issues concerning the need to design new models for virtual learning that engage a person's own ways of thinking and interacting with the educational content. For example, the instructional design for these projects is based on adapting the think aloud and means-end analysis research methods for evaluating how learning about human rights in a virtual environment might transfer to the real-world community. The projects have been presented over the past 10 years in the virtual worlds of Second Life and the Open Sims.

The focus is on how technology impacts the learner and educator identities, especially focusing on safety, privacy, and the cybersecurity of the technology-centric learning environments. Questions arise which will need to be resolved by designers of these systems. This chapter was completed at the end of the annual CES, Consumer Electronics Show, held January 2019 at Las Vegas. The justification for this approach was to assert the influences products displayed at this consumer show will have on future identities of the self among learners and educators. Concepts such as self-analysis technology are proposed and discussed, and challenges affecting learners and educators related to identity, authentication, authorization, and accountability are highlighted. It is concluded that solutions to these challenges are not a single entity but instead a combination of diverse continually evolving techniques.

Leaders seek models of healthy ecosystems to better foster systemic, predictable performance improvement for their learning enterprises. Ecosystems may be viewed narrowly, involving information technology architecture, content, and standards for interoperability or expansively where stakeholders connect to seek next-generation, transdisciplinary learning opportunities across society. Ecosystem stewardship is a responsibility of community/societal leaders and citizens who must collaborate to shape and harness forces and drivers of emerging technology. Mass collaboration is needed to push open simulation into an enterprise capability that monitors and models what was, what is, and can be. This chapter frames academic need and United States military use of open simulation suitable for exploring new ways to steward ecosystem wealth in the interest of learning enterprises and beyond.

Foreword

In this second edition book, the authors extend recent advances in applying identity and society awareness by interweaving multidisciplinary themes, insights, and applications with virtual learning. The book starts with an examination of currents and complexities of philosophical thought underpinning virtual learning. The influence of Plato, Descartes, Locke, Kant, Heidegger, and Buber are poignantly related to the evolving ways selfhood, community, and society are increasingly being shaped by people's experience with virtual reality. The reader can trace the influence of European idealism and American transcendentalism upon the educators contributing chapters to this book. Indeed, the influence of Ralph Waldo Emerson and Henry David Thoreau can be clearly perceived in the ways the authors offer new views of self and society for the reader to consider.

What is striking is the way the authors recast arguments for how individual character is molded by the environment in contemporary terms and context informed by identity theory and research to virtual learning. The principles and practices of education, using virtual reality, is framed around a refreshing form of progressive thought for designing virtual learning landscapes to help bridge between the isolated ways people can live and learn with learning in community for the common good in society.

It is immensely satisfying to see this 2nd edition on virtual learning advance the deep insights from the influence of eighteenth century German philosophy on the American mind for pragmatic applications of virtual reality for educating digital citizens. The updated chapters in the 2nd edition not only offer a solid foundation for understanding the emerging applications of virtual reality to learning but also reveal transparency not typically offered in scholastic publications. The authors offer straightforward revelations of struggles and lessons learned while pioneering innovative ways for developmentally shaping professional identity and growth, digital literacies, and learning communities. Collectively, the insights offered in this book, from the valorization prospects of virtual learning, suggests a hopeful future in ways people, community, and society can be transformed for the common good unimaginable by our current generation.

Arthur M. Langer
Columbia University, USA

Preface

Similar to the previous book, *Integrating an Awareness of Selfhood and Society into Virtual Learning*, this second edition is a multidisciplinary endeavor, a collection of chapters by philosophers, psychologists, sociologists, computer scientists, and medical researchers united in the common goal of sharing scholastic-based insights on virtual learning from their disciplines. The challenge facing the reader is to consider insights from a lens beyond one's academic specialty and ideological frameworks typically employed to interpret phenomenon occurring at the intersections of disciplines. Virtual reality is such a phenomenon since its features and applications make use of capabilities originating from a variety of disciplines. Virtual reality offers the means for a person to experience an immersive environment offering dimensional multi-sensory input. The level of sensory engagement plays a significant role in the suspension of disbelief for producing perceptions in the mind similar to real-life experiences. Virtual reality, by offering close proximity to reality via levels of sensory engagement, can convince the human mind that experiences and interactions with objects and other people in virtual spaces are just as meaningful as those in real life. The medium in which people interact, whether virtual or physical, can augment and alter how the mind perceives, interprets, and associates current views of identity and selfhood to evolving views being shaped by new experiences. The blending of human experiences across physical and virtual spaces introduces new pathways for developing identity and selfhood as creatively expressed in digital identities. Combining embodiment with social responsibility, the sense of self extends into a deeply personal and social awareness that leads to education within the contemplative mind.

Against this backdrop, interest is growing in researching the interconnectedness of identity, selfhood, virtual reality and learning. Virtual learning environments can lead to reduced isolation and rapid formation of social groupings independent of geography. This phenomenon can be seen as positive or negative depending on the beholder's perspective when interpreting its impact on identities, social structures, group formations, and the "art-of-the-possible" for designing and shaping the future with virtual learning. Overall, the consequences are likely to be positive and to include improved prospects for accessibility, diversity, geographic independence, and shrinkage of isolation.

The reader is encouraged to not read for a *right* interpretation about how identity, selfhood, and society ought to be developed and integrated in closer ways through virtual learning. The contributing authors are not attempting to convince readers about the *rightness* of a specific viewpoint, but are introducing new ways of thinking and reflecting on the connections between identity, selfhood, society, and learning from various perspectives from which interdisciplinary insights are offered for embracing the art-of-the-possible. The perspectives are offered as lines of thought to stimulate receptivity and inquisitiveness on the variety of meaningful ways people can develop, perceive, think, interact, and learn across physical and virtual spaces. Closer ties between identity, selfhood, and society through virtual learning offer prospects not from the basis of a future delivered by clever use of technology advances but rather from artfully crafted forms of transformative learning communities made possible by advances in new ways of thinking for bridging and using physical and virtual spaces.

The reader will discover a variety of ways educators can co-create as artists of reality across landscapes spanning physical and virtual learning spaces. Virtual learning landscapes can be crafted to offer aesthetic delight to a sojourner from which the interiority and exteriority of private and public expressions of identity and selfhood can be bridged for transversal journeys for the common good.

New forms of community and society, made possible with virtual learning, transforms not only symbolic order of constructs for what is possible in the mind, but also in society for the common good. The allelomorphs of virtual and real, theory and practice, and art and life no longer need to stay opaque and suspended in realms of provisional constraint for the educator. The art-of-the-possible for weaving closer ties between identity, selfhood, and society through virtual learning is neither entirely utopian nor dystopian in origin or outcome. Rather, virtual learning landscapes beckon the educator to map and navigate ways to bridge physical and virtual spaces for discoverable, translucent, and shareable learning passages for personal growth and the common good in society. The editors of this book call and invite the undecided educator to consider the insights offered by the contributing authors who are reporting back from their own identity growth, selfhood, and society transformational experiences with virtual learning.

The reader will find bold conjectures offered by authors from which progressive advancement is made possible with virtual learning. The book begins with chapters offering theoretical underpinnings supporting virtual learning on the basis of traditional philosophical claims about identity shaped by community and society social relationships. Major philosophical claims are introduced at the beginning of the book and, in many cases, threaded through chapters addressing organizational behavior, leadership, sociology, cognitive and assessment sciences, computer engineering, and transdisciplinarity efforts with virtual learning. Each chapter is introduced below.

Andrew Stricker and Cynthia Calongne (Chapter 1) introduce major philosophical claims underpinning the transformation of human experiences with virtual learning for enabling new forms of personal identity growth, selfhood, and society. The authors describe the ways people can perceive, think and interact across virtual and physical spaces from which fundamental changes occur to the mind, identity, social interactions, intellectual boundaries, and ways of knowing and learning in society. A discussion is also presented on ways to reconstruct stronger ties between an educators' professional identity to Aristotle's held view of the importance played by "civic friendship" to the common good of democracies nurtured and sustained by education. The authors highlight the ways virtual environments can offer benefits for supporting the development of an educators' professional identity around the common good by means of sustained "in situ" deliberations and engagement with virtual learning.

Andrew Stricker and his colleagues (Chapter 2) describe the philosophical basis of identity and outline contemporary research on identity theory. They offer important insights for helping to guide the development of professionals across the lifespan of service vital to the public's wellbeing. A developmental framework is introduced as a guide for professional identity growth along dimensions of cognitive and moral reasoning. The framework includes literacies, spanning the dimensions, associated with social intelligence, leadership, competencies, and mindsets. Insights from research are offered for supporting the use of the framework with developmental instruction of professionals to promote higher levels of identity growth and maturation associated with improved judgment and behavior. Instructional practices are also described for helping professionals transition effectively to higher growth levels for use by coaches, mentors, and instructors. The Profession of Arms is highlighted for illustrating and applying the developmental framework in the context of a profession.

Fil Arenas and Daniel Connelly (Chapter 3) build upon the insights offered in Chapters 1 and 2 by extending the broader concept of civic friendship to conviviality practiced in social interactions necessary for supporting beneficial face-to-face and virtual experiences. The educational context is introduced as one of many that can benefit from both types of experience. Impairment of the components of a shared learning experience (self, others, and teacher) does not have to occur if educators understand the unique combination produced by the content to be learned plus the markers of the type of learning experience selected. The authors conclude that conviviality in a specific application is not only possible, but, potentially highly productive in cyberspace, minimizing the logistical, high-risk, and cognitive constraints that can impair other forms of communication and specifically non-cyber learning experiences. This chapter contributes to a new era of human interaction literature in the age of virtuality.

Fil Arenas (Chapter 4) explores the impact of virtuality on leadership development in cyberspace and outlines new challenges encountered within an abstract interactive environment. The flexibility and versatility of virtual spaces offers many freedoms from ordinary rules and restrictions. The author addresses the development of individual character and provides guidance for virtual leadership. A case is made for aspiring authentic transformational leaders to continue their awareness of selfhood and society in cyberspace milieus by opening their human apertures while leveraging their signature character strengths.

Valerie Hill (Chapter 5) extends understanding of virtuality's impact on a global scale whereby a participatory digital culture can provide collaborative learning opportunities beyond physical walls and without time constraints. Learners connect across the planet in real time. The virtual representation of self requires understanding of personal responsibility for digital citizenship and information literacy. Both presentation of self and evaluation of content in all formats are new challenges for learners of all ages, including the youngest students born into an age of sharing and connecting. The author offers a transparent perspective on the ways virtual learning environments may transform education while also presenting challenges and potential disadvantages for educators and learners. Understanding personal responsibility for digital citizenship is imperative to best practices of education in virtual spaces. Overall, this chapter focuses on digital citizenship and information literacy in virtual worlds, virtual reality, and immersive learning environments.

Francisca Yonekura (Chapter 6) offers musings on co-designing identity aware realities in the virtual space focused on the individual self during a learning experience. While preserving the individual self of the learner for a comprehensive outlook, the chapter will expand on the exploratory journey looking into the identity of the collective self, the shared experiences of those co-creating the moment, and the potential for a community of practice to emerge while learning in virtual environments. In the spirit of the contemplative goal of the chapter, design considerations in the creation and facilitation of learning experiences inclusive of the community's self are postulated.

Fil Arenas and his colleagues (Chapter 7) discuss how several schools and colleges under Air University have found utility in using a mixed-reality approach to developing leadership acumen in this unique risk-free environment. The chapter describes the power of collaboration between Air University and Auburn University at Montgomery while demonstrating the impact of this mixed-reality approach on developing military leaders. These mixed-reality exercises (MRXs) leverage an environment that establishes a practical laboratory for developing leaders to interact with avatars using a combination of virtual immersion and human intelligence (live simulation engagement). This innovative approach to "real-play" allows real-time learning to take place in real time through virtual immersion.

Mary Kate Clennan and her colleagues (Chapter 8) describe the rationale for the virtual world features of an obesity prevention project that engaged middle school aged girls in a 3-week summer science enrichment program. The Get in the GROOVE! program was designed to promote self-efficacy for health behavior change, increase health knowledge, facilitate healthy behaviors related to physical activity and nutrition, encourage a healthy body image, and promote the development and consolidation of a health self-identity. The virtual world, which was explored by the girls via realistic and healthy avatars, supplemented experiences and reinforced curriculum and concepts learned in the physical world component of the program. Findings suggest that a virtual world is a promising platform to promote a health self-identity and healthy lifestyle in children.

Rachel Umoren and Natalia Rybas (Chapter 9) discuss how the U.S. healthcare delivery system relies on the formation of ad hoc teams of experienced, highly-trained providers of various specialties. The providers work in interprofessional teams that converge to address situations around acute patient care. Various models of virtual training provide structured opportunities for interprofessional education, whereby learners engage with roles and responsibilities essential for their professions and active collaboration with other team members. This learning is transformative as it influences the development of professional identity and teamwork skills needed for successful collaborative practice in interprofessional teams. This chapter explores the role of training health care professional students using virtual simulations and the emerging potential of virtual and augmented reality for health professional education.

Cynthia M. Calongne and her colleagues (Chapter 10) examine 10 years of virtual learning and reflect on the impact of presence. They explore how learning communities can develop when students assume roles while learning as part of their cognitive apprenticeship experience. The examples offered in the chapter reinforce the value of deep immersion and identity in situated learning. The software design learning activities illustrated in the chapter highlight the benefits experienced when students assume ownership and structure their activities. The authors advocate for why educators need to engage learners in self-reflection, to explore shared values, form into groups, and make personal discoveries. From their own experiences the authors offer examples to illustrate the power of design thinking during individual and group work. Applications to computer science education are also offered by Cynthia Calongne from her observations obtained by mentoring 400 eighth graders.

Kara Bennett (Chapter 11) discusses educational projects for learning problem-solving strategies in virtual worlds that encourage people to respect human rights as a lifelong learning experience. The discussion includes philosophical issues concerning the need to design new models for virtual learning that engage a person's own ways of thinking and interacting with the educational content. For example, the instructional design for these projects is based on adapting the Think Aloud and Means-End analysis research methods for evaluating how learning about human rights in a virtual environment might transfer to the real world community. The projects presented examples from the past ten years in the virtual worlds of Second Life and the OpenSimulator.

Themba M. Ngwenya and his colleagues (Chapter 12) focus on how the learner can approach the new technology-centric learning environments as an active participant and contributor. The chapter bridges with technologies from the annual CES, Consumer Electronics Show, held January 2019 at the Las Vegas Convention Center in Nevada, United States. The authors reflect on how technology impacts the future identities of the self among learners and educators. The main reason for this is to determine what influences products displayed at this consumer show will have on the future identities of the self among learners and educators, over the next twelve months. Themes highlighted in the first edition of the book serve as the foundation for the second edition's concepts, such as self-analysis technology and the impact of cybersecurity on the identity roles in the virtual learning environments. Challenges that will affect learners and educators are related to identity, authentication, authorization, and accountability of users and content in the virtual/online education systems.

Barbara Truman and Jaclyn M. Truman (Chapter 13) discuss how personal learning is an idiosyncratic ability built upon metacognition that fosters identity development. When supported with virtual learning using avatars, collaborative virtual environments (CVEs) and combinations of emerging technologies, personal learning advances identity exploration and community development. Virtual participation in groups and events fosters mentoring for community enrichment especially for vulnerable populations such as persons with disabilities, the elderly, and those in need of recovery. Emerging technologies such as extended reality (XR) and the Internet of Things (IoT) present opportunities to combine physical and virtual world media/interactions useful for improved learning engineering. New expressions of Gemeinschaft and Gesellschaft are possible to co-create the future when empowered stakeholders collaborate to design smart, enabled, blended physical and virtual cities/communities. This updated chapter explores how concepts from systems thinking, presence research, and Transdisciplinarity can advance personal learning and transcend human limitations.

Barbara Truman (Chapter 14) reviews how leaders seek models of healthy ecosystems to better foster systemic, predictable performance improvement for their learning enterprises. Ecosystems may be viewed narrowly, involving information technology architecture, content, and standards for interoperability or expansively where stakeholders connect to seek next-generation, transdisciplinary learning opportunities across society. Ecosystem stewardship is a responsibility of community/societal leaders and citizens who must collaborate to shape and harness forces and drivers of emerging technology. Mass collaboration is needed to push open simulation into an enterprise capability that monitors and models what was, what is, and can be. This chapter frames academic need and United States military use of open simulation suitable for exploring new ways to steward ecosystem wealth in the interest of learning enterprises and beyond.

Rachel Umoren and Barbara Truman (Chapter 15) discuss the need for collaborative, participatory exploration into emerging simulation technologies supportive of distributed, interdisciplinary practice to promote cultures of collaborative praxis. Higher educational institutions are adapting curriculum to support interprofessional education among healthcare students such as in medicine, nursing, and social work to build the ability to practice with greater safety for patient care. An analysis of critical supporting factors and challenges for distributed teams seeking to develop virtual simulations is presented with guidelines for distributed development and delivery using emerging simulation platforms applicable to healthcare teams and beyond.

Cynthia M. Calongne (Chapter 16) explores how immersion in virtual worlds presents opportunities for simulating the qualities valued in face-to-face classes with the flexibility afforded by online learning. Immersive learning engaged educators, curriculum designers, campuses, conferences, and educational community groups to devise new ways to collaborate and engage learners. Dreaming of opportunities that were not possible in the online classroom, educators saw the potential of building communities in virtual worlds. They gathered to share their and to employ novel approaches to address educational challenges. This chapter explores the phenomenon of selfhood and society integral to the development of a vibrant educational community. At the heart of virtual world education is an ecosystem of institutions, groups, and conferences comprised of the early adopters and pioneers who stimulated their imagination and pooled their resources to encourage and strengthen the community, and cast their eye to the future.

Andrew G. Stricker and his colleagues (Chapter 17) introduce a simulation design for using artificial intelligence (AI)-augmented developmental instruction for improving contemplative practices in the face of complexity. The focus of the design is on developmental instruction in the use of contemplative cognitive and moral reasoning practices to improve self-awareness and means to better discern and address complicated and complex challenges. Developmental instruction is supported by an AI-augmented tutoring aid provided during a simulated mission to Mars within an immersive 3D-world. A set of tasks are introduced during the Mars simulation to assist with the development of contemplative practices. The AI-augmented tutoring aid assists participants in the simulation to better understand and apply contemplative practices involving cognitive and moral reasoning meta-thinking suitable for each task. High levels of fidelity, involving visual, auditory, and interactive model-based reasoning (MBR) tools, help to embed the senses, thoughts, and actions of participants in the feeling of traveling and being on Mars.

The editors are pleased to offer the reader rich and wide-ranging topics on virtual learning from a juxtaposition of academic domains and applications. The transcendent greatness of imagination, more than any other insight offered by our authors, illuminates the unfinished, yet unfolding nature of the work ahead for educators. Virtual learning, like the unfinished Michelangelo sculpture depicting the human body emerging from stone, the elements that imprison it; the left arm of the *art-of-the-possible* is raised representing the will to evolve towards ever greater beauty in form and expression of identity and selfhood in society.

The Editors

Acknowledgment

First, we are deeply indebted to our editorial advisory board members for their keen insights and recommendations offered to our chapter authors from the 1st to 2nd edition: Anne-Marie Armstrong, Craig Cunningham, Lynda Rogerson, Bo I. Sandén, *and* Paul Thor.

We thank the wonderful visionaries who give us strength and challenge us to pioneer new pathways in virtual world education: Gerald Goodfellow, John Sosik, Jeanne Holm, Todd Westhauser, Patti Abbott, Nancy Lorenzi, Karen Cooper, Tami Griffith, Joyce Bettencourt, Michael Cerquoni (Nebadon Izumi), Kae Novak, Chris Luchs, Jeremy Bailenson, Jaron Lanier, Jeff Hiles, Chris Collins, Gentle Heron, Gwenette Writer, John Pathfinder Lester, Philip Rosedale, Larry Johnson, Narmotur Pendragon, Crista Lopes, Ubit Umarov, Grady Booch, Will Wright, Dave Fliesen, Nick Noakes, Balpien Hammerer, Astoria Luminos, Kay McLennan, Buffy Beale, Michael Hicks, Art Langer, Lee Knefelcamp, Caledonia Skytower, Shandon Loring, Ann Cudworth, Maria Korolov, Jared Bendis, Eric Hackathorn, Richard Hackathorn, Fred Fuchs, Hilary Mason, Peggy Sheehy, Marianne Malmstrom, Bronwyn Stuckey, Selby Evans, Alice Krueger, Lynne (Wisdomseeker) Berrett, Renne Emiko Brock, G. Ronnie Kraegel, Lori Bell, Mal Burns, Jeroen Frans, Michael Bailey, and James Attloud, AgileBill Krebs, and Terry Beaubois.

In addition, the editors would like to thank Air University, Columbia University, Harvard/MIT, Vanderbilt University, University of Michigan, Auburn University, Stanford University, Colorado Technical University, Colorado Community College System, Rockcliffe University, the New Media Consortium, the OpenSimulator Community, the Kitely Community, the ISTE educators, VSTE, Lori Bell, the Illinois' Alliance Library System, Suffern Middle School (the Ramapo Project), EdTech and Boise State University, Virtual Ability, Linden Research, the MacArthur Foundation, The Army Game Design Studio, Metanomics, and many more centers for learning in virtual worlds.

We also wish to thank our colleagues mapping new frontiers with immersive virtual learning: Cyrus Hush, Xhyra Graf, Sitearm Madonna, Douglas Maxwell, James McDermott, Aimee Weber, Jeroen Frans, Ruben Puentadora, Gardner Campbell, Kevin Feenan, Scott Merrick, Spiff Whitfield, Beth O'Connell (Ghostraven), Beverly McCarter, Larysa Nadolny, Chris Dede, Alan Levine, Bryan Alexander, Lev Gonick, Electric Sheep, Melanie Milland, Pooky Amsterdam, Nancy Sherman, Sendao Goodman, Shu Schiller, Justin Clark-Casey, Mark Sturgell, Sharon Tettegah, David Leasure, Douglas Gempel, Elizabeth Dorland, Mary Jane Willshire-Fairley, Richard Fairley, Charles Schroeder, Marijane Paulsen, and Steve LaVigne. We also want to express our deepest gratitude for the assistance offered to us by Claudia Poole, who finished editing her husband's (Matt Poole) chapter for the 1st edition. Matt tragically died from a rock climbing accident prior to the book's publication.

Special thanks to our spouses, family members, and close friends for their encouragement and support making our effort on this 2nd edition possible: Elizabeth Stricker (Algernon Loire), Jerry Richmond, Devlin Baker, Jason Harrison, Zo'e Arenas, Jaclyn Truman, Diane Martini, and David Truman.

Section 1

The Multidisciplinary Lens of Philosophy and Ethics

Chapter 1
Transformation and Development of Identity and Society With Virtual Learning

Andrew G. Stricker
https://orcid.org/0000-0002-4184-0554
The Air University, USA

Cynthia Calongne
Colorado Technical University, USA

ABSTRACT

The transformation of human experiences with virtual learning enables unprecedented forms of communication, connection, interaction, and mobility supporting new forms of selfhood and society. The ways people perceive, think, and interact across virtual and physical spaces are fundamentally changing the mind, identity, social interactions, intellectual boundaries, and ways of knowing and learning in society. This chapter introduces and explores philosophical claims for helping to interpret and shape the transformation and development of identity and society with virtual learning.

PERSPECTIVES OF THE GOODNESS FOR USING VIRTUAL LEARNING TO TRANSFORM THE SELF AND SOCIETY

Increasingly, people are very likely to spend each day spanning across physical and virtual spaces via electronic devices augmenting the human mind through means to digitally interact, communicate, and learn. The making and shaping of interconnected physical and virtual spaces in daily life introduces prospects for asserting the authority of goodness for transforming the self and society. One transformational perspective is to take Plato's metaphysical beliefs and assert the image of the Good with prospects ahead for shaping the interconnection for improving lucidity, diminishingly self-centered attention, and capacity for human growth. Though this perspective is not necessarily theistic, is does suggest the importance of moral, spiritual, or metaphysical beliefs for shaping the interconnection and developmental impact on a

DOI: 10.4018/978-1-5225-9679-0.ch001

Figure 1. Scene of public well in virtual 3D Pompeii

person's identity across physical and virtual spaces. This perspective, of course, would imply a person-shaping good external to human experience.

Another transformational perspective is centered on Descartes and Locke whereby the claim is made that the reality of the interconnectedness of physical and virtual spaces is simply what people make or project onto it as a matter of science. This so-called Anglo-American analytical philosophical claim brings with it a form of pragmatism for thinking about shaping the interconnection but also introduces anthropocentric humanism. Given these two polar claims, there is yet a third claim introduced by Heidegger. Under Heidegger's claim, the nature of the world (in whatever form it takes across physical and virtual spaces) becomes. In essence, the nature of becoming involves properties of shaping and revealing. There is an essence to the reality of human experiences. This essence is what Heidegger describes as the space of meaning. This space spans all spaces. Under this claim, within the space of meaning there are emergent properties not entirely subject to human will but becomes increasingly visible through human activities.

The space of meaning makes a claim on people through intrinsic worth. With this philosophical claim there is the introduction of a teleological perspective whereby a position is taken that there is an underlying purpose in nature, with its emergent, open-ended properties, made increasingly visible to people through active making and shaping. The adoption of this claim by educators would bring awareness that while people can make and shape the future of virtual learning environments, spanning physical and virtual spaces, there is sobering acknowledgement nature makes demands too. Heidegger described the role of people in the space of meaning as "shepherd of Being." This perspective introduces a sense of stewardship for the means to flourish in the world. Conversely, this claim also suggests poor stewardship would lead to diminished or disastrous prospects for people. The interpretation of this stewardship role takes place through discourse, stories, and other ecological- cultural sharing and passing on within and across generations.

Figure 2. Scene of private home in virtual 3D Pompeii

Consideration of Heidegger's philosophical claim offers educators an ecological viewpoint and context for guiding activities in making and shaping the art-of-the-possible for transformational use of virtual learning (see Abbey, 2004, for Charles Taylor's explication of Heidegger's thinking towards an ecological viewpoint). Assumption of this viewpoint brings a sense of responsibility, humility, and meaningfulness to one's role as an educator for engaging learners in making and shaping a sense of their learning selfhood across physical and virtual spaces. The assimilation of this viewpoint into one's identity and role as an educator also appeals to the importance of relationships and dependencies among people with each other and to nature if we expect to flourish together in making and shaping the art-of-the-possible with virtual learning.

THE STEWARDSHIP ROLE OF EDUCATOR ACROSS VIRTUAL LEARNING LANDSCAPES

The role of educator in the space of meaning can be represented as a steward or guide for learners to and fro across physical and virtual spaces bridged by their revealing connectivity enabled through human making and shaping. Heidegger used the bridge as a metaphor of the *Gathering* or essence of the space of meaning that is unlabeled (the "thing" or "*Versammlung*", pp. 356-357). Bridging activity by educators in the space of meaning between the banks of physical and virtual spaces of human experiences make visible emergent properties previously unperceived or understood. The bridge gathers elements of nature and provides for passage to and fro between physical and virtual banks of possibilities. Also, for

Heidegger, the bridge serves to enable the construction of locale. The human activity in the construction of locale transforms spaces into meaningful places.

Spaces get transformed to places through pervasiveness of human presence or dwelling therein. Our dwelling in the space of meaning, spanning physical and virtual spaces, makes visible the hereunto-unforeseen landscape for making and shaping. Similarly, Yi-Fu Tuan (1977) speaks of the transformation of spaces to places as a transcendental experience wherein people establish "homes" in meaningful locales and "camps" along journeys to future promise lands (p. 180). Whether homes or camps, people associate meaningfulness to spaces transformed into places through intimate experiences and the construction of tangible and recognizable structures. Human building in this landscape gives form to the essence and unfolding of nature. Educators, as designers of dwellings in the space of meaning between physical and virtual spaces, participate together in constructiveness or bringing forth of home- or camp-like dwellings for learning in spaces transformed into meaningful places. Similarly, Martin Buber (1947) spoke of education as a "foot-bridge" whereupon traversing brings forth the possibility of "communion" and for bringing together what is disintegrated and not in harmony (pp. 107-108).

Tuan's introduction of spaces, made meaningful through homes and camps (denoting meaningful places regardless of time spent), offers insights into human experiences filled with fluidity and transitory stays at camps on an emergent journey with prospects for intricate pathways connecting them to familiar homes. Traversing this landscape spans a person's lifetime journey between warmth of the familiar home cottage to the unknowns of unfamiliar regions extending beyond into larger society. Society can be initially perceived as lacking familiar and visible boundaries until the unfamiliar becomes familiar. With each venturing forth on a new journey a person seeks a way to associate or map meaningfulness with uncharted spaces. The larger constellation of harmony is sought from across the expanse of singular experiences, involving natural will associated with "a home place", leading to collective existence associated with larger society wherein rational will dominates and a sense of home place appears elusive.

Ferdinand Tonnies (1887) spoke of the familiar, home-community sense of fellowship, as the "Gemeinschaft"-like culture of natural will. The Gemeinschaft intimacies of close fellowship in community are contrasted by Tonnies to larger society dominated by a "Gesellschaft-life culture of rational will involving "loose relationships" governed largely by contractual rules. The tension between Gemeinschaft and Gesellschaft are dialectical in nature with human activity to harmonize the tension via making and shaping of community in society. Similarly, Hegel highlighted the ever-present dialectical nature between "Family-Society" and "Civic-Society." Even St. Augustine contrasted the "City of God" to the "society of man" as a constant churning of tensions shaping human activity (see last twelve books).

People want to construct meaningful locales of familiar places of home and community amidst the spaces of their contractual experiences in society. Without such locales of place in larger spaces of society, people sense alienation from one another and from nature. Perhaps this is the emergent "synthesis" or harmonizing of dialectical tension between community and society sought after by Young Hegelians during the 1830s in Germany (Singer, 1983, p. 110). The same appears to hold true for human experiences with learning, as noted earlier from Buber's views on education, wherein dialectical activity offers prospects for synthesis or harmony through effort that is authentically engaged in by participants to bring I and Thou closer together in oneness. A place is co-constructed wherein and whereby the other becomes thou to I of each, with fullness of presence for the appearing or revelation of a flourishing future. Thus, the harmonizing of Gemeinschaft with Gesellschaft, brought forth by a "letting go" associated with constructivist making and shaping of locales makes room for authentic presence in community dwelling

Figure 3. Scene of temple in virtual 3D Pompeii.

in society, comprehensible in appearance, and meaningful far beyond what is possible with a singular manifestation for a possible future.

The Greek for “to bring forth or to produce” is *tikto* from which techne (the verb’s root) means to “let” something “appear.” Here again, Heidegger’s claim offers tantalizing insights to educators on the importance of letting and dwelling between physical and virtual spaces for constructivist activity in meaningful locales spanning them. Constructivist activity brings together seemingly disparate emergent properties of physical and virtual spaces for learning and building oneness.

The oneness is the sense of meaning perceived, understood, and shared from flourishing experiences henceforth from the building and dwelling therein. The very teleological nature of human experience and being emerges from building and dwelling together in harmony with nature.

Putting Heidegger’s claim into practice by educators is possible. Several of the educators authoring chapters in this book are doing so through collaborative efforts to harmonize Gemeinschaft with Gesellschaft in the co-construction of virtual learning spaces designed to be integrated with experiences involving physical learning spaces. In particular, immersive 3D virtual learning environments offer unique affordances for co-constructed locales, on a community dwelling level, wherein participants experience persistence and presence of one another in shared spaces via avatars. For example, the Harmony Society town of New Harmony, Indiana, from 1814 to 1824, was co-constructed within a 3D virtual environment to offer learners experiential activity for perceiving, representing, and sensing daily activities of an early American utopian society offering Gemeinschaft-life communal fellowship.

A TALE OF TWO COMMUNITIES ACROSS TIME AND VIRTUAL LANDSCAPES

Educators and learners living in contemporary New Harmony, and from across the country, were invited to participate in co-creating of architectural appearances of the dialectical tension represented in the early origins of the creation of the community by the Harmony Society as it evolved over decades from influences in the making and shaping of the town by Owenites. The label Owenites became attached to philanthropists and scientists invited to the town under the sponsorship of Robert Owen (a wealthy textile industrialist with a new vision for society) after he had purchased the town from the Harmony Society in 1824 (Arndt, 1965, pp. 287-339). In similar fashion, members of the Harmony Society became known as Harmonists. Remaining and newly arrived residents to New Harmony, at the start of 1824, were introduced to broader Gesellschaft-like civic-social interconnections beyond those originally valued by the religious communal community of the Harmonists.

To this day, the two tensions are clearly visible in the distinctive architecture constructed by Harmonists and Owenites. The Owenites inherited the northern portion of the town through their purchase from the Harmonists and consequently built north towards the Wabash river with their distinctive scientific laboratories, auditoriums, museums, and art galleries. A laboratory, constructed by Owen's son (Robert Dale Owen) on the north side directly across from the Harmonist church became the model for the newly established Smithsonian Institution in Washington, DC. Interestingly enough, the Harmonist church stood on the dividing line between north and south New Harmony. It was a massive two-story brick structure constructed in the form of a Celtic cross. The dialectical tension took immediate appearance at the church location when the Owenites turned the building into a dance hall thereby prompting the Harmonists to buy back the property and sending a group from their newly constructed town of Economy in Pennsylvania to dismantle the church in New Harmony brick by brick (Arndt, 1978).

The co-construction of Harmonist and Owenite periods of New Harmony in an immersive 3D environment by educators and learners offered means to reveal, interpret, and sense manifestations of historical dialectical tensions still present in contemporary American society. Participants in the co-construction of virtual 3D New Harmony assumed Harmonist and Owenite roles in the building and shaping of a vast virtual space into an interpretable and meaningful place for them.

Harmonist participants constructed Harmony Society communal dormitories, dining areas, granary, stables, vineyards, and family homes.

Harmonist construction techniques were modeled down to virtual Dutch biscuits used to insulate the buildings from the harsh winters experienced in the Indiana wilderness by society members along the Wabash river.

Owenite role participants in Virtual Harmony co-constructed the Robert Dale Owen laboratory, residence of scientist Thomas Say (American entomologist and conchologist), the Poet's House cottage wherein the theologian Paul Tillich lived during his summer visits while composing his three-volume Systematic Theology (1951), assorted parks, sculptures, and public co-educational schools on the north side of the vast virtual space.

The massive Celtic cross-shaped Harmonist church was reconstructed to scale and once again Harmonist music from the time period was reintroduced into a meaningful dwelling place for people to hear, learn about the compositions, and share. Harmonist sermon notes from original Sütterlin script were translated and put on display revealing for the first time to the public the poetic expression of the society's views on ways to live in harmony with nature.

Figure 4. Images of New Harmony architectural representations

Figure 5. Scenes of Virtual 3D New Harmony architectural representations

Figure 6. Scene of virtual 3D new harmony church built by harmony society

Walking tours were offered to those at a 2-day resident retreat held in New Harmony, Indiana who had participated in the co-construction of virtual 3D New Harmony. Physically walking through existing buildings and pathways around contemporary New Harmony with the recent advantage of having experiences in virtually co-constructing and representing structures established by Harmonists and Owenites, long since demolished in some cases, had a profound impact on participants. They were able to engage in discourse among themselves about initial assumptions made about the Harmony Society and thereby deconstruct individual perceptions to build a common framework to better understand more sustainable lifestyles and community structures. Through dialogical deconstruction, they shared their deeper sense and understanding about not only the historical significance of New Harmony but its' continued relevance for transformative prospects in shaping the future of communities in society.

The church where the tension became manifested is no longer physically visible in contemporary New Harmony but nonetheless present for the participants in a very meaningful way beyond mere virtual reconstruction of its once manifested physical appearance. For co-constructive participants in virtual 3D New Harmony, the Harmonist church was transformed symbolically and became an abiding virtual dwelling place for them with associated deep insights and understanding about dialectical tensions between community and society. The making and shaping of virtual 3D New Harmony helped the participants to bridge and interconnect physical and virtual places and thereby make possible a flourishing future co-constructed from shared understandings about the art-of-the-possible for new forms of community in society.

Figure 7. Scene of virtual 3D new harmony church interior built by harmony society

CO-CONSTRUCTED FORMS OF COMMUNITY IN SOCIETY THROUGH VIRTUAL LEARNING

Enabling the means for participants to immerse into a shared 3D space depicting New Harmony, between 1814 and 1824, offered an engaging learning experience whereby they could visually and interactively encounter the problems encountered by the early Harmony Society at their settlement along the Wabash.

The canal system dug by the Harmonists in 1821 can now be seen and tracked from end-to-end across the community landscape and the questions explored by participants while actively problem solving within virtual 3D New Harmony: "Why were the canals dug along the perimeter of the town from one end of the Wabash bend in the river to the other?" "What was the relationship between the canals and health issues encountered by the community?" "Why did the society lose nearly 300 settlers within the first settlement year?" "Why were the graves of the deceased unmarked?" As immersive participants explore the recreated community of New Harmony they encounter clues pointing to the answers. They learn about the periodic flooding of the community along the banks of the Wabash. They learn about early medical symptoms recorded by the society's physician Dr. Christopher Muller as he struggled to understand and respond to a growing illness outbreak among society members complaining of fatigue, loss of appetite, only to briefly recover and then relapse quickly and die. Participants learn from historical Harmony Society accounts, the baffling illness and fear confronting the community:

"We were rather frightened. According to appearance the sickness did not seem the least bit serious, so the sick ones complained of no pain but a little "Durmel" in the head, until the heat had overpowered

Figure 8. Scene of Virtual 3D New Harmony canal system and doctor office.

them and they began to slumber so that one could scarcely bring them to consciousness for even a moment" (Arndt, 1965, p. 146).

Deeper understandings are made possible for participants in virtual 3D New Harmony as they grapple with the historic health epidemic encountered by the Harmony Society to make sense among the causes and effects. Using collaborative inquiry, participants are requested to figure out why the Harmonists got sick and what actions might have been taken to effectively address the epidemic. Working together, participants discover clues from dialogue with the virtual inhabitants of the society, read entries from diaries, and visit Dr. Muller's medical office to uncover further clues behind the outbreak. By traversing the virtual landscape of the historical Harmony Society community learners are engaged, with others, in ways not otherwise possible from sole use of traditional course readings about history.

Blascovich & Bailenson (2011) highlight the advantage of engaging learners in historical context with the use of virtual reality (p. 245). A variety of learning styles are supported in virtual 3D New Harmony for helping participants engage in historical context surrounding the two forms of community expressed in New Harmony. Within the immersive 3D environment, participants can develop relationships with others employing different learning styles. In participative ways, a person is able to learn first-hand how problems encountered in life can often be solved more effectively by collaborating with others employing a diverse range of learning styles. For example, one participant may employ a learning style whereby observations can be made, obtained from gathered information, and reflect upon the relevance and logic of insights to the problem; while others offer strength for taking risks, being adaptable, and discerning ways to choose the best solution given the observations. The give-and-take among participants, using various learning styles, helps to develop deeper awareness and value for being a flexible learner by consciously choosing to use learning styles suitable to the demands encountered in context of a real-life problem. The learning in virtual 3D New Harmony is not only transformative for promoting higher levels of engagement and meaningfulness, but also how virtual learning can transform social interactions.

TRANSFORMATION OF SOCIETY THROUGH VIRTUAL LEARNING SOCIAL INTERACTIONS

Returning again to Martin Buber, a case is made for the importance of virtue-based insights obtained from social interactions with others to cope with and address dilemmas in society by coming to terms with how people can see, believe, and place value across a polarity of issues, and yet be able to reconcile oneself to the 'other' for 'unconditional relation is the shibboleth of mankind '(1958, pp. 64-66). In this context, a Hebrew meaning of shibboleth serves as a community-social communion 'test.' The test is unconditional relation to others by means of shared virtuous bonds of brotherhood and sisterhood values even when faced with intractable dilemmas. The willingness to hold oneself true to virtuous values with others constitutes the core of human cultures (Wenden, 2004, p. 148). The Harmony Society strived for a state of mindedness among its members to hold true to virtuous values even under the harshest of circumstances. Participants in virtual 3D New Harmony are introduced to the social interactions employed by the Harmony Society to help build, nurture, and sustain the bonds of civic identity and cohesiveness among members.

Daily rituals and activities of historical Harmonists become visible to participants as they learn about the shared values held by the society: nonviolence, social justice, ecological sustainability, equity among members, and civic participation in governing. Using collaborative inquiry and critical reflectiveness, participants in virtual 3D New Harmony examine: "How were decisions made in the community to rapidly address the health crises and engage everyone in the solution?" "What values were represented by the decisions made and resulting behaviors of society members?" "In what form were disagreements among members brought forth and reconciled by the society for confronting the health crises?" "What is the comparison between the Harmony Society values exhibited during the health crises and one's existing values?" Providing a way for learners to collaboratively explore the answers to these questions within a situated context brings history alive and helps to illustrate the continued relevance of community participatory decision-making and action to modern-day and transformative forms of society. Such virtual learning experiences also help to bridge the passage of time between historical and contemporary viewpoints of society, culture, values, and practices.

It has been sixteen years since the publication of the *Reconstructing The Common Good in Education: Coping with Intractable American Dilemmas* (Cuban & Shipps, 2000). In this publication, honoring the retirement of David Tyack from Stanford in 2000, his colleagues and past students offered several essays on the theme of the common good in education. The underlying theme explored by the essays is the role of "civic friendship" for achieving the common good in America through education. Virtual environments can be used to reconstruct stronger ties between an educators' professional identity to Aristotle's held view of the importance played by "civic friendship" to the common good of democracies nurtured and sustained by education. Virtual environments offer benefits for supporting the development of an educators' professional identity around the common good by means of sustained "*in situ*" deliberations and engagement with the transcendent (nonmaterial) aspects of virtues in practice.

Figure 9. Scene of schoolhouse in virtual 3D new harmony

A POST-PROGRESSIVE VIEWPOINT OF THE EDUCATOR'S IDENTITY AND ROLE WITH THE PROMISE OF VIRTUAL LEARNING

An early post-progressive viewpoint advocating educators to help learners to connect directly to higher purposes that shape one's conduct and belief in the common good was offered by George Counts in a 1932 speech to the Progressive Education Association in Baltimore, "Dare Progressive Education Be Progressive?" Counts advocated for:

... Strengthening moral quality necessary to quicken, discipline, and give direction" to the energies of the young... 'which will create new enthusiasm and devotion'... 'which will unify and guide' ... 'men and women crave a tangible purpose towards which to strive and which lends richness and dignity and meaning to life'... 'They strive to belong in a culture which gives meaning, direction, and significance to life'...[which] 'lifts the person out of narrow personal interests'... 'to be touched by great passions'... 'The educator's role is to bring to the younger generation a vision which will call forth their active loyalties and challenge them to creative and arduous labors' (pp. 8-56)

Counts' post-progressive argument evolved from his concerns with educators holding progressive Depression-era viewpoints of education that placed emphasis on developing individual students above shared democratic commitments. It is worthwhile to quote Counts at length on his concerns:

"The weakness of Progressive Education thus lies in the fact that it has elaborated no theory of social welfare, unless it be that of anarchy or extreme individualism. In this, of course, it is but reflecting a viewpoint of the members of the liberal-minded upper middle class who send their children to the Progressive schools—persons who are fairly well-off, who have abandoned the faiths of their fathers, who assume an agnostic attitude towards all important questions, who pride themselves on their open-mindedness and tolerance, who favor in a mild sort of way fairly liberal programs of social reconstruction, who are full of good will and humane sentiment, who have vague aspirations for world peace and human brotherhood, who can be counted upon to respond moderately to any appeal made in the name of charity, who are genuinely distressed at the sight of unwonted forms of cruelty, misery, and suffering, and who perhaps serve to soften somewhat the bitter clashes of those real forces that govern the world; but who, in spite of all their good qualities, have no deep and abiding loyalties, possess no convictions for which they would sacrifice over-much, would find it hard to live without their customary material comforts, are rather insensitive to the accepted forms of social injustice, are content to play the role of interested spectator in the drama of human history, refuse to see reality in its harsher and more disagreeable forms, rarely move outside the pleasant circles of the class to which they belong, and in the day of severe trial will follow the lead of the most powerful and respectable forces in society and at the same time find good reason for so doing. These people have shown themselves entirely incapable of dealing with any of the great crises of our time—war, prosperity, or depression...Among members of this class… they wish their sons and daughters to succeed according to the standards of their class and to be a credit to their parents. At heart feeling themselves members of superior human strain, they do not want their children to mix too freely with the children of the poor or of the less fortunate races…According to their views education should deal with life, but with life at a distance or in a highly diluted form. They would generally maintain that life should be kept at arm's length, if it should not be handled with a poker… If Progressive Education is to be genuinely progressive, it must emancipate itself from the influence of this class, face squarely and courageously every social issue, come to grips with life in all of its stark reality, establish an organic relation with the community, develop a realistic and comprehensive theory of welfare, fashion a compelling and challenging vision of human destiny…" (pp. 7-9)

Counts' concerns, first articulated in 1932, inspired generations of educators to see themselves as shapers of social conditions by their leadership exercised in the design of learning environments whereby learners are brought into new forms of community offering greater diversity and encounters with contemporary concerns and democratic values. Counts' 1932 speech also generated considerable debate among educators about whether his "indoctrination" of values was a form of authoritarianism (Perlstein, 2000, p. 62). Even John Dewey weighed in on the debate about Counts' concerns with his stated view "social neutrality is an impossible and unworthy goal for teachers…the schools will surely, as a matter of fact and not of ideal, share in the building of the social order of the future according as they ally themselves" (1934, p. 12).

David Tyack, a historian of education, brought into focus a contemporary understanding of the role played by American educational leaders as "managers of virtue" (Tyack and Hansot, 1982). Tyack argues rather than social control strategies, placing emphasis on the transcendental components of education is a triumph of the American common school with roots going back directly to the purposes of education held in mind by the educational theories of Jefferson, Rush, and Webster…"these men sought to instruct Americans deliberately in schools. Having fought a war to free the United States from one centralized authority, they attempted to create a new unity, a common citizenship and culture, and an appeal to a common future" (1966, p. 31). Indeed, it can be argued that education can usefully be conceived as a

Figure 10. Scene depicting area view of virtual 3D New Harmony.

transcendental institution (Meyer, 2000, p. 208). The transcendental conception of education offers insights for reconstructing the professional identity of educators for the common good through purposeful design and use of virtual learning environments. Evolving ties between Positive Psychology and educational theory, placing importance on education as a very central good, provide the necessary scholarship on the virtue and character strengths associated of transcendence for application in practice. It has been 16 years since Martin Seligman and Mihaly Csikszentmihalyi (2000) introduced the field of Positive Psychology for supporting empirical studies across social and behavioural sciences of what actions lead to well-being, to positive individuals, and to thriving communities. In their view, psychology is not just the study of pathology, weakness, and damage; it is also the study of strength and virtue (Seligman & Csikszentmihalyi, 2000). Christopher Peterson (2006) offered the definition of Positive Psychology as "the scientific study of what goes right in life, from birth to death and at all stops in between" (p. 4). Positive Psychology emphasizes positive states and traits towards "making normal people stronger and more productive and making high human potential actual" (Seligman & Csikszentmihalyi, 2000, p. 8). The transcendental benefits obtainable for individuals and the common good in community ought to be situated in the context of meaningful learning experiences offering greater diversity and encounters with contemporary concerns and democratic values. A helpful framework for the purposeful design for obtaining transcendental benefits is suggested in the work of Etienne Wenger (1988).

He sees identity and practice as intertwined in the ways people live. His belief is that identity is produced and shaped as a lived experience from participation in specific communities:

Identity…is a layering of events of participation and reification by which our experience and its social interpretation inform each other. As we encounter our effects on the world and develop our relations with others, these layers build upon each other to produce our identity as a very complex interweaving of participative experience and reificative projections. Bringing the two together through the negotiation of meaning, we construct who we are. (p. 151)

Wenger defines the parallels between practice and identity with the following characteristics (p. 149):

- Identity as negotiated experience. We define who we are by the ways we experience our selves through participation as well as by the ways we and others reify our selves.
- Identity as community membership. We define who we are by the familiar and the unfamiliar.
- Identity as learning trajectory. We define who we are by where we have been and where we are going.
- Identity as nexus of multimembership. We define who we are by the ways we reconcile our various forms of membership into one identity.
- Identity as relation between the local and the global. We define who we are by negotiating local ways of belonging to broader constellations and of manifesting broader styles and discourses.

Chapter 2 offers a model and framework for helping to coach, mentor, and developmentally instruct identity growth and maturation.

Geographical boundaries can limit the forms and variety of experiences, types of community membership available, the inherent boundaries of limited physical space and place, and that nature of what is possible to experience across the familiar local and the larger unfamiliar global forms of society (the inherent tension described in 1887 by Ferdinand Tonnies in his classic Gemeinschaft und Gesellschaft). Virtual learning environments offer the educator the means to overcome the limitations of geographical boundaries to expand the types of community membership available, go beyond physical limitations of space and place, and bridge the familiar with larger constellations of relationships and discourses.

AN INTERFACE BETWEEN GEMEINSCHAFT AND GESELLSCHAFT LEARNING EXPERIENCES

Inhabitable-shared virtual spaces offer a Heidegger-like artistic realm of the "art-of-the-possible" for educators. As it was for Heidegger, the benefit of art works served as an interface to reveal which would not otherwise be discernable merely from the object itself. Likewise, this promise of revelation holds true for virtual spaces. The interface spans what is obvious from the object itself, in all its appearances, to what can be disclosed or revealed by its' artistic expression. In the case of virtual spaces used for learning then the placement of object exemplars in 3D spaces can become profound when offered in the context of inhabitable-shared virtual spaces whereby they can be engaged with by learners and made to find their place in constructed knowledge and understanding.

The means to construct knowledge among a small community of learners offers the gemeinschaft-like affective benefits of kinship, fellowship, and belief (as in it's believable because there is first-hand experience with and among kindred). Virtual spaces also offer the means to broaden or bridge participation beyond the small learning community to larger cosmopolitan populations offering gesellschaft-like

Figure 11. Scene of Art-of-the-Possible statue in virtual 3D New Harmony.

rational experiences whereby others from broader constellations provide public or civic negotiated appropriations, critique, and arguments of disbelief (as in finer discriminations offered by public discourse on interpretations and reconciliations of challenges addressing utility, value, or impact on existing doctrine). The means to creatively interface between benefits of gemeinschaft and gesellschaft learning experiences using virtual spaces is not merely an environmental convenience-of-choice offered to educators made possible by advances in technology; but rather, can be considered as beneficial for shaping identities and revealing new possibilities for how education can be strengthen to support the common good. Turning to Heidegger again, his use of the term "bridge" brings deeper definition and understanding of the significance virtual spaces can serve as an interface for use by educators.

Bridging between internal mental constructs made visible and shareable among others, together in real time, is made possible by immersive virtual spaces. As is the case with physical bridges that brings a stream, riverbank, and the land together to form connectable neighborhoods, so it is with immersive virtual spaces. From isolated, even lonely mental spaces of self-held constructs, emerges the means to gather them across individual landscapes of internal mental life for shareable or neighborly forms of expressions or revelation by means of the bridging service of immersive virtual spaces. In this way, virtual spaces take on deeper significance and become meaningful and inhabitable-shared places wherein presence is experienced and maintained by one's identity with co-constructed knowledge, meanings, and community.

From inhabitable-shared virtual places learning trajectories are made possible with the means to project beyond limits inherent with the physical limits of geography. The line of thinking about the importance and role of virtual space for educators is heavily influenced from the discipline of human geography and the insights offered by Yi-Fu Tuan (1977) in the ways people feel and think about space and place, how they form attachments to home, neighborhood, and nation. In particular to this discussion of virtual spaces, Tuan speaks to the importance of "purposeful activity whereby space and time become oriented with respect to the cogitating and active self" (p. 127).

Figure 12. Scene of cover bridge and mill in virtual 3D New Harmony.

The starting point for the cogitating self is "place" or that which is familiar and wherein one's identity is originally formed by and shaped in community (the gemeinschaft) to public-civic "space" (the gesellschaft) which one journeys towards in life, explores, and increasingly defines one's identity and roles in negotiated ways with others by participating in cosmopolitan society. The journey towards an identity increasingly shaped by participating in civic society is filled with the unfamiliar and greater levels of uncertainty.

Figure 13. Scene of Native American village in virtual 3D New Harmony.

At first, a new sojourner is very likely to be apprehensive about the unfamiliar and how best to grapple with uncertainty. It is quite natural for people to journey back and forth between familiar places and unknown new civic spaces in life to harmonize tensions naturally arising in how one's identity can be challenged when exposed to new ideas introduced from civic discourse and interactions. As an identity matures, however, the journeying between place and space is increasingly filled with movements forward in time.

A sojourner learns more about ways to assimilate though understanding or accommodate to the unfamiliar and uncertain. Thus, new journeys expand and shape one's identity through contacts and experiences not otherwise available from existing community affiliations bounded by local geography. Thus, for the educator, virtual learning offers a way to help bridge familiar life experiences and places to new horizons filled with civic spaces to be explored, understood, interpreted, and ultimately contributed to by the learning sojourner.

WAYS TO RECONSTRUCT THE PROFESSIONAL IDENTITY

Attention is turned to how the bridging use of virtual spaces can impact and help reconstruct the professional identity and practices of the educator. The work of Chris Argyris and Donald Schön (1974) offers important insights on the basis of how a professionals' identity is related to the ideology of the profession giving meaning to "professed" practices offered to society as values. For example, the societal values offered by "medicine is professed health; law professed justice; education professed truth; and ministry professed salvation" (p. 146). From the ideology of professed value a paradigm for practicing in the profession is offered on the basis of: an expected ethic that is binding on the professional; a set of arts or techniques that make up the profession's skills; membership in a guild of initiates (professional society) entitled to practice the special arts of the profession; a special relationship to lay people whereby deference, authority, and trust are accorded; an institutional setting (such as temple, hospital, court, or school) within professional activities occur; and a world-view or theory that sets forth the concepts of the world in which the professional practices and the ways professional activities are thought to lead to the better world envisioned in the ideology" (pp. 146-147).

How each part of the paradigm is applied in practice not only reveals key features of the practitioner's identity in the profession but also reinforces and shapes the identity and range of possibilities in how or whether expertise, skills or techniques are applied in the profession in novel or innovative ways. As it turns out, how techniques in a profession are practiced is very closely tied to institutional forms of organization and environments (e.g., hospitals, churches, courthouses, schools). Contemporary professions have strived to create controlled environments to better achieve predictable outcomes from practices. For example, hospitals offer laboratories and diagnostic services for improving medical treatments. Courthouses provide for standardized practices in court proceedings and application of law. And school settings offer grade-levels, curricular schedules, and proctored exams. Historically, the geography and physical properties wherein professionals applied their techniques promoted standardization, uniformity, and control.

In context with the environmental features of standardization, uniformity, and control the professional applied a theory of action that modeled the features: formal, structured interactions among themselves (often competitive) and with their clients (e.g., patients, plaintiffs, parishioners, students), spelling out the rules governing the procedures to be followed, sharp role differentiation, and expectations for how

Figure 14. Scene of St. Francis statue in virtual 3D New Harmony.

interactions were to be conducted. The expected consequence of the application of this theory of action in the profession was to realize objectives held by the professional, control the task, and render the behaviors of others predictable, and thereby control the outcome (Argyris & Schön, 1974, p.152). Argyris and Schön point out that while many of the features are desirable sometimes the controlling environment of the law courts interferes with justice; the controlling environment of the hospital can interfere with health, and controlling environment of schools can interfere with learning.

Increasingly, the localized physical environments, traditionally associated with the practices of professionals, are evolving into extended virtualized or hybrid-settings. Healthcare, legal, clergy, and education professionals can be called upon to practice across physical and virtual spaces. The expansion from beyond physical environments into virtual spaces places unique demands upon professionals. Techniques applied in physical settings may not work well or not at all in virtual contexts. Likewise, roles used for interacting with clients in physical settings may not only be ineffective in virtual spaces but detrimental to expected outcomes. And, in some cases, practices in virtual spaces may open up recognition in professional shortcomings and need for growth that otherwise would be unforeseen or understood apart from experiences with novel or innovative challenges when practicing in new environments. Argyris and Schön (1974) speak to the importance too for professionals to extend their practices beyond controlling environments to benefit from increased likelihood of engaging with double-loop learning. As often as not, they argue professionals can find themselves practicing in a 'self-sealing world' wherein it is rare to collaborate in practice and solicit diverse perspectives from which professional benefits to identity and growth in techniques/skills can occur. Double-loop learning involves willingness to examine one's current theory of action and on the basis of diverse feedback and follow-on discernments make appropriate adjustments (p. 19).

Engagement with open organizational boundaries and environments is also very likely to enlarge apertures, via communities of inquiry, for soliciting and receiving diversity of thought and viewpoints leading to new or innovative techniques in professional practices (Wenger, et. al., 2002).

Figure 15. Scene of home construction in virtual 3D New Harmony.

A TRANSCENDENTAL VIEWPOINT OF VIRTUAL LEARNING FOR THE COMMON GOOD

The importance served by the use of double-loop learning for professional identity and skills growth, while relevant for any profession, is certainly front-and-center to the ideology and reconstruction of theories of action employed by educators as role models for learners with the transcendental qualities of the common good. The concept of Kantian-based transcendentalism is used specifically here to speak to the qualities of the common good rather than usage of transcendent simply because the qualities of the common good are meant not to be understood as coming from beyond human experience, but rather are formed from the human mind. And when minds conjointly engage through discourse and co-construction of ideas then shared experiences can be formed.

The interplay of imperative transcendental forms by human minds co-create shared experiences which make possible unique and shareable insights and common bonds of unity that otherwise would not occur. Transcendentalism is associated with 19th century American literary, political, and philosophical movement led by Ralph Waldo Emerson and influenced by other important transcendentalists such as Henry David Thoreau, Margaret Fuller, Amos Bronson Alcott, Frederic Henry Hedge, and Theodore Parker.

The nature of transcendental insights can be thought of as perceptions that produce 'religious sentiment' not unlike inspiration wherein there is belief of endless forms of action made possible from openness of the human mind to new ways of thinking and perceiving. Transcendentalists have also been historically associated with new ways of thinking about community and forms for common good in society. Emerson's view of nature from a transcendental viewpoint conveys revelation through mediated molding through purposeful expressions of creativity. Nature is fluid, flexible, and changeable. These qualities speak to a universal experience with nature in overt and, in some cases, not so obvious ways. This line of thought is similar to Heidegger's views on human activities to unconceal the concealment of earth, or fundamentally nature, through art work which can serve as an interface between the known and concealed expressions of ideas leading to new forms and insights (Collins & Selina, 1998, pp. 133-137).

Extending this line of thinking to virtual learning, in the form of immersive and situated 3D spaces, educators co-create with learners shared experiences, insights, and common bonds that bridge between the familiar known associated with gemeinschaft-like experiences and new forms of knowing associated with unfamiliar gesellschaft-like experiences to construct deeper civic bonds for the common good. Thus, virtual learning in this form is ideally suited for double-loop learning whereby the identities of the educator and learners can simultaneously evolve and grow with co-constructed knowledge and shared understandings in a fluid, flexible artistic-like environment making use of high levels of authenticity not unduly constricted by controls. Virtual learning in this form of expression, making use of transcendental qualities, is in its nascent stage of usage among educators, but the authenticity and suitability of its form for reconstructing new ways of developing identities of professional educators for the common good are full of prospects.

PRINCIPLES OF DESIGN FOR TRANSCENDENTAL VIRTUAL LEARNING IN SERVICE OF THE COMMON GOOD

Merleau-Ponty (1962) advocated for the reconstruction of a person's ability to notice the transcendent world rather than merely as a set of "bracketed" or reduced isolated experiences wherein objects, people, events are taken for granted, go unnoticed. He placed emphasis on the importance of reflection (mindfulness) as means for arousing "forms of transcendence [to] fly up like sparks from a fire" (p. 8). The field of existential cognition makes a similar advocacy for the importance and role of mindfulness within situated context to reconceptualize and expand the opacity of how embedded our identity is with a shared, lived-in world (McClamrock, 1995, p. 189-191). Both Heidegger and Merleau-Ponty argued for the importance of shared environmental structures situated in context; in effect, a common objective phenomenology whereby importance is placed by educators on experiential-based transcendent landscapes offering "reachable" and "positional" places and spaces entirely co-constructed and experienced from direct impressions in shared ways. In effect, "being" and "appearance" become one. Thus, a person's "being," expressed in thought, reflection (mindfulness), and action is highly embedded, connected to, and shaped (impressed by) directly from interactions within situated environmental context, in the form of activity systems, and does not take place in isolation but is social (Lave & Wenger, 1991, p. 98).

Looking at virtual learning, from the lens of a common objective phenomenology, can illuminate transformative ways of thinking about the design of learning landscapes. Transcendental learning experiences, addressing civic-friendship for the common good, can be purposefully designed to support developmental growth of identity and practices using creative combinations of gemeinschaft–like places and gessellschaft-like civic spaces offered by virtual-learning landscapes.

The importance of virtual-learning landscape design takes into account the direct ways people experience a particular place or space, what is seen, heard, and felt while observing, moving around, and interacting. People form transcendental impressions and reactions to the "genius of the situated locale" as to whether there are "well-springs" offering sources of inspiration, stimulation, refreshment, beauty,

Figure 16. Scene of public meeting place in virtual 3D New Harmony.

and delight. The "well-springs" stimulate mindfulness to reconceptualize the "art-of-the-possible" to inspire new forms for developmentally shaping identity and practices in all the ways we construct who we are and who we are in communion with others.

The following principles are offered to help guide the design of virtual-learning landscapes for developmentally shaping identity and practices:

1. *Design focus is primarily on learning as a process of participation in communities of practice.* The purpose of the design is an initial landscape offering adaptive usage and evolvement overtime with meaningful, engaging, and interactive learning activities among communities of learners in situated and meaningful contexts of practice.
2. *Both function and aesthetics are satisfied.* The landscape exhibits excellence and offers forms of transcendent qualities of virtue and democratic values; are learners likely to experience transcendental qualities that are strong and influential for the common good? Does the design produce pleasure in the person experiencing it across gemeinschaft–like places and gessellschaft-like civic spaces?
3. *The landscape must provide for substantial shared experiences.* A strong sense of character, using iconographic forms, is observable for promoting mindfulness and render favorable impressions; represented by well-springs of activity for "in-situ" deliberations and engagement in conversations supporting divergent thought; public forums are offered wherein dimensions of civic daily life, in the form of learning communities, can take place across a variety of hybrid socializations regardless of originations from either virtual and physical sources

Figure 17. Scene of Roofless Church in virtual 3D New Harmony.

4. *The landscape supports creative interfaces and expansiveness of experiences.* Consideration is given to the "personality of the places and spaces", the "personality of expected users", the "personality of the function(s) served by experiential-based learning activities to the practices of application" and the "scale of the landscape" (does the expansiveness of the landscape offer familiarity with defined places as well as spaces for co-discovery and new constructions of knowledge and understanding with opportunity to apply in practice?

Collectively, the application of the guiding principles for purposeful design of transcendental virtual learning can help sustain fluid, dynamic, and evolving virtual-learning landscapes. The guiding principles serve as an alidade for taking bearings and for navigating with purpose in use of virtual learning for developing identity and practices for the common good through education.

Each of the following chapters in this edited book offer important insights for ways to flourish in making and shaping of selfhood and society with virtual learning. Insights are offered from authors spanning interdisciplinary viewpoints from education, psychology, theology, sociology, law, and computer sciences. Considerations from the collective viewpoints offered by the authors in this book can help shape and sustain a way of being for an educator in the natural world as it increasingly becomes and is made visible through our efforts for a flourishing future for the common good in society.

SUGGESTIONS FOR FUTURE SCHOLARSHIP AND RESEARCH

Scholastic investigations and research studies, strengthening the connection between theories of learning and practice in Positive Psychology, ought to be conducted to further extend understanding of the ways virtual environments can be used to not only shape professional identities of educators for the common good but also offer insights for progressive benefits to society at large for educating citizens. Developmental models of human development can be expanded to better account for how human identity and experiences can be nurtured in positive and constructive ways from the design and use of emerging learning landscapes spanning physical and virtual spaces.

REFERENCES

Abbey, R. (2004). Charles Taylor (R. Abbey, Ed.). Cambridge, UK: Cambridge University Press. doi:10.1017/CBO9780511610837

Argyris, C., & Schön, D. (1974). *Theory in practice: Increasing professional effectiveness*. San Francisco, CA: Jossey-Bass Publishers.

Arndt, K. (1965). *George Rapp's Harmony Society 1785-1847* (Revised Edition). Cranbury, NJ: Associated University Presses, Inc.

Arndt, K. (1978). *A documentary history of the Indiana decade of the Harmony Society 1814-1824* (Vol. 2). Indianapolis, IN: Indiana Historical Society.

Augustine. (412). *City of God* (H. Bettenson, Trans.). New York, NY: Penguin Books.

Blascovich, J., & Bailenson, J. (2011). *Infinite reality: The hidden blueprint of our virtual lives*. New York, NY: HarperCollins Publishers.

Buber, M. (1947). *Between man and man* (R. Gregor-Smith, Trans.). New York, NY: Routledge & Kegan Paul.

Buber, M. (1958). *I and thou*. New York, NY: Collier Books, Macmillan Publishing Company.

Collins, J., & Selina, H. (1998). *Introducing Heidegger*. New York, NY: Totem Books.

Counts, G. (1932). *Dare the school build a new social order?* New York, NY: The John Day Company.

Csikszentmihalyi, M. (2000). *Beyond boredom and anxiety*. San Francisco: Jossey-Bass.

Cuban, L., & Shipps, D. (2000). *Reconstructing the common good in education: Coping with intractable American dilemmas*. Stanford, CA: Stanford University Press.

Heidegger, M. (1964). Basic writings: from Being and Time and The Task of Thinking (D. F. Krell, Trans.). San Francisco, CA: Harper. (Originally published 1927)

Lave, J., & Wenger, E. (1991). *Situated learning: Legitimate peripheral participation*. New York, NY: Cambridge University Press. doi:10.1017/CBO9780511815355

McClamrock, R. (1995). *Existential cognition: Computational minds in the world*. Chicago: The University of Chicago Press.

Merleau-Ponty, M. (1962). *Phenomenology of perception*. London: Routledge and Kegan Paul.

Meyer, J. (2000). Reflections on education as transcendence. In *Reconstructing the common good in education: Coping with intractable American dilemmas*. Stanford, CA: Stanford University Press.

Perlstein, D. (2000). There is no escape...from the ogre of indoctrination: George Counts and the civic dilemmas of democratic educators. In *Reconstructing the common good in education: Coping with intractable American dilemmas*. Stanford, CA: Stanford University Press.

Peterson, C., & Seligman, M. E. P. (2004). *Character strengths and virtues: A handbook and classification*. Washington, DC: American Psychological Association.

Seligman, M. E. P., & Csikszentmihalyi, M. (2000). Positive psychology: An introduction. *The American Psychologist*, *55*(1), 5–14. doi:10.1037/0003-066X.55.1.5 PMID:11392865

Singer, P. (1983). *Hegel: A very short introduction*. Oxford, UK: Oxford University Press.

Tonnies, F. (1887). *Community and society* (C. P. Loomis & N. York, Trans.). Dover Publications, Inc.

Tuan, Y.-F. (1977). *Space and place: The perspective of experience*. Minneapolis, MN: The University of Minnesota Press.

Tyack, D. (1966). Forming of the national character: Paradox in the educational thought of the revolutionary generation. *Harvard Educational Review*, *36*(1), 29–41. doi:10.17763/haer.36.1.213504687324p76g

Tyack, D., & Hansot, E. (1982). *Managers of virtue: Public school leadership in America, 1820-1980*. New York, NY: Basic Books.

Wenden, A. (2004). Value-based perspective development. In A. L. Wenden (Ed.), *Educating for a Culture of Social and Ecological Peace*. Albany, NY: State University of New York Press.

Wenger, E. (1998). *Communities of practice: Learning, meaning, and identity*. Cambridge, UK: Cambridge University Press. doi:10.1017/CBO9780511803932

Wenger, E., McDermott, R., & Snyder, W. (2002). *Cultivating communities of practice*. Boston, MA: Harvard Business School Press.

KEY TERMS AND DEFINITIONS

Constructivist: From constructivism used to highlight a theoretical framework of learning holding that people construct knowledge and meaning from their experiences.

Dialogical Deconstruction: Addresses the importance of diverse perspectives coming from human discourse and conversations. Discourse among people can convey deeper meanings about the self, ways knowledge is constructed, and meaningfulness held by people of groups in society. Underlying assumptions regarding the meaning of words and context of usage are questioned (deconstructed) and new meaningfulness is "constructed" in active ways among people.

Existential Cognition: A framework of cognition placing emphasis on the interconnectedness between phenomenon of the perceiver with phenomenon of the thing wherein people sense perceptual consciousness. Perceptions are grounded from "existential" or places taken up by a person from whom object properties appear and organize in meaningful ways.

Progressive: A descriptive used to convey a perspective taken by a person advocating progress, change, or new way of thinking. A post-progression viewpoint is an adjusted progressive perspective taken on the basis of deeper insights from lessons learned from earlier change efforts.

Teleological: Relating to teleology, a philosophical perspective of nature from which objects are described in terms of their purpose, directive principle, or goal. The purpose can become evident from human use.

Tikto: Greek for "bringing forth or to produce." Used by Heidegger to convey emergent properties of human experiences.

Transcendental: Term used in the form proposed by Kant to convey a type of knowledge coming from intuitive-based human experiences. Meaning of experiences can take the form of the uncommon from deep reflections upon nature.

Versammlung: The genitive form used by Heidegger to address the concept of "gathering" whereby the essence of meaningfulness between objects lie in a revealing connectivity between them from the perspective of human experiences.

Virtual Learning: An education paradigm placing emphasis on the use of computers and the Internet for supporting the ways people can learn. Virtual learning environments can include 2D and 3D dimensions and degrees of presence, immersion, and volition offer.

Chapter 2
Identity Growth in the Professions

Andrew G. Stricker
https://orcid.org/0000-0002-4184-0554
Air University, USA

Todd Westhauser
Air University, USA

David J. Lyle
Air Education and Training Command, USA

Charles Christian Lowry
Air University, USA

Travis S. Sheets
United States Air Force, USA

ABSTRACT

Identity theory and research offer important insights for helping to guide the development of professionals across the lifespan of service vital to the public's wellbeing. A developmental framework is introduced as a guide for professional identity growth along dimensions of cognitive and moral reasoning. The framework includes literacies, spanning the dimensions, associated with social intelligence, leadership, competencies, and mindsets. Insights from research are offered for supporting the use of the framework with developmental instruction of professionals to promote higher levels of identity growth and maturation associated with improved judgment and behavior. Instructional practices are also described for helping professionals transition effectively to higher growth levels for use by coaches, mentors, and instructors. The profession of arms is highlighted for illustrating and applying the developmental framework in the context of a profession.

DOI: 10.4018/978-1-5225-9679-0.ch002

INTRODUCTION

Duty – Honor – Country. Those three hallowed words reverently dictate what you ought to be, what you can be, what you will be. They are your rallying points: to build courage when courage seems to fail; to regain faith when there seems to be little cause for faith; to create hope when hope becomes forlorn. General Douglas MacArthur

General Douglas MacArthur in his farewell speech to West Point Cadets in May of 1962, said "Yours is the Profession of Arms, the will to win, the sure knowledge that in war there is no substitute for victory, that if you lose, the Nation will be destroyed, that the very obsession of your public service must be Duty, Honor, Country."

From the perspective of the US military, as expressed by the Chairman of the Joint Chiefs of Staff, The Profession of Arms presents a calling requiring unique expertise to fulfill a collective responsibility to the American people, "provide for the common defense and secure the blessings of liberty. The Profession of Arms is distinguished from other professions in society because expertise rests in the justified application of lethal military force and the willingness of those who serve to die for country. The Profession of Arms is defined by values, ethics, standards, code of conduct, skills, and attributes. As volunteers, our sworn duty is to the Constitution. Our status as a profession is granted by those whom we are accountable to, our civilian authority, and the American people" (JCS, 2016).

The Joint Chiefs of Staff, white paper, *America's Military - A Profession of Arms* succinctly summarizes how all who enter the military join the profession: "All service men and women belong to the profession from the junior enlisted to our most senior leaders. We are all accountable for meeting ethical and performance standards in our actions and similarly, accountable for our failure to take action, when appropriate. The distinction between ranks lies in our level of responsibility and degree of accountability. We share the common attributes of character, courage, competence, and commitment. We qualify as professionals through intensive training, education, and practical experience. As professionals, we are defined by our strength of character, life-long commitment to core values, and maintaining our professional abilities through continuous improvement, individually and institutionally" (JCS, 2016, p. 4).

Another distinguishing feature of a professional is not only the internal nature of the individual but also the nature of their service. As stated above, a professional is defined by qualities addressing strength of character, life-long commitment to core values, and willingness to maintain and improve abilities (Hackett, 1962). What also distinguishes a practitioner in a profession is the practice of the professional in services vital to the public's well-being. Within a practice, professionals have a high degree of autonomy in deciding how to carry out their services, as authorized by legal rights, and are expected to conduct their behavior by a code of ethics. Thus, a professional is expected to not only engage in life-long development of their cognitive complexity associated with skillful abilities but also to developmentally grow and mature in moral reasoning dimensions impacting their judgment and behavior vital to the public's well-being. Recognition, understanding, and acceptance of the interdependence of these developmental dimensions is at the heart of a professional's identity and personal dedication to a course greater than oneself. The journey of developmental growth does not take place for a professional in social isolation but is highly dependent on social structures and networks involving peers, mentors, and coaches across the lifespan of service (Burke & Stets, 2009; Stryker, 1980).

In his foundational book *Mind, Self, and Society,* George Herbert Mead (1934) spoke of the integral role played by social interactions in the shaping of the mind and self. Our sense of personal identity within the context of group membership has a great impact on the subconscious thought processes that impact our thoughts and decisions, whether or not we're consciously aware of its impact. A critical milestone for identity development is the differentiation of how a person perceives the self while also able to reflect upon how others can perceive them. Over time, as a person interacts in social networks, structural symbolic adaptations with identity development occur as changes are made by a person to align closer to desired collective attitudes and behaviors modeled by others, in order to protect or enhance their sense of inclusion within those groups, and the degree of efficacy and control that the individual can bring to bear on impacting the collective direction of the group. According to Mead, a person begins to form a viewpoint of a public self gradually over time from the means to adjust their identity on the basis of perspectives of how they are viewed by others, serving as role models, as obtained via social interactions. The dynamic between the "inner self" and the perceived "public self" is developmental by nature and can evolve in healthy ways from early pre-teen years until late in life as a growth function - an ability to do so provides an evolutionary advantage for individuals who can retain inclusion within groups, and retain access to the collective benefits of membership. These insights are not completely new revelations - the core insights have been recognized and debated in precursor formulations of our modern constructs since the earliest days of deliberate inquiry on social issues in classical times. The growth function is best described from the ancient Greek viewpoint held by Plato and Aristotle (NE, 1999) about what makes for a worthy life lived by free people. As depicted in Figure 1, a worthy life lived by a free people is the embodiment of three features of the self: "theoria" (the thinking self), "poiesis" (the

The triangular structure of the ancient Greek viewpoint of the self encompasses interdependence among the internal moral elements of the self with resulting means by a person for reflective, virtuous contributions and behaviors necessary for a free society. Thus, for a person to dedicate themselves to a course greater than oneself, vital to the public's well-being, is to embark on a distinguishing developmental journey offering the highest levels of identity growth and maturation reserved for professional service in a free society. In this way, the professional journey becomes a vital part of the individual's "hero's journey", a resonant theme of personal growth and redemption that can be traced across history and across societies in the popular stories they record, as described by Joseph Campbell in *The Hero With A Thousand Faces* (Campbell, 1949; see Figure 2).

A professional identity is a person's viewpoint of who they are as a professional serving in a domain of expertise involving high expectations of excellence in the application of special knowledge and skills (Slay and Smith, 2011). As described above, the profession also expects the person to follow a code of conduct for ethical behavior. Collectively, a professional identity viewpoint consists of beliefs, values, motives and experiences that people possess and use to define themselves and guide their skillful practices in the profession (Schein, 1978).

A person's professional identity is influenced by the interpersonal interactions with peers and mentors in their profession. While stories and culture set the basic frameworks for cultural identity, people learn who they are and grow as a professional by seeing themselves in the eyes of others (Caza & Creary, 2016). An entering professional, through guild-like interactions with mentors, learns about role expectations and developmentally matures by engaging in reflective practice (Schön, 1983).

As suggested by the ancient Greek viewpoint of the self in a free society an entering professional in the Profession of Arms can expect to embark on a distinguishing developmental journey offering the highest levels of identity growth and maturation spanning interdependent elements of theoria, poiesis, and

Figure 1. Embodiment of a worthy life lived by a free people (Aristotle & Plato) making self), and "praxis" (the doing self). Each feature offers end goals of a worthy life (for true happiness): the end goal of "theoria" is a life guided by ethical truth; the end goal of "poiesis" is a productive life offering contributions to society; and the end goal of "praxis" is a life conducted by virtuous actions (NE, 1999).

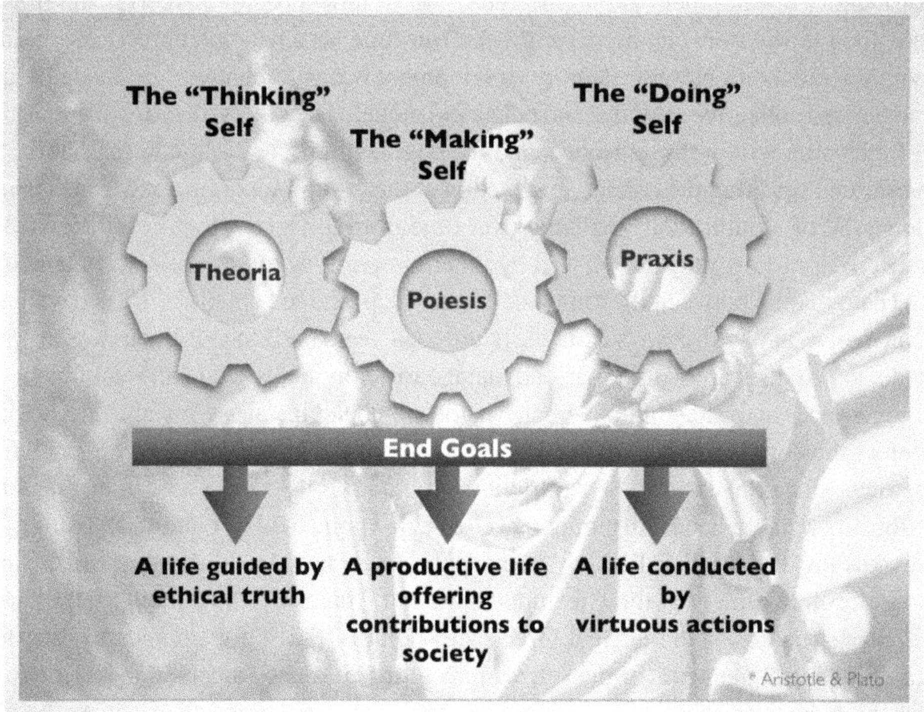

praxis. A framework is introduced to help convey service-span developmental levels of identity growth in the Profession of Arms. The framework offers a model for integrating skill literacies with maturation levels associated with professional identity development. Each part of the framework is briefly described below for helping to address developmental growth with professional identity.

PROFESSIONAL IDENTITY GROWTH FRAMEWORK

A professional identity growth framework helps to relate skill literacies and maturation dimensions associated with identity construction and growth in a profession (see Figure 3). Skill literacies cover moral, cognitive, and competence categories commonly attributed to professionals. Core literacies are mapped across moral and cognitive developmental dimensions to convey levels of maturation across a life-span of professional identity growth (Stricker & Lyle, 2018; Kohlberg, 1976, 1981; Langer, 2005; Knefelkamp, 1990).

Figure 2. Diagram of the hero's journey as described by Joseph Campbell
Source: diagram from Wikicommons, accessed 9 Nov 2018: https://commons.wikimedia.org/wiki/File:Heroesjourney.svg

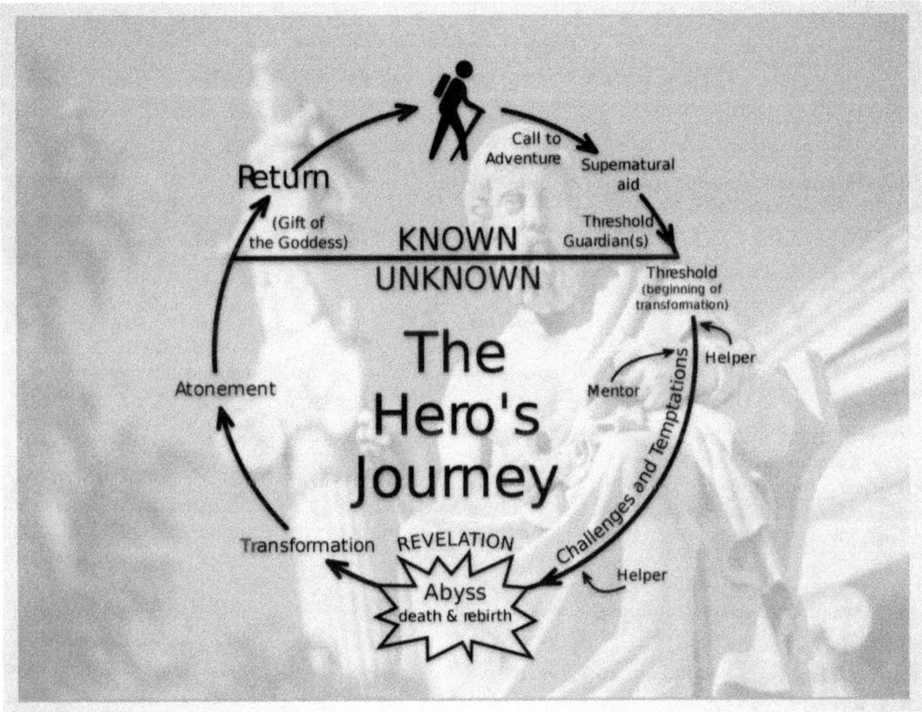

Core skill literacies and maturation dimensions associated with the framework are described below.

Skill Literacies

Effectance Competence (EC)

In 1959 Robert W. White wrote a classic article for *Psychological Review* titled, "Motivation Reconsidered: The Concept of Competence." In it, White proposed a new concept: effectance. Effectance was described as a "tendency to explore and influence the environment." White suggested that the "master reinforcer" for humans is personal competence. He defined competence as "the ability to interact effectively with the environment." Competence is the ability of an individual to do a job properly. A competency is a set of defined behaviors that provide a structured guide enabling the identification, evaluation and development of the behaviors in an individual. The term "competence" first appeared in an article authored by R.W. White in 1959 as a concept for performance motivation. Note: there is a subtle difference between (1) seeking life activities which "play to your strengths," which is certainly natural if people want to feel competent, and (2) the enjoyment of mastering new skills described as typical of successful entrepreneurs. These are not the same thing. If you merely seek situations that make you feel competent, you are likely to exercise old skills, and you are unlikely to advance (Dewey, 1938). Competence also implies mastery of a well understood and documented process or phenomenon, one that is relatively stable, so

Figure 3. Framework constructs of key interdependent elements of the self and the self in relation to others in service

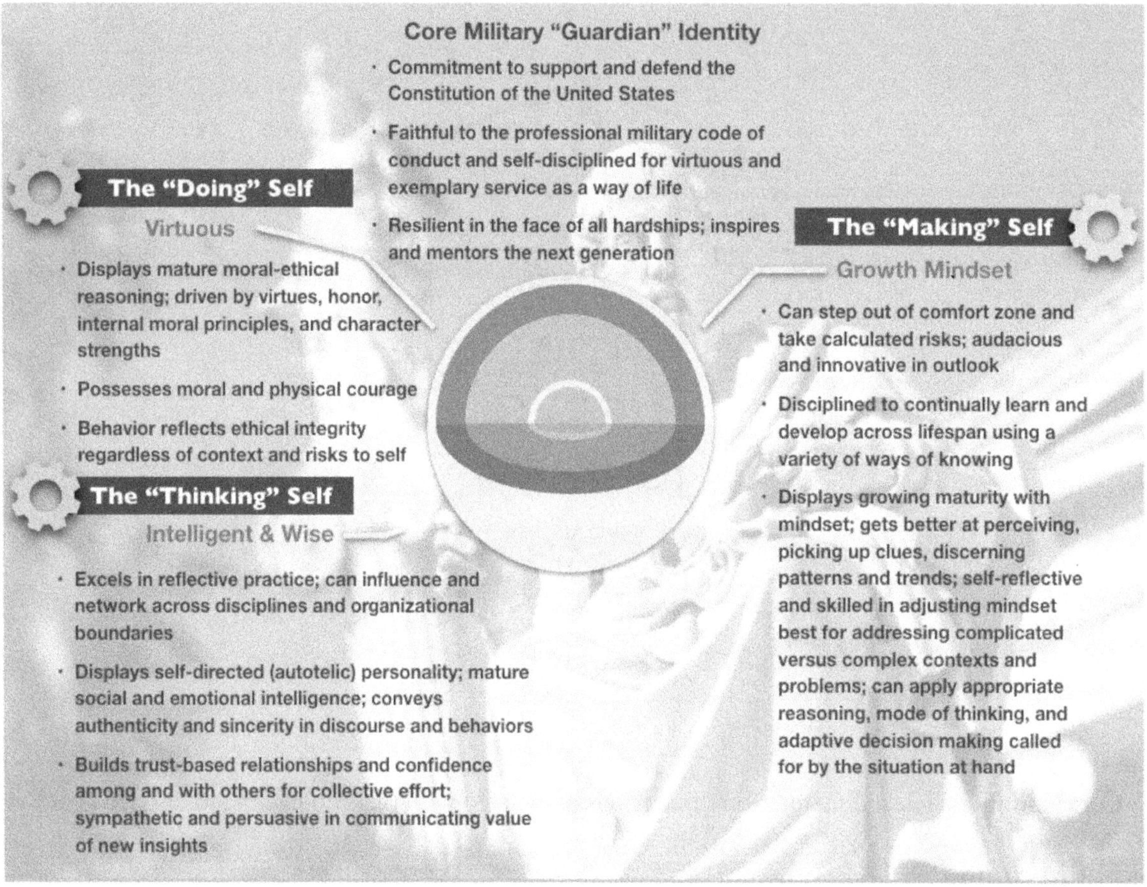

that the previously learned skills and competencies required to be effective in the past will continue to aid effectiveness in the future in similar conditions.

Social Intelligence (SI)

Social intelligence is primarily a learned skill, although some people may take to it more easily than others. A person with high social intelligence understands subtle etiquette, knows how to listen to people, and has a useful understanding of the internal motivations that are driving their behaviors and reactions. This person can typically motivate others to cooperate, and people generally enjoy being around him or her. Socially intelligent people know how to present themselves well, and can apply tact and discretion in sensitive dealings with others while still being genuine and authentic. Social intelligence is often linked with emotional intelligence, although they are two separate concepts. Emotional intelligence is a person's ability to analyze his thoughts and feelings, as well as control those reactions. Low emotional intelligence can affect a person's social intelligence, however. Social intelligence requires self-control and an ability to understand what other people are feeling, and people with low emotional intelligence are often unable to do that. Social intelligence is not an inherent part of a person's personality. While many think of an outgoing, energetic person as someone with high social intelligence, that level of energy is not essential. People can be quiet, calm and introverted while still being socially intelligent, while someone who is outgoing but too loud or rude has low social intelligence (Goleman, 2007).

Leading People (LP)

The other performance dimensions in this framework take visible expression in leading people. A key perspective to hold for leading people well is to appreciate how unity and diversity work together. Leaders build trust in people so as much freedom as possible is offered for people to be different while contributing to unified effort. Humility and transparency build trust, which is the glue of cohesive effort (Ellis, 2012). If there is enough trust and cohesion then creative conflict (Lencioni, 2000) can take place wherein people can engage in passionate discussions to better address a variety of challenges. Building trust and cohesion is especially critical for cross-functional efforts involving people separated by distance (Stricker, et. al., 2018). Balancing results and relationships is a major leadership challenge. Some leaders are naturally gifted with the head (logic) and not very good with the heart (feelings). Others are just the opposite. Only about 20 percent of the population has a natural ability with both (Ellis, 2012). Mature leaders balance accomplishment of the mission (results) and care for their people (relationships).

Moral Courage (MC)

Moral courage is the courage to take action for moral reasons despite the risk of adverse consequences. Moral courage is deeply connected to self-identity and how a person perceives the purpose of life, the benefit of learning from all experiences, and where strength can be drawn from in the face of difficulties. Life is difficult. Each person has a choice about how to respond to difficulties. Honor is key. Honor is intentionally modeling virtues, and associated character strengths, regardless of circumstances and who might be watching. Leading with moral courage and honor is about putting service vital to the public's well-being ahead of self interests. It means keeping your word and your commitments. It means serving sacrificially in a way that upholds possessed values. Reliably keeping commitments and consistently living espoused values is always challenging but essential for overcoming hardships while still doing what is right. Character is foundational for trust, and trust is the most essential ingredient for leading people (Ellis, 2015). And within the context of leadership and professionalism, moral courage might be best defined as the willingness to put forth positions or take actions which threaten the security of the individual's continued membership within the group - maintaining continued social conformity with the status quo group norms requires no moral courage.

Growth Mindset (GM)

"In a growth mindset, people believe that their most basic abilities can be developed through dedication and hard work—brains and talent are just the starting point. This view creates a love of learning and a resilience that is essential for great accomplishment," writes Dweck (2016). A mindset, according to Dweck (2016), is a self-perception or "self-theory" that people hold about themselves. Believing that you are either "intelligent" or "unintelligent" is a simple example of a mindset. People may also have a mindset related their personal or professional lives—"I'm a good teacher" or "I'm a bad parent," for example. People can be aware or unaware of their mindsets, according to Dweck (2016), but they can have profound effect on learning achievement, skill acquisition, personal relationships, professional success, and many other dimensions of life. People who embrace growth mindsets—the belief that they can learn more or become smarter if they work hard and persevere—may learn more, learn it more quickly, and view challenges and failures as opportunities to improve their learning and skills (Ibarra, 1999). There is a strong complex connection between a growth mindset, the body, and overall fitness. Identity maturation is not only highly interdependent with physical and psychological health but also with how the mind perceives the efficacy of self in relation to physical characteristics. Physical identity takes in self perceptions regarding the ability of the body to "work" and accompanied feelings of power, agility, and endurance (Whitbourne, 2002, p. 3). A growth mindset for professionals entails a deep sense of why it matters to not only keep oneself both physically and psychologically healthy but to purposefully engage in strengthening body and mind to better prepare for and address mental and physical hardships commonly associated with service. Applying and practicing a growth mindset under the most challenging of circumstances is of particular interest to the Profession of Arms. Research by the U.S. Army, investigating the complex connection between mind, body, and spirit (e.g., spiritual health and moral reasoning), reinforces the interdependent role played by physical, cognitive, and spiritual health for developing a person's overall resiliency and improved ability to self-regulate and perform optimally every day, and especially in the most challenging circumstances (Army Regulation 350-53, 2014).

Similarly to concepts of fitness, professionals stretch their limits in voluntary efforts to accomplish difficult and worthwhile tasks across all domains of their practice: cognitively, morally, and physically (Csikszentmihalyi, 1990). People with a growth mindset also possess curiosity leading to increased creativity (Csikszentmihalyi, 1996). Creativity is achieved through a mindset, involving the use of a systems perspective, that looks at the world from different angles and syntheses disparate thoughts into new revelations or approaches (Csikszentmihalyi, 1999). A systems perspective takes into consideration that systems represent interconnected parts, and when one part is changed it effects the entire system. Also, the structure of a system determines its behavior which in turn is driven by the connections among the parts. The behavior of a system is dynamic (continuously changing) due to the non-linear relationship among the parts. Thus, understanding the behavior of a system cannot take place merely by knowing its' structure. Rather, discernment takes place from systems thinking which is represented by an open mindset to the emergent properties and processes observed in system dynamics. Thus, systems thinking goes hand-in-hand with creativity. Such a mindset is distinguished by openness (Simonton, 2010). The more one is exposed (and open) to different ideas, thoughts, and concepts the better they are at creative thought and divergent thinking simply because they can make novel connections arising from discerning the "art-of-the-possible" when connecting ideas at the intersection of domains (Sternberg & Lubart, 1999). Often, the result is creative insight arising when initial analytic thought transcends the obvious from summations of domain knowledge to deeper levels of holistic thought associated with consideration of interdependencies and interconnections leading to transdiciplinary knowlege. Professionals with higher degrees of growth were often able to get there because of a natural tendency towards the growth mindset just to amass the knowledge needed to operate at those levels of cognitive complexity, but they're also more likely to be aware that continuous learning is not optional in an increasingly connected world that is changing rapidly, spinning off new ideas and inventions, which are being introduced much faster than many of our legacy social institutions and norms can keep up with. If leadership is about managing change, then awareness of both the changes and their systemic implications requires a constant engagement with the external environment, and also an awareness of the kinds of skill sets a team or organization requires in aggregate to even understand, let alone successfully address, modern challenges.

Maturation Dimensions

The literacies described above are semi-independent but get fused in application involving reflective practice by a professional. The combined skill literacies and maturation dimensions form a basis for judgment in the application of the literacies in reflective practice across levels of increasing identity maturation. The maturation dimensions address identity growth and ultimate ego integrity across the lifespan. Just as Erik Erickson's psychosocial model (Erickson, 1959) depict a person's evolving identity development and resolution of psychosocial crisis at critical stages of life towards ego-identity integrity (coherent sense of self across time), likewise, the maturation dimensions depict developmental levels of identity growth in a profession whereby at each higher level cognitive and moral reasoning increasingly mature and fuse in virtuous wisdom and practice depicting growing occupational and ideological commitment. There are close ties between social intelligence helping to facilitate interactions and individual structures of cognition and moral reasoning in all its acuteness for evolving developmental growth in virtuous wisdom. Jean Piaget spoke of the importance for healthy development to become increasingly co-operative and effectual in social relationships to help evoke and strengthen reciprocity of the self with and between individuals who know how to differentiate their viewpoints for ultimate shared understanding and effort.

Higher levels of human intelligence is highly correlated with co-operation out of which arises deliberation and reflectiveness, collaboration in work, exchange of ideas, constitution of logic involving complex states of awareness, intellectual feelings, and responses that are social in nature and carry a moral "categorical" imperative indispensable for intellectual interaction and co- operation in society (Piaget, 1950, pp. 178-179). Each maturation level, introduced and briefly described below, ought to be considered not only as successive developmental states, but also a lifelong form of growth involving intertwined cognitive and moral reasoning much more far-reaching in value and ultimate consequences for society than might be perceived or understood as well by an individual at earlier professional development levels. Appendix A provides an illustrative scenario with examples of interpretative reflections common with each level.

Familial Anecdotal

Level I addresses an entry point for early adulthood as a person's identity formation increasingly involves taking on or trying out various roles in society. There may be multiple social roles and public identities experimented with each presenting outcomes of rejection or acceptance by authority figures. Regardless of the range of role and identity experimentation a person at Level I relies primarily upon personal assumptions and experiences for making sense of new information and expected behaviors. When incongruities are encountered with ideas a person at Level I can consider assumptions and experiences of close family or associates but will rarely challenge social norms and rules held by self, family, and close associates. Expected moral development (under Kohlberg's model; see Appendix B) ranges from Stage 2 (Individual interest: behavior driven by self-interest and rewards) to Stage 4 (Authority: behavior driven by obeying authority and conforming to social order). Successful transition to the next maturation level is primarily driven by increased exposure and interaction with others in society resulting in greater clarity of likely and suitable social role(s) and public identities within reach as perceived by the young adult and encouraged by coaches, mentors, and accepted authority figures. At this level, the individual may be aware of the existing disciplines outside of their own, but no substantial knowledge of them, or how they tie into one's own discipline, are required to maintain one's position of identity within their discipline of origin, which is likely narrowly focused on a very specialized tactical skill set within the discipline itself, as implied by nearly any "starting position" job advertisement.

Disciplinary Analytic

It is at Level II wherein an adult is most likely to enter a formal developmental apprenticeship or program of study to meet expected knowledge and competencies associated with a profession. Developmental instruction in the profession plays an important role for introducing and preparing the adult for skillful performance involving cognitive and moral reasoning skills. Preparation for and entry into professions, particularly those relying upon scientific methodologies, helps the entering professional to be aware of personal bias and assumptions; be willing to reinterpret experiences on basis of input from 3rd-party observations from scientific disciplinary boundaries, collected data, and analysis. Expected moral development (under Kohlberg's model) for Level II ranges from Stage 3 (Interpersonal: behavior driven by social approval) to Stage 4 (Authority: behavior driven by obeying authority and conforming to social order). Successful transition to the next maturation level is primarily driven by a combination of increased experience with challenges cutting across disciplinary boundaries facilitated by being presented with incongruities of ideas and ways of knowing, thinking, and doing. Incongruities often take the form associated with analytic reasoning within the discipline, that fall short of satisfactory explanations and expected outcomes or results when facing challenges or phenomenon cutting across disciplines. Developmental instruction of professionals, in preparation for the next level, is to engage them with efforts to address challenges benefiting from collective areas of expertise spanning multiple disciplines. At this level, the member has likely mastered a number of skills within a defined discipline, and is beginning to gain the capability to supervise others within the discipline.

Multidisciplinary Analytic

At Level III a professional shows increased value for and willingness to consider knowledge and perspectives arising from multidisciplinary viewpoints, while still primarily nesting one's own sense of identity within one's family of origin discipline. It is also at this level that a professional can readily perceive there are multiple ways of knowing, accompanied with a greater appreciation for limits introduced by reductionist thinking and compartmentalization of knowledge when faced with different types of challenges. During this maturation level the professional shows signs of valuing and being able to use multiple ways of knowing to reframe challenges or problems spanning complicated and complex qualities. Expected moral development (under Kohlberg's model) at this level ranges from Stage 3 (Interpersonal: behavior driven by social approval) to Stage 5 (Social Contract: behavior driven by balance of social order and individual rights). Successful transition to the next maturation level is more challenging to make for the professional than the previous levels since it involves deeper commitment to engage with incongruities presented with overall analytic thinking when facing complexity and working with incomplete information and unknowns. Skillful coaches and mentors from Levels IV and V are necessary to help guide developmental instruction of the professional for making use of highly integrative usage of cognitive and moral reasoning skills in reflective practice wherein there are no text-book solutions for addressing complexity under high levels of uncertainty and risks. And, solution pathways are very likely to have emergent properties and require divergent ways of thinking and juxtaposition of opposing ideas and perspectives, with others involved in a distributive effort. Developmental instruction of professionals, in preparation for the next level, presents activities to engage them with distributive effort. Some forms of developmental activities could include live, virtual, and constructive (LVC) simulations to help present scenarios offering complex problems unlikely to be encountered in current practice or environments for level III (see Dörner, 1989, p. 192). LVC environments involve combinations of live and virtually-connected participants coupled with roles taken on by artificial intelligence (constructive) features. Combinatorial forms of LVC ought to involve experts across domains connected locally and virtually in teams within and across disciplinary boundaries and organization types (Stricker, et. al., 2016). Scenario designs should present complex challenges where solutions are not known and will very likely require new approaches involving interdependent sources of knowledge, thinking, and doing in a highly fluid context involving constant change, moderate levels of risk, shared sense making, commitment, and execution. At this level, the member is aware of the importance of the contributions of other disciplines to the larger collective enterprise, and also how they may need to compete with other disciplines for status and the apportionment of limited resources, but they still may not have the awareness of how one deliberately fuses those contributions into a cohesive effort.

Interdisciplinary Systemic

Level IV professionals are able to perceive porous connections among divergent ideas. They value network associations among disciplines; display understanding of systems and design thinking. In the face of complexity, involving interdependencies among opposing ideas, perspectives and observations they are capable of building coalition of effort requiring diverse areas of expertise and prolong effort where solutions are not known. The professional at this level places considerable value on multiple ways of knowing and sources of evidence and can collectively and distributively engage others for effective interdependent effort and results. A Level IV professional possesses capability to recombine new knowledge from across disciplines for new insights and interdisciplinary knowledge. Expected moral development (under Kohlberg's model) ranges from Stage 3 (Interpersonal: behavior driven by social approval) to Stage 6 (Universal ethics: behavior driven by internal moral principles). Instructional development of professionals, in preparation for Level V is similar to Level IV except for the in-depth inclusion of the professional into an existing transdisciplinary effort to observe and learn first-hand from interacting with highly skilled professionals making use of meta-skills, language, and symbols for communicating and working with complexity, via porous disciplinary and organizational boundaries, to synthesize and fuse ideas resulting in doing what has not been done before under high levels of risk. There is the element of pioneering and leading others into and through unknown frontiers often involving considerable ethical forced-choice options involving highly interdependent usage of cognitive and moral reasoning skills coupled with the means to wisely act with moral courage and commitment. Here again, LVC simulations can serve as adjunct tools to assist with developmental instruction of the professional. Senior coaches and mentors can supplement realtime inclusion activities of the professional with LVC simulations to help highlight incongruities and facilitate dialogue from simulation performance to address developmental needs associated with reflective practice for the next higher level. At this level, the member has gained a sense of identity that transcends their family-of-origin discipline's prevailing views and norms, and is willing to subordinate those priorities to ones that are more likely to help the larger organization succeed as a whole.

Transdisciplinary Synthesis

Level V is the pinnacle level for professionals who can envision and creatively leap to new insights and innovative problem reframing yielded from transdisciplinarity fusion (by sustained collective effort among people spanning porous disciplinary and organizational boundaries). Professionals at Level V are sympathetic and persuasive in communicating value of new insights and building trust-based relationships and dialogue among and across porous disciplinary boundaries to accomplish, with moral courage, what has not been done before involving synthesis-based, self-reflective transdisciplinary and ethical spirit for wise actions. Expected moral development (under Kohlberg's model) ranges from Stage 3 (Interpersonal: behavior driven by social approval) to Stage 6 (Universal ethics: behavior driven by internal moral principles). Professionals at Level V serve as senior coaches and mentors, steward the overall culture of the profession, guide the purpose and evolution of developmental instruction in the profession, and courageously lead engagement, with moral courage, of the professions in their service to society. It is incumbent of Level V professionals to also steward the next generation of leaders at this level to assume greater responsibilities for mentoring Level IV professionals for successful transition to Level V. At this level, the member not only can look across all of the subordinate disciplines of the organization they serve, but can also question if the current organizations structure and identity is still viable given the enterprise's stated goals and reasons for existence. At the highest level, the member's personal identity is not tied to any of the individual disciplines, but instead the collective effectiveness of the entire group, which facilitates the strategic choice of which disciplinary activities need to change - or cease completely - in order to realize the higher goals of the enterprise.

Overall, the levels of maturation presented above depict growth of a professional identity in the form of an epigenesis process involving increased differentiation and elaboration of various identities of self from simple forms to more complex states (see Figure 4).

The process revolves around social interactions and environmental influences interpreted by a person for assimilated or accommodative responses using evolving levels of maturing cognitive and moral reasoning skills (see Erickson, 1956; Kohlberg, 1976; Piaget, 1950; Perry, 1999). Assimilation processes, associated with identity growth, involves distorting facts that are inconsistent with one's present identity to protect positive views of the self (Whitbourne, 2002, pp 5-8). Psychological defense mechanisms of self- justification, identity projection (seeing one's own unacceptable feelings in others), defensive rigidity, and lack of insight are all forms of identity assimilation that distort present realities. Identity accommodation processes involves trying to arrive at a realistic appraisal of the self, which may ultimately change one's sense of identity. Self-doubt, looking at alternatives, and being responsive to external influences are all means of identity accommodation (Kroger, 2002, p. 85).

Growing maturity improves means to synthesize complex identifications in such a way that reciprocal relationships with society is discernible by professional identity integrity and practice (Marcia, 1966). Maladaptive development, on the other hand, results in identity diffusion (Erickson, 1956). There is a continuum associated with identity diffusion ranging from mild maladaptive foreclosure of further development to schizoid personality type at the other end (Marcia, 1966). The increasing levels of maturation depicted in the model represent positive growth potential across the lifespan. Generally, resistance to change and foreclosure of further identity growth are represented by level stagnation beyond expected

Figure 4. Professional identity growth and development model making use of the framework

Literacy \ Level	Familial Anecdotal (FA)	Disciplinary Analytic (DA)	Multidisciplinary Analytic (MA)	Interdisciplinary Analytic (IS)	Transdisciplinary Synthesis (TS)
Effectance Competence (EC)	Highly Important in very narrow scope	Very Important within branch/ department	Important as contributor with solid background	Less Important in individual areas of specialty	Less Important in individual areas of specialty
Social Intelligence (SI)	Less Important	Less Important	Important	Very Important	Highly Important
Leading People (LP)	Less Important during apprenticeship	Important as supervisor	Very Important	Very Important	Highly Important at level of setting vision
Moral Courage (MC)	Less Important	Important	Very Important as one breaks from "family of origin"	Highly Important	Highly Important
Growth Mindset (GM)	Less Important	Important	Very Important	Highly Important	Highly Important

timespans associated with normal psychosocial development stages across the lifespan (see Erickson, 1959). Foreclosure is likely to occur between levels I and II (and between II and III) when a person possesses a very high degree of fear of failure and self-esteem is exceptionally vulnerable to negative information (see Marcia, 1966).

Achieving maturation levels IV and V involves greater growth challenges and openness to change than previously encountered with earlier levels (see Figure 5). Higher degrees of assimilation and re-framing of mental sets and models used for sense making, are necessary when encountering new or divergent ideas that challenge existing ways of perceiving the self and understanding the world. Each higher maturation level introduces new demands for reflectiveness, employment, and integrative use of cognitive and moral reasoning skills. More so for achieving levels IV and V since the professional is expected to employ ways of knowing, thinking, and doing with others sufficient for addressing complexity in the face of incomplete information, no known solutions, and challenges to existing theories, doctrine, strategies, and operational practices. Also, complex challenges often present incongruities among known facts, knowledge, and practices. Professionals at levels IV and V are better able to discern the need for higher risk taking to make sense of opposing ideas, perspectives and observations to wisely address complex phenomenon. Thus, a moratorium with identity growth is likely to occur at levels II or III for some professionals unwilling or unable to address incongruities necessary to continue with identity growth and maturation (see Marcia, 1966, Perry, 1999). And, it is possible to regress from a higher level when encountering extreme and prolonged duress resulting in impairment of cognitive and moral reasoning skills (Gilbert, 1991, p. 111; Suedfeld, 1997). Toward the end of life a person is likely to regress to lower levels primarily due to impairments, but the effects of regression can be differential

Figure 5. Visual depiction of the five maturation dimensions as a growth function of professional identity development

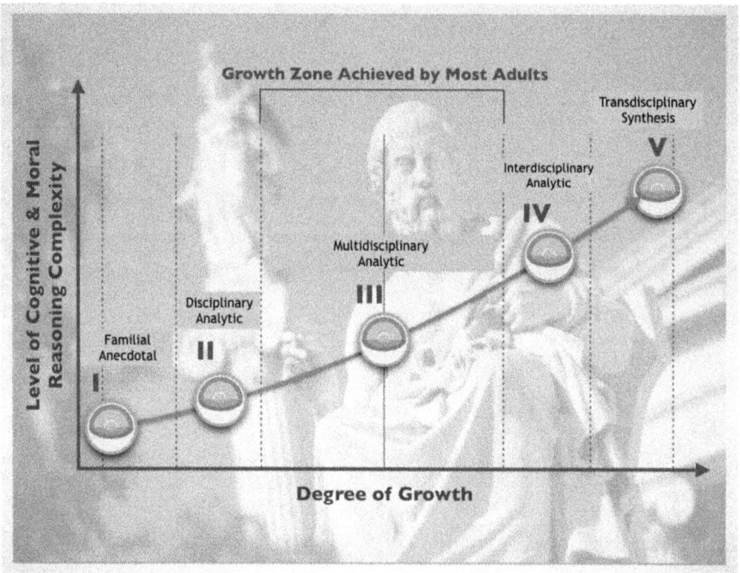

across skill dimensions (Kroger, 2002; Troll & Skaff, 1997). Attention is now turned toward a discussion of identity creation and ways for helping developmental identity maturation

SOURCES OF IDENTITY CREATION AND MATURATION

The creation and developmental maturation of an identity derive from general culture and experiences (Burke & Stets, 2009). A set of core beliefs held by a person about how they are seen in a role by others is known as an identity standard. In preparation for entering a profession a person engages in anticipatory socialization involving practicing and rehearsing a new role to acquire and reconcile new with previously held expectations of the profession with their core identity standard.

A healthy reconciliation results in congruence between the accuracy of how people see themselves (in light of expectations conveyed by mentors) and successful adaptations necessary for successful performance in the profession. Burke and Stets identified three sources instrumentally important for initially shaping a person's identity standard and accounting for developmental identity maturation: social learning, direct socialization, and reflected appraisals (p. 193). Each of the sources are briefly described below as related to the acquisition and maturation of a professional identity.

Social Learning

A person matures in their core standard conception of self, developed initially via social interactions among family and friends, by seeking out new roles and experiences which introduce adulthood elements of identity. The identity maturation process, picks up speed in young adulthood by social modeling (e.g., via mentors and coaches) and observing what takes place in contexts beyond the local familial community of family and friends.

Identity maturation accelerates through interactions with coaches and mentors because an increase in a person's awareness helps them connect internal perspectives to external environments. Relationships with coaches or mentors help model behaviors and share ideas about the roles and behaviors that are expected in contextual or organizational settings. It provides an element of certainty and confidence that was previously ambiguous. These interactions provide an understanding and ways to make sense of the situation by providing new mental models that make complicated issues more comprehensible, and the complex ones less mystifying. The increased awareness and understanding helps cultivate a new understanding of internal and external self. These iterative processes strengthen a person's confidence and ultimately their identity through an increased understanding of their profession and their own internal beliefs.

Coaching accomplishes identity maturity by doing two things – guiding a person's orientation to help to ask the right questions in hope they will find the right answers. Real growth comes from realizations that result from proper orientation provided by interactions with coaches or mentors. Coaching helps people realize not only who they are, but who they believe they can become. Whom a person strives to be is what gives personal growth a vector and life a considerable amount of meaning. Coaching is strategic foresight that connects external perspectives and internal identity with a journey of identity maturation or self-awareness. Relationships with coaches and mentors help accelerate understanding of self by increasing internal and external situational awareness and prioritizing moral options. Identity growth in the profession of arms is vastly dependent on the expectations and resulting orientation a person perceives from the interactions with the organization and the people of the organization. The identity they perceive to be successful will be the one they will pursue. In contrast, the exploration of these organizational interactions without coaches or mentors leaves a person dependent on their own biases, experiences, and interests to gain the proper orientation which greatly diminishes their growth potential or situational awareness. Coaching and mentoring help individuals embark on a distinguishing developmental journey aimed at better understanding of self, based on collaborative guidance and opportunities to develop a greater physical, social, emotional, and cognitive understanding that strengthens identity. Increasingly, identity maturation accounts for ways of perceiving self from social relationships and roles beyond family and friends. A fundamental adjustment occurs at this junction in the development and growth of a person's public self. A person grows into perceiving that one's identity entails both structure and process. The structure consists of core familial-based perceptions of self. Process involves accommodating and assimilating one's standard identity with new social roles and perceptions of how others see and accept them in those roles. Once a person's mind has arisen in the social process it makes possible the development of that process into much more complex forms of social interaction (Mead, 1934, p. 226). How well the process functions for constructive growth of identity depends upon direct socialization and reflective appraisals.

Direct Socialization

Successful accommodation and assimilation of new social identities with a person's core standard identity involves working out the correct identity standards expected of the professional role. Learning what is expected for fulfilling a new role and position in a profession involves formal education and direct socialization due to complexity of knowledge and skills expected of a profession, the inter-connectivity of positions, groups, and organizations, and the number of others that depend upon correct performance of the person in the profession (Burke & Stets, 2009, p. 194). Beyond knowledge and skill, the means to act correctly in a profession also involves reflectiveness about one's intentions to "be a particular kind of person" and care exercised in monitoring performance in the professional role. Developmentally, reflectiveness in professional practice is increasingly moral in nature (Argyris & Schön, p. 171).

Reflected Appraisals

Reflectiveness starts early in life by how a person thinks others define him or her. With growing maturity, reflectiveness takes into consideration moral qualities with the means to increasingly define perceptions of self and social identity on the basis of moral universals rather than singularly appraising one's social identity and behavior on the basis how those in authority see, validate, and judge. At higher levels of maturity, a person perceives with greater clarity a "categorical imperative" wherein a profession calls for the development of a larger self which identifies with the interests of others. There is awareness that when called upon to serve the interests of others by sacrifice, in the end, the self becomes larger. Association with a professional society makes possible the development of a social identity with means to fulfill the categorical imperative; and in reciprocal fashion, the mature self makes the professional society possible for the next generation (Mead, 1934, p. 386). Serving in a profession at this higher level of maturity is represented in better judgments, both cognitively and morally.

USAGE OF FRAMEWORK FOR DEVELOPMENTAL INSTRUCTION

Understanding the nature of transitions between levels in the framework's model is key for addressing how to help people orient and grow by means of developmental instruction involving teaching, coaching, mentorship and facilitating social/community interactions.

Research by Perry and colleagues (1999) highlight the following characteristics and instructional practices associated with helping a person transition from one level to the next (pp. 234-242):

- Development of meta-thinking about growth (insight about one's current situation to envision and value future growth and recognition that growth can take place along the dimensions of intellectual and moral levels throughout life) is facilitated by teaching that encourages groping (exploration) and reflection of present intellectual and moral incongruities and what higher levels of intellectual and moral development entails.
- The mindset from transitioning to one level to the next higher growth level is characterized by a felt need to address a perceived choice to either re-orient identity of self towards moving to the higher level or to "escape" by detaching or alienating from committing to growth.
- Committing to growth is more likely when there is a sense of membership in a community wherein there is perception that growth choices and struggle are commonly experienced by peers, mentors and teachers and there is openness among members about their intellectual and moral growth (see Argyris & Schön, 1974, p. 157).
- Mentors, coaches, and teachers should engage with junior members in the community to help integrate their learning with active and regular interpretation of their lives, as generally relevant to the student's construal of the world and their current level of growth maturation, and present the

intellectual and moral incongruities which best challenge the student at the leading edge of their growth level

- Each transition to a higher growth level requires courage by a student to assume risks for each forward movement (e.g., risks are associated with how the next growth level challenges an existing worldview, identity, and role in a community); consequently, although the student needs to make the decision to go forward, they ought to be encouraged and invited to take up new responsibilities in alignment with the higher level and be confirmed by members in a community representing the higher growth level

There is considerable distance between the ideal practices described above and the reality of current developmental practices offered via contemporary informal and formal education programs. There are many reasons for this current state. For one, while there is general recognition of the value of intellectual and moral reasoning growth in students, regardless of age, it is rarely addressed using a developmental scheme with the means to provide a basis for expected growth, accompanied with appropriate instructional practices, consistent with helping to transition students to higher levels of intellectual and moral reasoning. And, there is generally a lack of precision to introduce calculated incongruities required to instigate movement toward the next developmental growth level.

There is also the need to prepare instructors, coaches, and mentors with the means to steward students, at transition points, to better reflect on present intellectual and moral incongruities and assist with movement toward the next developmental level. At points of transition the student is likely to misconstrue what the teacher, coach, or mentor is doing; it is a crucial moment. Encouragement should be given to students to take risks to explore the incongruities. Less emphasis should be placed on correctness and procedures and more on patterns involved with the interplay of intellectual and moral reasoning required for addressing complexity wherein forms of knowing entwine with meta-thinking about uncertainty in highly trans-disciplinary, contextual, and socially interdependent ways.

THE MATURE PROFESSIONAL IN THE FACE OF COMPLEXITY

Professions depend on a relative degree of stability in order to justify their place and priority in the societies they serve - their skills built over time are based on regularities in the structure of problems that lend themselves to disciplined approaches to solutions, ones that enable an established body of knowledge and expertise to be continually relevant. But what if stability itself is inherently limited? Even the Pre-Socratic Greek philosophers realized the inherent limits of stability, famously captured in Heraclitus' observation captured in Plutarch's *On the El at Delphi* that "Ever-newer waters flow on those who step into the same rivers", which later morphed into the falsely attributed yet conceptually valid misquote, "No man ever steps in the same river twice, for it's not the same river and he's not the same man."

Ever since their outgrowth from the origins of natural philosophy introduced by the Greeks, the task of the sciences, professions, and strategy (which takes its very etymology from the Greek word *strategos*, or general) has been to propose and validate theories that help us understand, order, predict, and control the world around us. Since the Enlightenment, the tendency has been to seek order and regularity of structure in the world and capture it empirically, using the new sciences of mathematics and management to seek efficiencies in process and design. But many of the dominant management and leadership practices ignore that many of the things people care about can't be easily defined formally, or captured in an enduring process or algorithm, even if the psychological motivations that drive social interaction remain constant across the ages. As Gary Klein observed in his book *Streetlights and Shadows: The Keys to Adaptive Decisionmaking*, the traditional management and leadership methods taught in most schools work well even with complicated problems when those problems are well structured, but in the face of complexity - cases where the structure of the problem and the definition of "winning" is in flux - such deliberate methods fail, and usually create multiple problems for each one they attempt to solve (Klein, 2009). Both Anne Marie Slaughter and General Stanley McChrystal have recently pointed out that most of our senior strategic leaders mindsets are dominated by a "chessmaster mindset" that attempts to apply leadership approaches designed for well-ordered (complicated) problems to ill structured (complex) ones, which are increasingly leading to undesired results in an increasingly complex world (McChrystal, 2015, Slaughter, 2017). While there will always be the need to seek and even create the structure needed to coordinate and harness the various activities of diverse social communities towards the achievement of common aims, part of the task of leaders at the very top levels is to recognize that irreducible complexity - and the inherent levels of uncertainty that accompany complexity - are realities that must be accounted for in their leadership approaches. This was also recognized by business strategy guru Henry Mintzberg, who described the challenge of leaders as simultaneously planning "deliberate strategies" for the well-ordered parts of the challenge, while accommodating the "emergent strategies" that can accommodate the unforeseeable challenges and opportunities that will emerge from the complex elements of the task (Mintzberg, 1994). Figure 6 depicts Mintzbergs' forms of strategy. The challenge and opportunity arising from complexity and the emergence it creates was also referred to by Carl Von Clausewitz in his classic work *On War*, in which one of the three main components of the "Wondrous Trinity" at the center of his theory of war, the "the play of chance and probability within which the creative spirit is free to roam" (Clausewitz, 1832).

A professional at higher maturity levels is better able to cognitively discern differences between complicated and complex problems. Aristotle referred to this discernment as "virtues of thought." Importantly, Aristotle also highlighted "virtues of character" as critical for fine and right action. When faced with making decisions and acting in complex situations, wherein not all facts are known or can be known,

Figure 6. Forms of strategy (from Mintzberg, the rise and fall of strategic planning)

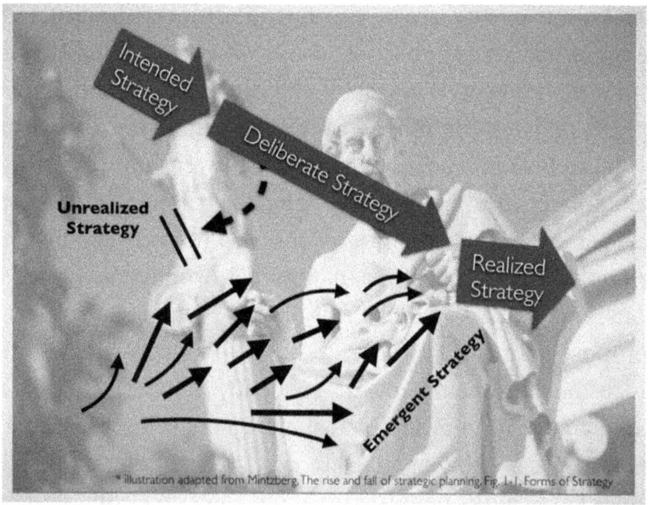

a professional will need to call upon both types of virtues. At higher levels of maturity a professional engages in a method of morality to better inform judgments and actions to address complexity. When faced with complex cases, a professional cannot be told what must be the form of their judgments. One cannot lay down in advance fixed rules as to just what should be done. More importantly, leaders at this level realize that they cannot possibly hope to deal with all of the issues on their own, and that their key task is to recruit and empower multidisciplinary teams that have the requisite variety of viewpoints, and diversity of skills, to define the most useful problems to solve, and tackle core issues rather than instantly jumping to treating for surface symptoms while the deeper sources of multiple problems go unaddressed. In a highly complex world, issues cannot be broken up into disciplinary silos and solved at one time - adjustments must be made at multiple points in the ecosystem - both simultaneously and iteratively - to drive its realized results into desired directions. In a free society the public places trust in the development of professionals to better enable them with means to proceed in the face of complexity. Development of professionals in a free society should prepare them with a plan of action executed in alignment with a method of morality that takes into account interests which make up a republic. There is societal expectation that a professional may from time to time be called upon to exercise judgement and action at a higher level than commonly practiced when essential to moral conduct. While this level of professional maturity is desired in all professions it is especially desirable for those in the Profession of Arms.

CONCLUSION

Identity theory and research offer important insights for helping to guide the development of professionals across the lifespan of service vital to the public's well being. A key insight is the significance for understanding and applying how a person's identity standard in a profession (coherent sense of self) undergoes transitions at key developmental thresholds associated with higher levels of cognitive and moral reasoning skills and abilities. Tied to this insight is research supporting the benefits for developmental instruction of identity growth to improve judgment and behavior by a professional. Judgment and behavior in professional practice are intertwined with developmental literacies associated with character, competence, moral courage, and growth commitment. Taking these literacies seriously by a professional requires a strong growth commitment to self for lifelong development and excellence in virtuous service. Another insight offered is the importance placed upon using a developmental scheme to coach, mentor, and instruct professionals for progress to higher levels of identity growth and maturation in the profession. Instructional practices have been identified for helping professionals transition effectively to higher growth levels along with importance for preparing coaches, mentors, and instructors to use developmental instructional practices known to be effective at each level. There is a profound need to better develop professionals for higher levels of maturity, with virtues of character, fine thought, and right action to act in alignment with values of a free society in a complex world.

SUGGESTIONS FOR FUTURE SCHOLARSHIP AND RESEARCH

Scholastic investigations and research studies, strengthening the connection between identity growth and maturation to professional education programs ought to be conducted to examine the correlation between the developmental levels of maturation with targeted literacies identified in this chapter. Also, further prototyping and validation of appropriate LVC simulation designs should continue accompanied with support for helping prepare coaches, mentors, and instructors in the use of developmental instructional models for guiding their efforts. Considerable advances have taken place with identity theory and research offering new insights, opportunities, and capabilities for guiding the development of professionals with much greater precision throughout their lifespan of service.

DISCLAIMER

The views and opinions expressed in this chapter do not necessarily reflect the views and opinions held by the U.S. Department of Defense, The United States Air Force, or The Air University. This chapter is cleared for public release; case number: AETC-2019-0056.

REFERENCES

Argyris, C., & Schön, D. A. (1974). *Theory in practice: Increasing professional effectiveness*. San Francisco, CA: Jossey-Bass.

Aristotle. (1999). Nicomachean ethics (T. Irwin, Trans.). Indianapolis, IN: Hackett Publishing Company, Inc.

Army Regulation 350-53. (2014). *Comprehensive soldier and family fitness*. Washington, DC: Headquarters, Department of the Army.

Burke, P. J., & Stets, J. E. (2009). *Identity theory*. New York, NY: Oxford University Press. doi:10.1093/acprof:oso/9780195388275.001.0001

Campbell, J. (1949). *The hero with a thousand faces*. New York, NY: Pantheon Books.

Caza, B. B., & Creary, S. J. (2016). *The construction of professional identity*. Retrieved from Cornell University, SHA School site: http://scholarship.sha.cornell.edu/articles/878

Clausewitz, C. V. (1984). On war (M. Howard & P. Paret, Trans.). Princeton, NJ: Princeton University Press. (Originally published 1832)

Csikszentmihalyi, M. (1990). *Flow*. New York, NY: Harper & Row.

Csikszentmihalyi, M. (1996). *Creativity. Flow and the psychology of discovery and invention*. New York, NY: Harper Perennial.

Csikszentmihalyi, M. (1999). Implications of a systems perspective for the study of creativity. In R. J. Sternberg (Ed.), *Handbook of Creativity*. Cambridge University Press.

Dewey, J. (1938). *Experience and education*. New York, NY: Macmillan.

Dörner, D. (1989). *The logic of failure: Recognizing and avoiding error in complex situations*. New York, NY: Basic Books.

Dweck, C. (2016). *Mindset: The new psychology of success*. New York, NY: Penguin Random House.

Ellis, L. (2012). *Leading with honor: Leadership lessons from the Hanoi Hilton*. Atlanta, GA: Freedom Star Media.

Erickson, E. (1956). The problem of ego identity. *Journal of the American Psychoanalytic Association*, *4*(1), 56–121. doi:10.1177/000306515600400104 PMID:13286157

Erickson, E. (1959). *Identity and the life cycle*. New York, NY: International Universities Press, Inc.

Gilbert, D. T. (1991). How mental systems believe. *The American Psychologist*, *46*(2), 107–119. doi:10.1037/0003-066X.46.2.107

Goleman, D. (2007). *Social intelligence: The new science of human relationships*. New York, NY: Random House, Inc.

Hackett, J. W. (1962). *The profession of arms. The 1962 Lees Knowles lectures given at Trinity College*. Cambridge. Washington, DC: Center of Military History.

Ibarra, H. (1999). *Provisional selves: Experimenting with image and identity in professional adaptation*. Boston, MA: Harvard University.

Joint Chiefs of Staff. (2016). Retrieved from http://www.jcs.mil/Portals/36/Documents/Publications/aprofessionofarms.pdf

Klein, G. (2009). *Streetlights and shadows: The keys to adaptive decision making*. Cambridge, MA: MIT Press. doi:10.7551/mitpress/8369.001.0001

Knefelkamp, L. L. (1990). *The development of the multi-cultural self: Integrating theories of intellectual, intercultural and identity development*. Portland, OR: Summer Institute for Intercultural Communication.

Kohlberg, L. (1976). Moral stages and moralization: The cognitive-developmental approach. In T. Lickona (Ed.), *Moral Development and Behavior: Theory, Research and Social Issues*. Holt, Rinehart and Winston.

Kohlberg, L. (1981). Essays on moral development: Vol. I. *The philosophy of moral development*. San Francisco, CA: Harper & Row.

Kroger, J. (2002). Identity processes and contents through the years of late adulthood. *Identity*, *2*(1), 81–99. doi:10.1207/S1532706XID0201_05

Langer, A. (2005). Responsive organizational dynamism: Managing technology using reflective practice. *Reflective Practice*, 2.

Lencioni, P. (2000). *The four obsessions of an extraordinary executive*. San Francisco, CA: Jossey-Bass.

Marcia, J. E. (1966). Development and validation of ego-identity status. *Journal of Personality and Social Psychology*, *3*(5), 551–558. doi:10.1037/h0023281 PMID:5939604

McChrystal, S. (2015). *Team of teams: New rules of engagement for a complex world*. New York, NY: Penguin Random House.

Mead, G. H. (1934). *Mind, self, and society*. Chicago, IL: Chicago University Press.

Mintzberg, H. (1994). *The rise and fall of strategic planning*. New York, NY: Simon and Schuster.

Perry, W. G. (1999). *Forms of ethical and intellectual development in the college years: A scheme*. San Francisco, CA: Jossey-Bass, Inc.

Piaget, J. (1950). *The psychology of intelligence*. New York, NY: Routledge and Kegan Paul.

Schein, E. (1978). *Career dynamics: Matching individual and organizational needs*. Reading, MA: Addison-Wesley.

Schön, D. A. (1983). *The reflective practitioner: How professionals think in action*. London: Temple Smith.

Simonton, D. K. (2010). Creativity in highly eminent individuals. In J. C. Kaufman & R. J. Sternberg (Eds.), *The Cambridge Handbook of Creativity* (pp. 174–188). Cambridge University Press. doi:10.1017/CBO9780511763205.012

Slaughter, A. (2017). *The chessboard and the web: Strategies of connection in a networked world*. New Haven, CT: Yale University Press.

Slay, H., & Smith, D. (2010). Professional identity construction using narrative to understand the negotiation of professional and stigmatized cultural identities. *Human Relations*, *64*(1), 85–107. doi:10.1177/0018726710384290

Sternberg, R. J., & Lubart, T. I. (1999). The concept of creativity: Prospects and paradigms. In R. J. Sternberg (Ed.), *Handbook of Creativity*. New York, NY: Cambridge University Press.

Stricker, A., Arenas, F., Westhauser, T., & Hawkins-Scribner, T. (2016). Positive education of stoic warriors as reflective practitioners in the profession of arms. *Reflective Practice*, *18*(1), 133–146. doi:10.1080/14623943.2016.1251415

Stricker, A., & Lyle, D. (submitted). The mind, personality, and networks of Henry H. "Hap" Arnold. *The Journal of Military History*.

Stricker, A., Westhauser, T., Sheets, T., Hawkins-Scribner, T., & Calongne, C. (2018). Values-based network leadership in an interconnected world. *The Journal of Values Based Leadership*, *11*(1), 1–21. doi:10.22543/0733.111.1210

Stryker, S. (1980). *Symbolic interactionism: A social structural version*. Menlo Park, CA: Benjamin/Cummings Publishing Company.

Suedfeld, P. (1997). Reactions to societal trauma: Distress and/or eustress. *Political Psychology*, *18*(4), 849–861. doi:10.1111/0162-895X.00082

The Arnold Project. (1961). *Oral transcripts. Oral History Research Office, Columbia University*. New York, NY: Columbia University Libraries Rare Books and Manuscripts.

Troll, L. E., & Skaff, M. M. (1997). Perceived continuity of self in very old age. *Psychology and Aging*, *12*(1), 162–169. doi:10.1037/0882-7974.12.1.162 PMID:9100277

Whitbourne, S. K. (2002). *The aging individual: Physical and psychological perspectives* (2nd ed.). New York, NY: Springer Publishing Company, Inc.

KEY TERMS AND DEFINITIONS

Cognitive Reasoning: Acquisition of knowledge, with improved means to associate and differentiate among and between knowledge constructs, drives processes of cognitive reasoning associated with comprehension, levels of understanding, and ultimately effectance competence. Cognitive reasoning growth is dependent not only upon developing intelligence but also the environment. The means to apply cognitive reasoning successfully for adaptation or accommodation to changes, introduced by the environment, varies considerably on the basis of developmental mental level. The maturity of mental level governs the nature and quality of interactions between a person and the social environment. The nature and quality of interactions are the basis of social intelligence, supporting reciprocity between individuals, are necessary for collaboration in work and exchange of ideas. The interactions, in turn, modify a person's mental structure. Since high levels of linear and nonlinear logic, reasoning, and problem solving (e.g., complicated and complex) involve ethical dimensions there exists a morality of thinking that is indispensable for intellectual interaction and co-operation necessary for healthy life adjustment, growth, and integrity of professional service to society.

Developmental Instruction: Developmental instruction, associated with professional identity growth, involves offering instructional practices making use of social learning, direct socialization, and reflected appraisals for helping a person to transition to higher levels of cognitive and moral reasoning. Instructional practices introduce calculated incongruities required to instigate movement toward the next developmental growth level.

Identity Maturation: Identity maturation posits the development of a person's core identity across the lifespan. This perspective comes from identity process theory and research highlighting the lifelong processes of identity assimilation, accommodation, and balance. These processes are responsible for addressing change in the sense of self, over the course of adulthood, in the person's sense of identity as increasingly represented to others in society. Although personality may be stable, a person's self-knowledge and relations with others undergo alterations throughout adulthood. Identity maturation in a profession is represented by the development of a cohesive viewpoint of the professional self and efficacy in practice from growth of cognitive and moral reasoning.

Moral Reasoning: Moral reasoning is developmental across the life span. As people grow older, and as their cognitive reasoning matures, their understanding of what is right or wrong, and under what circumstances, can also change. According to Lawrence Kohlberg's theory and research on moral development, there are levels of moral reasoning. At the lowest level a person's moral reasoning is driven primarily by avoidance of getting punished. As the person matures, this lower level evolves toward absolutism regarding right and wrong and associates the law as the final arbiter of what is moral. Higher levels of moral reasoning involve the means to associate ethical principles beyond self-interests along with commitments to choices on the basis of internal ethical principles.

Professional Identity: A professional identity is a person's viewpoint of who they are as a professional serving in a domain of expertise involving high expectations in the application of special knowledge and skills. The view of self in a profession consists of beliefs, values, motives, and experiences used to define and guide growth and skillful practices involving cognitive and moral reasoning.

APPENDIX A

Scenario (Operation Pointblank Cited From https://en.wikipedia.org/wiki/Pointblank_directive)

Operation Pointblank, was the code name for the primary portion of the Allied Combined Bomber Offensive intended to cripple or destroy the German aircraft fighter strength, thus drawing it away from frontline operations and ensuring it would not be an obstacle to the invasion of Northwest Europe. The Pointblank directive of 14 June 1943 ordered RAF Bomber Command and the U.S. Eighth Air Force to bomb specific targets such as aircraft factories, and the order was confirmed when the Allies met at the Quebec Conference, 1943. Up to that point the RAF and USAAF had mostly been attacking German industry in their own way – the British by broad night attacks on industrial areas and the US in "precision attacks" by day on specific targets. The operational execution of the Directive was left to the commanders of the forces and as such even after the directive the British continued in night attacks and the majority of the attacks on German fighter production and combat with the fighters was down to the USAAF. In practice the USAAF bombers made large scale daylight attacks on factories involved in the production of fighter aircraft. The Luftwaffe was forced into defending against these raids, and its fighters were drawn into battle with the bombers and their escorts. It was these battles of attrition that reduced the Luftwaffe strength despite increases in German aircraft production. At the January 1943 Casablanca Conference, the Combined Chiefs of Staff agreed to conduct the Combined Bomber Offensive (CBO), and the British Air Ministry issued the Casablanca directive on 4 February with the object of:

The progressive destruction and dislocation of the German military, industrial and economic systems and the undermining of the morale of the German people to a point where their capacity for armed resistance is fatally weakened. Every opportunity to be taken to attack Germany by day to destroy objectives that are unsuitable for night attack, to sustain continuous pressure on German morale, to impose heavy losses on German day fighter force and to conserve German fighter force away from the Russian and Mediterranean theaters of war.

On 14 June 1943, the Combined Chiefs of Staff issued the Pointblank directive which modified the February 1943 Casablanca directive. Along with the single-engine fighters of the CBO plan, the highest priority Pointblank targets were the fighter aircraft factories since the Western Allied invasion of France could not take place without fighter superiority. In August 1943, the Quebec Conference upheld this change of priorities. Among the factories listed were the Regensburg Messerschmitt factory (which would be attacked at high cost in August), the Schweinfurter Kugellagerwerke ball-bearing factory in tandem with Regensburg and (attacked again in October) and the Wiener Neustädter Flugzeugwerke (WNF) which produced Bf 109 fighters.

The Schweinfurt–Regensburg mission was carried out by Boeing B-17 Flying Fortress heavy bombers of the U.S. Army Air Forces on August 17, 1943, it was an ambitious plan to cripple the German aircraft industry. The mission was also known as the "double-strike mission" because it entailed two large forces of bombers attacking separate targets in order to disperse fighter reaction by the Luftwaffe, and was the first American "shuttle" mission, in which all or part of a mission landed at a different field and later bombed another target before returning to its base. After being postponed several times by unfavorable weather, the operation, known within the Eighth Air Force as "Mission No. 84", was flown on the anniversary of the first daylight raid by the Eighth Air Force.

Mission No. 84 was a strike by 376 bombers of sixteen bomb groups against German heavy industry well beyond the range of escorting fighters. The mission inflicted heavy damage on the Regensburg target, but at catastrophic loss to the force, with 60 bombers lost and many more damaged beyond economical repair. As a result, the Eighth Air Force was unable to follow up immediately with a second attack that might have seriously crippled German industry. When Schweinfurt was finally attacked again two months later, the lack of long-range fighter escort had still not been addressed and losses were even higher. As a consequence, deep penetration strategic bombing was curtailed for five months.

Of those involved with Operation Pointblank, how might perspectives taken late in August 1943 reflect maturation dimensions concerning deep penetration strategic bombing? Brief narrative perspectives are offered from the recall of individuals, directly or indirectly involved with Operation Pointblank, regarding elements associated with basic strategy, operations, and assessment of outcomes. Please note the following examples of perspectives are illustrative only and ought not to be viewed as definitive for accurate placement of the individuals into maturation levels simply on the basis of a single event and usage of short narratives from memory recall.

Level 1: Familial Anecdotal Perspective

Individual [M]: "I immediately found myself in a world alien to everything I had ever experienced. There were ME-109s and FW-190s leaping into existence from everywhere without warning. When they opened fire you saw sudden flashes of light winking at you from the distance. All at once there existed a canopy of cannon shells and bombs, aerial mines and rockets exploding everywhere. Each one was intent on hitting our pregnant bomb load and us. We are no longer in a stately march in tight formation through the upper heavens. We try desperately to return to the crisp efficiency of our tight formation, but it is impossible to achieve in this raging space of time. We find ourselves slogging our way through a thickening mass of exploding flame and smoke, with the equal determination of every member of the crew. We are driving ahead through a solid whirlwind of steel splinters, flame, and jagged chunks of red hot metal. The steel is everywhere; it crashes into wings, engines, bulkhead and airplane bodies; and into the bodies of men--spewing blood, tissues, intestines, and brains. The plane seemingly is alive with lights as all the guns are firing and the noise is deafening. There is the continued on the intercom shout of "incoming bandits" from all around the clock (fighters). The fourteen caliber 50 machine guns of our plane can be heard and felt above all the roar of the plane. Our world seems to plunge into insanity as the sounds of air battle are all around us seemingly merging into an inhuman shriek. Our ship doesn't seem to be occupied by men, we are transformed into beings from another world, with the strange breathing systems dangling beneath our faces…[Upon return from the mission]… As we all proceed to debriefing you look around and the faces this morning, which had the look of expectation, are now gray and blank. We are all thinking of too many friends who have gone down in flames before our eyes. What about tomorrow and the tomorrow after that? There are too many concrete handstands stained with oil and grease where the bombers had once stood so majestically are now standing empty, only a terrible aching void remains. A ground crewman is seen aimlessly walking off looking as if he had lost his brother. The German pilots knew all too well their effectiveness against our bombers. They witnessed the burning planes, bombers with the wings torn off, crews tumbling through the air, and the burning bodies. How could those bomber crews take such punishment and hand it back while continuing to fly towards the target? There never was a question of not reaching the target, no matter how many formations were split apart, how many bombers were in flame, and how cruel the test. We continued on with white knuckles and a tightened pucker string." (Source: http://www.kilroywashere.org/003-Pages/Hoffman/03-Harm--Hoffman.html)

Interpretation: The perspective held by Individual [M] displays a high level of effectance competence and commitment to performing one's duty. Direct observation, personal assumptions, and experiences are primarily driving interpretation of events and expected behaviors. The perspective conveys awareness of incongruities associated with intent and duty in tension with outcome and perseverance in the face of great cost and risk.

Level II: Disciplinary Analytic Perspective

Individual [S]: "I was concentrating so much on flying in formation. When I'd look up, the sky would be loaded with six or eight fighters coming at us. Over Schweinfurt, even flying at 25,000 feet, our crew braved what seemed like a solid wall of flak to drop their bombs. After the first bombing raid in August, the Nazis had beefed up anti-aircraft defenses around the city. Those crews fortunate enough to have reached the target found themselves chased by fighters for hundreds of miles home, across Germany, Holland and Belgium. The Germans shot down 60 Flying Fortresses that day, killing or capturing 639 airmen. An additional 121 had been damaged so badly they needed major repairs before they could fly again. We lucked out; brought the aircraft home with only one bullet hole.

It surprised me…I expected to be full of holes. We were constantly being shot at. The bombs took a fearful toll in Schweinfurt, killing 276 Germans, mostly civilians. All five ball-bearing factories had been hit, and Allied commanders at first labeled the raid a success. Only after the war did they learn the damage to the machines producing the bearings had been limited, and production quickly bounced back. The Nazis scattered the factories around the country, so there would be no crippling blows in the future." (Source: https://www.stripes.com/news/americans-germans-recall-deadly-wwii-raid-1.25148https://www.stripes.com/news/americans-germans-recall-deadly-wwii-raid-1.25148)

Interpretation: The perspective held by Individual [S] displays a high level of effectance competence, commitment to leading the bomber crew, and overall contribution to the intent of the mission and outcomes. Along with direct observation, personal assumptions and experiences, Individual [S] displays willingness to reinterpret experiences on basis of input involving data and analysis. Moral reasoning is also indicated from the usage of "fearful toll" in relation to the statistic: "276 Germans, mostly civilians." The perspective conveys awareness of incongruities associated with intent and duty in tension with outcome and perseverance.

Level III: Multidisciplinary Analytic Perspective

Individual [X]: "Nobody in industry, or in the scientific community, however, had brought in any drawings for one, or even suggested one. The first rumble that this might be possible was when the Mustang was first built by North American. A little earlier than the Lightning, a twin-engined Lockheed, had come along, with superchargers, and it looked as if we had a chance. It was very good for photographic reconnaissance on a long mission; but in most cases they even took the guns off it to give it more performance. If you hung wing tanks on it…The business of putting wing tanks on a plane extended the range of aircraft tremendously. But even when that came along the fighter people were very doubtful as to whether you ought to take that kind of an aircraft into Germany, because it was a vulnerable target. If the Germans hit those wing tanks, why, the ship was lost. So we were just experimenting with the Lightning and the Lockheed. In the earlier days they attempted to accompany the bombers several hundred miles inside Germany or inside the continent of Europe, and then they would drop their wing tanks if they were called upon to fight. They couldn't tarry long, however, because their fuel would just get them back. That was the first incubation of the new strategy in the long-range fighter. You will always find that the best tacticians, the best strategists, in a military area, deal with what they know to be the possibilities of weapons in those times. There is no point in their doing anything else. It would be a serious weakness on the part of a commander of a staff to plan some conflict or strategy with weapons which wouldn't be produced for several years. That would be stupid. You have to plan to use what weapons you have and can visualize as being available in your time span. We didn't have long-range fighters then.

Interpretation: The perspective held by Individual [X] displays an awareness of contributing factors and multiple disciplinary dependencies associated with mission options and likelihood of success. Individual [X] displays willingness to reinterpret experiences on basis of input involving data and analysis (e.g., from "the fighter people") there are are hints of recognizing that the problem associated with the lack of long-range fighters is both complicated and complex (incongruities associated with usage of extra fuel tank, coupled with dropping them to gain better performance when engaging in air-to-air combat with higher risks for not having enough fuel for a safe return). Options with engine performance enhancement, however, was not mentioned as means for addressing the incongruities. Moral reasoning is indicated from the expression of concern for safe return and exposure of pilots to greater vulnerabilities." (The Arnold Project, 1961).

Individual [Q]: "By the way, I'd like to stress that Schweinfurt also came out of my office. At this time, information tells us that this is the only point where he is building the small precision ball bearings…for precision instruments, and he's only building them in Schweinfurt, and he doesn't recognize the fact that we have listed that as a critical target. My plan for Schweinfurt is, 600 B-17's, no less, to be bombing the target as late in the afternoon as they can and still arrive home before sundown, because if you start coming home at night, this myopic mind of Goering's will chase you in, and he'll shoot you while you're there. If you want to be protected you've got to get your day bombers down before sundown. So they should bomb late in the afternoon…[xxxx] agreed to it—that he will follow up that day bombing raid with a fire carpet that night. See, we make tinder out of the target, and he puts the fire carpet on it. Now, that will warp every precision instrument that he's got. There may be some bricks still left standing, but the instruments will be gone, and they're precision instruments, and it'll be months before he has another plant, when he's got to start from scratch and build another plant. Now, the next one he's going to build underground, and I stressed that all you do when you take any target is to reduce the importance to the construction program for the period of time that it takes the enemy to replace that installation, and the German can do anything like that about twice as fast as we can. I don't think we would have kept the

Schweinfurt plant out—would have had this impact—for more than about six months. As I say, in about six months he'd have had another Schweinfurt. We thought we'd destroy him forever. You don't destroy anything forever; anything that was made by man can be remade by man and remade a little better. In fact, sometimes if you destroy old stuff, you make for better modern stuff. I don't think that we did too much permanent damage to the Ruhr, I think we helped them. The bastards have got a better installation in there now than they had when we knocked it down. They've built modern equipment. We threw away their obsolete equipment—we destroyed it. You look at the Ruhr right now; by God, it's in good condition, it's good. I think for instance that London might have been a little better had the Germans leveled it a little more. Those [xxxxxxxx] cow pasture lanes that you have to go through, and half of London you can't get around because you can't drive a car." (The Arnold Project, 1961).

Interpretation: The perspective held by Individual [Q] displays sense making of complicated challenges associated with the intent of the mission coupled with a sobering post-reflection of mission outcomes acknowledging German resiliency for rapid recovery and reconstitution of manufacturing capabilities. The post-reflection indicates awareness and appreciation of limits with holding the initial perspective that although the intent of the mission was to remove the means to construct small precision ball bearings, the outcome was the Germans were able to rebuild and improve upon their capability. Further developmental growth of Individual [Q] is indicated by the inconsistencies between cognitive and moral reasoning from the over-extension of the post-reflection with the view that the Germans ought to have leveled more of London for similar reconstruction benefits.

Level IV: Interdisciplinary Systemic Perspective

Individual (Y): "[X] First-rate chap. He was a very good officer. He was much more interested, of course—I think that was common among American air forces—in the purely air side of the operation than in the overall strategy. That was a difference, I think, between our two services, due to the fact that we'd had an independent air force for many years. I was a joint planner in 1928. For many years one had been accustomed to having a joint say and a joint responsibility in the overall strategic policy. [X] was not very interested in that side of it. He was also, of course, very much interested in things like Operation Strangle, the tactical air operations of Italy. But when it came to these strategic arguments about whether we should put forces into Yugoslavia or invade southern France, [X]'s attitude towards that sort of thing was much more detached than mine. His main interest in the operation was very different from mine. I was against operation Anvil because I thought that the important thing was to finish the war with a British-American force on the Danube. [X], I think, was mainly against it because he thought it would detract from Pointblank. So by the nature of his training and his whole background, by the fact that the American Air Force before the War had not been responsible for having anything to do with basic strategy, I think his attitude was much more centered on purely Air than we on the British Air Force side. Then, of course, it was purely explained by the American attitude to war (which is very different now). During the war, their attitude was, well, our business is to win this war, period, and to hell with anything else. We were always much more liable to think of the political effect of the war after it was over. I remember a great friend of mine in the Mediterranean, having violent arguments with him about the East and what's going to happen after the war in the Middle East. The American attitude was, "To hell with that, what's that got to do with us? Our job is to beat the Germans, then we'll go home and live happily ever after." Our attitude was, "What are we fighting a war for, if it isn't to create the situation you want to see after the war?" I think that would partly explain the differences of approach to these problems, between [X] and myself. Porter had a very good global outlook; I mean that he had an upbringing as a strategic thinker. He was a Joint Planner in the very early days, the late twenties, and he'd been brought up, as I was, as Brooks was, as many of us were, to be thinking about that sort of thing. The charter of the British Chiefs of Staff was that they were not only responsible for their own service, but they were responsible for joint advice on operations and policy as a whole. Porter wasn't only concerned with the air side. He always felt it a part of his job to take part in the major strategic decisions and influence major policies." (The Arnold Project, 1961)

Interpretation: The perspective held by Individual [Y] displays awareness of the porous connections among operational perspectives and approaches held, and taken, by military services. Individual [Y] also displays systems thinking and recognition of complexity associated with joint-interdependencies among military services impacting basic strategy. Highly integrative cognitive and moral reasoning is displayed by acknowledgment of interdependent strategic purposes associated with complex elements between war and consequential long-term political effects. High level of engagement is also displayed rather than "detachment" from consequential decisions and outcomes.

Individual (U): "…there was the strategic idea—not the 500 mile bomber range…there was some hemisphere thought involved in it, but I'm not sure which was the factor there. I'm pointing out that it was not one factor alone which brought out this desire for a long range bomber, which later became the strategic bomber. Then there was another element. I remember sitting on the Development Board, when the question of developing a big bomber came up, and we finally agreed in the board to build 500 mile bomber. The idea was beginning to develop that maybe we could develop something that would go as far as possible, instead of just putting an arbitrary short-range limit, and we reached out in the blue for something we thought was way beyond what they could do. What I'm trying to say is, in my opinion there's no one thing that produced all this. The Air Force people wanted to build something that would go a lot further that, and would operate beyond the sphere of the division and corps commander, and beyond the scope of the Army commander. As the result of that, the GHQ Air Force was born, which would be under the GHQ commander, not under the (Army) division and corps commander. The formation of GHQ was not a compromise; it was quite a step forward at that time, because GHQ had the responsibility for strategic targets, not for what they called tactical targets. The difference between them is that tactical targets affected the immediate battle and strategic affected the future battles of the war." (The Arnold Project, 1961).

Interpretation: The perspective held by Individual [U] displays systems and design thinking to help address complexity, surrounding challenges associated with what it takes to obtain strategic effects, by the expressed desire and willingness to explore what was possible with bombers to "go as far as possible…we reached out in the blue for something we thought was way beyond what they could do…there's no one thing that produced all this." There is also recognition of strategic value from collective and distributive engagement of diverse perspectives by going "beyond the sphere" of existing organizational models and structures.

Level V: Transdisciplinary Synthesis Perspective

Individual [R]: "They knew, …that he was sympathetic to the basic belief, which was that in fighting an enemy like Germany that had built up buffer captive states around it, you couldn't get at the heart of Germany by land. You didn't have the manpower. You couldn't do it in time. So you had to find some other way to get at the heart of Germany. Germany in all previous wars had made a profit—it had always fought the war on somebody's else's land, where the devastation occurred. Its own homeland had been free from it. This time, the only way to get at them was through the air, and we knew we could do it. We simply needed the machinery and the trust and the faith, and the manufacturing skills, which were ultimately developed. So once the relationship of complete solidarity of view was established, and once the competence of the individual had been tested, you were accepted by this top band of brothers. In being so accepted, there was none of this division between the civilian and the military. It simply did not exist. Individual [P] had this quality of profound optimism, of absolute certainty of victory in the future, of a dedication to this effective use of air power. If you choose to use an unfortunate word like "vision" he had enough vision to see that we could do with this field of things that had up to that time been thought impossible. He had a great deal of imagination, in its proper sense, and he inspired in others the confidence which he felt. Individual [P] was very enthusiastic about the ideas that they [British] had, in many fields. They were in a class by themselves. That's the great area in which they were of enormous, invaluable help to us. The other thing was that their Rolls Royce engine was, to our everlasting shame as the motor car center of the world, always better than our best liquid-cooled engine. But the liquid-cooled Allison [engine] was never as good as the Rolls Royce, and the proof was that we put the Rolls Royce American built into our Mustang P-51 fighters. That was a healthy thing to find out pretty early. The Air Force was red in the face, because they were the ones that had been pressing for this Allison engine, and in every known test—including the high horsepower out-take of those engines on what's called military power with water injection—Rolls was much better. There wasn't any question about it. That was a humbling experience. That was good for us. The radio was humbling. The radar was humbling. A lot of the night techniques, a lot of the landing techniques. We had a lot to learn. The British were very good about making that available to us, and it came awfully hard for some of those professional Army boys to admit that the British were better, but they were. So, profiting by the British experience in developing special target programs, when we got into this area, it was obvious that we needed to know everything that we could know about the German complex of industry and methods of road transport, water and rail transport—those areas, for example, where the canal ran on fills as compared to where it ran on cuts, because you could bomb the fill out. So we collected a group of those who had found it part of their business to travel in Germany—that is, American industrialists who had plants in Germany, American rail men who had traveled in Germany in connection with their business, and more particularly, consulting engineers and bankers who had spent a lot of time in Germany on joint projects. This became our target group, and we spent weeks and months developing the documentation leading to giving a priority order to the target command." (The Arnold Project, 1961).

Interpretation: The perspective held by Individual [R] displays systems and design thinking to help address complexity, surrounding challenges associated with what it takes to obtain strategic effects, by the expressed desire and willingness to explore what was possible with bombers "we knew we could do it." There is also recognition of strategic value from coalition of effort, involving distributive engagement of diverse perspectives, to go "beyond the sphere" by rethinking existing organizational models and approaches. The perspective taken by Individual [R] also displays very high levels of social intelligence, leading people, moral courage, and a growth mindset by reference between "trust and faith" with "skills" to the value of individual competence in alignment with coalition of effort (e.g., "band of brothers"). There is also acknowledgement of the importance played by imagination, inspiration, and belief in "doing the impossible" by referencing to Individual [P]. Humility is a driving force with Individual [R]'s growth mindset associated with a willingness to learn and obtain insights from a variety of sources and input necessary for "doing the impossible" resulting from a coalition of effort requiring diverse areas of expertise and prolong effort.

Individual [Z]: "He got along well with people. Individual [P] made it a point, you know, to talk to all kinds of people. If he would come out to visit the plant—during the War, or afterward—and walk around, he'd invariably grab a few mechanics and sit down and try to find out what their viewpoint was. I've been with him at a training base, outside of Ft. Worth, during the War, when he did the same thing. He had the commanding officer bring in all these boys who'd had various troubles in their training program, make them talk, and make them take their hair down and tell him just what they thought. Things like that. He had a very keen way of getting people to talk openly and honestly to him. He was very moral. I'd say he was an intensely curious man. If you traveled with him through a plant or a training base, he had to know everything. A great man for pulling information out of people. He was very intensely curious about everything. He was foresighted, about developing contacts between military and science. I went up to talk to him at Hamilton Field. At that time, he was thinking of the necessity of some sort of a research or thinking group, but not in government service. It was as a result of that thinking that this RAND Corporation was founded, that we first had under our wing. It was Individual [P]'s own idea. He was quite social. He wouldn't take criticism as reflecting on him personally. I think that's why people respected Individual [P]. He never held a grudge, not at all." (The Arnold Project, 1961).

Interpretation: The perspective held by Individual [Z] is shared to better convey insights about Individual [P] and importance towards overall strategic means enabled by the collective usage of literacies so effectively practiced at Level V to sympathetically communicate and persuade others the value of new insights. Individual [P] is used by Individuals [R] and [Z] as an exemplar of a professional with the means to build trust-based relationships and dialogue across networked, porous disciplinary boundaries (e.g., involving military and scientific communities), to accomplish what has not been done before.

APPENDIX B

Kohlberg's Moral Development Model

Figure 7. Kohlberg's moral development model depicting levels and stages across the lifespan.

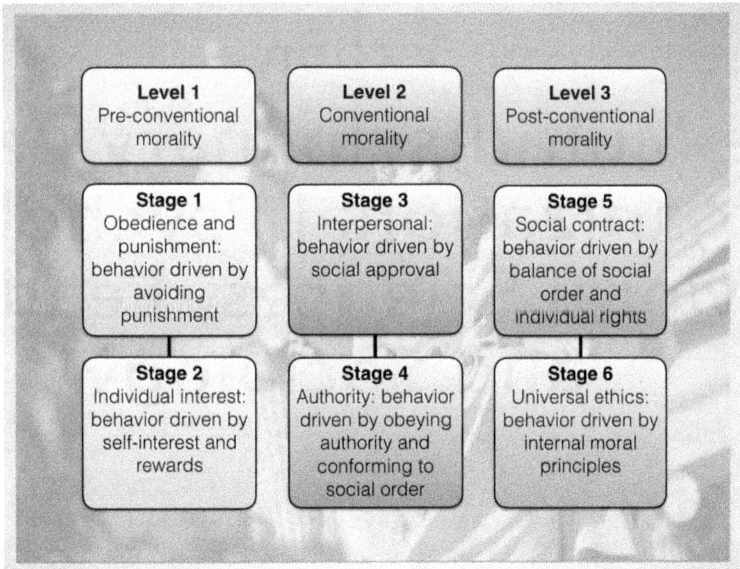

Section 2

The Multidisciplinary Lens of Organizational Psychology, Behavioral Sciences, Leadership, and Sociology

Chapter 3
The Claim on Human Conviviality in Cyberspace

Fil J. Arenas
https://orcid.org/0000-0003-1747-0706
The Air University, USA

Daniel A. Connelly
The Air University, USA

ABSTRACT

This chapter sets out by defining conviviality in a way that allows the term to be simultaneously applied to face-to-face and virtual experiences. The educational context is introduced as one of many that can benefit from both types of experience. Impairment of the components of a shared learning experience (self, others, teacher) does not have to occur if educators understand the unique combination produced by the content to be learned plus the markers of the type of learning experience selected. Matching the content to the medium produces the optimal results. The authors conclude that conviviality in a specific application is not only possible, but potentially highly productive in cyberspace, minimizing the logistical, high-risk, and cognitive constraints identified by Calandra and Puvirajah that can impair other forms of communication and specifically non-cyber learning experiences. This chapter contributes to new era of human interaction literature in the age of virtuality.

INTRODUCTION

Technology today is an overwhelming force. The available handheld information devices are becoming a necessity for those that need to remain connected for real-time information. According to Hopkins and Turner (2012), there are more handheld devices available in the world than toothbrushes! Although technology experts and futurists proclaim that we are still very much in the transformational stages of technological evolution, many feel that we are barely in the age of discovery (Bonk, 2010). Millenials, the next generation entering society after the turn of the century, have adapted the use of their electronic devices throughout their daily routines. Unlike generations of the past, they communicate through texts

DOI: 10.4018/978-1-5225-9679-0.ch003

Figure 1. Virtual West Point dining hall
(Image Credit: Andrew Stricker)

and instant messages as opposed to phone calls. For entertainment, millenials prefer to personally download their music, stream movies, and choose dating partners online. The Internet becomes the information center for inquiries about restaurants, cars, medical providers, electronics, or various appliances or services (Burstein, 2013).

A recent PEW Center survey of U.S. adults discovered that the social media preferences for 2018 were a mix of long-standing trends with emerging choices. Facebook and YouTube were the top two social media networks chosen by adults, while younger Americans (18 to 24-year-olds) desired platform diversity. Approximately 78% of this younger demographic use Snapchat, reporting that 71% visited multiple times daily. Additionally, 71% of this group also utilized Instagram, while nearly 45% leveraged Twitter as well. Although Facebook remains the most widely used social media by some 68% Americans today and YouTube the video-sharing platform as their next choice, no other social media sites were chosen by more than 40% Americans in this survey. Further, the PEW Center has inquired about five trending platforms from previous surveys and have focused on five choices by Americans: Facebook, Twitter, Instagram, LinkedIn, and Pinterest. The media preferences across the U.S. population remains constant since the 2016 survey with the exception of one platform; Instagram. This platform use has increased to 35% since the 2016 survey where 28% of the population chose this site previously (Smith & Anderson, 2018).

Social media is alive and well in the U.S., but how does that impact daily face-to-face interaction among Americans. Does this mean that our day-to-day human interaction has been decreased? How much of this human interaction have we lost each day? How may this affect overall human conviviality and relationships throughout our population. How much has social media impacted our culture? Does social media influence empathy, a key ingredient in human relationships?

A recent study has documented that Facebook and Twitter has affected the adolescent population based on their use of these networks. Moreover, these adolescents not only displayed high scores in the area of empathy, but with increased use of these specific platforms, reported lower self-esteem. Empathy has been an important connection to our ability to communicate with others. Empathy may be examined through affective and cognitive perspectives. Affective empathy describes the ability to feel and share

Figure 2. Virtual campus
(Image Credit: Andrew Stricker)

how another person may be feeling, whereas cognitive empathy refers to the rational explanation for *what* another person is feeling. Since our younger populations are dedicated users of social media networks such as Facebook and Twitter, their empathic abilities may influence their daily communication and relationships with others (Errasti, Amigo, & Villadangos, 2017).

The "information superhighway" of the early 1990s has evolved into a collection of colorful metaphors today attempting to define these technological spaces such as "cyberspace," "the Net," "online," and "the Web." Regardless of the term, these computer networks allow the creation of new social spaces allowing people to meet and interact with one another (Wellman, Salaff, Dimitrova, Garton, Gulia, and Haythornthwaite, 1996).

CONVIVIALITY AS A SOCIAL-COGNITIVE CONCEPT

Originally, the concept of *conviviality* was made popular by Illich's book entitled *Tools for Conviviality* (1973) whereby he defined conviviality as "… an individual freedom realized in personal interdependence" (p. 11).

Further, Illich defined a convivial learning experience as an occurrence where the teacher and the student may switch roles, allowing the teacher to become the student and the student become the teacher. This idea of role swapping recognizes reciprocity as a key component for conviviality. Such role swapping scenarios can directly be used in multi-agent systems (MAS).

According to Caire (2008), There are several reasons to add conviviality as a social-cognitive concept to multi-agent systems models and theories.

First, requirements for multi-agent systems expressed by politicians and managers say that systems must be convivial, whereas multi-agent system researchers and developers use other concepts. As an analogy, consider a manager requiring of her system developers to have a convivial attitude during a meeting, in order for example to make it more efficient. To model the requirement, the developers may interpret the conviviality requirement as being autonomous to make suggestions, being reactive to react the discussion in the meeting to reach their goals, being pro-active to take the initiative and being goal-directed, and most importantly being social by interact with others to reach their goals.

Second, the use of conviviality as an agent concept ensures that considerations on the user-friendliness of multi-agent systems get the same importance and considerations on the functionality of the system. In particular, using conviviality in multi-agent system models ensures that user friendliness is incorporated in the specification and design of multi-agent systems. There is a widespread belief that user friendliness is something which can be added to a multi-agent system once it has been developed. However, it is much more difficult to turn a non-convivial system into a convivial one, than developing a convivial system from scratch. Thus conviviality should be incorporated from the first design of the system.

Third, it is a useful high level modeling concept for organizations and communities, emphasizing the social side of them rather than the legal side. Erickson and Kellogg (2000) say: "In socially translucent systems, we believe it will be easier for users to carry on coherent discussions; to observe and imitate others' actions; to engage in peer pressure; to create, notice, and conform to social conventions. We see social translucence as a fundamental requirement for supporting all types of communication and collaboration."

Fourth, when developing user-friendly multi-agent systems, it is crucial to understand the inherent threads of conviviality. Whereas conviviality was put forward by Illich as a positive concept, also negative aspects were discussed. Agents are often not rational and cooperative to achieve conviviality (Sadek, Bretier, & Panaget, 1997) and unity through diversity (Hofkirchner, 2004) may lead to suppression of minorities. Taylor (2004) explores the contradiction that conviviality cannot exist outside institutions: i.e., the question "whether it is possible for convivial institutions to exist other than by simply creating another set of power relationships and social orders that, during the moment of involvement, appear to allow free rein to individual expression. Community members may experience a sense of conviviality which is deceptive and which disappears as soon as the members return to the alienation of their fragmented lives" (p. 1728).

In addition to MAS applications, conviviality for educators in Professional Learning Communities (PLCs) has reached a tipping point according to Dufour and Reason (2016), who claim that in high performing PLCs, educators:

- Focus on the critical questions that must be addressed in schools that profess a mission to ensure learning for all students
- Collaborate with one another to improve their professional practice
- Take collective responsibility for student learning
- Use evidence of student learning to inform and improve their professional practice
- Develop systems of intervention and enrichment to meet the needs of all students (pp. 1-2)

Further, the use of the PLC process has transformed the routine roles of classroom educators traditionally tied to isolated classrooms to collaborative teams of partners working together virtually to solve problems without any global or time restrictions. The impact of collaboration among educators continues to accumulate. Hattie (2012) has demonstrated through syntheses and meta-analyses that collaboration is not just a "congenial activity," but also a powerful process to improve both student and adult learning (p. 3). The emergence of this new evidence has proven that effective collaboration at the individual, school, and system levels leads to better student performance and increased professional satisfaction by teachers and leaders.

CONVIVIALITY: LIMITED UNDERSTANDINGS, UNLIMITED POSSIBILITIES

What is the range of settings in which human conviviality can occur? Can humans be convivial in cyberspace? The question of *conviviality* (the quality of being friendly and lively) versus strictly *utility* in a virtual environment quickly becomes confusing and unproductive due to an instance of the common logical fallacy of the *false dilemma*. This fallacy (McInerny, 2004) exposes as illogical the presentation of two alternatives as if those are the *only possible* alternatives (A and B) in a given scenario, when there are many more. In cases of deliberate manipulation, the presenter paints the alternative he does not want the audience to choose (A) as more unsavory than B, thus forcing the target to choose B. The alternatives for online conviviality when artificially reduced to two – either online interaction is identical to or completely unlike face-to-face interaction – are unproductive for scholars and a classic example of the false dilemma.

In this case the false dilemma works against those arguing for the possibility of online interaction that is conducive to human conviviality. In order to validate such beneficial outcomes of online interaction, the dilemma places this group in the unenviable position of having to somehow prove online shared experiences are exactly the same in every respect as face-to-face. This either-or construct neglects the rich variety along the spectrum of human sharing (Vygotsky, 1978) and imposes a reductive view of knowledge.

Scholars such as McLuhan (1964) recognized decades ago that people in the industrialized Western countries were passing out of the print age into the electronic age, with as dramatic consequences as those which followed the transition from oral to print culture. Three changes produced by these transitions are the diminishment of the handwritten letter, a reduction in the idea of knowledge as transferred by print and electronic media, and a loss of receptivity to being. These influences have undermined the common sense realization that *any environment in which human interaction occurs will contain more or less conviviality depending on the level of investment of the human participants.*

The philosopher Heidegger (1957) expressed two closely related concerns over the dominance of machine-printed text versus handwritten words: 1) the removal of the hand from the "realm of the word" and subsequent loss of written speech as an extension of the self and its being; and 2) the degradation of the word from its status as a sign of the being of the author to "mere means for the traffic of communication." In the midst of these changes, the handwritten letter changes in significance from a respectful and personal extension of the author's thoughts to an impractical time-waster that impedes rapid production and digestion. In the loss of the handwritten letter as an unwelcome anachronism, then, we lose the memory of centuries of routinely shared and enjoyed human conviviality through a distal medium – personal letters sent by post.

The loss of the handwritten letter and consequent weakening of direct *conscious* experience of other-than-face-to-face conviviality comes at the end of an upheaval similar to McLuhan's epochal changes in the dominant medium of culture – an upheaval in how humans viewed knowledge itself. The Baconian and Cartesian philosophical systems and their descendants, to protect (as they saw it) the use of human reason, separated reason from experience, since experience was seen as totally unreliable (Deneen, 2011; Merrill, 2008). Thus the practice of science, of proper knowing, was isolated from daily living. Whereas previous conceptions of knowledge combined philosophical wisdom (including knowledge of being) and empirical investigation (including mastery of physical processes), the above separation reduces knowledge to experimental research, and ascribes to the rest of living the status of sentiment.

CONVIVIALITY AND THE LOSS OF BEING

This change in the Western view of knowledge from a knowledge of being (the study of human activity in itself) as well as of processes, from an engagement with reality, with "what is" to a search for mastery over natural processes (Merrill, 2008), corresponds with the third change from shifts in medium – loss of receptivity to being. Deneen (2011) describes the transition: humans stopped emphasizing the practical study of human behavior, which amounted to discerning its operations, and by the time of the philosophers Hobbes and Locke, concentrated on the *theoretical* study of human behavior. Under this changed view, human beings were "predictable material entities" (Deneen, 2011, p. 94), and the goal of such study was no longer to know human beings "as they are," but to redirect their behavior toward desirable ends.

Why is this important to conviviality in cyberspace? With the separation of experience from the proper use of reason, any aspects of interaction between humans not universalized by theoretical study, such as in empirical psychological and sociological research, were trivialized as sentiment versus knowledge. No longer could people as a result of communicating *know* something substantive about themselves or others – this human sharing was relegated to the insubstantial and irrational realm of feelings and emotions. Conviviality, as a quality of human interaction, falls under the same ban, excluded from the realm of knowledge when it is not the topic of an empirical investigation, but simply occurs among particular people at a particular moment in history.

Therefore, when humans developed the technologies to extend their powers through the tools of the computer and the Internet, conviviality was never taken seriously as part of the project, aside from its money-making and social components. Conviviality's markers in face-to-face interaction are at least readily apparent – facial expressions, laughter, and pats on the shoulder. The lack of correspondence between these and their online facsimiles exacerbates the potential trivialization of online conviviality, directing serious attention away from this spatial and sometimes temporal extension of human expression. Instead, the focus is on the employment of computer technologies for utilitarian ends, specifically the aim of manipulating the equipment to extract data useful for other purposes, the character of the employment always being the *instrumental* use of knowledge.

This utilitarian view toward knowledge gained through computer technologies stands against a countervailing perspective which is the central argument of this chapter – that it is entirely plausible that the constant human desire for knowledge as an end in itself can cut across any medium which allows human expression, as in the case of conviviality (properly understood as knowledge versus "mere sentiment") which is related to the terminal good of friendship and can occur within the very same range of media. The most significant danger that attends this inappropriate restriction on conviviality's available media of expression – people will tend to remain unconscious of the range of effects of their human expression across computer technologies (Genosko, 2005, p. 357), and become increasingly irresponsible and unrestrained in what they express and how. Even more to our purpose, people will tend to marginalize the quality of virtual interactions in disciplines such as education. The overarching problem created here is the reduction of alternative media to "unreal experiences," facsimiles of reality governed by irrational forces rather than the person-to-person sharing of knowledge. In refutation of this mistaken judgment, the cost to victims of cyberbullying has been quite real!

Humans used to know this. Previous generations did not confine conviviality to the immediate and physically present, but giving it proper respect to its ability to transcend spatial and temporal gaps. Nor did they restrict the existence of conviviality to the presence of identical markers across media. Writing or reading a letter or a book did not demand identical markers because people did not expect them, and yet people regularly conveyed and experienced conviviality through distal media. Writers such as Flannery O'Connor (1970) and C.S. Lewis (2002) recognized this quality of other-than-face-to-face media. Csikszentmihalyi's (1992) work on flow and intersubjectivity reinforces this possibility, as do the contributions of phenomenology in restoring a broader, more meaningful definition of knowing and specifically validating a range of conscious experiences typically downplayed in empirical studies.

Moreover, the assumption of the inhuman-ness of cyberspace is not a recognition of reality so much as a function of the loss of confidence in our ability to express our humanity in meaningful ways across a range of media. This failure is complicated by the unwarranted expectation that markers of conviviality must be identical across media. The work of Derrida (1967) and other deconstructionists, given their thesis that texts cannot convey meaning, is both witness and participant in this growing loss of confidence. Interaction in other-than-face-to-face environments (sometimes spilling over into face-to-face) resembles a mere opportunity for manipulation or a power contest, rather than increased opportunities for human communion.

REGAINING THE INFINITE IN OUR HUMAN CAPACITIES: THE EXAMPLE OF EDUCATION

If, then, the possibility arises that people can share conviviality across a range of media from face-to-face conversation to personal letters and virtual experiences, then for further validation we can turn our attention to the practice of a communication-intensive discipline such as education, whose application across the range of media is still hotly debated today. Few would argue the educative power of print books and online texts as vital supplementary sources of education enhancing and for decades often replacing brick-and-mortar learning contexts. Just as few, on reflection, expect the learning experiences across these three media to be identical. The point, then, in prioritizing educative media is appropriateness to the learning goal in view, and this same reasoning applies to learning in a virtual, computer-generated setting. This awareness is far more productive than debates over the false dilemma outlined at the start of the chapter.

Extensive research programs have explored the relative merits of different learning environments. One of the most productive lines of research includes the work of Simonson (1999) on equivalency theory – the proposal that with careful instructional design different learning contexts can provide equivalent learning outcomes. Applying this theory to conviviality and the various learning contexts, we can establish three points of importance: 1) meaningful educational experiences can occur across a range of contexts and can combine more than one; 2) the three usual components of a shared (potentially convivial) learning experience are – self, teacher, others; and 3) the power of the learning experience is a function of the specific content to be learned related to the unique markers generated by the selected learning context. Wise instructional designers will match the content to their creation of unique markers in the learning context to reach equivalent learning outcomes.

In this vein the education of leadership principles is especially suited to provide a robust test of the conviviality of a virtual learning environment. Schlosser and Simonson (2010) argue that learning experiences include whatever is "observed, felt, heard or done." Avolio and Hannah (2008), following upon years of research programs on leadership education, indicate that optimal leadership development includes learning from experiences, specifically experiences of disequilibrium from "trigger events" that heighten self-awareness and generate re-evaluation of self-constructs. Slear's (in press) qualitative study on equivalency of distance learning education of leadership principles makes the case that instructional designers can generate sufficient disequilibrium to promote equivalent learning by providing text and other media with countervailing perspectives as part of the content distance learning students engage online.

Shared virtual experiences would seem in their potential for conviviality to generate disequilibrium even more effectively, bringing together people of diverse backgrounds and contrasting perspectives in a real-time learning event that additionally provides immediate, authentic feedback from teacher and peers. A shared, real-time virtual learning event as such with this last quality of authentic, immediate feedback "in the moment" meets Calandra and Puvirajah's (2014) definition of an optimal "fourth space" learning event that meets many learning outcomes mandated in professional development programs. Whereas spaces one through three range from reading texts to on-the-job training to brick-and-mortar group learning, the "fourth space" of virtual, synchronous shared learning achieves the additional benefits of realistic experience in a "free-to-fail" setting that often expends far less resources than a face-to-face equivalent, and that in some cases exceeds shared face-to-face contexts where the cognitive load may be too high to produce effective learning.

In Figure 3, four learning spaces are labeled displaying key learning attributes. The *first space* would appear as a traditional lecture-driven classroom seen in most learning institutions; the *second space* is where educators leverage micro-teaching efforts, simulations, and role-play exercises, often in a university settings; the *third space* is where educators actually practice teaching in learning environments; and finally, the *fourth space* is where teacher practice takes place in multi user virtual environments (MUVEs).

Further, these researchers describe why MUVEs may enhance partnerships and collaboration. MUVEs are typically described as 2D or 3D (two or three dimensional) computer simulated graphical environments where real-world participants represent themselves through online personification or avatars to interact with various digital structures, intelligent agents, and other avatars (Dede, Nelson, Ketelhut, Clarke & Bowman, 2004). In education, MUVEs are often intentionally designed to be a "form of socio-constructivist and situated cognition-based educational software" (Nelson & Ketelhut, 2007, p. 269).

It is important to note that multiple studies in recent years have addressed virtual collaboration. Duncan, Miller and Jiang (2012) reviewed over 100 published academic papers, reports, and educational websites on MUVE use in education, discovering that the most common types of educational and training activities reported were virtual quests, collaborative simulations, virtual laboratories, virtual fieldwork, role-play, game based learning, and lectures. Additionally, Hew and Cheung (2010) also compiled a literature review on the using MUVEs in educational contexts, claiming that they could be utilized as spaces for communication, as a simulation of space, and as experiential spaces.

CROSSING INTO CYBERSPACE

A continuing challenge for virtual learning environment (VLE) developers is the ability to capture the presence of real actors and avatars during face-to-face (F2F) interactions for realistic communication. Recently, the integration of virtual reality technology within social media platforms has generated much interest, F2F interactions has become a key component to these interactions. Various sensory organs provide relevant clues to effective F2F communication such as eye contact, agents facing one another, or talking to each other in close proximity creating many challenges for realistic interactions between virtual agents. One approach to address this issue is to utilize multi-agent navigation that facilitates F2F interactions between real users and virtual agents. Researchers at the University of North Carolina,

Figure 3. Hypothesized attributes of the four practice spaces for novices

	First Space	Second Space	Third Space	Fourth Space
Interaction	Mind	Mind-Body	Body-Environment	Mind-Body (Avatar)-(Virtual) Environment
Example	Reading, Listening to Lecture, Watching Videos	Micro-teaching practices, role plays	Experiences in real classrooms	Experiences in well- designed MUVEs
Learning Mode	Learning through others	Learning through doing	Learning through being-in	Learning through being
Authenticity of Experience	Low	Low	High	Medium-High
Relevance of Experience for Learning	Low	Low	Medium	High
Cognitive/ Sensory Load	Low	Low	(Too) High	Appropriate
Knowledge Acquired	Canonical	Canonical	Personally Constructed – Instinctual	Personally Constructed – Professionally Meaningful

Chapel Hill have proposed the interaction velocity prediction (IVP) algorithm to help predict whether a real user is approaching a virtual agent in order to determine if a F2F interaction is necessary. In a virtual environment, this is not always evident and considered critical information in many simulations. Further, the IVP combines human body motion constraints and facial actions to help improve realism of virtual agents for more meaningful communication experiences (Randhavane, Bera, & Manocha, 2017).

Chatbots are an emerging technology, which attempts to conducts human-like conversations with users, typically through messaging applications. A chatbot is a personalized, yet automated conversation between software and a user. These chatbots are typically programmed to anticipate human responses for a variety of applications. Such bots are completely unbiased, making them very unemotional during any tense user moments and are the current communication channels for contacting an assortment of users in any industry, commonly used in today's technology for many consumers. Some examples today may include: Expedia chatbot on Facebook Messenger to assist in hotel reservations, Taco Bell's future tacobot taking your lunch order on their website, or a friendly chatbot instructor checking up on student's progress during a training course. The popular messaging app for teens, Kik recently developed a Bot Shop to reach their audience. Organizations like the Washington Post and Quartz have created bots to deliver the daily news. Barbie has joined the world of chatbots with their latest addition of the Hello Barbie doll to interact with their customers.

The idea behind the evolution of chatbots ranges from a useful productivity tool to facilitating learning and development for all types of students. Most learners will not ignore messages from a friend and probably accept a message from a smart and friendly chatbot that strives to add value to their lives. Designing a chatbot is not only a relevant use of technology, but an art for the most creative instructional designers. Chatbots may be used as reminders, assistants, instructors, or facilitators for a multitude of tasks. The days of the cold machine-like conversations with virtual agents are over, a personalized, congenial chatbot can enhance conviviality in cyberspace for those hesitant users of virtual technology. Chatbots and their connection with artificial intelligence are still considered a nascent technology today, but expect them to permeate our daily lives over time (Han, 2017).

How does one practice communication in a virtual environment with the end goal of improving communication in a real environment? Is there a virtual laboratory for honing human communication acumen? Dakota State University, met these challenges by implementing their Virtual Avatar Learning Experience (VALE) for their preservice teachers. VALE is based on the TeachLivE (TLE) mixed-reality teaching platform developed at the University of Central Florida. The TLE mixed-reality technology uses a combination of live human interaction with virtual experiences. The technology leverages an Xbox Kinect for tracking developing teachers as they manage avatar students in a virtual classroom. Multiple avatar students are controlled by human actors behind the scenes creating various behavior issues by avatar students simultaneously to create classroom challenges for future teachers to manage. This VALE practice laboratory creates a risk-free environment allowing safe failure experiences for developing communication and classroom management skills. Additionally, this environment allows for further analysis and future responses to become more prepared in difficult situations. The scripts for the actors are at the discretion of the clients and may be adjusted to fit their unique organizational requirements or missions (Smith & Klumper, 2018).

At the College of Education at Auburn University, Montgomery campus in Alabama, the Virtual Avatar Laboratory was established to collaborate with Mursion Inc., in an effort to leverage a mixed-reality platform to allow teachers to interact with a variety of students and workers. Mursion's platform, utilizes a combination of artificial intelligence and live actors to produce powerful classroom simulations. These simulations can be personalized to include any specific learning content or levels of cognitive learning. This unique learning platform promotes learning at the cognitive and emotional levels, creating dynamic forms of interactive simulations unlike traditional role-playing scenarios (Virtual Avatar Laboratory Website, 2019).

CONCLUSION

What is the claim on human conviviality in cyberspace? Is it plausible? Is cyberspace a setting for productive human interaction and collaboration? Maybe cyberspace is too nebulous to assess such complex human relationships? Are we getting closer to crossing into cyberspace with human interaction? These are a few questions explored within this chapter. We have concluded that human relationships and collaboration in various virtual learning environments have a myriad of possibilities and have been an acceptable milieu for interaction and collaborative efforts for educators and researchers over the last decade.

Figure 4. Elementary classroom

Figure 5. Corporate lunch setting

REFERENCES

Avolio, B., & Hannah, S. (2008). Developmental readiness: Accelerating leader development. *Consulting Psychology Journal: Practice and Research*, *60*(4), 331–347. doi:10.1037/1065-9293.60.4.331

Bonk, C. J. (2010). For openers: How technology is changing school. In R. Dufour & C. Reason (Eds.), *Professional Learning Communities at Work and Virtual Collaboration* (p. 3). Bloomington, IN: Solution Tree Press.

Burstein, D. D. (2013). Fast future: How the millennial generation is shaping our world. In R. Dufour & C. Reason (Eds.), *Professional Learning Communities at Work and Virtual Collaboration* (p. 4). Bloomington, IN: Solution Tree Press.

Caire, P. (2008). Designing convivial digital cities. *Proc. of 7th Int. Conf. on Autonomous Agents and Multi-agent Systems (AAMAS 2008)*, 1727-1729.

Caire, P. (2009). How to import the concept of conviviality to web communities. *International Journal of Web Based Communities*, *6*(1), 99–113. doi:10.1504/IJWBC.2010.030019

Calandra, B., & Puvirajah, A. (2014). Teacher practice in multi user virtual environments: A fourth space. *TechTrends*, *58*(6), 29–35. doi:10.100711528-014-0800-3

Csikszentmihalyi, M. (1992). *Flow: The psychology of happiness*. London: Rider.

Dede, C., Nelson, B., Ketelhut, D. J., Clarke, J., & Bowman, C. (2004). *Design-based research strategies for studying situated learning in a multi-user virtual environment*. Academic Press.

Deneen, P. (2011). The science of politics and the conquest of nature. *New Atlantis (Washington, D.C.)*, *32*(3), 90–102.

Derrida, J. (1967/1997). *Of grammatology* (G. Spivak, Trans.). Baltimore, MD: Johns Hopkins University Press.

Dufour, R., & Reason, C. (2016). *Professional Learning Communities at Work and Virtual Collaboration*. Bloomington, IN: Solution Tree Press.

Duncan, I., Miller, A., & Jiang, S. (2012). *A taxonomy of virtual worlds usage in education*. Academic Press.

Errasti, J., Amigo, I., & Villadangos, M. (2017). Emotional uses of Facebook and Twitter: Its relation with empathy, narcissism, and self-esteem on adolescence. *Psychological Reports*, *120*(6), 997–1018. doi:10.1177/0033294117713496

Han, V. (2017). Are chatbots the future of training? *TD: Talent Development, Learning Technologies*, *71*(9), 42–46.

Hattie, J. (2012). Visible learning for teachers: Maximizing impact on learning. In R. Dufour & C. Reason (Eds.), *Professional Learning Communities at Work and Virtual Collaboration* (p. 3). Bloomington, IN: Solution Tree Press. doi:10.4324/9780203181522

Heidegger, M. (1957/2002). *Identity and difference* (J. Stambaugh, Trans.). Chicago, IL: University of Chicago Press.

Heim, M. (2005). Heidegger and McLuhan: The computer as component. In G. Genosko (Ed.), *Marshall McLuhan: Critical Evaluations in Cultural Theory* (Vol. 2, pp. 349–361). Routledge.

Hew, K. F., & Cheung, W. S. (2010). *Use of three- dimensional (3-D) immersive virtual worlds in K-12 and higher education settings: A review of the research.* Academic Press.

Hofkirchner, W. (2004). Unity through diversity: dialectics - systems thinking - semiotics. *Trans, Internet Journal for Cultural Sciences, 1*(15), 1728.

Hopkins, J., & Turner, J. (2012). Go mobile: Location-based marketing, apps, mobile optimized, and campaigns, 2D codes, and other mobile strategies to grow your business. In R. Dufour & C. Reason (Eds.), *Professional Learning Communities at Work and Virtual Collaboration* (p. 3). Bloomington, IN: Solution Tree Press.

Illich, I. (1973). *Tools for Conviviality*. London: Marion Boyars.

Kurtzberg, T. R. (2014). *Virtual Teams: Mastering Communication and Collaboration in the Digital Age*. Santa Barbara, CA: ABC-CLIO, LLC.

Lewis, C. (2002). *On stories: And other essays on literature*. San Diego, CA: Harvest Books.

McInerny, D. (2004). *Being logical: A guide to good thinking*. Random House.

McLuhan, M. (1964). *Understanding media: The extensions of man*. Cambridge, MA: MIT Press.

Merrill, T. (2008). Masters and possessors of nature. *New Atlantis (Washington, D.C.), 19*(1), 91–107.

Nelson, B. C., & Ketelhut, D. J. (2007). *Scientific inquiry in educational multi- user virtual environments.* Academic Press.

O'Connor, F. (1970). *Mystery and manners: Occasional prose*. Farrar, Straus and Giroux.

Randhavane, T., Bera, A., & Manocha, D. (2017). F2F crowds: Planning agent movements to enable face-to-face interactions. *Presence (Cambridge, Mass.), 26*(2), 228–246. doi:10.1162/PRES_a_00294

Sadek, M. D., Bretier, P., & Panaget, E. (1997). ARTIMIS: Natural dialogue meets rational agency. *International Joint Conferences on Artificial Intelligence,* (2), 1030–1035.

Schlosser, L., & Simonson, M. (2010). *Distance education: Definition and glossary of terms*. Charlotte, NC: Information Age Publishing.

Simonson, M. (1999). Equivalency theory and distance education. *TechTrends, 43*(5), 5–8. doi:10.1007/BF02818157

Slear, J., Slear, S., Connelly, D., Reames, E., & Maggard, P. (2016). A Qualitative Method to Promote Equivalent Learning Outcomes. *Quarterly Review of Distance Education, 17*(2), 1–14.

Smith, A., & Anderson, M. (2018). *Social media use in 2018*. PEW Research Center. Retrieved from http://www.pewinternet.org/2018/03/01/social-media-use-in-2018/

Smith, K., & Klumper, D. (2018). Virtually in the classroom: Virtual reality platforms can give preservice teachers opportunities to develop real classroom management skills. *Educational Leadership*, *76*(1), 60–65.

Smith, M. A., & Kollock, P. (1999). *Communities in Cyberspace*. New York, NY: Routledge Taylor & Francis Group. doi:10.5117/9789056290818

Taylor, M. (2004). Oh no it isn't: Audience participation and community identity. *Trans, Internet Journal for Cultural Sciences*, *1*(15).

Virtual Avatar Laboratory Website. (2019). Retrieved from http://www.education.aum.edu/VAL

Vygotsky, L. (1978). Mind in society: The development of higher psychological processes (M. Cole, V. John-Steiner, S. Scribner & E. Souberman., Eds.; A. R. Luria, M. Lopez-Morillas & M. Cole, Trans.). Cambridge, MA: Harvard University Press. (Original manuscripts published 1930-1934)

Wellman, B., Salaff, J., Dimitrova, D., Garton, L., Gulia, M., & Haythornthwaite, C. (1996). Computer networks as social networks. *Annual Review of Sociology*, *22*(1), 211–238. doi:10.1146/annurev.soc.22.1.213

Chapter 4
Character Strength Development of Leaders in Cyberspace

Fil J. Arenas
https://orcid.org/0000-0003-1747-0706
The Air University, USA

ABSTRACT

Leadership development in cyberspace presents new challenges within an abstract interactive environment. The flexibility and versatility of virtual spaces offers many freedoms from ordinary rules and restrictions. Examining relevant signature character strengths under the high six virtues of wisdom, courage, humanity, justice, temperance, and transcendence provide guidance for virtual leadership. Aspiring authentic transformational leaders must continue their awareness of selfhood and society in cyberspace milieus by opening their human apertures while leveraging their signature character strengths.

INTRODUCTION

The 21st Century has deluged humankind with a tsunami of technological advances that have placed an infinite amount of information at our fingertips anytime and anywhere. With the availability of notebooks, tablets, smartphones, or other mobile devices, anyone can remain "connected" all day long and never miss a minute of any type of informational updates. Furthermore, the technology required to generate virtual environments (VE) has matured at an accelerated rate over the last decade. Driven primarily by the gaming industry, users have sparked the demand for greater realism, intuitive interaction, and enhanced usability for today's virtual engagement (Hale & Stanney, 2015).

According to Moore's law, there have been multiple doublings of computer power in our current time span. Today, human-machine interfaces consist of a variety of multimodal display devices such as: visual, auditory, haptic, and olfactory displays used to provide information to VE users in addition to multimodal input devices used to control movement throughout the virtual world. These input sensors allow the ability to capture various physical responses such as eye gaze, gestures, facial expressions

DOI: 10.4018/978-1-5225-9679-0.ch004

Figure 1. Virtual campus
Source: Image Credit Andrew Stricker.

(Hale & Stanney, 2015). These trends pose unique challenges for the way we promote the leadership and character development of individuals who must interact with their followers in VE. Will human interactions be the same in these abstract environments? How will these trends affect future human interaction, engagement, ethics, character strengths, and the ability to lead in cyberspace? This chapter attempts to answer these questions by exploring the intersection of leadership and character development within the context of VE and other forms of advanced information technology (AIT).

CYBERSPACE

What is cyberspace? Maybe the real question is *where* is cyberspace? Some say it is the place where email conversations occur. Some say it is the space between the phones or the indefinite place where human beings meet and communicate online. The word "cyberspace" was coined by the science fiction writer William Gibson in his 1984 novel *Neuromancer* to refer to his vision of a global computer network linking people, machines, and multiple sources of global information, enabling one to navigate through a virtual space (Gibson, 1984). The word "cyber" refers to the science of *cybernetics* derived from the Greek verb "Kubernao" meaning to steer. Further, it describes the idea of not only navigating through a space of electronic data, but having control over much of the data as well. Additionally, Gibson's descriptions of cyberspace were not limited to passive spaces of data (such as libraries), but connected communication channels to the real world that permitted these cyberspace navigators to interact with that world.

Moreover, the word "space" provides several directions for this nebulous environment. First, it allows us to expect an infinite extension of information such as the existing levels of data available on the Internet. Next, space promotes the notion of freedom of movement without any restrictions. Lastly, space implies direction, movement, and dimension. This latter concept can be further illustrated in the use of *virtual reality*, whereby a three dimensional (3D) space is generated by a computer allowing the user to immerse and interact within a 3D space as they would in a real or physical world. Present day interpretations of *cyberspace* may include some of the descriptions described previously, reference for virtual reality, or an all-inclusive term for the Internet as a whole (Heylighen, 1994). "Virtual reality typically conjures up futuristic images of computer grids and intricate hardware. But…virtual reality begins in the mind and requires no equipment whatsoever." (Blascovich & Bailenson, 2011, p.18)

As society becomes more accustomed to interfacing with cyberspace in their daily routines, questions of one's selfhood and awareness within this milieu will arise questioning philosophical ideologies from the past. Timeless questions that mankind has pondered for thousands of years seem to complete the cycle as we assimilate into a new intellectual environment shaped by VE and other forms of AIT. As humans we are drawn back into familiar areas of philosophy once more: metaphysics, epistemology, and value theory. The study of reality or *metaphysics* has even more relevance when we are accepting cyberspace as our new learning environment, social environment, or work environment. What is real? What exists? What gives meaning to our existence? Are there nonphysical realities? How do we process ideas that are not associated with concrete entities? Metaphysical issues come into play today when we are discussing the utility of *virtual reality* platforms for learners, gamers, or real-world simulations. How does it differ from reality? Examining *epistemology* or the theory of knowledge, which concerns what we know and how we know it, is yet another philosophical area relevant to cyberspace discussions. How do we acquire knowledge? Do we only form ideas through our sensory perceptions? How do we develop our current human-related disciplines, such as logic or mathematics? *Value theory,* sometimes called "axiology" studies values and their distinction from facts (Van Camp, 2014, p. 4). What do we hold most important in our interactions in cyberspace? How does technology shape what we value most? Over time these rich discussions by philosophers, psychiatrists, psychologists and social scientists have led to the study of values in human behavior, or ethics. Let us examine a few of these areas of discussion.

According to Daneshi (2016), cybercrime is a global issue. Because of the "interconnectedness of our societies and the diversity of Internet users (ages, disciplines, education, political cultures, etc.), creating cyber ethics guidelines becomes an ongoing, global conversation" (p.1). One professor at Boston University insists on the need for more faculty intervention in this arena. He feels that "Cyberethics education is a way to address the need for teachers to gain knowledge and resources that help their students develop ethical practices in cyberspace" (Whittier, 2013, p. 225). Further, he asserts that teachers can share their background and experiences in addition to learning how they can become more effective at communicating with their students in this abstract virtual learning environment. Additionally, examining the impact on student performance and social equilibrium within cyberspace may lead to a better understanding on leading and instructing students in ethical behavior in all forms of electronic communication efforts. How does cyberspace influence leadership and its development? The inference that leadership and technology influence each other reciprocally is not a new concept. It has been linked to evolving leadership theory as well as research interests over the last decade to include connections with more recent conceptualizations of leadership (Avolio, Sosik, Kahai, & Baker, 2014).

Leadership

Leadership has evolved since the beginning of human existence, from the tenets of the Great Man Theory to Authentic Transformational Leadership behaviors utilized in today's most effective organizations (Bass, 2008). One recurring theme that continues to surface is the distinction between authentic and non-authentic leadership. What is the difference between these two choices? How does this leadership dichotomy impact followers? According to Bill George, author of *True North* (2007):

Authentic leaders are genuine people who are true to themselves and to what they believe. Rather than letting the expectations of others guide them, they are prepared to be their own person and go their own way. As they develop as authentic leaders, they are more concerned about serving others than they are about their own success or recognition. And they are constantly looking for ways to grow personally. Authentic leaders develop genuine connections with others and engender trust. Because people trust them, they are able to motivate people to high levels of performance by empowering them to lead. (pp. 205-206)

Additionally, George (2007) reiterates that an authentic leader is not a perfect leader and as human leaders, we all make mistakes. One way to help keep us on track is to incorporate what he refers to as the Five Dimensions of Authentic Leadership:

- Pursuing purpose with passion
- Practicing solid values
- Leading with heart
- Establishing enduring relationships
- Demonstrating self-discipline (p. xxxi)

PURSUING PURPOSE WITH PASSION

Authentic leaders must understand their leadership purpose by reflecting on their own preferences and passions. Incorporating one's passions will ensure that a genuine or authentic approach to leadership is adopted.

PRACTICING SOLID VALUES

All leaders are defined by their set of values, or personal beliefs that learned during early life-span development. These values help define who we are and how we respond to life's challenges. A key ingredient to authentic leadership is integrity, which begins with values.

LEADING WITH HEART

A true authentic leader is passionate and leads with heart. They believe in what they say or do. Some may consider leaders that take this approach to be weak or soft, but it is a genuine human quality that should be embraced. The ability to lead with heart and show empathy for followers illustrates courage to act on one's feelings. Courage is an important character strength for leaders making difficult decisions.

ESTABLISHING ENDURING RELATIONSHIPS

Good relationships are key to effective communication and essential to authentic leadership. Without effective dyadic relationships, followers may not feel connected to the organization. It is imperative that leaders establish rapport with their followers to ensure that they are approachable and open to ongoing relationships.

DEMONSTRATING SELF-DISCIPLINE

Authentic leaders are continuously self-regulating to control their wants and needs in life. Self-discipline is a major step to developing this element of authentic leadership. Followers typically emulate their leader's actions, so controlling those weaknesses or random impulses will ensure they are modeling excellence (George, 2007). The next section will continue our discussion of dyadic relationships as they build on transformational leadership behaviors.

Transformational leadership involves creating personal relationships with followers that raises their level of motivation and morality (Bass, 2008). A transformational leader is attentive to follower's needs and strives to help them reach their full potential. Raising the level of morality in others is a key tenet in this style of leadership according to Burns (1978). However, this may become complex when defining leaders such as Adolph Hitler or Saddam Hussein, who were transforming followers for unethical purposes. Bass (1998) referred to this type of transformation as *pseudo-transformational leadership*. Leaders who are self-consumed, exploitive, and power-oriented with unethical values and motivation fit this classification of leadership. When leaders are focused on their own self-interests over the interests of others, this is considered a personalized leadership approach. Personalized leaders leverage manipulation and punishment with disregard for their subordinate's feelings. Further, they are aggressive and narcissistic (Howell & House, 1992).

Another main focus of the transformational approach is addressing the follower's sense of self-worth. The challenge for all transformational leaders is to motivate their followers to accomplish more than they originally intended. This motivation helps followers to become self-actualized or reach their full potential. This outcome is accomplished by setting challenging expectations that allow followers to achieve higher standards of performance (Bass, 2008). However, transformational leaders go beyond simple exchanges and agreements with followers by employing one or more of the behaviors or components of transformational leadership. To some extent, these four behaviors have evolved through conceptualization and measurement of transformational leadership over time. Conceptually, leadership is *idealized* as exemplary role modeling of values and behaviors whereby followers identify and want to emulate their leader. Effective leaders *inspire* their followers with persuasion and challenging goals, providing meaning and understanding. Leaders *intellectually stimulate* their members to expand their knowledge, skills and abilities. Finally, leaders are *individually considerate* as they coach and mentor their followers. These descriptions highlight the four components of transformational leadership: idealized influence, inspirational motivation, intellectual stimulation, and individualized consideration. (Bass & Riggio, 2006; Sosik & Jung, 2010).

Sosik (2015) posits that when our character strengths are aligned with our transformational leadership behaviors outlined above, and they are considered to be virtuous, such alignment leads to *authentic transformational leadership.* "Virtues are core characteristics universally valued by moral philosophers and religious thinkers as exemplars of good character. Character strengths are positive traits or psychological processes or mechanisms for displaying the virtues" (pp. 50-51).

VIRTUES AND CHARACTER STRENGTHS

To provide a deeper level of understanding about how virtues and character strengths relate to authentic transformational leadership, Sosik (2015) considered each of the 24 character strengths classified under the 'High Six' virtues identified in Peterson and Seligman's (2004) research. For instance, *love of learning* is a character strength of the virtue *wisdom and knowledge*. Each of the High Six virtues and their associated character strengths are illustrated in Figure 2.

WISDOM AND KNOWLEDGE

When one exercises good judgment and the appropriate use of intelligence, this psychological process describes a virtue referred to as *wisdom and knowledge*. There are five associated character strengths that fall under this virtue: creativity, curiosity, open-mindedness, love- of-learning, and perspective (Peterson & Seligman, 2004). *Creativity* is typically characterized by someone's original or ingenuous abilities, displayed by the way he or she thinks, talks, or performs. Creativity has often been linked to non-conformity, unconventional behavior, flexibility, and risk-taking behavior. *Curiosity* describes someone who may have many interests, seeks novel ideas, or is open to new experiences. This character strength is often associated with general positive feelings and emotions, willingness to challenge stereotypes, and impulsiveness. *Open-minded* individuals will consider alternative viewpoints, examine all evidence, and typically do not jump to rash conclusions without weighing all of the facts. Those who are

Figure 2. Virtues and character strengths
(Peterson & Seligman, 2004).

motivated by an intrinsic desire to learn new things are exercising a *love of learning*. These individuals often experience positive feelings when considering new challenges and have high self- efficacy. *Perspective* describes the ability to consider all facets of a situation and integrate these views into one understandable solution for all to consider. Perspective is one of the key character strengths that can help to empathize with followers' needs (Peterson & Seligman, 2004; Sosik, 2015). Three specific character strengths imperative to any developing leader have been repeatedly highlighted by many researchers and scholars. The next section will describe *creativity, love of learning, and perspective*; and their tremendous impact in several virtual platforms. Sosik (2015) describes *creativity* as the opportunity for members of an organization to challenge the status quo and identify opportunities for improvement. Further, he suggests that a leader's creativity "fuels the inspirational motivation and intellectual stimulation" of your organization's followers (p. 84).

Many organizations struggle with methods to encourage creativity within the workplace. However, companies like Google have leveraged this creativity to benefit their cyberspace environments. Google founders Larry Page and Sergey Brin wrote the following in their 2004 IPO letter: "We encourage our employees, in addition to their regular projects, to spend 20% of their time working on what they think will most benefit Google." (D'Onfro, 2015, para 2) As a result, several model programs were created in this manner: Google News, Gmail, and AdSense This example at Google highlights the importance of not only leveraging creativity within organizations, but generating meaningful corporate or organizational knowledge. An organization's abilities to acquire knowledge have been regarded as critical sources of competitive advantage (Cohen & Levinthal, 1990; Davenport & Prusak, 1998; Grant, 1996). Additionally, not only is the form of knowledge important to the understanding of knowledge management (KM), but the process of how individuals or groups make use of the knowledge is important (Cook & Brown, 1999).

Incorporating practice-based and socially constructed knowledge challenges most information technology-based KM systems. Although multiple virtual communities and platforms exist, research indicates that real-life interactions are necessary to continue knowledge exchange and creation within these environments (Mueller et al., 2008; Tagliaventi & Mattarelli, 2006; Wasko & Faraj, 2000). The emergence of virtual technology platforms like Linden Lab's Second Life (SL) offers a virtual world for rich multimodal interactions and additional ways of connecting with others across the globe (Kohler et al., 2008; Schroeder & Axelsson, 2006). These types of virtual platforms offer SL residents opportunities to create their own avatars, organizations, and environments with limited parameters or restrictions. SL encourages the creation and collaboration of knowledge sharing through its media richness providing different lenses and perspectives for leaders. These virtual world platforms not only utilize simultaneous synchronous interaction, but create an exchange of tacit, context-bound knowledge.

Perspective is often utilized to allow followers to envision their performance goals. When leaders use this character strength to help articulate a vision, they are displaying inspirational motivation, intellectual stimulation, and individualized consideration for their followers (Sosik, 2015). Typical users or SL residents in these environments often report "flow-like" experiences keeping them interactively engaged while losing track of time, a positive psychology experience described by Csikszentmihalyi (1990) as a state of concentration or complete absorption. Incorporating these types of learning tools to offer multiple perspectives for curious followers become the impetus for innovation.

Although SL was one of the earlier virtual world platforms, there are more than 100 virtual worlds (de Freitas, 2008). Virtual worlds (VWs) have been defined as: "Any computer-generated physical space, represented graphically in three dimensions that can be experienced by many people at once" (Castronova, 2005, p. 22). Research has supported that VWs bring people virtually together for collaboration and creation of various projects, shared active databases, shared computer-aided design systems, use of photos, videos, and repositories of digital files. Interviews have revealed that friendship, respect, trust, and approval have been formed through ongoing social interaction in SL (Mueller, Hutter, Fueller, & Matzler, 2010).

Various Internet technologies and other visual platforms have been used in business, education, and academic life for over four decades. Multi-User Dungeon (Mud) games were originally created in the 1970s (Bartle, 1990). By the 1990s, fully graphical MUD systems were also developed with massively multiplayer online games (MMOGs); World of Warcraft is the most widely recognized MMOG with over 11 million subscriptions (Duncan, Miller, & Jiang, 2012). Additionally, a virtual learning environment (VLE) is a venue specifically designed to foster teaching and learning in cyberspace. These VLEs typically act as repositories for all relevant educational documents, assessment uploading, and other related tools allowing teachers and students to interact virtually (Browne & Walker, 2005). Multiple learning activities have been used in these virtual milieus: problem-based learning; inquiry-based learning; game-based learning; role playing; virtual quests; collaborative simulations; collaborative construction; design courses; language teaching and learning; virtual laboratories; virtual fieldworks; and attending lectures or classes (Duncan, et al., 2012).

One additional field that has taken advantage of immersive virtual learning environments has been nursing education. In this highly complex clinical and didactic content area, innovative learning experiences have been introduced through the use of risk-free 3D *simulations* in virtual environments. Gaba (2004) described these simulations as a technique, not a technology to replace real-life experiences with facilitated or guided immersive experiences that replicate real-world nursing procedures or tasks in a safe virtual environment. Simulations have become a popular means to meet the need for training and risk-management requirements for various high-risk industries such as aviation, nuclear power, and the military (Mattis, 2010).

Love of learning is a character strength leading organizations to identify new trends and strategies for their business challenges. Leaders can support this area by demonstrating inspirational motivation, intellectual stimulation, and individualized consideration to help their followers meet these challenges (Sosik, 2015).

Albeit an enriched interactive environment for creativity, varying perspectives, and multiple learning modalities, VWs offer advantages and disadvantages. Advantages include: presence of self and other avatars provides trust and reassurance; unlimited creativity for developers or innovators; multiple sources of information for learning or educational purposes; interactivity with other avatars or virtual games, simulations, or programs; global collaboration with partners anytime; and multiple perspectives may be arranged at will (weather, daylight, environments, avatars, etc.) Disadvantages include: technical hurdles for those that are technically-challenged; connectivity issues for organizations having limited Internet access; security issues that jeopardize sensitive information; poor graphics (depending on system capabilities); restrictions in certain private regions; cartoonish avatars; and travelling between virtual worlds not possible with same avatars (Mueller et al., 2010). Learning new possibilities and creating new forms of information, in addition to reframing old issues through new perspectives are cultivated in these virtual platforms.

COURAGE

Unlike all other virtues, *courage* has been a fundamental part of many philosophical discussions throughout history. Often referred to as "strength of the heart," courage is derived from one's will in the presence of opposing or dissenting opinions. Peterson and Seligman (2004) point out that despite disagreement, or even danger, persistence in the face of significant obstacles makes courage a core virtue. There are four related character strengths that reflect this virtue: bravery, persistence, integrity, and vitality. When someone speaks up for what is right in conflict with opposition or act on convictions regardless of how unpopular, this is an example of *bravery*. Bravery involves overcoming fear and requires an assessment of the situation, an understanding of the risk involved, and a decision to act despite potential undesired outcomes (Peterson & Seligman, 2004; Sosik, 2015).

Courageous people learn to persevere despite challenges, obstacles, or setbacks; this describes the character strength of *persistence*. In the military or law enforcement, we admire our members for "getting things done" despite the challenges. When one remains true to themselves and acts with honesty and authenticity, we are considering an individual's *integrity*. As described under many organizational core values, this signature strength has been inculcated among followers as "doing the right thing when no one is watching." When we say that someone has a "zest for life" or displays good physical and mental well-being throughout challenges in their lives, we call this character strength *vitality*. Because this strength has two components, physical and mental, there will be times due to illness, weakness, or fatigue, when we experience lower levels of vitality. How we bounce back and recharge ourselves during these challenging times defines our levels of vitality. History is fraught with stories of heroes overcoming harsh physical conditions, battle wounds, and mental warfare to meet their missions (Peterson & Seligman, 2004; Sosik, 2015). The next section will highlight how the character strength of integrity is tested in cyberspace.

Honesty and truthfulness become the hallmarks for not only integrity, but the essential foundation for authentic transformational leadership utilizing an idealized approach (Sosik, 2015). How has integrity been affected by online learning programs? Let us examine some unique issues in this flexible learning environment. The advent of educational technology has led to versatile online programs for college students today. Since 2003, online enrollments have swelled to 358% and 31% of all students take at least one course online (Allen & Seaman, 2011). By 2012, there were 6.7 million students that enrolled for at least one online college course (Allen & Seaman, 2013). These online assessments typically offer some attractive features for instructors: quick test creation (often from test banks), no paper copies, automatic grading (with student feedback), automatic grade book entries, testing analysis available upon test completions, and testing accomplished on student's time. On the flip side, faculty are concerned with integrity issues affecting online testing environments whereby cell phones and other technological devices (not allowed in traditional testing rooms) are available (Varble, 2014). The Internet provides unlimited resources and information for students to access for academic research, task assignments, and bibliography sources. Many students feel that the Internet then becomes their cognitive faculties and decision-making functions, incorporating the Internet as part of themselves (Alger, 2000). For many higher education administrators, this current trend presents concerns of what constitutes academic dishonesty and inappropriate behavior. Students today are exposed to sophisticated strategies for cheating with the current array of electronic aids like personal digital assistants, cameras, phones and instant messaging (Kiehl, 2006). A recent survey of online students discovered that 58% of the students felt that using an open book during the exam was not considered cheating and they assumed that personal class notes were permissible as well (Jones, Blankenship, & Hollier, 2013).

Virtual reality (VR) is a product of simulative technology, which makes it possible to create artificial environments whereby one can immerse to explore real situations in a computer-simulated environment, typically found in a variety of VR websites. Members of web communities are in a constant state of change, there typically are no written rules for this environment as such, these communities have no social norms to follow. The norms which are formed by the member's personalities, attitudes, and wishes, cannot be held accountable since no executive power in the traditional sense does not exist in virtual space. Does this VR context present a problem? Obviously, there are two ways to examine this situation; one side allows much member flexibility, while the other side weakens one's self-controlling barriers learned in society. Alter-egos or avatars (virtual self-representations) chosen in VR environments according to our media ideals are beautiful, handsome, smart, or just ugly, wicked, vengeful, or arrogant. They may not correspond to our own physical or psychological attributes, since cyberspace has created the illusion of a society lacking in rules or control (Parti, 2008). Does this freedom promote integrity erosion? Despite the teaching modality in cyberspace, educators must accept that cheating will occur using various sophisticated tools. Despite perpetual reminders and warnings by educators, "disintegrity" is quite common within academic settings. Deterrence of cheating in virtual learning environments will require new strategies from educators (Miller & Young-Jones, 2012).

Several universities offer courses in *cyberethics*, a growing topic that addresses some of the academic cyberspace deficiencies outlined previously. Cyberethics education is a path to help educators gain knowledge and resources to help their students develop ethical practices in cyberspace. Educators can share their experiences and discuss effective communication skills in cyberspace with their students to help alleviate integrity gaps or help define a social equilibrium (Whittier, 2013). As mentioned earlier, integrity is an essential ingredient for an idealized transformational leader, sharing open and honest feedback with followers is paramount to success.

HUMANITY

This virtue is one that we consider when we are defining "strengths of others" or more specifically interpersonal strengths that we use to protect or befriend others in our work or personal lives; what it means to be *human*. There are three character strengths associated with humanity: love, kindness, and social intelligence.

Peterson and Seligman (2004) refer to *love* as caring or valuing close relationships with others, particularly when sharing or caring are reciprocated. Since it is a human need to love and be loved, leaders should understand and demonstrate this strength to followers in the appropriate context. There are times when compassion and understanding are needed to comfort followers during a crisis, a loss of a family member, or during a stressful time in their lives. Valuing humanity while demonstrating generosity, nurturance, and compassion describe *kindness.* This strength has been linked to a variety of helping behaviors including volunteerism as it correlates to one's mental and physical health. Leadership includes building confidence, wisdom, and camaraderie in followers. When we recognize and control our emotions and engage in positive interactions with others, we are exercising the strength of *social intelligence*. Social and emotional intelligence has been linked with better life decisions, effective social functioning, more adaptive outcomes, and lower levels of aggression (Peterson & Seligman, 2004; Sosik, 2015). The character strength under the humanity virtue that tends to resonate in cyberspace environments readily today is social intelligence, the next section explores this potential leadership strength.

One of the character strengths that provides insight for developing leaders in the area of human relationships is *social intelligence.* Understanding the complexities of follower issues takes time and experience. The ability to recognize what motivates people, understanding political networks, controlling emotions, and self-awareness of one's own feelings and motivations, or the feelings of others is part of the role of social intelligence. Sosik (2015) posits that leadership is a social influence process within each organization. Further, he states that leaders that are "tuned in" (p. 141) to their own emotions can effectively influence followers. Additionally, leaders that comprehend organizational social systems become appropriate idealized leaders that provide inspirational motivation for their members, and through individualized consideration further develop their performance skills.

In less than two decades the Internet was shaped into a virtual space or cyberspace filled with various facilities and activities for users to enjoy, prior to that most of these activities were accomplished in physical spaces. Today, in conjunction with the Internet, fixed and mobile telephone services have been digitized providing various virtual arenas adopted to accommodate growing subscribers. This evolution has led to the satisfaction of basic needs for humans to achieve virtual communications and services in these new environments. According to Kellerman (2014), "double-space" (p. 538) has been formed, which allows humans that subscribe to the Internet and mobile phones to socialize in the traditional physical space or the virtual space on a daily basis as necessary. The virtual space has become a crucial environment for many seeking love and belonging and to lessen the burden of loneliness. Virtual correspondence and talks including video chats are popular online combined with traditional communications through postal letters. Recently, the Internet has expanded the opportunities for belonging with the creation of Facebook, a global social network. This choice for social belonging has become a daily routine for worldwide audiences. As of October 2012, Facebook reported one billion monthly active users, 81% outside of the United States (Facebook, 2012).

The skill of identifying group interaction patterns and collaborative framework can help leaders understand behaviors in virtual space. Recognizing and classifying patterns can help determine different forms of online collaboration. Patterns can take two forms; general or specific. Patterns were originally developed for the field of architecture, but are applied to a variety fields today: software engineering, human-computer interaction, education science, as well as technology-enhanced learning (Goodyear & Retalis, 2010). In a specific situation, the pattern concept was designed to solve a problem or reach a specified goal. Additionally, patterns were intended to help describe collaboration tasks in multi-user environments. Gottesdiener (2001) defined a collaboration pattern as a set of techniques, behaviors, and activities for people who share a common goal of working together in a group, to suggest a structure for collaboration. Furthermore, collaboration patterns may be tools, techniques, behaviors, and activities for people meeting together in specific locations or within certain groups or communities for interaction or completing a common goal (Schemell, Eppler, & de Freitas, 2012).

Typically, social cues that inactivate empathy in the physical world are often absent in cyberspace and the consequences of one's actions in cyberspace are usually invisible, remote, or delayed. It is helpful for educators and leaders to learn about empathy as a virtue in this context or as an ethical behavior, encouraging its development in virtual social interactions (Whittier, 2005). Social intelligence allows leaders to not only understand their own motives and actions, but knowing their follower's goals and concerns in order to become effective transformational leaders.

JUSTICE

Fostering a sense of fairness and righteousness describes the virtue of *justice*. There are three character strengths within this virtue: citizenship, fairness, and leadership. When we demonstrate a sense of loyalty, social responsibility, and teamwork, we are exercising *citizenship*. In many organizational situations, we must work well with other group or team members, display loyalty, and do our part of the workload to ensure harmony. Ensuring that we treat others the same without personal bias or preference describes *fairness*. This strength has been linked to a strong moral identity helping to foster trust among others (Peterson & Seligman, 2004; Sosik, 2015). Leaders must be fair in order to be trusted by followers. Peterson and Seligman (2004) describe a *leader* as someone that not only encourages a group to accomplish a goal, but also maintains good relations among the group. Utilizing transformational behaviors discussed previously will ensure effective leadership (Sosik, 2015). The character strength of *citizenship* or teamwork is the focus of the next section.

Encouraging followers to work together as effective teams or collaborators describe the importance of fostering *citizenship* as a pivotal character strength within any organization. An idealized leader has the ability to create loyalty and commitment among followers to help develop highly cohesive teams. Effective teamwork is the hallmark of any synergistic organization. When leaders value citizenship, they are building trust and loyalty among followers (Sosik, 2015). How does this work in cyberspace?

Cyberspace has become the new meeting point for many, whereby time and space may have blurred boundaries, but interaction occurs at various levels. The Internet has been referred to as social technology that allows users to meet social needs. According to Cohen and Willis (1985), when people engage in more social contact, they are happier and healthier both in a physical and mental sense. The flexibility of cyberspace has allowed people who may have never met physically to start new interpersonal relationships in a virtual setting regardless of global distances. Online chat relationships provide new and exciting opportunities for social contacts. Additionally, online chat rooms have become the new virtual meeting place for people to communicate regardless of time or space (Peris et al., 2002). When others are interacting in massively multiuser spaces, friendships, communities, and new societies and cultures may emerge, often very similar to real world interactions. Virtual worlds provide learning experiences, creative expression, and cultural interaction among unlimited groups and teams, which have been leveraged by many educators (Johnson & Levine, 2008). The amount of users or residents in the most popular VW communities (like Second Life) may exceed 5 million inhabitants with thousands online at any moment. This scale produces whole societies in many ways. Residents typically form into alliances, working groups, discussion teams, families, and peer groups, without limitations. These users choose their tasks or adventures and interact as easily as in the real world. Cultural rules and expectations may be simple or very sophisticated and socialization promotes learning processes of observation, reflection, and assimilation. Interpersonal relationships and collaborations are observable throughout virtual world settings. It is a fairly common sight to see groups interacting at various levels to ensure skills are increased by all, many tutorials are readily available in most virtual world settings for user convenience. Because these worlds encourage teamwork and partnerships, there are many rich forms of expression through the use of available tools and powers, communication may occur with text or voice in addition to objects, video, and demonstrations (Johnson Levine, 2008). Citizenship and teamwork offers leaders the ability to use idealized approaches to build trust and commitment among their followers.

TEMPERANCE

Temperance describes the ability to exercise self-control and consider boundaries and limitations on personal desires and aspirations. There are four character strengths associated with this virtue: forgiveness and mercy, humility/modesty, prudence, and self-regulation/control. A person that exercises *forgiveness and mercy* avoids the human impulse to become vengeful in certain situations. This involves displaying leniency and compassion for someone who may be in trouble or at a specific disadvantage. Additionally, utilizing forgiveness at the appropriate times may not only restore positive emotions, moods, and attitudes, it may also reduce anxiety, anger, and depression (Peterson & Seligman, 2004; Sosik, 2015).

The *humility and modesty* character strength involves remaining humble during one's achievements and not seeking the spotlight, or allowing one's performance to speak for itself. Typically, humble individuals are less likely to take unnecessary risks or make poor decisions and are usually excellent mentors. Leaders whose egos overpower their humility are prone to narcissism usually leading to career derailment, lack of follower trust, and low moral development. People exhibiting *prudence* are generally logical decision makers that make careful, thoughtful choices. They are considered conscientious, and demonstrate positive personality traits (agreeableness, extroversion, and emotional stability). *Self-regulation and control* describes the foundation of temperance as it relates to one's discipline and regulates one's appetites and emotions. Those leaders with high self-control typically inspire; better relationships, trust, fairness, and consistency with followers (Peterson & Seligman, 2004; Sosik, 2015). Self-regulation is the character strength that has a strong presence in cyberspace today, the next section will highlight further examples.

To achieve an idealized transformational approach, it is paramount that developing leaders display high ethical and moral standards at all times. These standards are derived from one's personal values, ideals, and beliefs. When we control our impulses and keep them in check against a self-imposed standard, we are *self-regulating* our behaviors. We take our cues from feedback around us in order to meet the social and acceptable norms of social groups, families, work settings, and other communities. Leaders that self-regulate their behaviors by observing social responses around them are exercising self-control by maintaining their feelings, thoughts, and emotions. This character strength promotes the display of idealized leadership, while inspirationally motivating followers to control their own behaviors, and showing individual consideration for those around them (Sosik, 2015). The next section will illustrate some relevant examples found in virtual environments today.

In the twenty-first century, it is hard to imagine a day without using the Internet. The Internet is all around us and according to Moor (2000), "computing technology is not running away from us as much as moving in with us. Computer sprawl, like urban sprawl, moves inexorably on many fronts unsupervised." (p. 35) Unfortunately, as unsupervised audiences grow in virtual communities, the unethical implications may become problematic. Cyberspace introduces new challenges to our ethical behavior probably because it offers a sense of invisibility, anonymity, and privacy (to a point). This environment offers freedom to pretend and explore and for some has led to hate speech and other unacceptable transgressions. As we examine these behaviors, we come to the realization that the targets of these foul behaviors rarely have the opportunity to hold these perpetrators accountable in cyberspace. Cyberbullying, theft, plagiarism, and fraud are just a few serious crimes that are commonplace in cyberspace today.

Unfortunately, cyberbullying and spreading rumors is popular misbehavior among younger groups. Cyberbullying is a term used when a perpetrator sends cruel or hateful messages to someone via the Internet or cell phone. The goal of cyberbullying is humiliation, intimidation, social or relational aggression such as social exclusion or ostracizing others (Whittier, 2006). Leaders today should be aware of these types of unregulated behaviors to ensure that their followers are not victims or practicing any bad habits that may lead to any similar transgressions. Willard (2005), describes some of the most common forms of cyberbullying:

- **Flaming:** Online fights using electronic messages with angry and vulgar language.
- **Harassment:** Repeatedly sending offensive, rude, and insulting messages.
- **Cyberstalking:** Repeatedly sending messages that include threats of harm or are highly intimidating. Engaging in other online activities that make a person afraid for his or her safety.
- **Denigration:** "Dissing" someone online. Sending or posting cruel gossip or rumors about a person to damage his or her reputation or friendships.
- **Impersonation:** Breaking into someone's account, posing as that person and sending messages to make the person look bad, get that person in trouble or danger, or damage that person's reputation or friendships.
- **Outing and Trickery:** Sharing someone's secrets or embarrassing information online. Tricking someone into revealing secrets or embarrassing information, which is then shared online.
- **Exclusion:** Intentionally excluding someone from an online group, like a "buddy list" or a game (Willard, 2005, pp. 1-2)

Other risky behaviors associated with virtual environments include: disclosing personal information, Internet addiction, suicide and self-harm communities, hate group recruitment and gangs, risky sexual behavior, and violent gaming.

Suggested programs to manage cyberspace misbehaviors include: policy and practice reviews, professional development, user education, cyberethics, and Internet management (Willard, 2005). Teaching cyberethics requires two types of leaders. The first are the administrators, community leaders, and taxpayers that make cyberethics a priority among followers and students. The second type of cyberethics leader are the educators who not only inculcate these principles in all relevant curricula, but ensure cyber awareness for all associated virtual platforms. Self-regulation directly impacts our organizations, as leaders we must set high standards for our followers to emulate to model authentic transformational leadership.

TRANSCENDENCE

Transcendence, is a virtue that is manifested in the "strengths of the spirit," and provides meaning to one's life by making connections to the larger universe or looking beyond oneself and toward relations with others. There are five related character strengths associated with this virtue: appreciation of beauty or excellence, gratitude, hope, humor, and spirituality. Transcendent individuals are often filled with awe, wonder, and elevation of spirit upon recognition of certain extraordinary people or things. These individuals learn to *appreciate beauty* or *excellence* in the skilled performance of others. Leaders utilizing this character strength support high goals for their followers and will often reward their followers for achieving increased levels of performance. Additionally, transcendent individuals are thankful for the good things in their lives and take the time to thank those that have had a positive influence, exercising *gratitude*.

Gratitude allows leaders the opportunity to recognize that their leadership outcomes are accomplished through their followers' efforts, which aids in fostering positive leader-follower relationships. Looking to the future with a positive vision or optimistic outlook describes *hope*. Typically, hopeful individuals are high achievers in academics, athletics, politics, and other industries as they have a positive vision for the future and will set loftier goals. Transcendent people often use *humor* to not only encourage creativity, but also relieve stressful situations. Studies have shown that self-deprecating and positive forms of humor may promote creativity, reduce stress, improve physical health, and promote good moods. *Spirituality* is associated with possessing faith in something greater than ourselves, or having beliefs relating to a higher purpose, meaning of life, or considering where one fits in the larger scheme of things. Research has shown that spirituality has positive influences on interpersonal relationships, social values, while promoting psychological and physical health (Peterson & Seligman, 2004; Sosik, 2015). The next section provides some spirituality considerations in cyberspace.

A growing recognition in organizations in recent years is the acknowledgement of employee's personal beliefs and businesses are recognizing the positive effects of *spirituality* in the workplace. The ethics, values, and beliefs of leaders is derived from many sources, including spirituality. To be clear, spirituality and religion are not the same issue. Religion is concerned with a person's divine feelings and experiences as they relate to an institution along with associated worship practices and service attendance. Spirituality examines an individual's connections or beliefs between human and metaphysical. Religion and spirituality may provide meaning and purpose for transformational leaders as they deal with their organizations, families, or life's challenges. Through idealized behaviors, inspirational motivations, and individualized leadership actions, one can help followers transcend through spirituality (Sosik, 2015). Is spirituality found in cyberspace? The following section examines how this virtual environment may be affecting the spiritual development of future followers – our youth.

Video gaming whether online or within one's home gaming center has become a popular pastime for youth. A Canadian study discovered that boys under 20 are more likely (80%) to engage in online games compared to girls in the same age group (20%) and the majority of these two groups play between 12 and 24 hours every week (Gladwell & Currie, 2009). Additionally, a U.S. study revealed that children between the ages of 11 – 14 years of age average 85 minutes a day playing video games, while those between the ages of 8 – 18 average more than an hour of daily gaming in a virtual environment (Rideout, Foehr, & Roberts, 2010). Reflecting on these results, one may wonder how this time in virtual gaming may affect the spiritual development of our young people? The most popular games (World of Warcraft, Halo, Ben 10, and Toon Sports) are centered in the area of fantasy. Typically, players enter the games as characters of a fictional society and are invited to escape the limits of real life and take on experimental traits that aid in their success of meeting a variety of goals or achievements. Furthermore, gaming scenarios include narratives involving quests, apocalyptic threats, heroism, social actions, spiritual, or religious issues (Hodge, 2010).

Players may embody avatars or self-representations as in most MMPORGs (massively multi-player online role-playing games) to engage in spiritual quests, battles between good and evil, or challenges to test their collaborative skills. One online study conducted by The Kids Help Phone, found that younger participants overwhelmingly admitted to the addictive nature of virtual gaming and over half agreed that their gaming habits conflicted with their school assignments and physical activities. Moreover, most of the participating respondents claimed that escaping reality was the main reason for their gaming behavior. One respondent claimed that it was easier to pretend to be someone else rather than face their own issues (Gladwell & Currie, 2009). The Kaiser Family Foundation study in the U.S., found that young people that

Figure 3. Transformational leadership-virtues-character strengths mind map relationships
Image Credit Fil Arenas.

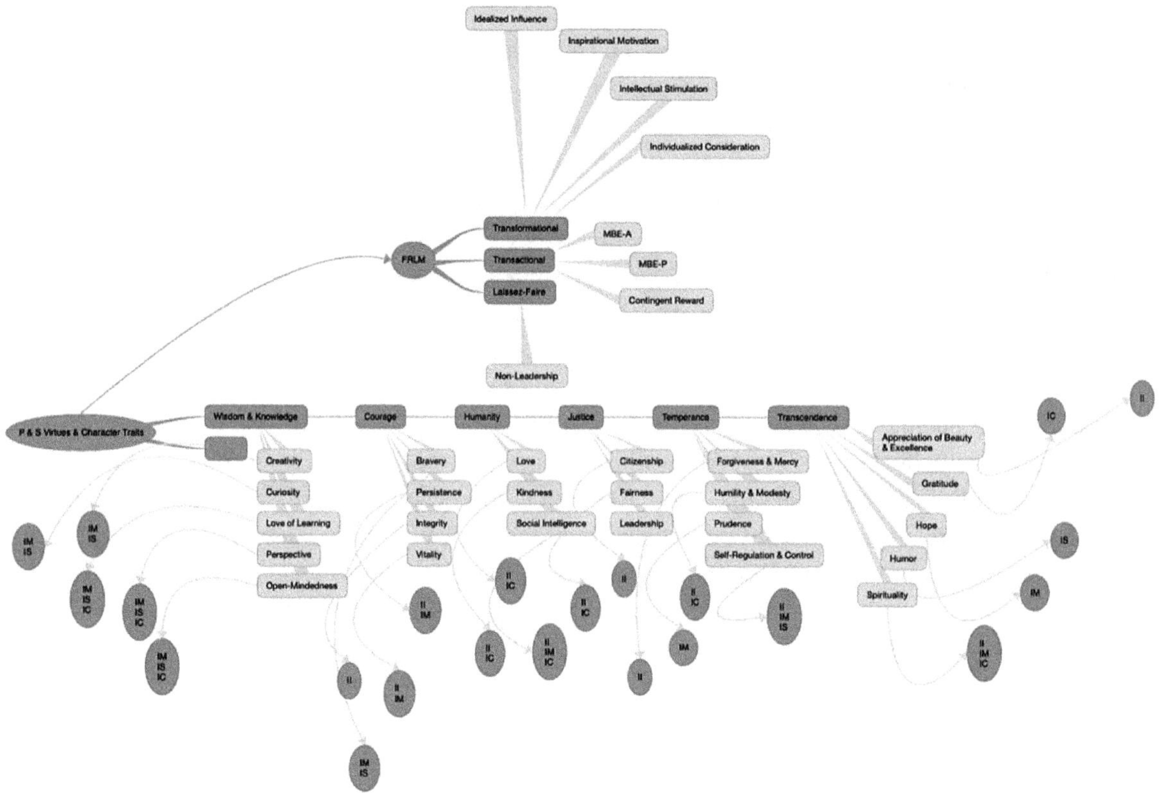

spend more than 16 hours a day involved with media-based content (including virtual gaming) are more likely to report sadness, unhappiness, or life boredom (Rideout et al., 2010). For this younger gaming audience, participating in virtual games may inhibit their spiritual development. Although significant questions remain regarding the long-term effects of gaming for young people, it is imperative that we continue to research this potential relationship. Considering the increasing number of virtual gamers that join these communities each year, exploring the correlation between youth's cyberspace adventures and spiritual development (Yust et al., 2011) could enlighten future leaders on this vital character strength.

Leadership researchers often focus on leadership styles and behaviors as they relate to accomplishing the mission or meeting a specific timelines or goals. In most dynamic and complex organizational environments, we often fail to consider the human aspects of leadership and followership. Utilizing the foundation of Peterson and Seligman's (2004) research and the transformational applications of Sosik's (2015) work, we can make more meaningful connections with our superiors, peers, and followers. Figure 2 illustrates a mind map connecting the above relationships from transformational leadership components to virtues and character strengths.

Many times in corporate decision-making, there is no black and white, only shades of gray. One lesson learned from modern warfare, especially in the war on terror, is that military officers are faced with decisions where all courses of action may have detrimental consequences. Understanding different models and strategies will give members a larger set of tools to use when they are faced with difficult

Figure 4. Virtual classroom

decisions. Each model has its own strengths and weaknesses and outcomes may vary depending on the situation. Additionally, as described by Peterson and Seligman (2004), the six virtues and associated character strengths shape each one of our decisions on an individual level. Comprehending these virtues and our own signature character strengths will not only help us grow into idealized exemplars, but help us relate to our follower's needs. Further, the most successful leaders will determine how to combine aspects of different sources to establish their own decision-making and character strength framework.

CYBERCHARACTER

The trials of bringing *character* into cyberspace is rapidly evolving as artificial intelligence, motion tracking, facial recognition, and avatar gestures are ameliorated over time. Displaying empathy in a virtual environment has been difficult to project given the abstract nature of most avatars actions. Although empathy is key to moral development, determining how our thoughts and actions impact others in cyberspace presents many challenges. Moreover, technology often limits communication by masking our affective cues that are prevalent in the physical world. These cues are integral to displaying how we feel and reflect how others feel, fostering moral and ethical interactions to take place (Goleman, 2006). At a recent conference in Alexandria, Virginia, a unique collaboration between educators and simulation designers set their sights on closing the gap on the *cybercharacter* challenge.

ASCD, a global leader of innovative programs for educators since 1943, joined forces with Mursion Inc. to leverage state-of-the-art technology to support leader dialogue and develop fledgling educators through immersive simulations. Mursion empowers organizations to create safe laboratory environments in order to practice engagement techniques in risk-free settings. This technology platform enables customized, authentic scenarios to address complex interpersonal situations. Through the use of cyberspace and live actors relevant interactions are created for real-time learning and coaching opportunities (ASCD Website,

Figure 5. Mixed reality exercise
Image Credit Andrew Clayton.

2016). One example of using this technology to develop character development has been implemented at the Air Command and Staff College, Air University, Maxwell AFB, Alabama for developing field grade officers. Participants signing up for the *North Star Leadership* elective experienced mixed-reality exercises (MRX) as they were immersed in multiple virtual scenarios involving subordinates requiring a variety of character strengths during their interactions. These scenarios were designed to enhance cognitive and emotional understanding of leader-follower relationships (Arenas, 2018).

Empathy is important to moral and ethical development, but learning about and thinking about how our actions affect others is a challenge. In the abstract environment of cyberspace, the consequences of our actions are not as readily apparent as they are in person. Technology mediates communication and reduces affective and social cues of the physical world, thereby distancing or removing people from the consequences of their actions in cyberspace. When we can see someone, we can more readily feel what he or she is feeling. In person, we react to people both consciously and unconsciously as social cues present in the physical world inform our ethical awareness. Neurobiologists suggest that empathy is a survival or evolutionary development that informs social interaction (Goleman, 2006). People have evolved to sense information about others. For example, we sense trustworthiness through facial expressions, body language, and other affective types of information absent or reduced in cyberspace.

CONCLUSION

Regardless of how we develop as humans, it is imperative that we continually embrace those profound principles passed on to us by our earliest philosophers, social scientists, and leadership scholars on what it means to be human. As cyberspace becomes ubiquitous in our society, leadership scholars and practitioners must remain vigilant since "what we know about the interaction between AIT and leadership still remains at the very nascent stages of development" (Avolio, et al., 2014, p. 121). Moreover, we must embody the efforts of those that that have introduced various cyber character awareness programs such as character education, cyberethics, and cybercharacter to meet the continual challenges for yet another abstract society; cyberspace.

REFERENCES

Alger, J. R. (2000). Classroom capitalism. *Academe*, *86*(1), 79–80. doi:10.2307/40252348

Allen, E. I., & Seaman, J. (2014). Changing course: Ten years of tracking online education in the United States. Atlantic Marketing Journal, 3(2), 131-149.

Arenas, F.J. (2018). *North star leadership course*. Air Command and Staff College, Air University.

ASCD Website. (2016). *ASCD announces partnership with Mursion to develop leadership institutes that leverage simulations in virtual reality*. Retrieved from http://www.ascd.org/news-media/Press-Room/News-Releases/ASCD-Announces-Partnership-with-Mursion.aspx

Avolio, B. J., Sosik, J. J., Kahai, S. S., & Baker, B. (2013). E-leadership: Re-examining transformations in leadership source and transmission. *The Leadership Quarterly*, *25*(1), 105–131. doi:10.1016/j.leaqua.2013.11.003

Bartle, R. (2012). Early MUD history. In I. Duncan, A. Miller, & S. Jiang. A taxonomy of virtual worlds usage in education. *British Journal of Educational Technology*, *43*(6), 949–964.

Bass, B. M. (2008). *The Bass Handbook of Leadership: Theory, Research & Managerial Applications*. New York: Free Press.

Bass, B. M., & Riggio, R. E. (2006). *Transformational Leadership*. Mahwah, NJ: Lawrence Erlbaum Associates, Inc.

Blascovich, J., & Bailenson, J. (2011). *Infinite Reality: Avatars, Eternal Life, New Worlds, and the Dawn of the Virtual Revolution*. New York: HarperCollins Publishers.

Castronova, E. (2010). *Synthetic worlds – The business and culture of online games*. Chicago University Press.

Cohen, S., & Willis, T. A. (1985). Stress, social support, and the buffering hypothesis. *Psychological Bulletin*, *98*(2), 310–357. doi:10.1037/0033-2909.98.2.310 PMID:3901065

Cohen, W. M., & Levinthal, D. A. (2010). Absorptive capacity: A new perspective on learning and innovation. *Administrative Science Quarterly*, *35*, 554-568.

Cook, N. S. D., & Brown, J. S. (2010). Bridging epistemologies – the generative dance between organizational knowledge and organizational knowing. *Organization Science, 10*, 381-400.

Csikszentmihalyi, M. (1990). *Flow: The Psychology of Optimal Experience.* New York, NY: Harper and Row.

D'Onfro, J. (2015, April 17). The truth about Google's famous '20% time' policy. *Business Insider, Tech.* Retrieved from www.businessinsider.com

Daneshi, T. (2016). *Cyber Ethics: A Global Conversation.* Retrieved from DeVry University blog website: http://www.devry.edu/blog/2014/02/cyber-ethics-a-global conversation.html

Davenport, T. H., & Prusak, L. (2010). *Working Knowledge – How organizations manage what they know.* Harvard Business School Press.

De Freitas, S. (2010). *Serious virtual worlds: A scoping study.* Academic Press.

Duncan, I., Miller, A., & Jiang, S. (2012). A taxonomy of virtual worlds usage in education. *British Journal of Educational Technology, 43*(6), 949–964. doi:10.1111/j.1467-8535.2011.01263.x

Facebook. (2014). Statistics. In A. Kellerman. The satisfaction of human needs in physical and virtual spaces. *The Professional Geographer, 66*(4), 538-546.

Gaba, D. (2004). The future vision of simulation in health care. *Quality & Safety in Health Care, 13*(suppl_1), 2–10. doi:10.1136/qshc.2004.009878 PMID:15465951

George, B. (2007). *True North.* San Francisco, CA: Jossey-Bass.

Gibson, W. (1984). *Neuromancer.* New York, NY: The Berkley Publishing Group.

Gladwell, C., & Currie, J. (2011). Online gaming: Child's play or obsession? In K. M. Yust, B. Hyde, & C. Ota. *International Journal of Children's Spirituality, 16*(1), 1–3.

Goleman, D. (2006). *Social intelligence: The new science of human relationships.* New York, NU: Bantam Dell.

Goodyear, P., & Retalis, S. (2012). *Technology-enhanced learning: Design patterns and pattern languages.* Academic Press. doi:10.17705/1jais.00309

Gottesdiener, E. (2001). Decide how to decide: A collaboration pattern. Software Development Magazine, *9*(1).

Grant, R.M. (n.d.). Toward a knowledge-based theory of the firm. *Strategic Management Journal, 17*, 109-122.

Guyette, R. W., King, C. G., & Piotrowski, C. (2008). Business faculty views of online course cheating: Evidence for a cohort effect. *Organization Development Journal, 26*(4), 25–31.

Hale, K. S., & Stanney, K. M. (2015). *Handbook of Virtual Environments: Design, Implementation, and Applications.* Boca Raton, FL: CRC Press.

Heiphetz, A., & Woodill, G. (2010). *Training and Collaboration with Virtual Worlds: How to Create Cost-Saving, Efficient, and Engaging Programs*. New York: McGraw-Hill.

Heylighen, F. (1994). *Cyberspace*. Retrieved from Principia Cybernetica Web: http://pespmc1.vub.ac.be/cybspace.html

Hinduja, S., & Patchin, J. (2009). Bullying beyond the schoolyard. Thousand Oaks, CA: Corwin.

Hodge, D. (2010). Role-playing: Toward a theology of gamers. In C. Detweiler (Ed.), *Halos and avatars: Playing video games with God*. Louisville, KY: Westminster John Knox.

House, R. J., & Howell, J. A. (1992). Personality and charismatic leadership. *The Leadership Quarterly, 3*(2), 81–108. doi:10.1016/1048-9843(92)90028-E

Ireland, J. L. (1999). *Provictim attitudes and empathy in relation to bullying behaviour among prisoners*. Academic Press.

Jenkins, M., Browne, T., & Walker, R. (2012). *VLE surveys: A longitudinal perspective between March 2001, March 2003, and March 2005 for higher education in the United Kingdom*. Academic Press.

Johnson, L. F., & Levine, A. H. (2008). Virtual worlds: Inherently immersive, highly social learning places. *Theory into Practice, 47*(2), 161–170. doi:10.1080/00405840801992397

Jones, I., Blankenship, D., & Hollier, G. (2014). Am I cheating? An analysis of online student perceptions of their behaviors and attitudes. *Proceedings of ASBBS, 20*(1).

Kellerman, A. (2014). The satisfaction of human needs in physical and virtual spaces. *The Professional Geographer, 66*(4), 538–546. doi:10.1080/00330124.2013.848760

Kiehl, E. M. (2008). Using an ethical decision-making model to determine consequences for student plagiarism. *Journal of Nursing Education, 45*, 199-203.

Kohler, T., Matzler, K., & Fuller, J. (2009). Avatar-based innovation: Using virtual worlds for real-world innovation. *Technovation, 29*, 395-407.

Mattis, P. (2010). Interactive immersive learning in higher education. *Creative Nursing, 16*(3), 106–109. doi:10.1891/1078-4535.16.3.106 PMID:20879617

Miller, A., & Young-Jones, A. D. (2012). *Academic integrity: Online classes compared to face-to-face classes*. Paper presented at the meeting of the Southwestern Psychological Association, Oklahoma City, OK.

Moor, J. (2006). If Aristotle were a computing professional. In R. Baird, R. Ramsower, & S. Rosenbaum (Eds.), *Cyberethics: Social and Moral Issues in the Computing Age*. New York, NY: Prometheus Books.

Mueller, J., Hutter, K., Fueller, J., & Matzler, K. (2010). Virtual worlds as knowledge management platform – a practice-perspective. *Information Systems Journal, 21*(6), 479–501. doi:10.1111/j.1365-2575.2010.00366.x

Mueller, J., Karr, A., & Renzl, B. (2010). Its not my community – insights from social identity theory explaining community-failure. *International Journal of Learning and Change, 3*, 23-37. doi:10.1111/j.1365-2575.2010.00366.x

Patri, K. (2008). Deviances in the virtual reality or the character-altering power of virtual communities. *European Journal of Crime Criminal Law and Criminal Justice, 16*(3), 325–343. doi:10.1163/157181708X333373

Peris, R., Gimeno, M. A., Ortet, G., Carrero, V., Sanchiz, M., & Ibanez, I. (2002). Online chat rooms: Virtual spaces of interaction for socially oriented people. *Cyberpsychology & Behavior, 5*(1), 43–51. doi:10.1089/109493102753685872 PMID:11990974

Peterson, C., & Seligman, M. E. P. (2004). *Character Strengths and Virtues:Handbook and Classification*. New York: Oxford University Press.

Schmell, A., Eppler, M. J., & de Freitas, S. (2012). A structured approach for designing collaboration experiences for virtual worlds. *Journal of the Association for Information Systems, 13*(10), 836–860. doi:10.17705/1jais.00309

Schroeder, R., & Axelsson, A. S. (2010). *Avatars at work and play: Collaboration and interaction in shared virtual environments*. Springer.

Sosik, J. J. (2015). *Leading with Character: Stories of Valor and Virtue and the Principles they Teach*. Charlotte, NC: Information Age Publishing, Inc.

Tagliaventi, M. R., & Mattarelli, E. (2010). The role of networks of practice, value sharing, and operational proximity in knowledge flows between professional groups. *Human Relations, 59*, 291-319.

Van Camp, J. C. (2014). *Ethics*. Boston, MA: Wadsworth.

Varble, D. L. (2014). Reducing cheating opportunities on online tests. *Atlantic Marketing Journal, 3*(2), 131–149.

Wasko, M. M., & Faraj, S. (2010). It is what one does: Why people participate and help others in electronic communities of practice. *Journal of Strategic Information Systems, 9*, 155-173.

Whittier, D. B. (2006). Cyberethics in the Googling age. *Journal of Education, 187*(2), 1–86. doi:10.1177/002205740718700202

Whittier, D. B. (2013). Cyberethics: Envisioning character education in cyberspace. *Peabody Journal of Education, 88*(2), 225–242. doi:10.1080/0161956X.2013.775882

Willard, N. (2005). *Educator's guide to cyberbullying and cyberthreats*. Retrieved from http://csriu.org, http://cyberbully.org

Yust, K. M., Hyde, B., & Ota, C. (2011). Cyber spirituality II: Virtual reality and spiritual exploration. *International Journal of Children's Spirituality, 16*(1), 1–3. doi:10.1080/1364436X.2011.564846

Chapter 5
Digital Citizenship in Virtual Environments

Valerie J. Hill
https://orcid.org/0000-0003-1508-8159
Texas Woman's University, USA

ABSTRACT

Virtual environments provide collaborative learning opportunities beyond physical walls and without time constraints. Learners connect across the planet in real time. The virtual representation of self requires understanding of personal responsibility for digital citizenship and information literacy. Both presentation of self and evaluation of content in all formats are new challenges for learners of all ages, including the youngest students born into an age of networked sharing and connecting. Virtual learning environments may transform education and certainly provide both advantages and disadvantages for educators and learners. Understanding personal responsibility for digital citizenship is imperative to best practices of education in virtual spaces. This chapter focuses on digital citizenship and information literacy in virtual worlds, virtual reality, and immersive learning environments.

INTRODUCTION

Learning in the 21st century has radically changed due to the toppling of the information hierarchy leading to a critical need for digital citizenship in participatory culture. We no longer live in an era of linear acquisition of knowledge by the individual with traditional publishing sources housed in libraries and carefully selected by "gatekeepers" at the top of the hierarchy. Participatory culture, a world where individuals have instant access to information on mobile devices and a vast array of content creation and curation applications, has allowed crowdsourced and user-generated content to overtake traditional sources in only a few years. In order to "participate" in participatory culture, through online tools and networks, digital citizenship has become critical. Without an understanding of the evaluation of information in the new gatekeeper-free era, an individual can be lost in an overwhelming flood of information. This chapter focuses on challenges presented by the change from a hierarchy of knowledge acquisition

DOI: 10.4018/978-1-5225-9679-0.ch005

to one of global instant access and a critical need for personal responsibility for learning. This awareness of digital citizenship is imperative to the future of learning both for the individual and for our society.

An example of participatory culture is Wikipedia, the largest encyclopedia in the world created by users across the globe which began with popular culture but (Joseph Deodato believes) is not fully embraced by politics and education. Deodato says, "However, the participatory culture of the Web, as constructed by online forums, blogs, social networks, and massively multiplayer games, empower users by offering opportunities to participate, create, interact, and engage in decision-making" (Deodato, 2014, p. 746). A new regime of collaboratively edited open content, according to Deodato, challenges traditional conceptions of knowledge and expertise covering a wide range of specialized and traditionally marginalized topics. The ability to participate in networked culture presents a need for responsible behavior.

Today, no matter which devices or technology applications we use, each one of us lives and learns in a virtual world more often than in a physical one. The walls of physical classrooms have been lifted and learners can communicate through social media, Skype, or numerous live online formats. The shift to learning in a virtual world has powerful advantages but also has disadvantages and obstacles both obvious and hidden. Awareness of the advantages and disadvantages of virtual learning is part of digital citizenship. Through exploring and reflecting on how literacy and learning have rapidly changed, the need for digital citizenship becomes clear for ourselves and for learners of the future. Whether or not one experiences global digital participatory culture with an avatar in a simulated environment, we all live in a virtual world with mobile devices at our fingertips taking us to places beyond our physical bodies. This chapter focuses on the need for digital citizenship with a focus on virtual environments for learning.

BACKGROUND OF VIRTUAL ENVIRONMENTS IN PARTICIPATORY CULTURE

Participatory culture can be defined as a culture in which private persons (the public) do not act as consumers only, but also as contributors or producers. "The term is most often applied to the production or creation of some type of published media" (Wikipedia, 2019). Learners in today's classroom live in global digital participatory culture and are digital citizens as well as citizens of a physical community and they participate as *prosumers* (a term first used by Alvin Toffler)- both consumers and producers of media (Toffler, 1980). Toffler, a futurist, predicted the movement toward producing media decades ago.

Schools and libraries are embracing participatory culture and the Web 2.0 tools that arose at the turn of the 21st century, such as image and video creation, mash-ups and curation tools. Librarians like Buffy Hamilton at Creekview High School in Georgia, believe strongly in participatory culture to promote inquiry-based collaborative learning through blogs, wikis, and building virtual learning portfolios. Hamilton says, "The participatory culture is also conducive to helping students create personal learning networks and environments to cultivate resources for accessing, evaluating, and sharing information locally and with the world" (Hamilton, 2011, p. 41). This move toward participatory culture has created a need for PLNs, Personal (or Professional) Learning Networks to learn and discover trends and changes because it is difficult, perhaps impossible, to keep up with the exponential growth and change of computer technology. A PLN can be considered as a personally curated network of individuals to share learning opportunities, particularly in online platforms.

Figure 1. Educator's tweet during Twitter chat about #DigitalCitizenship

Educators and librarians utilize Twitter for the development of global professional networks as well as for ongoing professional development. Information science professor, Judi Moreillion, conducted a netnographic case study of librarians using Twitter for professional development. Moreillion concluded, "As they appropriate Twitter purposefully to achieve desired outcomes—school librarian PD [professional development]— participants demonstrate and develop 21st----century literacy practices" (Moreillion, 2015, p. 136). A netnographic methodology is an ethnographic study done entirely online.

Through social media sites (Facebook, Twitter, Instagram and others) and curation sites (Pinterest, Tumblr, ScoopIt and others) older students have instant access to shared content on a global scale. Younger students can utilize apps for learning and creating content, such as ShowMe Interactive Whiteboard or Skitch for adding text to images. Even kindergarteners are creating video book reports using augmented reality apps to link images and video into presentations that can be shared. Participatory culture means students are no longer bound by physical classroom walls. Through Skype and numerous online tools, students can meet others all over the world and learn collaboratively. Tradition classrooms, only a few decades ago, were local, isolated and focused on physical world citizenship.

The vast array of apps available to create puppet shows, podcasts, edit mash-ups and add special effects is exciting but can also be intimidating to educators, often making them feel like there is no way to keep up. Not only are new technology applications arriving daily, the platforms and operating systems require constant upgrades and installations. Toffler is often quoted as saying, "The illiterate of the 21st Century will not be those who cannot read or write, but those who cannot learn, unlearn and relearn", however one may consider the irony of the difficult quest encountered in trying to find the actual source of that quote (Groom, 2009). While advocating the importance of 21st century information literacy, the flood of information we encounter online may practically wash away original source documentation. Respect for intellectual property, our own and others, is a value even young children can appreciate.

Much of the content created with technology tools could be classified as *disposable* since it is meant to be shared and viewed quickly without visitation or archival. The fast-paced interactive exchange of information across the globe sometimes makes deep learning and critical thinking a challenge. One of the biggest advantages of virtual worlds for learning is the ability to create learning content that is persistent and can be revisited time after time alone or with a community.

The definition of a virtual world has been evolving over the past decade and confusion has arisen. A virtual world is not necessarily a game and is considered a "subset of virtual environments". A virtual world may be viewed with a virtual reality headset or on a computer monitor. A thorough examination of the relationship of virtual worlds to other technologies culminated in the following definition. Virtual worlds can be defined as, "Shared, simulated spaces which are inhabited and shaped by their inhabitants who are represented as avatars. These avatars mediate our experience of this space as we move, interact with objects and interact with others, with whom we construct a shared understanding of the world at that time" (Girvan, 2018, p. 1099).

Figure 2. Learners, as avatars, manipulating thousands of math cubes in a virtual world

Learning Theories in Virtual Worlds and Participatory Culture

This shift from consumption of media to both consumption and production of media through collaboration on a global scale has brought new meaning to *connected learning*. Child development psychologist, Lev Vygotsky, believed learning is social and not accomplished in isolation (Vygotsky, 1978). The social connectivity of networked participatory culture aligns well with social constructivism theory and many educators embrace Vygotsky's pedagogical view. Yet, when we move from the "flat" web with sites and pages of shared content into 3D simulated virtual worlds, the potential for "hands on" learning is quite different. Virtual worlds, as computer simulated immersive learning environments, provide opportunities for students to learn in ways that are impossible in a physical classroom.

An example of virtual world learning illustrating what cannot be done in a physical classroom is "Math in 3D". An instructor can show millions of cubes and allow students to manipulate then in groupings. A physical classroom would not allow students to dump millions of cubes onto the classroom floor! (Hill, 2013). Students working in a virtual world simulation, with avatars representing themselves, are not physically picking up cubes with their hands, but are cognitively manipulating the cubes and exploring the math concepts. These students are constructing knowledge in a social environment within a virtual world which aligns with social constructivism (Vygotsky, 1978).

Loke (2015) conducted a systematic literature review to examine how virtual world experiences might bring about real-world knowledge and skills. Seven learning theories were found to adequately explain applicable learning in virtual worlds: Experiential Learning Theory, Situated Learning Theory, Social Constructivism, Constructivism, Self-Efficacy Theory, Projective Identity Model, and Presence Theory.

Through those seven theories, four modes of learning in virtual worlds were identified: learning through reflection, learning through verbal interaction, learning through mental operations and decisions, and learning through vicarious experiences. Loke concluded, "Knowing this, educators can more precisely determine what students can learn in virtual worlds: for example, in a virtual hospital, medical students can learn to decide when is an appropriate time to intubate a patient but cannot learn how to physically insert the tube into a patient" (Loke, 2015, p. 119). Loke suggests future research is needed to understand how learning in virtual worlds (and possibly through virtual reality) can best be achieved.

Whether learning in a physical classroom enhanced with technology and augmented reality or in a virtual world, learners are both physical and digital citizens. Digital citizenship is a critical element of information literacy requiring personal responsibility for choosing and evaluating content and experiences in all formats. Understanding and embracing this personal responsibility is important for both teacher and learner.

A NEED FOR DIGITAL CITIZENSHIP

Definition and Call to Action

The change from primarily physical world content to digital (virtual world) content happened rapidly without most individuals realizing how much time would be spent in connected online spaces. Access to quick answers on the Internet revolutionized learning and information seeking behavior. Although convenient, the quick answer is not always the best answer and learners are now required to evaluate sources through critical thinking. Mike Ribble, an educator with a focus on this change, says, "Digital citizenship can be defined as the norms of appropriate, responsible behavior with regard to technology use" (Ribble, 2016, para. 1).

This need to understand responsible use of technology is part of information literacy. The Association of College and Research Libraries (ACRL) defines information literacy as "… a set of abilities requiring individuals to "recognize when information is needed and have the ability to locate, evaluate, and use effectively the needed information" (ACRL, 2000). This includes respect for intellectual property, intellectual freedom, privacy and online security. In 2016, ACRL revised those standards with emphasis on "metaliteracy" which illustrates the fast-pace of our changing information landscapes and includes "an overarching, self-referential, and comprehensive framework that informs other literacy types" (Mackey and Jacobson 2011, p. 70). The new standards in the Framework for Information Literacy in Higher Education reflect the needed change, with the statement, "However, the rapidly changing higher education environment, along with the dynamic and often uncertain information ecosystem in which all of us work and live, require new attention to be focused on foundational ideas about that ecosystem" (ACRL, 2016, p. 2).

The American Association of School Librarians (AASL) presents standards for 21st century learning that include technology skills, inquiry, ethical behavior and a "disposition toward personal and aesthetic growth" (ALA, 2007). These standards were also changed in 2018 to include collaboration and curation in participatory digital culture (AASL, 2018), once again illustrating the revolutionary changes taking place in education, literacy and culture. Embracing personal growth and personal responsibility for information literacy and digital citizenship is essential for the future of learning.

Figure 3. 8 Digital intelligence competencies from DQ institute

DQ Institute presents a model for digital citizenship emphasizing 8 areas of digital intelligence, which include: digital identity, privacy management, critical thinking, digital footprints, digital empathy, cybersecurity management, cyberbullying management, and screen time management.

A program was created focusing on these 8 elements to develop "competencies for young children aged 8 – 12 because there is an urgent need to prepare them for the digital world when they actively start engaging in digital media and devices" (DQ Institute, 2019).

The convenience of *googling* for instant answers and the rise in crowd-sourced sharing of ideas and information led to Wikipedia, a great starting point for background on nearly any topic imaginable (Zahneis, 2018). While this wealth of knowledge and easy access to information is now commonplace and none the less amazing, it is not without concerns. The expectations of information to be free and individuals online to be trustworthy and authentic are misconceptions. Those misconceptions, alongside other issues surrounding digital citizenship, not only hinder learning but can lead to severe consequences.

How can we advocate and teach digital citizenship? Bolkan, an educator writing about technology's impact on youth, believes students are firmly entrenched in the digital world but are often unaware of the meaning of digital citizenship. Sharing thirteen resources for teaching digital citizenship, Bolkan states, "A complete digital citizenship curriculum should help students understand that their behavior on social media can be even more hurtful than the same behavior in the real world" (Bolkan, 2014, p. 22). One of the resources shared, Common Sense Media, provides a curriculum for educators and guides for parents including ratings for media and app (Common Sense Media, 2019). Utilizing these resources, educators and parents can understand how to teach digital citizenship to both children and adults.

Virtual Learning Tools

Learners in global participatory digital culture have access to numerous virtual learning tools including blogs, wikis. Web 2.0 creation apps, videogames, online learning management systems, and virtual worlds. 21st century students may not spend as much time reading and writing in traditional forms (with paper and pencil) as they did in the past, but they *are* reading and writing as much as before- if not more. The reading and writing of 21st century learners are often in short spurts and requires juggling media formats and platforms. The ability to reach across distance and share to a real audience is given to even the youngest of students.

Blogging

When students are prepared, informed digital citizens, they are equipped to share and participate online to authentic audiences on a global scale. Writing blogs is an effective way for young students to reach an authentic audience in participatory culture. A librarian and Spanish teacher collaborated on a blogging project through personal stories and cultural research in both English and Spanish. The experience not only gave the students a multicultural learning experience, the librarian reported:

They learned digital citizenship skills, including respecting intellectual property and giving credit, online etiquette, protecting privacy, and building a positive digital footprint. In fact, blogging serves as an ideal vehicle for providing instruction in all aspects of digital citizenship. The knowledge gained of appropriate behavior as an online publisher will serve them as a life skill (Lofton, 2015, p. 14).

Immersive Learning Environments

Beyond social media and sharing through Internet sites, virtual learning tools include online games and virtual worlds (immersive learning environments). Videogames and virtual worlds allow students to create avatars, virtual representations or embodiments for situating themselves within the computer simulation. Most online learning management systems, such as Blackboard or Canvas, and user-generated content tools cannot provide a "sense of presence" even when experienced simultaneously, such as in a live chat setting. The embodiment of an avatar in a shared 3D space creates the sense of *being there* together (Bulu, 2012).

An example of teaching digital citizenship in an immersive learning environment took place in a school library. Using the popular online videogame (considered a virtual world) of Minecraft, a librarian held an after-school technology club for 5th graders. The students were given resources on the topic of digital citizenship and challenged to create a Minecraft game to embed the concepts and teach them to younger students. The 5th grade team designed and built a virtual library in Minecraft with treasure hunt clues and questions on the topic of digital citizenship culminating with a digital citizenship crown prize (Hill, 2015). The students demonstrated constructive learning as prosumers in digital culture by not only "playing" an educational game to learn digital citizenship but by designing and building the game themselves to teach others. Combing play with work (labor) could be called "playbor", a portmanteau sometimes written as "playbour", first coined by Julian Kücklich stating. "… in the entertainment industries, the relationship between work and play is changing, leading, as it were, to a hybrid form of "playbour" (Kücklich, 2005 p. 1).

Augmented Reality

Even young kindergarteners are producing content in digital format with digital apps on mobile devices, such as images, videos, and multimedia or augmented reality projects. For example, students can use augmented reality (AR) to share original work and research projects. A kindergartener might make a video book report that is triggered to play through an AR app by holding a mobile device near a trigger

Figure 4. A virtual world library built by 5th graders in Minecraft

image. Fourth grade students created a virtual colonial wax museum using augmented reality to present their research through images, sounds and mixed media (Plemmons, 2015). Educators need to understand evaluation of apps and digital content creation platforms as well as privacy issues with sharing student projects online.

HISTORICAL SIMULATIONS AND ROLE-PLAY

Medieval Quest

Immersive learning environments, such as Second Life, allow users to enter historical eras and interact through role-play with objects and clothing of the time period. An international role-play was featured at the Virtual World Best Practices in Education Conference 2016 called "The Quest" in which participants experienced a treasure hunt built by Brant Knutzen, University of Hong Kong (VWBPE, 2016). The literature-based project presented hidden clues throughout a Medieval village, complete with King Arthur's court, a dungeon, towers, homes, a tavern, and numerous other interactive spaces. Learners in immersive spaces, such as the Medieval Quest, can explore alone or together with opportunities to build and share user-generated content. Librarians partnered with educators to role-play characters from medieval times (Hill & Knutzen, 2017).

Figure 5. Augmented reality application on a tablet

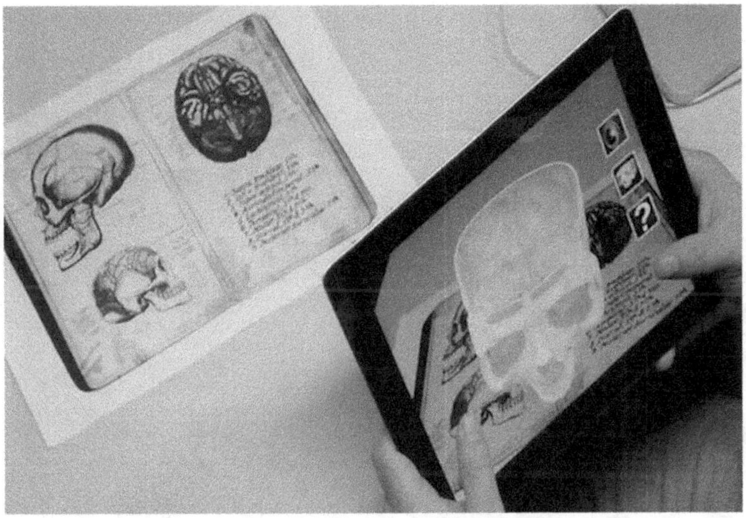

Figure 6. A medieval castle filled with literature-based clues in second life

The Dickens Project

For the past eight years, Seanchai Library has presented the Dickens Project, a simulation of Charles Dickens' A Christmas Carol set in London in Victorian times (Seanchai Library, 2018). Librarians, educators, and students at the Community Virtual Library in Second Life advocated authenticity and accuracy of historical content through shared research presentations. Topics included historical food

Figure 7. Research presentations at the dickens project 2018

and clothing, the legal system, debtor's prisons, Dickens' life, working conditions in London and other information about the Victorian era (Hill, 2017). Understanding the importance of accuracy and authenticity in virtual simulations is another aspect of digital citizenship.

The Digital Citizenship Museum in Kitely

Librarians are curating content on digital citizenship in the virtual world of Kitely, a "pay as you go" open source platform (CVL, 2019). The museum houses 16 rooms filled with topics on digital citizenship concepts such as privacy, cybersecurity, advocating digital citizenship for children, archival in digital content, terms of service, intellectual property, gamification in education and digital literacy. Marie Vans and colleagues share, "The mission of the CVL Digital Citizenship Museum in Kitely is to be a leader in the pursuit to make sure every person is digitally literate through education, raising awareness, and building community around the challenges and solutions of digital literacy" (Vans et al., 2018, p.22).

PROBLEMS DIGITAL CITIZENS FACE ISSUES, CONTROVERSIES, PROBLEMS

Problem 1: Evaluating Online Content (Authenticity, Accuracy and Authority)

Too often, teachers report, students rely on the Internet for research and believe everything online to be accurate. Social media sites allow users to share links and resources without documentation of the original source. Mashing up and remixing content, or creating animated GIF images to post memes online, has become commonplace in day-to-day digital culture. Students (and many educators as well) do

Figure 8. Digital citizenship museum in Kitely 2018

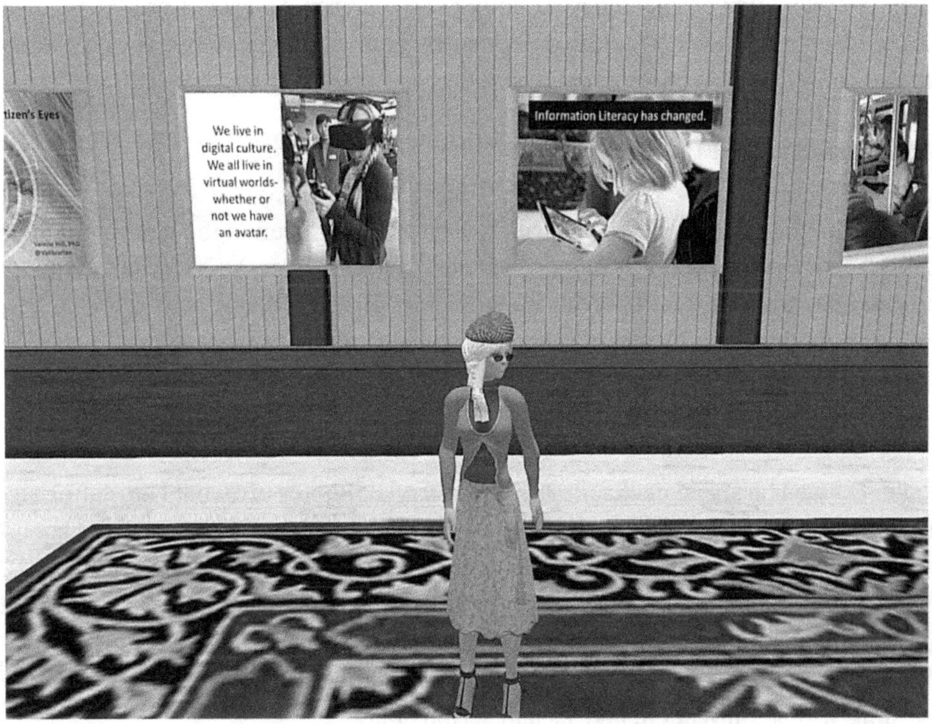

not realize why respect for intellectual property is so important. Without documenting where our ideas originate, the Internet could become a "book of sand". In, "Beyond the Blogosphere, writing professors state, "… [the book of sand] is the Internet, but without the possibility of organization, is information but with no system (or no discernible system), the centuries old-nightmare of the librarian and, today, of every serious researcher working through the web" (Barlow and Leston, 2012, p. 51).

Problem 2: Oversharing or Inappropriate Content

Educators are often worried about the online behavior of students, particularly with cyberbullying and sexting. Cyber researcher, Jason Ohler, believes school administrators should have a better plan for digital citizenship than dealing with "after the fact" consequences of rule breakers or arbitrarily blocking websites from students. He states, "The reality of students' cyber lives has thrust upon us a third approach: creating character education programs tuned to digital youth that are proactive and aggressive" (Ohler, 2012, p. 15).

Problem 3: Misleading Identity

An assumption of *anonymity* in online spaces can cause individuals to act in ways they might not in the physical world. Awareness of the personal responsibility to *be who you are* in both the physical and virtual world has become critical. Researchers examined online identity issues and found the major concerns: identity, traceability, privacy, accountability, and interoperability pointing to an identity federation need. "We clearly need to interconnect digital identities with physical identities, thus creating a unique federated identity system that can act independently from the virtual world of use" (Cruz et al, 2015, p. 33). The means of linking a person's electronic identity and attributes, stored across multiple distinct identity management systems in information technology is called a "federated identity" (Madsen, 2005).

Problem 4: Privacy and Cybersecurity

Clearly concerns about online privacy and security have recently been in the news with big companies such as Facebook and Google facing congressional hearings with accusations of collecting and sharing personal information (Roberts, 2018). Even the youngest digital citizens must learn to be personally responsible for online sharing with an awareness of privacy and security issues.

Problem 5: Disposable Media

Often the content shared on social media is meant to be trivial. Photos of "what I am eating right now" or silly comments teenagers share about clothing, favorite songs, or plans for the weekend are not meant to be archived. The Snapchat app was created to dispose of social media posts after ten seconds. The lines between personal disposable shared social media, educational content and marketing for business have all been blurred with the numerous tools that have become popular over the past decade. This blending of personal and professional content illustrates the need for digital citizenship as does the blending of work and learning with gamification, badges and serious play.

The interactivity within digital spaces and virtual worlds also merges personal trivia and fun activities with serious learning. Sifting out what is important from what is trivial (disposable) is an essential 21st century skill. The ACRL Framework for Information Literacy describes "Information Creation as a Process" with one of the knowledge practices to "develop, in their own creation processes, an understanding that their choices impact the purposes for which the information product will be used and the message it conveys" (ACRL, 2016, p. 5).

Problem 6: Personal Dashboards (Promoting Narrowmindedness)

Creating websites and personalizing the look of our dashboard on many sites has become commonplace with templates, profile pictures, and "about me" sections. Individuals can choose the color scheme, fonts, and styles of each site or account used online. Social media provides us with the ability to curate other individuals (friends, colleagues) for personal or professional reasons. We can "unfriend" or "unfollow" those who we don't agree with or find annoying or simply do not want to hear from at any time. This personally created network of incoming information can sometimes produce a narrow-minded perspective because we tend to follow and interact with those who agree with us. The tendency to accept only information that aligns with existing beliefs and ideas is *confirmation bias*. Ideas that challenge our own create deep thinking and align with Vygotsky's idea that learning is not done is isolation but in "collision" with others (Vygotsky, 1986).

Sherry Turkle believes we should *reclaim conversation*, particularly in face to face discussions with people on a deep level. She says, "First, the Internet gives us the possibility of sharing our views with anyone in the world, but it also can support information silos where we don't talk to anyone who doesn't agree with us" (Turkle, 2015, p. 50).

Immersive learning environments may lessen the isolation of the flat 2D web and provide opportunities for deep conversation across distance. A research study identified three types of presence in virtual worlds: place presence, social presence, and co-presence and the researcher found, "3D virtual worlds have different affordances than 2D virtual learning environments which would affect presence and satisfaction in a different way" (Bulu, 2012, p. 156).

Problem 7: FOMO and Addiction

Sherry Turkle, professor and researcher at MIT, has observed and researched the use of mobile technology with teens and found many, if not most, have their cell phones beside them at all times—even when they sleep. The first thing they do upon awakening each morning is check the phone for incoming information. Most young people feel strange and vulnerable if they do not have their device at hand. They check it throughout the day and understand when someone leaves a conversation to look at a device. Keeping up is a nonstop responsibility and they live with what some call FOMO (fear of missing out) because online life is as much (or more) of a reality than physical life (CNN, 2015). "Only half joking, people in their teens and twenties tell me that the most commonly heard phrase at dinner with their friends is "Wait, what?" Everyone is always missing a beat, the time it takes to find an image or send a text" (Turkle, 2015, p. 37).

Problem 8: Skimming the Surface (No Deep Learning or Deep Reading)

The nonstop skimming through blogs and social media barely resembles the deep reading one enters through print literature. Nicholas Carr depicts our dilemma of bouncing from link to link online in *The Shallows*, a book that shares the darker side of hyperlinked online media. One may recognize the changes in reading habits themselves when presented with his idea that thoughtful people may "…slip comfortably into the permanent state of distractedness that defines online life" (Carr, 2010, p. 112).

Problem 9: Nonstop Emergency (Breaking News)

Even young children often now either have cell phones or watch parents connected to cell phones constantly. Many parents, according to Sherry Turkle, believe in the importance of providing cell phones to their kids "in case of emergency". Turkle believes we send the message to young people that we live in a *state of emergency* because the media news crawl nearly always has *Breaking News* headlines scrolling. Turkle says, "If you see life as a stream of emergencies, this frames your life narrative" (Turkle, 2015, p. 299). Young people learn that framing things as emergencies attracts attention and ever since September 11, 2001, school children and their parents have felt a need to be "connected" in a "catastrophe culture". Turkle believes this problem can only be solved by opening up conversations about "being a self and a citizen in the world of big data" (Turkle, 2015, p. 301). That certainly sounds like digital citizenship.

Problem 10: Limiting Face to Face Conversation

Watch teenagers for only a few minutes and the amount of time they spend texting will become evident. This phenomenon has given rise to new lingo and acronyms such as PIR (parent in room). Sherry Turkle reports college students often avoid spontaneous conversation, especially from instructors. A college senior prefers email in a culture that has "zero tolerance" for making mistakes. This college boy is hoping to get into law school and says, "When you talk in person, you are likely to make a slip" (Turkle, 2015, p. 54).

Turkle argues that learning to speak in person, to see the reaction of another human being, builds empathy and texting does the opposite. As young people post mainly about themselves on social media, feelings of others are much easier to simply ignore. Good manners are part of citizenship in the physical world and, so too, in the virtual world.

Problem 11: The Edited Life (All About Me)

Cultivating one's image on social media is not a true representation of life but a *performance* of life. Understanding digital footprints and the permanent trail we each leave online is part of digital citizenship. Sherry Turkle tells us that this "edited life" for young people can be a burden when they constantly feel the need to "like" the status of friends or suffer the consequences of snubbing them. Teens may share problems on Facebook in order to feel less alone, but Turkle points out, "Online, even the statement of a problem is a performance" (Turkle, 2015, p. 117).

Problem 12: Hyperreality (the Simulation Trumps the Real)

French Philosopher Jean Baudrillard (1926-2007) wrote about postmodernism with an emphasis on the relationships among reality, symbols, and society. In *Simulacra and Simulation*, Baudrillard presents the hyperreal—a state in which reality and simulation are indistinguishable. As we move from postmodernism into post postmodernism, or metamodernism as a potential nomenclature, Baudrillard believed we have yet to glimpse the outcome for the media or the masses.

Building on McLuhan's concept of "*the Media is the Message*", Baudrillard suggests that the media (in many forms such as TV news and online sites) has created an "implosion" of meaning. He states, ""...--and this is where McLuhan's formula leads, pushed to its limit—there is not only an implosion of the message in the medium, there is, in the same movement, the implosion *of the medium and of the real* in a sort of hyperreal nebula, in which even the definition and distinct action of the medium can no longer be determined (Baudrillard, 1994, p. 82).

One might ask how hyperreality is applicable to virtual learning in education. In a study of virtual learning environments, researchers explain, "The appeals to reality, relevance and applicability, the case itself, and the ways in which it is mediated by the teacher or by technology, and the continued involvement of the student are parts of what Baudrillard describes, not as a social contract, but as a 'simulation pact' (Baudrillard 1990, p. 163) between teacher and student, at the centre of which is a system of symbols that employs the rhetoric of reality, but in fact offers not reality, nor a singular copy or representation, but a system of *simulacra*" (Carmichael and Tschollt, 2014, p. 36).

In reading works of fiction, we enter a suspension of disbelief (particularly in genres such as fantasy) which is like the concept of a "simulation pact" in which the entire concept of reality is altered by an acceptance of reality as being *in the mind* rather than limited by what our physical senses encounter. As educational pedagogies evolve alongside the Semantic web and computer technologies, certainly an understanding of hyperreality and simulacra will emerge with both advantages and perhaps consequences. Whether or not we understand the philosophical underpinnings, we can agree that digital citizenship includes an awareness of hyperreality and a balance of life in physical, virtual and augmented spaces.

SOLUTIONS AND RECOMMENDATIONS

One of the best ways to advocate and embrace digital citizenship, as mentioned earlier, is through building and participating in a PLN (either a personal or professional learning network). Life in global digital participatory culture can be overwhelming when individuals try to learn by themselves. The quest for learning includes respect for intellectual property created by all and a willingness to embrace new ideas and new perspectives (Moreillion, 2016). Students can create personal learning networks and certainly educators can continue professional development through PLNs.

Assessment of learning outcomes can be particularly challenging in virtual worlds because learners often use external sources in addition to collaboration with the immersive learning experience. Building a personal learning network (following blogs, forums, and social media) contributes to the learner's acquisition of knowledge and skills. Voulgari and colleagues conducted research on learning outcomes in massively multiplayer online games and believe further research on assessment is necessary.

External resources such as websites and fora constitute a major point of reference for players. These resources are, to a large extent, developed by spontaneous virtual communities of players. Players interact, exchange information, discuss, share game-related content, and improve their knowledge of the game beyond the limits of the designed environment. Such resources were considered by expert players in our sample as essential for progress in the game (Voulgari et al. 2016, p. 259).

The current need for digital citizenship includes many formats and online spaces in networked culture, including chat rooms, social media, videogames, augmented reality, virtual worlds and (possibly soon) virtual reality. With the purchase of Oculus Rift, one of many virtual reality systems, Facebook plans to make virtual reality social and connect individuals across distance (Wired, 2018). Certainly, gaming and social events are more profitable for virtual reality developers than educational applications; however, the potential for learning in immersive simulated environments continues to rise as both the hardware and software prices come down.

FUTURE RESEARCH DIRECTIONS

Will digital citizenship continue to be important? With virtual reality entering mainstream use and the release of Oculus Rift purchased by Facebook, digital citizens will continue to explore new learning experiences. A husband and wife team recently shared potential use of virtual reality, such as providing virtual experiences in the library. Michael and Constance Wiebrands demonstrated a head mounted display (HMD) at the Australian Library and Information Association, held in Sydney, Australia, which was predominantly librarian-led and well-attended (Lewis, 2015).

Virtual reality is often experienced through a head mounted device (HMD) using haptics, such as gloves or other wearable technology to enhance the realism of the experience. Instead of clicking on virtual objects using a mouse with your hand, the user interface is viewed through the headset and your own eyes "become the mouse". The potential for social presence across distance is appealing for a variety of reasons. Many simulated experiences, such as exploring underwater life, are presented through observation rather than interaction. This differs from virtual worlds- where users often interact and build collaboratively. Future research may study which types of experiences align to learning objectives for specific learning styles and needs. For the time being, it appears both virtual reality and virtual worlds hold potential for immersive learning.

Digital citizenship is critical to learning in the future as technology tools evolve to include virtual reality and applications of the Semantic web where boundaries of applications are lifted. Research on best practices for learning in virtual spaces will include assessment of information literacy skills and the ability to measure learning in physical, virtual, and augmented spaces. Understanding how to assess learners in multiple platforms, including mixed reality, will bring challenges as well as exciting research opportunities. The responsibility for becoming digital citizens rests upon each one of us and the roles we play in sharing that responsibility are essential as the world becomes one global community.

CONCLUSION

The future of education is exciting when viewed through the lens of exponential technological growth. That excitement is not without concerns about sustainability, cost effectiveness, and understanding of research-based practices for learning outcomes as we adapt to change. Often educators invest in technology tools only to find them quickly obsolete or outdated. At this date of publication, virtual worlds have not been fully utilized by educators as predicted a decade ago. Researchers believe another surge of interest is about to begin, in part due to the interest in virtual reality and the documentation of successful best practices by persistent educators (Gregory et al, 2015).

Conducting and keeping up with current research on technology trends will continue to be important in the future. Balancing the excitement of innovation with a clear understanding of information literacy and learning is a 21st century challenge which certainly includes digital citizenship. In fact, digital citizenship is imperative to the future success of everyone and cannot be over-emphasized.

REFERENCES

American Association of School Librarians. (2007). *Standards for the 21st century learner.* Chicago: American Association of School Librarians. Retrieved March 1, 2017 from http://www.ala.org/ala/mgrps/divs/aasl/guidelinesandstandards/learningstandards/standards.cfm

American Association of School Librarians. (2018). *AASL Standards framework for learners.* Retrieved February 17, 2019 from https://standards.aasl.org/wp-content/uploads/2017/11/AASL-Standards-Framework-for-Learners-pamphlet.pdf

Association of College & Research Libraries. (2000). *Information literacy competency standards for higher education.* Retrieved March 1, 2017, from http://www.ala.org/acrl/standards/informationliteracycompetency

Association of College & Research Libraries. (2016). *Framework for information literacy for higher education.* Retrieved February 4, 2019 from http://www.ala.org/acrl/standards/ilframework

Barlow, A., & Leston, R. (2012). *Beyond the Blogosphere: Information and Its Children.* Santa Barbara, CA: ABC-CLIO, LLC.

Baudrillard, J. (1990). *Seduction*. Montreal: New World Perspectives. doi:10.1007/978-1-349-20638-4

Baudrillard, J. (1994). *Simulacra and simulation*. Ann Arbor, MA: University of Michigan Press.

Bolkan, J. (2014). Resources to help you teach digital citizenship. *T.H.E. Journal*, *41*(12), 21–23.

Bulu, S. T. (2012). Place presence, social Presence, and satisfaction in virtual worlds. *Computers & Education*, *58*(1), 154–161. doi:10.1016/j.compedu.2011.08.024

Carmichael, P. M., & Tscholtt, M. (2013). Cases, simulacra, and semantic web technologies. *Journal of Computer Assisted Learning*, *29*(1), 31–42. doi:10.1111/j.1365-2729.2011.00459.x

Carr, N. (2010). *The shallows: What the internet is doing to our brains*. New York: W.W. Norton & Co.

CNN. (2015). *28 Internet acronyms every parent should know*. Retrieved February 1, 2019, from http://www.cnn.com/2014/12/08/living/internet-acronyms-every-parent-should-know/

Common Sense Media. (2019). *Common sense digital citizenship*. Retrieved February 20, 2019, from https://www.commonsensemedia.org/educators/digital-citizenship

Community Virtual Library. (2019). *Digital citizenship museum*. Retrieved February 18, 2019 from https://communityvirtuallibrary.org/digital-citizenship-museum/

Cruz, G., Costa, A., Martins, P., Gonçalves, R., & Barroso, J. (2015). Toward educational virtual worlds: Should identity federation be a concern? *Journal of Educational Technology & Society*, *18*(1), 27–36.

Deodato, J. (2014). The patron as producer: Libraries, web 2.0, and participatory culture. *The Journal of Documentation*, *70*(5), 734–758. doi:10.1108/JD-10-2012-0127

DQ Institute. (2019). *What is DQ?* Retrieved January 25, 2019 from https://www.dqinstitute.org/what-is-dq/

Girvan, C. (2018). What is a virtual world? Definition and classification. *Educational Technology Research and Development*, *66*(5), 1087–1100. doi:10.100711423-018-9577-y

Gregory, S., Scutter, S., Jacka, L., McDonald, M., Farley, H., & Newman, C. (2015). Barriers and enablers to the use of virtual worlds in higher education: An exploration of educator perceptions, attitudes and experiences. *Journal of Educational Technology & Society*, *18*(1), 3–12.

Groom, D. (2009). *To quote, unquote, and requote- 21st century illiteracy?* Retrieved January 15, 2019, from https://deangroom.wordpress.com/2009/12/21/to-quote-unquote-and-requote-21st-century-illiteracy/

Hamilton, B. J. (2011). Creating conversations for learning: School libraries as sites of participatory culture. *School Library Monthly*, *27*(8), 41–43.

Hill, V. (2013). *Math in 3D a library exhibit and tour.* Retrieved February 19, 2019, from https://youtu.be/DQ6783hYF8E

Hill, V. (2015). Digital citizenship through game design in Minecraft. *New Library World*, *116*(7/8), 369–382. doi:10.1108/NLW-09-2014-0112

Hill, V. (2017). *CVL Dickens research project 2017*. Retrieved December 27, 2018, from https://youtu.be/xT-vgR7eXU4

Hill, V. J., & Knutzen, K. B. (2017). Virtual world global collaboration: An educational quest. *Information and Learning Science*, *118*(9/10), 547–565. doi:10.1108/ILS-02-2017-0010

Kücklich, J. (2018). Precarious playbour: Modders and the digital games industry. *Fibreculture Journal*. Retrieved February 17, 2019 from http://journal.fibreculture.org/issue5/kucklich_print.html

Lewis, R. (2015). Virtual reality: Soon to become mainstream in libraries? (cover story). *Information Today*, *32*(4), 1–29.

Lofton, J. (2015). Blogging with students: A vehicle for writing, digital citizenship, and more. *School Librarian's Workshop*, *35*(5), 13-15.

Loke, S. (2015). How do virtual world experiences bring about learning? A critical review of theories. *Australasian Journal of Educational Technology*, *31*(1), 112–122. doi:10.14742/ajet.2532

Mackey, T., & Jacobson, T. (2011). Reframing Information Literacy as a Metaliteracy. *C&RL*, *72*(1), 62–78. doi:10.5860/crl-76r1

Madsen, P. (2005). *Liberty Alliance Project White Paper: Liberty ID-WSF People Service- federated social identity*. Retrieved December 27, 2018, from http://www.projectliberty.org/liberty/content/download/387/2720/file/Liberty_Federated_Social_Identity.pdf

Moreillion, J. (2015). #schoollibrarians Tweet for Professional Development: A Netnographic Case Study of #txlchat. *School Libraries Worldwide*, *21*(2), 127–137.

Moreillion, J. (2016). Building your personal learning network (PLN): 21st century school librarians seek self-regulatory professional development online. *Knowledge Quest*, *44*(3), 64–69.

Ohler, J. (2012). Digital Citizenship Means Character Education for the Digital Age. *Education Digest Readings Condensed for Quick Review*, *77*(8), 14–17.

Plemmons, A. (2014). *Expect the Miraculous*. Retrieved March 6, 2016, from http://expectmiraculous.com/2014/05/08/4th-grade-created-an-augmented-reality-wax-museum-using-layar-and-multiple-digital-tools/

Ribble, M. (2016). *Digital Citizenship: Using Technology Appropriately*. Retrieved February 21, 2016, from http://www.digitalcitizenship.net/

Roberts, M. (2018). *Google's day of reckoning is finally at hand*. Retrieved December 27, 2018, from https://www.washingtonpost.com/opinions/googles-day-of-reckoning-is-finally-at-hand/2018/09/14/782c6e26-b84c-11e8-a7b5-adaaa5b2a57f_story.html?utm_term=.bf524c108086

Seanchai Library. (2018). *The Dickens Project*. Retrieved December 27, 2018, from http://irelandslstory.blogspot.com/p/the-dickens-project-sl.html

Toffler, A. (1980). *The third wave*. New York: Morrow.

Turkle, S. (2015). *Reclaiming Conversation: The Power of Talk in a Digital Age*. New York: Penguin Press.

Vans, M., Hill, V., & Dunavant-Jones, A. (2018). Improving Digital Literacy: A Solvable Challenge Using Virtual Worlds. *Journal of Virtual Studies*, *9*(2), 14–24.

Voulgari, I., Komis, V., & Sampson, D. (2014). Learning outcomes and processes in massively multiplayer online games: Exploring the perceptions of players. *Educational Technology Research and Development*, *62*(2), 245–270. doi:10.100711423-013-9312-7

VWBPE. (2016). *Virtual Worlds Best Practices in Education Conference*. Retrieved March 6, 2016, from http://vwbpe.org/

Vygotsky, L. S. (1978). *Mind in society*. Cambridge, MA: Harvard University Press.

Vygotsky, L. S. (1986). *Thought and language* (A. Kozulin, Trans.). Cambridge, MA: MIT Press.

Wikipedia. (2019). *Participatory Culture*. Retrieved February 17, 2019, from https://en.wikipedia.org/wiki/Participatory_culture

Wired. (2018). *The Facebook Effect Hits Oculus: In VR Other People are Everything*. Retrieved from https://www.wired.com/story/facebook-oculus-connect-social/

Zahneis, M. (2018). Some Colleges and Scholars Cautiously Embrace Wikipedia. *The Chronicle of Higher Education*, *64*(39), A25.

KEY TERMS AND DEFINITIONS

Avatars: Computer-generated simulations of individuals in a virtual space.

Digital Citizenship: Demonstrating an understanding of appropriate ethical behavior in digital formats through consumption and production of media.

Immersive Learning Environments: A simulated space where participants feel a sense of presence through interacting with objects or others.

Information Literacy: The ability to locate, evaluate, and use information in all formats as a digital citizen in participatory culture.

Minecraft: A 3D computer video game in which users, alone or together, can build their own world using basic blocks "mined on their land."

Participatory Culture: The culture which encourages networked community sharing of information and artistic expression on a global scale.

Personal Learning Networks: A group of individuals collaboratively sharing learning experiences for common purposes particularly in networked culture.

Social Media: Websites and applications that allow users to communicate and share content in digital networked culture.

Virtual Reality: A 3D computer simulated environment situating the user in an altered reality usually with a head mounted display or other haptics, such as gloves to enhance the experience.

Virtual Worlds: A persistent computer simulated environment inhabited by avatars with a sense of presence and shared understanding of experience through interaction.

Chapter 6
Revisiting Musings on Co-Designing Identity-Aware Realities in Virtual Learning:
The Shared Experiences

Francisca Yonekura
University of Central Florida, USA

ABSTRACT

Previously, musings on co-designing identity-aware realities in the virtual space focused on the individual self during a learning experience. While preserving the individual self of the learner for a comprehensive outlook, the chapter will expand on the exploratory journey looking into the identity of the collective self, the shared experiences of those co-creating the moment, and the potential for a community of practice to emerge while learning in virtual environments. In the spirit of the contemplative goal of the chapter, design considerations in the creation and facilitation of learning experiences inclusive of the community's self are postulated.

PREAMBLE

Virtual learning in the third dimension presents many opportunities for meaningful learning to occur. Learning in which the learner's self and the collective self immerse in the co-creation of authentic experiences. The virtues of these 3D environments are best appreciated holistically through the visual and spatial perspectives. To do so, participating learners, designers, and facilitators have the capabilities to exert more control over the visual, spatial, and emotional aspects of immersive 3D virtual worlds. The learner's self and the communities in which this learner belong immerse and co-create their experiences. Some of these experiences extend the physical into the virtual and vice versa.

DOI: 10.4018/978-1-5225-9679-0.ch006

As previously posited, the evolutionary power to compute the human experience presents a myriad of opportunities to transform our self, society, and systems that govern us. The same guiding questions apply in contemplating design principles and process for immersive learning experiences in which the collective self is placed at the center of the design.

- What are the design considerations for integrating the individual and social selves in virtual learning?
- How do we facilitate meaning-making both in the physical and imagined realities?
- What are the value propositions of both the physical and virtual environments?
- How do we improve alignment to deliver beneficial learning experiences along the value chain proposed by both the physical and virtual?
- How do we facilitate an inclusive learning experience in which different perspectives are welcomed?

This book chapter addresses several of these questions and some of the prompts guiding the contemplations that follow.

VIRTUAL WORLD, VIRTUAL ENVIRONMENT, OR VIRTUAL REALITY?

Although similar and used interchangeably, throughout the literature the definition of the terms virtual worlds (VW), virtual environments (VE), and virtual reality (VR) are slightly different. Some definitions reflect the technological evolution this media form has undergone since its inception. Peachey and Childs (2011) define virtual worlds as "computer-generated environments in which participants adopt an avatar to interact with each other and with the virtual environment around them" (p. 1). Fox, Arena, and Bailenson (2009) define virtual environments as "a digital space in which a user's movements are tracked and his or her surroundings rendered, or digitally composed and displayed to the senses, in accordance with those movements" (p. 1). Schroeder (2011) defines virtual reality technology as "a computer-generated display that allows or compels the user (or users) to have a feeling of being present in an environment other than the one that they are actually in and to interact with that environment" (p. 4). In this chapter, the terms virtual worlds, virtual environments, and virtual reality are used interchangeably.

Many types of virtual worlds exist. Some worlds have predetermined common goals while others give their inhabitants the freedom to pursue and share their interests and purpose. The inhabitants' imagination is the limit in the latter type of worlds. These virtual worlds are persistent, always on for its inhabitants to participate and create shared experiences. Like the man-made imagined realities in the form of economic and political systems (Harari, 2015), we live and breathe in our physical worlds. We have the power to imagine and create learning experiences that blend our physical and virtual realities.

To gauge the capabilities the self can leverage in these 3D virtual worlds, Stephen Ellis' (1996), breakdown of virtual environments lend a helpful foundation. Ellis' three main elements compose the virtual world or environment: 1) content which consists of the objects with which the learner interacts and the actor which in our case is the learner, 2) geometry which portrays the dimensions, rules, and range of possible values that make up the environment, and 3) the dynamics that rule the interactions between the objects and the learner. Awareness of these elements is key in guiding the type of learning experience and interactions that can emerge.

Determining the continuity between these virtual worlds and other environments including the physical world is extremely important for a transparent learning experience. That is, the actors, learners, and facilitators define the degrees of fluidity and fidelity that are most fitting while functioning or co-creating experiences in and between these worlds. Fundamentally, the "learner" or user experience design must be orchestrated to allow for optimal interaction of the self in the virtual environment, the learner with others, the learner with the objects and spatial landscape, and the extension or spillover effect of these experiences into the physical world or the other way around. Also, continuity between the learner's personhood, prior experience, and tacit knowledge must be considered for meaningful personal learning to take place.

Lastly, the social aspect of these virtual environments brings forward the exponential power to spread values and ideologies across geographical boundaries and at a speed not possible before. Also, the intimacy that develops among the inhabitants of these virtual environments reveals the strength innate to close-knit communities which sensibly ushered with purpose can positively influence people in the masses or accomplish more together through social presence.

THE SELF

Understanding the self plays a fundamental role in the learning experience. Carl Rogers' concept of becoming a person provides a grounded perspective in facilitating experiences in virtual worlds. Rogers' (1961) interpretation of the self is best appreciated in the following passage:

... to be herself means to find the pattern, the underlying order, which exists in the ceaselessly changing flow of her experience. Rather than to try to hold her experience into the form of a mask, or to make it be a form or structure that is not, being herself means to discover the unity and harmony which exists in her own actual feelings and reactions (p. 114).

Based on Rogers' explanation of self, a point of potential contention surrounds the nature of avatars. To some, avatars might be construed as masks underneath which people hide; however, this notion constitutes a fallacy. Many studies have found that the technology of virtual environments has the extraordinary capacity to help with self-discovery, develop empathy to understand others, and to change beliefs and perceptions of ourselves and the world surrounding us. For instance, a study found that the affordances of anonymity in virtual environments allowed for adolescents to explore their identities through language and role play (Calvert, 2002). Yee and Bailenson (2007) studied the phenomenon of the Proteus effect in which they found evidence that people infer beliefs and attitudes from the avatar's appearance.

Furthermore, in a second study, these researchers found that people carried over these behavioral changes from the Proteus effect to the physical world (Yee & Bailenson, 2007). These examples are just a couple that substantiates that the "self" in virtual environments is as genuine and real as the "self" in the physical world for the very nature of self has to do with one's journey to find the harmony between our feelings and reactions to our overall life experiences. Therefore, reference to the physical world or experiences as "real" bears a cautionary consideration as this notion is farthest from reality.

Blascovich's and Bailenson's (2011) portrayal of the self and his or her footprints in virtual reality reinforces the matter. As individuals journey through the virtual worlds, they leave virtual footprints that reveal as much about the identity of the selves based on what they plan on doing, places they go, and whether they are going to be successful in what they were set to do.

In the generations to come, as technologies evolve and people imagine and participate in a myriad of virtual experiences, the identity of the inhabitants in these experiences will evolve into complex realizations of culture. A culture in which identities assumed in the physical and virtual spaces affect each other and therefore blurring spatial distinctions of the self. Virtual identities will become an extension of our physical selves with the capacity to influence people's behavior, educational, economic, judicial, and political systems.

THE COLLECTIVE SELF

Understanding the impact of the social aspect in virtual learning experiences and its potential to raise social awareness that leads into action, exhorts bringing to the forefront that an aspect of the learner's self seeks to define herself or himself based on the desire to feel connected to others and belonging to an affinity group. Turner, Hogg, Oakes, Reicher, and Wetherell (1987) describe social identity as "a shift towards the perception of self as an interchangeable exemplar of some social category and away from the perception of self as a unique person" (p. 50). As highlighted in Bobro (2018), "social identity is a collection of feelings, attitudes and emotions in the community that lead to unity, and ultimately, becomes part of the individual's identity" (p. 123).

The differences between the interpersonal and the collective identities of the learners require consideration in the facilitation of virtual environments as well. Brewer and Gardner (1996) explain that the essence and characteristic of the collective self lay in the degrees and self-representation manifestations of inclusiveness embodied both in the affective and cognitive domains of the self. From the differentiated self-concept, the relational self that manifests from the connections and relationships with others to the collective self that motivates the individual to participate for the welfare of the group. That is, in the collective self-representation, the *I* turns into *we* for self-reference (p. 84).

PRESENCE

Many aspects of presence in virtual environments have been researched, but more studies are needed. Some of the literature addresses the different dimensions of presence, presence as in situ, social presence, and co-presence (Bulu, 2012). Presence in the context of virtual environments has been defined as the sense of being in another place or space. A more comprehensive definition is put forth by Witmer, Jerome, and Singer (2005) who define presence as "... a psychological state of "being there" mediated by an environment that engages our senses, captures our attention, and fosters our active involvement" (p. 298).

As communication media have evolved from the textual to the more visually and spatially rich, the concept of social presence has evolved as well. Bulu (2012) indicated that some researchers view social presence as the individual's perception of the medium to connect with others to create sociable and intimate interactions. Co-presence deals with not only having a sense of being with other individuals but also having the feeling that others actively perceive them back as part of the group.

Witmer, Jerome, and Singer's (2005) presence questionnaire capture other important concepts to understand the nature of presence in virtual worlds and to seek optimal affordances in the facilitation of learning. First is the environment in which presence manifests itself, which are the physical, virtual, and symbolic spaces. Another critical element is the degree of presence the individual feels. According to Witmer, et al. (2005), the degree of presence is influenced by the fidelity of the elements the individual takes in through the senses and the nature and ease with which they interact in the environment. In the psychological plane, involvement and immersion are key in discerning presence. Involvement has to do with the state the individual experiences from focusing on meaningful stimuli, activities, or events. Immersion is the psychological state in which the individual perceives to be enveloped in or embraced by the environment which provides a continuous flow of stimuli and experiences (Witmer et al., 2005).

As the social presence literature review by Oh, Bailenson, and Welch (2018) revealed, many researchers have studied the matter at length and efforts continue to this day. These authors' review approach of studies on social presence included three lenses: 1) immersion, 2) context, and 3) psychological dimensions provides the facilitator of the virtual learning experience a great foundation for a socially aware and impactful outcome. The immersive qualities of an experience focus on technological affordances and visual representations that enable social presence. Conversely, the contextual and psychological dimensions address the subjective nature of social presence; in the contextual dimension, personality traits, social cues, agency, and type of task are the emphasis while the psychological dimension focuses on the demographic differences and the individual's traits (p. 4-10).

Many other aspects impacting our identity and feel of presence in virtual environments exist that cannot be included in the scope of a book chapter. As this medium and its techne evolve many other concepts and research agendas will emerge as well. With the above aspects surrounding virtual worlds and identity as the basis, the goal in the next section of this book chapter is to attempt to elicit and discern design matters when virtual worlds are part of the learning experience.

CONSIDERATIONS IN DESIGNING LEARNING EXPERIENCES IN VIRTUAL WORLDS

Guideposts

These non-determinant virtual worlds afford us three primary design components: the environment or space, the learner, and his or her sense of presence. An additional tenet to keep in mind before exploring what the design of meaningful learning experiences in virtual worlds entails is to recognize the importance of the learners' tacit knowledge in the process of learning. In other words, the learner's subjective insights, prior experience, and knowledge, as well as the opportunity to engage in practice go in parallel with the concepts of self, presence, and the virtual environment discussed above. Lastly, Mark Weiser's vision on ubiquitous human-centered computing which highlights that the most powerful experiences people will embrace and enrich them are those "that are effectively invisible in use" (Abowd, Mynatt, & Rodden, 2002, p. 48). Compared to previous iterations of virtual realities, today's technology allows us to co-create learning experiences that draw out the self and sense of presence from the learners with greater ease and fidelity as well as an empathic appreciation of those enduring the consequences of our many health, environmental, geopolitical, and societal problems.

As one starts to ponder on how to facilitate meaningful learning in virtual worlds, what comes to mind first and foremost is the importance of contextualizing the learning experience that is to take place. Also providing purposeful experiences is key. Telling learners to login into a virtual world and roam around on their own does not constitute a good example of meaningful learning. Such practice can be equated to the practice of asking students to make a specific number of posts and responding back to forum posts in an online course. Instead, we should ask ourselves how to provide purposeful, authentic experiences in the context of what the individual learner's goals are while taking into account the needs of the group or other selves and the affordances of the virtual environment in which the experience is to happen. One of the most common practices that take into account authenticity and context is that of asking learners to adopt a virtual self different from their physical self and interact in different areas of the virtual world. This activity is accompanied with a reflective element by asking the learner to document their experience via blogs, images, and machinima/art.

Reflection

Virtual worlds are also conducive for the reflective learner by creating an atmosphere in which he or she can move freely in, around, and between the spaces. As Carl Rogers (1961) indicated, for learning to take place, an atmosphere of freedom for the learner to move around in his thoughts, feelings, and being is necessary. The goal is to allow for self-discovery and reflection to take place. In this manner, the learner can personally visualize and assimilate the experience which will then lead into personal growth. Similarly, reflection is most useful in heightening an emphatic disposition to understand opposing or unexperienced perspectives. For instance, some of the most successful uses of virtual environments in learning have used Second Life and virtual reality headsets to experience the day-to-day life of someone with a psychological or physical condition.

Experimentation

Virtual worlds provide the environment in which experimentation can be cleverly facilitated in the learning process. Often, in the OpenSimulator grids and Second Life, "sandbox" areas are available for learners to create or prototype 3D objects that can be manipulated within the bounds of the physics engine behind the virtual world platform. Successful hackerspaces provide focused tutorials, resources such as objects, textures, and scripts to empower the novice learner to create 3D objects of their own in OpenSimulator. Furthermore, to support the birth of social identity for active participation, some of these hackerspaces facilitate periodic scheduled events and gatherings in which novices and experts interact to learn new skills or overcome challenges with a particular problem members bring forth. The experimental kind of virtual learning experiences with the most impact are those in which groups of learners work together on problem-based missions. Facilitators and participating learners must be attentive of their social and co-presence to be able to accomplish their mission successfully. Therefore, what matters in the design of these learning experiences is to empower learners to engage in active meaning making and sharing with others. A complementary key technique in facilitating problem-based learning in virtual worlds is to stagger moments and spaces for individual reflection and group work throughout the exercise.

Role Play

Another powerful instance of learning in virtual environments is that of contextualized learning via role play. In this practice, learners assume the different roles actors take part in a theatrical performance, or become the nurses and doctors who must handle an emergency in a hospital, or take on the role of military officers who must go on a rescue mission. This experiential learning can elicit the learner's sense of presence to immerse them in the role of their choice and interact with the other "selves" in the virtual environment that resembles the theater stage, the emergency room, or the location where the hostage is being held.

Collaborative Learning and Communities of Practice

When designing learning in virtual environments, it is important to design experiences in which meaningful active, varied, and frequent interactions among learners are facilitated to increase the chances of social identity to emerge. Social presence dimensions are also crucial in influencing a lasting collaborative learning experience that could evolve into a community of practice that influences in the larger stage of a discipline or field. Park and Seo (2011) state that "group identity shapes the motivation behind voluntary engagement in collaborative behavior and is linked to a person's desire to receive feedback from the group and to create, maintain, and enhance a favorable identity for the group" (p. 517). Some of the best instances of collaborative learning in virtual environments can be observed in groups such as the Non-Profit Commons in Second Life, an actively engaged community of non-profit organizations helping each other. Other examples include the OpenSimulator Community advancing the mission of an open source platform with annual conferences organized by volunteers, the Virtual Worlds Education Roundtable, an international group of educators discussing and sharing relevant issues on education in virtual worlds, and the Relay for Life in Second Life, a fundraising event to find a cure for cancer held since 2004. To effectively utilize the power of virtual environments, one must have social presence, an observable, on-going process rather than a subjective and stable condition in which the role of interaction in the process needs due consideration along the way (Sivunen & Nordbäck, 2015).

Transdisciplinary Abilities and Disposition

When the *I* turns into *we*, transdisciplinary approaches to education and research best practices are most powerful regardless of space and time. While facilitating learning in which consideration for the learner's own purpose and prior experience, opportunities for exposure and understanding on multidisciplinary perspectives and the integration of interdisciplinary approaches are brought together (McGregor, 2017). Learners experience a shift in their thinking. Transdisciplinary experiences involve how participants integrate ideas that consider a multitude of perspectives to ultimately reach a sound solution via collaborative learning. In this transdisciplinary approach, the process must be iterative. Learners must challenge basic assumptions and positions brought forth by all, articulate ideas, and carefully consider such ideas across disciplines and conventions. Essentially, shared vision, understanding of self both individual and collective, empowerment, advocacy, and inclusiveness to lead into transformative solutions must be designed into a transdisciplinary learning experience (p. 8).

Many of our complex societal problems can be dealt with the transdisciplinary habits of mind as presented by McGregor (2017). That is, the transdisciplinary approach encompasses a practice involving:

- The act of perceiving
- Pattern recognition
- Abstracting
- Embodied thinking where a key aspect is empathy
- Modelling to draw abstractions and analogies across the dimensions of space and time and
- Deep play to explore boundaries
- Synthesizing (page 12).

Virtual environments present us with opportunities to combine pedagogies through practicing habits of mind. McGregor presents nine potential transdisciplinary pedagogies for higher education:

- To adopt the proposed pedagogies of integrative curriculum
- Inquiry-based learning
- Transformative learning to help learners make the intellectual and emotional shift
- Authentic curriculum that is purposeful and relevant to the learners' lives and their society
- Learning communities that share vision and mission
- Deep education in which learners participate in a holistic, contextualized, and learner-centered experience
- Value clarification and analysis
- New ways to see and be in the world (paradigm shift)
- Question everyone's governing principles (double loop learning) (p. 14).

The chapter, *Advancing Personal Learning and Transdisciplinarity for Developing Identity and Community* by Truman & Truman provides a deeper understanding of the transdisciplinary discourse which presents principles to address many of our societal challenges including the much-needed transformation of higher education.

FINAL THOUGHTS

According to Harari (2015), the imagination of humans have created the story called economy, politics, religion, and many other forms of systemic environments that constitute the physical reality in which we have operated for thousands of years. Computational thinking is providing us the power to imagine the human experience in a manner not possible before. Virtual worlds/virtual reality will continue to evolve and iterate in ways we cannot imagine today. Linden Lab's Second Life virtual world platform, touted as long gone, is still making its reach known through its vibrant communities. As of 2015, Second Life's gross domestic product (GDP) was estimated to be around $500 million which is larger than that of some of the smaller countries in the world (Bryant, 2015). The power lies in imagining new empowering realities that intertwine and extend our selves between the physical and virtual worlds for the good of humanity. Technology affords us the Art-of-the Possible, and therefore we have the power to shape our future.

The key is to find the balance of imagined realities that is mindful and respectful of the learner's freedom to decide what is most suitable/desirable while considering the innate disposition of the collective self to belong and contribute to society as a whole. The tumultuous social and geopolitical world we currently live in, calls for us to immerse ourselves genuinely and to nurture the collective self to solve the many societal problems we face today whether environmental, health, education, or political. The prospects are exciting and filled with mindful and meaningful opportunities for learning afforded by the next iterations of virtual environments.

REFERENCES

Abowd, G. D., Mynatt, E. D., & Rodden, T. (2002, January - March). The human experience. *Pervasive Computing*.

Blascovich, J., & Bailenson, J. (2011). *Infinite reality - Avatars, eternal life, new worlds, and the dawn of the virtual revolution*. New York, NY: HarperCollins Publishers.

Bobro, M. (2018). Collective identity in the age of globalisation. *The Person and the Challenges*, *8*(1), 121–133.

Brewer, M. B., & Gardner, W. (1996). Who is this we? Levels of collective identity and self representations. *Journal of Personality and Social Psychology*, *71*(1), 83–93. doi:10.1037/0022-3514.71.1.83

Bryant, M. (2015, December). *Think Second Life died? It has a higher GDP than some countries*. Retrieved from http://thenextweb.com/insider/2015/11/07/think-second-life-died-it-has-a-higher-gdp-than-some-countries/

Bulu, S. T. (2012). Place presence, social presence, co-presence, and satisfaction in virtual worlds. *Computers & Education*, *58*(1), 154–161. doi:10.1016/j.compedu.2011.08.024

Calvert, S. L., Jordan, A. B., & Cocking, R. R. (2002). *Children in the digital age: influences of electronic media on development*. Westport, CT: Praeger.

Ellis, S. R. (1996). Virtual environments and environmental instruments. In Simulated and Virtual Realities (pp. 11-51). London, UK: Taylor Francis.

Fox, J., Arena, D., & Bailenson, J. N. (2009). Virtual reality - A survival guide for the social scientist. *Journal of Media Psychology*, *21*(3), 95–113. doi:10.1027/1864-1105.21.3.95

Harari, Y. N. (2015, July 24). Why humans run the world. *Ted Talks - London*. Retrieved from https://www.youtube.com/watch?v=nzj7Wg4DAbs

Hayles, N. K. (1999). How we became posthuman: Virtual bodies in cybernetics, literature, and informatics. Chicago: University of Chicago Press.

Knutzen, K. B., & Kennedy, D. M. (2012). Designing the self: The transformation of the relational self-concept through social encounters in a virtual immersive environment. *Interactive Learning Environments*, *20*(3), 271–292. doi:10.1080/10494820.2011.641680

Lombard, M., & Ditton, T. (1997). At the heart of it all: The concept of presence. *Journal of Computer-Mediated Communication, 3*. doi:10.1111/j.1083-6101.1997.tb00072.x

McGregor, S. L. T. (2017). Transdisciplinary pedagogy in higher education: Transdisciplinary learning, learning cycles, and habits of mind. In *Transdisciplinary Higher Education: A Theoretical Basis Revealed in Practice* (pp. 3–14). London, UK: Springer. doi:10.1007/978-3-319-56185-1_1

Oh, C. S., Bailenson, J. N., & Welch, G. F. (2018). A systematic review of social presence: Definition, antecedents, and implications. *Frontiers in Robotics and AI, 5*(114), 1–25.

Park, H., & Seo, S. (2013). Effects of collaborative activities on group identity in virtual world. *Interactive Learning Environments, 21*(6), 516–527. doi:10.1080/10494820.2011.604037

Peachey, A., & Childs, M. (2011). Virtual worlds and identity. In *Reinventing Ourselves: Contemporary Concepts of Identity in Virtual Worlds* (pp. 1–12). London, UK: Springer-Verlag. doi:10.1007/978-0-85729-361-9_1

Rogers, C. (1961). *On becoming a person. A therapist's view of psychotherapy*. Boston, MA: Houghton Mifflin Company.

Schroeder, R. (2011). *Being there together: social interaction in virtual environments*. New York, NY: Oxford University Press.

Sivunen, A., & Nordbäck, E. (2015). Social presence as a multidimensional group construct in 3D virtual environments. *Journal of Computer-Mediated Communication, 20*(1), 19–36. doi:10.1111/jcc4.12090

Turner, J. C., Hogg, M., Oakes, P., Reicher, S., & Wetherell, M. (1987). *Rediscovering the Social Group: A Self-categorization theory*. Oxford, UK: Basil Blackwell.

Yee, N., Bailenson, J. N., & Ducheneaut, N. (2009). The Proteus effect. Implications of transformed digital self-representation on online and offline behavior. *Communication Research, 36*(2), 285–312. doi:10.1177/0093650208330254

Chapter 7
Make It Real:
Presence and Immersion in Simulation Design

Fil J. Arenas
https://orcid.org/0000-0003-1747-0706
The Air University, USA

Andrew S. Clayton
The Air University, USA

Kate D. Simmons
Auburn University at Montgomery, USA

ABSTRACT

Several schools and colleges under Air University have found utility in using a mixed-reality approach to developing leadership acumen in this unique risk-free environment. This chapter will describe the power of collaboration between Air University and Auburn University at Montgomery while demonstrating the impact of this mixed-reality approach on developing military leaders. These mixed-reality exercises (MRXs) leverage an environment that establishes a practical laboratory for developing leaders to interact with avatars using a combination of virtual immersion and human intelligence (live simulation engagement). This innovative approach to "real play" allows real-time learning to take place in real time through virtual immersion.

INTRODUCTION

Air University (AU), Maxwell AFB, Alabama is known as the Intellectual and Leadership Center of the Air Force, graduating more than 50,000 resident and 120,000 non-resident officers, enlisted and civilian personnel each year (Air University Website, 2018). Air University provides professional military education, faculty development, and professional development for all ranks of Airmen and most of their courses have some *leadership* connection as well. Further, Air University continues to promote creativity

DOI: 10.4018/978-1-5225-9679-0.ch007

Figure 1. Virtual corporate setting

and innovation whenever possible inspired by the earliest roots of establishing airpower programs under the guidance of the Wright Brothers in 1910. The Air University mission focuses on producing leaders of character and critical thinkers, which strategically and jointly deliver airpower to support national security. AU's professional military education (PME) programs strive to educate Airmen to incorporate air, space, and cyberspace power to achieve their objectives. Additionally, specialized professional continuing educational programs provide scientific, technological, managerial, and other professional expertise to meet the needs of the Air Force.

Moreover, AU is the U.S. Air Force's center for professional military education (PME) and professional developmental education (PDE). Air University provides a full spectrum of Air Force education, from pre-commissioning to the highest levels of PME, including degree granting and professional continuing education for officers, enlisted and civilian personnel throughout their careers (Air University Website, 2018). Air Command and Staff College (ACSC) is one of several educational institutions within Air University. Air Command and Staff College is the intermediate Air Force professional military school. Annually, ACSC prepares about 600 resident and over 9,000 nonresident students from all US military services, federal agencies, and over 70 partner nations to lead in the operational environment - emphasizing the employment of airpower in joint operations (Air University Website, 2018). The core curriculum for ACSC focuses on several major learning areas to include; War Theory, Airpower, International Security, Joint Warfighting, and Leadership. It is this last learning area where the authors found themselves questioning the pedagogical approach to the curriculum. Recently, they have leveraged a new partnership with Auburn University at Montgomery (AUM), Alabama, a local university to expand on virtual learning applications in leadership. Cutting-edge technology utilized by AUM and the ACSC at Maxwell AFB have led to some very powerful classroom exercises.

Figure 2. Virtual avatar laboratory

VAL

VIRTUAL AVATAR LABORATORY

AUBURN UNIVERSITY AT MONTGOMERY • COLLEGE OF EDUCATION

The College of Education (COE) at Auburn University at AUM is proud to provide Alabama's only Virtual Avatar Laboratory (VAL) with Mursion, Inc. Through the capabilities and partnership with Mursion's mixed-reality platform, using a combination of artificial intelligence and live actors, they deliver realistic simulations that model the most challenging interactions that leaders may experience in their daily routines. Formerly, others may recognize VAL as the *TeachLivE* technology engineered by the University of Central Florida that has been successful in leading the research in teacher simulations. This blend of technology and human performance creates a fully immersive and challenging simulation environment that forces students into a risk-free learning environment. This type of learning has many advantages that will be described in greater detail within the chapter and supported by research that indicates that a kinesthetic or hands-on modality of learning may be most effective for some students. The VAL has partnered with various academic and non-academic organizations with the intent to create relevant immersive simulations for professional development in a variety of topics such as: teaching, budget negotiations, counseling, and leadership. During a coordinated VAL demonstration at AUM, members from the ACSC and other Air University school representatives met with other educators to continue collaboration in this unique learning modality. This led to an ongoing partnership between key members from AUM and Air University. AUM's partnership with Mursion, Inc. enables their VAL to service multiple organizational needs (College of Education VAL Website, 2018).

Mursion, Inc. develops a virtual reality environment where developing professionals are able to practice and master various complex interpersonal skills. The relevant organizational challenges provided by Mursion 's virtual reality platform delivers personalized simulations by using a combination of artificial intelligence and human intelligence (live actors)to customize real-time interactive scenarios. These designed vignettes provide a range of workplace environments in which to simulate challenging interpersonal exchanges; and forces learners to take risks from which they could learn how to improve their day-to-day performance. Originally designed as a virtual training platform for training STEM (science, technology, engineering, and mathematics) teachers. Teachers. Mursion's immersive training simulator is now being leveraged by a wide range of innovative organizations to improve their employees' interpersonal skills in multiple disciplines. In collaboration with client content experts, Mursion designs customized and personalized training simulations and performance-based assessments that match the unique learning objectives of their clients.

Difficult areas such as leadership behaviors, followership skills, and managing difficult peers or followers, providing complex counseling feedback are instantly duplicated in Mursion's simulator. Mursion also creates multi-avatar environments to allow trainees to practice facilitating teams or groups to hone team dynamics. Innovative educational institution are creating immersive mixed-reality exercises (MRXs)

Figure 3. Air command and staff college logo

within their professional development programs or curricula, while measuring teacher effectiveness . This new technological interactive approach is becoming a popular simulation alternative in a variety of industries (Mursion, Inc. Website, 2018).

Several schools and colleges at Air University have found utility in using a mixed-reality approach to developing leadership acumen in this unique risk-free environment. This chapter will describe power of collaboration between AU and AUM while demonstrating the impact of a mixed-reality approach on developing military leaders. These MRXs leverage an environment that establishes practical laboratory experiences for developing leaders to interact with avatars using a combination of artificial intelligence and live simulation engagement. This innovative approach to *real-play* allows real-time learning to take place at an accelerated pace through virtual immersion.

GENESIS

Leadership is a complex concept that may contribute to why leadership industry and higher education institutions appear to fall short in developing effective leadership curriculum. In his book *Leadership BS* (2015), Pfeffer makes the argument that the leadership industry has failed (p. 4). Further, he goes on to argue that part of this failure is the overabundance of leadership gurus, experts, and the array of so-called leadership conferences, symposiums, workshops, and development programs found throughout corporate, civilian, military, and higher education. Additionally, Pfeffer suggests that this failure is also due in part to the process that produces leaders and how we teach leadership (p. 3). The argument he provides may be valid and is not without its merit. How we teach leadership is a valid point. Does industry and higher education have the right pedagogical approach when it comes to leadership and leadership development? This is one of the central themes of this chapter. If leadership is failing as Pfeffer concludes, then what is the right approach to teaching, educating, and developing leadership within adult education? How do we assess the effectiveness of developing leaders and educators? The authors of this chapter suggest that in order to answer this question we must begin with a simple definition of leadership. We offer a

Figure 4. Air university mixed-reality exercise
(Image Credit Andrew Clayton).

simple definition of leadership – a practice in humanity. This simple yet powerful statement highlights the gap in higher education that is evident today. How do we develop effective leadership curriculum that allows the adult learner to practice their leadership behaviors? How should we teach leadership?

The practice of humanity infers the application of a spectrum of human behaviors that should exemplify the act or purpose of leadership, when applied. But within industry and higher education, the practice or act of leadership is not readily apparent within institutions' leadership curriculum, or within corporate leadership at writ large. The authors contend that the design process to allow for the practice of leadership behaviors is typically not part of higher educational approaches to leadership development. The foundation of the partnership between AU and AUM was based on addressing this gap in leader and educator development. A void in the practical application of leadership behaviors through interaction is not apparent in most leadership and higher education programs. This conundrum led AU's Air Command and Staff College (ACSC) to research a new pedagogical approach to leadership development.

The Department of Leadership at ACSC is one of several departments within ACSC that make up the core curriculum for ACSC. The Department of Leadership's curriculum is an 8-week course, preparing students for increased leadership responsibilities in the profession of arms (Air Command & Staff College Website, 2018). Students apply current doctrine and theory in considering leadership responses to problems posed by volatility, uncertainty, complexity, and ambiguity (VUCA). The Leadership Course is grounded on key principles of Harvard's Meta Leadership Model where organizations must consider three main elements for effective organizational leadership programs: leading people; leading organizations, and leading into the future. The goal of the Leadership Course is to help leaders know themselves better, lead more consciously, and contribute more abundantly to national security and the profession of arms.

Figure 5. Air university logo

The variety of topics and research that makeup up the Leadership Course come from the Joint Chiefs of Staff Joint Leadership Development, the Army Command and General Staff College, the United States Marine Core's Great Unit Study (2015), Stanford University Graduate School of Business, University of Cambridge: Judge Business School, Penn State University, and the University of Michigan: Ross Business School. The guiding themes throughout the course begin with knowing yourself to lead yourself; lead yourself to lead your team; create empowered organizations; and lead an enterprise into the future.

As mentioned earlier Pfeffer (2015) argues that the process of developing leaders and the pedagogical approach to teaching leadership has failed. Even in the ACSC Leadership Department with the abundance of leadership resources and experts who developed ACSC's graduate-level Leadership Course, something was still missing. The effectiveness of developing leaders at the graduate level was still not completely being met. The practice in humanity was not reaching the student body. The act of displaying transactional and transformational leadership through a myriad of virtues and character strengths was lacking. Students' ability to take leadership concepts, models, and theories from the classroom and operationalize them at the individual level was absent. The missing piece or failure as Pfeffer (2015) called it pushed the Department of Leadership at ACSC to question the approach and teaching method for leadership development. What aspect of the definition of leadership was missing from the course? How do you develop a graduate level course that allows students to practice humanity, to display the nature of human behaviors and then reflect on those behaviors and develop oneself into a more purposeful leader?

The authors contend that throughout AU and within ACSC, the approach to leadership development could become more effective with virtual engagement or the use of MRXs, especially at the application level of learning. According to Knowles, Holton, and Swanson (2012, p. 11), learning is the acquisition of knowledge or skills through experience, study, or by being taught. Combining the authors' definition of leadership – the practice of humanity, with learning as the acquisition of knowledge through experience, study, or being taught allows the author to question how students are acquiring knowledge to practice the act of humanity within courses offered at AU. Traditional methods are found throughout AU in an attempt to answer this question utilizing guided discussions in the classroom (Socratic method), formal and informal lectures, case studies, outdoor team building activities, role-playing exercises, or various written assignments. However, these educational approaches fall short under the definition of leadership – the practice or act of humanity. Is there an educational approach that puts students into situations that require them to practice or display behaviors of humanity, reflect on those behaviors, and adjust or create new behavioral approaches when put into the same or similar situation in the future? This was the question the authors struggled to answer until Air University discovered a new pedagogical approach to learning through AUM's College of Education and the Virtual Avatar Laboratory.

SIMULATIONS AND TEACHING: A POWERFUL COMBINATION

Simulations to most of the population sound complex, high-tech, and almost nerdy. However, simulations are a simple way to compress a scenario or teaching skill into a manageable exercise. Teacher candidates at AUM have had the opportunity to practice teacher interview skills, parent/teacher conferences, least prompts, verbal reprimands, lesson planning, and collaboration to name a few. Instructional leaders have had the opportunity to practice budget negotiations, interviews, enforcing zero tolerance policy, parent conferences, and bullying. The counseling program area has been working through scenarios of post traumatic stress disorder (PTSD), sexual assault training, and mental evaluations. The excitement of the simulation world is not in the technology, but in the experiences you are able to provide to the student or participant. When we teach we impart knowledge. What we want to know are three things: 1) did they obtain/understand the content (lecture), 2) do they remember the content (exam), and 3) can they apply the content (simulation). The third point is the hardest to practice and measure. Can they apply the content? Can they perform in a stressful or high stakes situation? A simulation can prepare them for those types of situations and mess up or crash and burn without causing harm to a real individual. A flight simulator of sorts for real life. Beyond COEs, virtual environments can be powerful tools to teach and train.

The innovative educational approach to learning utilized by VAL was a perfect fit for several schools and colleges at Air University. The VAL was the solution to Air University's search for immersive learning for the practice of leadership. The VAL provided students the opportunity to exercise human behavior skills, a key ingredient in professional military education (PME) and professional development education (PDE). The VAL's unique blend of technology and human performance fills the gap with two critical features. The first element that makes the VAL unique and shifts the paradigm for adult education is that the VAL is designed as an immersive virtual education and training simulator. Approaching the VAL as a simulation helps to view learning through different lenses in hopes of developing human skills such as emotional intelligence, social intelligence, virtues and character strengths, decision making, team dynamics, interpersonal communication, and transformational leadership behaviors. The second element is the use of live interaction through the use of a human simulation specialist. Both of these critical elements of the VAL need further explanation for the impact and new approach to developing immersive learning found within the VAL, which allows for the practice of humanity within higher education.

The VAL's unique design is due to the VALs ability to create an immersive environment that allows for the practice of educational content. The practice of educational content is not new in adult education. In fact, the practice of educational content is one definition for the term simulation. However, the VAL provides as used within Air University, the ability to develop immersive scenarios focused on leadership or soft skills. Traditionally, simulations were developed to allow for the practice of specific skills, sometimes called hard skills. Examples of hard skills found within simulations include but not limited to flying aircraft, practicing medical procedures, or executing law enforcement tactics. Further, the VAL allows for the development of leadership skills or behaviors known as soft skills. Examples of soft skills include Conflict resolution, feedback, emotional intelligence skills, empathy, or collaboration. The difference between hard and soft skills is critical to understanding the approach to leadership development and understanding the first element unique to the VAL, a simulation that allows for the development of soft skills.

This unique blend of a simulation approach to the practice of soft skills has multiple applications. VAL simulations promote several features found in most immersive learning environments such as authentic, relevant, and contextual scenarios and relevant environments sometimes creating suspension of beliefs to promote specific learning objectives. When applying the VAL as a simulation for leadership development, the VAL allows for students to interact in and practice authentic behaviors in a real-world environment. The VAL compared to other educational approaches to learning allows for a student-center approach to learning which allows the learner to engage in the learning process by going beyond remembering information, and instead allows the learner the ability to apply information in a realistic scenario and analyze and synthesize their experience and create new leadership behaviors. This process is known as experiential learning. Guthrie, Phelps, and Downey (2011) suggested that leadership development within immersive learning environments was possible through adult learning theories such as experiential learning.

Another adult learning theory found within immersive learning environment simulations such as the VAL is the use of situated learning or social learning. The VAL provides the ability for live interaction between the learner and the avatar requiring the learner to examine the situation at hand, adjust ones thought process, and develop solutions based on changes occurring in the VAL. This process is known as situated or social learning. The VAL requires the learner to learn or adjust based on the situation or scenario. This interaction and adjustment or learning by the learner requires the learner to observe, review information, and create a plan; actions which are part of demonstrating different aspects of leadership (Guthrie et al., 2011).

When focusing the VAL as a live simulation, the ability to develop leadership learning through experiential and situated learning sets the VAL apart from other simulations. The VAL allows for the development of soft skills through adverse, unfamiliar, and ill-defined problems where the solution to the simulation scenario is ambiguous. Siewiorek, Gregenfurtner, Lainema, Saarinen, and Lehtinen (2013), suggest that learning through simulations such as the VAL is one of the primary means for the practice of leadership. Through ill-defined and complex problems, learners can practice the behaviors of humanity such as conflict resolution, decision-making, problem solving, motivating others, ethical decision-making, transformational leadership, virtues and character strengths (Siewiorek et al., 2013). The application of the VAL as a simulation through experiential and situated learning is one element that makes the VAL unique. The other element that separates the VAL from other immersive learning simulations is the use of human intelligence or live interaction through a simulation specialist. However, there is a unique distinction in the approach to the VAL as a simulation compared to the traditional understanding of using simulations in higher education.

Since World War I, the need to train individuals on how to fly aircraft has been a vital requirement. However, training an individual to fly a plane is not an easy task and when mistakes are made during training the consequences can be life-threatening. The need to train individuals in a safer more controlled environment was inevitable. The advent of flight simulators became an alternative option to flight training and spurred a new form of education, the use of simulations for training and education. One of the

Figure 6. The Link trainer

most successful flight simulators was developed by Edwin Link called the Link Trainer (Page, 2000). *The Link Trainer* used electric driven suction pump motors and valves that controlled various aspects of the flight simulator to mimic certain aeronautical movements of a real aircraft. Over time as technology improved, so did the flight simulators and new types were being developed such as the electric simulator and the digital simulator as well as enhancements to make the flight simulators more realistic such as motion systems, and visual systems such as the use of virtual reality within flight simulators. Today flight simulators mimic every aspect of the real aircraft allowing more standardized and effective training for the student pilot.

Other occupations also use simulations and technology to enhance the simulation experience. The healthcare industry uses simulations similar to a student pilot using a flight simulator. Nurses and other health care professionals are using simulations to enhance the training and education for patient care. In "The Added Value of 3D Simulations in Healthcare Education" (2012), the authors posit that nursing students who use simulations as part of an accelerated nursing program have reduced anxiety during the simulation due to the opportunity to *fail* in a safe virtual simulation before engaging with real patients. Other nursing programs use high fidelity human patient simulators also known as mannequin-based simulations as developed at the Johns Hopkins Medicine Simulation Center.

These mannequin-based simulations use high fidelity simulators, developing mannequins that breathe, with breath sounds, heart tones, and palpable pulses for developing healthcare providers to experience the biological responses of human systems. Moreover, the mannequin patients are equipped with

Figure 7. Air university mixed-reality exercise
Image Credit Andrew Clayton.

monitors to display EKG, pulse oximeter, blood pressure, and many other vital medical signs. Using mannequins in clinical simulations allows future and current physicians to "practice on plastic" before treating live patients. By practicing clinical skills in a safe and regulated environment, future physicians can hone their skills and confidence before practicing medicine (Johns Hopkins Medicine Simulation Center Website, 2018).

The use of flight simulators and mannequin-based simulations validate the need for modeling and simulation in the learning environment. However, there is a critical element required to develop simulations with this level of fidelity. Simulations require the use of state-of-the-art technology and in most cases that technology is derived from mathematical computations, engineering design, software coding, mechanical inputs, electrical inputs, sophisticated software, and even the use of artificial intelligence. The input, output, and feedback from these types of simulations are limited to the technology that is available and constraints of artificial responses. Additionally, within these types of simulations the responses are artificial and generated by computer algorithms. The VAL minimizes the limitations of artificial responses by incorporating a unique element not found in most simulations; the use of live interaction through a simulation specialist.

The simulation specialist provides the human intelligence aspect to the VAL. As mentioned earlier, most simulations use non-human inputs, while the VAL provides a live interactive simulation specialist. A simulation specialist is an individual who is trained as a professional actor with specialties in impromptu acting and trained in high-speed gaming. This unique skillset when added to the VAL creates immersive, authentic, and realistic environments where the participant and the avatar (simulation specialist) are able to communicate in real-time through a mixed reality environment. So why does this formula of simulation design with a live simulation specialist enhance the application of leadership or practice in humanity? One possible explanation to this question is the concept termed *suspension of disbelief.*

When a participant interacts within the VAL (communicates with the avatar), dialogue is being created. However, within the VAL the dialogue becomes authentic and real as the participant realizes the responses from the avatar (simulation specialist) are not pre-programmed or being generated by some form of computer automation (e.g. the simulation specialist [avatar] notices the participant is wearing eyeglasses and responds "Are those new glasses you're wearing?" The participant begins to realize that what the avatar sees and hears influences how the avatar will respond. The participant communicates with the avatar as if the avatar is a real person or as a unique concept that the authors refer to as *real-play*. This concept of suspension of disbelief and interacting with an avatar as a real person allows an interactive relationship to develop between the participant and the avatar.

A recent Chief of Staff of the Air Force initiative is focusing on the revitalization of Air Force Squadron commands often referred to as the *heartbeat of the Air Force*. "To aid Airman in developing these qualities within their squadrons, the course's primary emphasis is to instill in them greater mastery of the 'human domain' skills." (Berube, 2018, p. 1) The idea is to enhance leadership acumen for future squadron commanders that are critical for developing meaningful dyadic relationships between leaders and follower such as personality dynamics, effective relationship behaviors, commander communication skills, and mentorship to name a few important tools. Many of these skills are captured at the Ira C. Eaker Center for Professional Development's newest Leader Development Course for Squadron Command (LDC-SC) at AU in their final *capstone experience* lesson. The capstone experience is an MRX designed form LDC-SC's key concepts that has students excited about learning at Maxwell AFB, Alabama.

To create a mixed reality simulation that allows a participant to apply leadership behaviors or soft skills, the simulation requires the participant to believe that the avatar is real resulting in an authentic, real, interactive dialogue. This suspension of disbelief creates an environment and scenario that is real for the participant. The authenticity and realness of the scenario creates a personal and intimate experience for the participant. A key to leadership development is the ability to reflect on our past experiences and adjust accordingly to future leadership events. If the experience in the simulation does not feel authentic and real to the participant, the learning intent will not be accomplished. The participant and avatar interaction is *real* because of the masterful skills of the simulation specialist. With this authentic dialogue capability, the variety of MRX scenarios within VAL are unlimited.

The application of leadership or the practice in humanity is now achievable within higher education. The design of the VAL at AUM provided AU and the Air Command and Staff College with a cutting-edge pedagogical approach to the application of leadership within higher education. Participants can now interact in a mixed-reality live simulation allowing participants to apply soft skills through the suspension of disbelief resulting in personal and authentic experiences for the participants. Incorporating the learning models of experiential and situated learning along with the unique educational design of the VAL, adult learners can now develop and apply leadership through the safety of virtual immersion opportunities.

CONCLUSION

What should educators consider when designing immersive exercises in cyberspace? Many institutions get lost in the *cool factor* and forget why they spent thousands of dollars on virtual learning simulations in the first place! We can now create higher levels of learning for our students by simply expanding the learning modalities. A mixed-reality approach offers a combination of virtual immersion and human intelligence by providing not only a kinesthetic learning modality, but leveraging experiential learning. Moreover, it is acceptable for students to think your immersive exercises are *cool*, but they must have relevance to the learning outcomes or they become simply entertainment.

REFERENCES

Air Command and Staff College Website. (2018). *Department of leadership syllabus*. Retrieved from https://www.airuniversity.af.edu/Portals/10/ACSC/curriculum/AY18_Leadership.pdf

Air University Website. (2018). Retrieved from https://www.airuniversity.af.edu/Command-and-Leadership/

Bai, X., Duncan, R., Horowitz, D., Graffeo, J., Glodstein, S., & Lavin, J. (2012). The added value of 3D simulations in healthcare education. *International Journal of Nursing Education*, *4*(2), 67–72.

Berube, P. (2018, Dec 28). *Air university's new leader development course helps squadron commanders 'thrive."* Air University Website news article. Retrieved from https://www.af.mil/News/Article-Display/Article/1721978/air-universitys-new-leader-development-course-helps-squadron-commanders-thrive/

College of Education Virtual Avatar Laboratory Website. (2018). Retrieved from http://www.education.aum.edu/VAL

Guthrie, K. L., Phelps, K., & Downey, S. (2011). Virtual worlds: A developmental tool or leadership education. *The Journal of Leadership Studies*, *5*(2), 6–13. doi:10.1002/jls.20214

John Hopkins Medicine Simulation Center. (n.d.). Retrieved from: https://www.hopkinsmedicine.org/simulation_center/training/mannequin_based_simulations/index.html

Knowles, M. S., Holton, E. F. III, & Swanson, R. A. (2012). *The adult learner*. Routledge. doi:10.4324/9780080964249

Page, R. L. (2000). Brief history of flight simulation. *SimTecT 2000 Proceedings*, 11-17.

Pfeffer, J. (2015). *Leadership BS: Fixing workplaces and careers one truth at a time*. New York: Harper Business.

Siewiorek, A., Gegenfurtner, A., Lainema, T., Saarinen, E., & Lehtinen, E. (2013). The effects of computer-simulation game training on participants' opinions on leadership styles. *British Journal of Educational Technology*, *44*(6), 1012–1035. doi:10.1111/bjet.12084

Section 3

The Multidisciplinary Lens of Cognitive, Learning, and Assessment Sciences

Chapter 8
Get in the GROOVE:
Using a Virtual World to Promote Health

Mary Kate Clennan
University of Miami, USA

Daniella Carucci
University of Miami, USA

Marissa D. Alert
Johns Hopkins School of Medicine, USA

Shannon Collins
SEC Prestige Consulting, USA

Erin N. Etzel
VA Maryland Health Care System, USA

Alyssa LaRoche
Aimee Weber Studio, USA

Maria I. Leeder
Miami-Dade County Public Schools, USA

Patrice G. Saab
University of Miami, USA

ABSTRACT

Over the last few decades there has been a rise in the prevalence of overweight and obesity in American youth. This chapter describes the rationale for the virtual world features of an obesity prevention project that engaged middle-school-aged girls in a 3-week summer science enrichment program. The Get in the GROOVE! program was designed to promote self-efficacy for health behavior change, increase health knowledge, facilitate healthy behaviors related to physical activity and nutrition, encourage a healthy body image, and promote the development and consolidation of a health self-identity. The virtual world, which was explored by the girls via realistic and healthy avatars, supplemented experiences and reinforced curriculum and concepts learned in the physical world component of the program. Findings suggest that a virtual world is a promising platform to promote a health self-identity and healthy lifestyle in children.

DOI: 10.4018/978-1-5225-9679-0.ch008

INTRODUCTION

While the prevalence of adult obesity has nearly doubled since 1980, the prevalence of childhood obesity has nearly tripled (Ogden, Carroll, Kit, & Flegal, 2014). Overweight and obesity prevalence is 33.4% among children and adolescents age 2-19 years and 69% among adults (Benjamin et al., 2017). The high prevalence of excess weight in youth is not unique to the United States but is also observed in many other countries contributing to a global epidemic (Friedrich, 2017; Wang & Lim, 2012). This situation is of considerable public health concern due to the well-documented health and psychosocial consequences associated with excess body weight together with the fact that overweight and obesity during childhood is likely to persist into adulthood (Haslam & James, 2005; Poirier & Eckel, 2002; Pulgaron, 2013; Thompson et al., 2007; Ward et al., 2017; Williams, Mesidor, Winter, Dubbert, & Wyatt, 2015).

The determinants of excess body weight are multifactorial and overweight and obesity have been linked to a number of lifestyle factors. Among children and adolescents, overweight and obesity have been associated with the consumption of sugar sweetened beverages, refined grains and high-calorie foods, and other poor nutrition choices, physical inactivity, and high levels of sedentary behavior (Bourke, Whittaker, & Verma, 2014; Drewnowski, 2004; Maher, Mire, Harrington, Staiano, & Katzmarzyk, 2013; Mitchell, Pate, Beets, & Nader, 2013). While data indicate engaging in healthy lifestyle behaviors such as improving diet, increasing physical activity, and decreasing sedentary behavior may contribute to a more optimal weight status and decreased cardiometabolic risk (Hagobian & Phelan, 2013), most American children and adolescents do not meet dietary (Banfield, Liu, Davis, Chang, & Frazier-Wood, 2016) or physical activity recommendations (Olvera, Kellam, Menefee, Lee, & Smith, 2010) and spend up to 8 hours each day in various sedentary pursuits (Lou, 2014; Tremblay et al., 2011).

Virtual reality technologies have the potential to improve eating habits, increase physical activity, and promote healthy lifestyle choices. A decade ago, experts identified several research and education priorities involving virtual world technologies to prevent and treat obesity and type 2 diabetes. These priorities include but are not limited to "making smarter food choices," "improving self-efficacy by virtual reality-guided practice of desired behaviors," and "using virtual reality to make behavior change more reinforcing and participatory" (Ershow, Peterson, Riley, Rizzo, & Wansink, 2011, p. 217). Virtual reality technologies, in general, and virtual world technologies, in particular, have the potential to augment learning experiences as they can immerse users in social learning environments (Johnson & Levine, 2008). Additionally, children of all ages enjoy engaging in virtual activities and are often familiar with virtual worlds and similar technologies (Coles, Strickland, Padgett, & Bellmoff, 2007; Prensky, 2001).

This chapter describes the virtual world features used in our obesity prevention randomized controlled trial, *Get in the GROOVE* (*Girls Realizing Options through OpenSim Virtual Experiences*)*!* The project compared two summer science enrichment program curricula that had similar health-related content addressing physical activity and nutrition but differed in the use of virtual world technology to reinforce health science concepts. *Get in the GROOVE!* was designed to investigate the extent to which a 3-Dimensional virtual world environment engaged and immersed middle school aged girls in a unique learning environment that promoted self-efficacy for healthy behavior change, increased health knowledge, facilitated healthy behaviors related to physical activity and nutrition, and encouraged a healthy, realistic body image. The *Get in the GROOVE!* virtual world environment, GROOVE Island, was explored in the context of 3-week summer programs held at the Phillip and Patricia Frost Museum of Science (in Miami) and the New York Hall of Science (in Queens, New York). The GROOVE Island virtual world component supplemented experiences, reinforced curriculum and concepts learned in the physical world component of the summer program, and extended the social environment of the summer program. GROOVE Island was designed to provide girls with opportunities for social support, learning, modeling and imitation of healthy behaviors, and the development of a salient 'health' self-identity. In our conceptualization, when an individual has a health self-identity, that individual incorporates health-related features as part of her or his identity and internalizes the value of health-related behaviors (Deci & Ryan, 2000; Strachan, Woodgate, Brawley, & Tse, 2005; Strachan & Brawley, 2009). For example, the individual may view herself as 'someone who is healthy,' 'someone who eats well,' 'someone who walks 11,000 steps a day,' 'someone who is motivated to learn about health,' and/or 'someone who embraces a healthy lifestyle.'

In designing the *Get in the GROOVE!* program, we took the position that what was learned about health and behavior in the virtual world and in the physical world would have reciprocal influences on the girls. To this end, girls participated in physical activities and healthy eating activities in the virtual world and in the physical world. On GROOVE Island, girls were able to customize and personalize age-appropriate avatars and receive virtual rewards for 'engaging in' and 'rehearsing' healthy behaviors. The GROOVE Island and the summer science enrichment program functioned as a community that spanned both the virtual world and the physical world. Within this community, there were opportunities to collaborate on joint projects, to compete, and to learn from each other. Girls could be influenced by agents in the virtual world who were rewarded for exhibiting healthy behaviors as well as by their own avatars' healthy behaviors. As such, a user's virtual identity had the potential to promote behavioral intention and the implementation of healthy habits in everyday life (e.g., Rise, Sheeran, & Hukkelberg, 2010). As girls adopted healthy lifestyle behaviors in the virtual world and the physical world and consolidated their health self-identity, self-efficacy for adopting and maintaining healthy behaviors in everyday life would be expected to increase.

This chapter discusses the rationale for key *Get in the GROOVE!* program perspectives and components. A previous version of this chapter was published in the first edition of Striker, Calogne, Truman, and Arenas (2017). We have updated the chapter by including additional information about GROOVE Island features, as well as by describing the contributions of immersion in the virtual world and identification with the avatar on program outcomes. The chapter begins with a brief review of literature discussing the use of virtual reality to motivate healthy eating behavior and physical activity. We then discuss the importance of promoting a healthy body image in the context of our obesity prevention/health promotion project. Next, self-efficacy and the role of modeling in the virtual world and its potential influence on health behaviors in the physical world are reviewed. This is followed by a consideration of whether the type of avatar matters. The reciprocal influence of the physical world and the virtual world in encouraging healthy behaviors is then presented. We next discuss how we addressed issues concerning creating healthy, realistic age-appropriate avatars, the role of individual differences, and linking activity in the physical world to the virtual world. The chapter closes by discussing future directions and providing conclusions.

CONSIDERATIONS FOR A VIRTUAL WORLD PROMOTING HEALTH IN GIRLS

Using Virtual Reality to Promote a Healthy Reality

Research has demonstrated that virtual reality technologies have the potential to modify health-related attitudes, behaviors, and health outcomes (Fox, Bailenson, & Binney, 2009; Johnston, Massey, & DeVaneaux, 2012; Kyoung Joo & Kim, 2017; Sullivan et al., 2013). Emerging evidence indicates that what occurs in virtual reality may impact behavior and health in the physical world. Yee, Bailenson, and Ducheneaut (2009) have described the Proteus effect and have demonstrated that avatars behaving in a virtual environment can change the behavior of the user in the physical world. With respect to relatively immediate behavior change, Fox and colleagues (Fox et al., 2009) showed that after participants viewed their avatar gaining and losing weight as a function of 'healthy' or 'unhealthy' food choices, women who had low presence (i.e., less likely to endorse that the virtual technology experience was 'real' for them) ate more candies in the physical world than women who reported high presence, whereas the opposite pattern occurred for men. This suggests that individual differences play a role in the response of both women and men to the virtual world.

In a study examining physical activity, participants who viewed their personal avatar exercising (serving as a virtual model) engaged in more physical activity in the following 24 hours than participants who viewed their personal avatar loitering or viewed a stranger avatar exercising (Fox & Bailenson, 2009). Recent research, however, suggests that some attributes of stranger avatars may affect adults' health behaviors. Men and women who observed a normal weight female avatar engaging in healthy behaviors in the virtual world were more likely to choose to exercise (rather than eat cookies) 30 minutes later than those who observed the same normal weight avatar engaging in unhealthy behavior or an overweight (and otherwise identical) avatar engaging in either healthy or unhealthy behaviors (Kyoung Joo & Kim, 2017). Research with 3rd through 6th grade children shows that participation in a virtual world can be reinforcing and contribute to increased physical activity. Children engaged in more physical activity over a 3-day period (as determined by an activity monitor) when 'rewarded' with the opportunity to 'exercise,' 'play with,' and 'train' an obese pet dog avatar (who lost weight as a function of these activities) relative to control students (Johnsen et al., 2014).

While the aforementioned studies are intriguing, they do not address whether virtual reality technologies have more sustained effects on attitudes, behavior, and health. Research looking at longer-term effects of weight management programs in Second Life has been reported (Johnston et al., 2012; Napolitano, Hayes, Russo, Muresu, Giordano, & Foster, 2013; Sullivan et al., 2013). Napolitano et al. (2013) showed that a health-focused virtual world promoted weight loss in overweight/obese adult women. Each participant customized the shape and skin color of her personal avatar. Participants then observed their avatars 'model' and engage in healthy weight behaviors (e.g., buying healthy foods at the supermarket, eating healthy foods, walking on a treadmill). After four weekly 30-minute sessions watching their avatar engage in healthy behaviors, the women lost an average of 3.5 pounds (Napolitano et al., 2013). Johnston and colleagues (Johnston et al., 2012) examined the effects of a 12-week virtual world weight loss program in Second Life with an in-person weight loss program. While both programs resulted in comparable weight loss, participants in the virtual world program significantly increased self-efficacy (for weight loss and physical activity), self-reported moderate and vigorous physical activity, and fruit and vegetable consumption relative to the physical world participants. Sullivan and colleagues (Sullivan et al., 2013) also compared the effects of a 12-week weight management program in Second Life with an in-person weight management program. Both types of weight management programs included a 6-month maintenance program in Second Life. While both conditions experienced similar, clinically meaningful weight loss, those who participated in the Second Life programs for the entire 9-month period continued to lose weight. Those who initially participated in the in-person condition, however, regained some weight. In addition, the Second Life only participants ate significantly more daily servings of fruit at the 9-month follow-up. Sullivan's (Sullivan et al., 2013) data are consistent with research suggesting that virtual worlds could continue to influence health behaviors after the virtual experience (Anderson & Bushman, 2001). Johnston's (Johnston et al., 2012) and Sullivan's (Sullivan et al., 2013) findings support the potential of virtual world programs to extend the reach of conventional health interventions and suggest that virtual world weight management programs may be associated with as much or more weight loss than programs in the physical world.

The potential of virtual worlds to promote diabetes self-management behaviors has also been examined (Rosal et al., 2014; Ruggiero et al., 2014). African American adults with pre-diabetes or diabetes were randomized to an 8-week diabetes self-care virtual world program or a face-to-face physical world program. In both conditions, the participants received eight 90-minute diabetes self-management sessions (adapted from the Center for Disease Control/National Institute of Health "Power to Prevent" program) (Rosal et al., 2014). The program, based on social cognitive principles, was designed to increase diabetes knowledge, attitudes, and self-management behaviors, and to promote healthy weight behaviors. In the virtual world condition, the curriculum was delivered in Second Life and included virtual food exhibits and exercise facilities. While both groups had reductions in glycosylated hemoglobin (i.e., a test that determines how well a person's diabetes is controlled), individuals who participated in the virtual world engaged in more physical activity. Ruggiero et al. (2014) also demonstrated that 6-month involvement in the Diabetes Island virtual world, which provided users with education on diabetes self-care and diabetes resources, was associated with increased physical activity in individuals with type 2 diabetes. Participation was also associated with significant reductions in body mass index, diabetes-related distress, and self-reported barriers to diabetes self-care. Taken together, the findings of Rosal et al. (2014) and Ruggiero et al. (2014) show that virtual worlds have the potential to promote diabetes self-management behaviors in adults.

Virtual world technologies may be particularly beneficial for those who may have perceived barriers for addressing health behaviors in the physical world (Morie & Chance, 2011), such as embarrassment associated with excessive weight, costs associated with joining a fitness club, or living in an unsafe neighborhood not conducive to outdoor activities. The health-related impact of the virtual world could be due to the ability of the virtual environment to foster an interactive style of learning and provide opportunities for collaboration, social support, and the exchange of information (Cowdery, Kindred, Michalakis, & Suggs, 2011; Dickey, 2005).

A Healthy Body Image in the Virtual World and Physical World

Rather than focusing on weight and weight loss, we share the view articulated by Neumark-Sztainer (2005) that it may be more beneficial to prevent childhood overweight and obesity by focusing on changing and promoting health behaviors, overall health status, and an identity that is deeper than physical appearance. It is especially important for girls to concentrate on healthy weight behaviors, rather than weight. Research shows that their physical activity steeply declines following puberty, they may spend more time engaging in sedentary behavior than boys, and unhealthy eating behavior during youth is associated with disordered eating in adulthood (Killen et al., 1996; Kimm et al., 2002; Pate, O'Neill, & Lobelo, 2008). Furthermore, evidence suggests that ruminating on weight concerns may have deleterious effects for girls and may lead to a distorted body image and body dissatisfaction, and these problems worsen with age (Davison, Markey, & Birch, 2003).

These findings are concerning considering body dissatisfaction in preadolescents and adolescents adversely affects identity and is associated with disordered eating, depression, social anxiety, stress, lack of sports participation, low self-esteem, and suicidal ideation (Chaiton et al., 2009; Cho, Han, Kim, & Lee, 2012; Izgic, Akyuz, Dogan, & Kugu, 2004; Kim & Kim, 2009; Slater & Tiggermann, 2011). The negative consequences of poor body image have been well established, particularly in girls (Bearman, Presnell, Martinez, & Stice, 2006; Delfabbro, Winefield, Anderson, Hammarstrom, & Winefield, 2011). While girls with a higher body mass index are likely to experience greater image dissatisfaction and emotional distress about their body (Vander Wal & Thelen, 2000), girls in general are vulnerable to body image concerns (Feingold & Mazzella, 1998). This vulnerability may be a function of socialization influences that emphasize adhering to traditional gender roles that prize appearance and attractiveness for girls and women (Hill & Lynch 1983). An unrealistic 'thin ideal' for female attractiveness is valued by many western societies and reinforced by media representations (Grabe, Ward, & Hyde, 2008). While this ideal may vary as a function of sociocultural group, this 'idealized' woman is portrayed at about 15% below the average weight of all women, and is tall, has narrow hips, long legs, a large bust, and thin thighs, akin to a 'Barbie Doll' (Wiseman, Gray, Mosimann, & Ahrens, 1992). However, attaining this 'Barbie Doll' body type is almost biologically and genetically impossible (Attie & Brooks-Gunn, 1989). Furthermore, adolescent girls may be particularly at risk of accepting this unrealistic ideal as their identity consolidates during this critical period (Botta, 2003; Yildirim, 1997). Researchers suggest that those girls who internalize this gender stereotype and unrealistic thin ideal are particularly at risk for body image dissatisfaction (Bearman et al., 2006).

Efforts need to be directed at countering the unrealistic ideal with realistic healthy representations of the bodies of girls and women in media and in digital applications. For instance, Dove's Campaign for Real Beauty, launched in 2004, utilizes women of various weights, sizes, and shapes to advertise their products. The campaign has been praised for its realistic portrayal of the average female body. Neumark-Sztainer and colleagues (Neumark-Sztainer, Story, Hannan, & Rex, 2003) showed that by exposing girls to a variety of role models of different shapes, sizes and ethnicities and by providing social support, girls' physical activity, healthy eating, and opinions of themselves improved. These findings are in line with Bandura's Social Learning Theory (1968) and Social Cognitive Theory (1986). Although both theories posit that behaviors are often learned via direct observation of models and may be imitated and maintained as a function of reinforcement received, Social Cognitive Theory also addresses the role of cognitive processes and their interaction with the social and physical environment (Tobin, Reynolds, Holroyd, & Creer, 1986), and by extension the virtual environment. Self-efficacy, the personal belief that one can successfully perform and sustain desired behaviors, is conceptualized as vital in changing and maintaining a behavior. Social Cognitive Theory posits that those who have high self-efficacy are more likely to engage in target behaviors, such as healthy lifestyle habits, while those who have low self-efficacy are less likely to perform those behaviors (Bandura, 1986).

Besides observational learning, efforts to increase self-efficacy would also involve opportunities for the practice of skills and behaviors, and, eventually, skill mastery. Social factors, such as social support from peers and valued others, are also powerful determinants of health behaviors and outcomes (Cohen, 2004; Umberson, Crosnoe, & Reczek, 2010), and affect self-efficacy, skill acquisition, and mastery.

Furthermore, like other identities, health self-identity would be expected to be influenced by social factors (Oyserman, Elmore, & Smith, 2012). Social support may take many forms, ranging from emotional support and encouragement to informational support to tangible support (Cohen & Syme, 1985). As self-efficacy and personal expectations for success increase and desired behaviors are acquired and mastered, self-concept and sense of identity also evolve. Bandura's theories serve as the theoretical foundation for the *Get in the GROOVE!* program, as well as for a large body of research addressing health promotion and health behavior change (Armitage & Conner, 2000; Bandura, 1998; Bandura, 2004; Schwarzer, 2008; Wallace, Buckworth, Kirby, & Sherman, 2000; Young, Plotnikoff, Collins, Callister, & Morgan, 2014).

Virtual Modeling

Evidence suggests that modeling can occur virtually, and the resulting behaviors may be expressed in the physical world (Fox et al., 2009). Modeling by means of virtual technologies can be viewed as an example of symbolic modeling. Symbolic modeling of health behaviors can be particularly beneficial, as models for desirable health behaviors may not always be available within girls' everyday social environments (Bandura, 2001). Symbolic modeling was initially conceptualized as the modeling of a desired behavior through the usage of video, images, or plays (Bandura & Menlove, 1968). However, in circumstances where the user is more 'present' in the virtual world or feels as though the virtual world is real (and that the sensations and feelings of their avatar in the virtual world are related to their sensations and feelings in reality), the modeling may be considered in-vivo rather than symbolic (Fox et al., 2009). In Bandura's conceptualization, behaviors that are modeled are likely to be imitated if the model is similar to the observer. Thus, when a computer user imitates the behavior of an avatar that she identifies as herself, she is demonstrating 'virtual imitation' (Fox et al., 2009).

The use of an avatar can make the virtual world experience more enveloping and genuine and may allow users to become profoundly engaged in the learning experience (Gazzard, 2009). Further, individuals are more likely to imitate the behavior of a model that they perceive as similar and similarity to the model can also influence self-efficacy (Rosenstock, Strecher, & Becker, 1988). Fox and Bailenson (2009) have shown that virtual world users' health behaviors are more influenced by avatars that are similar to their own appearance, body shape, and body size. Researchers have found that in an online learning environment (i.e., an online tutoring program), an avatar that is similar to the computer user is more influential in impacting self-efficacy (Kim & Baylor, 2006). Taken together, these findings suggest that change in a computer user's virtual self can lead to changes in the user's everyday life (Baylor, 2009; Fox et al., 2009). As such, there is a clear theoretical and evidence-based foundation indicating that realistic, relatable avatars can serve as models of healthy behaviors within the virtual world.

Avatar Appearance Matters

In light of the findings using doppelgangers in immersive virtual reality technologies described by Blascovich and Bailenson (2011), we believe that, by providing girls with options to choose age- and body size- appropriate realistic avatars, we would maximize the likelihood that girls would identify with their avatars. To this end, GROOVE Island gave girls the tools to develop healthy, realistic age-appropriate avatars.

The use of realistic age-appropriate avatars for middle school aged girls is in marked contrast to the unrealistic, sexualized avatars that are often used in virtual environments. Research suggests that exposure to sexualized avatars is damaging to users, particularly girls and women (Fox, Bailenson, & Tricase, 2013). Psychological consequences, such as increased body-related thoughts, unattainable body ideals, self-objectification, and negative attitudes toward women, are associated with embodying sexualized virtual characters (Fox et al., 2013). For example, Lara Croft, a popular character of the video game *Tomb Raider*, is reputed to reinforce a negative body image in female virtual users (Schleiner, 2001). In response to that report, recent versions of *Tomb Raider* have changed Lara Croft's appearance to reflect a more realistic body type. Her body size was increased, her breast size reduced, and she now appears to wear less makeup. Although the changes are laudable, we are not aware of an empirical evaluation examining whether Lara Croft's recent appearance change has had a desirable psychological effect on users.

Using the Virtual World to Encourage Healthy Lifestyle Behaviors

Given that increasing healthy lifestyle behaviors was a stated goal of the *Get in the GROOVE!* program, we provided girls with education about healthy eating and physical activity and time to engage in those behaviors in both the virtual world and the physical world. We capitalized on the use of GROOVE Island as a digital learning tool to offer the opportunity to acquire, reflect, and apply knowledge about nutrition and physical activity in new ways (Foss & Haraldseid, 2014) and to boost enjoyment in learning (Blakely, Skirton, Cooper, Allum, & Nelmes, 2009). The content development for the virtual world was informed by the research priorities outlined by Ershow and colleagues (Ershow et al., 2011) to use virtual world technology to improve food choices, to provide opportunities for rehearsal and practice of healthy lifestyle behaviors, and to make behavior change more rewarding. Below we describe emblematic physical activity and healthy eating activities that straddled both worlds.

Promoting Physical Activity

Our participants in Miami and New York were given FitBit pedometers to measure their daily steps in the physical world. At the same time, the girls were engaged in a virtual walkathon on Interstate 95, in which the girls from Miami walked north to New York and the girls from New York walked south to Miami. Each day, the collective number of steps walked by the girls at both locations was aggregated to calculate the total distance each team virtually travelled.

The concurrent use of the pedometer walkathon with the virtual world helped promote physical activity as the virtual world was a reinforcement tool for the program's physical activity goals. Progress was tracked and, when mileage milestones were achieved, rewards for activity were unlocked in the virtual world as prizes for the girls with which to personalize their avatars. For example, once the girls in New York collectively walked the first 212 miles toward Miami, the reward of a scarf was unlocked for them to add to their avatars' ensembles. When they collectively walked 1,277 miles, butterfly wings were made available for all the avatars from that location. Other rewards included sunglasses, backpacks, and bunny slippers. Research shows that the use of rewards in conjunction with goal setting has the potential to prevent decline in physical activity and increases in unhealthy weight gain that girls may experience in adolescence (Lubans et al., 2010). The use of incentives is supported by Bandura's (1968; 1986) work and by the Theory of Meaning Behavior (Spruijt-Metz, 1995). In the Theory of Meaning Behavior, both internal and external motivational incentives promote behavior change. Motivators include the unlocked 'prized' items in the virtual world that serve as rewards for increased physical activity in the study. Internal motivators include personal rewards, such as positive feelings from meeting the daily goal of 11,000 steps or walking the most steps on a given day (Arteaga, Kudeki, Woodworth, & Kurniawan, 2010). The pedometer walkathon provided the opportunity for both sources of motivation to encourage health behavior change.

Moreover, games that are contingent on exercise, like the pedometer walkathon, have the potential to facilitate increased physical activity in children (Southard & Southard, 2006). Game-like environments and competitions are also used to encourage physical activity by emphasizing the perception that engaging in those behaviors can be fun and rewarding (Arteaga et al., 2010). By demonstrating that physical activity could be fun and engaging, the virtual world pedometer walkathon had the potential to impact the girls' physical activity habits beyond the 3-week program.

Promoting Healthy Eating

We introduced the GROOVE Island food truck design challenge as a cooperative education strategy to engage girls in learning about healthy eating and portion control. This activity was designed to immerse girls in creative ways to think about food choices. Over the course of the 3-week program, girls in both locations collaborated by working in small teams to customize virtual food trucks and to create healthy menus for their food trucks. Although team members were encouraged to adopt different roles (e.g., nutritionist, marketer, chef, and artist), they were all involved in contributing to all aspects of the activity. The truck design was facilitated by a truck building system that allowed for quick and easy selection of visual designs, themes, colors, and patterns from a collection of presets. Teams functionally worked as health investigators to research the accurate nutritional information for their chosen menu items. To this end, they conducted Internet searches and used information from program lessons (e.g., pertaining to the USDA MyPlate food groups and 'Go, Slow, and Whoa' foods). In this way, the food truck design challenge was able to build the perceived personal relevance and importance of good nutrition. In so doing, an ideal virtual environment was created to foster persuasion for health behavior change to occur (Lotrean, Mocean, Laza, & Poledna, 2009).

During the final week of the program, the teams made brief virtual presentations about the choices they made in designing their food trucks and menus. The avatars then visited all the food trucks and made selections from the respective menus. To illustrate how menu choices conformed to the five MyPlate food groups (fruits, vegetables, grains, protein, and dairy), the avatars' food choices were represented on their food tray as colored 'gelatin overlays' indicating the choice and quantity. If too much of or too little of a particular food group was 'ordered,' the size of the overlay would appear either too large or too small, respectively. Once the avatars saw the visual representation, they could make changes to their food order. Following the activity, the girls discussed in the physical world what healthy choices they and others had made and brainstormed ways to improve the less healthy plates that had been constructed. Research has shown that engaging digital nutrition activities that use fun and creative methodologies, like the food truck design challenge, can be an effective approach to increase children's nutritional knowledge and positive dietary habits. Technology that allows for this type of interactive process can also further drive information and build self-efficacy during the learning process (Rosi et al., 2016).

A second nutrition activity that was presented in the virtual world and reinforced in the physical world was the scavenger hunt held in the virtual 'superfoods' farmers' market. Avatars visited stalls containing nutritious foods selected for their purported health benefits (e.g. quinoa, berries, pomegranates). The avatars used clues to find healthy food in the virtual farmers' market (e.g., "This food was introduced by the Incas of Peru and is high in protein and helps maintain blood pressure."). Upon finding the correct food for each clue, the avatars took virtual pictures of themselves eating the corresponding item. In the physical world, girls were also able to sample these foods. This activity exposed girls to foods that they may have not tried before and encouraged them to think critically about those foods, their nutritional properties, and their potential health benefits. This activity was designed to promote healthier eating behaviors and to foster higher-level thinking about the utility of food. As children's and adolescents' experience with foods influences preference as well as dietary intake, exposure to these healthy 'super-foods' was expected to increase the likelihood of healthier eating habits (Cooke, 2007).

Social Influences on GROOVE Island: Promoting Health Knowledge and Healthy Lifestyle Behaviors

The contribution of social influences in the virtual world warrants acknowledgement. Both the pedometer walkathon and the food truck design challenge introduced a strong, socially-oriented team element. The pedometer walkathon had the potential to fuel competition and raise physical activity levels. Each day of the program, the girls were able to track their personal progress by viewing their place on the leaderboard and also received information about the collective performance of the New York and Miami teams. This fostered a social environment in which girls were responsive to, and held accountable to, one another within their teams. In addition, they were mutually aware of one another across teams. Likewise, the food truck design challenge required the participants to cooperate in the virtual and physical worlds to research and create appealing menu items. Although the girls sometimes had differing opinions about themes and food to include, they worked together to address their common goal. Together, the pedometer walkathon and the food truck design challenge enabled girls to feel as if they inhabited a shared space with others and gave them the sense that they were a part of a group and process (Behm Morawitz, 2013). Seventy-two percent of girls endorsed the statement "When I spend time with the girls on GROOVE Island, I feel like I am with girls I know," suggesting the virtual world supported social connections. Thus, the social component that was facilitated through the support for teamwork in the virtual world potentially motivated participants to set physical activity and project completion goals and be more accountable in keeping those goals.

The social component of the virtual world is likely to have played a role in exercise motivation and increased physical activity. There is a large literature demonstrating the benefits of social support and connectedness on health and behavior (Cohen, 2004). The girls were often observed engaging in light-hearted competition when they encountered other girls in the virtual world and in the physical world. Research suggests that the social component may prompt individuals to appraise and adjust their physical activity in response to others within their environment, making comparisons between their own abilities and the abilities of those around them (Strauss, 2002). The girls in the *Get in the GROOVE!* program may have been motivated to adopt changes in health behavior as a result of the support and encouragement they received from others and by leveraging their natural drive to compete with others in their environment (Fogg, 2003).

As research shows that participants receive and process information through the virtual world as themselves (Cowdery et al., 2011), we believe that the pedometer walkathon and the MyPlate food truck dining choices made by avatars exemplified how educating through the virtual modeling of health behaviors by avatars could impact real-world behaviors. The virtual world and its activities were designed to increase the participants' awareness of their physical activity levels and food choices and potentially motivated them to improve their health habits in a way that was fun and engaging.

Individual Differences: Who Benefits Most From Participation in the Virtual World?

Research shows that individuals who feel more immersed in a virtual world are more likely to display the behaviors of an avatar (De Freitas, Rebolledo-Mendez, Liarokapis, Magoulas, & Poulovassilis, 2010). We were interested in determining whether Fox et al.'s, (2009) findings in adult women also generalized to middle school aged girls in the *Get in the GROOVE!* program. Specifically, we wanted to examine whether experiencing the virtual world as 'real' might influence health-related outcomes. To this end, we modified Fox's 10-item presence measure to tailor it to girls visiting GROOVE Island. The GROOVE Island measure was psychometrically sound and yielded an 'immersion in the virtual world' factor and an 'identification with the avatar' factor.

Girls who felt more immersed in GROOVE Island demonstrated healthier behaviors at the end of the program. They increased both their healthy eating behavior and their physical activity. Given the ample opportunities on GROOVE Island to engage in and learn about healthy eating and physical activity, it is likely that girls who were immersed more fully took the opportunities to learn about, rehearse, and imitate the healthy behaviors of their own avatars and those of the other participants.

We also found that identification with the avatar affected health attitudes. Girls who endorsed more identification reported higher self-efficacy for physical activity at the end of the program. This finding is encouraging as self-efficacy is one of the strongest predictors of physical activity (McAuley & Blissmer, 2000; Van der Horst, Paw, Twisk, & Van Mechelen, 2007) and would be expected to increase the likelihood of engaging in that health behavior (Bandura, 1986). In her work with adults, Johnston and colleagues (2012) showed that both self-efficacy for physical activity, as well as time spent engaging in physical activity, increased with participation in the virtual world. Taken together, these research findings suggest that virtual models are conducive to promoting self-efficacy. We believe that when individuals view their virtual representation participating in healthy behaviors, their confidence in their own ability to engage in said behaviors increases. This is encouraging as virtual worlds' capacity to increase self-efficacy through practice and rehearsal was previously hypothesized to be a way to prevent and treat obesity (Ershow et al., 2011).

It is important to underscore that our findings suggest that it may not be sufficient to merely participate in a health-oriented virtual world to achieve health benefits. Rather, it is critical to be both fully immersed and to identify with one's avatar. We expect that the personal attributes of the users affect their capacity for immersion and identification with their avatar. Notwithstanding, below we discuss our efforts to address avatar development as a means to maximize identification with the avatar (see section - Considerations in developing healthy age-appropriate realistic avatars).

SOLUTIONS AND RECOMMENDATIONS

As we have discussed, the *Get in the GROOVE!* summer science enrichment program offered health education and obesity prevention-focused activities. An array of experiences in the virtual world and the physical world were provided to enhance self-efficacy (physical activity, healthy eating, and science) and to practice and consolidate health behavior skills. Girls had the opportunity to participate in a pedometer walking program, choreograph dances, compete on teams, explore hiking trails, visit food markets (in the virtual world and in the physical world), learn about healthy 'superfoods,' collaborate on healthy food truck menus, and evaluate how meal choices conform with MyPlate.gov recommendations. Furthermore, girls were exposed to and received support from a community of models in the virtual and physical worlds that included peers, program teachers and mentors, and invited health professionals. As girls' accomplishments and self-efficacy increased over the course of the 3-week program, we anticipated that their health identity consolidated as they realized that they could engage in, be good at, enjoy health behaviors, and, ultimately, adopt a healthy lifestyle.

In designing the *Get in the GROOVE!* program, we gave careful consideration to how to create healthy realistic avatars and how to link the pedometer walkathon in the physical world to the virtual walkathon. A discussion of these issues follows.

Considerations in Developing Healthy Age-Appropriate Realistic Avatars

Our study's virtual world component, GROOVE Island, reinforced curriculum and concepts learned in the physical world component of the summer program. The limited available data on virtual worlds and health suggest that youth and adults are likely to benefit from virtual technologies that utilize avatars to manage weight and promote a healthy lifestyle (LeRouge, Dickhut, Lisetti, Sangameswaran, & Malasanos, 2015; Napolitano et al., 2013). The virtual world environment provided opportunities for girls to offer and receive support and encouragement and to model, imitate, and rehearse healthy behaviors displayed by one's own avatar and the avatars of other participants. Balancing the need to promote a healthy weight in children while also encouraging a healthy body image and health self-identity can be challenging, especially for girls. Thus, given the age and gender of the participants in the *Get in the GROOVE!* program, our efforts were directed at offering healthy and realistic avatar options for the participants to customize and make their own.

We wanted girls to enter the virtual world with an avatar that was uncontaminated by the implicit biases that might be communicated by the adult bodies and behaviors of the default avatars of OpenSim and Second Life. We did not want girls to make social comparisons to a default avatar. To this end, we first experimented with the 'gray' avatar that was featureless and race-less. This seemed to successfully remove any latent racial and ethnic expectations as well as cultural connotations carried by clothing style. However, the uniform color of the avatar created a silhouette that seemed to amplify any default messages communicated about the avatar's gender and body weight and accentuated the avatar's sexuality. We judged that priming the girls with the 'gray' avatar would undermine our efforts for them to develop age-appropriate avatars with healthy and realistic body images that would represent them on GROOVE Island. As a result, we abandoned the human form as a starting point.

Next, we explored the use of the invisible avatar. While resolving problems of bias, the invisible avatar created usability problems. It was difficult to navigate and control an avatar that could not be seen. More problematic, invisibility suppressed social interaction between users who could not see each other. This created a confusing, somewhat muted first impression of the virtual world that we were concerned could result in disengagement.

Finally, we used a common trope in television and film to create the 'energy beings' default avatar. This avatar consisted of a simple, glowing sphere of light that had the effect of eliminating any communication of anthropomorphic bias. While all 'energy being' avatars were geometrically identical, they were each assigned a color that was generated by using a simple hash algorithm against the user's selected name to create seemingly random RGB color values. This allows users to easily identify each other by the brilliant shades of red, green, blue, and yellow while understanding that these colors communicate nothing of relevance to their inner identity. These energy beings proved to be a successful solution.

The girls were instructed to navigate their energy beings to a kiosk on GROOVE Island that is marked by a 'billboard' with pictures of six ethnically and racially diverse middle school aged girl avatars that represent the sociodemographic characteristics of potential participants in Miami and New York (see Figure 1). In an easy, fun, and engaging process that could be accomplished in approximately an hour, the girls were given the tools to easily select and customize realistic age-appropriate avatars and make them their own. Girls were instructed to "make an avatar that is you." As a starting point, girls chose among the six avatar 'templates.' Once the avatar was selected, they could edit their avatars' physical characteristics (e.g., body shape, size, weight, hairstyle, and facial features) and choose clothing and accessories (see Figure 2). The avatars were also programmed to show various expressions and gestures such as laughing, clapping, and dancing. The avatars' appearance was not intended to be static. Over the course of the 3-week program, any girl could modify the avatar that embodied her virtual self.

Given our interest in offering healthy, realistic avatar options, the *Get in the GROOVE!* avatar templates described above were informed by a collection of body scans from Auburn University's Consumer Affairs Department. The scans, originally assembled for precise clothing sizing, included 100 actual 3-Dimensional body scans of adolescent girls of different ages and body sizes from different racial and ethnic backgrounds (Mahajan, 2009). We reviewed images of these scans to develop appropriate realistic virtual templates of girls of various ages, shapes, and weights.

We believe these efforts contributed to 70% of girls endorsing the statement, "When I visit GROOVE Island, my avatar is me," reflecting that a high proportion of girls identified with their avatar and, by extension, were 'present' in our virtual world. Furthermore, presence may also be viewed as the sense of being in the virtual world rather than in the place where the person is actually located (Sanchez-Vives

Figure 1. Various avatars that represent the sociodemographic characteristics of potential participants

Figure 2. An example of a GROOVE Island age-appropriate avatar of varying physical characteristics

& Slater, 2005). As we have indicated above, examining presence is important since an individual's subjective experience of presence may impact how well virtual experiences translate into behavior in the physical world (Fox et al., 2009). Eighty-five percent of the participants endorsed the statement, "I would like to spend more time on GROOVE Island," 60% agreed that "When I'm on GROOVE Island, I lose track of time," and 52% reported that "When I visit GROOVE Island, I forget that I am at the museum." These results suggest that the girls not only enjoyed spending time on GROOVE Island, but also were immersed and engaged in the virtual world. These findings are of importance as research suggests that an enjoyable learning task is likely to provoke intrinsic motivation, which is characterized by persistence, mastery, and general interest (Gottfried, 1990).

Considerations in Linking the Pedometer Walkathon to the Virtual World

The pedometer walkathon was presented as a friendly competition among the girls and museum sites. Research indicates that competitions encourage physical activity by emphasizing the perception that engaging in those behaviors can be fun and rewarding (Arteaga et al., 2010). The walkathon capitalized on social reinforcement, virtual world prizes, and personalized feedback to reward physical activity.

We used the Fitbit Zip pedometer to track the girls' activity. The Fitbit Zip engaged the participants through the emoji faces, step count, and other badge images that appeared on the pedometer screen daily. In fact, the Fitbit Zip's smiley face grew as the user increased physical activity throughout the day. This helped create the fun, dynamic environment that research suggests can motivate children to be physically active (Southard & Southard, 2006).

Unfortunately, we were unable to directly link the girls' pedometer data with the virtual world. To overcome this barrier, we created individual profiles for each girl on the Fitbit website and created community groups for each of the museums. The community groups showed updated aggregated steps walked by and, thus, the mileage covered by, the respective team each time a team member synchronized her pedometer. This information was available to each of the individual girls on a team and the program staff. A GROOVE Island administrator entered the activity information into the virtual world and distance covered was marked by footsteps on virtual Interstate 95. As such, the Fitbit website allowed girls to track their personal progress, view their team's leaderboard, and review their standing relative to their teammates. However, it was only on GROOVE Island where girls could compare the activity of their team with their competition at the other site, meet to hear announcements about the progress in the walkathon, learn about pedometer leaders at each of the sites, and receive the virtual world prizes that were unlocked as teams met activity milestones.

The Fitbit website was a useful supplement to GROOVE Island, as it provided girls with personalized information to better understand their physical activity. By viewing their steps, distance, and calories burned throughout the day, the girls knew if they were meeting, exceeding, or falling short of the 11,000 steps per day goal. If they did reach their benchmark of 11,000 steps a day, the girls received praise in the form of a shout out.

The *Get in the GROOVE!* teachers also facilitated discussion about the pedometers, what the girls had already done to be active, what they could do over the weekend to be active, and strategies for increasing activity. This may have encouraged the girls to be even more physically active, as research suggests that individuals appraise and adjust their physical activity in response to others within their environment (Strauss, 2002).

FUTURE DIRECTIONS

In our conceptualization, education functions as an intervention that gives individuals the tools to lead a healthy life. The findings of the *Get in the GROOVE!* program have the potential to inform what kind of educational experience is optimal to increase knowledge, promote better health, enhance self-efficacy for healthy behavior, and consolidate health self-identity in girls. Since education is a universal experience for American children and adolescents, our work has implications for both formal and informal science education settings. Furthermore, given the health status of American youth today (Ogden et al., 2014), we believe that there is a need to develop and utilize science-rich health education resources that motivate interest in adopting a healthy lifestyle for students of all ages. Furthermore, this may have the added benefit of promoting student interest in health-related STEM fields.

As girls in our program were from diverse socioeconomic and racial and ethnic backgrounds, it will be incumbent upon researchers to address whether virtual world strategies are effective in reducing health disparities. The generalizability of our findings in middle school-aged girls to boys or children in other age groups remains unknown. Opportunities to adapt the 90-hour summer curriculum for use in school and other settings should also be explored. Determining whether involvement with the curriculum over a few lessons, a quarter, a semester, or an academic year produces the same benefits as the summer program's virtual world and class-based experiences would likely inform future interventions.

Given the important contributions parents make to children's health, the availability of the virtual world technologies enables us to extend what happens in a 3-week summer program or classroom to the home and family. For example, a barrier to healthy food consumption often reported by youth is their lack of control over what food is offered at home. The availability of virtual technologies can facilitate exploration of healthy food choices by parents and children together. Thus, virtual world technology has the potential to increase the accessibility of health education and promote the adoption of health behaviors for children and their families. Likewise, virtual technologies can be employed to reinforce physical activity engaged in and encouraged by the family. Once aware of how to incorporate healthy options, parents can serve as role models for healthy behavior, provide social support, and function as agents of change for their children. Parents themselves will likely benefit from these experiences as a result of the bonding and communication with their children. Since approximately two-thirds of adults are overweight or obese (Ogden et al., 2014), parents are also an ideal target group to benefit from a health-oriented virtual world experience. Future work needs to be directed at designing research that addresses whether outcomes for children improve when both parents and children use health-oriented virtual technologies together.

A strength of virtual worlds is that they eliminate the geographic boundaries of the physical world. In light of the high prevalence of childhood overweight and obesity throughout the world (Wang & Lim, 2012), efforts directed at ensuring that health-oriented virtual technologies are accessible and acceptable to a diverse population are needed. However, this may be challenging as physical environments, diets, types of physical activity, and social norms vary across cultures. Thus, in future work, it will be critical to make readily available, culturally competent virtual world experiences that are sensitive to health-related beliefs and practices of users from different backgrounds.

Lastly, there are limitless opportunities to extend the reach of the *Get in the GROOVE!* program beyond research and education. Clinical applications of health-oriented virtual world technologies merit additional exploration. The potential benefits of offering a virtual world experience to students visiting school health clinics or to youth visiting pediatricians' offices could extend well beyond those provided by usual care. Future work involving clinical applications will need to expand outcomes beyond knowledge, self-efficacy, and behavior to health outcomes related to reducing metabolic and cardiovascular risk.

CONCLUSION

In light of the obesity epidemic affecting American children and adolescents, the *Get in the GROOVE!* program represents our effort to improve lifestyle habits, increase health knowledge, enhance self-efficacy for healthy behavior change, encourage a healthy, realistic body image, and promote a health self-identity in middle school aged girls. Research indicates that the use of avatars in virtual technologies may beneficially affect youth and adults attempting to manage their weight or adopt healthy lifestyle behaviors. Evidence also suggests that realistic avatars in the virtual world function as role models for users in the physical world. Realistic age-appropriate avatars are important for promoting a healthy body image for girls, as girls are vulnerable to social and environmental influences that place them at risk for body image dissatisfaction.

In our work, the virtual world augmented--and had reciprocal influences on-- activities, experiences, and learning that occurred in the physical world. The virtual world extended the physical world's social environment and offered girls additional opportunities to collaborate and compete, to both give and receive social support, and to acquire healthy behaviors and a healthy body image. As an engaging and novel intervention strategy, the virtual world seems to be an exceptionally promising social environment to motivate healthy habits and assist users in developing a health self-identity. Besides lending themselves to educational and research applications to promote health, the clinical applications of virtual technologies warrant further study.

ACKNOWLEDGMENT

This project is supported by SEPA NIH grant 5 R2OD010525.

REFERENCES

Anderson, C. A., & Bushman, B. (2001). Effects of violent video games on aggressive behavior, aggressive cognition, aggressive affect, physiological arousal, and prosocial behavior: A meta-analytic review of the scientific literature. *Psychological Science*, *12*(5), 353–359. doi:10.1111/1467-9280.00366 PMID:11554666

Armitage, C. J., & Conner, M. (2000). Social cognition models and health behaviour: A structured review. *Psychology & Health*, *15*(2), 173–189. doi:10.1080/08870440008400299

Arteaga, S. M., Kudeki, M., Woodworth, A., & Kurniawan, S. (2010). Mobile system to motivate teenagers' physical activity. *Proceedings of the 9th International Conference on Interaction Design and Children*, 1-10. doi: 10.1145/1810543.1810545

Attie, I., & Brooks-Gunn, J. (1989). Development of eating problems in adolescent girls: A longitudinal study. *Developmental Psychology*, *25*(1), 70–79. doi:10.1037/0012-1649.25.1.70

Bandura, A. (1986). *Social foundations of thought and action: A social cognitive theory*. Englewood Cliffs, NJ: Prentice-Hall.

Bandura, A. (1998). Health promotion from the perspective of social cognitive theory. *Psychology & Health*, *13*(4), 623–649. doi:10.1080/08870449808407422

Bandura, A. (2001). Social cognitive theory of mass communication. *Media Psychology*, *3*(3), 265–299. doi:10.1207/S1532785XMEP0303_03

Bandura, A. (2004). Health promotion by social cognitive means. *Health Education & Behavior*, *31*(2), 143–164. doi:10.1177/1090198104263660 PMID:15090118

Bandura, A., & Menlove, F. L. (1968). Factors determining vicarious extinction of avoidance behavior through symbolic modeling. *Journal of Personality and Social Psychology*, *8*(2, Pt. 1), 99–108. doi:10.1037/h0025260 PMID:5644484

Banfield, E. C., Liu, Y., Davis, J. S., Chang, S., & Frazier-Wood, A. C. (2016). Poor adherence to US dietary guidelines for children and adolescents in the national health and nutrition examination survey population. *Journal of the Academy of Nutrition and Dietetics*, *116*(1), 21–27. doi:10.1016/j.jand.2015.08.010 PMID:26391469

Baylor, A. L. (2009). Promoting motivation with virtual agents and avatars: Role of visual presence and appearance. *Philosophical Transactions of the Royal Society of London. Series B, Biological Sciences*, *364*(1535), 3559–3565. doi:10.1098/rstb.2009.0148 PMID:19884150

Bearman, S. K., Presnell, K., Martinez, E., & Stice, E. (2006). The skinny on body dissatisfaction: A longitudinal study of adolescent girls and boys. *Journal of Youth and Adolescence*, *35*(2), 217–229. doi:10.100710964-005-9010-9 PMID:16912810

Behm Morawitz, E. (2013). Mirrored Selves: The influence of self-presence in a virtual world on health, appearance, and well-being. *Computers in Human Behavior*, *29*(1), 119–128. doi:10.1016/j.chb.2012.07.023

Benjamin, E. J., Blaha, M. J., Chiuve, S. E., Cushman, M., Das, S. R., Deo, R., ... Muntner, P. (2017). Heart disease and stroke statistics—2017 update: A report from the American Heart Association. *Circulation*, *135*(10), e146–e603. doi:10.1161/CIR.0000000000000485 PMID:28122885

Blakely, G., Skirton, H., Cooper, S., Allum, P., & Nelmes, P. (2009). Educational gaming in the health sciences: Systematic review. *Journal of Advanced Nursing*, *65*(2), 259–269. doi:10.1111/j.1365-2648.2008.04843.x PMID:19032512

Blascovich, J., & Bailenson, J. (2011). *Infinite reality: Avatars, eternal life, new worlds, and the dawn of the virtual revolution*. New York: Harper Collins.

Botta, R. A. (2003). For your health? The relationship between magazine reading and adolescents' body image and eating disturbances. *Sex Roles*, *48*(9-10), 389–399. doi:10.1023/A:1023570326812

Bourke, M., Whittaker, P. J., & Verma, A. (2014). Are dietary interventions effective at increasing fruit and vegetable consumption among overweight children? A systematic review. *Journal of Epidemiology and Community Health*, *68*(5), 485–490. doi:10.1136/jech-2013-203238 PMID:24436339

Chaiton, M., Sabiston, C., O'loughlin, J., McGrath, J. J., Maximova, K., & Lambert, M. (2009). A structural equation model relating adiposity, psychosocial indicators of body image and depressive symptoms among adolescents. *International Journal of Obesity*, *33*(5), 588–596. doi:10.1038/ijo.2009.43 PMID:19274053

Cho, J. H., Han, S. N., Kim, J. H., & Lee, H. M. (2012). Body image distortion in fifth and sixth grade students may lead to stress, depression, and undesirable dieting behavior. *Nutrition Research and Practice*, *6*(2), 175–181. doi:10.4162/nrp.2012.6.2.175 PMID:22586508

Cohen, S. (2004). Social Relationships and Health. *The American Psychologist*, *59*(8), 676–684. doi:10.1037/0003-066X.59.8.676 PMID:15554821

Cohen, S. E., & Syme, S. (1985). *Social support and health*. San Diego, CA: Academic Press.

Coles, C. D., Strickland, D. C., Padgett, L., & Bellmoff, L. (2007). Games that "work": Using computer games to teach alcohol-affected children about fire and street safety. *Research in Developmental Disabilities*, *28*(5), 518–530. doi:10.1016/j.ridd.2006.07.001 PMID:16965894

Cooke, L. (2007). The importance of exposure for healthy eating in childhood: A review. *Journal of Human Nutrition and Dietetics*, *20*(4), 294–301. doi:10.1111/j.1365-277X.2007.00804.x PMID:17635306

Cowdery, J., Kindred, J., Michalakis, A., & Suggs, L. S. (2011). Promoting health in a virtual world: Impressions of health communication messages delivered in Second Life. *First Monday*, *16*(9). doi:10.5210/fm.v16i9.2857

Davison, K. K., Markey, C. N., & Birch, L. L. (2003). A longitudinal examination of patterns in girls' weight concerns and body dissatisfaction from ages 5 to 9 years. *International Journal of Eating Disorders*, *33*(3), 320–332. doi:10.1002/eat.10142 PMID:12655629

De Freitas, S., Rebolledo-Mendez, G., Liarokapis, F., Magoulas, G., & Poulovassilis, A. (2010). Learning as immersive experiences: Using the four-dimensional framework for designing and evaluating immersive learning experiences in a virtual world. *British Journal of Educational Technology*, *41*(1), 69–85. doi:10.1111/j.1467-8535.2009.01024.x

Deci, E. L., & Ryan, R. M. (2000). The" what" and" why" of goal pursuits: Human needs and the self-determination of behavior. *Psychological Inquiry*, *11*(4), 227–268. doi:10.1207/S15327965PLI1104_01

Delfabbro, P. H., Winefield, A. H., Anderson, S., Hammarström, A., & Winefield, H. (2011). Body image and psychological well-being in adolescents: The relationship between gender and school type. *The Journal of Genetic Psychology*, *172*(1), 67–83. doi:10.1080/00221325.2010.517812 PMID:21452753

Dickey, M. D. (2005). Three-dimensional virtual worlds and distance learning: Two case studies of active worlds as a medium for distance education. *British Journal of Educational Technology*, *36*(3), 439–451. doi:10.1111/j.1467-8535.2005.00477.x

Drewnowski, A. (2004). Obesity and the food environment: Dietary energy density and diet costs. *American Journal of Preventive Medicine*, *27*(3), 154–162. doi:10.1016/j.amepre.2004.06.011 PMID:15450626

Ershow, A. G., Peterson, C. M., Riley, W. T., Rizzo, A. S., & Wansink, B. (2011). Virtual reality technologies for research and education in obesity and diabetes: Research needs and opportunities. *Journal of Diabetes Science and Technology*, *5*(2), 212–224. doi:10.1177/193229681100500202 PMID:21527084

Feingold, A., & Mazzella, R. (1998). Gender differences in body image are increasing. *Psychological Science*, *9*(3), 190–195. doi:10.1111/1467-9280.00036

Fogg, B. (2003). *Persuasive Technology: Using Computers to Change What We Think and Do*. San Francisco, CA: Morgan Kaufmann Publisher. doi:10.1016/B978-155860643-2/50011-1

Foss, B., & Haraldseid, C. (2014). Improvement of Health Education: The Opportunities of Technology and Digital Learning Tools. *Journal of Biosafety and Health Education*, *2*(1), e114. doi:10.4172/2332-0893.1000e114

Fox, J., & Bailenson, J. N. (2009). Virtual self-modeling: The effects of vicarious reinforcement and identification on exercise behaviors. *Media Psychology*, *12*(1), 1–25. doi:10.1080/15213260802669474

Fox, J., Bailenson, J. N., & Binney, J. (2009). Virtual experiences, physical behaviors: The effect of presence on imitation of an eating avatar. *Presence (Cambridge, Mass.)*, *18*(4), 294–303. doi:10.1162/pres.18.4.294

Fox, J., Bailenson, J. N., & Tricase, L. (2013). The embodiment of sexualized virtual selves: The Proteus effect and experiences of self-objectification via avatars. *Computers in Human Behavior*, *29*(3), 930–938. doi:10.1016/j.chb.2012.12.027

Friedrich, M. J. (2017). Global Obesity Epidemic Worsening. *Journal of the American Medical Association*, *318*(7), 603. doi:10.1001/jama.2017.10693 PMID:28810033

Gazzard, A. (2009). *The avatar and the player: Understanding the relationship beyond the screen. In Proceedings from VS-GAMES'09, Coventry, 2009.* Washington, DC: IEEE. doi:10.1109/VS-GAMES.2009.11

Gottfried, A. E. (1990). Academic intrinsic motivation in young elementary school children. *Journal of Educational Psychology*, *82*(3), 525–538. doi:10.1037/0022-0663.82.3.525

Grabe, S., Ward, L. M., & Hyde, J. S. (2008). The role of the media in body image concerns among women: A meta-analysis of experimental and correlational studies. *Psychological Bulletin*, *134*(3), 460–476. doi:10.1037/0033-2909.134.3.460 PMID:18444705

Hagobian, T. A., & Phelan, S. (2013). Lifestyle interventions to reduce obesity and diabetes. *American Journal of Lifestyle Medicine*, *7*(2), 84–98. doi:10.1177/1559827612449600

Haslam, D. W., & James, W. P. T. (2005). Obesity. *Lancet*, *366*(9492), 1197–1209. doi:10.1016/S0140-6736(05)67483-1 PMID:16198769

Hill, J. P., & Lynch, M. E. (1983). The intensification of gender-related role expectations during early adolescence. In J. Brooks-Gunn & A. C. Petersen (Eds.), *Girls at puberty* (pp. 201–228). Boston, MA: Springer. doi:10.1007/978-1-4899-0354-9_10

Izgiç, F., Akyüz, G., Doğan, O., & Kuğu, N. (2004). Social phobia among university students and its relation to self-esteem and body image. *Canadian Journal of Psychiatry*, *49*(9), 630–634. doi:10.1177/070674370404900910 PMID:15503736

Johnsen, K., Ahn, S. J., Moore, J., Brown, S., Robertson, T. P., Marable, A., & Basu, A. (2014). Mixed reality virtual pets to reduce childhood obesity. *IEEE Transactions on Visualization and Computer Graphics*, *20*(4), 523–530. doi:10.1109/TVCG.2014.33 PMID:24650979

Johnson, L. F., & Levine, A. H. (2008). Virtual worlds: Inherently immersive, highly social learning spaces. *Theory into Practice*, *47*(2), 161–170. doi:10.1080/00405840801992397

Johnston, J. D., Massey, A. P., & DeVaneaux, C. A. (2012). Innovation in weight loss programs: A 3-dimensional virtual-world approach. *Journal of Medical Internet Research*, *14*(5), e120. doi:10.2196/jmir.2254 PMID:22995535

Killen, J. D., Taylor, C. B., Hayward, C., Haydel, K. F., Wilson, D. M., Hammer, L., ... Strachowski, D. (1996). Weight concerns influence the development of eating disorders: A 4-year prospective study. *Journal of Consulting and Clinical Psychology*, *64*(5), 936–940. doi:10.1037/0022-006X.64.5.936 PMID:8916622

Kim, D. S., & Kim, H. S. (2009). Body-image dissatisfaction as a predictor of suicidal ideation among Korean boys and girls in different stages of adolescence: A two-year longitudinal study. *The Journal of Adolescent Health*, *45*(1), 47–54. doi:10.1016/j.jadohealth.2008.11.017 PMID:19541249

Kim, Y., & Baylor, A. L. (2006). A social-cognitive framework for pedagogical agents as learning companions. *Educational Technology Research and Development*, *54*(6), 569–596. doi:10.100711423-006-0637-3

Kimm, S. Y., Glynn, N. W., Kriska, A. M., Barton, B. A., Kronsberg, S. S., Daniels, S. R., ... Liu, K. (2002). Decline in physical activity in black girls and white girls during adolescence. *The New England Journal of Medicine*, *347*(10), 709–715. doi:10.1056/NEJMoa003277 PMID:12213941

Kyoung Joo, Y., & Kim, K. (2017). When You Exercise Your Avatar in a Virtual Game: The Role of Avatars' Body Shape and Behavior in Users' Health Behavior. *Interacting with Computers*, *29*(3), 455–466. doi:10.1093/iwc/iwx003

LeRouge, C., Dickhut, K., Lisetti, C., Sangameswaran, S., & Malasanos, T. (2015). Engaging adolescents in a computer-based weight management program: Avatars and virtual coaches could help. *Journal of the American Medical Informatics Association*, *23*(1), 19–28. doi:10.1093/jamia/ocv078 PMID:26159466

Lotrean, L. M., Mocean, F., Laza, V., & Poledna, S. (2009). The Role of Information Technology in Health Education: Strengths and Weaknesses. In S. Vlad, R. V. Ciupa, & A. I. Nicu (Eds.), *International Conference on Advancements of Medicine and Health Care through Technology* (*Vol. 26*, pp. 73–76). Berlin: Springer Berlin Heidelberg. 10.1007/978-3-642-04292-8_16

Lou, D. (2014). *Sedentary Behaviors and Youth: Current Trends and the Impact on Health*. San Diego, CA: Active Living Research. doi:10.13140/RG.2.1.4294.8884

Lubans, D. R., Morgan, P. J., Dewar, D., Collins, C. E., Plotnikoff, R. C., Okely, A. D., ... Callister, R. (2010). The Nutrition and Enjoyable Activity for Teen Girls (NEAT girls) randomized controlled trial for adolescent girls from disadvantaged secondary schools: Rationale, study protocol, and baseline results. *BMC Public Health*, *10*(1), 652. doi:10.1186/1471-2458-10-652 PMID:21029467

Mahajan, A. (2009). *Comparing self and others' perceptions of adolescent girls' body size using figural stimuli and 3d body scans*. Retrieved from WorldCat.

Maher, C. A., Mire, E., Harrington, D. M., Staiano, A. E., & Katzmarzyk, P. T. (2013). The independent and combined associations of physical activity and sedentary behavior with obesity in adults: NHANES 2003-06. *Obesity (Silver Spring, Md.)*, *21*(12), E730–E737. doi:10.1002/oby.20430 PMID:23512825

McAuley, E., & Blissmer, B. (2000). Self-efficacy determinants and consequences of physical activity. *Exercise Sports Science Review, 28*(2), 85-88. Retrieved from: https://journals.lww.com/acsm-essr/pages/default.aspx

Mitchell, J. A., Pate, R. R., Beets, M. W., & Nader, P. R. (2013). Time spent in sedentary behavior and changes in childhood BMI: A longitudinal study from ages 9 to 15 years. *International Journal of Obesity*, *37*(1), 54–60. doi:10.1038/ijo.2012.41 PMID:22430304

Morie, J. F., & Chance, E. (2011). Extending the reach of health care for obesity and diabetes using virtual worlds. *Journal of Diabetes Science and Technology*, *5*(2), 272–276. doi:10.1177/193229681100500211 PMID:21527093

Napolitano, M. A., Hayes, S., Russo, G., Muresu, D., Giordano, A., & Foster, G. D. (2013). Using avatars to model weight loss behaviors: Participant attitudes and technology development. *Journal of Diabetes Science and Technology*, *7*(4), 1057–1065. doi:10.1177/193229681300700430 PMID:23911189

Neumark-Sztainer, D. (2005). Preventing the broad spectrum of weight-related problems: Working with parents to help teens achieve a healthy weight and a positive body image. *Journal of Nutrition Education and Behavior*, *37*, S133–S139. doi:10.1016/S1499-4046(06)60214-5 PMID:16246282

Neumark-Sztainer, D., Story, M., Hannan, P. J., & Rex, J. (2003). New Moves: A school-based obesity prevention program for adolescent girls. *Preventive Medicine*, *37*(1), 41–51. doi:10.1016/S0091-7435(03)00057-4 PMID:12799128

Ogden, C. L., Carroll, M. D., Kit, B. K., & Flegal, K. M. (2014). Prevalence of childhood and adult obesity in the United States, 2011-2012. *Journal of the American Medical Association*, *311*(8), 806–814. doi:10.1001/jama.2014.732 PMID:24570244

Olvera, N., Kellam, S. F., Menefee, K., Lee, J., & Smith, D. W. (2010). Physical activity in Latino children: Research and its implications. *Journal of Applied Research on Children: Informing Policy for Children at Risk*, *1*(1), 3. Retrieved from https://digitalcommons.library.tmc.edu/childrenatrisk/

Oyserman, D., Elmore, K., & Smith, G. (2012). Self, Self-Concept, and Identity. In M. R. Leary & J. P. Tangney (Eds.), *Handbook of Self and Identity* (pp. 69–104). New York, NY: The Guilford Press.

Pate, R. R., O'Neill, J. R., & Lobelo, F. (2008). The evolving definition of "sedentary.". *Exercise and Sport Sciences Reviews*, *36*(4), 173–178. doi:10.1097/JES.0b013e3181877d1a PMID:18815485

Poirier, P., & Eckel, R. H. (2002). Obesity and cardiovascular disease. *Current Atherosclerosis Report*, *4*(6), 448–453. Retrieved from https://link.springer.com/journal/11883

Prensky, M. (2001). Digital natives, digital immigrants part 1. *On the Horizon*, *9*(5), 1–6. doi:10.1108/10748120110424816

Pulgarón, E. R. (2013). Childhood obesity: A review of increased risk for physical and psychological comorbidities. *Clinical Therapeutics*, *35*(1), A18–A32. doi:10.1016/j.clinthera.2012.12.014 PMID:23328273

Rise, J., Sheeran, P., & Hukkelberg, S. (2010). The Role of Self-Identity in the Theory of Planned Behavior: A Meta-Analysis. *Journal of Applied Social Psychology*, *40*(5), 1085–1105. doi:10.1111/j.1559-1816.2010.00611.x

Rosal, M. C., Heyden, R., Mejilla, R., Capelson, R., Chalmers, K. A., DePaoli, M. R., ... Wiecha, J. M. (2014). A virtual world versus face-to-face intervention format to promote diabetes self-management among African American women: A pilot randomized clinical trial. *JMIR Research Protocols*, *3*(4), e54. doi:10.2196/resprot.3412 PMID:25344620

Rosenstock, I. M., Strecher, V. J., & Becker, M. H. (1988). Social learning theory and the health belief model. *Health Education & Behavior*, *15*(2), 175–183. doi:10.1177/109019818801500203 PMID:3378902

Rosi, A., Dall'Asta, M., Brighenti, F., Del Rio, D., Volta, E., Baroni, I., ... Scazzina, F. (2016). The use of new technologies for nutritional education in primary schools: A pilot study. *Public Health*, *140*(1), 50–55. doi:10.1016/j.puhe.2016.08.021 PMID:27756495

Ruggiero, L., Moadsiri, A., Quinn, L. T., Riley, B. B., Danielson, K. K., Monahan, C., ... Gerber, B. S. (2014). Diabetes island: Preliminary impact of a virtual world self-care educational intervention for African Americans with type 2 diabetes. *JMIR Serious Games*, *2*(2), e10. doi:10.2196/games.3260 PMID:25584346

Sanchez-Vives, M. V., & Slater, M. (2005). From presence to consciousness through virtual reality. *Nature Reviews. Neuroscience*, *6*(4), 332–339. doi:10.1038/nrn1651 PMID:15803164

Schleiner, A. M. (2001). Does Lara Croft wear fake polygons? Gender and gender-role subversion in computer adventure games. *Leonardo*, *34*(3), 221–226. doi:10.1162/002409401750286976

Schwarzer, R. (2008). Modeling health behavior change: How to predict and modify the adoption and maintenance of health behaviors. *Applied Psychology*, *57*(1), 1–29. doi:10.1111/j.1464-0597.2007.00325.x

Slater, A., & Tiggemann, M. (2011). Gender differences in adolescent sport participation, teasing, self-objectification and body image concerns. *Journal of Adolescence*, *34*(3), 455–463. doi:10.1016/j.adolescence.2010.06.007 PMID:20643477

Southard, D. R., & Southard, B. H. (2006). Promoting Physical Activity in Children with MetaKenkoh. *Clinical and Investigative Medicine. Medecine Clinique et Experimentale*, *29*(5), 293–297. doi:10.1037/bar0000029 PMID:17144438

Spruijt-Metz, D. (1995). Personal incentives as determinants of adolescent health behavior: The meaning of behavior. *Health Education Research*, *10*(3), 355–364. doi:10.1093/her/10.3.355 PMID:10158028

Strachan, S. M., & Brawley, L. R. (2009). Healthy-eater identity and self-efficacy predict healthy eating behavior. *Journal of Health Psychology*, *14*(5), 684–695. doi:10.1177/1359105309104915 PMID:19515684

Strachan, S. M., Woodgate, J., Brawley, L. R., & Tse, A. (2005). The relationship of self-efficacy and self-identity to long-term maintenance of vigorous physical activity. *Journal of Applied Biobehavioral Research*, *10*(2), 98–112. doi:10.1111/j.1751-9861.2005.tb00006.x

Strauss, B. (2002). Social facilitation in motor tasks: A review of research and theory. *Psychology of Sport and Exercise*, *3*(3), 237–256. doi:10.1016/S1469-0292(01)00019-X

Striker, A., Calogne, C., Truman, B., & Arenas, F. (2017). *Integrating an awareness of selfhood and society into virtual learning*. Hershey, PA: IGI Global. doi:10.4018/978-1-5225-2182-2

Sullivan, D. K., Goetz, J. R., Gibson, C. A., Washburn, R. A., Smith, B. K., Lee, J., ... Donnelly, J. E. (2013). Improving weight maintenance using virtual reality (Second Life). *Journal of Nutrition Education and Behavior*, *45*(3), 264–268. doi:10.1016/j.jneb.2012.10.007 PMID:23622351

Thompson, D. R., Obarzanek, E., Franko, D. L., Barton, B. A., Morrison, J., Biro, F. M., ... Striegel-Moore, R. H. (2007). Childhood overweight and cardiovascular disease risk factors: The National Heart, Lung, and Blood Institute Growth and Health Study. *The Journal of Pediatrics*, *150*(1), 18–25. doi:10.1016/j.jpeds.2006.09.039 PMID:17188606

Tobin, D. L., Reynolds, R. V., Holroyd, K. A., & Creer, T. L. (1986). Self-management and social learning theory. In K.A. Holroyd & T.L. Creer (Eds.), Self-Management of Chronic Disease (pp. 29-55). Orlando, FL: Academic Press. doi:10.1016/j.outlook.2008.10.004

Tremblay, M. S., LeBlanc, A. G., Kho, M. E., Saunders, T. J., Larouche, R., Colley, R. C., & Gorber, S. C. (2011). Systematic review of sedentary behaviour and health indicators in school-aged children and youth. *The International Journal of Behavioral Nutrition and Physical Activity*, *8*(1), 98. doi:10.1186/1479-5868-8-98 PMID:21936895

Umberson, D., Crosnoe, R., & Reczek, C. (2010). Social relationships and health behavior across life course. *Annual Review of Sociology*, *36*(1), 139–157. doi:10.1146/annurev-soc-070308-120011 PMID:21921974

Van der Horst, K., Paw, M., Twisk, J., & Van Mechelen, W. (2007). A brief review on correlates of physical activity and sedentariness in youth. *Medicine and Science in Sports and Exercise*, *39*(8), 1241–1250. doi:10.1249/mss.0b013e318059bf35 PMID:17762356

Vander Wal, J. S., & Thelen, M. H. (2000). Eating and body image concerns among obese and average-weight children. *Addictive Behaviors*, *25*(5), 775–778. doi:10.1016/S0306-4603(00)00061-7 PMID:11023018

Wallace, L. S., Buckworth, J., Kirby, T. E., & Sherman, W. M. (2000). Characteristics of exercise behavior among college students: Application of social cognitive theory to predicting stage of change. *Preventive Medicine*, *31*(5), 494–505. doi:10.1006/pmed.2000.0736 PMID:11071829

Wang, Y., & Lim, H. (2012). The global childhood obesity epidemic and the association between socio-economic status and childhood obesity. *International Review of Psychiatry (Abingdon, England)*, *24*(3), 176–188. doi:10.3109/09540261.2012.688195 PMID:22724639

Ward, Z. J., Long, M. W., Resch, S. C., Giles, C. M., Cradock, A. L., & Gortmaker, S. L. (2017). Simulation of growth trajectories of childhood obesity into adulthood. *The New England Journal of Medicine*, *377*(22), 2145–2153. doi:10.1056/NEJMoa1703860 PMID:29171811

Williams, E. P., Mesidor, M., Winters, K., Dubbert, P. M., & Wyatt, S. B. (2015). Overweight and obesity: Prevalence, consequences, and causes of a growing public health problem. *Current Obesity Reports*, *4*(3), 363–370. doi:10.100713679-015-0169-4 PMID:26627494

Wiseman, C. V., Gray, J. J., Mosimann, J. E., & Ahrens, A. H. (1992). Cultural expectations of thinness in women: An update. *International Journal of Eating Disorders*, *11*(1), 85–89. doi:10.1002/1098-108X(199201)11:1<85::AID-EAT2260110112>3.0.CO;2-T

Yee, N., Bailenson, J. N., & Ducheneaut, N. (2009). The Proteus effect: Implications of transformed digital self-representation on online and offline behavior. *Communication Research*, *36*(2), 285–312. doi:10.1177/0093650208330254

Yildirim, A. (1997). Gender role influences on Turkish adolescents' self-identity. *Adolescence*, *32*(125), 217–231. PMID:9105502

Young, M. D., Plotnikoff, R. C., Collins, C. E., Callister, R., & Morgan, P. J. (2014). Social cognitive theory and physical activity: A systematic review and meta-analysis. *Obesity Reviews*, *15*(12), 983–995. doi:10.1111/obr.12225 PMID:25428600

KEY TERMS AND DEFINITIONS

Behavioral Intention: An individual's expected probability of carrying out a behavior.

Body Image: A subjective opinion an individual has about her or his own body and appearance.

Eating Behavior: The patterns of an individual's food and beverage consumption habits, indicated by food choices, meal frequency, and portion size.

Health Self-Identity: When an individual incorporates health-related features as part of their personal identity, for example, "I am someone who is healthy."

Healthy Lifestyle: A consistent pattern of behaviors, including a nutritious diet, high levels of physical activity, and low levels of sedentary behavior, which lower the risk of health problems.

Go, Slow, Whoa Foods: The U.S. National Heart, Lung, and Blood Institute (NHLBI) groups food into three broad categories: Go Foods (healthy foods that should be eaten often), Slow Foods (foods that should only be eaten a few times a week), and Whoa Foods (foods that are high in fat, calories and/or sugar and should only be eaten once in a while).

Middle-School-Aged Girls: Girls aged 11-14.

Modeling: A learning process that occurs through the observation and replication of others' behaviors. It can occur "in-vivo" or symbolically.

MyPlate: A healthy nutrition guide published by the US Department of Food and Agriculture. The five core food groups (fruits, vegetables, grains, protein, and dairy) and the suggested portion sizes for each group are displayed on a place setting.

Pedometer: A device that can be worn to track activity (i.e., steps and distance walked, calories burned), such as a Fitbit.

Physical Activity: Movement of the body and muscles that results in an expenditure of energy.

Presence: The degree to which individuals believe that the virtual technology experience is "real" for them.

Self-Efficacy: The personal belief that one can successfully perform and sustain desired behaviors.

Social Cognitive Theory: Bandura's theory that suggests behavior is a result of an interaction between environmental and social, cognitive, and personal factors.

STEM Fields: The academic disciplines of science, technology, engineering, and math.

Theory of Meaning Behavior: A theory that proposes that incentives, either internal or external, imbue personal meaning to behaviors.

Virtual World: A digital environment that allows users to engage with their virtual surroundings, various activities, and interact with other users.

Chapter 9
Who Am I as a Healthcare Provider?
Identity and Transformative Learning in Virtual Environments

Rachel Umoren
University of Washington, USA

Natalia Rybas
Indiana University East, USA

ABSTRACT

The U.S. healthcare delivery system relies on the formation of ad hoc teams of experienced, highly trained providers of various specialties. The providers work in interprofessional teams that converge to address situations around acute patient care. Various models of virtual training provide structured opportunities for interprofessional education, whereby learners engage with roles and responsibilities essential for their professions and active collaboration with other team members. This learning is transformative as it influences the development of professional identity and teamwork skills needed for successful collaborative practice in interprofessional teams. This chapter explores the role of training healthcare professional students using virtual simulations and the emerging potential of virtual and augmented reality for health professional education.

INTRODUCTION

It is common for healthcare providers to work in ad hoc teams that converge around acute patient care situations to stabilize, diagnose, and treat illness or injury. These interprofessional teams must perform at a high level of reliability to deliver safe and appropriate patient care. Unfortunately, optimal team function may not be attained in every situation. Poorly functioning healthcare teams have a higher rate of adverse patient outcomes. Due to these concerns, health professional training programs have incorporated interprofessional educational activities to teach roles and responsibilities and encourage

DOI: 10.4018/978-1-5225-9679-0.ch009

positive interactions between learners in health professional programs. This chapter examines the role of virtual environments in training healthcare providers and addresses the following questions: 1) How do interactions occur in virtual environments created for learning? 2) How does professional identity emerge in virtual environments? 3) How do experiences in virtual environments provide opportunities for transformative learning?

We start by reviewing the healthcare team composition and types of virtual interactions that may occur for healthcare providers and learners in virtual environments. We then discuss the development of professional identity and suggest ways in which the transformative learning theory explains how learning in virtual environments may change attitudes and behaviors. We illustrate this approach by describing a learning activity set up for health professional learners across different virtual environments. We conclude by discussing the limitations of using virtual reality (VR) in health professional training and present future directions for the use of virtual and augmented reality (AR) technologies in health professional education.

VIRTUAL HEALTHCARE TEAM INTERACTIONS

Teamwork in healthcare settings is similar to teamwork in other disciplines with a few distinctions. Patient care demands 24/7 coverage by a team capable of efficient, high-quality care. Although team composition is fluid due to the constraints of shiftwork, team roles are often stable describing a job position, e.g. the role of surgeon or anesthesiologist; or a job function, e.g. the role of providing chest compressions or rescue breathing. In some cases, there is a need to rotate the leadership structure, for example, the anesthesiologist is the leader in the operating room when anesthesia is being administered, and the surgeon takes over the leadership role once the patient is under anesthesia (Hughes et al., 2016). Learners who are just beginning to understand their roles on the healthcare team are often part of the team. There is an established hierarchy, which is particularly evident when learners are working with senior physicians but may not be as obvious when there are multiple senior team members providing care.

All healthcare teams are at risk of making medical errors if team members lack strong communication and conflict management skills. For this reason, there is increasing attention to the role of teamwork at all levels, from training to practice. Teamwork training programs such as the Team Strategies and Tools to Enhance Performance and Patient Safety (TeamSTEPPS), developed by the Agency for Healthcare Research and Quality (AHRQ) and the Department of Defense have been used to train an estimated 1.5 million healthcare providers (Hughes et al., 2016). Even though these learning opportunities are available, they are still not sufficient to address the gap in the teamwork skills at all levels of healthcare systems. Virtual environments provide increased opportunity for instructors and learners to engage with each other from remote locations and across geographically separated campuses or other types of locations (Figure 1).

Learning in virtual environments is feasible and often beneficial for learners (Lemheney et al., 2016). Virtual environments allow for many more participants in the learning activity. They eliminate the need for travel and reservation of space in a simulation center, but ultimately the scheduling difficulties may still arise for educators and learners. Scheduling problems can only be eliminated with asynchronous learning though. While this approach also becomes more engaging in a virtual space, interprofessional learning activities should be structured to accommodate the conventional definition of involving students of two or more professions. Whether engaging learners or practicing healthcare providers, any interven-

Figure 1. Virtual team members interact in a multi-player team training environment.
Image credit: Rachel Umoren.

tion must be brief, interactive, and relevant to clinical practice with the goal of fostering experiential, collaborative learning that transforms attitudes and behaviors.

The nature of the virtual interaction is defined by who or what the learner engages with in the virtual space. Learners may engage with other healthcare providers, non-healthcare or research staff, and patients or families. Interactions can also occur with pre-programmed non-player characters (NPCs) for education or research. The role played by the learner in the interaction may also influence the experience and provide an opportunity to explore professional identity and to build relationships with other team members. In virtual contexts created for healthcare training, participants interact with game-like interfaces that simulate potential situations they may face in their clinical practice. Designers strive to program problems, dilemmas, and crises that prove problematic and complicated for real-life practice. Virtual characters appear as avatars that can be customized by the users regarding their physical appearance. Players interact with other users or other objects in the game, and in the process of such interaction, participants assume roles and play out scenarios constructed by instructional designers based on the scripts of professional behavior.

When we consider these factors, the types of user interactions in virtual environments can be categorized as shown in Figure 2. In a single player application, a single user interacts with objects in the virtual environment. In a simulated multiplayer application, the user interacts with non-player characters (NPCs) or avatars controlled by individuals who may or may not be colleagues, but who are role-playing as patients or other health team members. In a true multiplayer application, the user interactions are with team members in education or work-related activities.

- **Single Player:** These activities provide a single individual the opportunity to interact exclusively with a virtual environment. These activities could be pre-programmed or self-directed and involve a spectrum of engagement with basic objects through complex creations. In healthcare, laparoscopic trainers are a long-standing example of single player VR applications. Stand-alone robotic

Figure 2. Types of user interactions within virtual environments
Image credit: Rachel Umoren.

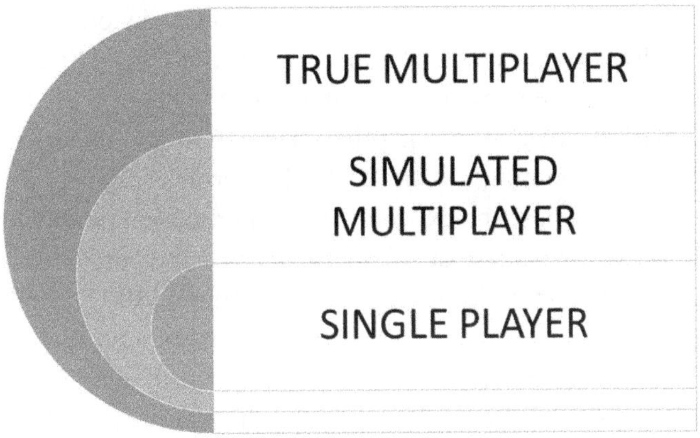

simulators provide access to training outside the operating room with exercises on basic and advanced surgical skills training and may include objective performance evaluation based on expert performance data. Screen-based single player activities are relatively straightforward to deploy and have few limitations on the number of players that can use each activity in the same way that thousands of users can browse an internet page.

- **Simulated Multiplayer:** Activities engage users in structured or unstructured role-play with non-player characters or human-controlled avatars. While the events are meant to be educational or entertaining, the human is always in a role. For example, non-medical personnel often play the role of standardized patients and nurses may play the role of physicians or pharmacists in the simulation. Sweigart & Hodson-Carlton (2013) describe a nursing interview trainer. Avatars controlled by trained actors portray standardized patients of varying ages and ethnicities. The student interacts with the avatar in a virtual environment to obtain a patient interview. Using human actors requires additional preparation and training for each role, but can provide more flexibility in the dialogue and experience than non-player characters. Such flexibility is particularly useful in working in particular subject areas particularly sensitive conversations and ethical dilemmas which may make pre-programming a non-player character difficult.
- **True Multiplayer:** Activities engage users in roles with which they are familiar. Heinrichs et al. (2008) described the development and implementation of virtual simulation for team training and assessment. Trainees found simulation exercises adequately realistic to "suspend disbelief," and they quickly learn to use internet voice communication and user interface to navigate their online character/avatar to work effectively in a critical care team (Heinrichs, Youngblood, Harter, & Dev, 2008). The performance of learners in the virtual simulation was similar to those who used a traditional simulation environment. The educational benefit of a true multiplayer activity is in the fidelity of allowing participants to be in their role, whether that is the role of a student nurse, practicing physician or some other professional. However, there is a potential lost benefit of exploring the experience of being in another role, even if it may come with the risk of feeling a "disconnect" with playing an unfamiliar role.

Development of Professional Identity in Healthcare Professional Students

Identity is a complex phenomenon. In general, the notion of identity denotes who a person is and how he or she actively engages with his or her identification (Woodward, 1997). Social scientists theorize that identity formation and career choice come together in the late teens or early twenties for most people (Albert, 1990), and that career choice represents the imagination and experiences of childhood, integrated with the person one is becoming (Gieryn, 2000). In a professional context, identity refers to the person's performances of roles, norms, and expectations of a profession with which he or she identifies. Professional identity is defined as the sense of self that is derived and perceived from the role healthcare providers take on in the work that they do (Erikson, 1968). Niemi (1997) conceptualizes professional identity as the knowledge of challenges and opportunities typical of a profession, individual choices in decision-making and behavior, as well as patterns of thinking, speaking, and relating to people. Thus, by the end of training students are expected to develop confidence in performing and thinking like healthcare providers.

Identity development is a continuous process that depends on multiple factors and influences. Similar to the general qualities of one's identity, professional qualities, skills, knowledge, and ethics develop through personal experiences, reflections, media exposure, formal and informal training opportunities, and interactions with members of the same and other professional groups. Even though elements of professional identity can be present before students commence their studies (Adams, Hean, Sturgis, & Clark, 2006), there is an agreement among researchers that training is an essential part in developing a professional identity. Professional identities in medical students change over time through the processes of socialization and identity work (Pratt, Rockmann, & Kaufmann, 2006). From their first days of training through graduation, all health professional students are exposed to strategically created curricula and experiences leading to positive and negative perceptions of their profession that form their professional identity (Chreim, Williams, & Hinings, 2007). The factors that determine the level of which a professional identity exists before any formal education include gender, previous work experience in healthcare environments, understanding of team function, knowledge of the profession and cognitive flexibility (Adams et al., 2006). Undergraduate student volunteers are exposed to values and behaviors that contribute to a student's sense of professional identity. This exposure occurs even before they start formal training in health professional schools. Specific professions internalize and practice professional culture at the workplace and possibly beyond. Thus, it is important to emphasize the process of professional identity development in training contexts as formal virtual curricula and training opportunities may impact the processes of identity development and allow health educators to target desired qualities in current and future health practitioners.

Training makes a significant impact on the development of professional identity of health providers. Even though professional identity formation occurs throughout a provider's career, the early years of training significantly affect one's sense of self in the profession (Johnson, Cowin, Wilson, & Young, 2012). The knowledge of the attributes and values of a particular profession fosters the development of professional identity. Also formed, whether intentionally or not, are biases and assumptions regarding other members of the health professions. Attitudes and behaviors developed during training carry into practice affecting team relationships, and the care patients receive in years of future practice (Eisenberg, 2008). Recent efforts to encourage positive professional interactions between individuals on health professional teams utilize interprofessional education to allow students to understand their professional role in the broader context of the healthcare team to ensure a successful transition into the healthcare workforce.

While there is a consensus that interprofessional education is important, the effects on professional practice and healthcare outcomes are variable and more research is needed in this area (Reeves et al., 2008).

The scholarship about identity performance online mostly focuses on categories or markers of difference, such as gender, race, sexuality or ethnicity in the environments of social play in online environments of socializing, for example, Youtube or Facebook (e.g., Anarbaeva, 2016). The researchers studying identities online argue that categories of identity shape one's experiences in online environments. Identity gets reformulated and constructed, articulated and rearticulated, similar to any other interaction online or offline. Users put themselves into being similar to other social environments, such as parks, work, school, or shopping malls both online and offline as they interpret themselves, the technology, and others (Rybas, 2012). In other words, technology-mediated environments serve as productive sites where cultural baggage norms about self-representation and self-performance get reiterated and reproduced despite that fact that the social site offers a seemingly free choice for content creation or other types of actions by users.

Despite the plethora of studies about identity in online environments, professional identity, as it is performed and developed in virtual reality, has rarely been explored. The previous research about cultural routines in online environments suggests that cultures offline would leak to online environments. In other words, social actors function at the intersections of online and offline contexts. We assume that participants of online interactions, including healthcare professionals, bring their ordinary and everyday logic of interaction to online environments. Thus, training opportunities targeting professional qualities have the potential to engage identities of participants. While the technical capabilities of the gaming environment may limit options for customization, the ability to customize one's avatar plays a significant role in user engagement and identity formation as we will discuss in the next section. By playing and participating in virtual contexts, individuals assume roles dictated by the game setup while also extending, reinforcing, transforming, or relating in other affective ways to their offline personalities (Markham, 1998; Poletti & Rak, 2014). Thus, the interconnections between the offline identity, the suggested game scenarios, and the actual movements and interactions with and within the training program environments allow identity performance and foster identity change.

Transformative Learning in Virtual Environments

Virtual team interactions use pre-programmed characters in the role of interprofessional team members. Such interactions can model and test knowledge of communication and teamwork skills, attitudes and behaviors, which provide a way to operationalize professional identity. Increased teamwork knowledge and attitudes can promote further engagement with interprofessional learning activities and collaborative practice. Debriefing sessions built into these scenarios explore virtual team members' motives and biases. Reflection on the scenarios can engage participants in discussions on how these biases can affect health care practice. These activities promote interprofessional socialization and can contribute to the development of professional identity so that to improve the skills of communication in interprofessional teams.

Transformative learning theory helps rationalize how virtual training may foster the development of a new professional identity and new ways of interaction. The Transformative Learning Theory, described by Jack Mezirow in 2000, is one of the most researched and discussed theories in adult education (Taylor, 2007). It is the process by which learners call into question accepted ideas, frames of reference or habits of mind. Major transitional experiences could be specific and intense like a crisis, or an accumulation of related experiences with progressive effects on the individuals' perspectives over time. Regardless of the nature of the experience, Mezirow's theory indicates that real learning occurs when the experience provokes changes in the learners' frame of reference allowing them to change how they interpret and interact with the world (Mezirow, 1997). Further, Illeris (2014) proposed that transformative learning should be re-defined as "changes in the learner's identity" (Illeris, 2014). Reports describe learning experiences that provide or support transformative learning. These range from exposure to extreme poverty in global health settings to the local community and classroom experiences.

There are parallels between virtual environments and physical simulations that support hands-on investigation and experimentation or role-play, which enable experiences and actions that may lead to transformative learning. This transformation occurs through the process of exploration of options for new roles, relationships and actions, planning a course of action and acquiring new knowledge and skills. The provisional trying of new roles and building of competence and self-confidence through multiple virtual interactions enables the process of exploration of options and perspectives and reintegration of the new perspectives (Figure 3). Virtual simulations tend to evoke less stress than in-person simulations, but there is evidence that they can be stressful to some users. The more immersive the simulation is, particularly with the use of head-mounted displays, the greater the potential for impact. Parker and Myrick (2010) proposed that high fidelity patient simulation experiences promote transformative learning (Parker & Myrick, 2010). As technology-based learning tools may be "unsettling to the rudimentary meaning schemes of new nursing students," they suggested that incremental exposure to low-stress scenarios be done, before the exposure to high-stress or emotional situations (Parker & Myrick, 2010). This recommendation while potentially appropriate to avoid excessive stress during learning sessions may actually be counter-productive to the transformative learning process as intense experiences may be required to trigger transformative learning.

The entry of the user into a virtual environment as an avatar triggers a dynamic process of identity formation, as though the physical or "non-virtual" world identity continually informs the virtual identity of the avatar (Waggoner, 2009). Even though a user is distant from the avatar, the user relates to the avatar

Figure 3. Role of virtual simulations in enabling transformative learning
Image Credit: Rachel Umoren.

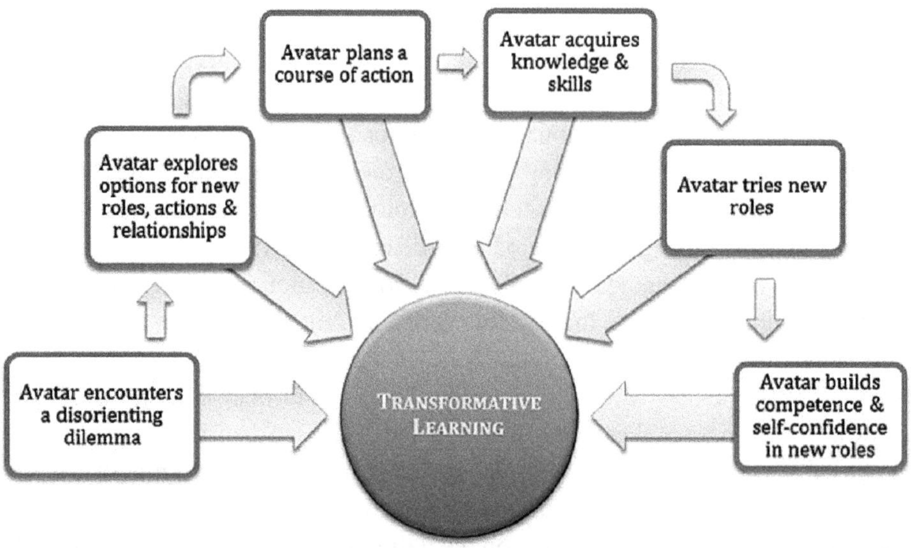

in complex ways through reflecting, adopting, and reinventing the rules of roles of particular groups and societies (De Zwart & Lindsay, 2012). This process alone or along with challenges encountered within the virtual environment constitutes a disorienting dilemma described as initiating the transformative learning process (Mezirow, 1991). At this point, the learner has the option to explore new roles, relationships, and actions through the avatar. In a single-player and simulated multiplayer activities, the learner engages with interactive objects and characters in the virtual space who may or may not have similar backgrounds, experiences, and goals. Interactions with the virtual space have the potential to influence the learner's decision to plan a course of action within the virtual activity. Through planning and executing a course of action in simulated activities, the learner acquires knowledge and skills necessary for situations in real-life. The application of this knowledge can be directly observed through the avatars' interactions with other avatars and objects within the environment. Following this, the avatar may choose to try on new roles that may have a dynamic impact on the non-virtual identity.

Implications for Professional Identity Development

Professional roles may vary by situation, and teams need to be adaptive to maintain optimal performance. As such cognitive flexibility regarding roles may need to be actively encouraged to improve team functioning. Virtual experiences that allow team members to experience their own and other team members' roles may facilitate this cognitive flexibility. The development of these kinds of scenarios should take into consideration the broad spectrum of health providers. For example, virtual teams should include nursing and medical providers as well as occupational therapy, physical therapy, and pharmacy students. Well-designed virtual scenarios appear to have a broad capacity to influence learner attitudes towards teamwork across professions (Sweigart et al., 2016). TeamSTEPPS Virtual Teams is a teamwork simulator that uses simulated patient care situations as immersive experiences with the user embedded within a virtual health-care team (Sweigart et al., 2016). The scenarios, based on the TeamSTEPPS program developed by the Agency for Healthcare Research and Quality and the Department of Defense, include virtual team members that model essential teamwork concepts and tools. After a brief exposure to this material, learners showed an increased recognition of TeamSTEPPS communication tools and improved teamwork attitudes ($p<0.05$) (Sweigart et al., 2016; Umoren et al., 2018).

While influence on learner attitudes is the first step towards impacting behavior, the ultimate impact needs to be felt at the level of patient care. Although patient care outcomes may be difficult to measure or relate to the team training, Hughes et al., (2016) described the connection between learning, attitudes, behaviors and impact on patient care and the healthcare system through a systematic review of the published outcomes of teamwork training (Hughes et al., 2016). However, consideration should be given to the differential impact that interprofessional education may have on students of various professions (Umoren et al., 2018). With ongoing practice, the learners are expected to build competence and confidence in their new roles increasing the potential for ongoing and long-term impact on the non-virtual identity, which is the essence of transformative learning (Mälkki, 2010).

Given the role of virtual environments in creating shared experiences, it is relevant to consider their impact on team communication. Shared understanding is higher in a virtual environment than in the text-based chat. Communication in virtual environments leads to higher task performance, consensus, satisfaction, and cohesion within the virtual team (Schouten et al., 2016). Research studies using virtual characters explore behaviors and actions through presenting a realistic situation or trigger to the participant. Robb et al. (2015) described a comparison of speaking up behavior during a conflict with real and virtual humans. Through various interactions with both human and virtual surgeons and anesthesiologists, the investigators found that while interactions were similar, users were more likely to ask the virtual anesthesiologist for input while working with the human surgeon ($p<0.05$) (Robb et al., 2015). These findings imply that in many cases, individuals will interact in similar ways with virtual characters as with human characters which have significant implications for the study of human behavior in virtual environments. These factors and the potential for the formation or enhancement of a professional identity may play a significant role in the outcomes of virtual learning.

SPH Places is a non-clinical case study that demonstrates the potential for transformative learning in a 3D virtual neighborhood that allows students of public health to explore and experience the impact of environmental and socioeconomic factors on health. The nature of the virtual space presents a variety of learning opportunities in such environments as an adequately staffed and equipped hospital room in an urban low-income clinic (Figure 4), an affluent suburban neighborhood (Figure 5), or resource-limited global health setting (Figure 6).

Students complete three knowledge-building modules before designing a public health intervention that addresses one of these factors. They can perform these activities individually or as a group. The students learn the increased risk of chronic disease and shortened life expectancy associated with living in a poor quality neighborhood through a review of the literature on the increased chronic disease and other health risks related to living in unhealthy neighborhoods. They then find clues at SPH Places locations: Places Urgent Care, Southside Apartments, the Bus Stops (both Northside and Southside), the Gas Stations, and others. using a heads-up display with Health and Stress trackers that provide clues when they are in range. Information stations provide participants with the article reference(s) supporting the clues provided. After finding as many clues as they can, the students test their knowledge with a quiz. Another objective of such training is to recognize the relationship between environment and stressors that can affect health. Students meet with two community members that they interview to determine the social and economic stressors that are related to living in an unhealthy neighborhood. Figure 4 shows a

Figure 4. Interviewing a member of the SPH Places Southside community
Image credit: Rachel Umoren

Figure 5. Identifying the characteristics of a healthy neighborhood in SPH places northside suburb
Image credit: Rachel Umoren.

Figure 6. A West African community at the peak of the Ebola crisis
Image credits: Rachel Umoren.

low-income public health setting in which the learner performs assigned tasks including interviews of NPCs representing community members to identify socioeconomic and environmental health risks. They report their conversation to the instructor. Next, students visit a bank in a suburban area of Northside to determine why individuals may have difficulty moving out of an unhealthy neighborhood. They report the requirements for getting a federally subsidized mortgage.

Students also compare and contrast the different environmental characteristics and qualities of healthy neighborhoods by visiting the SPH Places NorthSide neighborhood to identify locations on the list that indicate a healthy neighborhood. Their avatars' health score remains high or increases with locating healthy areas, and their stress level remains low or decreases. After discovering healthy locations, they take snapshots of themselves next to the locations and annotate them with descriptive sentences on why this is a healthy site. They then identify disease-causing physical and chemical agents by visiting the SouthSide neighborhood and what diseases they might cause, demonstrating their knowledge by annotating snapshots with descriptive sentences on why this is an unhealthy location. To identify the economic impact of unhealthy neighborhoods on health, they compare the cost of purchases in the grocery stores at the SouthSide and NorthSide neighborhoods.

The degree of the challenge posed by the characters and avatars that the user meets within the virtual space influences the planned course of action. The extent to which the user explores the environment increases the chances of interaction with objects, NPCs and other players increasing the knowledge and skills acquired. Switching between low-income and suburban settings (Figure 5) within the same learning activity accentuates the differences between healthy and unhealthy environments and may serve as an additional trigger for reflection and practice.

While socioeconomic and environmental factors may need to be tailored to specific circumstances, the broad objectives remain the same. Similar learning objectives take on new meaning when placed in widely disparate settings. For example, the challenges of obtaining healthcare in the SouthSide neighborhood may parallel those in sub-Saharan Africa (Figure 6). Such experiences in the virtual neighborhoods help participants of training acquire the knowledge and skills prescribed for their professions, therefore they transform identities of learners, who become healthcare providers.

LIMITATIONS

Limitations remain to the widespread use of virtual environments for health professional training. One of the most critical barriers is acceptance by educators, particularly those in health professional schools. Technological abilities of both teachers and learners need to be assessed before integrating virtual simulations into the curriculum. Health professional schools often lag in adopting and acquiring new technologies or may have aging IT infrastructure making the use of VR and AR by enrolled students and teaching faculty challenging. Engaging the Information Technology and Instructional Design staff in early conversations on the type, development, and deployment of virtual simulation is essential for success. These discussions will help to avoid common pitfalls and identify the best approach for the development and implementation of the simulations.

While this chapter has focused on the transformative learning theory as it applies to virtual environments, it is important to recognize that reflection, a major factor in Mezirow's transformative learning theory, is not an observable skill. More research on the user experience and assessment of learning outcomes are needed. Other adult education principles: experiential learning, collaborative learning, problem-based learning also have applications to training in virtual environments with an expectation to transform professional identities of participants.

Finally, it is important to note that every virtual environment created for training is not a neutral space and reflects the biases and worldviews of their creators. The technology matters beyond the notion of the tool to satisfy intentions, and a specific technical application emerges from the social constraints and possibilities of participants and other constituents of the learning process (Gillespie, 2010; Latour, 1992). The suggested geography of the crisis in the discussed case, in which SouthSide and NorthSide are set in opposition by the level of accessibility to resources and levels of well-being, can risk promoting and supporting social stratifications between and within societies and global zones. How such a representational structure does reiterates global inequalities and normalize social stratifications? Further discussions and attention to the nuances of the virtual environments will provide a complex understanding of how students learn about their profession and the contexts of work.

FUTURE DIRECTIONS

For healthcare institutions to be able to deliver safe, reliable patient care, healthcare preparation must focus on developing appropriate team-related skills and competencies. Placing individuals in situations where they can practice their teamwork skills is essential for fostering and encouraging these skills. As in-person simulation opportunities may be limited, educators should consider substituting realistic virtual environments and characters to enable team training as these environments are readily accessible, have low ongoing maintenance costs and provide an opportunity for ongoing coaching and refresher courses. Gamification encourages competition and learner engagement. The routine use of adaptive virtual environments that promote user engagement and planning will lead to increased knowledge and skill development. These simulations should portray typical clinical outcomes, and reward positive team behaviors. A variety of opportunities exist for the use of virtual simulation in healthcare including difficult conversations and conflict resolution. The potential for biofeedback as part of the game increases the options for users and may raise awareness of the impact of stress and emotions on everyday interactions with other providers and with patients.

Future studies should further assess the process of transformative learning, especially as it relates to personal and professional identity in virtual environments. Hu (2015) predicts that virtual reality and gaming promise to bring new studies in training and communication among healthcare workers. This study follows on this call, and suggests an emphasis on professional identity and attention to teamwork skills. Traditional perspectives on transformative learning focus on the individual learner. However, the experience of an individual learner may produce different outcomes from those of a group of learners, and the concept of group transformative learning requires further study. The in-depth exploration of participant choices and preferences within virtual simulations will advance team science through a greater understanding of how teams learn and apply group behaviors. The lessons learned will apply to clinical care and also to interdisciplinary research teams meeting the need for communication across disciplines in the discovery of new therapies.

CONCLUSION

Healthcare teams need to perform optimally in all settings and circumstances to ensure that they deliver safe patient care. It is becoming routine for healthcare providers to receive team training to meet the obligation to overcome challenges to communication that may impact patient safety. Some of the potential opportunities for team training are underutilized due to difficulties with engaging remote teams. Many critical lessons can be taught in virtual environments. Mezirow's theory of transformative learning supports the impact these lessons have on disrupting the learner's current world view to create new understanding and plans for action. On an individual level, personal and professional identity impact the way health professionals engage in teams. We used the transformative learning theory to explore how virtual environments enable users to explore and engage in new roles, build competence and apply new knowledge and skills. Exposing the learner to a variety of scenarios in multiple settings may accelerate this process. We continue to explore the impact of individual and team-based learning in virtual environments. As new virtual technologies continue to emerge, they promise to engage healthcare teams in new ways, and increase the potential for enhancing patient safety through transformative learning in virtual environments.

REFERENCES

Adams, K., Hean, S., Sturgis, P., & Clark, J. M. (2006). Investigating the factors influencing professional identity of first-year health and social care students. *Learning in Health and Social Care*, *5*(2), 55–68. doi:10.1111/j.1473-6861.2006.00119.x

Albert, R. S. (1990). Identity, experiences, and career choice among the exceptionally gifted and eminent. In M. A. Runco & R. S. Albert (Eds.), *Theories of creativity* (pp. 13–34). Newbury Park, CA: Sage.

Anarbaeva, S. (2016). Youtubing difference: Performing identity in video communities. *Journal of Virtual Worlds Research*, *9*(2). doi:10.4101/jvwr.v9i2.7193

Chreim, S., Williams, B. B., & Hinings, C. B. (2007). Interlevel influences on the reconstruction of professional role identity. *Academy of Management Journal*, *50*(6), 1515–1539. doi:10.5465/amj.2007.28226248

De Zwart, M., & Lindsay, D. (2012). My self, my avatar, my rights? Avatar identity in social virtual worlds. *At the Interface / Probing the Boundaries, 85*, 81-100.

Eisenberg, E. M. (2008). The social construction of healthcare teams. *Improving Healthcare Team Communication*, 9-20.

Erikson, E. H. (1968). *Identity*. Norton.

Gieryn, T. F. (2000). A space for place in sociology. *Annual Review of Sociology*, *26*(1), 463–496. doi:10.1146/annurev.soc.26.1.463

Gillespie, T. (2010). The politics of 'platforms.'. *New Media & Society*, *12*(2), 347–364. doi:10.1177/1461444809342738

Heinrichs, W. L., Youngblood, P., Harter, P. M., & Dev, P. (2008). Simulation for team training and assessment: Case studies of online training with virtual worlds. *World Journal of Surgery*, *32*(2), 161–170. doi:10.100700268-007-9354-2 PMID:18188640

Hu, Y. (2015). Health communication research in digital age: A systematic review. *Journal of Communication in Healthcare*, *8*(4), 260–288. doi:10.1080/17538068.2015.1107308

Hughes, A. M., Gregory, M. E., Joseph, D. L., Sonesh, S. C., Marlow, S. L., Lacerenza, C. N., ... Salas, E. (2016). Saving lives: A meta-analysis of team training in healthcare. *The Journal of Applied Psychology, 101*(9), 1266–1304. doi:10.1037/apl0000120 PMID:27599089

Illeris, K. (2014). Transformative Learning re-defined: As changes in elements of the identity. *International Journal of Lifelong Education, 33*(5), 573–586. doi:10.1080/02601370.2014.917128

Johnson, M., Cowin, L. S., Wilson, I., & Young, H. (2012). Professional identity and nursing: Contemporary theoretical developments and future research challenges. *International Nursing Review, 59*(4), 562–569. doi:10.1111/j.1466-7657.2012.01013.x PMID:23134142

Latour, B. (1992). Where are the missing masses: The sociology of a few mundane artifacts. In W. E. Bijker & J. Law (Eds.), *Shaping technology/building society: Studies in Sociotechnical Change* (pp. 225–258). Cambridge, MA: MIT Press.

Lemheney, A., Bond, W., Padon, J., LeClair, M., Miller, J., & Susko, M. (2016). Developing virtual reality simulations for office-based medical emergencies. *Journal of Virtual Worlds Research, 9*(1), 1–18.

Mälkki, K. (2010). Building on Mezirows theory of transformative learning: Theorizing the challenges to reflection. *Journal of Transformative Education, 8*(1), 42–62. doi:10.1177/1541344611403315

Markham, A. N. (1998). *Life online: Researching real experience in virtual space* (Vol. 6). Rowman Altamira.

Mezirow, J. (1991). *Transformative dimensions of adult learning*. ERIC.

Mezirow, J. (1997). Transformative learning: Theory to practice. *New Directions for Adult and Continuing Education, 1997*(74), 5–12. doi:10.1002/ace.7401

Niemi, P. (1997). Medical students professional identity: Self-reflection during the preclinical years. *Medical Education, 31*(6), 408–415. doi:10.1046/j.1365-2923.1997.00697.x PMID:9463642

Parker, B., & Myrick, F. (2010). Transformative learning as a context for human patient simulation. *The Journal of Nursing Education, 49*(6), 326–332. doi:10.3928/01484834-20100224-02 PMID:20210271

Poletti, A., & Rak, J. (2014). *Identity technologies: Constructing the self online*. University of Wisconsin Press.

Pratt, M. G., Rockmann, K. W., & Kaufmann, J. B. (2006). Constructing professional identity: The role of work and identity learning cycles in the customization of identity among medical residents. *Academy of Management Journal, 49*(2), 235–262. doi:10.5465/amj.2006.20786060

Reeves, S., Zwarenstein, M., Goldman, J., Barr, H., Freeth, D., Hammick, M., & Koppel, I. (2008). Interprofessional education: Effects on professional practice and health care outcomes. *Cochrane Database of Systematic Reviews, 1*(1). doi:10.1002/14651858.CD002213.pub2 PMID:18254002

Robb, A., White, C., Cordar, A., Wendling, A., Lampotang, S., & Lok, B. (2015). A comparison of speaking up behavior during conflict with real and virtual humans. *Computers in Human Behavior, 52*(C), 12–21. doi:10.1016/j.chb.2015.05.043

Rybas, N. (2012). Producing the self at the digital interface. *New media and intercultural communication: Identity, community and politics*, 93-107.

Schouten, A. P., van den Hooff, B., & Feldberg, F. (2016). Virtual team work group decision making in 3dvirtual environments. *Communication Research*, *43*(2), 180–210. doi:10.1177/0093650213509667

Sweigart, L., & Hodson-Carlton, K. (2013). Improving student interview skills: The virtual avatar as client. *Nurse Educator*, *38*(1), 11–15. doi:10.1097/NNE.0b013e318276df2d PMID:23222623

Sweigart, L. I., Umoren, R. A., Scott, P. J., Carlton, K. H., Jones, J. A., Truman, B., & Gossett, E. J. (2016). Virtual TeamSTEPPS Simulations Produce Teamwork Attitude Changes Among Health Professions Students. *The Journal of Nursing Education*, *55*(1), 31–35. doi:10.3928/01484834-20151214-08 PMID:26812380

Taylor, E. W. (2007). An update of transformative learning theory: A critical review of the empirical research (1999–2005). *International Journal of Lifelong Education*, *26*(2), 173–191. doi:10.1080/02601370701219475

Umoren, R. A., Scott, P. J., Sweigart, L., Gossett, E., Hodson-Carlton, K., Johnson, M., ... Das, R. (2018). A comparison of teamwork attitude changes with virtual TeamSTEPPS® simulations in health professional students. *Journal of Interprofessional Education & Practice*, *10*, 51–55. doi:10.1016/j.xjep.2017.12.001

Waggoner, Z. (2009). *My avatar, my self: Identity in video role-playing games*. McFarland.

Woodward, K. (1997). *Identity and difference*. London: Sage.

KEY TERMS AND DEFINITIONS

Agency for Healthcare Research and Quality (AHRQ): A U.S. government agency that functions as a part of the Department of Health and Human Services (HHS) to support research to help improve the quality of healthcare.

Augmented Reality (AR): A technology that superimposes a computer-generated image on a user's view of the real world, thus providing a composite view.

Debriefing: The process of sharing and discussing information after a mission, meeting, project, or another event that allows key players to obtain important information and leads to process improvement.

Disorienting Dilemma: The catalyst for perspective transformation, dilemmas usually occur when people have experiences that do not fit their expectations or make sense to them and they cannot resolve the situations without some change in their views of the world.

Gamification: The process of using game mechanics and game thinking in non-gaming contexts to engage users and to solve problems.

High-Fidelity Patient Simulation (HPS): The use of computerized manikins that simulate real-life scenarios.

Interprofessional Education (IPE): When students from two or more professions learn about, from, and with each other to enable effective collaboration and improve health outcomes.

Interprofessional Practice (IPP): Is a collaborative practice which occurs when healthcare providers work with people from within their profession, with people outside their profession and with patients and their families.

Laparoscopy: A surgical procedure in which a fiber-optic instrument is inserted through the abdominal wall to view the organs in the abdomen or to permit a surgical procedure.

Non-Player Character (NPC): Any character that is controlled by the computer through artificial intelligence, also known as a non-person character or non-playable character.

Simulated Multiplayer: Application, the user interacts with non-player characters or avatars controlled by individuals who may or may not be colleagues, but who are role-playing as patients or other health team members.

Single Player: An application in which an individual user interacts with objects in the virtual environment.

Standardized Patients (SP): Someone who has been trained to portray, in a consistent, standardized manner, a patient in a medical situation; also known as a simulated patient.

TeamSTEPPS (Team Strategies and Tools to Enhance Performance and Patient Safety): An evidence-based framework to optimize team performance across the healthcare delivery system.

True Multiplayer: An application in which the user interactions are with team members in educational, or work-related activities.

Virtual Environment: A computer-generated, three-dimensional representation of a setting in which users perceive themselves to be, and within which interaction occurs, also called virtual landscape, virtual world, or virtual space.

Virtual Reality (VR): The computer-generated simulation of a three-dimensional image or environment that can be interacted with in a seemingly real or physical way by a person using specialized electronic equipment, such as a head mounted display or gloves fitted with sensors.

Virtual Simulation: The use of 3D objects and environments to create immersive and engaging learning experiences.

Chapter 10
Cognitive Apprenticeship for Teaching Computer Science and Leadership in Virtual Worlds

Cynthia Calongne
Colorado Technical University, USA

Andrew G. Stricker
https://orcid.org/0000-0002-4184-0554
The Air University, USA

Barbara Truman
https://orcid.org/0000-0002-7839-1772
University of Central Florida, USA

Fil J. Arenas
https://orcid.org/0000-0003-1747-0706
The Air University, USA

ABSTRACT

Cognitive apprenticeship refers to the development of skills under the guidance and tutelage of a domain expert. This chapter covers the theory and highlights 10 years of virtual learning experiences and 52 classes using the cognitive apprenticeship model. It reflects on the impact of presence and explores how learning communities develop as students assume roles and learn by working next to skilled faculty. The examples reinforce the value of deep immersion and identity in situated learning. The software design activities illustrate the benefits experienced when students assume ownership and structure their activities. Through self-reflection, learners illustrated the power of design thinking through group and individual design studios. The chapter concludes with observations from 400 eighth graders and reflections on future work in the design of sustainable learning programs for computer science and leadership education.

DOI: 10.4018/978-1-5225-9679-0.ch010

INTRODUCTION

How do students learn? How do they apply the knowledge they acquired to address future problems and tasks? This chapter explores several cognitive theories and the use of cognitive apprenticeship through ten years and 50 classes held in a virtual world. The examples begin with middle school experiences from 8th grade students in Suffern, New York studying in a virtual world and shifts to address every level of higher education in a computer science degree program with a concentration in emerging media as the evolution of Web science. The chapter reflects on how design thinking within the technology strengthened teamwork and leadership skills through deep immersion, and presents recommendations for future work.

BACKGROUND

Learning blends the pedagogy of facts and rules to form cognitive models for how learners think, reason, and respond to apply them in present and future situations. Craik and Lockhart (1972) turned cognitive models of learning upside down by introducing the levels of processing that describe memory recall and the depth of memory processing. Their model featured two categories: shallow processing and deep or semantic processing.

Memories decay under shallow processing and sensory data establishes connections in the mind.

- How an object looks through structural processing
- How something sounds using phonemic processing
- How letters are symbols that when grouped together, become words as graphemic processing
- How the shape of objects appear under orthographic processing

In contrast, the construct of semantic processing through deep immersion provides connections that support applied learning.

- The relationship between objects or experiences
- The deeper meaning of the experience
- The importance of the experience

Craik and Lockhart (1972) researched deep learning and applied semantic processing theory to explain how the exposure to immersive experiences serve as patterns for memories that persist. Computer science education seeks to map the pedagogy related to programming languages and software engineering practices to applied learning activities to give students the tools needed to create and evaluate their products.

Cognitive apprenticeship blends the sensory data experienced in virtual worlds with design thinking practices (Brown, 2008) to form relationships with experts. Students work next to faculty experts, observing the skills and testing them in their early efforts. The practice benefits from the struggle learners experience when the project challenges them to exceed their current capabilities during its design. If the domain expert blends instruction and support with observation, the learner gains the skills, feedback, and support needed during the initial design and later refinement efforts to achieve a sense of accomplishment and mastery that Csíkszentmihályi (2008) described as the mental state of flow.

Experiencing the state of flow occurs when the challenge slightly exceeds the learner's abilities, giving a challenge that is within reach, yet a stretch to achieve. McGonigal (2011) related the experience of flow to accomplishments within games as the feeling of fiero, the highest levels of excitement experienced when the player feels *on fire* or *in the zone*. Fiero describes an effervescent sense of accomplishment that excites and transforms players. In an educational context, a student who is new to learning within virtual worlds feels a sense of accomplishment that inspires further activity, leading to a sense of accomplishment.

When applying the theory behind cognition and memory (Craik & Lockhart, 1972) to understand how the states of flow and fiero (Csíkszentmihályi, 2008; McGonigal, 2011) lead to transformation learning experiences due to situated learning (Glick, 1997), the blend of constructivism or applied learning and meaningful play (Hamari, 2013; Huizinga, 1955) helps learners to understand the complex concepts and express them in their projects created in 3D spaces. Students express their designs under the watchful eye of faculty mentors. Instead of focusing solely on places and spaces, they create imaginative expressions of emotional constructs through stories that pull the observer through experiences, such as the tough choices made after experiencing cyberbullying, invasions of privacy, social injustice, or encounters with friends who suffer from bulimia. Their designs featured probing questions that shaped diverse ways of thinking about the situation, reminiscent of performance art, only set within computer science education. The insights gained from experiencing their designs led to uneasy feeling akin to discomfort as well as an appreciation of their deeper meaning that persisted long after the class ended. The benefits of mapping these connections within the mind went beyond remembering the task to identifying new design strategies to address future problems.

The search for deeper meaning through comparing and contrasting related experiences provides opportunities to reflect on the value and lessons learned from the experience. In over 50 virtual world higher education classes, students met in synchronous class sessions or worked asynchronously with 3D holograms that provided opportunities to explore and synthesize the course content. Faculty domain experts or knowledgeable guests demonstrated the concepts and how to model them in 3D designs called holograms. The holograms resembled places, like buildings and settings as well as indoor and outdoor spaces. They also represented abstract concepts, emotions, or illustrated complex designs.

How does this work for applying cognitive apprenticeship today? Faculty mentors as domain experts observe the development of the projects and watch students struggle without interfering for the struggle is an important part of the learning experience. Identifying how long to let students struggle is part of the artistry behind cognitive apprenticeship in education. The cycle of demonstration, practice, observation, struggle, feedback and refinement is critical to the personal transformation learners' experience, leading to the feeling of flow and fiero.

Virtual worlds are ideal environments for observing the struggle and gauging when it is time to provide demonstration and analysis in the feedback. Educators can observe students from afar surreptitiously, and not interfere with their concentration or intrude on their group discussions. When needed, educators offer guidance through voice and text communication features and share information in public, private, or group voice channels depending on the situation. The ability to demonstrate the skills, work in a natural setting next to students, and demonstrate by example applies the cognitive apprenticeship model into a practice that feels seamless and natural for skill development.

Students have an opportunity to study the process and to practice it in a relaxed, natural setting after class lectures, demonstrations, and discussions. Students work in groups on their project themes, each designing individual parts of the collective project. They construct 3D designs using a variety of shapes, symbols, textures, and media that when combined, create an experience that comes alive within a situated learning environment.

The design process, struggle, and discoveries made by learners become pathways for present and future learning practices. Instead of thinking of the class as a set of rules and facts to apply, the process becomes intrinsic as learners evolve it to fit their own preferences, beliefs, and habits. They refine and improve their technique or recognize that their skills reside in other areas, such as integration and testing rather than creation and design. The benefits of group work allow learners to use their strengths, experience the entire process, yet to recognize the divide that separates the theory from applying it to address new problems and situations.

In each project, the focus was less on a single class concept, but instead on how to communicate complex ideas through 3D modeling. The difference between a class focused on lecture or on project development is the cooperative and intimate nature of working next to experts and to gain real-time feedback after a suitable struggle. Applied learning is not new to computer science education. Programming classes use labs to give students opportunities to apply the syntax and theory to the creation of simple programs. The different between computer labs and virtual world education projects is the difference between guided steps to complete the labs and the power of creation when faced with a theme and little guidance on how to express it through a sensory experience in a virtual world.

Deep immersion occurs when the learners apply the principles of design thinking (Brown, 2008) to imagine and reflect on the art of the possible as learners apply the course concepts using situated cognition (Glick, 1997), critical thinking and problem-based learning challenges. They imagine a variety of possible scenarios, and create 3D projects as if designing a scene for a stage play. Stepping into the scene and interacting with the objects engages the visitors in probing, immersive experiences. The power of creation by students reinforces the connection and the benefits of the learning experience, and learners retain memories of how it felt as fiero, while some remember the details while others focus primarily on the outcome.

It is tempting to focus solely on the benefits of cognitive apprenticeship, but how much time and attention is reasonable? What happens when the feeling of flow and fiero extend inspire learners and educators to spend inordinate amounts of time pursuing these transformative feelings? Questions arise, such as the concerns related to flow, addiction, safety and identity (Hoffman & Novak, 2009).

How much exposure to project development within virtual worlds is safe? Table 1 presents a proposed model that identifies the levels of deep immersion and their relationship to identity confusion and safety in virtual worlds.

Exceptions to the levels noted in Table 1 exist, in particular for embodied avatars of persons with disabilities who feel a sense of personal transformation (Davis & Boellstorff, 2018). Represented by avatars, their physical bodies may experience constraints and boundaries that do not exist in virtual spaces, giving them a freedom of movement or an abandonment of sensory boundaries that constrict them outside the virtual world (Drax, 2018).

When thinking of the cognitive apprenticeship process, the deeper levels foster a suspension of disbelief to form relationships that establish the optimal conditions for shaping identity. Interesting questions come to mind, illustrated using the analogy of a scuba diver:

1. "What immersive social and environmental features are sufficient for reaching a suspension of disbelief level as one goes deeper with immersion?"

Table 1. Levels of immersion, benefits, and VR identity confusion for safety risks

Depth Level	Immersive VR and User Experience Features	Sensory Benefits to Immersive Learning	VR Identity Confusion Safety Risks
1	• Offers limited interaction with others and objects • Minimal control offered to user to shape environment • Person's sense of presence is low • Realistic fidelity of objects minimal • Immersive time is minimal • Suspension of disbelief is low • Positive impact on learning from flow immersion is minimal	• Little to none	• Little to none
2	• Offers regular interaction with others and objects • Medium control offered to user to shape environment • Person's sense of presence is believable • Realistic fidelity of objects is apparent • Immersive time is periodic • Suspension of disbelief is medium • Positive impact on learning from flow immersion is sporadic	• Noticeable effects of benefits	• Little
3	• Offers frequent interaction with others and objects • High control offered to user to shape environment • Person's sense of presence is highly believable • Realistic fidelity of objects is impressive • Immersive time is significant • Suspension of disbelief is high • Positive impact on learning from flow immersion is optimal	• Positive effects of benefits	• Balanced
4	• Offers high level of interaction with others and objects • Dominant volitional control offered to user to shape environment • Person's sense of present begins to rival real life • Realistic fidelity of objects is nearly indistinguishable from reality • Immersive time is preferred during person's waking hours • Suspension of disbelief is very high • Impact on learning from flow immersion shows signs of distress	• Noticeable negative effects	• Elevated
5	• Offers continuous interaction with others and objects • Total volitional control offered to user to shape environment • Person's sense of presence rivals real life • Realistic fidelity of objects is indistinguishable from reality • Immersive time dominates person's waking hours • Suspension of disbelief is extremely high • Impact on learning from flow immersion is distressed	• Mostly negative effects	• Extreme

2. "At what point of deeper levels does it become counter-productive? When does a person lose perspective between virtual and physical aspects of their identity?" The scuba diver wants to go deeper, but there are increased health risks and extraction procedures to follow to avoid the deleterious side effects.
3. "What might be the extraction features for a person who regularly deep dives in immersive environments?"
4. "Can there be indicators for immersive divers to help them monitor their time, oxygen levels, depth level so they can maintain healthy buoyancy and get back to the surface safely?"

Deep immersion in virtual learning reflects on the value of the experience and how to refine it.

TEN YEARS OF VIRTUAL WORLD EDUCATION

The chapter explores lessons from the past to reflect on what deep immersion means in the context of mapping online classes to a virtual learning delivery model. The classes taught over a ten year period featured a wide range of topics, primarily related to software engineering, game design, robotics, and emerging media (Calongne & Hiles, 2007; Calongne, 2016). The classes spanned 14 course subject areas with projects developed using cognitive apprenticeship as featured in a video commemorating 33 of the classes (Calongne, 2012, August 21).

- User interaction design and usability
- Software requirements engineering
- Software design
- Systems engineering methods
- Robotics
- Advanced game design
- Games, gamification and serious games
- Introduction to virtual worlds
- Virtual world simulation
- Virtual and cloud computing architecture
- Virtual economics and business
- Information accountability and web privacy
- Socio-technical futuring and studies in futuring and innovation
- Web science and augmented reality

The case studies featured later in the chapter illustrate the tactics employed early in the virtual world classes and their adaptation from software engineering models, middle school classes, and the immersive use of chat bots to enhance the sense of realism and presence (Calongne, 2008). The concepts applied in the class design studios (Brown, 2008; Stricker & Calongne, 2015) bridge the discoveries from Scharmer's (2000) research at MIT's Presencing Institute on why presence matters with regard to communication within virtual spaces, and Wenger's (1998) work on communities of practice and understanding how virtual education communities strengthen both the practice and the educators as they share strategies, explore problems, envision and evaluate new ways of teaching and assessing the value of virtual world education. These thoughts also embrace Ward, Smith, and Finke's (1999) recognition of the power of creation and its effect on cognition. Deep immersion is not relegated to a momentary experience, but causes learners to form a connection with the world around them and to feel transformed by the experience when it is shared.

At the NMC 2007 summer conference, a National Science Foundation staffer asked what virtual worlds could offer that the recent redesign of the NSF website could not. The answer was simple, yet also complex. Virtual worlds offer the intersection of content and the people who interact with it, an awareness of others and their presence. The awareness of other users as avatars around the visitor and the feeling of connectedness matters in ways that are profound and that have the potential to transform the learners who experience it. In contrast, a virtual world region without other users, despite how beautiful it may be, is like an empty wasteland. Regions devoice of people lack the feeling of presence that is vital to feeling transformed by the shared experience. Truman (2013) explored these qualities in her doctoral research, evaluating virtual-physioception and virtual intersubjective presencing using resources from Otto Scharmer's (2000) work on presencing and guidance from Andrew Stricker.

COURSE DESIGN AND DELIVERY APPROACHES

Thinking back to those early days, the approaches that describe the practices and adaptation of the course design and delivery strategies favored four methods: 1) appreciative inquiry; 2) agile methods; 3) formative design; and 4) participatory design. The cognitive apprenticeship approach blended all four methods and demonstrated how they worked by demonstration and example throughout each virtual world class. This section introduces the methods and then explores their application.

Appreciative inquiry seeks to understand what works well and to leverage the early successes. In virtual learning and early pioneering efforts, appreciative inquiry offered an opportunity to identify the strengths and leverage them, and opportunities to modify or abandon the tactics that did not work. While effective for building momentum, the method when used alone does not provide sufficient guidance on how to explore the issues and challenges that need reflection, assessment and action. By employing a software engineering process for iteratively scrutinizing and evaluating teaching and learning strategies through a formative evaluation, the opportunity for symmetry strengthened the learners' understanding of the software engineering principles and how to repurpose them for a virtual learning context. It was not unlike learning inside out and seeing evidence of the learning artifacts through firsthand experience and personal involvement in the refinement efforts.

Agile methods describe a lightweight software project management process that centers on close involvement with the stakeholders (Fowler, 2005, December 13). In software engineering, it encourages design and development activities with frequent assessments to confirm that the design meets the requirements and to identify the need for change early in the process. The emphasis on building the right product and gaining stakeholder approval through close involvement are key elements of the method. For learning in a virtual world, the focus on quality and process improvement offered an opportunity to practice it with the learners evaluating the activities and offering refinement suggestions using formative design. In essence, this method embodied the *practice what you preach* approach to teaching software engineering. The abstract software design theories seem less useful and lack relevance until learners experience it through discovery and made observations on the process and product of learning. The method presented further opportunities for exploration and community building, which are featured in the case studies.

Formative design focuses on evaluating the product and the process early and iterating the design and evaluation in frequent quality assessments. In contrast with summative design, formative design focuses on building a product and assessing its strengths and requirements for refinement. By addressing the need for change early, corrective actions implemented immediately reduce the likelihood of creating an undesired software product. An example of summative design is beta testing, which occurs late in the process after the software becomes a product. Making changes late in the process has a far greater impact on the time, energy and costs required to improve it.

Participatory design for virtual learning involved a self-aware examination of the course content, the design and use of 3D instructional content, and the process of learning. Learners are not only stakeholders in the process, but become agents for change, making recommendations and offering insights that are critical to the success of the program.

One benefit is to iterative evaluations and refinement is that it supports change management efforts when the requirements determine the need for change and adaptation. The synergy experienced when agile methods blend with a formative design approach to involve the entire class in the course redesign efforts offers great rewards for strengthening the class design, delivery and assessment and allows educators to align the virtual world learning activities with the online and campus curriculum.

How do these four methods apply to virtual world classes? Hosting classes in a virtual world offered a potential for rich learning experiences, but the risks and potential challenges were high. Stakeholder involvement, frequent course assessments throughout the term, participatory design through an exchange of ideas and corrective actions, and iterative refinement and adaptation helped the educators to identify and address issues fast and under the observant eye of the learners.

Since the early classes featured usability and software engineering classes, the symmetry between the evaluation style and the subjects taught made implementation feel natural and the method easy to employ. One of the strengths of any assessment method is to make it easy to use and adapt to the needs of learners and educators.

The adoption and application of this process did not happen by accident. The first class, comprised of doctoral students, was not a simple task. The stakes were high, and gaining stakeholder support and a shared vision of the usefulness and advantages required going back to middle school.

Case Study: Ramapo

In 2006, Peggy Sheehy, a media center specialist and visionary at Suffern Middle School in New York earned support from her school board to purchase and design three regions for designing a learning environment for 8th grade students participating on the Ramapo project (Calongne, Sheehy, & Stricker, 2013). Linden Lab hosted the regions on the Second Life Main grid for a few months before moving them to a private location on the Teen grid. The concept was simple. Sheehy created a group, invited the world to join it, and used a barn raising motif to encourage experts in 3D design to help her to raise a virtual schoolhouse for 400 8th graders. Spread across three regions, the schoolhouse extended beyond a single building to encompass a music conservatory, a space observatory, castles, parks, 3D design tutorials, classrooms, and much more.

After working on a robotics project called The Big Robot on Campus, sponsored by the Electric Sheep Company, Wired Magazine and the Lego Mindstorms NXT project, just prior to its release, a mentor for the Ramapo project created an avatar to accompany the regions on their exodus to the Teen grid. What started as a volunteer effort to support the use of robotics on the project became instead an opportunity to work with the younger learners. It presented an opportunity for discovery and reflection on how to use diverse approaches to virtual world instruction.

In 8th grade classes, the students logged into the virtual world and participated in learning activities for 40 minutes until the bell rang. To compartmentalize and transition their activities, they logged off, ran down the hall to the next class, and logged back into the virtual world, ready to participate in a different subject and set of class activities. One hour, they worked on geometric shapes and studying math through a visual and tactile exploration of math in action, and how it behaved on a useful object, like a vehicle, a plane, or a ball. The next hour, they discussed the books they read and enacted the character roles using deep immersion.

One particularly important example centered on the John Steinbeck (1937) novel Of Mice and Men. In the learning activity, the students read the book, and then put it aside and enacted the roles from it. The scene they studied was not in the book, but instead, they hypothesized what might happen after the story ends. They asked probing questions. *Was George guilty of killing his friend Lenny?* If so, *should they charge him with manslaughter or murder?*

At the beginning of the courtroom trials, all of the students said that George was not guilty. After all, he loved his friend and only shot him to save him from torture murder. During the four days of trials in one of two courtrooms, the students assumed the roles of the court reporter, the judge, the prosecuting attorney, the defense, or they served on the jury or as witnesses. They blogged the courtroom proceedings and grew engrossed in the trials, which took four days to complete with eight trials held in two courtrooms each day. At the end of their deliberations, the verdict from the students was surprising: guilty!

When asked what changed their minds, they noted that due process does not reflect on the intentions of the defendant, but on whether there was a reasonable doubt. Since George admitted to shooting and killing Lenny, they convicted him, but recommended a lighter sentence because he meant well. The transformation of thought was profound, and the students did not reach this decision lightly.

On the fifth day, they removed the courtroom furniture, to make room for museum exhibits. The students hung posters of famous people, and inserted within them their biographies, written on notecards. When guests clicked on a poster, they received a notecard with a short biography and interesting facts about the subject. The students invited another middle school to visit and tour the exhibits on the following Monday.

During a final sweep of the museum, one poster featured a young girl smiling expectantly. Upon inquiring about the image, a student spoke up and said that it was her, and her notecard listed what she planned to accomplish in the next 15 years when she would join the ranks of the famous. Stunned by the power of this pronouncement, the educator noted that vision and empowerment were among the benefits of these simple, yet profound learning experiences.

Among the lessons learned from 400 thirteen-year-old students were how to compartmentalize the lessons into 40-minute segments, how to complete an activity, write a software script or create a 3D design within a single session. The opportunities for team activities, collaboration on 3D designs and building an ecosystem for a virtual world version of Junior Achievement, complete with student-run businesses, condos and custom designs provided a forum for discovery and bringing back the techniques to share with adult learners. When senior students expressed concerned over the challenges, they reviewed the discoveries and marveled, noting if children could do it, they could do it.

The challenge added another dimension to the next set of classes, increasing the opportunity to test new strategies and strengthen the virtual learning program.

Case Study: Curiosity and Creativity in Student Projects

In a single term, three classes were held in Second Life that shared a deep immersion learning experience: an undergraduate third year software design class, and two graduate classes that studied software requirements engineering and systems engineering methods. The students in all three classes on campus one night each week and online the rest of the time to complete their assignments. Early in the term, the educator offered the software design class an opportunity to design and build their software in the virtual world, test it, and evaluate the correctness of their designs.

The curriculum centered on designing software diagrams using the Unified Modeling Language by Rumbaugh, Jacobson, and Booch (1999), a good-parts version of their three different modeling styles. The models described the timing, transitions between different software states, the processes and use cases that illustrate how the software, once it was developed, should behave. On campus, they went to the whiteboard to draw out a design for a capture the flag game, set in a 250x250 meter floating maze (see Figure 1). They discussed alternative approaches and completed software models to place within a software design document. In addition to creating the project, they grew curious about how it might look and feel.

Outside of class, the students visited the virtual world and selected different pieces of the 3D design. One student modeled and applied textures to the maze, assembling it on a platform created by the instructor. Another created traps modeled after the popular massively multiplayer online roleplaying game (MMORPG) by Blizzard Entertainment (2004) called The World of Warcraft. A third student created prizes, and a fourth created the flag with a sensor to attach it to a player whenever the player drew near. The other seven students created different design elements, worked on refining the class project, and helped to evaluate and modify the game.

Meanwhile, the graduate classes noticed the activity. Not to be outdone, the software requirements class explored the requirements for an amusement park with games and rides. In the campus class sessions, they took turns roleplaying as software requirements engineers and customers as the users.

The students eliciting the requirements discussed strategies for designing each ride. For their online activities, they met in Second Life and created 17 theme park attractions, including a roller coaster, a train system, variety of amusement park rides, a duck shooting gallery, a merry-go-round, a Ferris wheel, and a fun house. The class met for 5.5 weeks, and by the end of the term, they had draft designs and a software requirements specification.

Figure 1. The maze for the capture-the-flag game

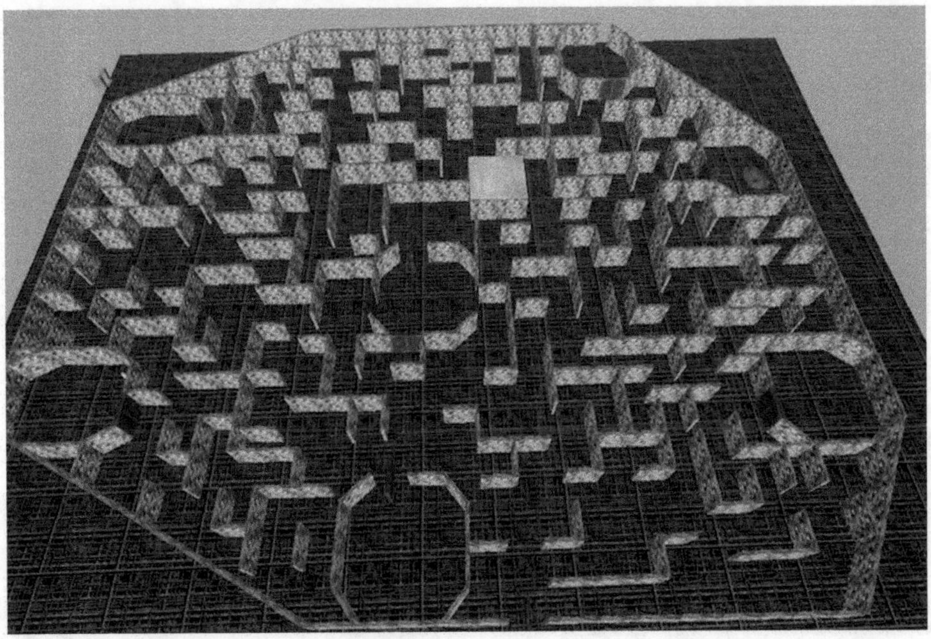

The students who served as users were demanding, and requested fanciful designs, ranging from a train to traverse the amusement park to a rollercoaster. At one point, they noted that the ride was not very exciting, and the designer added corkscrews to the track and turned on physics, giving the riders a thrill when they went upside down and crashed into water, only to snap back onto the track as the train returned to an earlier state.

Most of the same students attended the systems engineering methods class and explored the behavior of products, and a variety of methods for modeling, developing and testing them. Several students focused on state machines, a subject that mapped nicely to the behavior of many of the attractions that started and stopped, changing state upon demand. Timing issues caused them to reflect on different strategies for addressing them.

The train designer grew curious about the software design class, which built its game design maze 300 meters above the amusement park on the ground level. He created a track (see Figure 2) that travelled vertically up to the platform, did not activate physics, and the train hugged the track as it soared upward on the vertical track. Avatars riding the train clicked on the car and sat, attached to it while it soared up the track. At the top, the class could play the maze game and study the game design elements.

This curiosity between classes and their activities seemed like a virtual method of running down the hall to see what was happening in the next room. While unlikely on campus, it presented an opportunity for demonstration, usability testing, and sharing ideas across the classes. It is important to note that no grades or graded feedback was exchanged in the virtual world. Sensitive to FERPA issues, the designs and creativity focused on an inquisitive exploration of the capabilities. The mechanics of grading and sharing feedback occurred on the course management tool using a secure, compliance controlled process.

The behavior of these early classes combined with their inquisitiveness and discovery methods served as a model for future classes. In those early years, communication focused on text as Second Life did not integrate voice communication within the virtual world until later. The early designs might seem crude by today's capabilities, yet were magical, designed by students who had no graphic arts, scripting or animation background.

Figure 2. The track leading up to the Maze game from the amusement park

The last week of the software design class, the students played the game and discovered an issue with the timing of the flag. When it attached to an avatar, the sensor triggered a line of text that hollered to the text chat log that player x had the flag. Unfortunately, it did it several times a second, making the chat log scroll fast like the blades of fan, spinning out of control. The students picked up the flag, silencing it, studied their 2D UML designs, made q quick modification, opened the script with the flag, adjusted the timing, saved it, and started a new game. Within a few minutes, they learned that their initial design had an issue that wasn't apparent from the diagrams. By seeing the software in action, they learned how to map the models to the 3D design, scripts and overall behavior of the game.

As part of their final work, the students created t-shirts with the slogan "I survived the Maze game," a scoreboard, a teleportation device for getting into the game quickly, and a penalty for losing the flag. The guns they used shot monster-sized bullets the size of a toaster and by turning on the health meter on the region, the players took damage when hit. Dying in the game resulted in a time penalty, sending the victim to their home location. A plot of land was set aside for the game design group to own, and allowed the players to join the group and set their home location to that plot. When players died in game, they teleported to the amusement park on the ground and appeared on their group's plot of land. To get back into the game, they ran over and clicked the teleporter.

Observing their progress during the term, the amusement park team created a few games, including the duck shoot, a chess game, an egg hunt, and later, Clue. The camaraderie and gentle rivalry transformed the class activities from assignments to enjoyable designs, and class presentations became opportunities to play and evaluate the lessons learned. These early virtual world class experiences strengthened the students and educators, making the tasks a great joy to support.

How did cognitive apprenticeship impact the success of these classes? To learn how to design the maze walls, the traps, the flag and the treasure, the students learned via demonstration, instruction, by example, and by working alongside the educator, emulating the apprentice to journeyman to master relationship and process. They quickly learned tips related to 3D modeling, how to texture the bare primitive shapes, how to repurpose and revise scripts, and how to integrate, link, evaluate and model their designs. The educator worked next to the students, creating similar, but different designs, demonstrated the concepts, and offered design tips when needed. The students mastered the design techniques quickly, benefiting from 40-minute design sessions modeled after the 8th graders, and modular design techniques for completing each lesson.

The difference between this experience and working in a computer lab on campus was the educator as a creator, working next to the learners. The shared experience combined with opportunities to witness and practice diverse strategies led to a fast game design and opportunity for deep reflection on how the 2D UML design models relate to the code and the behavior of the finished product.

One quality worth mentioning is how the energy level, excitement, and commitment of everyone in the class involved soared. Teaching in a virtual world was exciting, pleasing and full of surprises.

Case Study: A Space and Place in the Cloud

A virtual architecture and cloud computing class adopted a unique perspective to explore the vast opportunities and architectural structure of the cloud. Instead of focusing solely on the concepts that define cloud computing, the class design employed a liberal arts approach with Renaissance thinking to reflect on the qualities and poetics of space (Bachelard, (1964) and how communities design their most sacred and profane places (Tuan, 1977) to support diverse ways of thinking, enlightened behaviors, or patterning the living spaces after their hopes, their dreams or in alignment with their function and their values.

The class project featured Bachelard's topoanalysis, adapted by the educator and instructional designer to be represented as a poignant Cloud Topoanalysis montage seen in Figure 3. It features five of the spaces that learners in the class explored, wrote reflective papers to analyze and searched the Web and the virtual world for examples to weave into their class projects. The five spaces include the Discovery (research) space, the Actuality-of-being space (accomplishment), the Private space (intrinsic,

Figure 3. The cloud topoanalysis montage

deep, probing and self-reflective), the Daydreaming space (a place of dreams and creativity), and the Friendship space (a place for community).

Learners in the class were initially stunned by the focus on these five spaces and were at a loss for words to blend them with the constructs associated with cloud computing, such as software as a service. At first, several students did not see the value in exploring the five perspectives of space as intrinsic to their understanding of the research and their personal discovery and accomplishments. They did not see the value of reflecting on the private, shared, and inner reflective experience of the cloud. Mapping the behavior of cloud computing to how early civilizations structured their villages, homes and environment seemed inconsequential.

Only by asking probing questions about why villages, cities and the home is structured in a particular way were students able to suspend their disbelief and reflect on how their world evolved into today's architecture and how it behaves. After working with them, demonstrating examples, and getting them to think about their connection to the cloud, they pondered how the world was designed, why their homes have a particular organizational structure to sustain them, and the questions spewed from them like water from a floodgate. Deep immersion provided students with perspectives that led to a new awareness of the world around them, shifting to an analysis of why these qualities matter, how these connections between places and how their spaces were organized.

The quest continued by reflecting on an identification of their character strengths (Peterson & Seligman, 2004) for they reside at the heart of the organism they were studying, and what matters most to them helps to frame their values and how they organize their lives.

Cloud computing no longer looked like a distant technology, but instead, as the universe that surrounds them, serving as an extension of themselves and life around them. The connections formed when reflecting on their inner strengths helped them to recognize their values and how these values shape their life decisions, work and everything that they do. They reflected on the philosophy behind these spaces and why matter. In their projects, they explored their relationships and thoughts about how they sustain their lives. Shifting from the mundane examination of the topic to deep immersion led to critical thinking and very satisfying observations. The feeling of transformation was not unique to a course, subject or school, but common across diverse schools, use of technologies, and diverse instructional methods, as noted by the next example.

Deep Immersion in Leadership Studies

The students at The Air University's Squadron Office College were ecstatic about teleporting back in time to 12 May 1962 to West Point and listening to a virtual avatar of Gen MacArthur deliver his famous *Duty, Honor, Country* speech after receiving the Sylvanus Thayer Award. This prestigious West Point award is presented to an outstanding citizen whose national contributions exemplify the Military Academy motto, "Duty, Honor, Country." During the creation of this 3D learning environment, the designer acquired the actual audio recording from the MacArthur Memorial in Norfolk, VA and integrated the audio recording of the speech to a 3D interface object for the instructor to wear as a facilitation delivery tool.

During the lesson, the instructor wore a heads-up display (HUD) device and launched 5-minute segments from the famous speech for discussion. Transfixed, the students stepped back in time and listened to the powerful thoughts of Gen MacArthur as his avatar, a representation of the great leader within the virtual world, delivered his speech. They experienced the power of his insights while standing in his presence. After reflecting on Gen MacArthur's message, the class analyzed various lines from his speech using the full range leadership model to identify and connect the powerful thoughts to leadership behaviors. "However horrible the incidents of war may be, the soldier who is called upon to offer and give his life for his country is the noblest development of mankind," was described by one student as the epitome of self-sacrifice illustrating the transformational leadership behavior; *idealized influence*. The power of 3D immersion in this instance allowed students to experience history first-hand! It was one of the students' favorite experiences in the virtual world, forming a connection between experiences with the past and the intimacy of the shared experience.

DELIVERY METHODS AND TECHNOLOGICAL CHALLENGES

Back on campus, it is worthwhile to note that the virtual learners explored the same curriculum covered in other delivery methods: 1) in the campus classroom; 2) in a hybrid class that met on one day a week on campus and the rest of the week online; 3) in a class held only online. For virtual world classes, they used the online learning management system, posted discussion board posts, downloaded activities, and uploaded assignments. The difference featured the opportunity to attend synchronous meetings in a virtual world, to work next to the instructors on their designs, and to get support after a reasonable period of struggling, reflecting and discovering alternative approaches.

In the virtual classes, the project content included images from 3D buildings and exhibits designed by the students as well as links to student-created videos. They created self-reflective presentations for conferences, like the Virtual Worlds Best Practices in Education and the TCC Worldwide Online Conference, sharing their awareness of the process of learning in addition to offering observations about their challenges and accomplishment.

Another difference between online and virtual classes featured the use of the virtual environment and client software, called a 3D viewer. Similar to a 2D Web browser, the 3D viewer provides access to online content located. The difference displays the 3D setting and the avatar within it, integrated communication tools, an inventory of content the avatar owns or uses, and a 3D content creation tool for rendering primitive shapes, called prims, and texturing them. Instead of making the technology invisible and transparent to the learner so it did not intrude with the course objectives, virtual world classes explored how to use the technology and were expansive in sharing the process of learning as well as course concepts and activities.

A benefit of this extra dimension to the class was that some students rose to the challenge, assumed ownership of the world, and became self-determined learners, adopting the new learning environment and methods with considerable ease. Students started bringing their families and considered some of the landscape as a community space for informal learning. At the end of the term, classes met in world to celebrate and share their accomplishments, and a DJ came by to host dances. These opportunities to relax, socialize and share their discoveries strengthened the learning experience. Years later, graduates visited the virtual world to share their recent discoveries, exchange designs, and reflect on how those early experiences helped to transform their way of thinking, knowing and doing.

OPPORTUNITIES FOR TRANSFORMATION AND DEEP IMMERSION

A virtual world simulation class may best illustrate some of the principles and benefits of deep immersion. In a series of games set in the period of Greek Mythology, four students took different approaches in their simulations. One examined the role of identity and confidence in virtual worlds, asking questions about the feelings of inadequacy and confidence after traveling through the labyrinth in Medusa's Lair (see Figure 4).

After touring the Labyrinth, the temple, and Medusa's Lair, guests visit Pandora's garden to reflect on the qualities that were let loose on the world within the story. In the example seen in Figure 3, Barbara Truman reinforces the story through firsthand experience in the garden, through shared media and by transforming into the Phoenix as a bird on fire (see Figure 5) to illustrate how the perspective shifts as visitors view the experience from several dimensions. The presentation offered a connectedness, an appreciation of constructionism (Resnick, 1996) and creativity (Smith, 1995) that is illustrated throughout her research and philosophy on life (Truman, 2013).

CHALLENGES

Not every virtual world learning experience was rosy. In contrast, at least 5-15% of the students in some classes had bandwidth issues due to their connection speeds, use of satellite connectivity for Internet, which suffers from interruptions, or DSL at lower access rates. Others had rendering issues and could not see high quality graphics, hardware lighting, or communicate using voice. Configuring low end laptops for smooth access to the virtual world was easier in the early years with settings built-into the viewer's preferences for graphical adjustments. Students on campus or when they attended a symposium the second week of a term met with instructors to configure their equipment.

Figure 4. The survey next to Medusa's lair explores self-image and self-assessment

Figure 5. Transforming into the Phoenix during a class presentation

The barriers to learning to use the 3D viewer and design 3D projects were significant for students who had inadequate graphics and bandwidth resources. It was easier to address these disconnects using an earlier version of the Viewer than it was with the full-featured viewers that require additional resources and bandwidth. To address the diverse set of needs, third party viewers created by residents offered lightweight viewer capabilities as well as custom ways of personalizing and using the modern viewers, not unlike using Firefox or Chrome instead of Internet Explorer or Edge.

Future classes experience the challenges of change. Many users prefer 3D mesh designs and how they support realism in the aesthetics, but 3D mesh requires external resources, advanced design skills, and take longer to develop. To create 3D mesh, students cannot use the built-in object creation and texturing tool, but instead, need to learn how to create objects using vector geometry, connect them via a wireframe, and learn to assign materials and textures to the various faces or sides of a mesh creation. This is a barrier to entry that the modern virtual world tools find acceptable. But for students to experience the depth of engagement needed for transformation, the power of creation is recommended.

Early work in Second Life class project designs did not incorporate 3D mesh content, making it easier for every student to create designs or integrate content from other designers in their projects. Once the costs of commercial virtual worlds exceeded school budgets, some educators moved their classes to virtue worlds that use OpenSimulator, an open source alternative to the commercial tools. Some host them in the classroom at the school's campus while others use low cost hosting services. Change brings growth, and in this case, it led to a departure from the carefree and easy manner in which students created content and shared it.

The shift from the educational use of Second Life to the advances in the use of open source tools like OpenSimulator occurred when Linden Lab, the creator of Second Life, experienced an economic downturn and cancelled the educator discount in the middle of the school year. Most schools had a hard time handling budgets that doubled in mid-year, and the school boards could not maintain the budget increases that occurred with 2-3 months' notice.

Critics say that education in virtual worlds failed, but what failed was the shift to an unsustainable economic plan. Many of the universities and schools that had regions could no longer afford them. Moving to open source tools required educators to assume yet another technology role, that of either IT support to host the server-side virtual world grid or to contract with service providers for a new configuration, often barren of content. The problem of content creation started anew as many could not extract their designs from Second Life due to digital rights and copyright restrictions. Owning content in a virtual world is limited to use when in world, and does not include export rights.

FUTURE WORK

A few of the schools who continue to offer classes set in a virtual world, including The Air University, identified the need for integrated learning management tools, open source solutions, cloud computing flexibility with low cost pricing models, data analytics for evaluating the benefits and challenges of virtual learning, and easy movement between virtual world grids using a technology called the Hypergrid by Crista Lopes from the University of Southern California at Irvine. Proquest/UMI dissertations features thousands of studies related to virtual worlds research, yet most offer exploratory or less than generalizable results. The educational community is eager for studies that architect and analyze the benefits using discreet measurements and larger populations. Certain problems exist in the design of quantifiable studies, as measuring the cause and effect of some of these experiences is not a simple nor guaranteed to be a useful task.

For future virtual worlds that rely heavily on mesh designs, learners need built-in mesh design tools and game design resources that make it easy to model their ideas and complete class projects. Holodeck (Roddenberry et al., 2007) capabilities extending beyond the simple housing and recall of interchangeable scenes may offer dynamic opportunities to engage learners and draw into dramatically different spaces. Without the tools needed to adapt the world and transform it from a barren landscape or a space one visits to a place of wonder, the learner may not experience the deep probing sense of immersion and involvement. The applied learning benefits gained from *practice by doing* projects, learning through cognitive apprenticeship and deep immersion may be reduced to thought provoking discussions and viewing the content created by other designers. The power of creation transforms the learner from a tourist to a maker.

CONCLUSION

In summary, nothing beats the power of creation for illustrating lessons that last and form deep connections within the learner. Remembering the details from ten-year-old learning activities feels as fresh as it did when the experience was new. The reason is due to the reciprocal nature of learning in a virtual world. Just as learners form deep connections and remember what they have learned, the same is true for educators. The discoveries form connections and relationships within the mind to evoke memories that are distinct and serve as triggers when recalled.

The tactics worth applying feature the principles of participatory design, to regularly evaluate the requirements to determine the need for change and adaptation, and to practice iterative refinement. All things change, and by keeping a finger at the pulse, the educator remains flexible and open to try and assess new tactics. The synergy experienced when agile methods blend with a formative design approach is learner centric, yet rewarding for the instructor.

Despite the challenges and issues users face with the future of 3D mesh worlds, virtual worlds continue to offer a compelling landscape for hosting imaginative learning spaces. The possibilities are limited only by the imagination of students and educators.

REFERENCES

Bachelard, G. (1964). *The poetics of space*. New York: Orion Press.

Blizzard Entertainment. (2004). *The World of Warcraft* [Computer software]. Austin, TX: Blizzard Entertainment.

Brown, T. (2008). Design thinking. *Harvard Business Review*. Retrieved from https://hbr.org/2008/06/design-thinking

Calongne, C. (2008). Educational frontiers: Learning in a virtual world. *EDUCAUSE Review*, *43*(5), 36–48.

Calongne, C. (2012, August 21). *Highlights from 33 classes with Lyr Lobo* [Video recording]. Retrieved from http://ctusoftware.blogspot.com/2012/08/highlights-from-33-classes-with-lyr.html

Calongne, C. (2016, June). *Future of games in education.* Keynote address at the International Society for Technology in Education Conference Games & Simulations Network Playground, Denver, CO. Retrieved from https://www.slideshare.net/lyrlobo/future-of-games-iste-ven-gsn-calongne-keynote

Calongne, C., & Hiles, J. (2007). Blended realities: A virtual tour of education in Second Life. *Proceedings of the 12th Annual Technology, Colleges & Community (TCC) Worldwide Conference.*

Calongne, C., Sheehy, P., & Stricker, A. (2013). Gemeinschaft identity in a gesellschaft metaverse. In R. Teigland & D. Power (Eds.), The Immersive Internet: Reflections on the entangling of the virtual with society, politics and the economy (pp. 180-191). Basingstoke, UK: Palgrave Macmillan.

Craik, F. I. M., & Lockhart, R. S. (1972). Levels of processing: A framework for memory research. *Journal of Verbal Learning and Verbal Behavior*, *11*(6), 671–684. doi:10.1016/S0022-5371(72)80001-X

Csíkszentmihályi, M. (2008). Flow: The psychology of optimal experience. New York, NY: Harper Collins.

Davis, D., & Boellstorff, T. (2018). *Virtual worlds, disability, and new cultures of the embodied self.* Retrieved from http://www.ourdigitalselves.com/

Drax, B. [Draxtor Despres]. (2018, May 17). *Our digital selves: My avatar is me* [Video file]. Retrieved from https://youtu.be/GQw02-me0W4

Fowler, M. (2005, December 13). *The new methodology*. Retrieved from http://www.martinfowler.com/articles/newMethodology.html

Glick, J. (1997). Discourse and development: Notes from the field. In L. B. Resnick, R. Säljö, C. Pontecorvo, & B. Burge (Eds.), *Discourse, Tools, and Reasoning: Essays on Situated Cognition*. Berlin: Springer. doi:10.1007/978-3-662-03362-3_11

Hamari, J. (2013). Transforming homo economicus into homo ludens: A field experiment on gamification in a utilitarian peer-to-peer trading service. *Electronic Commerce Research and Applications*, *12*(4), 236–245. doi:10.1016/j.elerap.2013.01.004

Hoffman, D., & Novak, T. (2009). Flow online: Lessons learned and future prospects. *Journal of Interactive Marketing*, *23*(1), 23–34. doi:10.1016/j.intmar.2008.10.003

Huizinga, J. (1955). *Homo ludens: A study in the play element in culture*. Boston, MA: Beacon Press.

McGonigal, J. (2011). *Reality is broken: Why games make us better and how they can change the world*. London: Penguin Books.

Peterson, C., & Seligman, M. E. P. (2004). *Character strengths and virtues: A handbook and classification*. American Psychological Association.

Resnick, M. (1996, July). Distributed constructionism. In *Proceedings of the International Conference on the Learning Sciences Association for the Advancement of Computing in Education*. Northwestern University.

Roddenberry, G., Hurley, M., Baron, M., Barry, P., Beimler, H., & Black, J. D. F.Paramount Pictures Corporation. (2007). *Star trek, the next generation: Season 1* [Television series]. Hollywood, CA: Paramount Pictures Corporation.

Rumbaugh, J., Jacobson, I., & Booch, G. (1999). *The unified modeling language reference manual*. Reading, MA: Addison-Wesley.

Scharmer, C. O. (2000). *Presencing: Learning from the future as it emerges*. Presentation at the Conference on Knowledge and Innovation, Helsinki School of Economics, Finland. Retrieved from http://www.ottoscharmer.com/docs/articles/2000_Presencing.pdf

Smith, S. M. (1995). Fixation, incubation, and insight in memory and creative thinking. In S. M. Smith, T. B. Ward, & R. A. Finke (Eds.), The creative cognition approach (pp. 135-156). Cambridge, MA: MIT Press.

Steinbeck, J. (1937). *Of mice and men*. New York: Covici-Friede.

Stricker, A., & Calongne, C. (2015). Remapping mental models of collaboration using immersive 3D design thinking studios. In A. Kok & H. Lee (Eds.), *Cultural, behavioral, and social considerations in electronic collaboration*. Hershey, PA: IGI Global.

Truman, B. (2013). *Transformative interactions using embodied avatars in collaborative virtual environments: Towards transdisciplinarity* (Doctoral dissertation). Available from ProQuest Dissertations & Theses Global. (Order No. 3628698)

Tuan, Y. (1977). *Space and place: The perspective of experience*. Minneapolis, MN: The University of Minnesota Press.

Ward, T. B., Smith, S. M., & Finke, R. A. (1999). Creative cognition. In R.J. Sternberg (Ed.), The handbook of creativity (pp. 189-212). Cambridge, MA: MIT Press.

Wenger, E. (1998). *Communities of practice: Learning, meaning, and identity*. New York, NY: Cambridge University Press. doi:10.1017/CBO9780511803932

KEY TERMS AND DEFINITIONS

Agile Methods: A lightweight method that reduces the tasks to small segments and centers on stakeholder involvement and evaluation early and often throughout the development process.

Appreciative Inquiry: Seeks to identity the successful outcomes and leverage them to build upon success. Discover what works and strengthen it.

Avatar: Representation of the person within a virtual world. A person's virtual identity.

Deep Immersion: Explores the deeper meaning behind a lesson after modeling life experiences and reflecting on why the experience matters. When the experience is life changing, it leads to what Morris Massey called a significant emotional event.

Design Thinking: Focuses on problem solving, modeling ideas, and creating action-oriented outcomes. It builds on instructional systems design (ISD) to engage collaborators with a meta-awareness of the performance and behavioral goals of the task.

Formative Design: The process of iterative design and evaluation early and often through the design process, continuing to refine, evaluate, and iterate the design and testing phases until it converges into a product. When used in virtual learning, it is the formation, creation, and evaluation of teaching and learning strategies in virtual worlds.

Participatory Design: The act of creating a product by involving the stakeholders and users of it, engaging their ideas and incorporating them in later versions of the design.

Presence: The understanding and experience of self and others in the virtual world, based on dialog with individuals, an exchange of ideas with a class, shared perspectives with individuals, groups, institutions, or the world. Presence builds upon Otto Scharmer's research at MIT's Presencing Institute.

Virtual World: A simulated space located on the web or on a local grid that provides a view of the simulator from the server's perspective. The virtual world is comprised of parcels of land, regions, and 3D content that residents create within them.

Chapter 11
Learning Problem-Solving Strategies in Virtual Worlds That Encourage People to Respect Human Rights

Kara Bennett
Elder Voices Inc, USA

ABSTRACT

This chapter will discuss educational projects for learning problem-solving strategies in virtual worlds that encourage people to respect human rights as a lifelong learning experience. The discussion includes philosophical issues concerning the need to design new models for virtual learning that engage a person's own ways of thinking and interacting with the educational content. For example, the instructional design for these projects is based on adapting the think aloud and means-end analysis research methods for evaluating how learning about human rights in a virtual environment might transfer to the real-world community. The projects have been presented over the past 10 years in the virtual worlds of Second Life and the Open Sims.

INTRODUCTION

How can people choose to act in ways that respect human rights in a 21st century global society?

Whether our information is represented as images on cave walls thousands of years ago, or in contemporary 3D virtual worlds, the kind of knowledge that encourages a person to choose humanitarian values is not well understood. For example, the Universal Declaration of Human Rights was adopted by the United Nations in 1948 with the hope of preventing crimes against humanity that occurred during World War II. However, seventy years later dictators and terrorists continue to threaten our lives and can now communicate their plans through the internet and social media.

At the same time, information technology could create new possibilities for people to learn problem-solving strategies to explore ideas about human rights in a virtual world and discover guidelines for their

DOI: 10.4018/978-1-5225-9679-0.ch011

expression in the real world community. This chapter will discuss the projects designed by the author and her colleagues in the virtual worlds of Second Life and the Open Sims that offer this kind of education (Bennett & Patrice, 2013; Bennett, 2017; De Leon & Bennett, (in press). The discussion will include;

1. The philosophy and rationale for the educational content, instructional design, and research methods for evaluating the virtual learning experience.
2. Descriptions of example projects.
3. Summary and suggestions for future virtual education about human rights.

BACKGROUND

Educational Content and Instructional Design

The Educational Content

The projects involve learning about the thirty universal human rights listed by the United Nations by exploring problem-solving strategies that assist in translating these ideals into individual and community actions. (see Appendix for a description of these rights).

For example, Eleanor Roosevelt asks people to think about how to bring humanitarian values into their daily life in her community guide entitled, *In Your Hands.*

Where after all do human rights begin? In small places, close to home -- so close and so small that they cannot be seen on any map of the world. Yet they are the world of the individual person, the neighborhood he lives in, the school or college he attends, the factory, farm or office where he works. Such are the places where every man, woman, and child seeks equal justice, equal opportunity, equal dignity without discrimination. Unless these rights have meaning there, they have little meaning anywhere. Without concerted citizen action to uphold them close to home, we shall look in vain for progress in the larger world (Roosevelt, 1958).

A virtual world offers the chance to learn about a subject at both a conceptual level of knowledge and as an immediate sensory experience. This is important for understanding the meaning of human rights in ways that can be expressed as a philosophical inquiry, as well as how they affect daily life relationships.

The Instructional Design

When a person uses an Avatar designed to represent them in the virtual world, there is the opportunity to learn and share information as a real time interaction. To take part in an immersive experience that includes the possibility of communicating through voice, text, images, and animation. Educational content can be offered in the form of stories, science, art, games, theater, lectures and new genres invented for a digital Metaverse. The person/Avatar can also connect to information from video, web sites, and social media. Over the past ten years, the author and her colleagues have designed places in the virtual worlds where a person represented by their Avatar can try out problem-solving strategies that encourage the expression of human rights. (see the references for the virtual world project locations.)

The problem-solving strategies designed for people to explore in the virtual world projects are based on the adaptation of the Think Aloud data collection and Means-End analysis introduced by Drs. Herbert Simon and Alan Newell in the 1960's for studying human and artificial intelligence problem-solving abilities. These methods capture the dynamic goal-directed behavior of the individual as they try to achieve a desired goal and learn about their choices and reasons for the actions they take (Simon, 1969; Newell & Simon, 1972). The information obtained from the Think Aloud protocol is like an unedited documentary of the person's strategies for achieving their goals. The protocols can be examined using a Means-End analysis to describe the person's strategies for trying to reduce any differences between their present situation and the goal state (Ericsson & Simon, 1993). These methods also give the opportunity for the person to learn how to analyze their own problem-solving abilities and continue to explore their ideas after participation in the education and research studies.

Although the Think Aloud protocols and Means-End analysis have not been previously designed for human rights education in virtual worlds, they have been adapted for the author's education research, psychotherapy practice, and community psychology projects that include human rights concerns. These methods were learned by the author in her work with Dr. Howard Barrows, a professor and neurologist at the University of Southern California who wanted his neurology and psychiatry residents to understand their problem-solving abilities for making a clinical diagnosis and ethical decisions (Barrows, 1980).

For this work, actors were trained to simulate a real patient's symptoms and then the physician was asked to Think Aloud as they performed their examination of the patient (Barrows & Bennett, 1972; Elstein, Shulman, & Sprafka, 1978). The unique thinking styles of the physician, as well as their common problem-solving strategies were described using a Means-End analysis. For example, physicians must have ways of transferring their medical knowledge to the personal experience of the patient's symptoms. Although instruments for recording vital signs can help locate the patient's symptom values such as for temperature and blood pressure, the physician must rely on their cognitive tools to identify how the different symptoms fit to a particular disease category. It is in the study of the physician's problem-solving strategies that ways of relating their medical knowledge to the patient can be suggested (Bennett & Barrows, 1972).

The author continued this research for her dissertation entitled; A Construction of a Diagnosis: a study of a Physician's Mental Strategies for fitting a Patient's Symptoms and Signs to a Disease Category (Bennett, 1981). This study used the Think Aloud/Means-End analysis to suggest a model for these problem-solving strategies. The model describes the stages for building the physician's knowledge of the best fit of the patient's health to possible diagnostic categories. For example, physician's report using mental tools such as using images of where an injury might be located to decide on physical exams for the patient. The model was also compared to the artificial intelligence diagnostic programs being designed for medical diagnosis. The computer programs were capable of suggesting diagnoses of illness and injury that could be represented with specific information, but did not have the ability to compare more complex or general categories such as found in psychiatry and neurology, or illnesses which present with nonlinear patterns of symptoms (Sacks, 1990; Bennett, 2000).

The problem-solving strategies suggested in the model include; 1.Defining the goals and values to be achieved, e.g. making a medical diagnosis of the patient and learning if their human rights are being protected. 2. Identifying the present state of the physician's knowledge that includes sensory level information, e.g. of the patient's symptoms. 3. Designing a cognitive map to discover any distance between the defined goals and the present knowledge, e.g. recording the patient's symptoms over a period of time. 4. Using this map to discover possible paths to reduce any distance between the goal state and the physician's present level of knowledge of the patient's illness. 5. Performing the actions to change the present state of knowledge into the desired one, based on the person's map and choice of path to try out. 6. Using feedback from these actions to decide how close the desired goal fits to the knowledge of the patient's diagnosis, and what needs to be discovered. 7. Sharing the information with others.

For psychotherapy, the Think Aloud/Means-End analysis was adapted for the person to record their problem-solving strategies at any time they wanted to Think Aloud, while trying to achieve the goals and values they thought were important for their mental health. For example, the strategies could be asked as questions such as how to discover ways to live with the loss of a loved one and hold onto the person's values when they are challenged by adversity. Their recordings could then be discussed with the therapist to explore how the person translates their definition of their values into daily life experiences.

For community projects, human rights issues such as discrimination and gang violence were explored in small theater environments that offered a place for a person to try different ways of expressing themselves, and learn about the kind of character who could act in ways that respect humanitarian values (Los Angeles gang intervention, 1985; Moore, 1974; Trotter, 1985). For our work, a story was written called, *The Galaxy Language,* that adapted the seven problem-solving strategies from the nonfiction content to try ways of learning about the strategies in a fiction environment. The story was about discovering a language that encouraged a person to hold onto their deepest values without using violence even in the worst of times. People were asked to create a character and a story that could be presented as part of the ancient tradition of building a Community Drum to share music and stories (Hart, 1990).

When the virtual worlds became accessible in the beginning of the 21st century they presented the opportunity to design educational material for learning problem-solving in a virtual place similar to real world simulations and theater spaces. The origin of the concept of an Avatar came from the Hindu philosophy that a deity could descend to Earth in the incarnate form or manifest shape of an "Avatar." The Sanskrit definition is listed as Avatara; to be a passing down or across (Ava=down) and (Tara=a passing). The meaning of "Avatar" was also defined as an embodiment or concrete manifestation of an abstract concept, for example, in a person's expression of a particular quality of themselves, such as their movement, physical style, and emotions. Both definitions are listed in The Random House College Dictionary (Random House Dictionary, 1982).

With virtual world Avatars we can embark on a mythic journey for the information age. A journey to discover the problem-solving strategies that support learning how the ideals of human rights can become guides for community interaction.

THE VIRTUAL WORLD EDUCATION PROJECTS

The author and her colleague Dr. Susan Patrice Weiner began their virtual world human rights journey in 2008 with the Second Life program as avatars Dancers Yao and Kasuku Magic.

When The Virtual Tech Museum of Innovation invited people to build exhibits for their Tech laureates this offered a chance to learn how to adapt the author's work about human rights and problem-solving strategies to virtual world education. One of their laureates was the Witness organization concerned with documenting and bringing awareness to violations in human rights using cameras and sharing the stories on the Internet.

Figure 1.

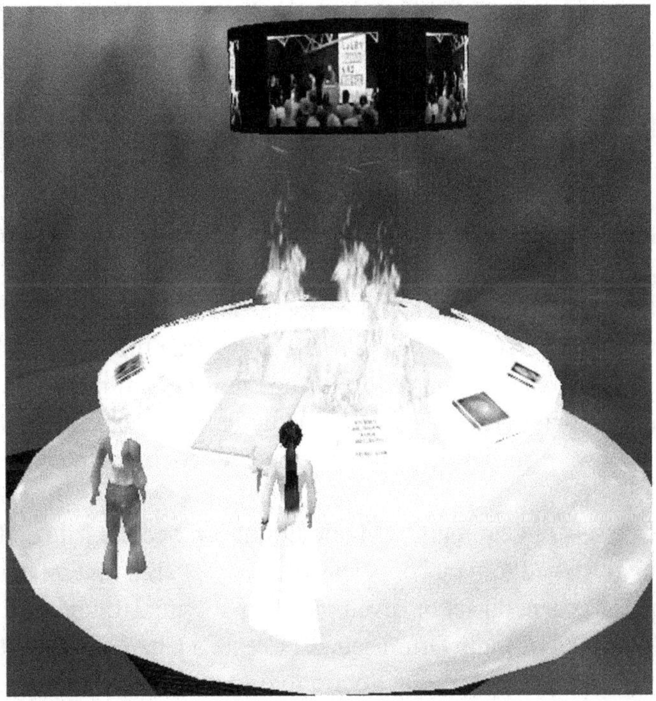

Create a Universal Language

The exhibit was called "Create a Universal Language" and begins with video stories from the Witness organization shown on a screen above a fire. Surrounding the fire is a simulation of a touch screen computer shaped like a large Community Drum. The Drum displays a virtual book to read the Universal Declaration of Human Rights from the United Nations and a link to read the declaration in the person's preferred language. Other images and text around the top of the Drum offer questions about how to create a universal language that people could use to express these rights in a global society. Each question relates to one of the seven problem-solving strategies learned from the author's previous research and practice. The visitors can share their ideas and stories by recording them on a notecard and dropping it into the fire which was linked to the museum web site and the Witness.org web site.

For the projects since 2008, the author and her colleague joined the Non Profit Commons on Second Life with their organization, Elder Voices, whose mission is to explore ways of bringing human rights to health care with education, prevention, and intervention (see www.eldervoices.net). The projects use the concept of the Community Drum and have six individual Drums, called Magic Drums, to represent each of the seven problem-solving strategies. They are designed to;

1. Engage a person in an introspective and interactive learning experience that will not only offer information about the subject of human rights, but will encourage finding how this information can be applied to their own lives and community.
2. Explore different ways of knowing about a subject, such as using art, science, common sense, story-telling, to offer the freedom to look at the same subject from different points of view. This

can involve how a person sees themselves and others from different perspectives, so when learning how to express respect for human rights is the goal, people can try out ways to do this in a virtual environment and then choose what might work in their community.

3. Give the person a chance to explore questions about their own values, so the concept of human rights becomes a personal exploration about their rights, as well as an opportunity to ask the same questions with an international group of people in the virtual world.
4. Use different levels of abstraction as symbolic representations of the information necessary to discover ways of crossing the distance between where a person is in their present circumstances, and the goals they want to achieve.
5. Offer the chance to record the person's expression as an Avatar as they interact with the Drums. In the virtual environs the person can be recorded at the time they are involved in a goal directed activity, for example, as a chat log, machinima, and audio recording. This is a way to learn about the person's problem-solving processes as they actually try to achieve their goals. Then they can compare whether they were successful, or if they need to continue to create more steps to take.

There are currently five sets of Community/Magic Drums on Second Life and one set at the Avacon Grid Open Sim. They are designed to focus on a specific subject area that relates to human rights concerns, while offering the same general set of seven problem-solving strategies.

These include the Community/Magic Drum sets of; Create a Character that respects Human Rights for basic survival goals, Searching for Borrelia: a quest to find a cure for a new illness, Create a Character that respects Human Rights for the education of preservice teachers, Create a story about your Digital Citizen Character, a science fiction version called The Quest for the Galaxy Language. The following is a description of each project.

Create a Character Who Respects Human Rights

This adventure is called "Create a Character who Respects Human Rights." The setting for this quest is a volcanic crater. Near the Community Drum are six individual drums (Magic Drums) with information about a problem-solving strategy the person will need to learn to create their character. The first drum asks the person to choose the kind of human rights they want to learn how to express from among the thirty rights listed by the United Nations.

The drums are "played" with the person's imagination, as they add their images and text to offer answers to the questions. Using a derivative of a virtual slide show script, these can be displayed on the tops of the drums, and kept as personal notecards. The Magic Drums also link to examples of strategies for achieving basic survival needs, like a video showing how to perform Cardio Pulmonary Resuscitation (CPR) for physical survival. Or, the story of the invention of a way to bring solar energy to a community that previously had no electricity, this story offers a way of respecting the human right of living in a safe environment (CNN Heroes, 2010).

The following is information people will have to participate in their virtual learning experience, given as notecards that become their Journey Guide.

Figure 2.

Notecard Example for Create a Character Who Respects Human Rights

We can try out ways in the virtual world to discover problem-solving strategies for bringing human rights to our personal life. By playing the seven Magic Drums with your imagination, you can explore how you might create a character who can respect individual diversity and our common human values.

When you touch the Base of each Drum you will receive a notecard with a question that can help to create your virtual character. The Top of the Drum displays an image that links to information from video stories, text, and music to explore possible answers. Make notes, take pictures, and record your ideas to make a personal Journey Guidebook with your notecards.

For your quest, touch the globe with the circle of lights to take a Solar Light with you. The light sparkles and moves into different designs as you move your Avatar.

Begin with the drum that has an image of the sun shining through the trees where you will find suggestions for defining the values and goals of your character.

Drum 1 How Would You Define the Values of Your Character?

Touch the image of the sun shining through the trees to link to a story about the invention of a solar light for people who did not have electricity in their village in Kenya. Many of the steps important for defining your values are illustrated in this story.

To apply the story example to your character, here are some questions to ask;

What are the values most important for your character to have in order to achieve the human rights you have chosen to express?

Figure 3.

You might want to look at qualities in yourself, people you know or have read about in real life or fiction stories. Like someone who has the courage to stand up against prejudice, or a person who can invent something to help people survive in their community.

How would your character solve the problems that might occur while trying to achieve their goals? For example, do you like to have a big picture view of the problem, be able to break it down into smaller parts, keep track of what happens over a period of time? Try another point of view if an idea is not working? Enjoy playing with your imagination? Write poetry? Design a research study? Try common sense?

The ways you choose for your character to think about and express their human rights become the guides, the standards of conduct for how you might act.

With your goals in mind, look for a drum with a multicolored image on top to explore how you might express the values you have chosen as a sensory experience.

Drum 2 Where Are You Now? Learn Ways to Express the Goals of Your Character as a Sensory Experience

This drum will help you explore ways to experience with your senses how the abstract ideals of human rights might be applied in real life situations. To make the images in your mind an experience to see, hear, touch, feel.

Touch the top of the drum to link to Wiki information about each of our senses. Try out different ways of using your sensory information in Second Life. Maybe flying could be an expression of freedom, waving hello to show respect. An animation as a dance that makes you feel the joy that could be shared with someone. Talking to other Avatars about prejudice to try and find ways of preventing it.

Your selections can be documented as guides for your character and noted in your Journey Guidebook.

Now you might need a map to see how close or far you are from the character you want to be. Find the drum with a digital message on top.

Figure 4.

Figure 5.

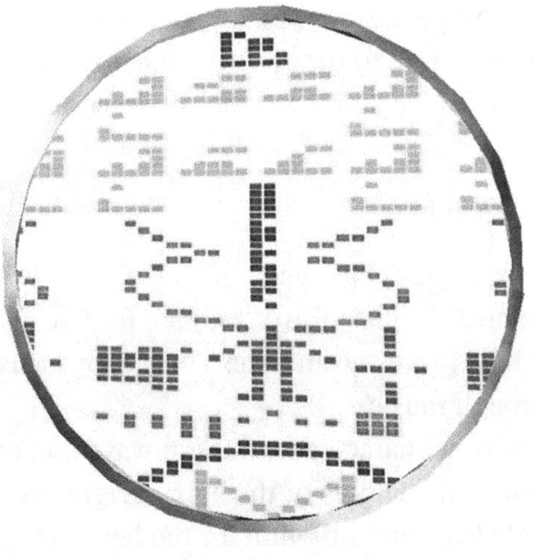

Drum 3 Design a Map to Cross the Distance Between What You Know How to Express About Your Human Rights and What You Want to Learn

How would you create a map to cross the distance between the goals you want to accomplish and what you are experiencing now? A map that will help you become the character you want to be?

Maps can be created in many different styles. It is important to include the essential values you want to keep no matter what the distance you may need to travel to reach your desired destination. These are the guides, the choices that must be held no matter what happens.

A drum with a link to a story about the "Message from Arecibo" gives an example of a map sent from scientists on Earth to try and contact intelligent life in the universe. The message was sent in a binary code and shows how someone might travel to Earth from wherever they are in our galaxy.

Figure 6.

Create a map that represents the distance your character might need to travel to reach their goals and add this to your Guidebook. What kind of path could your character take to reach their goals? Looking at your map, see if you can imagine a path, steps you might take to become the character you want to be.

The next step is to find a path you want to travel across the distance you have estimated. Look for the drum with an image of a crowd of people and the names of some of the human rights.

Drum 4 Creating a Path

The Drum with the image of a crowd of people and words like, Freedom, Health Care, Justice, links to a segment of the video from the documentary film, "Playing for Change". While you listen to different versions of the song, "Stand by Me" played around the world, enjoy this experience of how we can find a path to relate to each other through music.

Think how you might express your character's values in ways that can be adapted to different situations, while holding onto the essential qualities of the human rights you have chosen.

Then look for the Drum that helps learn a rhythm for the heart, and Learn to Save a Life.

Drum 5 Try Expressions as an Avatar That Might Be Applied to Real Life Situations

The drum with the picture that says "Learn to save a life" suggests ways of expressing human rights in real life situations as an example of how you could bring health care to someone. This drum connects to the Wiki link for how to perform hands on Cardio-Pulmonary Resuscitation.

The last drum is a place to look at the problem-solving strategies you have explored, and choose the best examples for the character you want to create. This drum shows a picture that connects the images from all the other drums.

Figure 7.

Drum 6 Are You the Character You Want to Be?

Now you can use all the problem-solving strategies suggested in each Drum to decide the best guidelines for your character and what to explore for the future.

Besides telling a story about your personal character in your Journey Guidebook, you can share ideas for ways of respecting human rights. An example is to place them in the Community Drum.

Drum 7 The Community Drum

Add your own images as textures by right clicking the Top of the Drum and then click Edit and Content. Drag the texture from your inventory with full permissions and place it in the content. You should then see your image as one of the community images.

From your experiences with the virtual Magic Drums you can decide if you want to express any of your choices as a character in real life situations.

Searching for Borrelia

For this project, the Magic Drums are designed as part of a role playing experience to help find a cure for Lyme Borreliosis. This illness has been very difficult to diagnose early enough to avoid life threatening complications, and is now considered a global health epidemic (Open Eye Pictures, 2008). Because of years of controversy surrounding the correct guidelines for making a diagnosis and deciding on the

Figure 8.

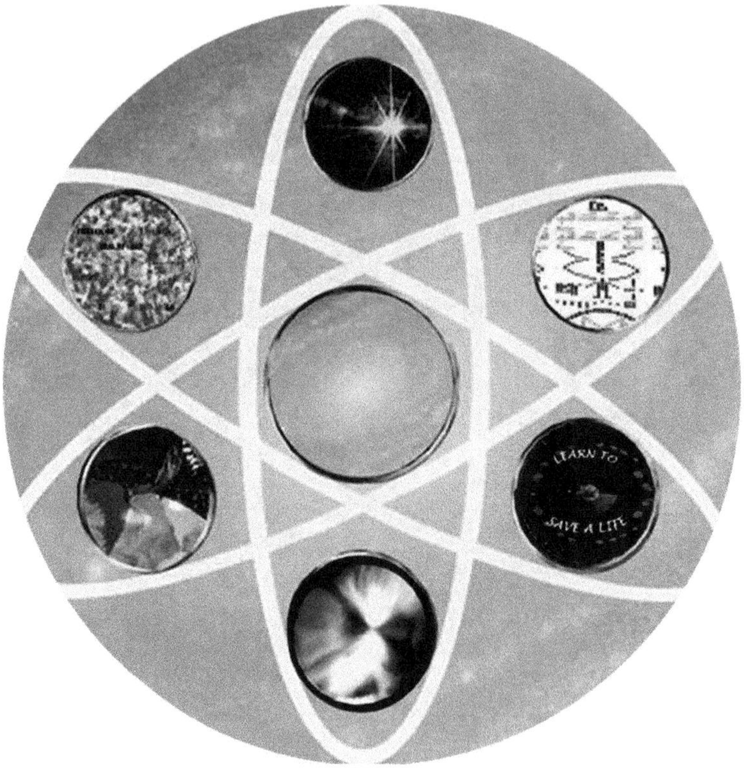

Figure 9.

Figure 10.

best treatment, violations in the human rights of patients and doctors have been reported to the United Nations World Health Organization (CanLyme, 2018).

Avatars can learn the different kinds of knowledge necessary to make a diagnosis, such as from research, health care practitioners, microbiology, insurance companies, government agencies, and find how they can become involved in the search for a better understanding of this mysterious illness (Bennett, 2000).

Avatars could also learn to act as simulated patients to teach health care professionals in the virtual environment about their clinical diagnostic strategies. They can try out new ways of making a diagnosis such as with patient wearables, augmented reality, home care robots,(Mataric, 2018) and artificial intelligence diagnostic programs (Gluck, 2018).

Create a Character Who Respects Human Rights Adapted for Pre-service Teachers

See Figure 11.

The Magic in the Drums: Using Imagination and Think Aloud Processes to Develop Humanitarian Identities

To demonstrate in a research study if the virtual Magic Drums learning experience could transfer to real life situations, the Drums were adapted for Dr. Leticia De Leon for her undergraduate pre-service teachers. Her students participated in the first virtual study using the combination of the Think-Aloud and Means-End Analysis for teaching problem-solving strategies on Second Life

The Drums were given a special place in a Sky Dome where her students could visit. They were asked to create a character who could respect human rights as they explored their problem-solving strategies with the questions in each of the drums. The first question was to choose one of the human rights they want to learn ways of expressing as a person, and to help teach their future students.

Dr. De Leon has obtained preliminary data suggesting a transfer between the virtual world and how her students could apply this learning experience to human rights projects in their community (De Leon

Figure 11.

& Bennett, in press). This study was also presented for the Second Life Science Circle (De Leon & Bennett, 2013). Some examples of the responses to the questions in the Magic Drums are listed below;

Values that are important for my character to have are the ability to listen and hear criticism. My character should be open-minded and should be able to hear what others think about the situation without judgment to that person.

As well, my character will break problems into smaller parts in order to visualize and analyze them first to find multiple ways to solve those problems. She will write poetry to let her emotions flow through the words and maybe solve any problems.

The goal I want to reach is the one of equality among people in the world, where everyone has the same rights and freedoms, and in order to make that possible, I would have to travel around the world, so that's the reason for which I chose a world map, where I would be able to become the character I want to be, a character that is so wise, that can have the ability to change people's mind, and make them think of humans as one kind.

Some of the Community projects that were encouraged by the virtual learning experience were;

1. Boys and Girls club meetings to discuss issues of change and idea expression.
2. Special Olympics volunteer and discussions with parents regarding the value of the event.
3. Engaged with a student organization to do a drive for needy families and then distribute these.
4. Engaged local community to share experiences of discrimination.
5. Taught a class of second graders what it was to be good citizens.

Dr. De Leon is continuing her research for this project.

Exploring Ways of Being a Digital Citizen by Sharing Our Stories Around a Community Drum

A Community /Magic Drum set was designed for Dr. Valerie Hill for her virtual Community Library on Second Life. People will learn about the problem-solving strategies for creating the kind of character they want to be and interact with as a digital citizen. After exploring the questions in the Drums, people can share their stories in the Community Drum.

What Is a Digital Citizen?

The rights and responsibilities we each have now that much of our life is spent in digital "online" spaces are called Digital Citizenship. This includes understanding privacy, security, respect for intellectual property, digital literacy, and much more. Our "digital footprints" mean we have an online persona with responsibilities for civil behavior (Common Sense Media, 2018).

Digital citizenship has become essential for learners of all ages as technology has revolutionized how we learn. Access to information across the globe brings benefits to education but also presents challenges. Learning to evaluate information, part of digital literacy, can be challenging and is now

Figure 12.

the personal responsibility of each digital citizen (Common Sense Media, (2018); Digital Citizenship, 2018; Hill, 2017).

The Quest for the Galaxy Language

The science fiction version of the Magic Drums called "The Quest for the Galaxy Language," is presented on Inspiration Island in Second Life and the Open Sim Avacon Grid. These locations are dedicated to promoting whole brain health through offering specially designed immersive activities and programs.

For example, having a sense of purpose is an important ingredient for brain health, as are creative play and engagement with the world. Dramatizing the quest for the Galaxy language draws on all these elements in powerful ways. A group of avatars from Inspiration Island performed the quest as a theater piece at an Open Sim conference in 2014 (OSCC, 2014). The avatar cast included Thuja Hynes, Francisco Koolhoven, Ixmal Supermarine, Letty Luckstone, Lissena Wisdomseeker, and Dancers Yao. Each avatar was given a general script that was structured around the drums' questions. Each chose their own personal images to place into each drum, guided by two avatar extraterrestrials who descended from a spaceship to assist them in learning the Galaxy language. The theater can be found on the Avacon Grid (see www.avacon.org).

The Quest continues with an invitation for people to visit Second Life and the Avacon Grid to help discover what kind of language we need to communicate with Extraterrestrials if we receive a message from outer space or they visit us! Learning about The Galaxy Language is a chance to explore a universal language based on what an intelligent life might need to survive with meaning and purpose. A language

Figure 13.

that could involve common problem-solving abilities for respecting the value of life, no matter where you live.

SUMMARY AND SUGGESTIONS FOR FUTURE DIRECTIONS IN VIRTUAL EDUCATION AND RESEARCH FOR LEARNING PROBLEM-SOLVING STRATEGIES THAT ENCOURAGE RESPECT FOR HUMAN RIGHTS

The educational projects discussed in this chapter offer suggestions for learning about the basic human rights necessary for personal survival and being part of a global society. The suggestions are based on adapting a model of the essential problem-solving strategies for relating the ideals of human rights to a person's daily life actions. The hope is to encourage ways of learning these strategies in the virtual environment that could transfer to real life situations.

The focus of the educational content is to learn about the meaning of human rights both as a concept, and how the conceptual level of understanding can offer guidelines for the person's actions. The problem-solving strategies that are necessary to create this connection are explored in the projects presented in the Second Life and Open Sim virtual worlds. This gives the opportunity to try out ideas and actions, and then select what the person might choose to transfer to their real life environment.

To investigate how this problem-solving model is working to accomplish these educational goals, the Think Aloud and Means-End analysis research methods are adapted for each project These methods offer a way to study how a person represents information as guidelines for the actions they take to achieve their goals, and includes the dynamics and complexity that can occur in real life problem-solving situations. Equally important, this approach gives the person a voice, a way to express how they like to try and solve problems.

SUGGESTIONS FOR FUTURE RESEARCH DIRECTIONS

Asking a person to define what human rights mean to them in a virtual world environment offers a way to begin a global dialogue about the problem-solving processes involved in creating a society that can interact in ways that respect individual diversity and universal humanitarian values.

The ability to have this kind of society is especially important with the increasing number of artificial intelligence machines that can make decisions for people's daily life activities (Groth & Nitzberg, 2018). Scientists also wonder how a computer program could be designed to have artificial general intelligence and be able to make judgments that respect human values (Goertzel, 2014; Soares, 2014; Pineau, 2018). For example, Dr. Joelle Pineau, an Associate Professor at McGill University, states that the environments many AI researchers use to train their machine learning systems do not include dynamic and complex real life situations. Consequently, they may be too restrictive for the diversity of human expression.

However, no matter how brilliant artificial and human intelligence may become, the ability to have a conscience, a moral compass, and care about life remains essential for our existence.

What if robots with an autonomous and general problem-solving ability could end up acting like humans who do not care about humanitarian values? These questions have resulted in research to address these concerns (Armstrong, 2014; Markoff, 2015; Omohundro, 2014; Malle, 2014). For example, in 2014, Brown University began investigating how robots can be designed to ensure they will act in ways that are beneficial for people. Dr. Bertram Malle stated; "To design a morally competent robot that interacts with humans, we need to first get clear on how moral competence functions in humans."

Virtual world environments can offer complex and dynamic environments where people can interact and share their own ideas and stories about their values. Perhaps future projects can include creating a global Community Drum where people share and think aloud about their questions concerning human rights. A chance to appreciate there can be different kinds of answers, but that we share common problem-solving strategies and questions.

CONCLUSION

The educational projects presented in this chapter suggest that offering a virtual world environment can encourage people to learn about their problem-solving strategies for making choices of humanitarian values and ways of expressing alternatives to violence and prejudice. By adapting the Think Aloud and Means-End analysis for these projects it is possible to begin to evaluate how a person can learn about human rights in the virtual worlds and explore ways of transferring their knowledge to real world environments. The journey continues.

REFERENCES

Armstrong, S. (2014). *Smarter Than Us: The Rise of Machine Intelligence.* Berkeley, CA: Machine Intelligence Research Institute (MIRI).

Avacon Grid. (2018). Retrieved from http://www.avacon.org

Barrows, H., & Bennett, K. (1972). The diagnostic (problem-solving) skill of the neurologist: experimental studies and implications for neurology training. *Archives of Neurology,* 26, 273-277. Retrieved from http://archneur.jamanetwork.com/article.aspx?articleid=571194

Barrows, H., & Tamblyn, R. (1980). *Problem-Based Learning: An Approach to Medical Education.* New York, NY: Springer.

Bennett, K. (2000). Perceptions of Lyme Borreliosis. *Journal of Spirochetal and Tick-borne Diseases,* 7, 42–51. Retrieved from https://www.academia.edu/12300945/Perceptions_of_Lyme_Borreliosis_Kara_Bennett

Bennett, K., & Barrows, H. (1972). An investigation of the diagnostic problem-solving methods used by resident neurologists. *Mathematical Biosciences, 15*(1-2), 63–181. doi:10.1016/0025-5564(72)90071-5

Bennett, K., & Patrice, S. (2013). Exploring the Virtual World of Second Life to help bring Human Rights to Health Care. In D. Baldwin & J. Achterberg (Eds.), *Women and Second Life*. London: McFarland and Co. Inc.

Bennett, K. S. (1981). *A construction of a diagnosis: a study of a physician's mental strategies for fitting a patient's symptoms and signs to a disease category* (Doctoral Dissertation). UCLA. Retrieved from 2018 http://search.proquest.com/docview/303106298/abstract

BerrettL. (2018). Retrieved from https://agelessmindproject.org https:VirtualInspirationIsland.org

CanLyme. (2018). Retrieved from https://canlyme.com/2018/06/14/corruption-and-human-rights-violations-against-lyme-doctors-scientists-and-parents-now-on-united-nations-record/

CNN Heroes Solar Light. (2018). Retrieved from http://www.cnn.com/2010/LIVING/02/11/cnnheroes.wadongo/index.html

Common Sense Media. (2018). Retrieved from https://www.commonsense.org/education/digital-citizenship

De Leon, L., & Bennett, K. (2015). *The Magic in the Drums: Using Imagination and Think Aloud Processes to Develop Humanitarian Identities*. Presentation, The Science Circle Second Life.

De Leon, L., & Bennett, K. (in press). Human Rights, Think Aloud Protocols and Magic Drums: Revealing Character in Pre-Service Teachers. *Journal of Interactive Learning Research.*

Elder Voices, Inc. (2018). Retrieved from www.eldervoices.net

Elstein, A. S., Shulman, L. S., & Sprafka, S. A. (1978). *Medical problem solving: an analysis of clinical reasoning*. Cambridge, MA: Harvard University Press. doi:10.4159/harvard.9780674189089

Ericsson, K. A., & Simon, H. A. (1993). *Protocol analysis: verbal reports as data.* Cambridge, MA: MIT Press.

GluckJ. (2018). Retrieved from http;//AIinHealthCare.net https://healthitanalytics.com/features/artificial-intelligence-promises-a-new-paradigm-for-healthcare

Goertzel, B. (2014). *Between Ape and Artilect: Conversations with Pioneers of Artificial General Intelligence and Other Transformative Technologies*. Create Space Independent Publishing Platform.

Groth, O., & Nitzberg, M. (2018). *Solomon's Codes: Humanity in a World of Thinking Machines*. New York, NY: Pegasus Books.

Hamilton, E., & Cairns, H. (1961). *Plato*. Princeton University Press.

Hart, M. (1990). *Drumming on the edge of magic*. San Francisco, CA: Harper.

Hill, V. J. (2017). Digital Citizenship in Participatory Culture. In A. Stricker, C. Calongne, B. Truman, & F. Arenas (Eds.), *Integrating an Awareness of Selfhood and Society into Virtual Learning* (pp. 60–73). Hershey, PA: IGI Global. doi:10.4018/978-1-5225-2182-2.ch005

Los Angeles Gang Intervention. (1985). Retrieved from www.edutopia.org/no-gangs-here- stage

Malle, B. (2014). *Can robots be trusted to know right from wrong? Tufts University, Brown University, and Rensselaer Polytechnic Institute, and the U.S. Navy explore technology that would help develop robots capable of making moral decisions*. Retrieved from www.kurtzweilai.net

Markoff, J. (2015). *Machines of Loving Grace: The Quest for Common Ground Between Humans and Robots*. New York: Ecco/HarperCollins Publishers. Retrieved 2018 from http://www-robotics.usc.edu/~maja/

Moore, S. (1974). *The Stanislavski System*. New York: The Viking Press.

Newell, A., & Simon, H. A. (1963). GPS a program that simulates human thought. In E. Feigenbaum & J. Feldman (Eds.), *Computers and thought* (pp. 279–297). New York: McGraw Hill.

Newell, A., & Simon, H. A. (1972). *Human problem solving*. Englewood Cliffs, NJ: Prentice-Hall.

Omohundro, S. (2014). Autonomous technology and the greater human good. *Journal of Experimental & Theoretical Artificial Intelligence*, *26*(3), 303–315. doi:10.1080/0952813X.2014.895111

Open Eye Pictures. (2008). *Under Our Skin Trailer*. Retrieved 2018 from https://www.youtube.com/watch?v=sxWgS0XLVqw

Pineau, J. (2018). *The Reproducibility Problem: AI Agents should be trained in more realistic environments*. Retrieved from https://futureoflife.org/2018/12/05/neurips-2018/

Roosevelt, E. (1958). *In Your Hands: A Guide for Community Action for the Tenth Anniversary of the Universal Declaration of Human Rights*. Retrieved from http://www.udhr.org/history/inyour.htm

Sacks, O. (1990). Chaos and awakenings. In Awakenings. New York: Harper Perennial.

Second Life Virtual World. (2018). Retrieved from www.secondlife.com

Simon, H. A. (1969). *The sciences of the artificial*. Cambridge, MA: M.I.T. Press.

Simon, H. A. (1979). *Models of thought*. New Haven, CT: Yale University Press.

Soares, N. (2015). The Value Learning Problem. Berkeley, CA: Machine Intelligence Research Institute.

The Magic Drums. (2018). Retrieved from http://maps.secondlife.com/secondlife/Aloft%20Nonprofit%20 Commons/240/126/23

The Quest for the Galaxy Language. (2018). Retrieved from http://conference.opensimulator.org/2018/ program/learning-lab/

The Random House College Dictionary. (1982). New York: Random House, Inc.

The Tech Virtual Museum Exhibit. (2008-2015). Retrieved from http://legacy.www.thetech.org/about-us/media-room/tech-museum-innovation-announces-winners-ucantu-virtual-exhibit-creation-contest

Trotter, R. (1985, September). Profile: Muzafer Sherif, a life of conflict and goals. *Psychology Today*, 55–59.

Universal Declaration of Human Rights. (1948). Retrieved from http://www.ohchr.org/EN/UDHR/Pages/ SearchByLang.aspx

Witness Organization. (2018). Retrieved from http://hub.witness.org

KEY TERMS AND DEFINITIONS

Avatar: A 3D representation of a person in a virtual world that offers the possibility of expressing oneself through voice, text, images, and animated movements in real time interaction.

Human Rights: The right to have access to the essential needs of human survival such as the 30 human rights adopted by the United Nations in 1948.

Open Sims: Open source virtual worlds.

Problem-Solving Strategies: Ways of thinking and acting that help achieve a person's values and goals.

Second Life: A virtual world where avatars from anywhere on earth can interact in an immersive 3D environment.

Think Aloud and Means-End Analysis: Research methods for studying problem solving while the person is actively engaged in trying to achieve a desired goal.

Values: The desired experiences and choices of character a person acts to create and to keep, such as their human rights.

Virtual World Learning: Using the 3D environment for education that offers new ways of representing and experiencing information.

APPENDIX

United Nations Universal Declaration of Human Rights: Summary of Adopted Agreement on December 10, 1948 (http://www.ohchr.org/En/udhr/Pages/SearchByLang.aspx)

A world in which human beings enjoy freedom of speech and belief and freedom from fear and want has been proclaimed as the highest aspiration. It is essential that human rights should be protected by the rule of law. Member States have pledged to promote universal observance of human rights and fundamental freedoms.

Article 1

All human beings are born free and equal in dignity and rights.

Article 2

Everyone is entitled to all the rights without distinction of any kind, such as race, colour, sex, language, religion, political or other opinion, national or social origin, property, birth or other status.

Article 3

Everyone has the right to life, liberty and security of person.

Article 4

No one shall be held in slavery or servitude

Article 5

No one shall be subjected to torture or to cruel, inhuman or degrading treatment or punishment.

Article 6

Everyone has the right to recognition as a person before the law.

Article 7

All are equal before the law and are entitled to equal protection of the law.

Article 8

Everyone has the right to an effective remedy for acts violating rights

Article 9

No one shall be subjected to arbitrary arrest, detention or exile.

Article 10

Everyone is entitled to a fair and public hearing by an independent and impartial tribunal

Article 11

1. Everyone has the right to be presumed innocent until proved guilty
2. No one shall be held guilty of any act which did not constitute a offence at the time it was committed.

Article 12

No one shall be subjected to arbitrary interference with his privacy, family, home or correspondence, nor to attacks upon his honour and reputation.

Article 13

1. Everyone has the right to freedom of movement and residence in their country
2. Everyone has the right to leave any country and to return to his country.

Article 14

Everyone has the right to seek and to enjoy asylum from persecution.

Article 15

1. Everyone has the right to a nationality.
2. No one shall be arbitrarily deprived of his nationality

Article 16

1. Men and women have the right to marry and to found a family.
2. Marriage shall be entered into only with free and full consent
3. The family is entitled to protection

Article 17

1. Everyone has the right to own property
2. No one shall be deprived of his property.

Article 18

Everyone has the right to freedom of thought, conscience and religion;

Article 19

Everyone has the right to freedom of opinion and expression

Article 20

1. Everyone has the right to freedom of peaceful assembly and association.
2. No one may be compelled to belong to an association.

Article 21

1. Everyone has the right to take part in the government of his country
2. Everyone has the right to equal access to public service in his country.
3. The will of the people shall be the basis of the authority of government; expressed in periodic and genuine elections which shall be by universal and equal suffrage and shall be held by secret vote

Article 22

Everyone has the right to social security and realization of the economic, social and cultural rights for the free development of his personality.

Article 23

1. Everyone has the right to work, to free choice of employment, to just and favourable conditions of work and to protection against unemployment.
2. Everyone, without any discrimination, has the right to equal pay for equal work.
3. Everyone who works has the right to just remuneration ensuring of an existence worthy of human dignity, and supplemented, if necessary, by social protection.
4. Everyone has the right to form and to join trade unions

Article 24

Everyone has the right to rest and leisure, including reasonable limitation of working hours and periodic holidays with pay.

Article 25

1. Everyone has the right to a standard of living adequate for the health and well-being including food, clothing, housing and medical care and necessary social services, and the right to security in the event of lack of livelihood .
2. Motherhood and childhood are entitled to special care

Article 26

1. Everyone has the right to education. higher education shall be equally accessible to all on the basis of merit.
2. Education shall be directed to the full development of the human personality and shall promote understanding, tolerance and friendship and peace.
3. Parents have a right to choose the kind of education that shall be given to their children.

Article 27

1. Everyone has the right freely to participate in the cultural life of the community, to enjoy the arts and to share in scientific advancement
2. Everyone has the right to the protection of interests resulting from any scientific, literary or artistic production of which he is the author.

Article 28

Everyone is entitled to a social and international order in which the rights can be realized.

Article 29

1. Everyone has duties to the community
2. Everyone shall be subject only to legal limitations ensuring respect for the rights and freedoms of others and meeting morality, public order and the general welfare.
3. Rights and freedoms may not be contrary to the purposes and principles of the United Nations.

Article 30

No one has any right to act to destroy any of these rights and freedoms.

Chapter 12
Self-Analysis Technology, Roles, and Cybersecurity in the Virtual Learning Environments

Themba M. Ngwenya
Parker University, USA

Roxanne Kemp
Parker University, USA

Festus Elleh
Parker University, USA

Renee Carrillo
Parker University, USA

Coleman McKoy
Parker University, USA

Mayra Quezada
Parker University, USA

Frankie Lloyd
Parker University, USA

Twana Cochran
Parker University, USA

ABSTRACT

The focus is on how technology impacts the learner and educator identities, especially focusing on safety, privacy, and the cybersecurity of the technology-centric learning environments. Questions arise which will need to be resolved by designers of these systems. This chapter was completed at the end of the annual CES, Consumer Electronics Show, held January 2019 at Las Vegas. The justification for this approach was to assert the influences products displayed at this consumer show will have on future identities of the self among learners and educators. Concepts such as self-analysis technology are proposed and discussed, and challenges affecting learners and educators related to identity, authentication, authorization, and accountability are highlighted. It is concluded that solutions to these challenges are not a single entity but instead a combination of diverse continually evolving techniques.

DOI: 10.4018/978-1-5225-9679-0.ch012

INTRODUCTION

The ever-evolving computer technology has dramatically changed how the World, Society, and Individuals in general interact. An annual barometer is the CES, Consumer Electronics Show, held from January 8th to January 11th, 2019, in Las Vegas, (CES, 2019). At a 'high-level,' some of the main topics from the show were related to 5G and Internet of Things, Accessibility, Blockchain and Crypto technology, Artificial, and Machine Intelligence, Augmented and Virtual Reality, Gaming, Content, and Wearables.

At the detailed level, we look at a few of these products and how they might affect the identities and roles of Learners and Educators as well as the associated learning environments, once implemented. Figure 1 is a word cloud of the trending learning, technology and cybersecurity concepts during the year 2019 and beyond.

Figure 1. Trending concepts in 2019 and beyond

CHAPTER FLOW

The chapter flow is arranged in the following manner:

1. An overview of CES 2019 trending products and services.
2. A summary of the Future Identities of the Self and how they could relate to the current trends, especially cybersecurity.
3. A flashback review of computer security concerns from the 1960s and 1970s, which later evolved to the cybersecurity concept we now know.
4. Current and future cybersecurity forecasts based on industry trends.
5. A review of the policies and regulations that have been established for online education by the US Department of Education. The focus is on the privacy and security aspects, (FERPA, PII, PPRA), of Learner's information which need to be adhered to by current and future Online/Virtual Learning Environment service providers.
6. A Summary of the current state of Learner, Educator and Impact of Cybersecurity on Online/Virtual Learning Environments. The proposal of Self-Analysis Technology (SAT) concept as a component of the solutions to identified challenges. Advantages of the PIES architecture.
7. Summary of three cases studies which are snapshots of industry work in dealing with cybersecurity challenges in Online/Virtual Learning Environments: Attack Tree simulations and possible solutions; Online/Virtual Learning Environments as part of a nation's cybersecurity strategy; Understanding Learner privacy in MOOCs.
8. A look at the Five Questions that have arisen as to how best implement cybersecurity in Online/ Virtual Learning Environments. Some of the research reviewed could offer solutions.
9. Putting it altogether which recommends possible solutions which can be synthesized from the study ideas and concepts that have been highlighted in this chapter.

BACKGROUND: CURRENT CONCEPTS THAT AFFECT LEARNERS, EDUCATORS AND EDUCATION ENVIRONMENTS

Impact of 5G and Internet of Things

The end of 2018 saw the introduction of 5G technology trials, by the large service providers such as AT&T, Verizon, in the United States, Korea Telecom in South Korea and NTT Docomo in Japan, (5G Launch, 2018). 5G is touted to be faster as compared to 4G/LTE and will be the driver for expansion of the Internet of Things as more devices will now be connected, (5G Launch, 2018). The Keynote from the Verizon CEO highlighted how 5G connectivity would blend the physical and digital worlds, (CES, 2019). The stance resonates with the Future Identities educational goals across physical and virtual spaces. The current 5G deployments are for fixed networks, with mobile versions being made available in late 2019 to 2020-time frames. This introductory period will be crucial for device manufacturers, software developers and content providers to ensure compliance with standards in the final products. The goal to create ubiquitous Online/Virtual Learning Environments accessible on multi-devices such as smartphones, laptops, tablets, and wearables will benefit from these developments. The ultra-wide bandwidth that 5G offers (5G Launch, 2018), will allow use cases such as holography in education, immersive learning, and other learning areas that require real-time connectivity, i.e., Labs, (Holography, 2019), or are data-dependent, i.e., research & processing. The data from Learners and Educators collected from sensors and wearables will be available for analytics and will utilize these networks. Of the 20-30-billion connected devices forecasted to be connected by the year 2020, (Connected Devices, 2016), Education system designers are challenged to ensure devices related to online/virtual environments form a sizeable percentage.

Improvements to Accessibility

The incorporation of Accessibility in the design process, (CES, 2019), was visible in the solutions that were on offer. Instead of "re-inventing the wheel," some solutions can be repurposed to focus on education. Just as there are seniors and people with disabilities living in various diverse communities, ranging from urban to remote, so are Learners and their Educators who would benefit from these innovations related to mobility, sight, and sound. The use of driverless vehicles, drones, AI and AI assistants, data analytics, telemedicine, and sensors are some benefits. For interactive lessons, virtual and augmented reality, as well as Gaming for learning, would allow immersive absorption of content. Online and Virtual learning environment designers cannot afford to omit Accessibility in all forms or scenarios if they still want to be in business offering their services. Rewriting the catchphrase for the 1970s action drama 'The Six Million Dollar Man,' (SMDM, 1973), as "we now have the technology and capability to make all the online and virtual World Accessible."

Blockchain Technology for Education Systems

G. Chen, Xu, Lu, and N. Chen (2018) discussed the potential use of blockchain technology in education due to the advantages offered by the concept's features including, decentralization, traceability, immutability, and currency characteristics. The benefits provided by blockchain technology were reliability, trust, security, and efficiency. Chen et al. (2018) referenced several uses of blockchain technology in the education environment including the reduction of degree fraud. These qualities appear to embrace the foundation goals of Online/Virtual Learning Environments. In terms of immutability, could Blockchain be used to ensure the authentication and integrity of educational content? Concerning openness, can improvements to online/virtual learning systems be driven by a diverse team on the local, national and global levels? In terms of fairness, the critical factor is to encompass all contributors and participants and never discriminate against any Learner or Educator or relevant content. The call is for education system designers to explore and hopefully include the potential stability and security that Blockchain technology appears to afford.

Artificially Intelligent and Machine Learning Education Environments

The future trends in the online/virtual system require that these environments utilize AI and Machine Learning as catalysts to revolutionize the education frontier. Coupled with data analytics, the fusion of these technologies takes learning to the highest levels. Memories from some decades ago highlighted in Chapter 17 of Book 1 (Stricker et al., 2017), of the traditional classrooms and learning environments, of the need to physically visit the library for any scholarly information, and access to data available to the privileged few are becoming a very distant fantasy. The use of AI assistants, as well as the research results based on pattern recognition by Machine Learning software, should improve teaching and learning. Smart education systems should make available to students and teachers feedback metrics to help improve their participation and contribution. Education system designers will require guidelines related to relevant standards, ethics, authentication and authorization to create those 'ideal' learning environments. Cooperation by Education authorities, equipment manufacturers and software developers will assist this endeavor.

Augmented Reality, Virtual Reality, and Gaming

Augmented Reality, (AR), Virtual Reality, (VR) and Gaming Techniques are revolutionizing how users embrace technology and indicate how general society is now willing to interact. Transforming the experience in immersive entertainment toward immersive education may appear a daunting task for online/virtual system designers. One key factor that assists in overcoming this challenge by leveraging AR, VR and Gaming techniques is that humans are the target recipients in both cases. Discovering those characteristics in products that appeal to audiences in all aspects of entertainment provides guidelines on what Learners and Educators seek in online interactions, (Chapter 17: Stricker et al., 2017). The ability to virtually travel back or forward in time, or to be able to teleport to locations as part of a course requirement practically is possible.

Content

The adage "Content is King," rules supreme not only at CES but in the constant evolution of technology. The consumers of content directly drive the demand, which appears insatiable. The announcement of mutual ventures such as Verizon partnering with Disney studios, (CES, 2019), highlights this phenomenon. The need for educational content that is both stimulating, immersive and teaches is one of the main tenets of the Online/Virtual Learning Environments. The designers of these systems have several challenges that need solutions, most of them related to one principal question, "does this content stimulate the user and create effective teaching or learning?" The list of devices on which educational content is available on is in an upward trend and based on chip design associated with nanotechnology, (Quero, Perdigones, & Aracil, 2018). Real-time analytics of educational content subscriptions and access will be an invaluable feedback tool in designing online/virtual curriculum, and alert to which areas require additional emphasis.

Wearables

The following is a compilation of titles of some of the conference sessions at the Wearable Tech Summit during CES 2019, (CES, 2019): BYOW (Bring Your Own Wearable), Powered Clothing (Intelligent Wearable Strength), Modern Wearable Lifestyle, Environmental Fashion, Interactive Intuitive and Intimate, Putting Wearables to Work, Later Years/Sight and Sound, Managing Myself, Advancing Performance Analytics in Wearables, Wearables that Work. The focus in 2019 was on fashion, sports and health, but this assortment of use-cases could be repurposed for education systems as well. The same requirements related to the legal, privacy and safety issues of users of Wearables would equally have to apply to Learners and Educators. The ability to use sensor technology to measure specific metrics and traits of the human system to create data and feedback information for personal or legal decision making is a step ahead, (Yang, 2018). From the earliest recorded times, Humans have been striving for ways to improve their participation and performance in a variety of challenges including in sport, in war, in health, and education. The advent and evolution of technology have assisted this demand for "perfection." "For Education," Wearables systems designers would need to formulate solutions which incorporated to some extent vital sign data with Eye-tracking techniques used to measure cognitive development, (Yang, 2018), to give a real-time assessment of participants in the Online/Virtual Learning Environments.

Figure 2 illustrates the concepts impacting Learners and Educators in 2019 and beyond.

CES is not the only show highlighting trends in technology. Several other events are occurring monthly during the year, such as the Future of Education Technology' or, 'Mobile World Congress in Barcelona, (MWC19, 2019). The ability for online/virtual environment designers to understand the 'bigger picture' and not lag when synthesizing learning systems is key to effective education. A very critical aspect affecting all these developments is Cybersecurity. Unfortunately, the current security solutions related to the Online/Virtual Learning Environments appear not to be adequate or are non-existent in some cases. This fact exposes both participants and institutions to cyber threats which will tend to diminish online safety, lower the quality of the programs and remove data integrity. This discussion on Cybersecurity highlights its importance and forms the bulk of the contribution of this chapter. A brief recap of the identities of the self and the associated roles mentioned in Book 1, (Chapter 17: Stricker et al., 2017), is given in the following section.

MAIN FOCUS OF THE CHAPTER: CYBERSECURITY AND THE FUTURE IDENTITIES OF THE SELF

The concept of the Future Identities is summarized in Figure 3, reproduced from Book 1, (Chapter 17: Stricker et al., 2017). This diagram describes how the identities are related to the possible Species, (Human, Animal, Machine), and the Sub-identity roles these species could assume, (Temporary/Current

Figure 2. Concepts impacting learners and educators in 2019 and beyond

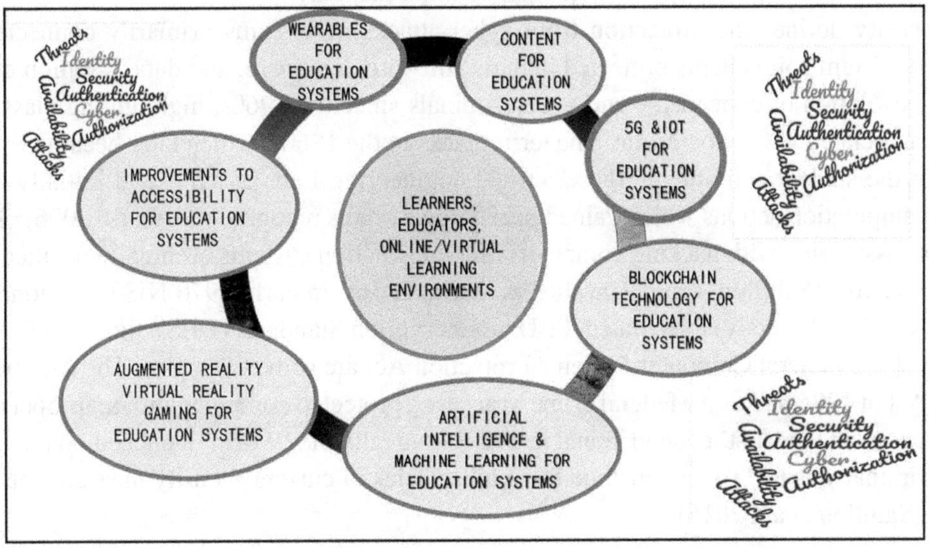

Figure 3. Learner sub-identity roles, sub-identities and interaction modes

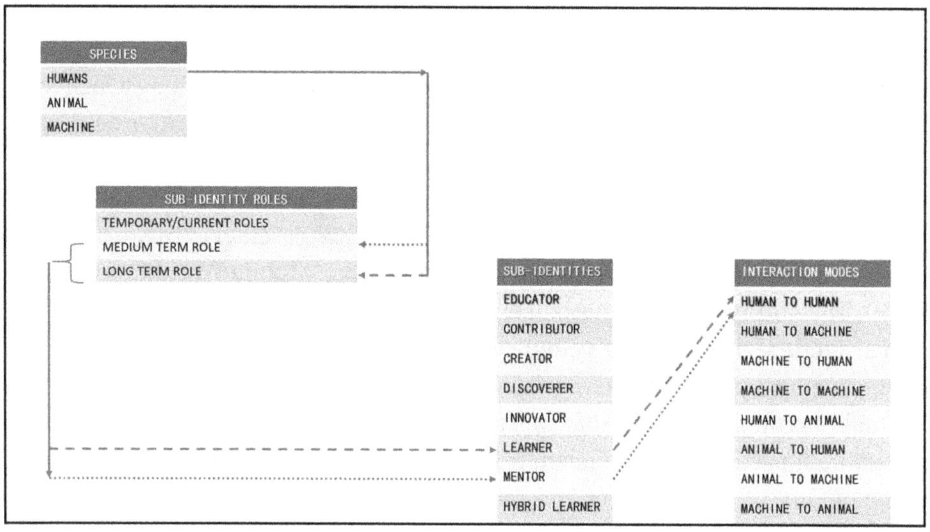

Role, Medium Term Role, and Long-Term Role). The list of Sub-identities and how they could interact, (Interaction Modes) illustrates the concept indicated by the lines and arrows, and in this scenario focused on that between humans, (Learners and Mentors).

The review of CES new product offerings above highlights the significance of the Identities and the roles they assume. In all the solutions mentioned it is apparent how participant contribution is mandatory during implementation for success. For example, in the products related to 5G, both a Learner and Educator will access a holographic system environment for studies, or in the Wearables, the privacy guidelines need to be adhered to include legal permission to use data obtained from the sensors. The Cybersecurity impact on users of technology innovation is now in the forefront. Resolving this challenge is crucial to creating safe and legitimate Online/Virtual Learning Environments. Questions arise such as, investigate which areas related to education Cybersecurity? Which aspects of online security should be a priority, and how should proposed solutions be implemented?

Cybersecurity defines the protection from cyber-attacks of systems primarily connected via the internet. The system components protected include software, hardware, and data. Sabillon et al., summarized the evolution of cybercrime and cybercriminals since the 1960s, highlighting classifications, definitions associated with cybercrime. The term ‘hack’ in the 1960s, which later became hacker’, was coined from the student activities in the electrical engineering Labs at MIT, and initially referenced computer manipulation actions which gained peer-to-peer status recognition, (Wark, 2006). The illegal connotations associated with hacking computers and information systems eventually resulted in formal laws and standards, (Sabillon, Cano, Cavaller, & Serra, 2016). In early 1970 NIST (National Institute of Standards and Technology) formulated the Data Encryption Standard, (DES), the 1973 Swedish data Act, and the 1977 Federal Computer Systems Protection Act are some examples. The Computer Fraud and Abuse Act of 1986 makes it a federal crime to access a protected computer without proper authorization, helped convict the ‘first’ cybercriminal in 1989. Ironically the ‘Worm’ launched on the internet by this cybercriminal was to “To demonstrate the inadequacies of current security measures on computer networks,” (Sabillon et al., 2016).

A REVIEW OF SECURITY CONCERNS FROM 1960s, BUT RELEVANT IN 2019 AND BEYOND

Figure 4 summarizes some key milestones related to technology evolution and cyber threats.

The computer security report 'Security Controls for Computer Systems' published in 1970, (Ware, 1970), identified a series of inadequacies which combined to create a security problem and is still relevant today. Ware (1970) described how geographically diverse computer equipment and networks raised issues related to the protection of classified information. The four vulnerabilities flagged were:

- Human-related and associated with accidental or deliberate actions to the systems
- Hardware related and based on insecure equipment and networks
- Software related, especially in the operating systems and applications
- The user involved and connected to identification, authentication, authorization, and accountability

Ware (1970) mentioned that the vulnerabilities were present in both government and industrial environments which processed classified data. The areas of security concern that required critical attention focused on:

- Physical protection of computer equipment and data storage facilities. The report recommended the establishment of physical security standards to ensure secure locations for the overall computer system.
- Hardware points of failure ranging from malfunctioning equipment to deliberate misconfiguration issues. Designers were encouraged to consider all implementation scenarios when designing systems.

Figure 4. Milestones illustrating the impact of cyber threats as technology evolves

- Software points of failure due to operating systems and application software lacking proper security protections including introducing strict user access controls. The 'bugs' in software systems was the most significant risk highlighted.
- Communication nodes and networks points of failure due to issues such as unauthorized access or interception of information.
- Organizational points of failure related to institutional, operational procedures and personnel security clearances.

The report recommended the following characteristics to create a secure system environment, (Ware, 1970). The safe environment needed:

- To be responsive and flexible to constant change in terms of requirements, skills, hardware, software, and standards.
- To be accountable and reliable for both the users and processes.
- To possess integrity, to ensure it complies with the required standards.

The lack of adequate security in computer systems is directly proportional to the evolution of computer technology. This scourge is impacting Online/Virtual Learning Environments as well. The next section gives an overview of the latest trends that affect Learners and Educators.

Cybersecurity Trends Impacting Learners and Educators

The report on the predictions of the global cybersecurity market from 2014 to 2024, (Global Cybersecurity, 2014), highlighted demand drivers, growth stimulators, market size, modernization techniques and associated spending in cybersecurity across the globe. The report forecasted a compound annual growth rate (CAGR) for the cybersecurity market of 4.6% with network security having a 35.1% market share impact. The Global IoT in Education Markets, 2018-2023, (Global IoT Education, 2019), highlighted growth opportunities mainly due to the increase in Online/Virtual Learning Environments, the ubiquity of connected devices and the decreasing cost of connectivity. The market size for the IOT related to Education was forecasted to have a CAGR of 18.8% from an amount of USD 5 billion in 2018 to around USD 11 billion by 2023, (Global IoT Education, 2019).

Most importantly, Global IoT Education, 2019, stressed that cyber-attacks would hamper the growth on educational institutes including online/virtual environments, issues related to product interoperability as well as insufficient industry standards. The proposed structure of the IOT for education industry comprised of system integrators, platform providers, service providers, software providers, solution providers, and equipment manufacturers. Also, the gamification of the educational sector would provide increased opportunities, (Global IoT Education, 2019). Figure 5 illustrates the envisaged IOT in Education ecosystem.

The work by Bandara, Loras, and Maher (2014) focused on E-Learning cybersecurity concerns and provided an overview of critical cybersecurity problems affecting Higher Education systems including online/virtual environments. The focus areas of the study included detection of threats, security requirements and protection in distributed e-Learning systems. The research proposed a security management model to assist educational institutions in managing their information security risks. Bandara et al.

Figure 5. Envisaged IOT in education ecosystem highlighting providers and stakeholders

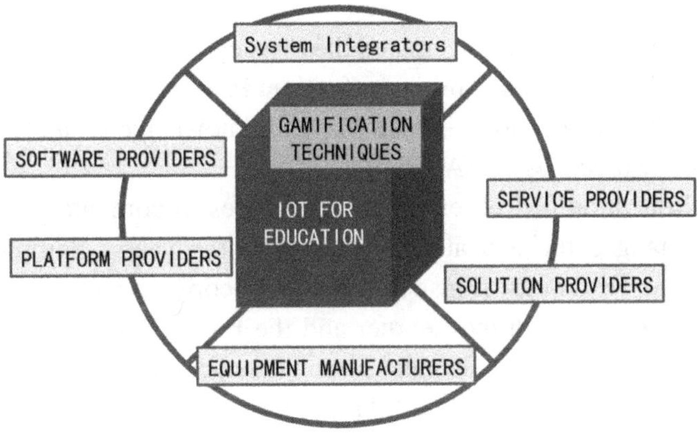

(2014) noted the impact on e-Learning operations due to application non-uniformity, diverse systems, and learning environment interoperability issues.

In general, the Online/Virtual Learning Environments directly depended on the availability of the internet for existence. The leveraging of technology related to computers and networks for E-Learning systems was not only innovative, but it offered a paradigm shift over the traditional education systems described in Book 1 (Chapter 17: Stricker et al., 2017). Besides, the high levels of engagement and participation by Learners and Educators was a testimony to the changing educational demands and requirements. This development opened opportunities centered around knowledge share, collaboration and contribution for participants to acquire and develop education and life-long skills, (Bandara et al., (2014)). The bad news though was that developments in cybercrime were occurring in parallel with Information related to the Online/Virtual Learning Environments and their participants becoming sought after by evil hackers. The irony was the open systems approach which encouraged different inputs from collaborators to make a robust product was now its Achilles heel. The exposure to cyber threats of confidential, protected or personal information was a rising trend, (Bandara et al., (2014)).

Bandara et al. (2014), highlighted some items which impacted the goal of building digital trust in the Online/Virtual Learning Environments. The concept of BYOD (Bring Your Device) was being implemented enthusiastically due to the low connectivity cost to education systems and the ability to study anywhere anytime. Despite the guidelines afforded by the 1998 Data Provision Act about meaningful ways to handle information, the non-ownership of the devices by the data controller meant own gadgets such as smartphones or tablets were more likely to be compromised. The main threats identified by Bandara et al. (2014), were:

- Malware, viruses and social media
- Virtualized environments have increased risks due to more users
- The non-secure practices of users, especially those with multiple devices

The security threats to Online/Virtual Learning Environments described by Bandara et al., (2014) ranged from integrity and confidentiality attacks to authentication and system availability. Amazingly, these threats were almost like those discovered over four decades earlier in the Ware (1970) report.

Protecting Student Privacy: Best Approaches

The United States Department of Education created the Privacy Technical Assistance Center (PTAC) in 2010 to focus mainly on upholding student privacy, (Student Privacy, 2019). This development is known as a "one-stop" resource for the education industry to gain knowledge related to student data privacy, confidentiality, and security practices, (PTAC, 2014).

The Department of Education had observed how advances in computer technology and telecommunications strikingly changed the education system over the years. Computers, scanner devices, and networks now replaced Textbooks, filmstrips, and photocopying methods. The typical classroom required the physical presence of both the Learner and the Educator but reestablished in the form of virtual interactive forums that offered on-demand personalized content to enhance the learning process by encouraging participation. Compared to the 'old' systems, the online environment allowed fast dissemination of information to Learners as well as the ability to customize learning solutions for students, (PTAC, 2014). The advantages that technology was bringing to the education arena such as information sharing, web-hosting and the increased surface area of education content various devices triggered the Department of Education's 'red flags.' The creation of PTAC was to counter the cyber threats especially those impacting student privacies, and to offer guidelines and best practices to include when evaluating Online/Virtual Learning Environments, (PTAC, 2014).

PTAC (2014) defined online educational as those services that Learners use to access class content, to view their learning progress and grades, to watch video lessons, to give feedback on class activities, or to complete homework deliverables such as discussions, assignments or quizzes. The privacy and security focus was on software and applications for computers and mobile devices as well as third-party applications provided to schools and learning institutions. The four main questions that PTAC attempts to answer are described next.

Question 1: Does FERPA Protect Student Information Used in Online Educational Services?

PTAC (2014) discovered that because of diversity in online/virtual educational environments it was almost impossible to offer an exact response to the question but relied on stakeholders to follow the general guidelines and make specific decisions on a case-by-case basis.

FERPA, (The Family Educational Rights and Privacy Act), sought to protect personally identifiable information (PII) of Learners from their education records from unauthorized access and disclosure. Education records defined as documentation:

- Related to a Learner.
- The maintenance accomplished by an institution, educational agency or a proxy on behalf of institution or agency.

Question 2: What Are the FERPA Requirements When PII From Learners' Education Records Get Disclosed to a Provider?

Like the response approach recommended for Question 1, the diversity of Online/Virtual Learning Environments required the case-by-case approach, PTAC (2014). The general guideline prohibited a school or district from sharing Learner PII with a provider without written consent from parents or eligible Learners 18 years of age or older. The two common exceptions to this rule were the Directory Information Exception and the FERPA School Official Exception. The FERPA School Official Exception was found to appeal more to the needs of Online/Virtual Learning Environments offered by schools and districts.

Question 3: Does the Protection of Pupil Rights Amendment (PPRA) and FERPA Restrict What Providers Can Do With Received Learner Information?

The general response in terms of FERPA was that any Learner PII information supplied to the provider via the FERPA School Official Exception was to be used only for the specific disclosed purpose. Also, the school or district had direct control over how the provider used and maintained the PII. This fact meant the provider could not use the information for other activities such as marketing new products to Learners or selling the PII to other parties.

Like FERPA, the Protection of Pupil Rights Amendment (PPRA) governed what providers could do with Learner information. PPRA applied to K-12 institutions, and though it did not restrict the use of data collected from college students, it did limit the use of collected Learner information while still in high school even after graduation. PPRA required that:

- The School districts had to, with exceptions, directly inform parents of Learners whose information was collected and used in activities ranging from disclosure, to selling the data, to marketing, as well as offer the parents the opt-out option.
- The School districts had to consult with parents when developing and adopting policies.

Question 4: Which Best Practices Protect Learner Privacy When Using Online/Virtual Learning Environment Services?

The best practices approach related to privacy, transparency, and security and recommended by the US Department of Education when implementing either FERPA or PPRA required Schools and districts to:

- Also consider the impact of other laws related to local, tribal, state and federal requirements which affected information sharing with providers, aside from FERPA and PPRA. For example, for children under age 13, Children's Online Privacy and Protection Act (COPPA) had to be considered. COPPA covered activities where commercial Web sites and online services had collected personal information from children after obtaining verifiable parental consent. In limited circumstances, COPPA granted permission to Schools and districts to exercise consent on behalf of parents.
- Be up to date with online/virtual learning environment services available to them from providers. The advantages of a master list of updated services on offer would assist educational authorities in collaboration, and consultation activities with parents to ensure useful products for Learners.

- Have clear processes in place which considered policies and procedures required for the evaluation and approval of educational services before implementation in the Online/Virtual Learning Environments. The clarity needed applied to all stakeholders and included formal contracts and Click-Wrap agreements. The latter method, akin to signing a contract, used "Click-Wrap" software acquired by the end-user (School/District) simply clicking "accept" to the provider's Terms of Service (TOS).
- Using written or legal agreement always when possible assisted Schools and Districts to enforce and maintain the" direct control" requirement with the provider.

The discussion above informs on some of the important input required by system designers to create Online/Virtual Learning Environments that comply with regulations in terms of structure and administration. The next section reviews the current state of cybersecurity within the last five years, related to Online/Virtual Learning Environments and what it means for the identities of the self.

THE CURRENT STATE OF LEARNER AND EDUCATOR ROLES AND CYBERSECURITY FOR ONLINE/VIRTUAL LEARNING ENVIRONMENTS

In the ever-evolving world of technology, the emphasis has shifted toward the individual, with services and products being customized to suit the needs of a person. We saw in the CES 2019 summary whether it was from the introduction of 5G technology, the use of AI or adoption of Wearables, the focus is on how individuals can leverage technology to improve their experiences. Exploration occurs in this paradigm shift in the Online/Virtual Learning Environments.

Xu, Li, Sun, Yang, Yu, Manogaran, Mastorakis, and Mavromoustakis (2019) discussed the use of 5G when implementing a smart online/virtual learning and teaching platform. An operation model based on four initiatives (Government/Education Authority-led, Educational Institutes, Educators, Learners), was adopted when creating the online teaching platform. The high 5G network data transmission rates, the increased number of connected devices and the reduced time delay were crucial components to the success of this teaching approach, (Xu et al., (2019).

Self-Analysis Technology (SAT)

Self-Analysis Technology, (SAT), in this context, would be defined as a participant using a feedback system based on technology and sensors to gather information about themselves to make informed decisions mainly related to education. Self-Analysis Technology models which need formulation for Learners and Educators to actively participate in all aspects of their personal, professional and social development. Next, an integrated educational system concept informs on its main features, and how some of the functionality described could be leveraged for SAT.

Reigeluth, Aslan, Chen, Dutta, Huh, Lee, Lin, Lu, Min, Tan, S. Watson, and W. Watson (2015) highlighted the Personalized Integrated Educational System, (PIES) concept which utilizes technology for education solutions centered around the Learner. The resourceful use of technology created a Learner-centered teaching approach concept that differed significantly from the traditional teacher-centered method. Four significant functions were identified and all related to advancing the abilities of the Learner. These were Recordkeeping, Planning, Instruction, and Assessment. The secondary duties ranged from administration and improvement of PIES to communication and collaboration techniques.

Record Keeping Function of PIES

This function focused on three inventory records governing a Learner's standards, personal attainments, and personal characteristics, (Reigeluth et al., (2015)):

- **Learner's Standards Inventory**: This consisted of all the achievements, (academic and non-academic), a Learner must or could attain.
- **Learner's Attainment Inventory**: This included all attainments and related learning analytics each Learner had obtained.
- **Learners Personal Characteristics Inventory**: This comprised of the Learner's characteristics relevant to their learning. The PIES instruction assessment functions automatically collected these characteristics ranging from career goals, interests, special needs, learning styles, major life events, etc., and determined which approach was useful for each Learner. A similar proposal in terms of security and privacy allowed the Learner to control access to this information.

Planning Function of PIES

The PIES planning function integrated aspects of learning and allowed Educators/teachers/facilitators to customize their knowledge sharing approach toward each Learner and learning space. Additional advantages included collaboration techniques between Learners and Educators, tools available to gauge and address social, academic and emotional issues, learning plans with goals and how to attain them for the Learner. A Learner's advisory committee comprising the Learner, parents, mentors, facilitators, Educators, etc. could collaborate to decide on learning contracts, Learner career and long-term goals, Learner short-term goals, Leaner projects, teams, supporting roles, (Reigeluth et al., (2015)):

The Instruction Function of PIES

The instruction function promoted by PIES comprised Project and Scaffolding sub-functions, supported by an integrated database platform coordinating the project, coaching, and instructional sub-functions, (Reigeluth et al., (2015)):

- The Project sub-function characteristics involved connecting a Learner to appropriate projects; ensuring project environment (virtual or real) was available; allowed collaboration and offered conflict resolution skills; assisted Learners in managing project time and resources; and allow Educators to monitor progress.
- The Scaffolding sub-function always utilized the Just in Time (JIT) concept to provide Learners with customized mentoring and instruction at any location and. PIES promoted the use of Open Education Resources (OER) such as simulations, assessments, textbooks, research publications, and visual content. Aside from the lower costs of these educational materials which were typically license free, OERs could be available as apps to use on a variety of connected devices.

The Assessment Function of PIES

The assessment function of PIES assessed not only the Learner but also the similar educational activities. Accurately, the sub-functions assessed both project performance and instructional modules learning outcomes. PIES also allowed non-teachers such as parents, community members, and peers to take part in determining non-academic issues related to emotional, social, and character development, collaboration and communication skills; work ethic, and metacognitive skills.

The Secondary Functions of PIES

The critical role played by the Secondary functions of PIES was to support the four primary features and the Learners and focused on communication and collaboration, as well as administration and improvement of PIES, (Reigeluth et al., (2015)):

- **Communication and Collaboration as Secondary Functions of PIES**: The service supported blended or virtual learning environments by advocating effective communication and collaborative tools, like discussion forums during projects. The channels of communication such as phone calls, emails, social networking, and video conferencing, ensured users created and maintained their contact lists, especially for future collaborations. Leveraging the cloud computing technologies meant customizable communication between Learners, parents, Educators, peers, community members, etc.
- **Administration and Improvement as Secondary Functions of PIES**: The PIES Administration function revolved around access management, general Learner data, and educational institute personnel data:

Advantages of the PIES System Architecture Concept

The concept of the PIES system architecture offered numerous advantages, mainly related to leveraging technology innovations as the foundation building block, with this future-proofing this proposed paradigm shift in Online/Virtual Learning Environments. This Cloud-based system housed within PIES servers offered access to Learners, parents, Educators and other authorized people. Databases related to Education standards, Learner profiles, teammate selections, projects, and instructional modules connected the primary and secondary functions. Interoperability with Open Education Resources (OERs) systems and other external databases allowed modularity and customization of educational materials, (Reigeluth et al., (2015)).

Self-Analysis Technology, (SAT), would benefit from implementing various aspects of the PIES system, including functions involving improvement. More significant and active Learner and Educator participation and collaboration would constitute part of the desired results. Figure 6 illustrates the high-level implementation of the SAT concept which leverages the advantages described by the PIES approach. The other goals would include the ability to apply cybersecurity solutions, (discussed in the next section), to these systems.

Figure 6. SAT concept implementation leveraging the PIES Concept

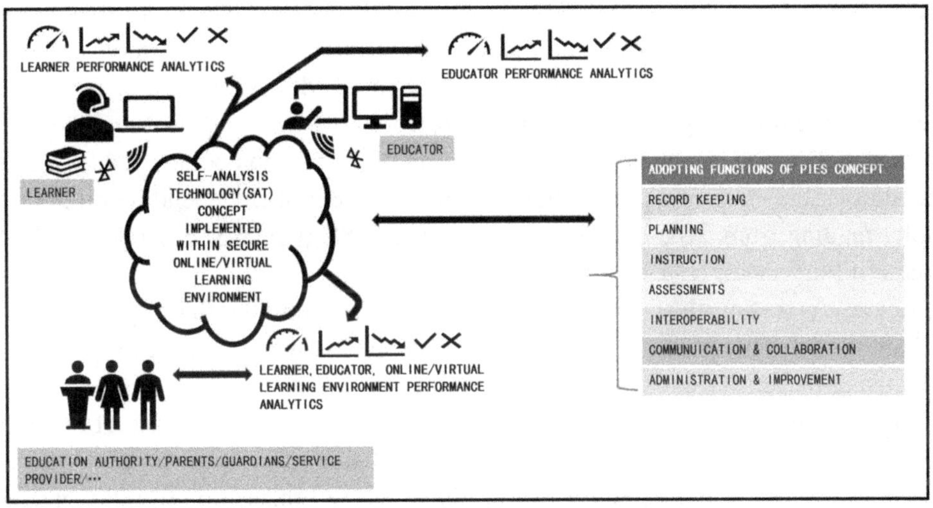

ADDITIONAL CYBERSECURITY CASE STUDIES FOCUSING ON ONLINE/VIRTUAL LEARNING ENVIRONMENTS

Case Study 1: Attack Tree Simulations

Mihai and Giurea (2016) discussed the need to make online/virtual environments safer by using techniques related to prevention, detection and responding to cyber-attacks. Mihai et al. (2016) concluded that compromised online/virtual learning environment platform security was due to strikes, (such as malware infections, redirections to infected websites, phishing, smapping, etc.)

The Attack Tree Overview

The Attack Tree simulator demonstrated the impact of different cyber-attacks on Online/Virtual Learning Environments. The experiments comprised both real and simulated attacks, and the results offered insight into creating countermeasure strategies. This method allowed in depth of attack paths to generate website intrusion scenarios, (Mihai et al., (2016)).

The Attack Tree was made up of the root or central node and as well as multiple nodes on various levels. The cyber-attack process involved the root node and the action of traversing each edge to the internal node structure of the Attack Tree. There were internal nodes, (seven stages of the Cyber Kill Chain), of the Attack Tree and outer edges connecting the leaf nodes, (optional attack vectors):

- Surveillance (Reconnaissance), was the first stage of the attack tree representing the first phase of the intrusion Kill Chain model. This phase allowed attackers to discover vulnerabilities in the online/virtual Learning environment platform's security. The cybercriminals could try to seek vulnerabilities in associated platforms and servers, attempt to obtain administrative credentials by identifying user access rights via methods like social engineering attacks on their accounts.

- Weaponization was the second stage of the attack tree representing the second phase of the intrusion Kill Chain model. The weaknesses identified in the first phase could further be exploited by attackers who could identify tools or software to use the flaws. Sources of tools or weapons could range from purchasing from the Dark Web or could be self-developed.
- Delivery was the third stage of the attack tree representing the third phase of the intrusion Kill Chain model. This phase addressed the distribution of the weapon configured by the attackers in the second phase. Different types of attacks would be undertaken depending on the weapon tool available, ranging from SQL injection, Brute Force, XSS (Cross-Site Scripting), CSRF (Cross Site Request Forgery) or (D)DoS attacks.
- Exploitation was the fourth stage of the attack tree representing the fourth phase of the intrusion Kill Chain model. This phase illustrated the exploitation of vulnerabilities identified in the first stage by using the attacks launched in the third stage.
- Installation was the fifth stage of the attack tree representing the fifth phase of the intrusion Kill Chain model. The step described the attackers' installation of harmful scripts or iFrames to the online/virtual learning environment platform. The impact of this action resulted in dangerous activities such as infecting website users.
- Command and Control was the sixth stage of the attack tree representing the sixth phase of the intrusion Kill Chain model. The scene described the ability of the attackers to access and control the online/virtual learning environment platform, via administration or database portals.
- Action on the Target was the seventh stage of the attack tree representing the seventh phase of the intrusion Kill Chain model. At this stage, the vulnerable system allowed the attackers to achieve their objectives including infecting other systems, introducing malware or redirecting to malicious sites via clickjacking. The attacker objectives could also include stealing database information, as well as modifying data integrity and decreasing availability to the platform.

Possible Remedies for Managing Online/Virtual Learning Environment Platform Security

Mihai et al. (2016) proposed solutions for cyber threats on online/virtual learning environment platforms channeled into three processes involving the detection of intrusions, malware infections, and suspicious activity monitoring. Mihai et al. (2016) recommended an integrated cyber-threat prevention approach using a combination of the tools or solutions:

1. The use of IDS (Intrusion Detection System). A device/application that monitors the system for malicious activities as well as scan files and their content for integrity.
2. Use of cryptography and hash functions like SHA2 (Secure Hash Algorithm 2), to monitor file integrity
3. The method of Web Application Firewall (WAF) to restrict and record access attempts and using platform security administration techniques like changing default locations and access credentials to avoid brute force attacks.
4. The Investigation of suspicious files for malware by uploading them to Virustotal.com, a platform with more than 60 anti-malware scanners with the ability to scan a file or a URL.
5. The use of Sucuri.net platform to detect suspicious activities like suspicious redirections, by scanning and displaying links, iFrames or the scripts. The Webmaster toolkit extracts and analyzes

hyperlinks and website scripts and determines suspicious redirections from the online/virtual learning environment platform.

6. Detecting spamming or phishing e-mails by checking if the affected domain marked in the spam lists or blacklists. Using the blacklistalert.org website for spam list domain verification by the tool checking in an extensive database list of compromised areas used in generating spamming and phishing attacks.
7. To counter the use of cookies employed to monitor visitors to a compromised website, the use of the Cookie-Checker.com tool informs of the types of cookies associated with the site.
8. Monitoring DDOS (Distributed Denial of Service) attacks using the tool monitor.us

Case Study 2: Online/Virtual Learning Environments as a Component of National Cybersecurity

Udroiu (2017) described the critical aspects of the Cybersecurity of online/virtual learning environment platforms and how they could impact the security of a nation. The low security that affected several Online/Virtual Learning Environments made them prone to cyber-attacks from both state and non-state actors. These environments were used as gateways for lethal attacks on other more essential networks such as local and state government, institutions, infrastructure, utilities, the federal government, and military systems, (Udroiu, 2017).

Udroiu (2017) recommended some possible approaches to deal with security in online/virtual educational systems. It was critical for both private and public entities involved with online/virtual learning systems to collaborate on the best security approach to take. The private organizations, overall, were the service providers for the educational systems, while the public, including institutions like universities as well as individuals, were generally the users and consumers of the learning services. Two ways were identified to address the security challenges:

1. Firstly, in terms of policies and actions to protect all aspects of the connected network (including software, hardware, data, stored or transmitted information) from unauthorized access and use.
2. Secondly, in the form of a feedback process of continuous monitoring and evaluation of the policies and actions, keeping up with the ever-changing threats.

Udroiu (2017) described a potential cyber-attack scenario on an online/virtual learning environment platform, such as a company's ERP (Enterprise Resource Planning) system with training modules used to train employees. The scenario involved an employee accessing the ERP modules remotely from their home, and the steps were:

1. The employee accessed a training module via their smartphone or tablet or computer to conduct their training remotely, i.e., from home.
2. Their smartphone or tablet or computer previously infected with malware that triggered when it detected specific IP addresses.
3. The only access control available to access the training modules was the employee's username and password.
4. The activated malware multiplied and infected the company's ERP system or was able to steal access credentials and information when the employee connected to the training modules.

5. The malware allowed the attacker to penetrate and access the company's information system, including access to human resources and personnel data assets.

The reasons Udroiu (2017) gave for the success of this attack were related to possible vulnerabilities of the ERP information system such as:

1. Potential security deficiencies in the planning of the training modules typically located within the human resources management system. This weakness would allow compromise of the ERP and other infrastructure.
2. Non-existent, or ineffective, employee training in information security.
3. Ineffective IT department and company enforcement of security policies and rules in terms of behavior on company intranet as they would typically focus on external attacks instead.
4. Company deficiencies, in terms of the management of enterprise information security and protection.

Udroiu (2017) concluded that despite the complexity of cybersecurity challenges, it was the obligation of all the stakeholders in online/virtual educational learning systems to identify and develop effective countermeasure solutions.

Case Study 3: Protecting Learner Privacy in MOOCs and Virtual Education Environments

Zeide and Nissenbaum (2018) expanded on the need to protect Learner privacy in Massive Open Online Courses (MOOCs) and Virtual Education environments. The study highlighted trends in Online/Virtual Learning Environments that offered to teach experiences and credentials directly to users, but in some cases, independent providers were also able to collect information directly from Learners without any form of mediation. This practice exposed Learners to security vulnerabilities as a result of providers not being compliant with institutional authority regulations.

Zeide et al. (2018) described the functionalities offered by Online/Virtual Learning Environments compared to the traditional institutes of education. The use and manipulation of data was the foundation utilized by online/virtual learning environment providers to convey instruction, allow Learner discussion and collaboration, management of assessment tools, and bestow certifications and credentials. Zeide et al. (2018) noted with alarm how the providers' adoption of commercial non-effective privacy norms into their learning systems was a danger to this form of educational endeavor. To better perceive and evaluate information practices of Online/Virtual Learning Environments. Zeide et al. (2018) used the contextual integrity (CI) framework. Benthall, Gürses, and Nissenbaum (2017) discussed privacy and context in computing and elaborated that CI brought forward three concepts related to privacy:

- Contexts.
- Contextual informational (privacy) norms.
- Contextual ends, purposes, and values.

Contextual Integrity (CI) defined privacy as the proper movement of information flow as stated by the norms specific to social contexts or spheres, (Benthall et al., (2017)).

Zeide et al. (2018) gave an account of the rise of commercial independent online/virtual learning providers and educational platforms when discussing Learner privacy. A comparison between the traditional schooling environment and the economic ecosystems revealed diverging approaches to the handling of educational information and data. While the former exhibited the traditional information practices and privacy norms based on agreed standards and regulation, the latter's commercially regulated entities did not strictly abide by rules related to proper educational data use, user confidentiality, consent, and access.

Zeide et al. (2018) summarized the data practices and regulation of Learner information in MOOCs and Online/Virtual Learning Environments to expose their relatively recent privacy standards. Zeide et al. (2018) observed that Learner data was treated as a commodity with value, due to the ability to sell it, and was without similar protections afforded to Learner records in traditional educational environments.

The features of information exchange in Online/Virtual Learning Environments comprised:

1. Subjects or Learners, individuals occupied with educational experiences.
2. The Actors or online/virtual learning environment providers.
3. The Contractors, typically third-party student information processors that ran facility operations supplied systems to manage data, provided e-textbooks and courses. The online/virtual learning environment providers reserved the right to share Learner information with subcontractors, business partners, affiliates, as well as marketers and product developers.
4. The Researchers comprised both internal to providers and external, that Learner information could be shared with to trigger innovation and improve end-user experiences. Other uses of the data ranged from the production of Learner metrics to ways to better understand Learner cognition, motivation, or language.
5. The Purchasers were online/virtual learning environment entities that bought and sold Learner information for uses ranging from creating customized advertising or marketing for Learners.
6. The Attributes referred to the field of information types online/virtual learning environment providers collected, demographic information, formal and informal Learner performance results.
7. The Entered information comprised Learner information users submitted to the platform, like discussion posts, assignments, quiz responses, and chat room interactions.
8. The Administrative and learning data was collected to authenticate Learner identity, track Learner attendance, progress, completion, and contribution. Other information gathered ranged from demographic data to prior experiences with Online/Virtual Learning Environments.
9. External data typically mined from other sources such as geolocation data from communication networks, or social media presence.
10. The Biometric information about Learners relied on sensor-based technologies in Wearables and the Internet of Things (IoT) to confirm accuracy when using remote proctoring applications. The products collected digital, audio, visual, and biometric (biometric signatures, head placement, sounds, eye movement, and facial recognition), data to verify Learners' identities and detect cheating behavior patterns.

Zeide et al. (2018) stated online/virtual learning environment providers needed to emulate their traditional education partners by similarly promoting measures that maintained or encouraged the values reinforced by Learner privacy norms. Besides, the role undertaken by online/virtual learning environment providers required acknowledgment of their responsibility toward Learner vulnerabilities related to pervasive scrutiny, regular assessment, and continued possession of data. This critical challenge would require detailed examination of the role online/virtual learning environment played, the data they had access to for teaching, assessments and Learner credentials. Zeide et al. (2018) concluded these issues would impact both Learners and learning environments, especially the private, non-accredited educational system types.

QUESTIONS ARISING ON HOW TO IMPLEMENT CYBERSECURITY IN THE ONLINE/VIRTUAL LEARNING ENVIRONMENT

The three studies discussed above, Mihai et al. (2016), Udroiu (2017), and Zeide et al. (2018) shed light on the safety and security requirements of Learners, Educators, and the Online/Virtual Learning Environments. The current challenges are related to Identity Management, Authentication, Authorization, and Accountability, (IAAA), of users and content in the online/virtual education systems. These problems will tend to evolve in tandem with technology and cyber-threat advances unless paradigm countermeasure solutions can be discovered and put in place. The five questions that the challenges raise and directed toward Learners, Educators and the Online/Virtual Learning Environments, include:

1. "Are you who you claim to be?"
2. "What unique authentication, authorization and accountability techniques need implementation?"
3. "Is this instance of the online/virtual learning environment I am accessing legitimate?"
4. "What integrity measures are in place to protect educational content, databases, etc. from fake information?"
5. "How is the data collected via the educational platforms and wearables handled and protected and who owns it?"

The guidelines described by PTAC (2014) when implementing either FERPA or PPRA are a starting point for creating compelling solutions dealing with IAAA. The following summaries depict additional research work which offer ideas on how to potentially respond to the five questions.

Toapanta, Gallegos, and Trejo (2016) described Identity Management as controlled access to resources by utilizing authentication, authorization and accounting schemes. Toapanta et al. (2016) developed an identity management model to assist mitigation of security risks and vulnerabilities to a national population database. Metz (1999) described the following:

- Authentication as involving the validation of the user's identity before granting network access. The unique characteristics attributed to the user such as their biometric data like iris scans or fingerprints or secret key parsed by the IAAA server and compared to user associated information in the database. A decisive match resulted in network access granted.
- Authorization stated the rights and services available to end user after granting network access. Authentication and authorization were typically conducted simultaneously in the IAAA environment.
- Accounting outlined the methods to collect data from the user used for processes related to billing and auditing of the services they consumed.

Babic, Kresic, and Kucel (2014) discussed the impact of 2.0 on e-learning and the challenges related to Learner privacy, responsibility, trust, and security. The study concluded that digital identity and online reputation management were essential factors to the Learners. Thakur and Gaikwad (2015) conducted a survey focusing on user Identity and Access Management systems and proposed the Federated Identity Management (FIM). The automated FIM process could be used to manage users across distributed systems.

Naik and Jenkins (2016) studied identity and access management (IAM) service, IDentity-as-a-Service (IDaaS) and proposed evaluation criteria for effective IAM standards for Mobile Cloud Computing (MCC). The requirements were:

1. The ability for extensive authentication and authorization.
2. The ability of user-friendly single sign-on capabilities.
3. The necessity to have a lightweight standard/protocol for mobile applications.
4. The features such as being platform independent, vendor-neutral and open standard.
5. The ability to be a scalable standard without impacting security, cost, and performance.
6. The ability to support web and native mobile apps.
7. The ability to support consumers and enterprise.
8. Permitting the immediate revocation of access when dealing with security threats.
9. Offering end user delegated authorization.
10. Exhibiting data integrity and confidentiality.
11. The ability to incorporate mobile standards.

Katsikogiannis, Mitropoulos, and Douligeris (2016) presented a model to manage the multilevel integration of identity, authentication, and authorization. The policy-based model processes included analyzing and integrating identity modules, allowed authentication and authorization, dealt with user roles and access control levels, and used rule validation techniques. Yang, Chen, Wang, and Cao (2014) advocated the use of security as a service to achieve a standardized and scalable architecture, to solve a series of security problems related to identity and access management in cloud computing environments. Moghaddam, Wieder, and Yahyapour (2017) evaluated a policy-based authentication plan via scientific performance, security and competitive analysis methods to examine the identity management in cloud-computing environments for reliability and efficiency. The policy-based schema mapped cloud users' permission requests with the stated policies of cloud-computing servers. Suguna, Anusia, Shalinie, and Deepti (2017) developed a secure identity management (SIDM) model to mitigate attacks in the consolidated identity management (CIDM) system. The proposal used methods to enhance identity privacy and strengthen authentication using a two-step process involving token validation and zero-knowledge proof (ZKP). Damon and Coetzee (2018) suggested an evaluation method to assist organizations in creating features for their identity and access assurance (IAA) component model. The aspects of the model's heat map included items related to identity federation, authentication and authorization mechanisms, as well as on security auditing and logging.

Raju, Boddepalli, Gampa, Yan, and Deogun (2017) proposed a privacy-increasing user identity management system utilizing blockchain technology. The system offered end-to-end management from user identification to usage billing with emphasis on anonymity and allowed network access using pseudonymous identities. Lin, He, Huang, Khan, and Choo (2018) designed a cryptographic membership authentication scheme that supported blockchain-based identity management systems (BIMS) and allowed the binding of a digital identity object to its real-world entity. The study proved the security capabilities of the transitively closed undirected graph authentication (TCUGA) scheme. Dunphy and Petitcolas (2018) described distributed ledger technology (DLT)-based identity management (IdM) which depended on the blockchain data structure. The work utilized a framework to evaluate the impact of using DLT schemes to enhance identity management processes. Othman and Callahan (2018) proposed Horcrux1 protocol which relied on decentralized identifiers (DIDs). The approach was based on IEEE 2410-2017 Biometric Open Protocol Standard (BOPS) and implemented the decentralized biometric credential storage option via blockchains using DIDs. Mikula and Jacobsen (2018) described the application of blockchain in identity and access management for electronic health records when using the hyper ledger fabric framework, (HFF).

Naik and Jenkins (2017) identified a solution to deal with the security challenges associated with transmitting and sharing sensitive information affecting user privacy and security over insecure channels. The proposed Federated Identity Management (FIdM) standard used to authenticate and authorize users across multiple organizations to obtain access to their networks and resources while mitigating security risk. The study assessed the following standards:

- Security Assertion Markup Language (SAML)
- Open Authentication (OAuth)
- OpenID Connect (OIDC)

Vo, Fuhrmann, and Fischer-Hellmann (2018) introduced Identity-as-a-Service (IDaaS) that gave users a federated identity to access multiple Cloud services while protecting their privacy. The method integrated purpose-based access control and attribute-based encryption with multi-authorities support to preserve user privacy and PII. Schanzenbach, Bramm, and Schütte (2018) presented 'reclaimID,' a model that allowed users to recover their digital identities via a secure attribute sharing scheme without using a centralized service provider. Y.Gao, Li, X., Li, Yun. Gao and Philip (2019) proposed Info-Trust, a multi-criteria trustworthiness calculation mechanism to assist validating information sources and mitigate incidents related to cyber fraud. Trust factors related to identity, behavior, relation, and feedback were the main constituents in this trustworthiness evaluation model. The results indicated the accuracy of this method when used to identify the trustworthiness of information from network sources.

It is evident from the literature reviewed that the nature and rate of technology evolution unleashes a slew of developments that tend to benefit the end user, but which simultaneously trigger similar challenges related to privacy and security. The highlighted studies represent a minute snapshot of the overall attempt to ensure safety, especially in the Online/Virtual Learning Environments. The methods outlined could be leveraged in solutions which also attempt to answer the five questions mentioned above.

RECOMMENDATIONS AND POTENTIAL FUTURE SOLUTIONS: PUTTING IT ALTOGETHER

Figure 7 offers a high-level view of how a secure learning environment could leverage technology. This study proposes the use of the Self-Analysis Technology concept in a secure environment, as one of the main components of solutions to challenges identified.

This chapter built on the first edition chapter 'Future Identities of The Self Among Learners Across Physical and Virtual Spaces'. The focus is on how the Learner could approach the new technology-centric

Figure 7. A proposed secure learning environment leveraging technology

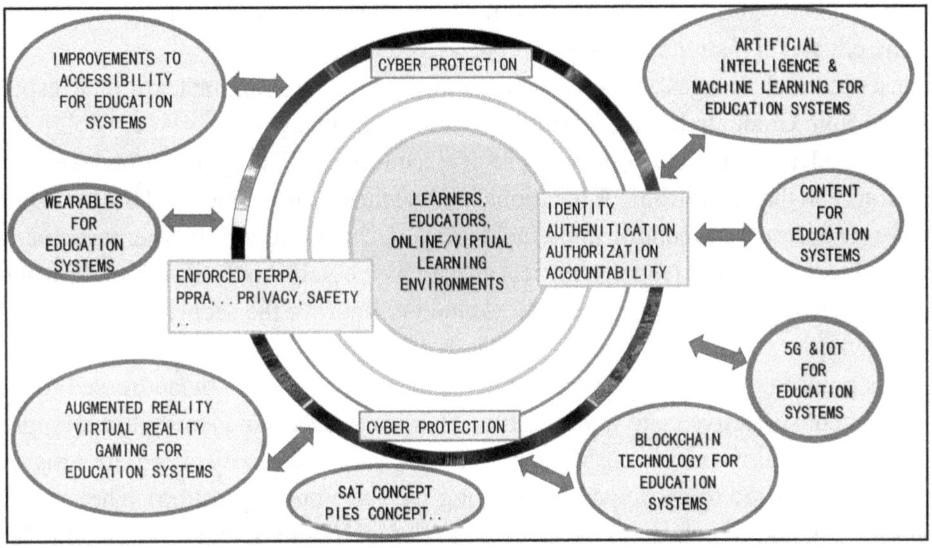

learning environments as an active participant and contributor without worrying about online safety. Trends related to Artificial Intelligence and Data Analytics will continue to play a significant role in current and future online or Virtual teaching. These learning methods will require timely (real-time) and critical input from the Learners to ensure the systems were in a constant state of improvement and compliance with the relevant educational standards. Cybersecurity will persist impacting these learning systems running on network environments built in the Cloud or which may be available over newer technologies such as 5G, Fifth Generation Fixed and Mobile Technology networks. Effective security countermeasures in virtual education will require participant awareness of the role they must play to mitigate and even in some cases eliminate these challenges including identity authentication of participants, measurement of learning metrics and authentication, authorization and accountability related to learning resources.

The 'big picture' view on Cybersecurity looks for the weakest link in a system or network and finds ways to prevent attacks. The creators, participants and the virtual learning environments need similar scrutiny to instill correct protections. Discussions and debates on online user privacy in response to the need to ensure current laws keep up with the changes in online interaction due to technology evolutions. Authentication will play an essential role in all aspects of communication. What measures need to be put in place to ensure the correct participant is responding as well as to provide access to accurate content?

As data becomes an ever-valuable 'commodity' the approach used in handling or processing, storing and accessing will be important. Educational database administrators will need to ensure availability, and the need to maintain data Integrity. Methods of detecting illegal or fraudulent activities in virtual education environments will be needed to comply with standards. Events such as 'hack-a-thons' where activities related to security like penetration and testing of educational systems will be required periodically. This approach is like the round the clock security afforded to Financial, Federal institutions or big companies. Remote individuals or communities on a local or global scale would tend to be impacted severely by unauthorized intrusions into their online education systems. The question, "how do they prove who they are?" comes to light among other things. The use of AI techniques such as in the search engines from Google, or virtual assistants Siri from Apple and Cortana from Microsoft has triggered projects which will bring about the use of bots that could masquerade as students or Educators. How can this phenomenon be detected and prevented from compromising virtual learning environments? How can legal online education institutes be differentiated from illegal ones?

The responses to the challenges would need to cater to all aspects of online learning irrespective of the level, i.e., K1 through Graduate Higher learning, as well as ensuring there is Accessibility for all types of scenarios and students. AI, Data Analytics and IOT (Internet of Things) will be leveraged to create practical solutions and that the relevant Educational and Security Authorities and System Designers will be able to assess, approve and monitor implementations. Critical too will be the participants, Learner and Educator and their roles and responsibilities, as well as the Self-Analysis Technology models. This study evaluated at the higher-level the use of Blockchain to improve the security aspects of virtual education environments.

Observations point to the apparent enormity of the tasks that need to be addressed to make online learning environments effective, safe and reliable. This study recommends a phased approach when assessing and implementing priorities. Most importantly as in any project undertaking, the correct stakeholders must be invited to participate, (including Learners and Educators). The evaluation of the proposed solutions should be scheduled so that the 'easier' solutions such as 'Awareness Training' for participants can implement first. These can be followed by the more complex ones which may involve equipment and network designers and the relevant regulatory bodies. An essential requirement is that the Federal or State Educational Authority maintain overall control of the whole project implementation to ensure fair participation and accountability.

ACKNOWLEDGMENT

This study would like to acknowledge the authors from Parker University Computer Information Systems (CIS) department, Online Education department and General Education department for their valuable contributions.

This research received no specific grant from any funding agency in the public, commercial, or not-for-profit sectors.

REFERENCES

Babic, S., Kresic, M., & Kucel, K. (2014, May). E-Education 2.0: Students' digital identity and online learning activities. In *Information and Communication Technology, Electronics and Microelectronics (MIPRO), 2014 37th International Convention on* (pp. 756-761). IEEE.

Bandara, I., Ioras, F., & Maher, K. (2014, November). Cybersecurity concerns in e-learning education. *Proceedings of ICERI2014 Conference.*

Benthall, S., Gürses, S., & Nissenbaum, H. (2017). *Contextual integrity through the lens of computer science.* Now Publishers Incorporated. doi:10.1561/3300000016

CES. (2019, January). *Consumer Electronics Show Las Vegas Jan 8 – Jan 11.* Retrieved from https://www.ces.tech/About-CES.aspx

Chen, G., Xu, B., Lu, M., & Chen, N. S. (2018). Exploring blockchain technology and its potential applications for education. *Smart Learning Environments*, *5*(1), 1. doi:10.118640561-017-0050-x

Cybersecurity, G. (2014). *The Global Cybersecurity Market 2014-2024*. Retrieved from https://www.globaldata.com/store/report/gd-df0053sr--the-global-cybersecurity-market-2014-2024/

Damon, F., & Coetzee, M. (2018, August). Evaluation of Identity and Access Assurance Component Model Dimensions. In *The 2018 International Conference on Advances in Big Data, Computing and Data Communication Systems (icABCD)* (pp. 1-6). IEEE. 10.1109/ICABCD.2018.8465126

Devices, C. (2016). *Popular Internet of Things Forecast of 50 Billion Devices by 2020 Is Outdated*. Retrieved from https://spectrum.ieee.org/tech-talk/telecom/internet/popular-internet-of-things-forecast-of-50-billion-devices-by-2020-is-outdated

Dunphy, P., & Petitcolas, F. A. (2018). *A first look at identity management schemes on the blockchain*. arXiv preprint arXiv:1801.03294

Gao, Y., Li, X., Li, J., Gao, Y., & Philip, S. Y. (2019). Info-Trust: A Multi-Criteria and Adaptive Trustworthiness Calculation Mechanism for Information Sources. *IEEE Access: Practical Innovations, Open Solutions*.

Global IoT Education. (2019). *Global IoT in Education Markets, 2018-2023*. Retrieved from https://globenewswire.com/news-release/2019/01/23/1704060/0/en/Global-IoT-in-Education-Markets-2018-2023-Potential-Growth-Opportunities-for-System-Integrators-Declining-Cost-of-Connectivity-and-Connected-Devices.html

Katsikogiannis, G., Mitropoulos, S., & Douligeris, C. (2016, December). An Identity and Access Management approach for SOA. In *Signal Processing and Information Technology (ISSPIT), 2016 IEEE International Symposium on* (pp. 126-131). IEEE. 10.1109/ISSPIT.2016.7886021

5G. launch: The Top Countries Most Likely to Launch 5G First – SDXCentral. (2018). Retrieved from https://www.sdxcentral.com/5g/definitions/5g-network-countries/

Lin, C., He, D., Huang, X., Khan, M. K., & Choo, K. K. R. (2018). A New Transitively Closed Undirected Graph Authentication Scheme for Blockchain-Based Identity Management Systems. *IEEE Access: Practical Innovations, Open Solutions*, *6*, 28203–28212. doi:10.1109/ACCESS.2018.2837650

Metz, C. (1999). AAA protocols: Authentication, authorization, and accounting for the Internet. *IEEE Internet Computing*, *3*(6), 75–79. doi:10.1109/4236.807015

Mihai, I. C., & Giurea, L. (2016). Management of eLearning platforms security. In *The International Scientific Conference eLearning and Software for Education* (*Vol. 1*, p. 422). "Carol I" National Defence University.

Mikula, T., & Jacobsen, R. H. (2018, August). Identity and Access Management with Blockchain in Electronic Healthcare Records. In *2018 21st Euromicro Conference on Digital System Design (DSD)* (pp. 699-706). IEEE. 10.1109/DSD.2018.00008

Moghaddam, F. F., Wieder, P., & Yahyapour, R. (2017, November). A policy-based identity management schema for managing accesses in clouds. In *Network of the Future (NOF), 2017 8th International Conference on the* (pp. 91-98). IEEE. 10.1109/NOF.2017.8251226

MWC19: Mobile World Congress. (2019, February). Retrieved from https://www.mwcbarcelona.com/

Naik, N., & Jenkins, P. (2016, March). A secure mobile cloud identity: Criteria for effective identity and access management standards. In *Mobile Cloud Computing, Services, and Engineering (MobileCloud), 2016 4th IEEE International Conference on* (pp. 89-90). IEEE.

Naik, N., & Jenkins, P. (2017, May). Securing digital identities in the cloud by selecting apposite federated identity management from saml, oauth and openid connect. In *Research Challenges in Information Science (RCIS), 2017 11th International Conference on* (pp. 163-174). IEEE. 10.1109/RCIS.2017.7956534

Othman, A., & Callahan, J. (2018, July). The Horcrux protocol: a method for decentralized biometric-based self-sovereign identity. In *2018 International Joint Conference on Neural Networks (IJCNN)* (pp. 1-7). IEEE. 10.1109/IJCNN.2018.8489316

Privacy Technical Assistance Center (PTAC). (2014). *Protecting Student Privacy While Using Online Educational Services: Requirements and Best Practices*. Retrieved from https://nces.ed.gov/programs/PTAC/

Quero, J. M., Perdigones, F., & Aracil, C. (2018). Microfabrication technologies used for creating smart devices for industrial applications. In Smart Sensors and MEMs (2nd ed.; pp. 291-311). Academic Press. doi:10.1016/B978-0-08-102055-5.00011-5

Raju, S., Boddepalli, S., Gampa, S., Yan, Q., & Deogun, J. S. (2017, May). Identity management using blockchain for cognitive cellular networks. In *Communications (ICC), 2017 IEEE International Conference on* (pp. 1-6). IEEE. 10.1109/ICC.2017.7996830

Reigeluth, C. M., Aslan, S., Chen, Z., Dutta, P., Huh, Y., Lee, D., ... Watson, S. L. (2015). Personalized integrated educational system: Technology functions for the Learner-centered paradigm of education. *Journal of Educational Computing Research*, *53*(3), 459–496. doi:10.1177/0735633115603998

Sabillon, R., Cano, J., Cavaller, V., & Serra, J. (2016). Cybercrime and cybercriminals: a comprehensive study. *International Journal of Computer Networks and Communications Security, 4*(6), 165.

Schanzenbach, M., Bramm, G., & Schütte, J. (2018). *reclaimID: Secure, Self-Sovereign Identities using Name Systems and Attribute-Based Encryption*. arXiv preprint arXiv:1805.06253

Six Million Dollar Man (SMDM): NBC Episodes. (1973). Retrieved from https://www.nbc.com/the-six-million-dollar-man

Stricker, A., Calongne, C., Truman, B., & Arenas, F. (Eds.). (2017). *Integrating an Awareness of Selfhood and Society Into Virtual Learning*. IGI Global. doi:10.4018/978-1-5225-2182-2

Student Privacy. (2019). *Protecting Student Privacy*. Retrieved from https://studentprivacy.ed.gov/about-us

Studies, H. (2019). *WPI Center for Holographic Studies & Laser micro-mechatronics*. Retrieved from http://chslt.wpi.edu/

Suguna, M., Anusia, R., Shalinie, S. M., & Deepti, S. (2017, March). Secure identity management in mobile cloud computing. In *Nextgen Electronic Technologies: Silicon to Software (ICNETS2), 2017 International Conference on* (pp. 42-45). IEEE. 10.1109/ICNETS2.2017.8067894

Thakur, M. A., & Gaikwad, R. (2015, January). User identity and Access Management trends in IT infrastructure-an overview. In *Pervasive Computing (ICPC), 2015 International Conference on* (pp. 1-4). IEEE. 10.1109/PERVASIVE.2015.7086972

Toapanta, S. M. T., Gallegos, L. E. M., & Trejo, J. A. O. (2016, September). Analysis to define management of identities access control of security processes for the registration civil from Ecuador. In *Smart Cities Conference (ISC2), 2016 IEEE International* (pp. 1-4). IEEE. 10.1109/ISC2.2016.7580753

Udroiu, M. (2017). The cybersecurity of e-learning platforms. In *The International Scientific Conference eLearning and Software for Education* (*Vol. 3*, p. 374). "Carol I" National Defence University.

Vo, T. H., Fuhrmann, W., & Fischer-Hellmann, K. P. (2018, February). Privacy-preserving user identity in Identity-as-a-Service. In *2018 21st Conference on Innovation in Clouds, Internet and Networks and Workshops (ICIN)* (pp. 1-8). IEEE. 10.1109/ICIN.2018.8401613

Ware, W. H. (1970). *Security controls for computer systems. Report of defense science task force on computer security (No. RAND/R-609-1)*. Rand Corp.

Wark, M. (2006). Hackers. *Theory, Culture & Society*, *23*(2-3), 320–322. doi:10.1177/026327640602300242

Xu, X., Li, D., Sun, M., Yang, S., Yu, S. J., Manogaran, G., ... Mavromoustakis, C. X. (2019). Research on Key Technologies of Smart Campus Teaching Platform Based on 5G Network. *IEEE Access*.

Yang, G. Z. (Ed.). (2018). *Implantable Sensors and Systems: From Theory to Practice*. Springer. doi:10.1007/978-3-319-69748-2

Yang, Y., Chen, X., Wang, G., & Cao, L. (2014, December). An Identity and Access Management Architecture in Cloud. In *Computational Intelligence and Design (ISCID), 2014 Seventh International Symposium on* (Vol. 2, pp. 200-203). IEEE. 10.1109/ISCID.2014.221

Zeide, E., & Nissenbaum, H. (2018). Learner Privacy in MOOCs and Virtual Education. *Theory and Research in Education*, *16*(3), 280–307. doi:10.1177/1477878518815340

KEY TERMS AND DEFINITIONS

5G: Fifth generation telecommunication technology deployments for fixed and mobile networks.

Accountability: This process outlines the methods to collect data from the user used for processes related to billing and auditing of the services they consumed.

AI: Artificial intelligence is intelligence demonstrated by machines in computer science.

Authentication: This process involves the validation of the user's identity before granting network access. The unique characteristics attributed to the user such as their biometric data like iris scans or fingerprints or secret key parsed by the IAAA server and compared to user associated information in the database.

Authorization: States the rights and services available to an end user after being granted network access.

Educator: The individual carrying out the functions associated with a teacher or lecturer.

Environments: The online and virtual spaces were teaching and learning occur.

IOT: Internet of things, a system of interconnected computing devices, machines, people, animals transferring data in some cases directly between themselves.

Learner: The student in an online/virtual learning environment.

Machine Learning: An automated analysis technique performed by advanced computing devices using pattern recognition methods.

Chapter 13
Fostering Collaborative Open Simulation for Next-Gen Enterprise Learning Ecosystems

Barbara Truman
https://orcid.org/0000-0002-7839-1772
University of Central Florida, USA

ABSTRACT

Leaders seek models of healthy ecosystems to better foster systemic, predictable performance improvement for their learning enterprises. Ecosystems may be viewed narrowly, involving information technology architecture, content, and standards for interoperability or expansively where stakeholders connect to seek next-generation, transdisciplinary learning opportunities across society. Ecosystem stewardship is a responsibility of community/societal leaders and citizens who must collaborate to shape and harness forces and drivers of emerging technology. Mass collaboration is needed to push open simulation into an enterprise capability that monitors and models what was, what is, and can be. This chapter frames academic need and United States military use of open simulation suitable for exploring new ways to steward ecosystem wealth in the interest of learning enterprises and beyond.

INTRODUCTION

Academic institutions and military organizations are part of an interdependent ecosystem facing similar challenges to obtain rapid value from emerging technologies involving simulation. While academic institutions exist to improve the quality of life within societies, military organizations must secure and defend them. Computer-based simulation has been an effective training strategy for the United States military and means are sought for educational uses as well. Determining the optimal fit for integrating simulation use across curriculum requires consistent use of terms for studying effectiveness. Transfer of technological innovation from the military to the educational domain is viewed as a return on investment for public funding, yet few institutions have enterprise simulation capabilities.

DOI: 10.4018/978-1-5225-9679-0.ch013

Innovative, cost-effective means is sought by organizations across industry sectors to educate and train learners. Organizations try to identify elements that contribute to a learning ecosystem necessary to support next-generation solutions. This chapter describes recent examples of open simulation used by the United States military and how advances may translate for use in higher education.

The feasibility for higher education to adopt and adapt open source software technology for open simulation is becoming within reach of institutions which can commit to partnering on next-generation learning efforts. Besides the benefit for higher education to use open simulation within online learning programs, the technology can support the core teaching, learning, and research missions on university campuses. In fact, to learn how to apply knowledge flexibly in authentic situations requires users to learn first how to handle routine situations to progressively tackle complex scenarios and solve complex problems (Clark, 2008, p. 5). Simulations can help bridge the gap between synthetic and authentic environments. These principals of handling routine to complex tasks apply to support faculty as well. "So that each new project does not have to forge the exact same path, there needs to be a community of practice at each institution, even if that only consists of a small but accessible team" (Gregory et al., 2015, p. 10).

HIGHER EDUCATIONS NEED FOR OPEN SIMULATION

Three primary sources were used to obtain the most recent trends and issues in higher education related to learning online in the United States. These sources include Grajek & Grama (2018) an EDUCAUSE Center for Applied Research (ECAR) report; the Babson Survey Research Group (2018); and Seaman, Allen & Seaman, J. (2018). "Grade Increase: Tracking Distance Education in the United States", also produced by the Babson Survey Research Group. The word 'simulation' does not appear in these reports.

As of fall 2016, there were 6,359,121 students taking at least one distance education course, comprising 31.6% of all higher education enrollments. "The majority of students taking distance courses (3,356,041 of the total 6,359,121, or 52.8%) also took at least one course on campus. These students may take their "distance" courses while sitting in their dorm room or in the campus student center, and are just as likely to be on the institution's physical campus as students taking only on-campus courses (Seaman et al., 2018, p. 16). Faculty have held mixed views of online learning due to a variety of factors such as inexperience and unfamiliarity with emerging technology. In order to engage in using, creating, and shaping the evolution of open simulation, faculty will need assistance from centers of academic technology whose maturity comes from more constant, cross-institutional collaboration using simulation technologies.

As campuses created faculty development programs and staffed their support centers to adopt online learning, attitudes to experiment became more favorable; although the 2016 scorecard report of online learning indicated that faculty skepticism is slipping and worse, only 29.1% of chief academic officers believe their faculty accept the value and legitimacy of online education. This rate is lower than the rate recorded in 2004 (Allen et al., 2016, p. 6). Technology-mediated learning is a continually moving target where new digital literacies are required to master pedagogical techniques. If faculty become isolated in their discipline, practice, and brick and mortar classrooms, they risk missing opportunities to improve learning outcomes, especially for those learners that need intervention to persist. If institutions outsource their online learning solutions, they may not benefit from organizational learning and the digital literacies that could flourish across disciplines.

The term open simulation is inherently social as referred to in this chapter, and can be used for experimentation among faculty and support staff to build a new transdisciplinary field of learning engineering described by EDUCAUSE (2019) as:

Sitting at the confluence of learning science, learning technology, and instructional design, learning engineering can be framed as the application of engineering design methodologies in developing learning technologies and infrastructures. Learning engineers have the skills needed to integrate engineering and systems thinking with learning science in support of better learning technologies and, ultimately, improved learning outcomes. Learning engineers provide architectures and techniques that can help us develop new and better tools to apply what we are learning about learning, cognition, and human development. (para. 1)

The field of learning engineering may offer the ability for academics and trainers to collaborate in new ways with IT professionals to better serve curricular and operational technology requirements. This new collaboration will not replace face-to-face meetings; instead it will combine them with an ongoing, social virtual world (VW) capability. "The five trends exerting the most influence on higher education's IT strategy are (1) complexity of security threats, (2) student success focus/imperatives, (3) data-driven decision-making, (4) contributions of IT to institutional operational excellence, and (5) increasing complexity of technology, architecture, and data. Each of these trends is influential at 61% or more of colleges and universities" (Grajek & Grama, 2018, p. 5).

At least 30% of institutions are tracking these 15 technologies in 2018:

- *Next-generation Wi-Fi (e.g., 802 11ah, HaLow) (42%)*
- *Integration platform as a service (37%)*
- *Next-generation LMS/digital learning environment (36%)*
- *Content-aware data loss prevention (34%)*
- *Software-defined networks (34%)*
- *End-to-end communications encryption (33%)*
- *Digital microcredentials (including badging) (32%)*
- *Privacy-enhancing technologies (e.g., limited-disclosure technologies, anonymous credentials) (32%)*
- *Adaptive learning (31%)*
- *Predictive learning analytics (course level) (31%)*
- *Applications of analytics to security (such as user behavioral analytics) (30%)*
- *Cloud access security broker (30%)*
- *Games and gamification (30%)*
- *High-precision location-sensing technologies (30%)*
- *Mobile apps for institutional BI/analytics (30%) (Grajek & Grama, 2018, p.17).*

Dalgarno and Lee (2010) summarized five learning affordances for 3D virtual learning environments as spatial knowledge representation, experiential learning, engagement, contextual learning, and collaborative learning (p. 24). Faculty and instructors must orient toward these 3D learning affordances.

If faculty are not enthusiastic about using technology for teaching and learning, their attitudes will be transferred to learners whether knowingly or not. The same is true for leaders who communicate informal rules influencing the culture and practice of an organization creating heuristics whether or not they were deliberately intended or evolved (Truman, 2014, p. 221). Two primary factors contribute to the ability to identify and comprehend the intangible value of emerging technologies, especially for simulation. One factor is the time or support provided to play with technology to explore its applicability, the other factor is professional development support to integrate and apply the technology into curricula to achieve desired learning outcomes for individual learners. Bower and Richmond (2016) found that providing time for learners to get familiar with the technology was desired in order to build a meta-competency, virtual world efficacy comprising three distinct, yet related, dimensions 1) autonomous learning 2) multiple level operation, and 3) collaborative adaptability (p. 24). Likewise, Goh, Truman and Barber (2018) found the more practice that participants were allowed within the modality of technology, the less stress was experienced by the participants (p. 7).

Virtual worlds using simulation involve sensory use of cognitive, psychomotor, and affective domains. In the ECAR 2016 Report listed under the What We Don't Broadly Understand, Number 10 described *affective computing* indicated by 16% of survey respondents. Affective computing refers to computing in relation to affects, or emotions. It includes technologies that can recognize as well as those that can influence emotions (Grajek, 2016, p. 34). Social virtual worlds represent an affective computing technology. Herlig, Taylor-Nelms, Bliton and Reyher (2011), described engaging 3DVWs framed by Gagne's events of instructions using virtual environments:

The ability to present the stimulus to learn in a creative, engaging, and immersive way is one of the significant advantages of 3DVWs. The art of cinematography, creative writing, and the role of architecture can help to deliver a compelling training experience, especially if the elements included in the environment support the learning material. The stories that entice the participants to want to know more, and the active nature of the 3DVWs makes presenting the stimulus extremely engaging. (p. 6)

The term 3DVWs is not commonly used, and the nomenclature varies significantly to the point that a practitioner may seek guidance from the literature on what they think involves immersive simulation, only to find that the term 'avatar' actually represented a character that was fundamentally limited. The same is true for the type of platform. In this chapter, the terms *open simulation* is used interchangeably with social, virtual worlds and collaborative virtual environments. Improved nomenclature, or at least the translations between definitions was suggested by Truman (2017) in a proposed Computer-Based Simulation (CBS) Spectrum (p. 1) as seen in Figure 1. A two dimensional illustration cannot capture the intricacies of 3D immersive worlds. Truman made a CBS Spectrum project in an OpenSimulator virtual world on the Kitely Grid to explore how a 3D representation could illustrate platform differences. Researchers possessing OpenSimulator avatars may join in on the construction and association of learning strategies and theories associated with the nomenclature. The Spectrum involves serious games and virtual worlds for use across informal learning, education, performance support, and training. The open simulation described in this chapter involves non-determinant worlds on the right that may have realistic, simulated elements or may be fantastic representations of things not-possible-in-real-life.

Morgado et al. (2016) found that requirements for corporate training can get confused with affordances found in serious games that offer a simulation-type approach to learning; the added that virtual worlds as a simulation approach enable cooperative learning and situated learning activities with visual,

Figure 1. Computer-based spectrum
Source: Truman (2017).

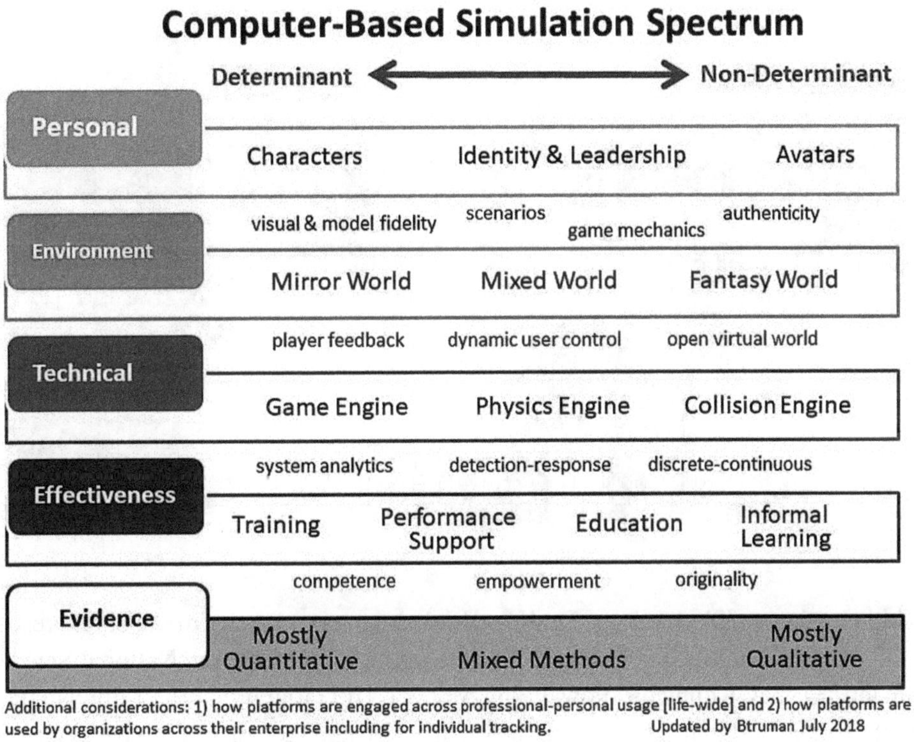

concrete contexts for actions and concepts, and group learning dynamics in distance learning contexts (p. 19). Military uses of blended learning/training may employ a mirror world approach recreating physical environments within the simulation. In these worlds photo-realistic avatars are preferred to more creative expressions of identity often preferred by civilians.

Physical Labs and Virtual Simulation

In higher education, physical laboratories are often costly, dangerous places, reserved for faculty researchers and students who are majors or graduate students. Physical labs have become inaccessible in some general, undergraduate curriculum where severely limited time on machinery and experiments gives way to online videos and quizzes. Virtual laboratories modeled on physical environments will become more practical and valuable for blended learning/training scenarios that may increase recruitment and retention of STEM majors. Figure 2 represents specialized curriculum and research dependent on place-bound, time-bound access. Some specializations in higher education are also dependent upon the ability for faculty to supervise lab access and usage. Virtually-simulated laboratories may increase the ability for institutions to recruit, retain, and build the ranks of the professoriate. The creation of a virtual representation of a working environment allows learners to make mistakes safely and inexpensively or prepare for rare or dangerous events (Maxwell & McLennan, 2012, p. 1).

Figure 2. Physical laboratory used for training
Source: Photo credit CC-BY-SA 3.0

At the Florida Institute of Technology, Dr. Kurt Winkelmann is a faculty member and researcher who has co-created virtual labs in Second Life and has obtained funding from the National Science Foundation. Winkelmann, Keeney-Kennicutt, Fowler and Macik (2017) found that their pilot study of general chemistry demonstrated that experiments conducted in a VW had the potential to be a valid substitution for real world experiments. An analysis of the project showed that students performing experiments in a VW made reasonable learning gains. "Of particular note is that students in the control group and SL group performed equally well on a laboratory practicum. Students performing the virtual world experiments held positive attitudes about virtual experiments" (p. 856). Virtual preparation using virtual worlds could result in truncating time needed to complete the onsite instruction or be used to provide additional advanced instruction during the initially allotted time (Maxwell, 2015, p. 124).

University of Central Florida's Online Learning Enterprise

When an institution commits to explore and build systemic support for promising emerging technologies, the transformation of the enterprise is possible. The University of Central Florida in Orlando is an example of enterprise transformation. As a young, rapidly growing institution, UCF sought blended learning technologies to achieve its mission. Experiential and authentic learning activities and assessments can provide greater support for online learning, especially for blended learning that has been shown to have the highest success rates over face-to-face and fully online learning (UCF Center for Distributed Learning, 2017). Building brick and mortar fast enough to accommodate growth was impossible. Kitchenham (2011) described UCF where:

...the data suggest that when blended learning aligns itself with institutional strategic initiatives and the proper support infrastructure is in place for student and faculty cohorts, success will be substantial and withdrawal percentages will be minimal. At UCF, this success has manifested in measurable faculty satisfaction and significant growth in the delivery of blended learning courses and programs. (p. 31)

UCF exemplified how face to face and online programs were supported using a blended learning strategy. UCF was initially chartered to support the space industry in central Florida and helped the region become the national center for simulation. A recurring, key institutional goal for UCF was to be a partnership university and as this chapter suggests, learning from the military using collaborative simulation technology offers the potential to shape the development of open simulation. It is impossible to institutionalize support for emerging technologies without administrative commitment, systematic involvement and systemic support for faculty who contribute to building a learning organization. Figure 3 illustrates a place-based, time-based use of simulation for the UCF College of Nursing.

UCF is such a university that could create an enterprise, open simulation capability if the administrative will existed to align strategy. The use of virtual worlds enables the ability to learn vicariously and observe open source software development as part of a dynamic, learning ecosystem (Truman, 2004, p. 95). Virtual worlds can also provide the distributed rehearsal that prepares learners for using simulators like the mannequin shown in Figure 3.

Learning Ecosystem Drivers and Elements

Enterprise needs for incorporating open simulation for military/educational applications are similar on the enterprise level, whether for training or educational uses. Military services are continually scouting how to save lives, time, and funding using simulation. In the United States, the Department of Defense created the Advanced Distributed Learning (2019) Initiative as a coordinating resource. The ADL Initiative provides R&D into standards development, funding for prototypes, and facilitates the diffusion of effective practices through events and social media. Some of the ADL Initiative's efforts have led to greater interoperability of instructional systems and reusability of media content. One of the priorities of the ADL Initiative is to research next-generation learning ecosystems.

Figure 3. UCF College of Nursing simulator photo credit UCF

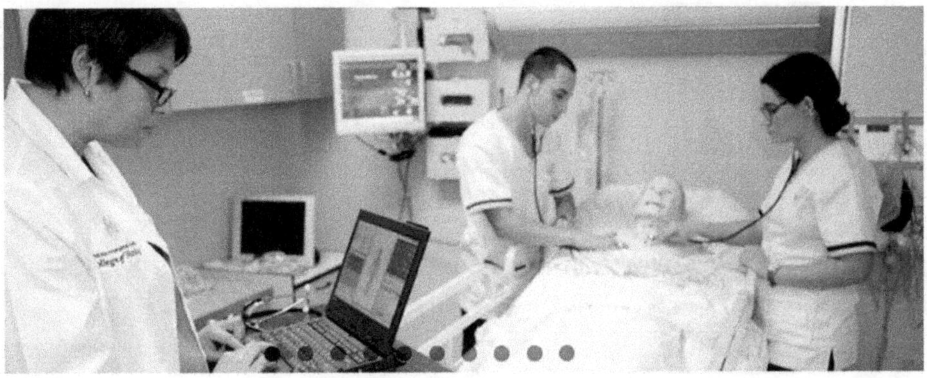

Next-generation learning refers to a vision for breaking down technical barriers between different learning technologies so that learners and instructors can transition seamlessly between them, increasing usability and impact on learning. The Advanced Distributed Learning (ADL) Initiative proposes an open-source set of specifications together called the Total Learning Architecture (TLA) to achieve this vision. (Folsom-Kovarik & Raybourn, 2016, p. 1)

Several ADL projects are included in their evolving ecosystem. These include the Total Learning Architecture (TLA), Experience API (xAPI) development, Competency-Based R&D, learning record store repository development, and Transmedia Learning (Raybourn 2018). A virtual world R&D effort called the Virtual World Framework (VWF) existed, but was retired. The VWF had an architecture that involved peer-to-peer technology, which is much different from the open simulation advocated in this chapter. Within higher education, there is no coordinating organization like the ADL Initiative. The IMS Global Learning Consortium helps higher education in coordinating and validating technical needs for the enterprise. In 2018, The ADL Initiative and the IMS Global Learning Initiative were coordinating on the topic of learning analytics.

This book has several chapters describing the importance of using avatars and their influence on identity development. Figure 4 illustrates several elements that make up a virtual world ecosystem. One area often overlooked in ecosystem health is content development. Recent developments of social, virtual world platforms have not advanced as rapidly as expected. Many of these platforms have disabled in-world, user-generated content. Learning enterprises must address where to obtain content or pursue efforts to teach the literacies needed to supply environments. One option is to use Open Educational Resources (OER).

Content development also means the strategic use of open educational resources (OER) that may be freely licensed for educational uses. Learning how to take advantage of such resources and feed simulation-based ecosystems is a new digital learning literacy.

Figure 4. Virtual world ecosystem components

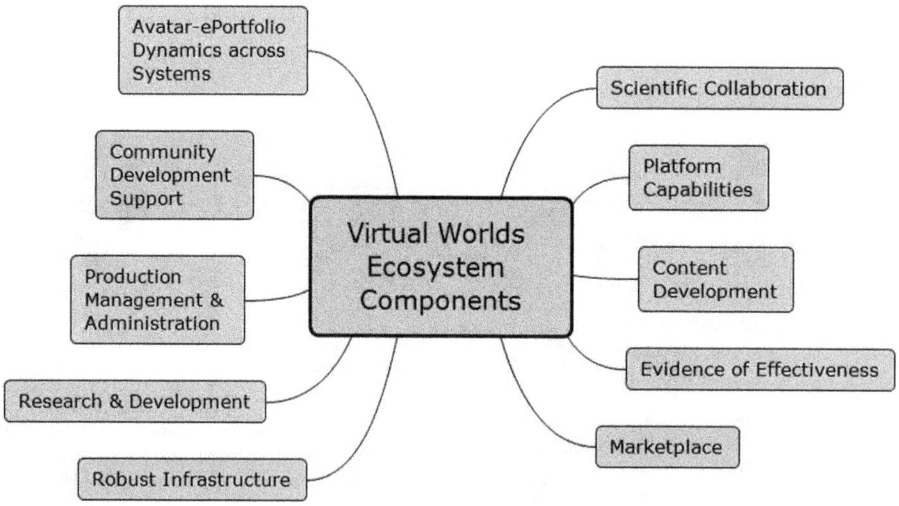

The William and Flora Hewlett Foundation defines OER as follows: OER are teaching, learning, and research resources that reside in the public domain or have been released under an intellectual property license that permits their free use and re-purposing by others. Open educational resources include full courses, course materials, modules, textbooks, streaming videos, tests, software, and any other tools, materials, or techniques used to support access to knowledge. (Babson Survey Research Group, 2018, p. 4)

Immersive Simulation for Education and Training

A key benefit of training and education conducted in virtual worlds is the experiential aspect. Performance can be elicited if the goal of the training is behavioral. Greater insight into the knowledge transferred can also be obtained (Herlig et al., 2011, p. 7). Well-designed 3D virtual world learning experiences should result in better retention and transfer than activities performed in a traditional classroom or webinar setting based on the affordances simulations and immersive learning strategies (p. 8). Learning how virtual worlds can support blended learning/training using open simulation may be best applied with innovation management strategies that encourage participatory design afforded by the platform itself with stakeholder involvement. "…not only does collaboration lead to more expansive virtual world landscapes but the rapidly changing platforms for virtual worlds makes collaboration essential to sustaining a viable virtual world presence" (Maxwell & McLennan, 2012, p. 10). New forms of collaborative pedagogies are possible to explore across disciplines involving faculty, support staff, and learning across the enterprise. Reiners, Gregory and Knox (2016) report that their blended approach supported transfer to cognitively prepare pre-service teachers for real classroom experiences, supporting the transfer of knowledge and skills learned in virtual environments to real classrooms" (p. 171).

Educators occasionally downplay the role of training favoring more holistic educational approaches that prepare learners for broader applications of knowledge. Training performed in the military often combines education for improving situational awareness required to demonstrate knowledge in context. The use of virtual worlds can provide authentic scenarios designed to increase military readiness for missions that may require warfighting and cultural sensitivity in the same situation. Simulation enables practice, accelerating development of experience that can lead to adaptive expertise under appropriate guidance. The military seeks to create adaptive experts who are highly successful under novel conditions (Clark, 2008, p. 2). Virtual world technology also offers users the ability to co-construct prototypes. The U.S. Navy employs design teams to convert traditional schoolhouse courses into simulated environments rapidly (Mazzone & Aguiar, 2017, p. 2). Constructive simulation, where scenarios and environments can be adjusted on the fly, create adaptive learning models and flexible delivery methods that allow users to engage in critical thinking for complex, irregular situations (Maraj, Lackey, Badillo-Urquiola, Ogreten & Maxwell, 2015).

U.S. ARMY: VIRTUAL WORLD TRAINING FOR INFANTRY SOLDIERS

The US Army Research Lab (ARL) researched the effectiveness of a blended learning/training program using a mixed approach of classroom-based simulation activities as preparation for physical simulation exercises. The program focused upon an open-source simulation platform for which the Army has developed with assistance from academia as part of an interdependent, virtual community. The Army provided the modified software code, 3D content, and studies to the community as benefits of technical knowledge transfer. Research was conducted into gaming and virtual world technology to align with training priorities. ARL and the University of Central Florida conducted studies involving over 500 soldiers to determine how effective virtual training methods compared to traditional training methods for dismounted infantry soldier skills (Maxwell, 2016, p.1). In support of the training research, ARL adapted and forked an open source platform, OpenSimulator, to modify affordances in support of creating a secure blended education/training platform. The project and platform was called The Military Open Simulator Enterprise Strategy (MOSES) and sought: "… to foster an "ecology of learning that provides context to data, generates repeated exposure of the data to facilitate knowledge transfers and retention, and provides a social network for online mentorship" (Maxwell & McLennan, 2012, p. 5).

The MOSES initiative was open to virtual world educators and interested researchers for participation in weekly meetings within the open simulation environment. An intervention strategy was used to incorporate MOSES using a simplified interface as part of a 21-day leadership training course to evaluate training effectiveness for infantry soldiers. Data collection activities were conducted to determine baseline training effectiveness comparison of simulation-based training methods versus traditional classroom and physical walkthrough means (Maxwell, 2016, p. 1). Soldiers experienced greater practice of leadership skills through role-play compared to use of a more complex game-based learning simulation, Virtual BattleSpaces 3, an approved Army program of record. Instructors were able to influence the use of MOSES as seen in Figure 5 in a National Guard Training Classroom.

The MOSES Initiative sought to make a turn-key package called MOSES-in-a-box that was available to agencies with specifications for server hardware, software configuration, and grid management

Figure 5. Blended classroom configuration and instructor support
Source: Photo credit Barbara Truman

capabilities. A version of the package was provided for the UCF College of Engineering and Computer Science where at least two dissertations were conducted using the capabilities to support engineering leadership. One of the areas of research for using simulation in blended education/training involves exposing learners to appropriate stress to create automaticity in reactions within high stakes scenarios. In higher education, the scenarios may involve responding to a toxic spill within a Chemistry laboratory or for medical staff members dealing with crisis in a healthcare setting. Maraj et al. (2015) found training that required higher complexity skills using virtual worlds involve some level of previous experience or familiarity of the operational environment. "The complexity of the task and the participants' inexperience contribute to greater mental demand, while the novelty of the VW training environment may increase task engagement" (p. 8).

Common interfaces across devices and technologies are consistent with the aims of the IMS Global Accessibility effort mentioned earlier to support persons with disabilities. Infantry soldiers do not have disabilities unless they have experienced traumatic injuries. Curriculum is often thought of in terms of lifecycle, rather than users' self-efficacy, strengths, and adaptable expertise. "…a common user interface for synthetic training environment using simulation-based training for infantry must be considered…it makes sense to teach it in basic training. This common user interface needs to be introduced early and reinforced often throughout the soldier's career" (Maxwell, 2016, p. 8).

The infantry soldier blended learning/training example also applies to higher education for the need to reinforce the concept of learning, practicing, and working in teams. Distributed, simulation-based training and education can be performed remotely, for soldiers this could be performed in the barracks or at home station for pre-deployment. Acclimation of concepts and skills maintenance can also be practiced asynchronously at any time if the environment supports it. Synchronous distributed access supports teams at a distance, and while the scope of this article does not permit discuss of the role of identity development using avatars, there is some related literature on the development of a professional identity for engaging in teams using collective intelligence. "Organizations can harness identities in the physical world as well as embodied avatars acting in virtual environments all acting as sensors to collaborate using collective intelligence" (Truman, 2014, p. 222).

Maxwell (2016) sums up the potential for a distance learning approach to improve performance on the individual and team level while saving costs:

Distributed training is key to the next generation of infantry soldier skills training, as even current technology allows for collective skills development. Since most tasks infantry soldiers are trained for are collective in nature, a simulation technology that allows for remote participation coupled with task coordination may be a more appropriate medium to use. Time spent in the simulators will allow for the soldiers to gain tool expertise as well as provide opportunity for self-paced learning. Allowing soldiers to access the simulators from home station offers a cost effective means for training by allowing collective activities without the need for physical co-location at a battle training center. (p. 5)

In 2017, the MOSES Initiative was retired when the principle architects took positions within industry. Calls for civilian management led to further collaboration and exploration of enterprise uses of the OpenSimulator platform among community members. More leaders are needed who can work at the intersections of academic-military boundaries. In 2017, the U.S. Army Research Lab's priorities shifted to create the Synthetic Training Environment resulting in a new UCF-partnership located on the campus's research park (UCF Today, 2019).

U.S. NAVY: VIRTUAL WORLD SCHOOLHOUSE

The U.S. Submarine Learning Center (SLC) and the Naval Undersea Warfare Center (NUWC) have been exploring the use of virtual world (VW) technology using open simulation. Some use required classified clearance to participate. Approved developments were shared at the 2015 Federal Consortium of Virtual Worlds (FCVW) Workshop, an online conference held within a virtual world sponsored by the Army's MOSES Team. NUWC staff was able to load copies of their immersive learning simulations by bringing their OAR (archive region) files onto the conference grid (Truman & Metcalf, 2015, p. 3). The goal of the NUWC program is to significantly change the way instruction is delivered to United States Navy sailors (Mazzone & Aguiar, 2017, p. 2) and increase the methods by which instruction at the learning sites can be delivered and training hardware accessed (Mazzone & Aguiar, 2017a, p. 2). The virtual laboratory provides full fidelity remote access for students to operate the tactical trainer from workstations in the student's local training center. Twelve course convenings were delivered involving up to five learning sites participating from the East and West Coast. Results were positive leading SLC and NUWC to continue the use of virtual world technology to build a highly capable Fleet training environment (p. 11). The VW courses create a force multiplier for instruction and is unique in that VW courses can support the hardest content to teach in a traditional classroom setting such as performance-based training (Mazzone & Aguiar, 2017a, p 2). Figure 6 shows an early version of the NUWC Virtual World Schoolhouse.

Supporting instructors is a challenge due to the two-year rotation of duty station that must be managed with course delivery cycles. The NUWC staff developed a comprehensive 22 hour VW apprentice

Figure 6. Steven Aguiar's avatar in the virtual world schoolhouse

training course covering the following topics: Understanding the benefits of VW technology, Common VW skills, Object manipulation, Scene composition, Texture generation, Scripting, Rapid prototyping, Integrating with other applications, Applications for modeling and simulation, and Applications for training (Mazzone & Aguiar, 2017a, p. 3). Sailors want to leverage virtual environment capabilities that are not possible in a tactical training environment (Mazzone & Aguiar, 2017, p. 11). Figure 7 illustrates the construct of *virtual world efficacy* discovered as part of a study on the effective use of the Virtual World Schoolhouse conducted by officers at the Naval Post Graduate School.

U.S. Navy Role Play in Second Life

The United States military has had multiple presences in virtual worlds including Second Life and OpenSimulator. The Services have also streamed some face-to-face conferences such as the Defense GameTech Conference and the Federal Consortium of Virtual Worlds Conference. An active role-play group exists in Second Life where civilians and military veterans engage in role play using models of ships and aircraft to conduct simulated training activities. Second Life community members as seen in Figure 8 are still enthusiastic after significant hype and ultimate collapse of expected transformation from promised innovations such as educational discounts and an enterprise service that could be installed behind institutions' firewalls.

U.S. AIR FORCE: BLENDING PROFESSIONAL AND PERSONAL IDENTITIES

The United States Air Force (USAF) has also used virtual worlds extensively, including OpenSimulator at The Air University located at Maxwell Air Force Base in Alabama. The focus involved USAF officers who explore character and leadership development, virtual heritage, and Connectivism (Stricker et al., 2017, p. 2). The Squadron Office College affects the lives of all USAF captains across occupations in

Figure 7. Virtual world efficacy
Source: Bower and Richmond, 2016, p. 40

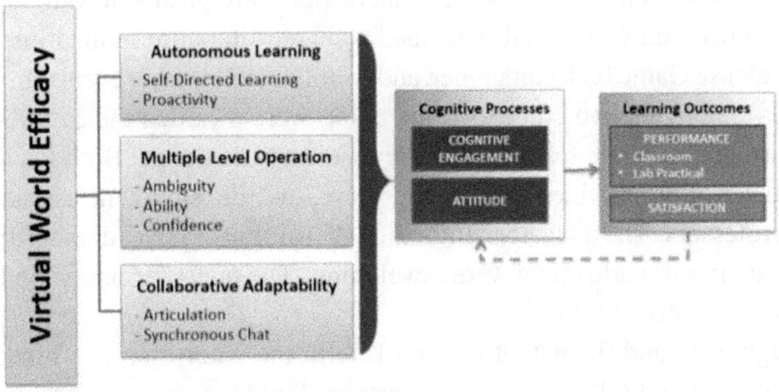

Bower-Richmond Model of Student Competencies in the Virtual Learning Environment

Figure 8.
Source: Photo credit B-) by Nesca Fey (CC BY 2.0) https://www.flickr.com/photos/nescafey/33782348233/in/dateposted/

the USAF. At one point, 600 students each semester at The Air University were oriented to using virtual worlds to obtain their professional education.

The USAF VW activities were shared regularly through participation in scholarly communities where leaders made presentations and taught university classes using virtual worlds. Events have included brown bag lunch presentations and Global Learning Forum sessions where leaders such as Dr. Margaret Wheatley have used an avatar shown in Figure 9 to come in world and share recent research activities. Other guest presenters included Dr. Jeremy Bailenson, Dr. Art Langer, and Dr. Kenneth Stanley. The editors of this book have been directly involved in orchestrating these VW events or participating. This book and its predecessor are products of the lessons learned from collaborative efforts that involve continual activities within the VW platforms described for adapting to enterprise uses.

Each year, the VW environments got more sophisticated with combining mesh models and user-generated content. Design Studio sessions were held to produce rapid prototyping of ideas and content among collaborators. The boundaries of instructional design were pushed toward learning engineering approaches. Designs provoked dialogue that formed a shared literature foundation. The USAF group participated in the Defense GameTech conference and in online, immersive events. In 2010, Drs. Andrew Stricker and Cynthia Calongne, two editors of this book, were awarded the $25,000 first prize award from the Federal Virtual Challenge for their Mars Expedition Challenge. Both leaders taught doctoral students using virtual worlds provided mentoring, tours, and development assistance. The teaching roles were not just professors. The educators embodied their values to live, demonstrate, and share their experiences using the virtual worlds they were developing. The quest for praxis on how to apply VWs in a cost-effective manner is ongoing.

When budgets tightened and the use of Second Life in the enterprise was hindered with constant updates of viewer software and rolling restarts, leaders explored the use of OpenSimulator as well. Design thinking for virtual worlds was the topic of a massively open online course (MOOC) Stricker and

Figure 9. Dr. Wheatley presents at the USAF global learning forum
Source: Photo Credit Barbara Truman

Calongne produced in 2013 that used Moodle as the learning management system. The USAF digital heritage was carried forward and translated into new VW realms in a personal grid Dr. Andrew Stricker made called Virtual Harmony. The Virtual Harmony grid included the ability to hypergrid allowing educators, scholars, and VW developers to visit. Virtual Harmony became a collaboration platform for seeking next-generation learning opportunities that spanned history while looking toward the future. The grid was inherently transdisciplinary because its leaders represented scholarly life experiences of living History, Philosophy, Learning Science, Engineering, Computer Science, and arts and sciences. When cloud computing became available the Virtual Harmony grid was adapted as a hybrid environment. The cloud enabled the inclusion of other instructional and informational software systems. Dr. Stricker was able to combine open source software involving social media, gaming, and analytic development using a learning record store as part of a broad, Integrated Learning Environment testbed. Lessons learned were shared with USAF leadership and educators were invited to participate during online, virtual world conference events like the OpenSimulator Community Conference (OSCC), Federal Consortium of Virtual Worlds (VCVW) Workshop, and Virtual Worlds Best Practices in Education (VWBPE) Conferences.

The Virtual Harmony grid was much more than a professional outgrowth of USAF activities. The grid also originally was modelled after the town of New Harmony, Indiana, located not far from where Dr. Stricker and Dr. Calongne grew up and went to college together. Virtual Harmony represented both a religious, harmonist community and a scientific community originating from early American colonial efforts beginning in 1824. Virtual Harmony's digital heritage expanded with additional regions such as an Indian village (genealogy research), a maritime harbor (oceanographic research), Vesuvius volcano region (modeled after a USAF duty tour), English university cloister (USAF fellowship), and more recently the addition of games and simulations used in USAF officer education.

Recent OpenSimulator additions include a French Village called Loire, and survival research environments for Antarctica and Mars. The rich, immersive environments combined with cross-disciplinary activities led to weekly salon-type meetings representing a collaborative brain trust. The Virtual Harmony fellowship of research is akin to literary notables who gathered in pubs rubbing elbows, sharing ideas, and garnering inspiration. The use of open simulation provides rich fodder. Figure 10 shows the editors of this book convening in world in the Virtual Harmony Loire salon. Librarians are now involved adding new dimensions of scholarship and promise to catalogue VW development for future generations and digital heritage.

The chapter, *Identity Growth in the Professions* by Stricker, Westhauser, Lyle, Lowry, and Sheets contains the framework promised in a progress report regarding Squadron Learning Commons submitted for The Air University (2017):

A team-of-teams interactive fluency learning framework will be offered for squadron leaders to help guide and interpret progress made with building a natural learning culture wherein Airmen experience and commit to personal growth, doing the right things, and assisting each other interactively in small teams with their development...leading and being led at the same time. A natural learning experience at the squadron level, infused by design thinking, will turbocharge Airmen with deeper levels of buy-in from the heart as well as the head. (p. 4)

BARRIERS AND CHALLENGES

Gregory, Lee, Dalgarno and Tynan (2016) produced a book on virtual learning illustrating multiple use cases of effective learning strategies that complement their findings on barriers. The challenges to building enterprise support around open simulation are not trivial. Pockets of innovation exist on most university campuses where a single faculty champion may lead research and development efforts not considered viable for institutional applicability. Gregory et al. (2015) conducted a study to ascertain why educators were not using virtual worlds for teaching and learning. Findings surrounded four themes: technological issues, potential student difficulties, institutional issues, and personal perceptions. Lack

Figure 10. Book editors manage publication activities
Source: Photo credit Barbara Truman

of funding and teaching support were also significant barriers (Gregory et al., 2015, p. 7). Publishers have had limited success in producing simulation platforms, environments, and authentic assessments as well. Subcontractors are hired to offer specialized services as part of textbook packages. While attaining learning effectiveness is possible, organizational learning for the enterprise is lost with bolt-on technology solutions.

The list below represents some of the major challenges facing the adoption of open simulation among enterprises whether for education or military:

- Awareness
- Security
- Accessibility
- Knowledgeable Administration
- Distributed Installation
- Usability
- Interoperability
- Professional development for 3D digital literacies
- Learner support
- Content development
- Assessment support
- Intellectual Property Management
- Project management & estimation

Of these challenges, foremost is security. Cruz, Costa, Martins, Goncalves and Barroso (2013) reported that virtual world technology is moving upon standardization. Identity federation has been neglected by most of the standard-setting efforts, preventing widespread adoption by educational institutions (p.1). Cruz et al. (2013) proposed user-centric identity management to provide an effective way to build trusted communities in virtual worlds allowing attribution of different kind of roles and permissions, under a digital rights and intellectual property policy basis (p. 2).

Platform Characteristics

Figure 11 illustrates specific capabilities required for enterprise development of open simulation as an integrated platform.

The open simulation platform used in the Army blended education/training scenario permits uploading regions that represent immersive environments called OAR (OpenSimulator archive) files. When a digital OAR file is uploaded, all ownership and permissions can be assigned incorrectly purging any permissions and attribution at the same time. The ability to move files around must be secured (Heilmann & Maxwell, 2016, p. 6). Gregory et al. (2015) cited, "It is imperative to have a sustainability plan in place if virtual worlds are to be a viable resource in future education" (p. 10). Managing the life cycle of virtual world use becomes critical when part-time faculty or instructors are hired just in time without proper training and orientation. Diffusing 3D digital literacies is imperative to support the sustainability of the open simulation platform.

Figure 11. Platform characteristics of open simulation
Source: Image credit Barbara Truman

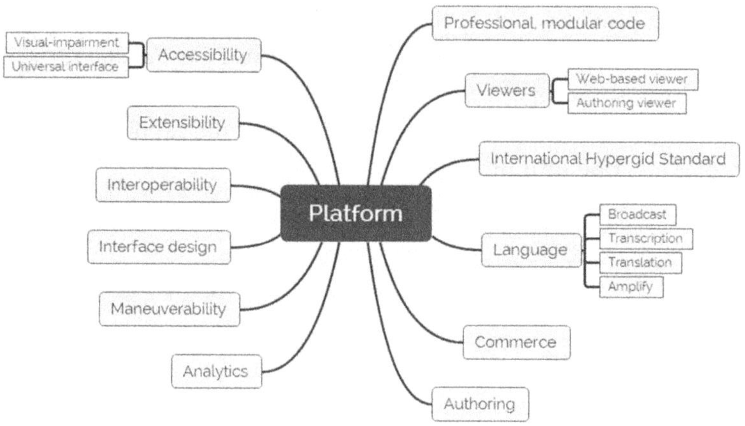

In the ECAR 2016 Report listed under the What We Don't Broadly Understand, Public key infrastructure (PKI) described in Number 9 was cited by 16% of survey respondents. PKI supports secure data exchange and authentication over the Internet via the distribution and identification of public encryption keys. PKI generally includes "hardware, software, policies and standards to manage the creation, administration, distribution and revocation of keys and digital certificates" (Grajek, 2016, p. 34). The open simulation platform (OpenSimulator) grid administration is difficult, and it is tempting to take shortcuts to get up and running quickly increasing the likelihood of overlooking security threats (Heilmann & Maxwell, 2016, p. 5).

The Next-Generation Digital Learning Environment (NGDLE) initiative from EDUCAUSE is over two years old. The NGDLE efforts is raising consciousness on many issues including accessibility. The draft standard from IMS Global on Access for All (v.3.0) will allow users to set preferences that will be shared across other applications by integrating accessibility into all tools and content in a way that can be personalized. "What is required is to get campuses providing feedback on the Access for All standard and then joining together to get vendors to adopt this effort" (Kelly, 2016). As academic institutions assume leadership for the stewardship of open simulation, a consortial approach can be used to support people with differing abilities in ways not thought possible before stakeholders were able to contribute.

FUTURE RESEARCH DIRECTIONS

The military examples examined in this article involved a modified use of the virtual world, OpenSimulator, that can also be considered a distributed virtual environment (DVE) that connects multiple users instantly with each other and with a shared virtual space over a network. Other examples of DVE applications include: "World of Warcraft, Second Life, Google Hangouts, shared online editors, and advanced instant messaging systems (e.g., Slack), among many others" (Valadares, Gabrielova & Lopes, 2016, p.3292). To date, commercial interests have driven the development of DVEs where research has been fairly ad hoc. Calls for making DVE development more systematic have appeared (p. 3307). Open simulation integration will be an area of research that includes data analytics and visualization.

In late 2016, a presentation was made on the U.S. Army's MOSES as shown in Figure 12. The event was in Second Life and hosted by the NonProfit Commons group. The future research recommendation involved integrating OpenSimulator with a learning management system, such as Instructure's Canvas.

Morgado et al. (2016) investigated the integration specifications for conjoining the virtual world OpenSimulator and a proprietary LMS. Their research found no published data on actual requirements for virtual world use from a software engineering perspective for corporate training (p. 20). When a virtual world using a web-based viewer can be nearly seamlessly integrated with an LMS, the potential for enterprise adoption of open simulation appears likely.

NextGen Learning as Digital Learning Commons

The term *Learning Commons* was made popular on college campuses as a call to modernize meeting spaces to promote study, collaboration, informal learning, and socialization. Another variation of modernization on campuses involved *Tech Commons* where technical support is available nearby. Figure 13 shows learning spaces created with rich technology designed to support informal, non-classroom-based learning and collaboration.

What is a Digital *Learning Commons?* Campuses are trying to define what makes up a Digital Learning Commons to connect and serve users at a distance and to integrate information technology and physical services. Concerning the military examples in this chapter, the U.S. Air Force has had the broadest vision for how a digital learning commons can transform professional military education for squadron officers: "Each squadron can employ a "Squadron Learning Commons" uniquely tailored for their mission, organization structure, location, and membership without disrupting underlying learning services, learning data collection, analysis, and reporting tools offered to any Air Force squadron" (The Air University, 2017, p. 7). In higher education, co-curricular learning could be primarily supported to improve retention and success of learners, especially for vulnerable populations using a digital learning commons approach similar to how the USAF seeks to keep officers connected forever wherever they

Figure 12. Army MOSES presentation in NonProfit commons meeting
Source: Photo credit Barbara Truman

Figure 13. Learning commons
Source: Mosborne01 CC BY-SA 3.0 via Wikimedia Commons

are stationed. Figure 14 shows a diagram of architectural components commonly found in universities. Open simulation represents a platform that could be incorporated in this architecture.

Investigating what constitutes a Digital Learning Commons could be viewed as when institutions created centers for teaching and learning or when they crafted a professional web site representing full-spectrum activities. Finding new ways to involve stakeholders and support decision-making would be accelerated with a web-based virtual world viewer that could have its data connected to an enterprise LMS. "New generations of scholars possessing CVE [collaborative virtual environments] meta-literacy skills may emerge to partner with university faculty in research specializations that may accelerate and improve interdisciplinary research using a strengths-based approach" (Truman, 2014, p. 222).

Creating self-directed learners using virtual world simulation will support the needs of the military and academia by discovering how to steward motivation for when complex tasks require extraordinary perseverance. Deci & Ryan (2008) described self-determination theory (SDT) as focusing on types, rather than just amount, of motivation. SDT pays particular attention to autonomous motivation, controlled motivation, and amotivation as predictors of performance, relational, and well-being outcomes (p. 182). As more stakeholders use open source virtual worlds to collaborate, the possibility of shared efficacy among its users increases. Open science may be the benefactor. "Open collaborative projects involve users and others who share the work of generating a design and also reveal the outputs from their individual and collective design efforts openly for everyone to use" (Wielsch, 2010, p. 2). The quest to support open science is another call for support staff to engage in the playful exploration of virtual worlds to practice digital literacy skills necessary to support the development of a Digital Research Commons.

Figure 14. Digital learning commons architecture
Source: Image credit Barbara Truman

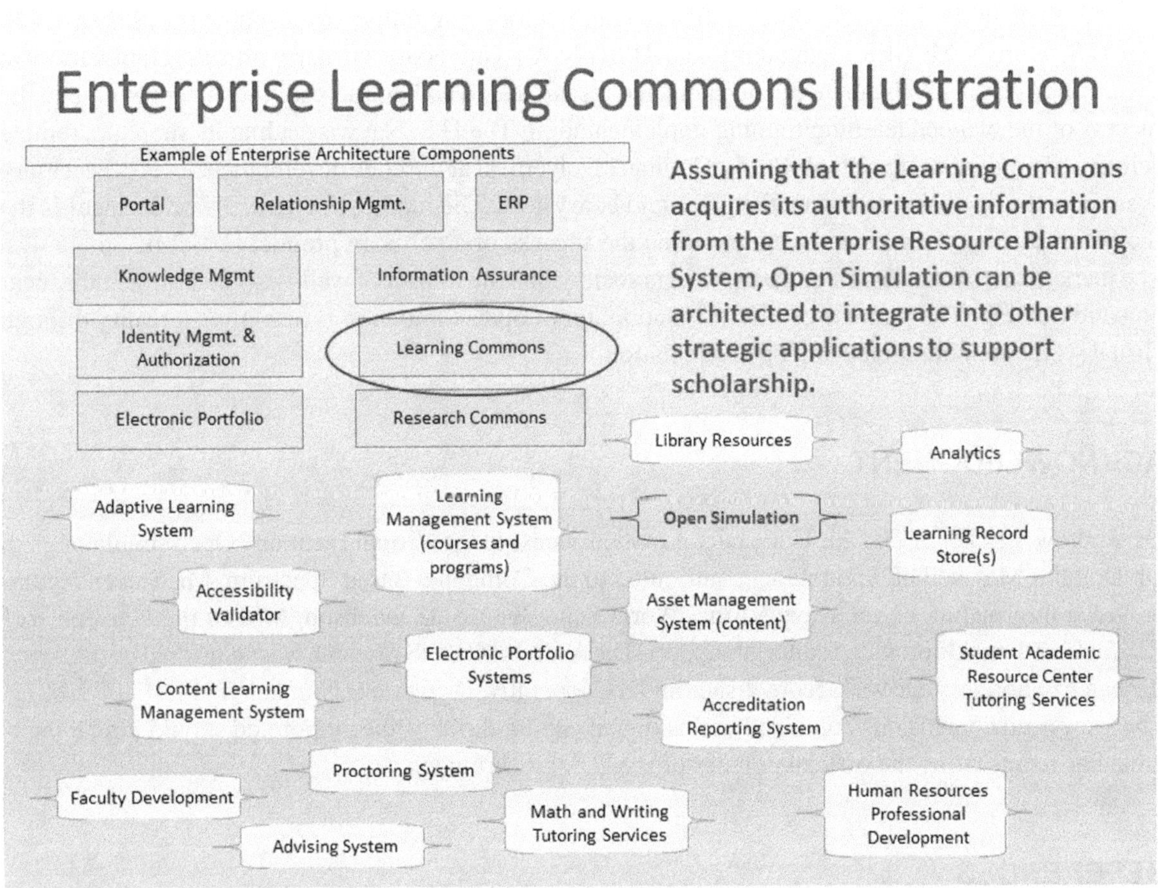

CONCLUSION

The U.S. military's blended learning/training examples illustrated modified, open source virtual world software that educational institutions can participate in and use to shape the technology. These military virtual world examples serve as prototype models to higher education for the potential to achieve enterprise needs in support of teaching, learning, and research missions. The involvement of actual soldiers in studies to validate the instructional fit of simulation uses in a variety of contexts suggest that pragmatic gains can be translated through technical and knowledge transfer. It is possible that inter-institutional use of virtual worlds can improve recruiting and retention, including within STEM fields. The U.S. National Science Foundation is creating a community of practice for STEM faculty researching the use of virtual worlds. Finally, open simulation virtual worlds may engage more faculty to support strategic visions of online learning.

Governance of an open source virtual world platform cannot be managed and sustained by the United States military alone "… effective governance and work practices that are appreciated by community members is fundamental for long-term sustainability" (Gamalielsson & Lundell, 2014, p. 130). Leaders in higher education must step forward to participate and shape the virtual world technology to meet higher education's social contract and mission to support communities and society. Models of open source governance exist to support diverse community involvement. Gamalielsson & Lundell (2014) found in their study that open source software communities can outlive open source projects (p. 144). The U.S. Army's MOSES Community and USAF's Air University virtual world development team have embraced the involvement of educators and researchers who have helped test and contribute to the success of the blended learning/training implementation. The U.S. Navy is scaling its strategic, remote delivery of training using virtual worlds. Civilian involvement at the code development level is necessary to support the open simulation marketplace and ecosystem. The market [for virtual world usage] is the ecosystem's energy source and can determine the success of a software product (Yu, 2013, p. 46-47). The market for virtual world simulation affects society like the impact of well-designed, strategic education and training. The promise of enterprise adoption of open simulation is becoming a reality through virtual world collaboration using open simulation.

ACKNOWLEDGMENT

Dr. Andrew Stricker of The Air University provided access to the Virtual Harmony OpenSimulator grid. Dr. Douglas Maxwell of Aptima Inc. contributed to the Computer-Based Spectrum. Mr. Steven Aguiar provided information on the Navy Virtual World Schoolhouse. JJ Jacobson, MSI of the University of California, Riverside provided editorial support. The Army's MOSES research was sponsored by the Army Research Laboratory and was accomplished under Cooperative Agreement Number W911NF-14-2-0012. The views and conclusions contained in this document are those of the author and should not be interpreted as representing the official policies of the U.S. Government.

REFERENCES

Advanced Distributed Learning Initiative. (2019). Retrieved from https://adlnet.gov

Affective Computing. (2016). Retrieved from: http://affect.media.mit.edu

Allen, I. E., Seaman, J., Poulin, R., & Straut, T. T. (2016). *Online Report Card: Tracking Online Education in the United States*. Retrieved from: http://onlinelearningsurvey.com/reports/onlinereportcard.pdf

Babson Survey Research Group. (2018). *Freeing the Textbook: Educational Resources in U.S. Higher Education*. Released under a Creative Commons Attribution-ShareAlike 4.0 International license. Report available at: www.onlinelearningsurvey.com/oer.html

Bower, J. M., & Richmond, J. R. (2016). *Learning competencies used in the U.S. Navy's Virtual Schoolhouse learning environment*. Naval Postgraduate School Monterey United States. Retrieved from: https://apps.dtic.mil/dtic/tr/fulltext/u2/1030717.pdf

Clark, R. (2008). *GEL, Adaptable Expertise and Transfer of Training*. U.S.C Center for Cognitive Technology.

Cruz, G., Costa, A., Martins, P., Goncalves, R., & Barroso, J. (2013, September). Federation Technology and Virtual Worlds for Learning: Research Trends and Opportunities Towards Identity Federation. In *Games and Virtual Worlds for Serious Applications (VS-GAMES), 2013 5th International Conference on* (pp. 1-4). IEEE.

Dalgarno, B., & Lee, M. J. (2010). What are the learning affordances of 3-D virtual environments? *British Journal of Educational Technology*, *41*(1), 10–32. doi:10.1111/j.1467-8535.2009.01038.x

Deci, E. L., & Ryan, R. M. (2008). Self-determination theory: A macrotheory of human motivation, development, and health. *Canadian Psychology*, *49*(3), 182–185. doi:10.1037/a0012801

EDUCAUSE. (2019). *7 Things You Need to Know about Learning Engineering*. Retrieved from: https://library.educause.edu/resources/2018/9/7-things-you-should-know-about-learning-engineering

Folsom-Kovarik, J. T., & Raybourn, E. M. (2016, November). Total Learning Architecture (TLA) Enables Next-generation Learning via Meta-adaptation. *Interservice/Industry Training, Simulation, and Education Conference Proceedings*. Retrieved from: https://www.adlnet.gov/public/uploads/Total-Learning-Architecture-TLA-Enables-Next-generation-Learning-via-Meta-adaptation.pdf

Gamalielsson, J., & Lundell, B. (2014). Sustainability of open source software communities beyond a fork: How and why has the libreoffice project evolved? *Journal of Systems and Software*, *89*, 128–145.

Goh, J., Truman, B., & Barber, D. (2018). Exploring individual differences as factors to maximize interactive learning environments for future learning. *Interactive Learning Environments*, 1–11.

Grajek, S. (2016). *Higher Education's Top 10 Strategic Technologies for 2016*. Research report. Louisville, CO: ECAR. Available from http://www.educause.edu/ecar

Grajek, S., & Grama, J. L. (2018). *Higher Education's 2018 Trend Watch and Top 10 Strategic Technologies*. Research report. Louisville, CO: ECAR. Available from http://www.educause.edu/ecar

Gregory, S., Lee, M. J., Dalgarno, B., & Tynan, B. (Eds.). (2016). *Learning in Virtual Worlds: Research and Applications*. Athabasca University Press.

Gregory, S., Scutter, S., Jacka, L., McDonald, M., Farley, H., & Newman, C. (2015). Barriers and Enablers to the Use of Virtual Worlds in Higher Education: An Exploration of Educator Perceptions, Attitudes and Experiences. *Journal of Educational Technology & Society*, *18*(1), 3–12.

Heilmann, M., & Maxwell, D. (2016). Securing the Hypergrid. *Hypergrid Business*. Retrieved from: http://www.hypergridbusiness.com/wp-content/uploads/2016/09/Securing-the-Hypergrid-Michael-Heilmann-and-Douglas-Maxwell.pdf

Herlig, K., Taylor-Nelms, L., Bliton, D., & Reyher, T. (2011). *Recommendations for Designing Effective Learning Events in 3D Virtual Worlds*. Paper presented at the Inter-Industry Training Simulation and Training Conference, Orlando, FL.

IMS Global Learning Consortium. (2019). Retrieved from https://www.imsglobal.org/activity/accessibility

Kelly, R. (2016). 9 Ed Tech Trends to Watch in 2016. *Campus Technology*. Retrieved from: https://campustechnology.com/Articles/2016/01/13/9-Ed-Tech-Trends-to-Watch-in-2016.aspx?p=1

Kitchenham, A. (2011). *Blended learning across disciplines: Models for implementation*. Hershey, PA: Information Science Reference.

Maraj, C., Lackey, S., Badillo-Urquiola, K., Ogreten, S., & Maxwell, D. (2015). Empirically derived recommendations for training novices using virtual worlds. In *Interservice*. Orlando, FL: Industry Training, Simulation, and Education Conference.

Maxwell, D., & McLennan, K. (2012). Case study: leveraging government and academic partnerships in MOSES (Military Open Simulator [Virtual World] Enterprise Strategy). In *Proceedings of World Conference on Educational Multimedia, Hypermedia and Telecommunications* (pp. 1604-1616). Academic Press.

Maxwell, D. B. (2015). *Gauging Training Effectiveness of Virtual Environment Simulation Based Applications for an Infantry Soldier Training Task* (Doctoral dissertation). University of Central Florida, Orlando, FL.

Maxwell, D. B. (2016). Application of Virtual Environments for Infantry Soldier Skills Training: We are Doing it Wrong. In *International Conference on Virtual, Augmented and Mixed Reality* (pp. 424-432). Springer International Publishing.

Mazzone, L. A. L., & Aguiar, S. (2017, December 30). *U.S. Navy Virtual World Schoolhouse Case Study*. Paper presented at the Interservice Industry Training Simulation and Education Conference, Orlando, FL.

Mazzone, L. A. L., & Aguiar, S. (2017a, December 30). *Rapid Prototyping Innovative Virtual Worlds that Include the WOW Factor*. Paper presented at the Interservice Industry Training Simulation and Education Conference, Orlando, FL.

Morgado, L., Paredes, H., Fonseca, B., Martins, P., Antunes, R., Moreira, L., . . . Santos, A. (2016). Requirements for the use of virtual worlds in corporate training: perspectives from the post-mortem of a corporate e-learning provider approach of Second Life and OpenSimulator. In *iLRN 2016: Immersive Learning Research Network Conference. Workshop, Short Paper and Poster Proceedings from the Second Immersive Learning Research Network Conference* (pp. 18-29). Technischen Universität Graz.

Reiners, T., Gregory, S., & Knox, V. (2016). Virtual Bots as seen in Gregory, S., Lee, M. J., Dalgarno, B., & Tynan, B. (Eds.). (2016). Learning in Virtual Worlds: Research and Applications. Athabasca University Press.

Seaman, J. E., Allen, I. E., & Seaman, J. (2018). *Grade Increase: Tracking Distance Education in the United States, Babson Survey Research Group*. Released under a Creative Commons Attribution-ShareAlike 4.0 International license. Report available at: http://www.onlinelearningsurvey.com/highered.html

Stricker, A. G., Westhauser, T. C., Sheets, T., Hawkins-Scribner, T., Calongne, C., & Truman, B. (2017). Values-Based Network Leadership in an Interconnected World. *The Journal of Values Based Leadership*.

The Air University. (2017). *Squadron Learning Experience*. Prototyping Effort Status Report. Unpublished report.

Truman, B. (2017). *Computer-Based Simulation Spectrum*. Retrieved from: http://barbaratruman.com/cbs-spectrum

Truman, B., & Metcalf, D. (2015). Advancing Interagency Collaboration through Constructive Simulation: Results from the 2015 Federal Consortium of Virtual Worlds Workshop. In *Proceedings of the HCI International 2015 Conference*. Springer.

Truman, B. E. (2004). UCF's Exemplary Faculty Support: An institutionalized ecosystem. *Journal of Asynchronous Learning Networks*, *8*(3), 89–96.

Truman, B. E. (2014). *Transformative interactions using embodied avatars in collaborative virtual environments: Towards transdisciplinarity* (Doctoral dissertation). Colorado Technical University.

UCF Center for Distributed Learning. (2017). *Distributed Learning Impact Evaluation*. Retrieved from https://online.ucf.edu/research/dl-impact-evaluation

UCF Today. (2019). *UCF's Partnership IV Building to be New Home for Army's Synthetic Training Environment*. Retrieved from: https://today.ucf.edu/ucfs-partnership-iv-building-new-home-armys-simulation-training-environment/

Valadares, A., Gabrielova, E., & Lopes, C. V. (2016). On designing and testing distributed virtual environments. *Concurrency and Computation*.

Wielsch, D. (2010). Governance of Massive Multiauthor Collaboration – Linux, Wikipedia, and Other Networks: Governed by Bilateral Contracts, Partnerships, or Something in Between? JIPITEC, 1.

Winkelmann, K., Keeney-Kennicutt, W., Fowler, D., & Macik, M. (2017). Development, implementation, and assessment of General Chemistry Lab experiments performed in the virtual world of Second Life. *Journal of Chemical Education*, *94*(7), 849–858.

Yu, L. (2013). The market-driven software ecosystem. *IT Professional*, *15*(5), 46–50.

KEY TERMS AND DEFINITIONS

Avatar: An electronic image that represents the embodiment of a person in a virtual world that can be manipulated in appearance, movement, and gesture.

Collaborative Virtual Environment: A virtual space where people can interact with each other using avatars and create sharable content while distributed anywhere in the world through internet access.

Constructive Simulation: Social, virtual environments/worlds that allow users to create and interact with content in the world.

Ecosystem: An interconnected, complex system that represents multiple elements that combine to form a holistic environment.

Extended Reality (XR): Current and future virtual reality (VR), augmented reality (AR), mixed reality (MR), and other XR technologies for supporting and enhancing learning and human performance in evidence-based and research-grounded ways.

Identity: The distinguishing characteristics that make up a person's qualities, values, and beliefs.

Internet of Things: Networked/embedded physical objects that collect and exchange data across devices, society that make up smart cars, homes, cities, communities, etc.

Learning Engineering: An effort to combine learning science with engineering to improve the design of environments using multiple media and applications to improve learning outcomes.

Open Simulation: Computer-based simulation that is built upon open source software and open standards enabling users to co-create content simultaneously while the software operates.

Persona: An individual's image or personality that makes up a social façade that someone projects to others.

Section 4

The Multidisciplinary Lens of Computer, Information Technology, Systems Thinking, and Transdiscipliarity Sciences

Chapter 14
Advancing Personal Learning and Transdisciplinarity for Developing Identity and Community

Barbara Truman
https://orcid.org/0000-0002-7839-1772
University of Central Florida, USA

Jaclyn Truman
Columbia International University, USA

ABSTRACT

Personal learning is an idiosyncratic ability built upon metacognition that fosters identity development. When supported with virtual learning using avatars, collaborative virtual environments (CVEs), and combinations of emerging technologies, personal learning advances identity exploration and community development. Virtual participation in groups and events fosters mentoring for community enrichment especially for vulnerable populations such as persons with disabilities, the elderly, and those in need of recovery. Emerging technologies such as extended reality (XR) and the internet of things (IoT) present opportunities to combine physical and virtual world media/interactions useful for improved learning engineering. New expressions of Gemeinschaft and Gesselschaft are possible to co-create the future when empowered stakeholders collaborate to design smart, enabled, blended physical and virtual cities/communities. This chapter explores how concepts from systems thinking, presence research, and transdisciplinarity can advance personal learning and transcend human limitations.

DOI: 10.4018/978-1-5225-9679-0.ch014

INTRODUCTION

This chapter explores the notion of generating greater responsibility and empowerment for a concept of personal learning framed through the use of embodied avatars, collaborative virtual environments, metacognition, and emerging technologies. The catalyst for cultivating identity will be shown as a function of learners' interaction socially where mentoring abounds. The authors posit that improved self-discovery, self-efficacy, self-regulation, self-determination, and self-leadership contributes to the development of authenticity and ownership of identity made possible through immersive, virtual learning. These qualities, when habitually practiced contribute to involvement in communities that serve as brokers of practical innovation impacting quality of life in the virtual and physical world. Several words in this chapter appear to have improper punctuation. Familiar concepts are shown with differences in meaning when applying new lenses such as self-Self, being-Being, and nature-Nature.

Future developments in the IoT are discussed for applications of personal and environmental uses that when combined and integrated into virtual and physical environments provide the potential for transformative benefits. Extended reality (XR) is described as expressions of augmented, virtual, and mixed realities that will blur boundaries between worlds and activities undertaken for personal and professional uses. Implications for supporting under-served populations such as persons with disabilities are considered within the frame of an enabled, smart community.

Reciprocal sharing and appreciation are necessary to create a community. Communing within communities involves a spiritual dimension of hope and optimism that transcends wealth and social status. Across cultures, there is a wide disparity of economic wealth, and yet, people freely learn together in some cases creating a learning community, the bedrock of society. Practicing mindfulness has been widely attributed to promoting spiritual health, and while digital technologies have cause greater human separation in some, on the whole, these technologies have provided the basis for connecting more people continuously from most anywhere. As media exposure from augmented reality becomes more common in everyday life will our awareness diminish due to distraction or will we aspire to create new understanding through new forms of communication? Tuan (1977) said, "People tend to suppress that which they cannot express" (p. 6) and "Exceptionally talented people can live for art and science and go wherever they thrive" (p. 138). Will we create our own safe, virtual havens and dare to discover feelings that which are in us? And then, will we be open to sharing with others creating new forms of intimate understanding? Mentors have a leading role to play, and we can all be mentors in virtual world communities, "Feelings and intimate experiences are inchoate and unmanageable to most people, but writers and artists have found ways of giving them form" (p. 202).

BACKGROUND

Practicing the development of habits of mind require embracing *personal mastery* so that we shape technology more than it shapes our humanity. An essential component of the discipline of personal mastery involves taking the time to focus and reflect on our vision so we can see objectively (Senge, 2006, p. 136). Oelofsen (2012), describes personal learning as how you interact with the experiences you have that involve self-awareness and clarity on how your personal history, past experiences, and personality affect your approach to your work role (p. 295). Social learning is not distinct from personal learning and is often intertwined. Seeing the connections between one's role and job to others involves interdependence.

Lankau and Scandura (2002) refer to this type of personal learning as relational job learning. Another type is personal skill development that leads to improved working relationships based on the acquisition of new abilities and skills (p. 3). Frequently in the workplace, professional development organizations try to capture and emulate scenarios to promote the acquisition of the types of personal learning that cannot be trained. Personal learning is directly related to what constitutes a person's individuality and identity, i.e., their selfhood.

Emerging technologies include a wide range of devices and platforms. For this chapter, the authors examined the Internet of Things (IoT) especially smart sensors that when used personally can improve health and fitness such as when using wearables. The explosion of IoT technologies made up of often inexpensive and miniaturized components are resulting in the development of smart cities where services are created to support safety, sustainability, and economic development. Emerging IoT capabilities can be used for advancing the development of human-computer abilities when we can answer the question, "How does an individual create and use his own assistive service from the various devices present in the environment?" (de la Guía et al., 2015, p. 64). As IoT matures, new capabilities to bridge health, wellness, and education will be possible through the additional information offered from data obtained from our states in varied contexts. This IoT-enabled information can lead to improved personal mastery when combined with what Stephen Covey (2006) describes as the Eight Habit, a commitment to continuous improvement of the whole person, or Kaizen (p. 156). The whole person paradigm is what distinguishes the educational offering of institutionally-offered personalized learning and organically-developed personal learning. In order to fully take advantage of the discovery and development of IoT-enabled abilities, a personal learning approach is required. Educational institutions often provide support to build learning capability from workshops, and instructional content focused on metacognition, but personal learning encompasses the whole person over time and across contexts of learning. Downes (2016) cites personal learning as, "like shopping at a grocery store. You need to assemble the ingredients yourself and create your own meals…you control the experience, and you control the outcome" (p. 3).

The authors assert that in order to promote a theme of this book, Gemeinschaft (community), personal awareness of and connection to nature is required to acknowledge oneness with community. When we experience this connection of being and recognize and contribute to our ability author our future, this actualization contributes to a state of *Being*. Nicolescu (2014) describes the characterization of this state, "… understanding means fusion of knowledge and being" (p. 212). Previously Nicolescu had cited Jakob Boehme's work *Aurora*, as showing how the multiple 'splendor of Being' is reflected in the 'mirror of Nature' (Nicolescu, 2013, p. 66). He goes on to state that a new Philosophy of Nature can only be modern science, demanding an opening to being, which only takes place through a transdisciplinary approach, a new type of scientific and cultural approach. He says this approach opens an 'incredible space' for a free dialogue between the past and the present, between science, art, Tradition, and all other forms of knowledge (p. 66). As individuals tinker with new IoT-discovered abilities and participate in their communities to exchange and validate contributions, the positive impact for society can be dramatic. The potential to create *enabled*, smart communities using IoT capabilities designed to integrate the physical world with cyberspace and virtual environments poses the affordance of radical inclusivity for involving everyone irrespective of age or disability (p. 63). Not everyone may benefit without facilitated inclusion. "People living with a sensory or cognitive impairment may have even more difficulty when attempting to start using a wearable health monitoring device" (Schwartz, Oppold, & Hancock, 2019).

Learning together also builds *community*. When members have deep humility and respect the dignity of others, community is apparent. The learning can be formal or informal so long as it is shared learning. Hall et al. (2012) described a learning process as, Team learning, an evolving process that encompasses reflection and action. Team learning and mental models make up two of five disciplines defined by Senge (1991) contributing to learning organizations. The other three are personal mastery, shared vision, and systems thinking. Sharing information, asking questions, seeking feedback, experimenting with team processes, reflecting on results, and discovering and discussing errors or unexpected consequences are all behaviors of team learning (Hall et al., 2012, p.423). Dialogue is also a key enabler of community development, and even companies that use dialogue to focus on shared mental models and cultural assumptions are believed to be more flexible. The key variables associated with flexibility involve action, structure, and processes (Scharmer, 2000). True dialogue does not follow structure, yet promotes understanding without sound. "…cultures emerge from the silence between the words…" (Nicolescu, 2014, p. 10). Capturing silent meaning in immersive, collaborative environments is a technological challenge.

Key Factors that Contribute to the Development of Personal Learning

Formal education has the potential to diminish the curiosity and creativity of learners over time. Attaining a sense of self-mastery may also be fleeting as the neuroscientist Damasio (2012) states, "The self permits a view of the mind, but the view is clouded (p. 13). Even in medical school where candidates are selected for their abilities appear to experience erosion of professionalism during their training (West & Shanafelt, 2007, p. 2). The personal factors were grouped into 1) personal well-being 2) individual characteristics and 3) interpersonal qualities and skills. These elements were described as being combined with the environmental factors of 1) institutional culture 2) formal/informal curricula on professionalism and 3) practice characteristics. All six factors and their sub-elements combine to create professionalism among physicians (p. 3). While it is often not possible to directly influence the environmental factors within organizations in the physical world, it is possible to model environments in the virtual world to explore how the personal and environmental factors can be construed. West and Shanafelt (2007) concluded that "Modeling of and support for desirable behaviors in the informal and hidden curricula should support the formal curriculum for professionalism" (p. 6). The findings did not envision the use of personal learning combining the use of avatars, collaborative virtual environments, extended reality (XR), and the Internet of Things.

Virtual world environments are steadily maturing. The graphical, 3D representations of physical spaces enable a person to experience a realistic or fantastic environment using avatars to explore a space, manipulate objects, and, when networked together, interact with other avatars (Cooke & Hilton, 2015, p. 164). Collaborative virtual environments (CVEs) enable users to create and maintain situation awareness across remote and local sites creating and maintaining a sense of presence, or "being there" regardless of physical location (Sonnenwald, 2006, p. 68). Ratan (2011) describes presence as a concept within the field of Communication that grew out of the need to understand the effects of technologies and media that increasingly embody the user, namely robotics and virtual reality (p. 7). The question of attachment to the avatar and the milieu of virtual reality arise for how some individuals become empowered to participate in virtual communities of practice. For some people, empowerment and awareness of selfhood become a force that transfers to the physical world. Ratan (2011) describes a similar finding from his research:

> *When the experience of self-presence is strong, interactions between the avatar and the virtual environment are treated to some extent as unmediated, and this may increase the strength of physiological responses during avatar use. Thus, people who are induced to feel a stronger connection to their avatar, via avatar customization, gender consistency, or the interaction between these variables, may exhibit more physiological arousal or stronger emotional responses during avatar use. (p. 82)*

Taking ownership of one's self and identity poses the question of the chicken and the egg. Which comes first, assuming responsibility for one's self or exercising personal learning? The two are directly related and when exercised lead us in most circumstances to ask, "...what is the best thing I can do under these circumstances?" (Covey, 2006, p. 133). Can we effectively learn without being self-responsible to influence everything in our power to improve? The motivation to improve is also a factor that develops personal learning. Integrating motivation, specifically autonomous motivation into the sense of self represents the idea of incorporating both intrinsic and extrinsic motivation. "When people are autonomously motivated, they experience volition, or a self-endorsement of their actions." (Deci & Ryan, 2008, p. 182). Virtual learning sometimes referred to as learning online with non-immersive learning management systems or conferencing systems. We differentiate our use of virtual learning to include transmedia learning elements that connect learning more seamlessly across experiences and involve the use of avatars as a reflection of ourselves as protagonists. Raybourn (2018) cited that successful habits of transmedia learners as self-regulated and self-directed. We include self-efficacy as a desired habit to suggest that imagining and rehearsing competencies can be achieved prior to physically doing activities in many cases.

Understanding our self is the opportunity posed in delving deeply into personal learning practices in order to identify fears and negative associations that may create a bias that impedes our abilities. The practice of presencing advocated by Senge, Scharmer, Jaworski, and Flowers (2005), improves understanding of self and others. Building a habit of listening and observing openly is key to experience presencing. "If we can simply observe without forming conclusions as to what our observations mean and allow ourselves to sit with all the seemingly unrelated bits and pieces of information we see, fresh ways to understand a situation can eventually emerge" (p. 31). Practicing presencing can lead to greater wellbeing through understanding. Improved wellness contributes to personal learning across life within activities that span work, school, leisure, and personal domains. These domains involved cognitive, social, affective, physical, emotional, and spiritual health.

Mounting evidence illustrates the value of embracing the whole person paradigm to enact personal learning for self-health, especially with the data offered by using IoT personally. "... Widespread advances in technology, enabling researchers to track the pathways of mind and immunity, are finally overcoming the resistance of the scientific community to the notion that the brain and the immune system can and do communicate" (Sternberg, 2001, p. 6). One pathway of communication involves emotions and how we respond to translate them into feelings. Emotions scientist, Barbara Frederickson (2013) quotes Harvard psychiatrist George Vaillant who summarized, "Love is the shortest definition of spirituality I know" (p. 182). Frederickson also asserted that how we think about love reshapes the way our bodies experience love (p. 189). More scientists are scrutinizing the impact of positive emotions on health to obtain patterns across societies and cultures. How we as individuals calibrate our emotions through deliberate awareness exercises will improve the potential for including others in meaningful experiences and interactions, especially love. Frederickson cited a worldwide collapse of imagination when love comes to our limited view of obtaining the health benefits from experiencing micro-expressions of love with anyone (Frederickson, 2013, p. 189). She also cited that love is compassion and when it is focused on others, the person most changed is us (p. 153).

Taking ownership for one's identity requires self-awareness and courage to take leadership of stewardship over what is possible to improve under given circumstances. The relationship between identity stewardship and the development of authenticity becomes apparent as personal learning matures. Authenticity goes beyond understanding and involves acting, doing, or behaving. Gardner, Cogliser, Davis and Dickens (2011) reported on a literature review performed on authenticity and conclusions that authenticity documents a range of mental and behavioral processes. Over time and across situations, people discover and construct a core sense of self where four central themes emerge: "authentic functioning of people's (1) self-understanding, (2) openness to objectively recognizing their ontological realities (e.g., evaluating their desirable and undesirable self-aspects), (3) actions, and (4) orientation towards interpersonal relationships" (p. 1121). Authenticity is not associated with securing rewards or avoiding punishment and involves a relational orientation of achieving and valuing truthfulness and openness in close relationships (Gardner et al, 2011, p. 1121). Self-awareness is seen as a key component of authenticity informed by the true self (Ladkin, & Taylor, 2010, p. 5). The true self must be discovered using personal learning.

Maintaining a commitment to self as an entity in its own right was described as a serious concern more so than in performing role identities such as a parent, teacher, volunteer, etc. (Erickson, 1995, p. 126). Considering how the self is simultaneously shaped and is shaping by social interactions within environments, the self must be seen as a social force within environments in order to participate in social construction (p. 127). The authors assert that this is especially true when learners are engaged in using an avatar within collaborative virtual environments where users have constructive power over the environment. Maintaining commitment to self as an entity was described by Erickson as evidenced by relative authenticity, the extent of fulfilling expectations one has for self (p. 13). The chapter, *Identity Growth in the Professions* by Stricker, Westhauser, Lyle, Lowry, and Sheets propose social intelligence (SI) as one of five skill literacies necessary for identity maturation. The other literacies are Effectance Competency (EC), Leading People (LP), Moral Courage (MC), and Growth Mindset (GM) that follows the research of Carol Dweck (2008). Stricker and co-authors also propose a transdisciplinary framework advancing identity maturation for the profession of arms that can be translated to civilian professionalism. Story vignettes are described in the appendix as examples of identity progression based on World War II aviation warfare that led to the development of the United States Air Force.

Another key factor that contributes to the development of personal learning is self-affirmation. Cohen & Sherman, (2014) report that barriers and psychological threats are lifted in a situation when affirmation is used (p. 358). The effect is similar to outcomes within resiliency research such as stress reactivity, self-regulation, and information processing. "The core areas typically affirmed—relationships, family, and spiritual and religious values—dovetail with the hot spots for intervention in resilience research" (Cohen & Sherman, 2014, p. 360).

Creating New Abilities through Combining Emerging Technology

The use of immersive, virtual environments within the last decade has created dynamics impacting professional identity and personal learning, especially in higher education. Stanford's Virtual Human Interaction Lab is one example of a university that has performed research on the relationship of avatar use, empathy, awareness of self, and community interactions (Yee & Bailenson, 2009). In many cases, creating an avatar leads to the development of a persona that is used across social media and various virtual worlds. The avatar can also be construed as a learning artifact representing expression and evidence of the cultivation of identity.

The avatar also represents a kind of mirror to the self. Sparrowe (2005) describes seeing oneself as an other as a means of narrating our selves. By creating the avatar as an object of self, we can reflect upon and examine our authentic life as suggested in leadership theory (p. 429). The question of: "Is the authentic self the self that is constant (sameness) or is it the self that is faithful to its promises though fluid and changeable (selfhood)?" Sparrowe suggests that it is neither one alone. The narrative unites them [*self that is constant and self that is faithful*] (p. 430 emphasis ours). The notion of creating a story arc for our self could have transformative implications for resiliency and wellness as we hone the ability to see what is happening through personal learning. Raybourn (2014) appealed to a military audience to employ transmedia learning approaches:

Similarly, serious games for homeland security and defense training can be interactive scenarios in which the learner is engaged by being the protagonist of his or her own story. Live Action Role Play (LARP) and multi-player games often involve the learner from the first-person perspective. This first person buy-in is also key to transmedia learning storytelling. When learners are emotionally invested in the story and, in the case of training and education, see themselves as protagonists of their own training story, they remember it better and continue to respond to new or strategically repurposed content that is associated with familiar emotional triggers. (p. 473)

The translation for civilians applies for persons in need of recovery or assistance who when empowered can imagine and create more optimal, potential outcomes, or the *art-of-the-possible*. Sparrowe (2005) cites examples from cognitive science based on the research of Roser & Gazzaniga (2004), Turner (1996), and Dennett (1991, 1992) that suggest a convergence between interpretative and functionalist paradigms in relation to understanding self and identity. Narrative identity need not and should not be constrained by the limits of either paradigm, although research from a functionalist paradigm on autobiographical memory can illuminate how individuals, including leaders, misrepresent themselves to themselves (Sparrowe, 2005, p. 434).

For some people attachment to the avatar does not occur and for others, embodiment is readily felt. There is insufficient research on which persons and their associated factors contribute to avatar attachment. For some users, somatic flexibility, a means of transcending the physical body but not, embodiment is achieved (Young & Whitty, 2011, p. 537). Somatic flexibility is thought to be appreciated most by persons with disabilities who enjoy the affordances of using an avatar in a collaborative virtual world where parity is impossible in the physical world. Social interaction using avatars is enhanced by presence, which Ratan (2011) describes as the way people connect to their avatars on three levels: body, emotion, identity (p. 1). Social interaction plays a significant role in the establishment of positive traits in individuals. Sustainment of positive traits is supported within virtual communities where individuals engage in social presence (Stricker, McCrocklin, Calongne, Scribner, & Holm, 2010, p. 5). These interactions are significant for persons in need of recovery such as cancer survivors.

It is hard to imagine the artistic and creative abilities that may become possible through new forms of human-computer ability made possible by emerging technology. Clark (2007) suggests that our choices of biotechnological unions create soft selves, new forms of hybrid cognitive and physical being that represent who and what we are (p. 279). The emphasis on choices is key. The question of deliberation remains of whether choices have been made with deliberation as a manner of creativity and stewardship of identity. Csíkszentmihályi (1997), the researcher who developed the Theory of Flow, said: "It is easier to enhance creativity by changing conditions in the environment than by trying to make people think more creatively" (p. 1). In constructive, virtual worlds, the dynamic change of the environment can be a means of expression and dialogue. When learners accelerate learning from participating in virtual communities, they will combine IoT sensor-based data to form new forms of identities. "There is no doubt that emerging technologies have raised the quality of life globally for Deaf individuals, allowing for new connections to be made across borders" (Truman, 2019, p. 198).

Learning Engineering and Embodiment for Advancing Personal Learning

Concurrent with the design and development of physical communities and measures of well-being, emerging technologies surround the use of virtual reality and the Internet of Things (IoT). Virtual reality is experiencing a renaissance due to new authoring abilities of rich content and for the use of consumer-grade head-mounted displays. Many of these technologies converge when virtual worlds become a sort of middleware between applications. In 2017, the Institute of Electrical and Electronic Engineers (IEEE) created an industry consortium called ICICLE that seeks to advance learning engineering as a curricular and pedagogical approach reliant upon interoperable devices and platforms that can make learning more seamless (2019). Several special interest groups are gathering resources to illustrate possible future applications, including for extended reality (XR), the blend of augmented, virtual, and mixed reality across media, time, and environments. Google Cardboard is an example of a low-cost innovation that can be used in public schools, nursing homes, and developing nations to experience existing virtual reality. EDUCAUSE (2019) described learning engineering as:

Sitting at the confluence of learning science, learning technology, and instructional design, learning engineering can be framed as the application of engineering design methodologies in developing learning technologies and infrastructures. Learning engineers have the skills needed to integrate engineering and systems thinking with learning science in support of better learning technologies and, ultimately, improved learning outcomes. Learning engineers provide architectures and techniques that can help us develop new and better tools to apply what we are learning about learning, cognition, and human development. (para. 1)

The question of embodiment arises concerning the attachment to an avatar and whether the emerging virtual reality compares with existing virtual world uses. The phenomenon of embodiment involves developing interaction not only in the virtual environment but with the physical world. "It is not simply our beliefs or behaviours; rather, it is our ways of living and experiencing our world that 'involves our sensory and motor processes, perceptions, and actions'" (Johnson, 1989, pp. 362–363) as found in (Li, 2010, p. 407). Fundamentally, the issue of reality in terms of physics and Nature has a reoccurring theme of being plastic and at our discretion because of our free will to choose. Nicolescu (2014) states that "Reality is not something outside or inside us: it is simultaneously outside and inside. We are part of this Reality, which changes due to our thoughts, feelings, and actions. This awareness means that we are fully responsible for what Reality is" (p. 215). The shift from reality to Reality may be viewed as this awareness of continual choice, a co-emergence or enactivism. Co-emergence involves the change of a living system and its surrounding environment. The change depends on the interaction between this system and the environment as a means of coupling, hence co-emergence of interaction, but no guarantee of greater or lesser adaptation to each other (Reid, 1995)" as seen in (Li, 2010, p. 407).

IoT, also referred to the Internet of Everything (IoE) is 'staggeringly transformational' and highly disruptive at the same time (ISACA, 2015, p. 4). Goldman Sachs (2014) represents IoT as the third wave in the development of the Internet itself (p. 1). Sensor-enabled technologies will allow us to take greater charge of our health in the physical world. When we combine the use of these technologies with the virtual world, our identities will aspire to new abilities on the neurological level that are hard to imagine. "This new generation of quantified-self experimentation allows individuals to heal, fix, optimize, tinker, and engage in curiosity-driven research in new ways than were possible previously, and which may have deeply meaningful solutions" (Swan, 2012, p. 239). Smart sensors fuel the potential for societal transformation within the Internet of Things, especially when individuals practice the discipline of presencing to become more informed, inclusive, open (smart) citizens.

Enabling Technology for Improving Abilities

Technology has been demonstrated to assist with learning in a variety of contexts, but what about improving the basic conditions upon which people must live? Emerging technology such as the Internet of Things represents new opportunities to improve the quality of life at home, school, work, and beyond. Smart devices incorporating sensors are gaining popularity and may be personalized for specific needs among persons with disabilities, the elderly, and persons needing recovery like cancer survivors. Improved quality of life can impact personal security, wellness, economic livelihood, and educational attainment. Educators must recognize the opportunity to explore and test new ways to use IoT capabilities that can result in breakthrough empowerment for themselves, their organizations, and communities. Institutions must enable stakeholder involvement to improve the accessibility and usability of their environments. An ethos of radical inclusivity made possible with IoT initiatives may unlock cognitive capabilities and appreciation for minds that are trapped in frail bodies. IoT creates enabling environments by offering people with disabilities assistance in access to buildings, transportation, information and communication (Domingo, 2012, p. 594). Collaborative virtual worlds offer a platform for including members of vulnerable populations to contribute to the design of IoT-based innovations.

Living with a disability, whether temporary or permanent affects families who may also face economic challenges due to the inability to access health services, education, and employment opportunities. Gaining family and community support is critical to reducing barriers to engaging in personal learning. If assistive technology services are not received at an early age, opportunities may be severely limited later when challenges are greater due to differences in the ages of peers. For example, deaf children often need additional exposure to American Sign Language (ASL) because most parents of deaf children are hearing and not fluent in ASL. An interactive IoT system is available for deaf children to take with them from school to home. The most challenging vocabulary can be reviewed until it is understood and memorized, perhaps involving other family members. Learning barriers are reduced with the innovative, game-based learning system. Can IoT-enabled services provide an intervention capability to serve cross-generational learning? A strong correlation exists between early signed language exposure for deaf children and later academic achievement (Domingo, 2012, p. 594). Aging in place at home for the elderly and support for vulnerable persons needing care is possible through using IoT-enabled combinations of physical and virtual environments.

Another opportunity for educators is the fact that physical world environments can be modeling virtually to provide a low-cost means of designing assistive technology capabilities using IoT. Insights on usability and ergonomics can be discovered before implementation to improve an environment that supports personal learning. The physical and virtual world may be linked through the use of extended reality (XR) to view visualized data and dashboards produced from data received by IoT in the physical environment. The ability to participate in communities will increase as more physical environments have corresponding virtual representations that people can access easily online. As spaces are networked, new forms of communities will be possible offering options for participation face-to-face or electronically. Greater independence and interdependence will become more affordable. Full participation of persons with disabilities in everyday activities is achieved through support for mobility, accessibility, place of residence, transportation and education (Peraković, Periša, & Prcić, 2015, p. 22). Other vulnerable populations can benefit as well using technologies that are embedded in the environment or worn.

Stricker, Holm, Calongne, and McCrocklin (2011) found the use of an immersive virtual reality (IVR) ecosystem for collaborative-design based (CDB) -prototyping can help foster a sense of place, purpose, and community identity. "Innovation prototyping, using an IVR landscape to span physical and virtual geography, offers breadth, depth, and endless frontiers for enhancing learning, instruction, and discovery" (Stricker et al., 2011, p10). One such community is the Nonprofit Commons (NPC) group that meets in the virtual world Second Life every week. Colorful avatars of many non-profit groups gather to learn and share innovations applicable for personal learning and for improving the quality of life, Figure1 represents an anniversary poster for the NPC group. Virtual Ability is a nonprofit group that regularly participates in the NPC meetings. Virtual Ability was created for members to obtain support and celebrate different abilities. The outreach of the Virtual Ability community would be too costly and

Figure 1. Nonprofit commons in second life
Source: Photo credit Barbara Truman

time-consuming to replicate and participate in the physical world. For some members, there would be a physical risk to participate as well. Virtual participation affords a low-cost, low-threat alternative to refine personal learning. Communities like Virtual Ability exhibit 'eudaimonia' a form of happiness that seeks happiness and pleasure as desired end states in contrast to hedonism (Gardner, Cogliser, Davis, & Dickens, 2011).

Ironically, nonprofit organizations operating in physical spaces such as churches are not required to comply with federal disability laws to provide reasonable accommodation for parishioners with disabilities. Churches frequently do not have funds at their disposal to make significant building renovations, but they also enjoy tax-free status. Truman (2015) reported on how some deaf persons in the church are reduced to objects for which 'ministry' is offered rather than individuals deserving of access to emotional support delivered in the complexity of their native sign language by qualified interpreters (p. 2). Churches often take care to preserve their cultural affiliation using scriptural stories, songs, and psalms to cultivate a cultural identity. Diehl and Prins (2008) describe how when people actively mobilize through communication, the community is shaped based on the economic, historical, social and political contexts. Cultural identities are not fixed entities encompassing differences that move beyond region and ethnicity as the chief sources of cultural identity (p. 108). The most positive impact and interaction with individuals with disabilities result from an approach incorporating virtue-based ethics (Truman, 2015, p. 5). Generation differences affect culture as well. Human rights and activism is a priority to enable communal gathering in spaces made available to persons with different abilities "… an organized, collaborative effort to generate a highly sophisticated, technologically advanced community center can facilitate integrating where Deaf people operate daily, also bridging the generational gap" (Truman, 2019, p. 199).

The combination of identities and communities imply that new forms of expression will be created adding richness to language and meaning. It will be a challenge to remember the person behind the dynamic forms of avatar expressions that will also carry over into the physical world with augmented reality. Networked communities that visit each other in person and with embodied avatars will play a vital role in translating meaning between groups. Figure 2 shows an event in the virtual world Second Life that included the option to use avatars in world and video conferencing.

Senge et al. (2005) describe an ability of seeing from the whole attained from practicing the discipline of presencing, an activity requiring full attention to listen and open heart, mind, and will. "The key to 'seeing from the whole' is developing the capacity not only to suspend our assumptions, but to 'redirect' our awareness towards generative process that lies behind what we see" (Senge et al., 2005, p. 42). Active, iterative, experiential engagement provides an understanding of new information with the constructivist learning view, "People construct understanding based on life experiences and beliefs to help associate new knowledge" (Stricker et al., 2010, p. 10). Using a combinatory approach, educators have the potential to pioneer new forms of enabled, experiential learning communities that generate inclusivity and cross-cultural understanding.

Beyond Presence to Presencing and Transdisciplinarity

The Presencing Institute, located in Cambridge, Boston in the United States, is an awareness-based action research community for profound societal innovation and change. Scharmer (2011) described the presencing process as a journey that connects us more profoundly both to what wants to emerge in the world and to our emerging, higher self The Presencing Institute originates research, conducts professional development and facilitates community building in the pursuit of actualizing Self. The discipline

Figure 2. Playcamp in Second Life
Source: Photo credit Barbara Truman

of presencing does not necessarily take into account the value of technology to add to Self-actualization. For educators, who choose to experience and experiment (play) with emerging technologies, greater discovery will lead to cultivating identity.

This presencing notion of listening to develop Self is consistent with the experience of Being when unified with Nature. The question for us is how do we make this awareness and integration harmonious? As science advanced, the term 'Nature' began to disappear from science vocabulary and yet, Nicolescu asserted that Nature could only be conceived in terms of being human. The awareness required to understand, and by extension-thrive-is to conceive as if the book of Nature were being written, understanding it is not to be read, rather it is to be experienced as if we freely choose to participate in the writing of the book of Nature (Nicolescu, 2002, p. 65) as seen in (Truman, 2014, p. 4). With the recognition of this ability to author, we are all artisans, able to live artfully through the transparency of our choices. Through awareness of Nature and Being and the practice of presencing advocated by Scharmer for the development of Self, thriving is more likely to become common as a uniquely- human ability to choose is exercised and practiced. As we participate in virtual learning where we can create 'place' together, we may create *enlightened* communities as well as smart communities.

Many cities are evaluating technologies to purchase as part of smart city/community development. The creation of smart communities using the Internet of Things is enhanced when citizen participation is incorporated and when open government and data are used in combination (Pellicer et al., 2013, p. 442). Organizations such as the National Institute for Standards and Technology (NIST) and the National Science Foundation (NSF) are mobilizing research universities as well as municipalities to promote innovation and intelligence orchestration across people, devices, and data. NIST has an ongoing global cities challenge that includes potential funding to support municipal participation. Most of these organizations are relying upon the use of Web 2.0 technologies and face to face meetings to move the change management agenda forward.

Appreciating Complexity

The International Council on Systems Engineering (INCOSE) defines a system as an artifact created by humans. A system consists of components that pursue a common goal unattainable by each of the single elements (Karwowski, Ahrem & Amaha, 2013, p. 4). Key researchers cited in this chapter advocate self-awareness as a function of Being and embrace Nature to participate in the art of living. Emerging technologies are inherently complex. Calls for simplicity have villainized complexity requiring us to take a closer look at the beauty of complexity and its relationship with our awareness of selfhood and society.

Abandon the urge to simplify everything, to look for formulas and easy answers, and to begin to think multidimensionally, to glory in the mystery and paradoxes of life, not to be dismayed by the multitude of causes and consequences that are inherent in each experience -- to appreciate the fact that life is complex. (M. Scott Peck)

Daniel Goleman, author, and researcher of emotional intelligence also wrote about the power of attention in a book called, *Focus*. Goleman later teamed up with systems scientist Peter Senge and expanded and integrated the concepts in a book called *The Triple Focus*. Goleman and Senge cited that achieving the opportunity to perform and sustaining the performance are two different things. What gives some people more ability than others who have similar intelligence quotients? Some of the abilities include discipline, confidence, persuasiveness as a team member, and empathy. They advocate three abilities that should be taught by educators. The focus of these abilities is referred to as *inner*, *other*, and *outer* (Goleman & Senge, 2014, p. 6). More explicitly these become 1) Focus on yourself for self-awareness and connecting to purpose and aspirations 2) Focus on others for empathy, communication, and persuasion, teamwork and 3) Focus on systems to understand organizational dynamics, economies, industries, and technologies to see the interconnectedness for systems understanding. In elementary school, the exercise of naming emotions accurately helps children become clearer about what is going on within them emotionally (p. 13).

Previously Goleman (2013) had been studying how companies use cognitive models to identify how to hire better and promote employees. In a talk made to an audience at Google, Goleman described how his MIT colleague, John Sterman, said systems blindness is the number one challenge facing people today (31:00). Is it possible that system blindness causes the inability to see the effects of weather changes, environmental degradation, and poverty? Wicked problems encompass global and local environments that interact with each other in a myriad of ways, and they are ill-defined problems that are uniquely configured. They involve multiple constituencies and interdependencies. "Because of their multidimensional nature, the problems engendered by climate change cannot be solved by a single disciplinary approach——for example, by technologists——but must also incorporate social, cultural, environmental, economic, legal and political dimensions" (Miller, 2016, p. 40). Goleman and Senge (2014) identified nine habits that characterize someone who is a systems thinker:

Habits of a Systems Thinker

- Recognizes the importance of time delays when exploring cause and effect relationships.
- Finds where unintended consequences emerge.
- Changes perspectives to increase understanding.
- Identifies the circular nature of complex cause and effect relationships.
- Recognizes that a system structure generates its behavior.
- Uses understanding of systems structure to identify higher leverage action.
- Surfaces and test assumptions.
- Checks results in changes actions if needed: successive approximation.
- Seeks to understand the big picture (p. 53-54).

Transdisciplinarity and Networked Societies

Alfonso Montuori is a Professor of Transformative Leadership at the California Institute of Integral Studies in the United States. Montuori said that the challenge of our networked society and the emerging technologies is how we organize the new and existing data to make it into valuable knowledge to use wisely. "This is the challenge of complexity and Transdisciplinarity" (Montuori, 2013, p. 226). Perceiving Transdisciplinarity increases the potential awareness of Self in Nature within the context of others and the outer systems that make up our society. The choices we make within the realm of Transdisciplinarity of how we self-regulate and interact with others determine our collective power to continuously and consciously create Society. Basarab Nicolescu, considered to be the father of Transdisciplinarity, described it one way as a duality that is transcended by the open unity that encompasses both the universe and human beings. Transdisciplinarity involves the transgression of duality in opposing binary pairs such as simplicity-complexity, reductionism-holism, nature-divinity, and diversity-unity (Nicolescu, 2014, p. 209). For educators, Choi and Pak, 2006 describe and illustrate Transdisciplinarity in contrast to interdisciplinary and multidisciplinary stating its qualities are holistic, transcendental, integrative, and collaborative" (p. 356).

Integrating Mindfulness for Harmonization

Tuan (1977) whose writings describe the relation of space and place, said that nearly all learning is at the subconscious level (p. 200). Using emerging technology such as collaborative virtual environments (CVEs) extended reality (XR), and the Internet of Things provides us more space and data about what is happening inside of us physiologically as we shift between environments. In order for us to make learning more visible to us, we must become more mindful to listen and reflect on the subtle nuances and patterns of preferences and biases that make up our habits. Mindfulness practice requires attentional training and involves the ability to be aware of one's thoughts, feelings, and experiences in general and non-judging terms (Proulx, Todorov, Aiken & de Sousa, 2016, p. 7). Mindfulness is consistent with the emphasis on focus as called for by Daniel Goleman and the practice of presencing advocated by Otto Scharmer. Nicolescu's (2014) views concerning education are similar, and he said that a viable education could only be an integral education of the human being. Nicolescu added that this integral education requires a new type of intelligence that harmonizes mind, feelings, and body (p. 134).

Enactivism may help bridge the gap to this new form of intelligence needed for an integral education. Li (2010) referred to enactivism as a "philosophy based on two important premises: cognition and environment are inseparable, and 'systems' enact with each other from which they 'learn'" (p. 405). Holton (2010) referred to Begg (2000) who described enactivism: "thinking and cognition are grounded in bodily actions: "it is not knowledge as-object but knowledge-as-action" (p. 3). Another approach championed by Seymour Papert focuses more on the art of learning, or 'learning to learn,' and on the significance of making things in learning" (Ackermann, 2001, p. 1). This making represents Constructionist learning. Constructing virtual environments for learning using avatars within collaborative virtual environments is a powerful tool for educators to practice learning to learn. Papert's constructionism is highly dependent upon context similarly to situated learning. Jean Piaget, who worked and studied with Papert viewed knowledge as experience that is acquired through interaction with the world, people and things (Ackermann, 2001, p. 3). Li described the difference in an enactivist learning world compared to typical constructivist approaches. Using enactivism, learners would immerse themselves in rich and stimulating learning experiences while the intentionally built-in constraints foster learners' development towards the set of intended co-evolving patterns. "Learners, therefore, are coauthors of their learning environments, their learning and knowledge" (Li, 2010, p. 415). Could the designer/educator be the same as the learner? If so, this is consistent with the model for personal learning advocated by the authors. Enactivist, constructionist, and constructivist approaches will benefit from integrating these strategies with immersive, virtual learning that is constructive and social. The authors have advocated an awareness of systems to appreciate complexity and appreciate Transdisciplinarity.

Risks and Limitations

The gains for personal learning, identity maturation, inclusivity, and community development made possible from combinations of virtual worlds, physical meetings, avatar use, learning engineering approaches, extended reality (XR) and IoT-enabled environments do not come without their challenges. Viewing one's self as an object online in a virtual world may lead to what Young & Whitty (2011) describe as *idealized self* rather than *ideal self.* Marginalization may result when one's offline self does not compare and fulfill the need for identity development and authenticity. "With regard to the phenomenal self, the line between the authentic and inauthentic is somewhat fuzzy because, in each case, one's embodied experience is a genuine *experience*" (p. 553). The absence of attachment to avatar usage is a hindrance to participating fully in social virtual worlds and may hinder inclusion within communities.

Interoperability standards for technology and systems are being worked on by leaders in several nations and professional associations. The most significant challenge involves *privacy, trust, and security*." (de la Guía, et al., 2015, p. 60). For vulnerable populations, authentication into their trusted, IoT-enabled, extended reality (XR) applications requires research and development. Continuous stakeholder participation must be facilitated. Providing greater flexibility in how authentication in managed will allow more people to connect to secure services, information, and communities. Such security is necessary for members of the community to thrive (Griffin, 2015, p. 5).

FUTURE RESEARCH DIRECTIONS

A future area of study involves the exploration of how people dynamically adapt, recover, and evolve into new realms of identity development when using IoT-enabled collaborative virtual environments in a combinatory approach with face-to-face, extended reality (XR) environments. Attentional focus on and awareness of internal body sensations involve a construct of body awareness (Mehling et al., 2009, p. 1). Smart vests are an example of an IoT-enabled wearable currently being used for military, law enforcement, and astronauts. As smart vests become available to consumers to wear as part of daily living, the wearable physiological monitoring system that measures heart rate, blood pressure, body temperature, galvanic skin responses will add to the available information that makes up body awareness. Smart vests can even perform an electrocardiogram (Appelboom et al., 2014, p. 2).

Mehling et al. (2009) described a theoretical model for the body awareness construct made up of following four inter-related dimensions 1) Perceived body sensations 2) Quality of attention 3) Attitude of body awareness 4) Awareness of mind-body integration (p. 12). With sensor data available using the Internet of Things it may be possible to have a much greater understanding of the brain. Insights on mental performance optimization techniques and a variety of emotion reading, mapping, and management programs may be possible to track over time and within various contexts (Swan, 2012, p. 224).

Cultivating identity and stewardship of self requires a behavioral change that may break habits and form new ones. Swan (2012) suggested a possible progression of the personal monitoring required to invest in behavior change as 1) start tracking 2) obtain data 3) analyze data in infographics 4) interpret and determine meaning 5) try a behavior change 6) maintain the behavior change through the three week required for new habit development 7) produce a long-lasting change (p. 240). Including the use of XR- and IoT-enabled CVEs will enable new forms of data visualization that may become possible to engage in real-time decision-making where our avatars serve as a form of mirror to our self. Behavior change may be more possible from having access to the more fundamental drivers of human behavior, both at the individual (self) and overall human (society) level. "In the near-term it may be possible to have 24/7 access to more rigorous neural data streams, emotion-mapping information, motivation triggers, productivity determinants, and other transformative new data flows" (Swan, 2012, p. 243).

An additional area of future research will surround how communities combine the use of social media, virtual worlds, and emerging technologies for the participatory design of smart communities. Micro-electro-mechanical systems (MEMS) or very small devices will interact with human biology and interconnect within smart communities across society. MEMS and sensors are ubiquitous in products such as cars, kitchen appliances such as toasters and wearables. Philosopher Charles Taylor (2011) asked a question that represents another primary area of future research when he spoke at an academic gathering, "Now comes the questions of how we suppose to agree upon our value horizon?" (1:15).What will be our commitment to one another?

CONCLUSION

In summary, Figure 3: *Advancing Personal Learning Concept Map*, depicts the interdependent associations related to the elements described in this chapter and book.

Personal learning represents a frontier to develop an aspirational, authentic, yet dynamic identity. Practicing authentic self-leadership is predicted to become easier from IoT-enabled data that shapes identity made available from body awareness and body image. Practicing authentic self-leadership may become more of a challenge as environments shift more frequently due to the extended reality (XR) layers that provide more significant expression of self across physical and virtual contexts. For educators, engaging in experimentation with personal learning using avatars, collaborative virtual environments, and emerging technologies for personal use represents an opportunity to practice personal mastery. The authors believe mentoring will result in greater wellness for the whole person: physically, cognitively, emotionally, and spiritually.

This chapter summarizes many of the key themes in this book with a culminating call to seek Transdisciplinarity through creative uses of personal learning. The potential for creating new forms of community using virtual learning will result in interwoven Gemeinschaft and Gesselschaft principles. Nicolescu (2008) said that Transdisciplinarity requires a discipline of self-inquiry that integrates the knower in the process of knowing in order to get to the roots of knowledge to challenge our ways of thinking and our construction and organization of that knowledge (p. xvi) as seen in (Truman, 2014, p.44). Transdisciplinarity involves levels of Reality possessing multidimensional and multireferential

Figure 3. Advancing personal learning concept map
Source: Barbara Truman.

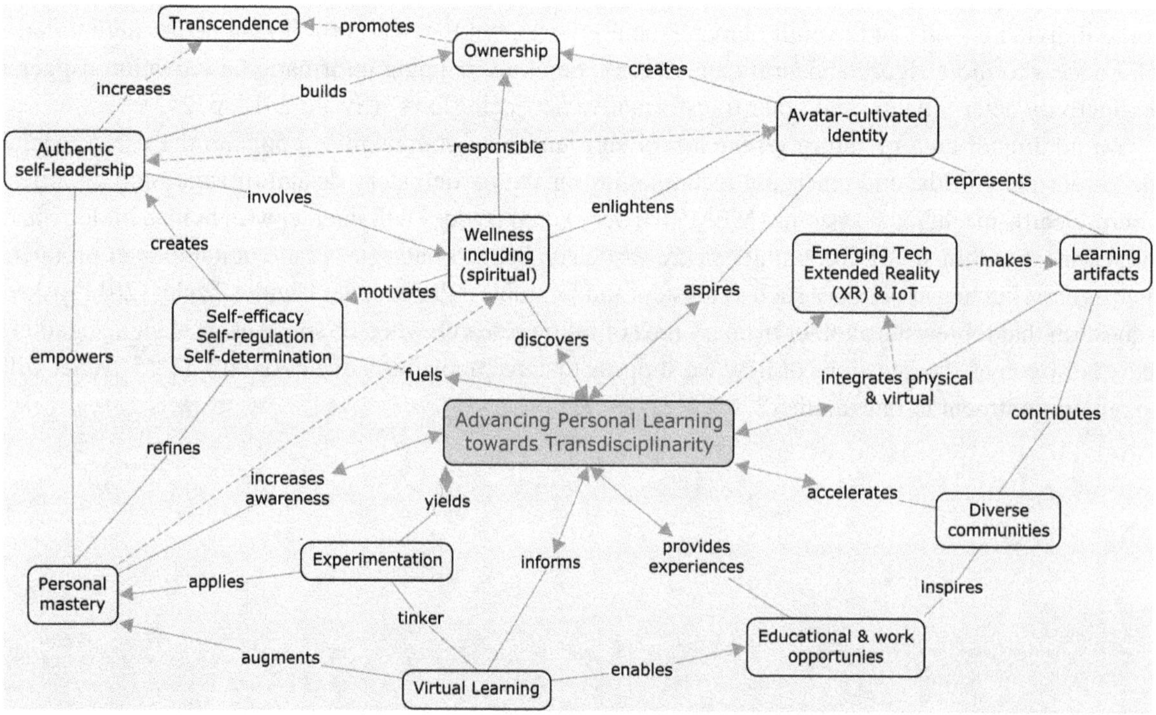

properties that relate to the "natural" and the "social" thereby applying to the study of nature and society (Nicolescu, 2014, p. 207).

When applied to advance personal learning using collaborative virtual environments (CVEs), Transdisciplinarity becomes possible to practice through engaging in the discipline of presencing within a virtual community. This discipline involves dialogue with Self then with others to increase understanding. As virtual learning increasingly spans physical and virtual spaces, leaders using avatars and dialogue can influence awareness of society through new forms of local and global (glocal) communities as illustrated in Figure 4. These communities can form the basis of aspirational Societies.

As Shane Lopez (2013) said, "While it may be hard to believe, your hope, in a small but meaningful way, is related to the hope of someone you may never meet" (p. 205). Transdisciplinarity offers a means of self-transformation. It orients towards the knowledge of the self and the unity of knowledge. Transdisciplinarity also offers the creation of a new art of living (Nicolescu, 1997) that can extend to virtual communities and society to transcend limitations. Communitarian, philosopher Charles Taylor has the last word as the final thought for this chapter: "Cherish your own confusion; don't flee from it or try to resolve it too soon. The creative process can be painful; but out of these pains come the deepest new insights" (KyotoPrize, 2012, 3:30).

Figure 4. Virtual and blended community of practice
Source: Barbara Truman

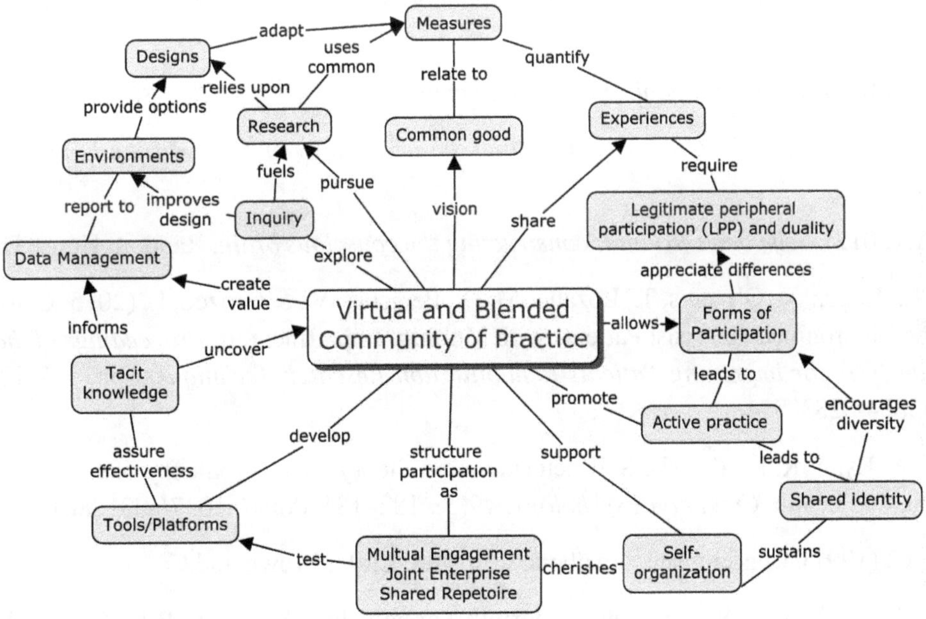

REFERENCES

Ackermann, E. (2001). Piaget's constructivism, Papert's constructionism: What's the difference. *Future of Learning Group Publication, 5*(3), 438.

Appelboom, G., Camacho, E., Abraham, M. E., Bruce, S. S., Dumont, E. L., Zacharia, B. E., ... Connolly, E. S. (2014). Smart wearable body sensors for patient self-assessment and monitoring. *Archives of Public Health, 72*(1), 28. doi:10.1186/2049-3258-72-28 PMID:25232478

Begg, A. (2000). *Enactivism: a personal interpretation*. Unpublished manuscript. Retrieved July 20th, 2009 from http://www.emr.vic.edu.au/Downloads/enactivism_andybegg.doc

Choi, B. C., & Pak, A. W. (2006). Multidisciplinarity, interdisciplinarity and transdisciplinarity in health research, services, education and policy: 1. Definitions, objectives, and evidence of effectiveness. *Clinical and Investigative Medicine, 29*(6), 351.

Clark, A. (2007). Re-Inventing Ourselves: The Plasticity of Embodiment, Sensing, and Mind. *The Journal of Medicine and Philosophy, 32*(3), 262–281. doi:10.1080/03605310701397024 PMID:17613705

Cohen, G. L., & Sherman, D. K. (2014). The psychology of change: Self-affirmation and social psychological intervention. *Annual Review of Psychology, 65*(1), 333–371. doi:10.1146/annurev-psych-010213-115137 PMID:24405362

Cooke, N. J., & Hilton, M. L. (Eds.). (2015). *Enhancing the Effectiveness of Team Science*. National Academies Press.

Covey, S. R. (2006). *The eighth habit*. Simon and Schuster.

Csíkszentmihályi, M. (1997). *Creativity: flow and the psychology of discovery and invention*. Harper Perennial.

Damasio, A. (2012). *Self comes to mind: constructing the conscious brain*. Random House Digital, Inc.

de la Guía, E., López, V., Olivares, T., Lozano, M. D., Penichet, V., & Orozco, L. (2015, October). Easy Smart-Home Environment to Assist Patients with Mobility Impairment. In *Proceedings of the 3rd 2015 Workshop on ICTs for improving Patients Rehabilitation Research Techniques* (pp. 122-125). ACM. 10.1145/2838944.2838974

Deci, E. L., & Ryan, R. M. (2008). Self-determination theory: A macrotheory of human motivation, development, and health. *Canadian Psychology, 49*(3), 182–185. doi:10.1037/a0012801

Dennett, D. C. (1991). Consciousness explained. Boston: Little, Brown and Co.

Dennett, D. C. (1992). The self as a center of narrative gravity. In F. S. Kessel, P. M. Cole, & D. L. Johnson (Eds.), Self and consciousness: Multiple perspectives. Hillsdale, NJ: Lawrence Erlbaum Associates.

Diehl, W. C., & Prins, E. (2008). Unintended outcomes in Second Life: Intercultural literacy and cultural identity in a virtual world. Language. *Intercultural Communication Language and Intercultural Communication, 8*(2), 101–118. doi:10.1080/14708470802139619

Domingo, M. C. (2012). An overview of the Internet of Things for people with disabilities. *Journal of Network and Computer Applications*, *35*(2), 584–596. doi:10.1016/j.jnca.2011.10.015

Downes, S. (2016). *Personal and Personalized Learning*. Retrieved from: http://www.downes.ca/post/65065

Dweck, C. S. (2008). *Mindset: The new psychology of success*. Random House Digital, Inc.

EDUCAUSE. (2019). *7 Things You Need to Know about Learning Engineering*. Retrieved from: https://library.educause.edu/resources/2018/9/7-things-you-should-know-about-learning-engineering

Erickson, R. J. (1995). The importance of authenticity for self and society. *Symbolic Interaction*, *18*(2), 121–144. doi:10.1525i.1995.18.2.121

Fredrickson, B. L. (2013). *Love 2.0: Finding happiness and health in moments of connection*. Penguin.

Gardner, W. L., Cogliser, C. C., Davis, K. M., & Dickens, M. P. (2011). Authentic leadership: A review of the literature and research agenda. *The Leadership Quarterly*, *22*(6), 1120–1145. doi:10.1016/j.leaqua.2011.09.007

Goldman Sachs. (2014). *IoT Primer The Internet of Things: Making sense of the next mega-trend. Equity research*. Author.

Goleman, D. (2013). Focus: the Hidden Driver of Excellence. In *Talks at Google* [Video file]. Retrieved from: http://bit.ly/264GIvu

Goleman, D., & Senge, P. (2014). The Triple Focus. *Reflections: The SoL Journal*, *14*(1).

Griffin, P. H. (2015). *Security for Ambient Assisted Living: Multi-factor Authentication in the Internet of Things*. Paper presented at the IoT Ambient Assisted Living Workshop (IoTAAL), IEEE Globecom 2015 Conference, San Diego, CA.

Hall, K. L., Vogel, A. L., Stipelman, B. A., Stokols, D., Morgan, G., & Gehlert, S. (2012). A four-phase model of transdisciplinary team-based research: Goals, team processes, and strategies. *Translational Behavioral Medicine*, *2*(4), 415–430. doi:10.100713142-012-0167-y PMID:23483588

Holton, D. L. (2010). *Constructivism + Embodied Cognition = Enactivism: Theoretical and Practical Implications for Conceptual Change*. Paper presented at the American Educational Research Association, Denver, CO. Retrieved from: http://usu.academia.edu/edtechdev/Papers/168218/Constructivism_Embodied_Cognition_Enactivism_Theoretical_and_Practical_Implications_for_Conceptual_Change

IEEE. (2019). *ICICLE Extended Reality (XR) Working Group*. Retrieved from https://www.ieeeicicle.org/xreality-sig/

ISACA. (2015). *Internet of Things: Risk and Value Considerations (registration required)*. Retrieved from: http://www.isaca.org/knowledge-center/research/researchdeliverables/pages/internet-of-things-risk-and-value-considerations.aspx

Johnson, M. (1989). Personal practical knowledge series: Embodied knowledge. *Curriculum Inquiry*, *19*(4), 361–377. doi:10.1080/03626784.1989.11075338

Karwowski, W., Ahram, T., & Amaba, B. (2013). A system-of-systems engineering approach to leadership and innovation: Sustainable STEM education and workforce development through the Smart Cities initiative. In *QScience Proceedings (World Congress on Engineering Education 2013)* (p. 12). Academic Press.

KyotoPrize. (2012). *Dr. Charles Margrave Taylor* [Video file]. Retrieved from: https://youtu.be/ayi8n-lZQkDo

Ladkin, D., & Taylor, S. S. (2010). Enacting the 'true self': Towards a theory of embodied authentic leadership. *The Leadership Quarterly*, *21*(1), 64–74. doi:10.1016/j.leaqua.2009.10.005

Lankau, M. J., & Scandura, T. A. (2002). An investigation of personal learning in mentoring relationships: Content, antecedents, and consequences. *Academy of Management Journal*, *45*(4), 779–790.

Li, Q. B. I., Clark, B., & Winchester, I. (2010). Instructional design and technology grounded in enactivism: A paradigm shift? *British Journal of Educational Technology*, *41*(3), 403–419. doi:10.1111/j.1467-8535.2009.00954.x

Lopez, S. J. (2013). *Making hope happen: Create the future you want for yourself and others*. Simon and Schuster.

Mehling, W. E., Gopisetty, V., Daubenmier, J., Price, C. J., Hecht, F. M., & Stewart, A. (2009). Body awareness: Construct and self-report measures. *PLoS One*, *4*(5), e5614. doi:10.1371/journal.pone.0005614 PMID:19440300

Miller, C. Z. (2016). Towards Transdisciplinarity: Liminality and the Transitions Inherent in Pluridisciplinary Collaborative Work. *Journal of Business Anthropology*, *1*(1), 35–57. doi:10.22439/jba.v1i1.4959

Montuori, A. (2013). Complexity and Transdisciplinarity: Reflections on Theory and Practice. *World Futures*, *69*(4-6), 200–230. doi:10.1080/02604027.2013.803349

Nicolescu, B. (1997). *The Transdisciplinary Evolution of the University Condition for Sustainable Development. Presentation to the International Congress "Universities' Responsibilities to Society*. Bangkok, Thailand: International Association of Universities, Chulalongkorn University. Retrieved from http://ciret-transdisciplinarity.org/bulletin/b12c8.php

Nicolescu, B. (2002). *Manifesto of transdisciplinarity*. State University of New York Press.

Nicolescu, B. (Ed.). (2008). *Transdisciplinarity: Theory and practice*. Cresskill, NJ: Hampton Press.

Nicolescu, B. (2014). *From Modernity to Cosmodernity: Science, Culture, and Spirituality*. SUNY Press.

Nonprofit Commons in Second Life. (2019). Retrieved from http://www.nonprofitcommons.org/

Oelofsen, N. (2012). Developing practical reflective skills (1/2): Personal learning. *British Journal of Healthcare Assistants*, *6*(6), 294–297. doi:10.12968/bjha.2012.6.6.294

Pellicer, S., Santa, G., Bleda, A. L., Maestre, R., Jara, A. J., & Gomez Skarmeta, A. (2013, July). A global perspective of smart cities: a survey. In *Innovative Mobile and Internet Services in Ubiquitous Computing (IMIS), 2013 Seventh International Conference on* (pp. 439-444). IEEE. 10.1109/IMIS.2013.79

Peraković, D., Periša, M., & Prcić, A. B. (2015). Possibilities of Applying ICT to Improve Safe Movement of Blind and Visually Impaired Persons. In *Cutting Edge Research in Technologies*. Intech. doi:10.5772/61080

Proulx, M. J., Todorov, O. S., Aiken, A. T., & de Sousa, A. A. (2016). Where am I? Who am I? The relation between spatial cognition, social cognition and individual differences in the built environment. *Frontiers in Psychology*, *7*. Retrieved from http://www.ncbi.nlm.nih.gov/pmc/articles/PMC4749931/

Ratan, R. A. (2011). *Self-presence: Body, emotion, and identity extension into the virtual self* (Ph.D. 3477991). University of Southern California. Retrieved from https://login.ctu.idm/oclc.org/?url=http://search.proquest.com/docview/901452620?accountid=26967

Raybourn, E. M. (2014). A new paradigm for serious games: Transmedia learning for more effective training and education. *Journal of Computational Science*, *5*(3), 471–481. doi:10.1016/j.jocs.2013.08.005

Raybourn, E. M. (2018). Harnessing Transmedia Learning: How to Optimize Your Productivity with Learning Science, Media, and Technology. *Interservice/Industry Training, Simulation and Education Conference Proceedings*. doi: 10.6084/m9.figshare.7149383

Reid, D. (1995). *Enactivism*. Retrieved November 20, 2006, from http://plato.acadiau.ca/ courses/educ/reid/enactivism/EnactivismDef.html

Roser, M., & Gazzaniga, M. S. (2004). Automatic brains—Interpretive minds. *Current Directions in Psychological Science*, *13*(2), 56–59. doi:10.1111/j.0963-7214.2004.00274.x

Scharmer, C. O. (2000). *Presencing: Learning from the future as it emerges*. Presentation at the Conference on Knowledge and Innovation, Helsinki School of Economics, Finland. Retrieved from http://www.ottoscharmer.com/docs/articles/2000_Presencing.pdf

Scharmer, O. (2011, October 24). *Entering the field of the future*. Presentation made at the First Presencing Global Forum, Boston, MA. Retrieved from: http://www.presencing.com/sites/default/files/page-files/2011_ForumOpening_0.pdf

Schwartz, M., Oppold, P., & Hancock, P. A. (2019). Wearables and Workload. In H. Lum (Ed.), *Critical Issues Impacting Science, Technology, Society (STS), and Our Future* (pp. 145–170). Hershey, PA: IGI Global. doi:10.4018/978-1-5225-7949-6.ch007

Senge, P. M. (1991). The fifth discipline, the art and practice of the learning organization. *Performance+ Instruction, 30*(5), 37-37.

Senge, P. M. (2006). *The fifth discipline: The art and practice of the learning organization*. Broadway Business.

Senge, P. M., Scharmer, C. O., Jaworski, J., & Flowers, B. S. (2005). *Presence: An Exploration of Profound Change in People social, Organizations, and Society*. Crown Publishing Group.

Sonnenwald, D. H. (2006). Collaborative virtual environments for scientific collaboration: Technical and organizational design frameworks. In R. Schroeder & A. Axelsson (Eds.), *Avatars at Work and Play* (pp. 63–96). Springer. doi:10.1007/1-4020-3898-4_4

Sparrowe, R. T. (2005). Authentic leadership and the narrative self. *The Leadership Quarterly*, *16*(3), 419–439. doi:10.1016/j.leaqua.2005.03.004

Sternberg, E. M. (2001). *The balance within: The science connecting health and emotions*. Macmillan.

Stricker, A., Holm, J., Calongne, C. M., & McCrocklin, M. (2011). Collaborative Prototyping of Learning Innovations Across Loosely Coupled Educational Communities. *International Journal of Learning and Media*, *3*(1). doi:10.1162/ijlm_a_00064

Stricker, A., McCrocklin, M., Calongne, C., Scribner, T., & Holm, J. (2010). *The rise of avatars in positive psychology: Enabling military cultures in a 3D world for strengths of character development*. DTIC Document. Retrieved from http://www.dtic.mil/cgi-bin/GetTRDoc?AD=ADA516864

Swan, M. (2012). Sensor mania! The internet of things, wearable computing, objective metrics, and the quantified self 2.0. *Journal of Sensor and Actuator Networks*, *1*(3), 217–253. doi:10.3390/jsan1030217

Taylor, C. (2011). Charles Taylor: Solidarity and Diversity in a Secular Age. *SweatmanMedia*. Retrieved from: https://youtu.be/96u-ijmn_uI

Truman, B. E. (2014). *Transformative interactions using embodied avatars in collaborative virtual environments: Towards transdisciplinarity* (Doctoral dissertation). Colorado Technical University.

Truman, J. (2015). *Case Study on Church Ethics and exemption from ADA Law* (Unpublished report). Asbury Theological Seminary.

Truman, J. (2019). *Intersectional Deaf Spirituality in America: Imagining a Next Generation Intercultural Deaf Community Center* (Unpublished doctoral dissertation). Columbia International University, Columbia, SC.

Tuan, Y. F. (1977). *Space and place: The perspective of experience*. U of Minnesota Press.

Turner, M. (1996). The literary mind: The origins of thought and language. Oxford University Press.

West, C. P., & Shanafelt, T. D. (2007). The influence of personal and environmental factors on professionalism in medical education. *BMC Medical Education*, *7*(1), 29. doi:10.1186/1472-6920-7-29 PMID:17760986

Yee, N., & Bailenson, J. N. (2009). The difference between being and seeing: The relative contribution of self-perception and priming to behavioral changes via digital self-representation. *Media Psychology*, *12*(2), 195–209. doi:10.1080/15213260902849943

Young, G., & Whitty, M. (2011). Progressive embodiment within cyberspace: Considering the psychological impact of the supermorphic persona. *Philosophical Psychology*, *24*(4), 537–560. doi:10.1080/09515089.2011.556606

KEY TERMS AND DEFINITIONS

Authenticity: Genuine, accurate, true to one's own character and spirit.

Avatar: An electronic image that represents the embodiment of a person in a virtual world that can be manipulated in appearance, movement, and gesture.

Being: Being with a capital B refers to living as reflected and connected to everything in nature.

Collaborative Virtual Environment: A virtual space where people can interact with each other using avatars and create sharable content while distributed anywhere in the world through internet access.

Complexity: Principle of universal interdependence.

Constructionism: A paradigm of teaching and learning that involves building knowledge structures through progressive internalization of actions.

Constructivism: A paradigm of teaching and learning that involves how humans generate knowledge and meaning from an interaction between their experiences and their ideas.

Cosmodernity: A paradigm that states all entities (existence) in the universe is defined by its relation to all other entities. Concerning education, cosmodernity involves knowledge through a complex, creative, transdisciplinary, polysemous, transcultural, transnational, and transpolitical approach.

Enactivism: Argues that cognition arises through a dynamic interaction between an acting organism and its environment.

Extended Reality (XR): Current and future virtual reality (VR), augmented reality (AR), mixed reality (MR), and other XR technologies for supporting and enhancing learning and human performance in evidence-based and research-grounded ways.

Identity: The distinguishing characteristics that make up a person's qualities, values, and beliefs.

Internet of Things: Networked/embedded physical objects that collect and exchange data across devices, society that make up smart cars, homes, cities, communities, etc.

Learning Engineering: An effort to combine learning science with engineering to improve the design of environments using multiple media and applications to improve learning outcomes.

Micro-Electro-Mechanical Systems (MEMS): Technology of very small devices made using microfabrication such as microsensors and microactuators that convert a mechanical signal into an electrical signal.

Nature: Nature with a capital N is an indivisible, substantial whole of which everything is a part and is interdependent. The term Nature has been neglected in the literature of recent centuries.

Persona: An individual's image or personality that makes up a social façade that someone projects to others.

Personal Learning: Idiosyncratic, self-guided, and self-motivated synthesis and mastery of knowledge, skills, and experiences that result in an individual's growth.

Personal Mastery: One of the five disciplines created by Peter Senge representing continuous clarifying and deepening of personal vision, focus of energy, development of patience, and seeing reality objectively.

Self: Self with a capital S represents your highest future potential that you can develop based on the research of the Presencing Institute.

Society: Society with a capital S refers to new forms of technology-enabled, participatory communities that span local and global physical and political boundaries constantly challenging laws, culture, and identity.

Chapter 15
Transdisciplinary Collaborative Development of Healthcare Virtual Simulations

Rachel Umoren
University of Washington, USA

Barbara Truman
https://orcid.org/0000-0002-7839-1772
University of Central Florida, USA

ABSTRACT

There is a need for collaborative, participatory exploration into emerging simulation technologies supportive of distributed, interdisciplinary practice to promote cultures of collaborative praxis. Higher educational institutions are adapting curriculum to support interprofessional education among healthcare students such as in medicine, nursing, and social work to build the ability to practice with greater safety for patient care. An analysis of critical supporting factors and challenges for distributed teams seeking to develop virtual simulations is presented with guidelines for distributed development and delivery using emerging simulation platforms applicable to healthcare teams and beyond.

BACKGROUND

Higher education curricula must be up-to-date, relevant, and feasible, especially where technology is involved. Complexity in curricular development increases as interdisciplinary faculty become involved in efforts to combine and integrate curriculum for students of different disciplines. Technology evolution is even more complex but has resulted in benefits for distributed, interdisciplinary education. Higher educational institutions are adapting curriculum to support interprofessional education among healthcare students such as in medicine, nursing, and social work to build the ability to practice with greater safety for patient care. In-person simulation is a strategy used in training and current advances in virtual simulation use immersive technologies to create virtual characters and teams for education and

DOI: 10.4018/978-1-5225-9679-0.ch015

professional development in remote and geographically-separated campuses. Successful integration of virtual simulation holds the promise of applying lessons learned toward building a culture of readiness to adapt to future challenges.

Méndez (2015) referred to a joint problem-solving using "Prevention through Design," a cross-disciplinary initiative to "understand the impact on the environment and nearby communities of people to guide reiteration of their designs" (p. 131). West et al. (2016) reviewed IPE curriculum and practices conducted at higher education institutions across the United States. They reported that the format of IPE included didactic instruction, simulation, and team-based learning. The latter were popular methods since they are "...conducive to role exploration, application of various communication techniques and "hands-on" team development" (p. 44). Meeting the instructional needs of each discipline requires faculty development even for shared didactic instruction. "Faculty development efforts ranged from limited or non-existent, to very sophisticated; however, the schools uniformly expressed the need for faculty development resources" (West et al., 2016, p. 42).

This chapter provides a glimpse of what is possible to construct as models of environments where designers can gain insights from accelerated experience when they have learned to interact and even build in the virtual world environment where simulated scenarios can be performed. This chapter explores the benefits and challenges of integrating virtual technology into healthcare curricula as well as the enabling processes and lessons learned in the collaborative development and deployment of virtual simulations using a transdisciplinary action research approach (Stokols, 2006, p. 66).

Integrating Technology Into Healthcare Curricula

A variety of 2D and 3D collaboration technologies are available for distributed teams. Figure 1 illustrates typical tools such as Skype, Google Documents, and learning management systems. These tools do not rely upon 3D capabilities. Lacerenza, Zajac, Savage and Salas (2015), reported that global virtual teams must communicate through technology-mediated tools cited as a disadvantage or challenge to team process. "However, with continual technological advancements and increased usage, these tools may actually represent an advantage" (p. 100) for example in creating a record of revisions that can be referred to later. The best collaboration approach involves identifying and combining the use of technologies that permit display and joint authoring capabilities.

Mature, campus departments engaged in learning technologies that support innovative faculty development may have all three platform capabilities in their repertoire. Managing digital media assets can also

Figure 1. 2D collaboration technologies

be reused and repurposed among environments so long as digital rights and intellectual property factors are understood. Figure 2, 3D Simulation Technologies, illustrates three primary platforms explored.

Nomenclature in the literature commonly refers to immersive, 3D environments as virtual worlds or virtual environments. For this study, Second Life and OpenSimulator were considered virtual worlds since they offer flexibility for building new content in world among users while providing the ability to create or change the environment in real time (Wong, Nguyen, & Ogren, 2012, p. 5). These types of virtual worlds are considered collaborative virtual environments, mainly when voice over IP is available as well as social networking features within the environment. Popular game engines such as Unity3D and Unreal can be used to create single and multiplayer virtual environments. The technology that supports access to these virtual platforms is rapidly evolving with improved user experiences and a significant reduction in technical difficulties with access and experience. Research into the educational affordances of evolving immersive platforms is needed.

Second Life, created by Linden Lab was explored for its ability to hold class meetings where inter-professional education was facilitated. Figure 3, also illustrates exploratory action research efforts to explore methods of design and delivery. The virtual world environment has been used and reported upon by educators in particular programs such as for courses in Science, Technology, Engineering, and Mathematics (STEM). Few universities have adopted the platform most likely to its costs and requirement to frequently update client viewers, requiring IT professionals to manage computer lab updates on campuses. Early technical difficulties related to platform stability and issues related to security, confidentiality, and intellectual property, as well as the broad user-base that utilized the environment for non-educational social pursuits also played a role as well in hindering widespread adoption by educational institutions.

Figure 2. 3D simulation technologies

Figure 3. Classroom lecture and role play on teamwork in Second Life

OpenSimulator is an open-source variation of Second Life that was reverse engineered by volunteer developers when Linden Lab released its viewer code for public modification in 2007. The ability to obtain the software to manage grids and regions provides flexibility, but requires technical know-how. While this platform is attractive to educational users because of the ability to control privacy, security, and retain intellectual property rights on virtual objects and experiences, it requires a local server and technical support. Along with OpenSimulator, the Second Life virtual world can connect to various websites through Hypertext Transfer Protocol (HTTP).

Unity Technologies offers a licensed game engine that includes Unity 3D, a browser-based plugin to access virtual environment content. Unity Technologies is reported to support 24 platforms that include mobile devices and head mounted display technologies. A large developer community is also supported by an asset store. The capacity for multi-user collaboration requires sophisticated support which is provided through synchronizing user location and text-based communication (Unity Technologies, 2017). This platform required more technical support for development and maintenance but had advantages in allowing for the web-based distribution of aesthetically pleasing interactions that were easily accessible through a browser by end-users. In-built analytics software allowed for anonymous tracking and reporting of user interactions. Unity was therefore considered a final platform for development and distribution of experiences that had been pilot tested in the other two platforms described.

Transdisciplinary Co-Creation of Virtual Simulations

Pohl and Hadorn (2008) described the transdisciplinary challenge with the complexity of problems as: "… interrelating the broad range of factors to come up with an integrated understanding of the problem and integrated suggestions for dealing with the problem" (p. 114). This case study describes the selection and development of interprofessional team training scenarios. In the U.S. medical system, an estimated one million medical errors occur each year. These errors lead to the death of 440,000 people with an estimated annual cost to the healthcare system of more than 17 billion dollars. (Donaldson, Corrigan & Kohn, 2000; Mallow, Pandya, Horblyuk, & Kaplan, 2013; Van Den Bos et al., 2011). While there has been a modest reduction reported in patient deaths from medical error, healthcare organizations look towards a future of "zero patients harmed" must continue to prioritize patient safety (Ghormley, 2015). Human factors and poor team communication are the primary causes of most sentinel events, near misses and close calls (Leonard, Graham, & Bonacum, 2004). Teamwork is an essential component of high-reliability organizations that can sustain a high level of safety over long periods of time (Baker, Day, & Salas, 2006). To improve teamwork, health professionals receive training in strategies to improve the structure and quality of information exchanged.

The nationally-recognized TeamSTEPPS program is effective in enhancing patient safety under clinical situations. TeamSTEPPS has been studied across a variety of healthcare settings such as community health centers, large hospitals, and even on the military battlefield. Availability and accessibility of master TeamSTEPPS training were initially limited to in-person training at six TeamSTEPPS implementation centers across the United States, but recently online training options have become available. Umoren et al., (2014) cited 3D virtual simulations are increasingly taught to learn skills difficult to acquire in-person through healthcare education settings such as simulation centers due to limitations in cost and scheduling (p. 2). Maguire, Bremner, Bennett and VanBrackle (2015), reported in a longitudinal study: " Developing team-based simulations for nursing students offer not only a risk-free environment to practice team skills but the opportunity to participate in creating a culture shift to teamwork" (p. 137).

Factors related to integrating the understanding of complex challenges using a 3D immersive learning approach are described in Table 1.

An inter-institutional initiative was created using an action research approach to enable transdisciplinary practice and theory with core team members representing several disciplines. The project had a "diversity of stakeholders in the production of relevant knowledge for promoting specific changes; and that aims more fundamentally at democratizing knowledge" (Streck, 2017, p. 1). The team began its work in 2011 with two healthcare faculty, a physician, and nurse, each supported by a small faculty instructional technology grant and in-kind resources to collaboratively develop a healthcare-oriented virtual environment learning experience. This project attracted broader participation and funding over time as project goals became more manifest. Testers were needed, and in some cases, members joined the team with interest in adapting the scenarios.

In the example shown in Figure 4, the project leader introduced a new contributor to simulation delivery options provided in the Second Life platform. The environment employed a simple pedagogical approach where learners viewed slides similarly to didactic instruction.

The team consisted of faculty members from Medicine, Nursing, Neurology, Social Work, Physical Therapy, Occupational Therapy, and Communication Studies. The team is also supported by members contributing expertise in research administration, multimedia production, and instructional design.

The interdisciplinary team members sought professional development activities often on their own to learn digital literacy skills necessary to attain self-efficacy for participation in virtual world environments. Through trial and error, connecting with certain key individuals, and exploration of the literature, application possibilities became apparent for teaching, learning, and research. After successful simulation prototypes were created, piloted, and evaluated, review of the process of development was possible to consider which transdisciplinary research principles were used and how they could be adapted for further development. The process used to create the simulation scenarios required negotiating and compromising mostly within constraints of time and budget. Méndez (2015) cited differences in arguments among transdisciplinary researchers who favored different tasks and issues to be taken into account as research developed and the possibility of identifying various commonalities among approaches. Klein

Figure 4. Authors met for the first time in a virtual world

also called for the definition of flexible principles including the coexistence of different goals, which in this study could be the development of product and process as explored from a transdisciplinary action research strategy.

Participatory action research provided informal professional development experiences among team members who experienced platforms. Figure 5, Exploring teamwork and conflict resolution in an OpenSimulator region, shows the authors investigating the feasibility of how interaction design could be prototyped and how a simulation exercise surrounding conflict could be addressed.

As a result of action research and inquiry into 3D platforms, the research team created TeamSTEPPS Virtual Teams, a virtual simulation resource that allows for multi-user and individual participation within a virtual simulation of a hospital environment, along with other educational areas. These simulation scenarios involved a series of preprogrammed interactions with a virtual healthcare team to simulate safe and effective participation in team-based clinical experiences. "Each of the scenarios features a health care team consisting of nurses, physicians, occupational and physical therapists, interpreters, and social workers interacting with patients and with the learner in ways that illustrate common issues one may encounter in clinical settings" (Umoren et al., 2017, p. 185). Figure 5 shows a scenario delivered on a stand-alone Unity 3D application or a web-based experience. The platform provided enhanced graphics, ease of use for learners and instructors, and adaptability to a variety of devices. Scenarios play like a video where scripted nonplayer characters in the roles of professionals, including nursing, medicine, and radiology speak to learners. Prompts are provided to choose among menu options providing feedback. The virtual simulation allows assessment of learners' understanding of how to apply the components and application of each TeamSTEPPS tool, so that learner's do not have superficial recognition (Umoren et al., 2017, p. 188).

Sweigart et al. (2016) conducted a cross-sectional feasibility study of individual and group activities for training health professional students located at remote campuses. Two objectives were explored to test the utility and acceptability of a virtual learning environment (VLE) immersive training using the TeamSTEPPS curriculum, and to examine the change in teamwork attitudes regarding interprofessional communication (p. 32). Iterations of virtual simulations were incorporated into classroom-based sessions (Umoren et al., 2017). The initial experience was positive of using the conceptual framework of TeamSTEPPS in a VLE for interprofessional team training in health professional students (p. 33). Results from the Virtual TeamSTEPPS simulations produced in association with this study have been published previously in health-care journals and cited in this paper regarding curricular integration

Figure 5. Exploring teamwork and conflict resolution in an OpenSimulator region

Figure 6. Virtual TeamSTEPPS simulation example

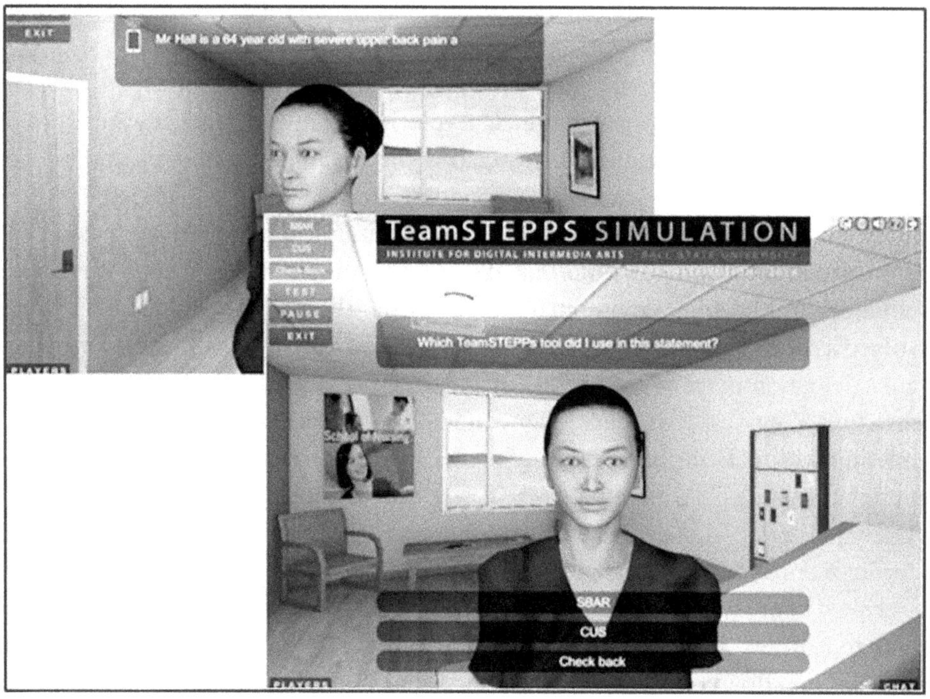

(Umoren et al., 2018). Those results were based on comparing learner attitudes across disciplines to explore leadership using TeamSTEPPS validated measures and instruments. Umoren et al. (2017) summarized the findings in terms of interprofessional education that may have value for other disciplines requiring teamwork at a distance:

A brief intervention which placed learners into virtual interprofessional teams allowed for the rapid dissemination of teamwork knowledge in health professional students. The intervention also allowed the practice of TeamSTEPPS principles in context and identified differences in approaches to a patient care safety concern. Practice in teamwork and communication skills gained through the virtual simulations may prepare learners for interprofessional practice and help them become better advocates for their future patients (p. 189).

Lessons learned from this multi-year, inter-institutional, inter-disciplinary action research inquiry into how emerging 3D simulation platforms can provide learning opportunities not possible or practical previously can be grouped into three primary themes:

- Transdisciplinary collaboration enabled educators to develop technically sophisticated virtual experiences across distance and institutions without prior face-to-face relationships in some cases (see Table 1)
- The exploratory process to distinguish pros and cons of different platforms was enhanced through participatory, experiential learning and sharing among investigators
- Successful deployment of interprofessional virtual scenarios resulted described in the Virtual TeamSTEPPS Simulation section as shown in Figure 5. Users around the world accessed these simulation scenarios.

Interprofessional Education to Promote Praxis

Regardless of technology usage, higher educational institutions and faculty seek means to promote praxis evidenced in processes supporting enactment and embodiment of lessons and skills among interdisciplinary learners. This study involved participatory action research imagining how designing interventions can be simulated virtually for use in practice. In the United States, health science departments are trying to build or relocate facilities to enable students from differing disciplines the opportunity to participate face-to-face in more problem-based challenges. The curriculum is being revised requiring teams of aspiring healthcare professionals to learn together using interprofessional education (IPE).

Buring et al. (2009) provide a definition of IPE: Interprofessional education involves educators and learners from 2 or more health professions and their foundational disciplines who jointly create and foster a collaborative learning environment. The goal of these efforts is to develop knowledge, skills, and attitudes that result in interprofessional team behaviors and competence. Ideally, interprofessional education is incorporated throughout the entire curriculum in a vertically and horizontally integrated fashion (p. 2). Praxis become more favorable when IPE includes a strategy that involves what Greenfield, Nugus, Travaglia & Braithwaite (2010) described as the combination of Interprofessional Learning (IPL): "…a collaborative, interdisciplinary education and learning process designed to produce effective, multidisciplinary patient centred care'', and Interprofessional Practice (IPP): "…the enactment of competencies required to attain this" (p. 437). These kinds of educational experiences may provide opportunities for greater integration of virtual world simulation and identity development. Informal professional development using virtual worlds may assist in the identification of interprofessional education (IPE) theoretical approaches such as described by West et al. (2016). "…cooperative, collaborative, or social learning; experiential learning; education of the reflective practitioner; epistemology and ontology of interdisciplinary inquiry…" and collect details of IPE interventions (p. 42). The collaborative virtual environment may empower the ability for individuals and teams to develop knowledge through action and purposeful thinking within a social context that can acknowledge prior learning experiences as embodied knowledge …" (p. 364).

Production methods used by the research team involved 2D collaboration tools shown in Figure 1 to discuss concepts of how to annotate team-based case studies through interaction design. Paper-based scenarios provided challenges for how to inexpensively design 3D scenarios. The research team members, mostly healthcare educators, explored affordances of immersive virtual environments while explaining the communication interaction requirements among simulated patients and healthcare teams. Figure 7 illustrated an example of how interdisciplinary researchers who possess digital literacy for using virtual worlds can speak and modify the environment in real time to share mental models.

The experience of meeting other professionals committed to deriving the benefits of virtual worlds for praxis promotes motivation to shape the technology collaboratively. Figure 7 also illustrates how avatars can reflect the role of professional identity providing a reflective mirror to one's self. Attachment to using an avatar to create identity can also promote professional development similar to the notion Anderson (1959) described involving human creativity:

Growth is a continuing process of differentiating, of self-producing, moving on to more and more complexity; it is integrating and harmonious, not disintegrating nor disharmonious; it is confronting, not conflicting; it represents the free interplay of differences, spontaneous abandoning, yielding of present structures and functions. (p. 281-282)

Figure 7. Simulated healthcare environment

Anderson description of creativity extends to the use of avatars in virtual worlds where dynamic appearance can be exotic when users adapt their representation in various contexts. For professional development, the role of building reputation requires further study to identify factors that build trust. For students engaged in health-care scenarios, faculty seek to focus on a more specific avatar appearance to promote virtual role play using specific language choices. "The creativity with which we shall be concerned here is a form or manner of relating to others which admits of one's own uniqueness and dignity and at the same time respects a uniqueness and dignity in others" (Anderson, 1959, p. 278).

Refining Distributed Simulation Co-Production Practice

Stokols (2006) stated that in addition to evaluating tangible products of transdisciplinary collaboration, assessing various interpersonal and inter-organizational processes that either facilitate or hinder a group's efforts to produce outcomes is essential (p. 73). Participating in virtual worlds to create virtual simulations offers an opportunity to create conceptual artifacts. Capturing interaction ideas are still elusive unless there is a combined approach of using 2D and 3D tools such as exploring prototype modeling in the virtual world while writing ideas on a shared Google Document. Salas et al. (2005) propose that the big five components of teamwork are essential in all team contexts. These components include leadership, adaptability, mutual performance monitoring, back up behavior, and team orientation. Shared mental models, closed-loop communication, and trust are necessary for effective teamwork (as seen in Salas, Rosen Held & Weissmuller, 2008, p. 344). Conceptual artifacts also include dialogue in virtual worlds that may include captured chat that promotes understanding and accessibility for persons unable to unwilling to use the voice capabilities. Lotrecchiano (2011) reported that transdisciplinary environments provide mechanisms to promote human agency, self-efficacy that can be translated into leadership (p. 42).

The ability to conjure mental models using constructive, virtual worlds creates the possibility of increasing shared mental models rapidly if users have self-efficacy to create content in the world. Such conjuring in game engines is more limited and may not be possible at all. Determining the fit of the pedagogy among the tools is a critical success factor that must be explored using a participatory action research approach. Burke, Stagl, Salas, Pierce, & Kendall (2006) described what relates to the ability to co-create conceptual artifacts as shared mental models (SMM), a dynamic, simplified, cognitive representation of reality that team members use to describe, explain, and predict events. These SMMs enable team members to react quickly to stressful situations. On the curricular level, the distributed co-production of simulation scenarios required involving team members to contribute a design process described by Umoren et al. (2017). Six stages were involved in the design process as shown in Table 1 with corresponding examples:

Cultivation of Collaborative Praxis

Project leadership must facilitate the development of shared mental development of shared mental models for desired outcomes to promote sustained engagement, especially among loosely connected volunteers. Figure 8, Stakeholders involved in transdisciplinary action research, indicate the type of individuals involved in co-production and the relative proportions that make up an ecosystem necessary to support the inquiry necessary to refine ideas, processes, and product outcomes. An ecosystem may be bound by a department, an institution, a network representing communities of practice, and may also include loosely connected volunteers participating across virtual worlds who relay information about the availability of resources and feasibility. Process models need further research using collaborative virtual environments. Stokols (2006) reported that alignment of contextual factors at the outset results in more likely prospects for achieving and sustaining effective collaboration across multiple fields to support the goals and activities of transdisciplinary research teams (p. 26). Researchers exploring innovative practices like making virtual simulations should coordinate with campus departments engaged in teaching and learning, and faculty development. The output of coordination could assist with the dissemination of innovation on campus within an institution.

Concerning health-care delivery, West et al. (2016) cited the need for effective faculty development as well as "… measures to examine the link between IPE learning outcomes and patient outcomes" (p. 41). Conceptual development of shared mental models is often messy. Time and distance contribute to conceptual decay among diverse team members. Care must be taken to avoid a surgical project management approach such as used in rapid prototyping when transdisciplinary communication is sought to build trust and influence the development of professional identity and culture toward collaborative praxis. Lacerenza et al. (2015) stated that trust develops within teams when each member "a) makes a

Table 1. Design process stages and examples

Stage	Example
Stage 1 – Discuss learning objectives and typical scenarios	Demonstrate closed-loop communication in the context of a newborn resuscitation
Stage 2 – Define specific, measurable learning objectives for scenarios	Use the TeamSTEPPS tool "check-back" prior to epinephrine administration
Stage 3 – Expand typical scenarios to feature multiple professions	Scenario features at a minimum a nurse, a physician, and a pharmacist.
Stage 4 – Collaboratively write and refine dialogue for scenarios	Interprofessional team co-writes the script for the dialogue between health professional characters
Stage 5 – Insert multiple choice questions with feedback throughout the dialogue	e.g., What TeamSTEPPS tool did I just use?
Stage 6 – Write debrief based on learning objectives and questions	Debrief emphasizes learning objectives

Figure 8. Stakeholders involved in transdisciplinary action research

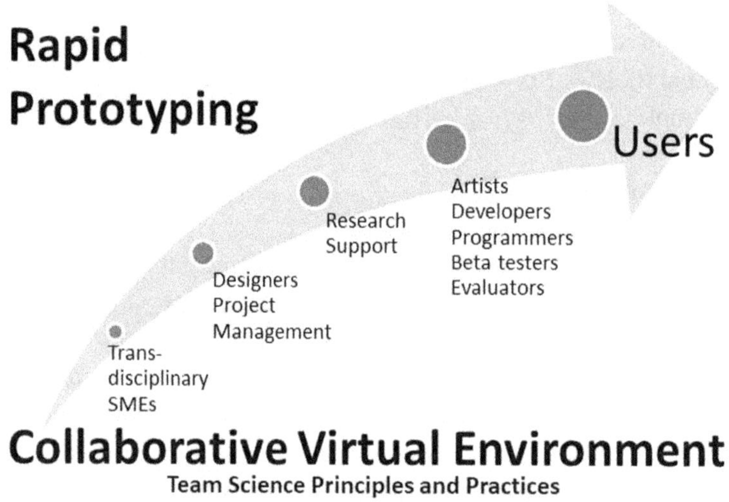

good-faith effort to behave in accordance with any commitments both explicit or implicit, b) is honest in whatever negotiations preceded such commitments, and c) does not take excessive advantage of another even when the opportunity is available" (p. 94). While virtual world platforms enable team members to frequently gather, spontaneously, and even instantaneously, the challenge of exemplifying character and intent is an ongoing area of research.

The development of adaptability, as needed for effective communication within diverse groups was found using virtual simulation and immersion (Umoren et al., 2014, p. 3). Sustainability of teams and development of communities into communities of practice is necessary for educational institutions to bridge practice. Busciglio (2015) cited that ultimately, a transdisciplinary approach is a way to foster sustainable education. The approach was reported to cultivate students' "sense of agency and power based on their life discourse and their processes of identity development" (p. 20).

The results found merits in three platforms used in the development of the virtual simulations. These platforms included Second Life, OpenSimulator, and Unity3D. Ideally, a multi-user simulation capability can support the following factors to promote interprofessional education using immersive 3d platforms:

- Advanced scenario experiences and exercises
- Debriefing
- Social development
- Creative expression
- Identity development
- Mentoring

If feasible to manage multi-user simulation capabilities, support for exploration into theory and practice for enculturating interdisciplinary education into praxis is thought to be possible. Umoren & Rybas (2017) reported the educational benefit of real multiplayer activity is in the fidelity of allowing participants to be in their role, whether that is the role of a student nurse, practicing physician or some other professional.

Strategic institutional support for creating and using virtual simulations may support training and research in healthcare and other disciplines. The action research experiences of the project team provided glimpses into the possibilities of how institutions can benefit from using each of the simulation platforms explored including for combination in a process of development that spanned concept to product. The project team was able to manage their own equipment sufficiently to gain access to viewer software and plugins necessary to experience the affordances offered between platform approaches. The team was frequently forced out of their comfort zones through the technology and discourse surrounding how different disciplines approached challenges our scenarios were designed to illuminate. Members maintained openness and through transdisciplinary collaborations fundamentally new conceptualizations of scientific and societal phenomena were discovered. The downside of community benefits was labor intensity and that it may take several years to realize the potential of the collaboration (Stokols, 2006, p. 68).

One challenge in the design of the simulated scenarios involved the ability to have after-action reviews or debriefing sessions. "Previous research has shown that regular team interaction and team debriefs facilitate the development of team cognition; however, the opportunity for such collaboration is often absent in virtual teams" (Tannenbaum et al., 2012 as seen in Lacerenza et al., 2015). This absence may be due to the use of 2D technologies. Alston and Schatz (2013) found that in using VLE, the environment provides context and intrinsic feedback for the experience. Scenarios are the events that challenge, teach, and test the learners to facilitate a more holistic learning cycle (Sweigart et al., 2016, p. 32). Virtual worlds could meet the need for continuous debriefing if the software were mobile-friendly. Regular briefs and debriefs among team members have shown to promote guided team self-correction (p. 95). Ultimately, individual learners played single-user formats of the gaming platform that used pre-programmed debriefing. Some group sessions were tried using the Unity web player but were found not to be as practical. Virtual worlds used in education have a few unique properties that make them particularly advantageous when compared to 3D games, and more spontaneous debriefing is one (Umoren et al., 2014, p. 2).

The project team had little ability to observe the interactions of students in the virtual world due to technical challenges with software complexity. Limited availability of time in classes also prevented virtual world use with students during classes. Professional technical assistance is usually required for feasibility exploration, design, development, and sustainability to use the technology over time. The transdisciplinary communication challenges persist with interaction with the programmers, architects, software developers, and systems designers who create the code used in the simulation platforms. This challenge cannot be understated as developers participate from around the globe using different languages. Some companies do not open source their software code and therefore do not allow communication with core developers.

RECOMMENDATIONS

As a result of the action research conducted for this study the following recommendations are made:

- Promote transdisciplinary action research oriented processes that inform platform selection necessary to promote transdisciplinary collaborative research

- Promote the development of simulation products to offer practice in building appreciation for transdisciplinary culture
- Promote non-threatening opportunities for team members to build self-efficacy skills that may lead to collaborative praxis
- Capture desired requirements while using emerging technologies and make them known to technical staff members who may be able to influence the development platforms/technology
- Enable innovative ideas and suggestions for improvement to come from as many stakeholders as possible, especially students
- Consider the type of system data requirements that can improve learner performance with richer feedback, increase the simulation visualization capability, and possibly improve accessibility and accommodation
- Appeal to leadership to self-organize and engage in transdisciplinary communication to collaborate and shape technology, especially open source technology to overcome the challenges of multiplayer capability.

West et al. (2016) recommended collaboration among consortium schools to generate consensus on outcome measures for IPE (p. 44). We suggest including the use of immersive, distributed simulation usage for developing some outcome measures.

CONCLUSION

This chapter describes the participatory design nature and evolutionary, cross-disciplinary team-based development needed to create virtual simulations by a distributed, group of educators. The action research findings were illustrated revealing mixed results for using immersive simulation platforms. Component elements for achieving collaborative praxis were identified. A game engine platform supported individual training uses for virtual scenarios while the virtual world technologies provided a means for exploring and developing applicable, shared mental models for project development. The support of multi-user simulation is desired for its potential to serve students and faculty with transdisciplinary communication opportunities and valuable professional development activities. The ability to extend and disseminate the benefits of collaborative praxis across and between organizations will depend on how collaboration is practiced to promote transdisciplinary communication. Further research is needed on the study of transdisciplinary leadership practices that encourage Transdisciplinarity using and influencing the development of 3D virtual worlds and game engines. Table 1 provided a conceptual illustration of how an additional level of digital intelligence for leadership may influence positive organizational development. Self-leadership is also of interest to identify which practices while engaged in virtual community learning organizations lead to the development of habits that can be transformative. Identifying the factors that enable enterprises to integrate immersive simulation into their operations and professional development offerings will accelerate the 3D ecosystem evolution opening up new ways to pursue action research.

Finally, new technological capabilities need research that involves web worlds. These worlds enable users to create scenes such as when building the virtual world OpenSimulator. The scene is baked and translated into JavaScript and WebGL to make the world accessible through the web browser Google Chrome. Web worlds may add another capability in the conceptual-to-product pipeline enabling greater user access and sustained participation that lead to collaborative praxis.

ACKNOWLEDGMENT

The authors acknowledge Martina G Solas Allen, Kay Hodson-Carlton, Rohit Das, Evalyn Gossett, Miles Johnson, James A Jones, Heather McCabe, Patricia J Scott, Linda Sweigart, Julie A Poore, and Natalia Rybas for their participation on the distributed team described in this article.

REFERENCES

Alston, A. L., & Schatz, S. (2013, December). *Beyond scenarios: Designing holistic experiences for simulation-based training*. Interservice/Industry Training, Simulation, and Education Conference.

Anderson, H. H. (1959). *Creativity as personality development. Creativity and its cultivations*. Academic Press.

Baker, D. P., Day, R., & Salas, E. (2006). Teamwork as an essential component of high-reliability organizations. *Health Services Research, 41*(4p2), 1576-1598.

Buring, S. M., Bhushan, A., Broeseker, A., Conway, S., Duncan-Hewitt, W., Hansen, L., & Westberg, S. (2009). Interprofessional education: Definitions, student competencies, and guidelines for implementation. *American Journal of Pharmaceutical Education*, *73*(4), 59. doi:10.5688/aj730459 PMID:19657492

Busciglio, D. F. (2015). *Not Covering but Discovering: Agency and Shared Autonomy in Deep Project-Based Language Learning* (Doctoral dissertation). The University of Wisconsin-Madison.

Ghormley, Y. (2015). Medical Errors In US Healthcare Organizations: Have We Made Any Progress? *American Journal of Health Sciences*, *6*(1), 45–52. doi:10.19030/ajhs.v6i1.9269

Greenfield, D., Nugus, P., Travaglia, J., & Braithwaite, J. (2010). Auditing an organization's interprofessional learning and interprofessional practice: The interprofessional praxis audit framework (IPAF). *Journal of Interprofessional Care*, *24*(4), 436–449. doi:10.3109/13561820903163801 PMID:20377396

Klein, J. T. (2008). Evaluation of interdisciplinary and transdisciplinary research: A literature review. *American Journal of Preventive Medicine*, *35*(2Supplement), S116–S123. doi:10.1016/j.amepre.2008.05.010 PMID:18619391

Lacerenza, C. N., Zajac, S., Savage, N., & Salas, E. (2015). Team training for global virtual teams: Strategies for success. In *Leading Global Teams* (pp. 91–121). Springer New York. doi:10.1007/978-1-4939-2050-1_5

Leonard, M., Graham, S., & Bonacum, D. (2004). The human factor: The critical importance of effective teamwork and communication in providing safe care. *Quality & Safety in Health Care*, *13*(suppl 1), i85–i90. doi:10.1136/qshc.2004.010033 PMID:15465961

Linden Lab. (2017). Retrieved from https://www.lindenlab.com

Lotrecchiano, G. R. (2011). Complexity leadership in transdisciplinary (TD) learning environments: A knowledge feedback loop. *FormaMente: Rivista internazionale di ricerca sul futuro digitale*, (1), 103.

Maguire, M. B. R., Bremner, M. N., Bennett, D. N., & VanBrackle, L. (2015). Evaluation of TeamSTEPPS integration across a curriculum regarding team attitudes: A longitudinal study. *Journal of Nursing Education and Practice*, *5*(7), 131–138. doi:10.5430/jnep.v5n7p131

Mallow, P. J., Pandya, B., Horblyuk, R., & Kaplan, H. S. (2013). Prevalence and cost of hospital medical errors in the general and elderly United States populations. *Journal of Medical Economics*, *16*(12), 1367–1378. doi:10.3111/13696998.2013.848210 PMID:24063367

Méndez, F. (2015). Transdiscipline and research in health: Science, society and decision making. *Colombia Médica (Cali, Colombia)*, *46*(3), 128–134. Retrieved from http://www.scielo.org.co/pdf/cm/v46n3/v46n3a07.pdf PMID:26600628

OpenSimulator. (2017). Retrieved from http://opensimulator.org

Pohl, C., & Hadorn, G. H. (2008). Methodological challenges of transdisciplinary research. *Nature Sciences Sociétés*, *16*(2), 111–121. doi:10.1051/nss:2008035

Stokols, D. (2006). Toward a Science of Transdisciplinary Action Research. *American Journal of Community Psychology*, *38*(1), 63–77. doi:10.100710464-006-9060-5 PMID:16791514

Streck, D. R. (2017). *What Can Action Research and Transdisciplinarity Learn from Each Other? Integration and Implementation Insights*. Retrieved from: https://i2insights.org/2017/08/29/action-research-and-transdisciplinarity/

Sweigart, L. I., Umoren, R. A., Scott, P. J., Carlton, K. H., Jones, J. A., Truman, B., & Gossett, E. J. (2016). Virtual TeamSTEPPS® simulations produce teamwork attitude changes among health professions students. *The Journal of Nursing Education*, *55*(1), 31–35. doi:10.3928/01484834-20151214-08 PMID:26812380

Umoren, R., & Rybas, N. (2017). Who am I as a Healthcare Provider?: Identity and Transformative Learning in Virtual Environments. In A. Stricker, C. Calongne, B. Truman, & F. Arenas (Eds.), *Integrating an Awareness of Selfhood and Society into Virtual Learning* (pp. 148–163). Hershey, PA: IGI Global; doi:10.4018/978-1-5225-2182-2.ch011

Umoren, R., Stadler, D. J., Gasior, S. L., Al-Sheikhly, D., Truman, B., & Lowe, C. (2014). Global collaboration and team-building through 3D virtual environments. *Innovations in Global Medical and Health Education, 1*. Retrieved from: http://www.qscience.com/doi/full/10.5339/igmhe.2014.1

Umoren, R. A., Poore, J. A., Sweigart, L., Rybas, N., Gossett, E., Johnson, M., ... Das, R. (2017). TeamSTEPPS Virtual Teams: Interactive Virtual Team Training and Practice for Health Professional Learners. *Creative Nursing*, *23*(3), 184–191. doi:10.1891/1078-4535.23.3.184 PMID:28789739

Umoren, R. A., Scott, P. J., Sweigart, L., Gossett, E., Hodson-Carlton, K., Johnson, M., ... Das, R. (2018). A comparison of teamwork attitude changes with virtual TeamSTEPPS® simulations in health professional students. *Journal of Interprofessional Education & Practice*, *10*, 51–55. doi:10.1016/j.xjep.2017.12.001

Unity Technologies. (2017). Retrieved from https://unity3d.com

Van Den Bos, J., Rustagi, K., Gray, T., Halford, M., Ziemkiewicz, E., & Shreve, J. (2011). The $17.1 billion problem: The annual cost of measurable medical errors. *Health Affairs*, *30*(4), 596–603. doi:10.1377/hlthaff.2011.0084 PMID:21471478

West, C., Graham, L., Palmer, R. T., Miller, M. F., Thayer, E. K., Stuber, M. L., ... Joo, P. A. (2016). Implementation of interprofessional education (IPE) in 16 US medical schools: Common practices, barriers and facilitators. *Journal of Interprofessional Education & Practice*, *4*, 41–49. doi:10.1016/j.xjep.2016.05.002 PMID:28184380

Wong, J., Nguyen, A., & Ogren, L. (2012). *Serious Game and Virtual World Training: Instrumentation and Assessment*. Newport, RI: Naval Undersea Warfare Center. doi:10.21236/ADA582033

KEY TERMS AND DEFINITIONS

Action Research: Inquiry into how to improve the quality of an organization and its performance within an authentic or simulated context to improve practice.

Collaborative Virtual Environment: A virtual space where people can interact with each other using avatars and create sharable content while distributed anywhere in the world through internet access.

Interprofessional Education: Experiences where learners from two or more professions in healthcare learn together with the object of cultivating collaborative practice for providing patient-centered care.

Praxis: Practical applications of theory as practice.

TeamSTEPPS: Team strategies and tools to enhance performance and patient safety. An evidence-based framework to optimize team performance across the healthcare delivery system.

Transdisciplinary: Representative of a holistic, inclusive approach to go beyond disciplines into new realms of inquiry, practice, and research.

Virtual Learning Environment: Web-based platform often referred to as a learning management system that relies on 2D interactions and content.

Web Worlds: 3D, immersive content that is accessed via the web without special software. May serve multiple users and is made from WebGL or OpenGL. Some regions made in OpenSimulator are being converted into web worlds.

Chapter 16
Pioneering in the Virtual World Frontier

Cynthia Calongne
Colorado Technical University, USA

ABSTRACT

Immersion in virtual worlds presented opportunities for simulating the qualities valued in face-to-face classes with the flexibility afforded by online learning. Immersive learning engaged educators, curriculum designers, campuses, conferences, and educational community groups to devise new ways to collaborate and engage learners. Dreaming of opportunities that were not possible in the online classroom, educators saw the potential of building communities in virtual worlds. They gathered to share their and to employ novel approaches to address educational challenges. This chapter explores the phenomenon of selfhood and society integral to the development of a vibrant educational community. At the heart of virtual world education is an ecosystem of institutions, groups, and conferences comprised of the early adopters and pioneers who stimulated their imagination and pooled their resources to encourage and strengthen the community and cast their eye to the future.

INTRODUCTION

With the decline of learner motivation and engagement in the study of science, technology, engineering, and math (STEM), education sought to find novel ways to engage and inspire interest in STEM disciplines. Increases in software capability, social virtual worlds, and high speed internet access made it possible to offer classes set in virtual environments where students studied within 3D spaces.

Similar to any historical record, identifying the beginning of virtual world education is a challenge. Perspectives vary depending on the role, technology used, and the level of immersion experienced during online classes. The narrative offered here is internal and employs an ethnographic lens to report the events and to share how it felt to experience the early discoveries in 3D situated learning.

From the fictional roots found in Neal Stephenson's (1993) book Snow Crash, the Metaverse emerged as the 3D Web, a collection of virtual worlds comprised of grids, which are interconnected regions that reside on servers, often within virtual machines (VMs) to optimize their resources and processing re-

DOI: 10.4018/978-1-5225-9679-0.ch016

quirements. Within the Metaverse resides the technologies that make the worlds come alive, including commercial virtual world servers, and a wealth of software for 3D design, animation design, scripting languages, compilers, interpreters, and libraries, physics engines that simulate the real world behavior, and the people, represented by avatars. The avatars, as educators, came into these worlds, encouraged by institutions and inspired by early adopters and their successes.

What were the forces that drew educational institutions to issue a call to action that stimulated attention from over 150 countries? Highlights from the early work explore how the culture evolved and the people within them formed into communities and support networks. While thousands of groups exist, the ethnographic lens features the major events and group work and shares insights into their early goals, challenges, and discoveries. The summary reflects on the future, and the ongoing work in developing programs that first assess the character strengths that define selfhood and society within a virtual community.

BACKGROUND

The River City project (Dede, 2003) fueled the imagination of educators with a historical multiuser virtual environment (MUVE) created for middle grade science students. Designed within a commercial virtual world called Active Worlds®, the science-oriented learning environment was funded by National Science Foundation grants led by Harvard's Chris Dede (2003) in collaboration with the Virtual Environments Lab at George Mason University, the Smithsonian's National Museum of American history, and research partner Thoughtful Technologies, Inc.

The goal was to help learners discover a love of science. The curriculum mapped to established assessment methods and gave educators tools for studying the *cognitive audit trails*, which served as both a metaphor and a method of assessing when learners were ready for the next level. River City represented the early promise of virtual world education and employed a team-based approach to using scientific methods to analyze and address serious problems while increasing interest and a desire to study science.

The River City simulation featured traveling back in time to address 19th century problems and in particular, three diseases using 21st century tactics. It wove historical, social and geographical content amid the threat of diseases that stemmed from airborne, water-borne, and insect-based sources within the immersive landscape. Harvard University's Graduate School of Education coordinated the design, with pilot tests conducted with Boston public schools and the implementation of the immersive MUVE (Dede & Ketelhut, 2003). The project reflected on scalability issues and how to offer the environment to schools throughout North America. Over 100 teachers and 5,000 students studied in River City across twelve states during the first two years. The River City project inspired the educational community and served as a road map for what might be possible for teaching other subjects. Active Worlds was a popular tool with educators, but a variety of forces, including financial and ownership changes led educators to seek other opportunities.

There®, a virtual landscape that encouraged the public to join the developers' community, encouraged educational use during their beta test that led to a small, but devoted group of educators. The strengths included access to diverse content and technological affordances that supported safe use (dressing rooms appeared when changing the avatar's appearance, classroom animations, vehicle physics, and an education special interest group), but also implemented a content creation and submission system that required review board approval to ensure that the content met community standards, after which, the creator pre-paid for a volume of copies. Mapping the virtual community's goals with the curriculum and school district requirements was for some educators, a challenge.

Philip Rosedale, founder and former CEO at Linden Research (known as Linden Lab), adapted the software tool that they used for haptic interface design and launched it as LindenWorld, and the next year renamed it to Second Life® with 16 regions (Second Life History, 2017, December 29). The sparse user population, known as residents, grew slowly through the first few years.

Major growth in the educational use of Second Life occurred when the New Media Consortium with over 225 universities, schools, and museums invited its members and conference attendees to join their NMC Virtual Worlds group in Second Life.

A CALL TO ACTION

The New Media Consortium (NMC, 2005) and Learning Times, a Web conferencing partner, hosted a conference on educational gaming and invited the attendees to meet in Second Life (SL). The conference attendees were a blend of NMC members, EDUCAUSE members and educational professionals with an interest in online learning, including members of the TCC Worldwide Online Conference. Learning Times provided the hosting service for both the NMC and TCC conferences, and the feeling of community and openness flourished under the TCC Hawai'i Ohana, a Hawaiian word for family, aptly characterizing the TCC close knit community.

NMC's leadership under CEO Larry Johnson and Lev Gonick, former NMC Board Chair and NMC Campus Project partner, envisioned the potential of the virtual landscape as a place for blending the liberal arts and education, for stimulating Renaissance thinking through playful exhibits, gardens, and as a landscape for learning and creativity. The first taste of the promise of this imaginative playground intrigued the attendees, yet frustrated some as the early software tools used to experience the world demanded a steep learning curve and sufficient bandwidth. Despite the initial challenges, the New Media Consortium (NMC, 2006) worked with the creative genius of the Electric Sheep Company to design and launch their virtual NMC Campus (Levine, 2008) for meetings and educators events as seen in Figure 1. The inaugural event attracted campus leaders from their 200 campuses, museums and libraries, who in turn started work on developing an archipelago of educational regions, representing the technology champions from each member institution to realize the NMC's mission of sparking creativity and innovation.

Bryan Alexander (2006), a researcher at the NMC, senior fellow and futurist known for hosting a playful think tank for forecasting predictions called NITLE, the exploration found its roots in shared objects. Engeström (2005, April 13), Alexander (2006), and Da Silva (2015, February 17) noted that what brings people to participate in a social network or an online community is the focus on a shared object that frames the experience, such as photos and images on a photo sharing service. In virtual learning, the shared object serves as a catalyst for connecting social spaces, virtual content, curriculum, and the feeling of presence for the residents within them. Shared objects provide a raison d'etre for community development and participation in virtual spaces. Educational content extends beyond curriculum, rubrics, and 3D designs to feature a sense of place (Bachelard, 1964) that meets certain behavioral expectations and organized by the perceptions of architecture and space (Tuan, 1977). Bachelard noted how objects serve a purpose and fit within their environment while Tuan reflected on the historical view of how communities organize their living spaces within communities, their work environments, and extend that world view from within the community and out to characterize the world around them.

Figure 1. Educators at the NMC Campus

Within these virtual spaces, the terrain, setting, animations, and objects within it presented an environment for learning and are detailed instantiations of the unifying shared objects that define the community's goals. For some educators, learning spaces resembled the physical campus and the familiar look and feel of the classroom. Others envisioned dramatically different learning spaces designed to stimulate the mind and evaluate novel learning techniques.

Amidst the reflections on how to nurture virtual education, external forces were at work that strengthened the call to action and opened the flood gates for educators worldwide.

Community Development

Figure 2 illustrates some of the institutions, communities, conferences, technology, and character strengths (Peterson & Seligman, 2004) that encouraged the virtual pioneers to persevere. The mind map highlights the major groups and events from ten years in virtual world education and the three character strengths most evident in them. The selection of a mind map was intentional as it is order independent, yet suggests the relationships between the groups.

Gartner's Prediction Opens the Floodgates

Gartner Research made a bold pronouncement that generated a flurry of activity and made skeptics wonder if it would be a self-fulfilling prophecy. Long respected for their skillful forecasts on the evolution and maturation of novel technologies, Gartner (2007) made a bold prediction: "By the end of 2011, 80 percent of active Internet users (and Fortune 500 enterprises) will have a "second life", but not necessarily in Second Life, according to Gartner, Inc."

Figure 2. Virtual world communities and conferences

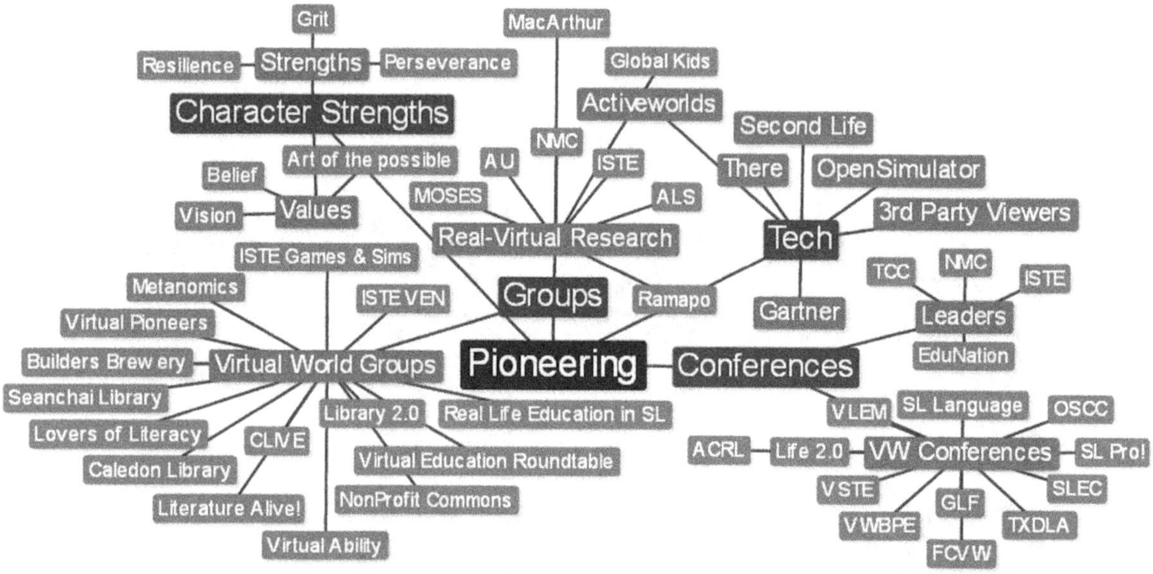

Gartner spoke of collaborative communities and transaction-based commercial opportunities as well as the five laws for business use in virtual worlds. Of interest to educators was the quest for identity and development of selfhood in virtual spaces as represented by the avatar, and to be relevant and add value. Gartner stated the need for cultural development and understanding the (as yet) unwritten rules for behavior, critical for enterprise users and to protect their corporate reputations, equally important for educators and for creating safe learning environments. With regard to relevance, rethinking online education required exploring a shift from asynchronous to synchronous class activities provided a forum for teamwork, for meeting minds and for collaboration.

The fourth law focused on branding and recognizing the threats and affordances within a virtual world. Misconduct and mischievous disruptions were considerations that made educational leaders wonder if a safe learning environment was possible. The fifth law noted the issues with avatar scalability and environment stability as well as the desire to merge virtual worlds and their assets while preserving the rights of content creators while managing the transfer of assets between avatars. These rules stimulated great discussion among the virtual education community.

To understand the power of this prediction, consider for a moment how the Hype Cycle works. The Gartner Hype Cycle reports the inception and evolution of an emerging technology based on practitioner and scholarly interest and use and movement along the Hype Cycle depends on news from the media. The media attention speculates about the technology and suggests the promise of success, yet for the technology to evolve, it needs a history of use, promising test results, and a period of continuous refinement, and a sufficient number of features for the technology to mature into a productive and successful solution.

Gartner tracks the progress of the innovative idea as it moves from the initial Technology Trigger and charts the results on the Gartner Hype Cycle. They track the rise of a technology through the Peak of Inflated Expectations, which by its title suggests that the media promises more than the technology can deliver. After considerable use and criticism from the early adopters and users who try it, only to discover that it does not meet their expectations, Gartner tracks the criticism and shows how it travels down from the Peak to the Trough of Disillusionment, where interest in it declines until the champions of the technology identify successful applications, test their merits and report the results. Some technologies become obsolete before they mature, while others compete with other technological solutions, such as the decline of the Sony Betamax in favor of VHS as an early video recording medium.

The time it takes to move from disillusionment to enlightenment can be slow, and depends on numerous factors, including use cases and a proven record of use, measurement, and success reports followed by papers and studies that study whether the benefits outweigh the risks. The technology moves through the Hype Cycle after achieving certain milestones. The next area in the Hype Cycle is called the Slope of Enlightenment. It offers renewed interest, growth in media attention and the promise of success. It generates keen interest in the technology, which builds momentum and further discoveries as the technology evolves and matures. With growth through continued use, the technology completes the cycle in the Plateau of Productivity, and benefits from widespread acceptance until a new technology trigger challenges it.

When Gartner issued this news release, it magnified virtual world interest among educators and early adopters. The next section reflects on the pioneering efforts and how the communities formed and shared their discoveries.

VIRTUAL WORLD SYMPOSIA AND CONFERENCES

The MacArthur Foundation Digital Media event (Boyd, 2006; NMC, 2006) brought the community together to reflect on the next five years in digital media design and on the current work across different groups. One of the recipients of the MacArthur grants featured Global Kids, whose heart wrenching exhibit on the topic of Child Trafficking awareness and activism was modeled in the virtual world as a maze on the SL Teen Grid. Other attendees included Joyce Bettencourt and Jeroen Frans of the Vesuvius Group, LLC, who also support the Nonprofit Commons, Avacon and the OpenSimulator Community Conference. Peggy Sheehy of the Ramapo project for Suffern Middle School inspired educators to contribute to the project's content. Terry Beaubois of Montana State encouraged collaboration and thoughts on architecture, while Howard Rheingold gave the keynote address on his first day in a virtual world. Boyd (2006) blogged the event and Kanter (2006) shared insights on what it was like to attend a blended reality event in person and online in a virtual world. From the live meeting, Katie Salen and Eric Zimmerman sat with the MacArthur briefing and answered questions from 65 virtual attendees on game development in education during the blended reality question and answer session (Calongne & Hiles, 2007; Kanter, 2006; Levine, 2008).

Technical conferences in these early days included Dr. Dobb's Journal's event, Life 2.0 with more than 1,000 software developers attending either logged in as an avatar in the virtual world or watching the event from a streaming website while sitting in a physical conference room in Silicon Valley. The use of a Chat Bridge allowed virtual and physical conference attendees to ask questions and offer observations during the sessions, and the topics ranged from software engineering issues to security and scalability concerns (AdvertisingAge, 2007, September 10). At one event, the author sat next to an avatar who at the physical conference was sitting next to Bill Gates. Sharing ideas across boundaries, technologies and without regard for ones circle of influence is part of the magic of virtual world events.

EduNation with their emphasis on Language Learning evolved from the early Yahoo Group called Webheads to host meetings and community events as well as the annual SL Languages conference and the Virtual Roundtable. The EduNation region featured a beach-themed build, filled with music videos and conversation nooks to inspire imaginative and relaxing spaces for teaching English as a second language and promote language learning.

The English Village by pioneer Fire Centaur featured language learning games, roleplay and later, the use of Holodecks as conversation nooks. He invited the educational community to participate in their events over the Real Life Education in Second Life group.

Libraries in Second Life

The Community Virtual Library bridges virtual worlds and technologies to offer library services and a virtual world database for education and research use (Community Virtual Library, 2019). For K-12 as well as higher education, the Illinois' Alliance Library System and support from an educational grant led to the design of Info Island, extended into additional regions, including in creating a space for librarians and educators to explore and obtain technology resources on Info Island, and later, HealthInfo Island and additional regions, including the Eduisland regions. The various 3D designs blended the creative efforts of educators and talented designers, including Aaron Griffiths from the Kiwi Educators' group, who wove a picnic rug with animations from the author's designs into a space that appeared on demand, a technology used in later game simulations. The scene appeared when visitors drew near for them to enjoy and disappeared when they left.

The community of librarians from around the world also featured prominently in several conferences, including the Virtual World Library, Education and Museum (VLEM) conference and the Association of College Research Librarians (ACRL) conferences.

The NMC held two virtual world conferences in addition to their summer conference for several years and the topics ranged from digital media and learning or the symposium for the future. After the inaugural campus event in June 2006 (Levine, 2008), they held a fall southwest regional conference in San Antonio and John Lester, known as Pathfinder Linden, gave the keynote address. The presentations ranged from Ruben Puentedura's (2006) session on the Third Place, a social place where everyone knows your name which is vital to life balance and informal learning, to mirror Tuan's (1977), Bachelard's (1964) and Maslow's thoughts (McLeod, 2016; Maslow, 1943) on the needs within the First Place (home) and Second Place (work) as defined and coined by Ray Oldenburg (2002).

Why did these topics matter? The underlying notion of virtual spaces rests in how they sustain individual and social needs. Once selfhood and identity within a virtual world is grounded with a sense of community (Oldenburg, 2002), it is easier to design, evaluate, revise and implement educational programs that blend the playful and social qualities of 3D spaces with curriculum and assessment.

Best Practices in Education and the VWBPE

In 2007, the first Best Practices in Education in Second Life, hosted by Chris Collins (Fleep Tuque) and Beth Ritter-Guth (Desideria Stockton) brought educators together to share their experiences and designs. The BPE in SL conference set the tone for later educational conferences, including the Education Support Faire, and the annual Virtual Worlds Best Practices in Education (VWBPE), hosted by Rockcliffe University under the guidance of Kevin Feenan. In 2009, the SL Education Support Faire under John Lester (Pathfinder) featured 3,785 unique visitors from 93 countries with 50 poster displays and 50 presentations over a five day period (Calongne, 2009).

VWBPE spans several days and supports attendees from up to 150 countries who are passionate about learning. The sessions extend beyond Second Life to embrace other MUVEs, including Unity3D, Blizzard's World of Warcraft®, and Minecraft®. The conference features many sessions, games, social events, tours, and demonstrations of projects and otherworldly educational content.

Virtual Ability and the Nonprofit Commons

Selfhood focuses on how a person's identity emerges and the shared human experience. Virtual worlds attract users from all walks of life and capabilities, and few regions are more welcoming than Virtual Ability (2019a). Gentle Heron at Virtual Ability offers support, acceptance and a warm welcome for all users, and provides particular support and sessions for users who may not be able to walk, hear, or see in the physical world. Virtual world tools are complex to use, yet offer an amazing experience for users. To be able to fly, to run, and to dance when movement is no longer an option is a grand experience. The video called Better Life by Rob Wright (2006), who is well known as SL music and sound pioneer Robbie Dingo, illustrates the opportunity for escapism and transcending physical boundaries in a virtual world.

Virtual Ability hosted conferences on the International Disability Rights Affirmation Conference (IDRAC) (Virtual Ability, 2019b), the Mental Health Symposia (Virtual Ability, 2019c), and strengthen the mentorship and educational programs held weekly at the Nonprofit Commons (2007), a Second Life social good community of the global nonprofit organizations that meets on Friday mornings. Over 150 nonprofit and social good agencies support the Nonprofit Commons in Second Life.

The Military Archipelago

An archipelago of military regions connected The Air University and Squadron Officer College, two centers of learning for the U.S. Air Force, the U.S. Army's Simulation and Training Technology Center with the Team Orlando group, the U.S. Navy, and quite possibly, the U.S. Marines, although they were a lot quieter. Some of these regions were open to the public while others were private.

After publishing an EDUCAUSE Review article in their back-to-school edition on teaching in virtual worlds (Calongne, 2008), The Air University (AU) initiated a collaborative effort that loosely coupled researchers, educators and military enthusiasts across several projects and two events: the Global Learning Forum and bi-weekly lunch and learn meetings. These events welcomed the community and military residents in a wonderfully connectivist fashion, crossing over boundaries and encouraging the use of innovative strategies. The GLF speaker sessions held 2-4 times a year featured Jeremy Bailenson from the Stanford Virtual Human Interaction Lab GLF, the Dean of the Vanderbilt Medical School, Art Langer from Columbia University and Nancy Sherman from Georgetown University, who spoke on moral injury.

From the collaboration came experiments using a custom-designed game simulation kit by Andrew Stricker and Michael McCrocklin called The Hostage Rescue Game: Operation Anaconda with playtesting by community educators and students from Colorado Technical University. Linda Hamons featured the game in her study of shared leadership.

The Mars Expedition Strategy Challenge used a challenge-based method for analyzing a complex problem while flying the learner to Mars. Participants began on a rocket and flew up to the Huffman Prairie Red Lion Deep Space Explorer where they stepped into the role of a science officer en route to Mars. On board, they toured four science stations, reviewed videos, completed a survey and reflected on where the U.S. Congress should direct its budget for the future of the U.S. space program.

The team's innovative design received recognition and the Grand Prize in the first Federal Virtual World Challenge at Defense GameTech. The simulation of a journey to Mars mirrored the self-cleaning behavior and efficiency of a Holodeck from Star Trek (Roddenberry et al., 2007) as it rendered the spacecraft and mining colony when the users drew near and deleted them when they left. They won the $25,000 Grand Prize in the competition. The simulation also rendered space phenomena (a meteor shower, a comet, and a satellite) and different versions of a mining colony on Mars as well as a self-assessment quiz in the form of a trivia game that reminded the participants of the key points from the Mars Expedition Challenge.

One of the advantages of The Air University simulations and games are how the designs focus on identifying the character strengths of the participants and how to leverage them and strengthen other characteristics (Peterson & Seligman, 2004). Strengths-based education reflects on challenging situations and how to call upon the inner strengths in times of crisis and draw upon them to make good decisions. They also center on self-assessment and continuous refinement in addition to formal assessment.

The U.S. Army Simulation and Training Technology Center (STTC) hosted a project called the Military OpenSimulator Enterprise Strategy (MOSES). While the project resided outside of Second Life, two STTC regions offered a site for blended reality conference sessions between the attendees at Defense GameTech in Orlando and the virtual world attendees. The MOSES project designed a custom implementation of the OpenSimulator software and integrated it in a solution called MOSES in a box that simplified the installation and use of custom virtual worlds at educational sites. Volunteers from the MOSES project hosted the Federal Consortium of Virtual Worlds (FCVW) conference, supporting the shift from a physical conference with virtual events to a fully virtual conference in 2015.

During their weekly meetings and in-world activities, the MOSES group researched avatar scalability, open source virtual world stability, physics engine alternatives, avatar realism, and photogrammetry. The MOSES community featured 200 researchers, educators, military personnel, contractors, game designers, businesses, students, and artists collaborating for eight years to advance the state of research in avatar realism, avatar scalability, realism in training, and education in a virtual world. The culture, protocol, and even the avatar names reflect real world practices, and the conference featured tracks in security, modeling and simulation, metacognition and education and training.

One of the differences between MOSES and the AU Metaverse is the perception of education and the community needs. AU focuses on critical thinking, while an important project in MOSES focuses on providing environments and support for military training and familiarization exercises set in realistic landscapes under the leadership of Douglas Maxwell from the STTC. MOSES Community Manager Barbara Truman works closely with the University of Central Florida, while Maxwell coordinates the efforts of simulation experts in the design of a resource fork to the OpenSim software that integrates with Halcyon in its server software and on the development of a custom browser-based viewer.

OpenSimulator Community Conference

Since 2013, the annual OpenSimulator Community Conference bridges open source enthusiasts with the core developers, third party viewer developers, educators, business users, Hypergrid Business, and artists, scripters, musicians, videographers, nonprofits, and entertainers. The conference celebrated the current state of the Metaverse and recommendations for future work. Guest speakers from past conferences featured the CEO from High Fidelity, Steve LaValle, who has two patents for the Oculus Rift, and IBM Fellow Grady Booch, famous for his work on the Unified Modeling Language (UML).

What was amazing was the stable performance of the simulators during the conference, which was designed to support 350-400 users across four main stage regions. Past conferences featured an entire grid for shopping and avatar customization, a sandbox, four expo regions with exhibits and the speaker booths, and four landing points for load distribution and balance.

Virtual reality and its manifestation in virtual worlds changed dramatically over the past 15 years. Rosedale (2015, January 13) in his keynote address from High Fidelity noted the future directions for virtual reality research, including natural gestures, facial expressions, and other techniques designed to strengthen the interaction between avatars.

With over 400 universities and thousands of educators, only highlights appear in this description. Other notable mentions include the Nanotechnology Lab, host of the National Physical Laboratory's launch of nanotechnology innovations during their physics events in Second Life and the Science Circle (2019), an 11-year-old community of scientists and STEM educators from around the world.

See Table 1 for a list of institutions, groups, educational conferences and events.

Notably absent from the list are the early work by 400 universities, including Iowa State University, Boise State University, Ball State University, University of California at San Diego, Princeton University, Stanford University, Wright State University.

Interest in Virtual Worlds and Education

It is hard to characterize all of the major influences on virtual learning due to amount of research and diverse work in the area, but one indicator was the rise in maturity noted on the Gartner (2016) Hype Cycle. The growth in virtual world environments and their capabilities rose steadily. Over 200 virtual world technologies attracted educators due to the need for K-12 friendly environments Calongne, 2009). The most popular worlds offered great content, free student accounts, and a large, diverse community with over 40 daily classes and community events. The various forms of virtual worlds shared elements in common, such as the concept of presence and a unique name for residents. Most important was the concept of an avatar, which served as a representation of self and how other residents observed and interacted with other residents. The avatar modeled real world capabilities and then extended them with flying, elaborately scripted movements, and with the abilities that transcend what is possible in everyday life.

Characteristics in common between virtual worlds include the ability for the avatar to move, animate, gesture and communicate with other avatars within the shared space. Truman's (2013) research elaborated on the importance of these behaviors. What motivates people to feel vested in a virtual community through their group participation and shared presence? She explored two concepts that further define the experience: virtual physioception as an awareness of self, identity and selfhood and virtual-intersubjective presencing which grows from a shared awareness of others that extends out from the individual experience of identity development to shape the avatar's selfhood and emergence as a member of a society. These concepts elaborated on the work of Otto Scharmer (2000) at MIT's Presencing Institute and extended them beyond the interactions between people and the virtual environment.

Early Campus Designs

What did educators do when faced with a barren virtual landscape? They reflected on different strategies for encouraging familiarity, recognition, and preserving the values that matter with the search for motivational alternatives and novel approaches to online education. They examined opportunities to

Table 1. A sample of educational institutions, groups, conferences and meetings

Institution	Mission and Groups	Conferences and Meetings
ISTE	K-12 & Higher Education, ISTE VEN, ISTE Games & Simulations Network, Virtual Pioneers, VSTE affiliate	ISTE annual conference, ISTE NECC, VSTE, Weekly Meetings
EDUCAUSE with the New Media Consortium	Sparking Creativity & Innovation in Higher Education, K-12, Museums, NMC Virtual Worlds Group, NMC Horizon Report with EDUCAUSE eLearning Initiative (ELI)	NMC Educational Gaming, Digital Media & Learning, Symposium for the Future, SL Pro! (with Linden Lab)
Libraries in Second Life	ALS, ACRL Virtual Worlds Interest Group, Seanchai Library, Library 2.0, Caledon Library, Lovers of Literacy, CVL	VLEM, The Future is Now, ALA Annual Conference, SLymposium, Virtual Confs.
EduNation	Language Learning, English as a Second Language, English as a Foreign Language	SL Languages, Virtual Round Table
OpenSimulator	Open source virtual world software development	OpenSimulator Community Conference
Virtual Ability	Research projects, community dances, support for persons with disabilities	MHS, Int'l Disability Rights Affirmation Conference
The Air University	US Air Force education, StudioX, game & simulation design, character strengths, big data analytics	Global Learning Forum, AU Metaverse Lunch & Learn
MOSES	US Army & civilian research, avatar scalability, photogrammetry, realism, military education	Federal Consortium of Virtual Worlds, Defense GameTech (Team Orlando)
State Groups in VWs	Texas, Oregon, North Carolina	TXDLA, CLIVE, SLEC
Dr Dobb's Journal, Sun, IBM	1,000 Software Developers studying development in a virtual world conference	Life 2.0
Virtual Education Roundtable	Virtual Education Roundtable	Weekly educator meetings
Metanomics	Economics in the Metaverse	Weekly Shows & Meetings
Nonprofit Commons	Nonprofits & educators meeting since 2006	Weekly speakers
Rockcliffe University	Virtual Education, K-12, Higher Education	VWBPE
Science Circle	Science archipelago, Science Fridays	Weekly Speakers
Builder's Brewery	Virtual world education in design	Daily classes and events

break out of the real-world mold and to reflect on the art of the possible. At a high level of abstraction and not all-inclusive by any means, the early work in the design of virtual learning spaces fell into two categories: 1) emulating the campus to encourage familiarity and recognition for online, hybrid and campus students, often coupled with campus decorum and behavior; and 2) re-imagining the look and feel of the virtual campus as a place to evaluate new strategies and methods.

The institutions that favored emulating the real world campus recognized that they needed support from their champions and to address the concerns of their critics. They saw the virtual world as an extension of the campus traditions and values. To support the classroom emulation model, educators sought out designers or developed their modeling skills to design virtual campuses that resembled the school's physical campus. For tools in class, some featured hand-raising animations consistent with the campus decorum and mirrored the values and classroom behavior best conducive to learning in the classroom designs. The second group reflected on the opportunities presented by the virtual landscape and the virtual reality simulator's potential. Some envisioned unusual, permanent settings or rotating exhibits and buildings for learning spaces, while others preferred an open palette or the use of interchangeable settings packaged as a hologram that appears and disappear upon request, similar to the Holodeck described by Gene Roddenberry and featured on the television series Star trek: The Next Generation (Roddenberry et al., 2007).

Educators fell into three main groups: 1) pioneers as risk takers; 2) settlers who evaluated adapting the real world methods and applying them within the new technology; and 3) the early adopters who reflected on a balanced approach, blending elements from both perspectives. All three of these tactics offered advantages for evaluating the art of the possible while managing risk. In the face of media hype and criticism (Gartner, 2007), each group tested their organizational boundaries and educational opportunities while helping to define social and cultural norms.

Whether the campus was a tribute to the real world environment or an imaginative permanent or interchangeable space, this described only the setting for learning. Educators faced enormous challenges with regard to mapping the curriculum, instructional methods, delivery styles, managing and evaluating student work, performing learning assessments, and reflecting on how to improve the process. The requirements for providing an environment suitable for learning ranged from content creation, delivery styles, ensuring quality instruction, planning for assessment, balancing public versus private access, managing the risks associated with virtual campus misconduct, and concerns over instructional quality as well as compliance with the Family Educational Rights and Privacy Act (FERPA) on the need for privacy and protection of student education records (U.S. Dept. of Ed., n.d.). FERPA compliance includes privacy in the classroom, an affordance that raised concerns over written and spoken communication in virtual world classes. The challenges seemed enormous for some campuses.

CHALLENGES AND STRENGTHS FOR PIONEERS

The cognitive and technological challenges disenfranchised talented educators who saw the appeal, but felt that virtual world technologies were not ideal for certain classrooms. Using the SL or Third Party Viewers required a steep learning curve due to the feature-rich interface. Educators struggled to design 3D tutorial simulations to support the training needed to orient novice learners and educators. The most significant challenge was not resident misconduct (called griefing), inappropriate content, or concerns over safe learning environments, but instead, a major disruption in the economic model for education (Mark, 2014). When Linden Lab announced the end of the educational discount, many schools and educational programs had few options for extending their educational technology budgets in the middle of a school year. A widespread panic, followed by an exodus either to open source virtual worlds or different technologies led to a disruption in the community (Mark, 2014; Young, 2010, October 14). When the furor stabilized, the community remained, but some of them could no longer afford to host educational regions in Second Life and instead, gave up their regions and either moved to Kitely or another open source world, left SL, or used the community and group areas as a social space for attending conferences and connecting with friends and colleagues.

While some wonder what might have happened without this economic pressure, on the positive side, it stimulated growth in open source virtual worlds and challenged educators to find new solutions. In contrast, some abandoned their previous work, noting that the world failed to support them and that the technological hurdles associated with hosting were too steep. Contracting with another service, like Kitely, offered an archipelago of regions devoted to education and like-minded community members.

The changes led to growth, but the timing of the disruption slowed the progress along the Gartner Hype Cycle until the renewed interest in 3D virtual reality (VR) wearable devices and 360 degree video gained media attention.

The Power of Script Creation: Autoscript

During the 2007 NMC Summer Conference, Hilary Mason asked conference attendees to test her design of an automated tool for writing custom scripts for Second Life called Autoscript (Mason, 2007). Hosted on a website, it supports nine main functions and asks 2-3 questions about when the script should execute and how it should behave. Users click three options and then the *Make My Script* button to see their custom script before selecting it, copying it, and pasting it into a new script in Second Life.

The Autoscript tool gave educators, students and virtual world residents the power of creation and taught some basic algorithmic procedures used in software design. Later versions featured the tool in several languages.

Virtual World Technologies

OpenSimulator (2016) was the open source alternative to the Second Life server software, designed by a talented team of volunteers. The content within an OpenSim grid looked similar to SL, but behaved differently. The Third Party Viewers (TPVs) used to access SL also worked in OpenSim with the OpenSim TPV versions. Most TPVs supported Windows, Mac and Linux users.

Crista Lopes, one of the core developers and a founding member of the Women in Virtual Reality, saw an opportunity for strengthening the need to meet in different virtual worlds and to avoid logging into additional avatar accounts to visit different worlds. To provide greater mobility and connectedness, she introduced features into the OpenSimulator server software to permit users who enabled it on their servers to visit different worlds without needing an account on them. Moving between virtual worlds by entering the address and port number of the destination grid in the world map she called the Hypergrid.

The Hypergrid capability brought the community closer together and the Hypergrid Safari conducted tours of three Hypergrid destinations each week (Lester, 2014; Ember, 2011).

In Pursuit of Selfhood: The Sweet Spot

Think back to that first attempt at riding a bicycle. Teetering, trying to find a sense of balance, the rider struggles and falls, groaning with frustration. Determination and encouragement from others fuels the spirit and causes the would-be rider to get back on the bicycle and try again. For some, the struggle is longer and more arduous, while others slip into balance with a surprising grace.

The magic occurs when that mysterious sweet spot, so elusive before, clicks into place and the rider soars forward, amazed and gratified by the feeling of centeredness and balance. At first, a fragile experience, the rider wavers at the beginning and the end of the ride, and wonders if the feeling of success was accidental, just a moment in time, or whether it can be repeated. With praise and practice, the rider soars, gliding as if flying for the first time.

The feeling of joy that educators shared when they entered the virtual world makes the effort worthwhile. The awareness of others within this magical place transforms them. It is an otherworldly feeling, and like the first bicycle ride, not a simple task nor one that feels natural. Novices often think about the technology, the steep learning curve, and how strange it feels to move, look around and interact with objects, but it is comparable to the early attempts to use the mouse, fumbling and frustrated as the mind wills the hand to respond, yet the cursor goes awry.

Coupled with the technology challenge were the cognitive hurdles. Once the avatar moved, communicated, and manipulated objects, the next decision was what to do and how to translate curriculum and activities into 3D representations that supported education in virtual spaces. In the early days, assessment was one of the challenges, stimulating the need for rubrics and prior planning.

Selfhood, Presence, and the Shared Experience: Community

When asked what the virtual world provides that a well-constructed website cannot, the answer is presence and the intersection and awareness of people and content. It is the connection between people and their shared objects that makes the experience of the world come alive (Alexander, 2006; Truman, 2013). Without other avatars, which are representations of self within these spaces, and their awareness of one another, the experience is lifeless, and the user wanders alone, cut off from the world. Gartner (2007) warned against the use of beautiful, empty spaces, noting that they do not strengthen the brand nor satisfy user expectations.

The awareness of others requires more than bumping into other avatars or seeing them from a distance. It is the shared experience, the interaction of people with the content, and the joyful discoveries as well as those awkward moments when the culture, behavior and social norms within these spaces seem make the users wonder if they are welcome and if they will look or feel foolish. It is the development of a community that struggles together and shares their successes.

The early concerns mirrored life experiences, such as going to school for the first time, meeting new people, teaching those first few classes and having knowledgeable students who exude more confidence than the educator feels. What is it that causes pioneers to overcome these hurdles, master their fears, or to adopt a playful reaction to each stumble, to falter and pull themselves upright, persevering until they feel that connection with the world and others within it?

It is the experience of community, of a society that transforms individuals into a cohesive group, and confirms their connection with the world around them. Extending the analogy, it is the feeling of joining a group, such as a bike-a-thon or a race, and riding with hundreds of other riders, gliding, feeling the shared joy of the ride. It is less about being first, but instead, about feeling the connection with other riders and the beauty of the land around them, the hazards overcome and the feeling of connection.

Pioneers see opportunities and apply the character strengths of perseverance, resilience and grit to study the art of the possible. Educators also include settlers who define pathways for a sustainable practice and document their strategies for mapping the curriculum to a virtual world delivery model.

They are the heroes, transforming minds and encourage motivation and engagement to support lifelong learning. But the individual efforts are even more satisfying when they take shape within the educational community.

FROM CURRENT TO FUTURE WORK

Virtual reality languished for years on the Gartner Hype Cycle for Emerging Technology (Gartner, 2016) in part due to over 20 years of work trying to overcome the technological hurdles and deleterious side effects users experienced when wearing a head-mounted display (HMD) device. In 1995, the General Reality Cyber Eye was comfortable to wear, but suffered from registration issues (objects staying faithful to their location in 3D space), and the fixed focal point of 11' from the user's body. No matter how close a user moved to the content, it rendered 11 feet from the user's body, making it a poor candidate for reading text on screen. In 2016, some users reported feeling dizziness or motion sickness while wearing the Oculus. Aside from wearable technology, the perception of virtual reality resulted in disagreement among members of the community on what defined VR and how VR applications.

In 2016, manufacturers and VR enthusiasts distinguished the technologies and classified them into several categories: 1) VR that used a HMD or smartphone running a 3D VR app, visible using Google Cardboard or a more expensive presentation device; 2) the 3D VR apps featured either 360 degree video with head tracking that allowed users to turn and view content beside or behind them on 3D games; 3) VR simulations for training, research and niche markets.

One of the challenges with 3D games was the need for interaction support and better interfaces. VR games used a controller to interact with objects on screen, such as firing weapons and interacting with non-player characters or other players, and interactive virtual spaces, designed as simulations, museums, learning environments, research, military education, entertainment, or social use. While fine for games, educators needed robust interfaces with additional capabilities to create content, position it, and adjust the environment as well as integrate with external Web resources.

When Mark Zuckerberg, co-founder and CEO of Facebook, acquired Oculus VR in 2014, the virtual reality company that manufactured the Oculus Rift, the world reflected on the implications (Bailenson, 2018). His thoughts mirrored what many educators considered. Will immersive virtual reality require a HMD for full immersion and serve as the next computing platform? If so, how will it work, what will it do, and how can educators and designers contribute and help to shape the future?

Not everyone agreed that the technology was ready for the market, much less ready for widespread use (Sung, 2015). The lack of interfaces to support interaction within the virtual environment as well as support for multiple users coupled with the need to reduce the feeling of motion sickness and nausea led to different perspectives on use in 2016, much less the next few years.

At the 2016 Virtual Worlds Best Practices in Education (VWBPE) conference, educators discussed VR technologies and their implications for virtual worlds, distinguishing the two technologies as if they had little in common. The perception of the differences suggested that VR required a HMD while virtual worlds did not. In this sense, VR represented immersive virtual reality, and for some, focused on 360 degree video with head tracking while 3D VR games used a controller for interaction.

The distinction of virtual worlds as social spaces rather than part of the current definition of virtual reality was surprising. In 2016, virtual worlds like Second Life were hard to use with a HMD, in part due to the wide disparity of content, the user interface and how text appeared on screen. Some of the problems experienced in the past still existed with regard to rendering text, setting a fixed focal point for HMD comfort and to minimize the sense of vertigo when the focus shifted as new objects appeared on screen. Despite these interface limitations, the immersive property of educational virtual worlds made it less dependent on visual representation and more dependent on a sense of avatar involvement and the feeling of engagement and presence.

Driven to third party worlds and open source solutions, educators straddled Second Life compatibility versus the need for new and dramatically different alternatives that appealed to future learners and educators. If not HMDs and 360 video, what was the next viable direction?

With an eye toward the future, Linden Lab designed Project Sansar, a working title for a 3D mesh alternative to Second Life that at this time was not launched. While it may offer better compatibility with VR HMDs, the challenges for use in education may outweigh the high quality graphics and sense of realistic spaces. The desire to stay relevant and current with technology contrasts with the need for content creation tools that allow educators and students to create 3D designs, class objects and projects.

Solutions like High Fidelity by CEO Philip Rosedale (2015) who presented a keynote address at the OpenSimulator Community Conference, integrated community development with high quality strategies for content creation. To handle the processing requirements for use in the future on mobile devices, High Fidelity proposed a distributed peer-to-peer processing architecture with something similar to crypto currencies for compensating users for their off-duty processing support, a concept similar to SETI-at home, only with a modern twist.

What were the implications for educators? As mobile technology use became a vital part of online learning, drawing learners further away from campus classroom into the realm of ubiquitous education, lightweight client tools, such as 3D mobile viewers, may reduce some of the complexity and make it easier and affordable for students and educators to use. Certain challenges remain, particularly for content creation by students and educators as well as hosting class projects that require students to create 3d content that either models their ideas or represents a blended reality example of the problem or the solution.

The power of creation in 3D virtual worlds is breathtaking and a vital component in learning activities that reinforce the concepts through practice by doing activities and projects. If the technology shifts to elegant environments that favor high quality visuals over usability and creation, then the next item on the wish list for the future is the need for easy-to-use tools that demystify how to create mesh content and design 3D environments.

Otherwise, current 3D technologies, like Second Life, OpenSim, Inworldz, Kitely, and other educational grids will continue to flourish until the next technological shift. Once a learner or educator embraces the power of creation, it is hard to step back into cruise control.

CONCLUSION

Ray Oldenburg (2002) observed that community development and time spent in the Third Space contributes to social and psychological health. A lifestyle divided solely between home and work (or school) becomes a routine that does not account for social and psychological needs. A community provides a place for playful banter in contrast to the serious business of work, yet in a fast-paced world, the time spent with a community grows shorter without groups, events, champions and a commitment.

It is with regret that the chapter did not recognize the thousands of amazing educators, librarians, curriculum designers, administrators and technology evangelists who pioneered and shaped virtual world education. Faced with economic pressures, when they closed their educational programs in Second Life, many found alternative paths and developed societies in open source virtual worlds or game worlds as MUVEs.

The rapid growth and large number of groups and communities within Second Life have yet to be rivaled in open source or commercial worlds, but the numbers are steadily growing. Maria Korolov of Hypergrid Business (2016, November 15) reported record high numbers of regions in open source worlds and steady growth, and noted that the size rivals Second Life.

What will tomorrow bring to shape the future of virtual world education? The successes of the past ten years indicate the promise of a bright future, and this time, driven by technology-enhanced educators, curriculum designers, librarians, administrators, and learners who understand the value of selfhood and society.

REFERENCES

AdvertisingAge. (2007, September 10). Second Life has some firms second guessing [Weblog post]. Retrieved from http://adage.com/article/btob/life-firms-guessing/268564/

Alexander, B. (2006). *NMC 2006 regional* [PowerPoint slides]. Retrieved from http://www.slideshare.net/BryanAlexander/nmc-2006-regional

Bachelard, G. (1964). *The poetics of space*. New York: Orion Press.

Bailenson, J. (2018). *Experience on demand: What virtual reality is, how it works, and what it can do*. New York, NY: W. W. Norton & Company.

Boyd, D. (2006, October 21). Announcing the Macarthur Foundation's digital media and learning initiative [Weblog post]. Retrieved from http://www.zephoria.org/thoughts/archives/2006/10/21/announcing_the.html

Calongne, C. (2008). Educational frontiers: Learning in a virtual world. *EDUCAUSE Review, 43*(5), 36–48.

Calongne, C. (2009). Virtual worlds: Explorations and implications [PowerPoint slides]. *Association for Information Technology Professionals*. Retrieved from http://www.slideshare.net/lyrlobo/aitp-keynote-on-virtual-worlds

Calongne, C., & Hiles, J. (2007). Blended realities: A virtual tour of education in Second Life. *Proceedings of the 12th Annual Technology, Colleges & Community (TCC) Worldwide Conference*.

Community Virtual Library. (2019). *Real librarianship in virtual worlds*. Retrieved from https://communityvirtuallibrary.org/

Da Silva, M. (2015, February 17). The meaning of social objects [Weblog post]. Retrieved from http://abcofinternetmarketing.co.za/blogging/social-media/meaning-social-objects/

Dede, C. (2003). Multi-user virtual environments. *EDUCAUSE Review, 38*(3), 60–61.

Dede, C., & Ketelhut, D. J. (2003). Designing for motivation and usability in a museum-based multi-user virtual environment. *American Educational Research Association Conference*, Chicago, IL.

Ember, T. (2011, October 19). HG safari [Weblog post]. Retrieved from https://hgsafari.blogspot.com/2011/

Engeström, J. (2005, April 13). Why some social network services work and others don't -- Or: the case for object-centered sociality [Weblog post]. Retrieved from http://www.zengestrom.com/blog/2005/04/why-some-social-network-services-work-and-others-dont-or-the-case-for-object-centered-sociality.html

Gartner. (2007). *Gartner says 80 percent of active internet users will have a "Second Life" in the virtual world by the end of 2011*. Retrieved from http://www.gartner.com/newsroom/id/503861

Gartner. (2016). *Gartner's 2016 hype cycle for emerging technologies identifies three key trends that organizations must track to gain competitive advantage*. Retrieved from http://www.gartner.com/newsroom/id/3412017

Kanter, B. (2006, October 19). The birth of a field: Digital media and learning [Weblog post]. Retrieved from https://beth.typepad.com/beths_blog/2006/10/the_birth_of_a_.html

Korolov, M. (2016). *November a solid month for opensim growth.* Retrieved from http://www.hypergridbusiness.com/2016/11/november-a-solid-month-for-opensim-growth/

Lester, J. (2014, July 29). Hypergrid safari -- The evolution of exploration across the interconnected Metaverse [Weblog post]. Retrieved from https://becunningandfulloftricks.com/2014/07/29/hypergrid-safari-the-evolution-of-exploration-across-the-interconnected-metaverse/

Levine, A. (2008). The NMC campus. *EDUCAUSE Review*, *43*(5).

Mark, C. L. (2014). *Growth and decline of Second Life as an educational platform* (Doctoral dissertation). Available from ProQuest Dissertations & Theses Global. (Order No. 3584527)

Maslow, A. H. (1943). A Theory of Human Motivation. *Psychological Review*, *50*(4), 370–396. doi:10.1037/h0054346

Mason, H. (2007). *Script Me!* Retrieved from http://3greeneggs.com/autoscript/

McLeod, S. A. (2016). *Maslow's hierarchy of needs*. Retrieved from www.simplypsychology.org/maslow.html

NMC. (2005, December). Symposium on Games in Education. *Learning Times*.

NMC. (2006). *Symposium on digital media and learning*. MacArthur Foundation.

Nonprofit Commons. (2007, January 30). Welcome to the NPSL blog! [Weblog post]. Retrieved from http://nonprofitcommons.org/node?page=97

Oldenburg, R. (2002). *Celebrating the third place: Inspiring stories about the "great good places" at the heart of our communities*. New York: Marlow & Company.

OpenSimulator. (2016, October 27). *OpenSimulator* [Software]. Retrieved from http://opensimulator.org/

Peterson, C., & Seligman, M. E. P. (2004). *Character strengths and virtues: A handbook and classification.* American Psychological Association.

Puentedura, R. R. (2006). *Game theory revisited: Third places and the new web* [Podcast]. Retrieved from http://hippasus.com/resources/thirdplace/

Roddenberry, G., Hurley, M., Baron, M., Barry, P., Beimler, H., Black, J. D. F., . . . Paramount Pictures Corporation. (2007). *Star trek, the next generation: Season 1*. Paramount Pictures.

Rosedale, P. (2015, January 13). OSCC14 - Philip Rosedale keynote: What is the metaverse? *Second Annual OpenSimulator Community Conference*. Retrieved from https://youtu.be/iR3uUVPyjhU

Scharmer, C. O. (2000). *Presencing: Learning from the future as it emerges*. Presentation at the Conference on Knowledge and Innovation, Helsinki School of Economics, Finland. Retrieved from http://www.ottoscharmer.com/docs/articles/2000_Presencing.pdf

Science Circle. (2019). *Lectures, debates, excursions and symposia*. Retrieved from https://www.sciencecircle.org/lectures-debates-excursions-and-symposia/

Second Life History. (2017, December 29). Retrieved February 20, 2019 from the Second Life Wiki: http://wiki.secondlife.com/wiki/History_of_Second_Life

Stephenson, N. (1993). *Snow crash*. New York: Bantam Books.

Sung, D. (2015, November 13). *Virtual reality realism: Why 2016 might not be VR's big year. Three experts fail to agree on whether 2016 will be the year VR breaks through*. Retrieved from http://www.wareable.com/vr/is-2016-the-year-vr-goes-mainstream

Truman, B. (2013). *Transformative interactions using embodied avatars in collaborative virtual environments: Towards transdisciplinarity* (Doctoral dissertation). Available from ProQuest Dissertations & Theses Global. (Order No. 3628698)

Tuan, Y. (1977). *Space and place: The perspective of experience*. Minneapolis, MN: The University of Minnesota Press.

U.S. Dept. of Ed. (n.d.). *Family educational rights and privacy act (FERPA)*. U.S. Department of Education. Retrieved from http://www2.ed.gov/policy/gen/guid/fpco/ferpa/index.html

Virtual Ability. (2019a). *Virtual Ability, Inc*. Retrieved from https://virtualability.org/

Virtual Ability. (2019b). *International disability rights affirmation conference (IDRAC) 2012-2018*. Retrieved from https://virtualability.org/idrac/

Virtual Ability. (2019c). *Mental health symposia 2012-2018*. Retrieved from https://virtualability.org/mental-health-symposia/

Wright, R. (2006). *Better life* [Video file]. Retrieved from https://youtu.be/8_4dW1rZBhI

Young, J. R. (2010, October 14). Academics discuss mass migration from Second Life, The Chronicle of Higher Education [Weblog post]. Retrieved from http://www.chronicle.com/blogs/wiredcampus/academics-discuss-mass-migration-from-second-life/27672

KEY TERMS AND DEFINITIONS

Archipelago: A group of regions that look like islands with a related theme. The NMC hosted an educational archipelago of 110 islands.

AU: The Air University hosts open source virtual worlds for education that feature both practical and playful spaces designed to stimulate thinking and creativity, blending the art of the possible with a passion for excellence. The learning activities to support research in signature character strengths and evaluation of serious games as well as data analytics.

CTU: Colorado Technical University, a for-profit higher education institution that featured doctoral, graduate and undergraduate classes in computer science, emerging media and virtual worlds that met and designed projects in a virtual world from 2006-2016.

Grid: A collection of regions that comprise the virtual landscape. Architecturally, two of Second Life's largest grids featured the Main Grid in which the regions are connected and look like a continent. In the early years, Linden Lab operated a Teen Grid for approximately 6,000 residents ages 13-17.

Hypergrid: Including the ability to move between virtual worlds using the same account.

ISTE: The International Society for Technology in Education offers conferences and year-round support for over 21,000 educators around the world. Each year, ISTE hosts a conference for many of their members, and in the early years, held regional exhibits and a virtual conference simultaneously in Second Life with live speakers presenting from the SL or Virtual Environments Playground.

MUVE: A multiuser virtual environment includes a variety of online shared spaces for large groups of people. Examples include a virtual world, a massive multiplayer online game (MMOG), a massive multiplayer online roleplaying game (MMORPG) like the *World of Warcraft*, or smaller multiplayer games like *Minecraft*, or other shared spaces, like multiuser dungeons (MUDs), chat rooms, and online social spaces.

New Media Consortium (NMC): A consortium of over 200 museums and schools devoted to innovation in technology and education. The NMC and EDUCAUSE published the Horizon Report, a publication that forecasted the next five years for technology in education. Several editions of the Horizon Report are published each year, including Higher Education, K-12, and several international publications.

OpenSimulator: Open source virtual world server software that looks and behaves in a manner similar to Second Life. The code has features that differ from SL, and visitors log into these worlds using a third-party viewer.

OSCC: OpenSimulator Community Conference, held annually to nurture the open source community. The first conference was in 2013.

Region: A virtual world simulator, often installed on a virtual machine that processes and displays the virtual landscape. A single server can host multiple regions.

Second Life: A commercial virtual world operated by Linden Research, which conducts business as Linden Lab.

TCC: The TCC Worldwide Online Conference began in 1995 under the original title Technology in Community Colleges. Over the years, the mission of the TCC conference has evolved, yet continues to foster research and sharing the best practices in online education. The TCC held preconference events in Second Life, and held after hour's events on the Squirrel Island hosted by their conference partner, Learning Times.

Virtual Worlds: A simulated environment where people and 3D content converge. The setting can look like an island, a parcel of land, reside underwater or float high in the air, and the content can vary from realistic objects and buildings to imaginary spaces. The virtual worlds come to life when people interact with one another and the world around them through communication and content sharing.

VWBPE: Virtual Worlds Best Practices in Education, an annual conference since 2008 hosted by the Rockcliffe University Consortium, a virtual world university.

Chapter 17

AI-Augmented Developmental Instruction for Improving Contemplative Practices in the Face of Complexity

Andrew G. Stricker
https://orcid.org/0000-0002-4184-0554
The Air University, USA

Cynthia Calongne
Colorado Technical University, USA

Barbara Truman
https://orcid.org/0000-0002-7839-1772
University of Central Florida, USA

David J. Lyle
Air Education and Training Command, USA

J. J. Jacobson
University of California – Riverside, USA

ABSTRACT

A simulation design is introduced for using artificial intelligence (AI)-augmented developmental instruction for improving contemplative practices in the face of complexity. The focus of the design is on developmental instruction in the use of contemplative cognitive and moral reasoning practices to improve self-awareness and means to better discern and address complicated and complex challenges. Developmental instruction is supported by an AI-augmented tutoring aid provided during a simulated mission to Mars within an immersive 3D-world. A set of tasks are introduced during the Mars simulation to assist with the development of contemplative practices. The AI-augmented tutoring aid assists participants in the simulation to better understand and apply contemplative practices involving cognitive and moral reasoning meta-thinking suitable for each task. High levels of fidelity, involving visual, auditory, and interactive model-based reasoning (MBR) tools help to embed the senses, thoughts, and actions of participants in the feeling of traveling and being on Mars.

DOI: 10.4018/978-1-5225-9679-0.ch017

INTRODUCTION

Since the second half of the twentieth century, physics has gradually lost the concision and simplicity of its classical theories. Modern theoretical models have become more and more complex, vague, and uncertain. Experimental verifications has become more difficult as well. (The Three-Body Problem, Cixin Liu, 2014)

In Cixin Liu's science fiction novel, *The Three-Body Problem*, he introduces to readers several big questions related to complexity facing science and the developmental journey among key scientists in the novel about how their self-awareness grows in discerning and addressing complexity. Liu's novel, winner of the Hugo Award for Best Novel, interweaves hard science with speculative fiction. Indeed, the title of the novel itself is a plot device for the unfolding story making use of the hard science that there is no solution to the general three-body problem in quantum mechanics. In general terms, the motion of three bodies in relation to each other is generally non-repeating, except in special cases. A complete solution for a particular three-body problem would provide the positions for three particles for all time (across time), given three initial positions and initial velocities. Unfortunately, no closed-form solution can be definitively offered for such a problem. This phenomenon is inherent to the chaotic nature of the time evolution of three-body or "n-body" (more than 2-body) systems. On a larger scale, for example, the three-body problem represented by the Moon, the Earth, and the Sun, takes a restrictive form whereby periodic calculated approximations are used to make predictions of trajectories of orbiting objects. In the case of space flight, a four-body problem (spacecraft, Earth, Sun, Moon), for example, can shift approximately to a three-body problem when gravity becomes negligible as the spacecraft travels further from a large mass and reverts back to a four-body problem when approaching an additional large mass such as another planet (e.g., Jupiter) and a moon (e.g., Europa) in addition to the Sun. In this example, the periodic calculated approximations require a computer to continuously analyze the calculated solutions.

The three-body problem helps to highlight the nature of some challenges encountered with evolving complex human-activity systems wherein no known solutions exist and the time evolution of system features is generally non-repeating and in flux (irreducible complexity). Such situations call for regular sense-making, approximations, and emergent strategies for solutions that cannot be tested in advance and will need to be adapted over time. But, not all challenges encountered by people with human-activity systems take the speculative form of a three-body problem. Rather, there are two-body problem forms (e.g., in classical mechanics; for example, a satellite orbiting a planet wherein the center of mass is always constant) involving the means to obtain a correct solution even though the system possesses complicated features (e.g., calculating the central force upon the satellite in orbit over time; uncertainty can be reduced given enough time and discovery of key features for a closed-form solution). Thus, some people can expect to encounter challenges representing forms of two-body problems (complicated) and three-body problems (complex). Generally speaking, post-secondary education can prepare most people with the means to initially address complicated challenges and offer the means for developing skills to improve over time. Unfortunately, however, most people are not well prepared to address challenges involving multidimensional aspects of irreducible complexity. This explains the need for developmental instruction for improving contemplative practices in the face of complexity. The following sections in this chapter explore in greater depth the nature of complexity, why there is a need to help people learn about differences between complicated and complex challenges, and describes a simulation design making use of developmental instruction to assist discernment and improving upon practices for addressing both challenges.

COMPLEXITY

Complexity is an evolving scientific theory addressing properties and behavioral phenomena of systems not well understood, explained, or predictable by means of conventional analysis of its' parts or subsystems (Gleick, 1988). Complexity can be inherent to both structure and behavior of the system. And, interestingly, a complex system can have a complicated structure that is ultimately understandable but display behavior that cannot be regularly predicted across size and time scales (see Figure 1).

Network social structures, involving diffusion of authority, is representative of this type of complex system wherein the organization of the network structure can be defined but the range of behaviors and interaction patterns among members accounting for behaviors may not be regularly predictable for predetermined controlled action (Mitchell, 2009; Ferguson, 2017). Generally, there is also greater independency among components of an open complex system making the overall system usually more

Figure 1. Multidimensional aspects of complex systems at different scales

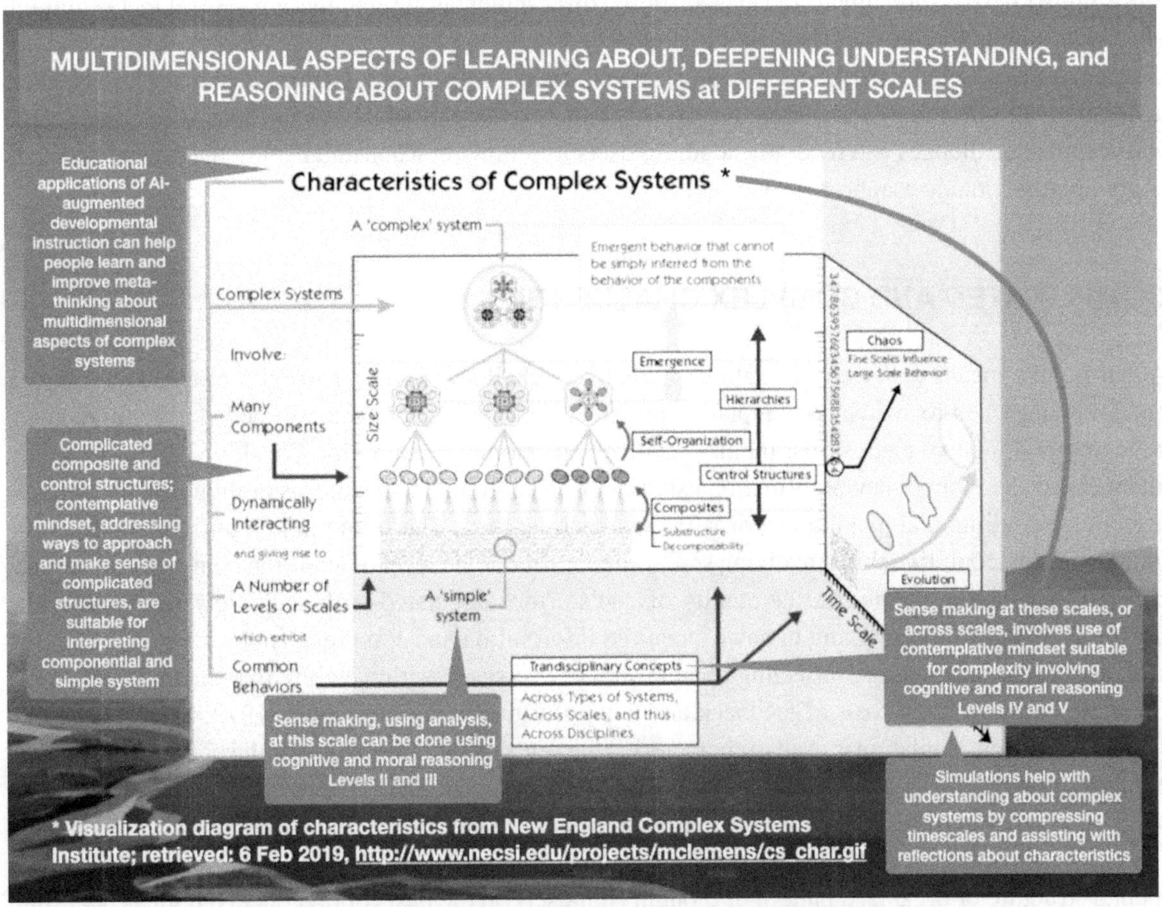

resilient to unexpected events via dynamic interactions and self-organization (Checkland, 1981, p. 87). Conversely, even though complex systems exist in nature and display problems to human observers with no apparent closed-form solutions, models can offer computational close approximations. It is important, however, to keep in mind that although rule-based computational models of complex systems may offer close approximations, involving powerful deductive logic machines (e.g., using high performance computers), there are complex systems producing emergent behavior displaying more inductive-like in-world self-organization and adaptations to unforeseen perturbations and cascading events over long periods of time.

A point of contemplation, when dealing with problems associated with emergent complex systems, is that although the resulting adaptations of the system may appear to be chaotic there could very well exist lower-level composite patterns not discernible to the observer. And conversely, observable and episodic simple behaviors may very well be related to even lower-level complex interactions yet to display new emergent and adaptive behaviors that are random differentially across very long periods of time and therefore not truly "deterministically-random" as would be expected of actual chaotic systems (e.g., some systems in nature are highly sensitive to initial positions and states with resulting fractal pathways of emergent characteristics). The best course of action, when initially facing a challenge or problem presenting considerable unknowns, is to contemplate the degree or level of complexity from a transdisciplinary perspective involving consideration (inquiry) for types of systems, scales, and disciplines likely to help with informing, interpreting, and making sense of the challenge or problem (Checkland, 1981, pp. 100-101; Churchman, 1971). This initial discernment will set in motion several meta-thinking points of contemplation or reflection associated with how the challenge is further perceived and addressed along accepted practices or in some combination with improvisation, discovery, and regular adaptations to unfolding or emergent behaviors. The next section addresses the nature of complicated and complex challenges and recommended mindsets for knowing when and having the means to switch contemplative practices appropriate for each.

COMPLICATED AND COMPLEX CHALLENGES

Acquiring the means to discern the nature of whether a challenge is inherently complicated or complex and knowing when to switch contemplative practices appropriate for each, as needed over time, is dependent upon inquiry meta-skills. Inquiry involves questioning assumptions, seeking out information, and making sense out of new information using existing contemplative patterns of thought for interpreting, understanding, and making use of what has been learned. These internal cognitive processes are guided by metacognitive skills involving self awareness about the level of attention being given to a task, personal bias and assumptions, the quality of one's effort associated with accurately interpreting the nature of the task, sense-making of newly acquired information and comprehension of whether or not to seek additional information, reflecting on appropriate courses of action, acting in a timely fashion, and correcting action on the basis of feedback and new information (Flavell, 1978, 1979; Sternberg, 1983, 1985, 1986). Contemplation is used to characterize the deep and holistic nature of the cognitive processes involved with reflective inquiry and strategic thinking employed in the face of challenge. Inquiry meta-skills are highly dependent on context, experience, and maturation of cognitive and moral reasoning. Collectively, inquiry meta-skills operate as a strategic-thinking contemplative process making use of a mental structure or organized pattern of thought (mindset) on the basis of preconceived ideas regarding some aspect of what is being faced. Sternberg's (1988) research on human intelligence helps to understand how people manage their cognitive resources to monitor, control, and evaluate one's performance on cognitively demanding tasks. His triarchic theory of human intelligence links cognition to context of challenges being faced. Sternberg's theory distinguishes among three types of human intelligence components: meta, performance, and knowledge-acquisition:

Metacomponents are used to decide what to do, to monitor it while it is being done, and to evaluate what one has done after it is completed. Performance components are used in the actual execution of a task. And knowledge-acquisition components are used to learn how to perform a task in the first place. Metacomponents activate performance and knowledge-acquisition components, which in turn provide feedback to the metacomponents. (Sternberg, 1994, p. 282)

When facing complicated and complex challenges a person employs metacomponents in the form of contemplative or reflective patterns of thought (collectively referred to as mindsets; see Slaughter, 2017; Klein, 2009 for examples):

Complicated Challenge Mindset (Contemplative Patterns of Thought)

- Using procedures are helpful to perform tasks more skillfully in alignment with accepted practices for addressing complicated challenges
- Although the challenge is complicated all elements needed for a correct or closed-form solution can be discovered and fitted together given enough time and expertise
- Successful decision making when addressing complicated challenges relies primarily upon logic and statistics
- To make a decision, generate several options and compare them to pick the best one
- Reduce uncertainty by gathering more information
- It's bad to jump to conclusions—wait to see all of the evidence
- To make sense from a complicated situation draw inferences on the basis of data
- The starting point for any effort to address a complicated challenge is to get a clear description of the goal
- A plan will succeed more often for addressing complicated challenges if the biggest risks are identified and ways are found to eliminate them

Complex Challenge Mindset (Contemplative Patterns of Thought)

- What may be necessary isn't the right information but the right way to understand the information at hand
- With complex challenges it is not possible to figure out all that is going on (irreducible complexity)
- Sense-making is at the heart of addressing complexity; it's not just acquiring new knowledge, but also about changing the way things are seen and the thinking about them;
- Comprehension involves asking: Is it possible to make sense of conflicting and confusing data by asking what led up to the events that are happening with the challenge? What can be anticipated about how actions are likely to influence future events?
- Potential action and goals for complicated challenges become clearer over time (emergent goals)

- Breakthrough insights about a complex challenge depends on the ability to learn by making new connections, not on doggedly pursuing the original goal; networking matters for creative insights via divergent perspectives
- It is important to be able to discern what is not controllable and not to dismiss its importance because it is uncontrollable; might need to adapt
- There is the need to be mentally prepared to recover from disappointments, to be resilient, to improvise, and to discover workarounds when facing complexity

As briefly mentioned above, how well a person determines the need for and employs a contemplative mindset and can appropriately switch, as necessary, to the other is based on context (e.g., the degree of mixture between complicated and complex elements requiring switching of mindsets for addressing a challenge or set of challenges), experience (e.g., whether a person has previously encountered and worked with others on the challenge at hand or similar challenges in the past), and a person's developmental maturation level associated with intertwined literacies making use of cognitive and moral reasoning (e.g., ranging from Levels 1 to V as described in the maturation framework introduced in Chapter 2). The degree to which a person can benefit from developmental instruction to acquire, deepen self-awareness about their cognitive and moral reasoning skills, and improve upon each contemplative mindset is related to their maturation level and preparedness for transitioning to a higher level with assistance (Perry, 1999). Dietrich Dörner (1989) refers to this form of self-awareness and contemplativeness as *operative intelligence*:

...operative intelligence, the knowledge that individuals have about the use of their intellectual capabilities and skills. In dealing with complex problems we cannot handle in the same way all the different situations we encounter. Sometimes we must perform detailed analyses, at other times it is better simply to size up a situation. Sometimes we need a comprehensive but rough outline of a situation, at other times we may have to give close attention to details. Sometimes we need to define our goals very clearly and analyze carefully, before we act, exactly what it is we want to achieve; at other times it is better simply to go to work and muddle through. Sometimes we need to think more 'holistically,' more in pictures, at other times more analytically. Sometimes we need to sit back and see what develops; at other times we have to move very quickly...Everything at its proper time and with proper attention to existing conditions. There is no universally applicable rule, no magic wand, that we can apply to every situation and to all the structures we find in the real world. Our job is to think of, and then do, the right things at the right times and in the right way...And it seems to me that the ability to deal with problems in the most appropriate way is the hallmark of wisdom rather than of genius. (pp. 192-193)

Assistance with operative intelligence can take many forms involving formal intervention by mentors, coaches, and teachers; and, informally by interacting with others from higher maturation levels. Generally, formal assistance works best when provided on the basis of a zone-of-proximal development (ZPD) aligned to support expected growth (Vygotsky, et. al., 1978). A ZPD consists of determining what a person can do without and with assistance. Assistance is offered to best scaffold the degree of help necessary to develop a person, in alignment with their ZPD, and is adjusted over time on the basis of demonstrated levels of improved understanding and performance. Determining and using ZPD can be done systematically using assessment tools and instructional assistance or intelligent tutoring programs with the means to scaffold the degree of help in the zone, over time, using assessment data. Research from the interdisciplinary field of augmented cognition provides support for using environments wherein people can be paired with computer assistance tools to help augment thinking and performance (Engelbart, 1962; Reeves, et.al, 2007; Kobus, et.al., 2005). The design of computer assistance tools and aids, in support of augmented cognition for a person, has evolved over the years from hard-coded electronic performance- and decision-support systems embedded in actual physical devices to now include systems making use of artificial intelligence to better adjust ZPD augmentation necessary for an individual, as well as for teams, in both physical and virtual environments (Turban, et.al., 2005). Using the same augmentation aids and tools across training, education, and work improves authenticity of learning experiences and helps with transferring new skills across usage settings (Klopfer, 2008; Brown, et.al., 1989). Scenario-based learning, offering real-life challenges, has also been shown to help with both authenticity and learning transfer (Bransford & Schwartz, 1999; Klopfer, 2008). Consequently, combining intelligent ZPD-based augmentation aids and tools with scenario-based learning offers compelling capabilities in support of enhancing and delivering developmental instruction. There are even greater prospects offered for presenting complex challenges, via scenario-based learning, by using virtual environments, with benefits provided by immersive 3D and interactive tasks and tools associated with a simulated real-life challenge, to strengthen suspension of disbelief and authenticity (see Shaffer and Resnick, 1999). Immersive 3D-virtual environments are also very suitable for promoting activity flow associated with high levels of engagement marked by improved concentration, focus, receptivity to feedback, adjustment to difficulty and intrinsic motivation (Csikszentmihalyi, 1990, 1996). And, in line with research by Lave and Wenger (1991), another benefit is support for sharing the environment with other people via participatory embodiment roles involving mentors, coaches, and teachers assisting with developmental instruction within the immersive 3D-world space (see Rambusch & Ziemke, 2005).

Embedding scenario-based simulations, within immersive 3D worlds, offers additional benefits by means to expose participants to a variety of demands posed by scenarios with capability to observe planning processes and consequent actions to better pinpoint cognitive errors, identity their psychological determinants, and help make visible the kinds of mistakes made, and probable causes (Dörner, 1989, p. 197). Dietrich Dörner (1989) highlights the importance and role played by simulations to help people learn to think in terms of systems:

We must learn that in complex systems we cannot do only one thing. Whether we want it to or not, any step we take will affect many other things. We must learn to cope with side effects. We must understand that the effects of our decisions may turn up in places we never expected to see them surface. Can we possibly learn all this? We can't, in the real world, where expanses of time and space hide our mistakes from us. Hence my plea for simulations. Time passes quickly in a computer, and distance doesn't exist. A simulation can make apparent the consequences of our decisions and plans. And in this way we can develop a greater sensitivity to reality. Mistakes are essential to cognition. But when we are dealing with real complex systems, it is hard to pinpoint our errors. (pp. 198-199)

Learning to think in terms of systems, involving the use of metacomponents taking the form of mindsets, is a framework of thought associated with systems thinking and science that helps to deal with complex things in a holistic way (Flood & Carson, 1993). Attention is now turned to on-going development and prototyping of a simulation design, embedded in an immersive 3D world, making use of artificial intelligence (AI)-augmented developmental instruction for helping to improve contemplative practices with the use and switching of mindsets associated with addressing complicated and complex challenges.

ARCHITECTURE OF DEVELOPMENTAL-INSTRUCTION SIMULATION DESIGN

The focus of the simulation design is on social-cognitive developmental instruction in the use of contemplative cognitive and moral reasoning practices to better discern and address complicated and complex challenges. Emphasis was placed on social-cognitive design features to promote benefits with authentic learning, social participation, and virtual embodiment of participants with real-world challenges situated in an immersive environment supporting high levels of interactivity and engagement. The intent of the design was to provide an immersive environment for the simulation where participation is deep, meaningful, and built to support interaction with others and tutoring aids via engaging activities that help participants grow in their understanding to better discern and address complicated and complex challenges using contemplative practices supporting sustained cognitive and moral reasoning.

The early prototype for the simulation was started in 2009 by a team of researchers from Air University, Colorado Technical University, University of Central Florida, and NASA Jet Propulsion Laboratory (JPL). Mars was selected as the context for the simulations' immersive environment for tutoring on complex-problem solving due to the richness of data obtained from NASA robotic missions to Mars, since the Viking missions of the 1970s, and from extensive studies relating to human space exploration options stewarded by the Mars Exploration Program Analysis Group (MEPAG) sponsored by NASA JPL (see https://mepag.jpl.nasa.gov/index.cfm). MEPAG is an organization of approximately 100 scientists who represent collectively the Mars science community. Work on the simulation (Mars Expedition Strategy Challenge) spanned a year involving the construction and testing of interactive 3D models (e.g., space travel training devices, launch control mechanisms, rockets, and an assortment of devices supporting interactive exploration of NASA Mars studies and data) necessary to engage participants. During the simulated mission to Mars participants were introduced to the tools, procedures, and mental and physical challenges that a real future Mars mission might face. The variety and nature of challenges introduced in the simulation were obtained from NASA and National Academy of Sciences studies regarding Mars exploration. The simulation was the grand prize winner of the inaugural Federal Virtual Worlds Challenge at the 2010 Defense GameTech Users' Conference (see https://www.army.mil/article/37034/army_announces_federal_virtual_worlds_challenge_winners). Since 2010, a team of researchers and developers has continued to evolve and improve upon the original Mars Expedition Strategy Challenge simulation using a collaborative design-build prototyping process (CDB) first introduced by RAND (Stricker, et.al., 2011). The team supported the use of CDB with virtual salon meetings, hosting interdisciplinary faculty and students from around the world, for soliciting and encouraging the juxtaposition of ideas to improve upon the simulation (see Figure 2).

Several improvement prospects were identified from the salon discussions and were ultimately put into the simulation using CDB:

- Moving the original simulation to the Open Simulator platform
- Making the simulation accessible to the Open Simulator community spanning several participating universities using hyper-grid technology
- Moving the simulation code to Linux virtual machines on the Cloud
- Employing a robust physics engine to simulate real-world physics in the simulation
- Using interactive mesh models for all major 3D components and tools in the simulation for improving realism and fidelity of materials supporting better shadowing and particle effects to help

Figure 2. Simulation design and prototyping pathway supported by CDB

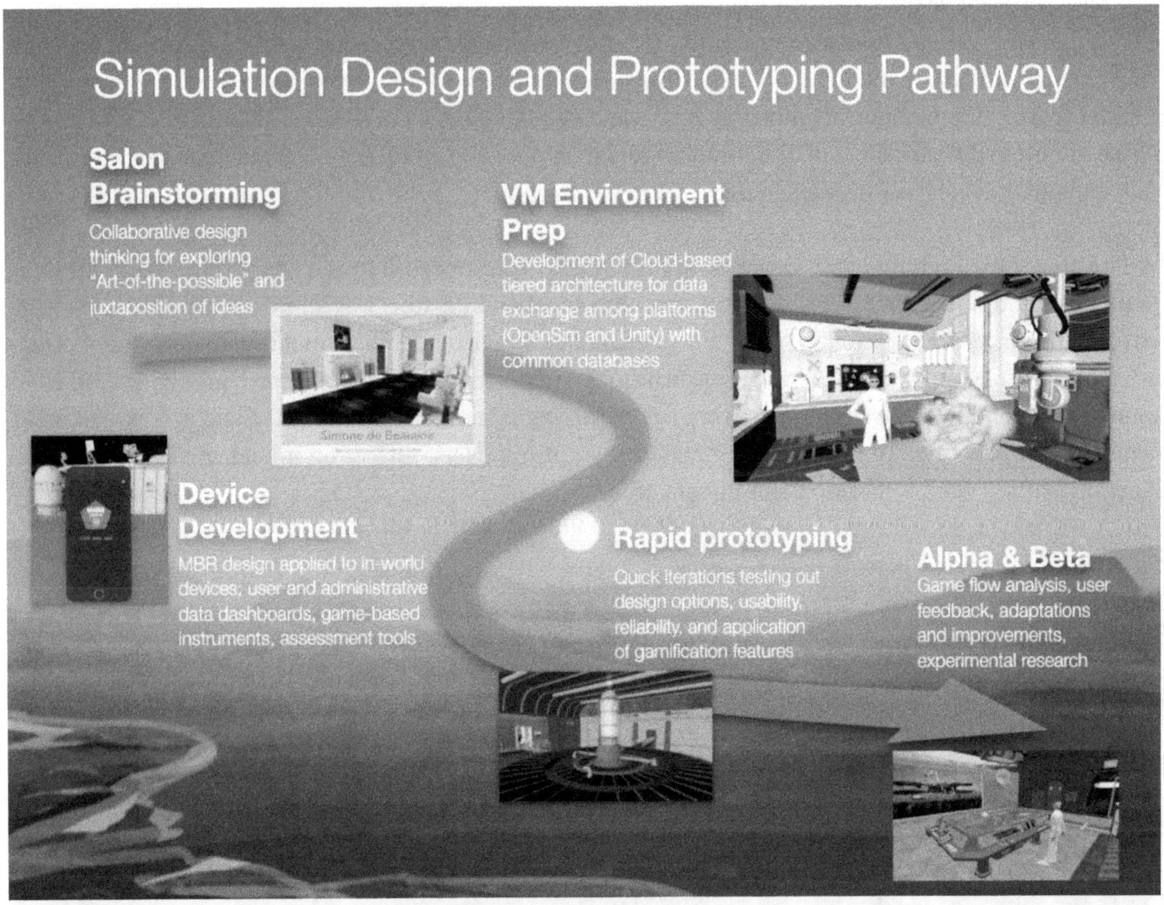

embed the senses, thoughts, and actions of participants in the feeling of traveling and being on Mars

- Implementing a web-based dashboard interface for viewing simulation data (see Appendix)
- Applying Cloud Lambda services for specified code execution on task or tool demand
- Improving APIs for linking and data sharing with Open Simulator and other supporting game engines (e.g., Unity 3D)
- Introducing an AI-augmented tutoring aid, using the Web Ontology Language (OWL) to assist with coaching on contemplative patterns of thought and offering feedback specific to task performance by examining participant input regarding complex knowledge about things, groups, and relations between them
- Linking the AI-augmented tutoring aid to John Bransford's *Learning Challenge Cycle*, (Bransford, et.al., 1999; 1986), for structuring and sequencing tasks presented in the simulation
- Inclusion of a Heads-Up-Display (HUD) supporting game features offered by the simulation (e.g., health scores associated with activities in space; performance assessments)
- Support for team or individual participation in the simulation; embedded team survey assessment tool added for supporting team discussions

- Improved temporal flexibility by offering sustained simulation participation options over hours, days, or even weeks
- Improving the model-based reasoning (MBR) tools with server-side data connections and processing of participant "what-if" experimentations
- Increasing the number of gameplay levels and task challenges
- Enriching the storyline of the simulation for supporting nonlinear learning pathways through gameplay levels and task challenges

The above list highlights the range of improvements introduced into the Mars Expedition Strategy Challenge simulation since 2010. Overall, the high-level architecture was significantly changed to improve software, engine platforms, tools, enrichments to the virtual environment, and gameplay options and quality (see Figure 3). Discussion now turns to the importance placed for improving the overall Mars context of gameplay in the simulation to engage participants in sustained cognitive and moral reasoning, manage the levels of complexity, contemplate usage of mindsets, reflect upon and implement courses of action as they work with imperfect information.

Figure 3. High-level architecture of the mars expedition strategy challenge simulation

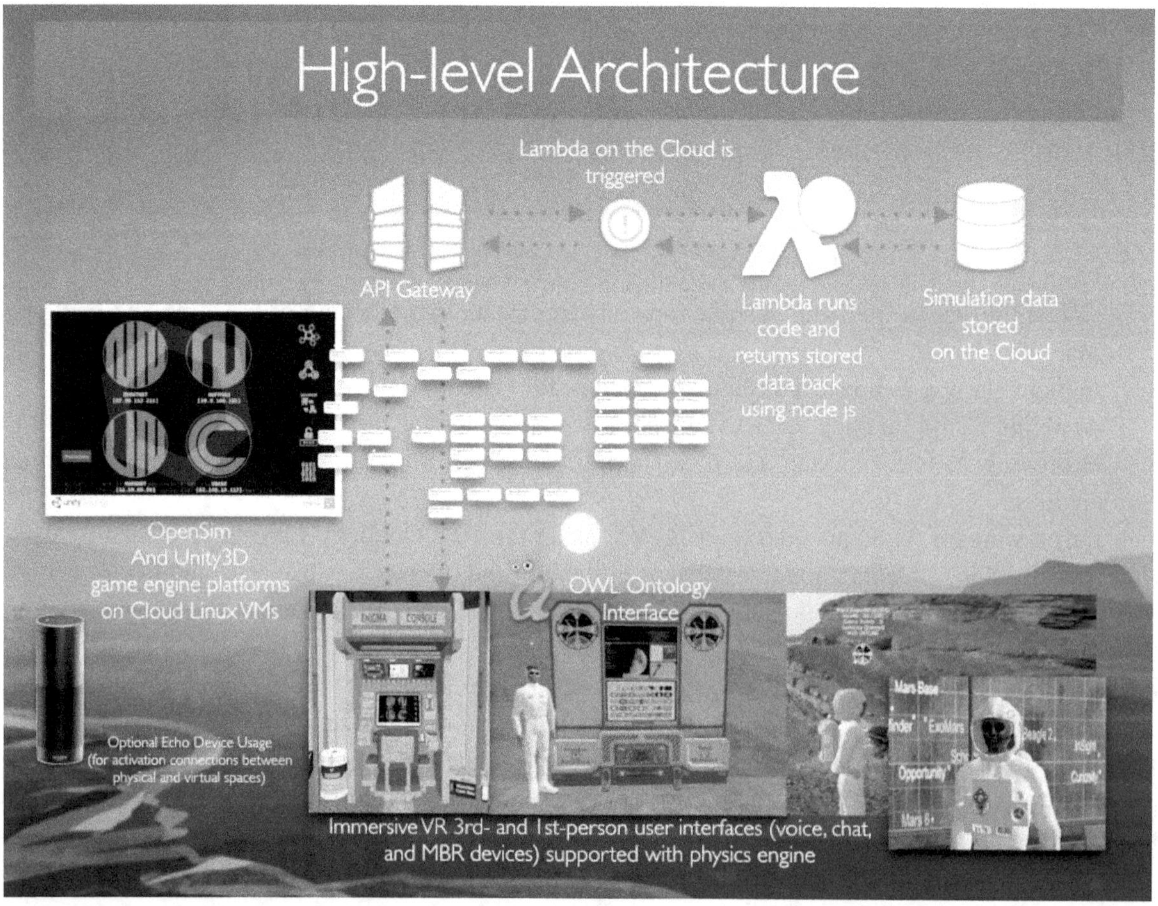

MARS CONTEXT FOR SIMULATION CHALLENGE TASKS AND TUTORING

Participants in the simulation start gameplay at an in-world launch training facility. A simulation facilitator provides orientation assistance to gameplay and helping participants put on astronaut clothing, usage of the simulator HUD and various space equipment (e.g., rocket launch systems, space station consoles, Mars scientific machines), how to operate various types of devices for acquiring information and cues from environmental sources across levels of gameplay (e.g., how to interact with the AI-augmented aid named "Red Queen", how to access simulated networks, responding to Red Queen questions and receiving responses using kiosks, means to interact with instructional 3D models and tools). Interactive 3D model-based reasoning (MBR) tools are embedded in the simulation to help participants uncover important relationships about systems and how concepts are used and relate to each other for developing deeper understanding (see Nersessian, 1999, 2002, 2007; Glenberg, 1997). Figure 4 depicts a MBR device offered to participants at the Launch Control facility to help orient them about usage of MBR tools for deepening understanding about NASA research, and related studies, addressing geothermal energy and human habitation on Mars (Fogg, 1997; Morgan, 2009).

Kenneth Craik (1943) introduced the concept of mental modeling as a form of reasoning. Craik proposed that, in general, people reason by carrying out thought experiments on internal models. Mental modeling has been investigated in a wide range of phenomena, including: reasoning about causality in physical systems (De Kleer & Brown, 1983); the role of representations of domain knowledge in reasoning (Gentner & Stevens, 1983); analogical reasoning (Gentner & Gentner, 1983); deductive and inductive inferencing (Johnson-Laird, 1983) and comprehending narratives (Perrig & Kintsch, 1985).

Figure 4. MBR tool for learning about prospects for geothermal energy on Mars

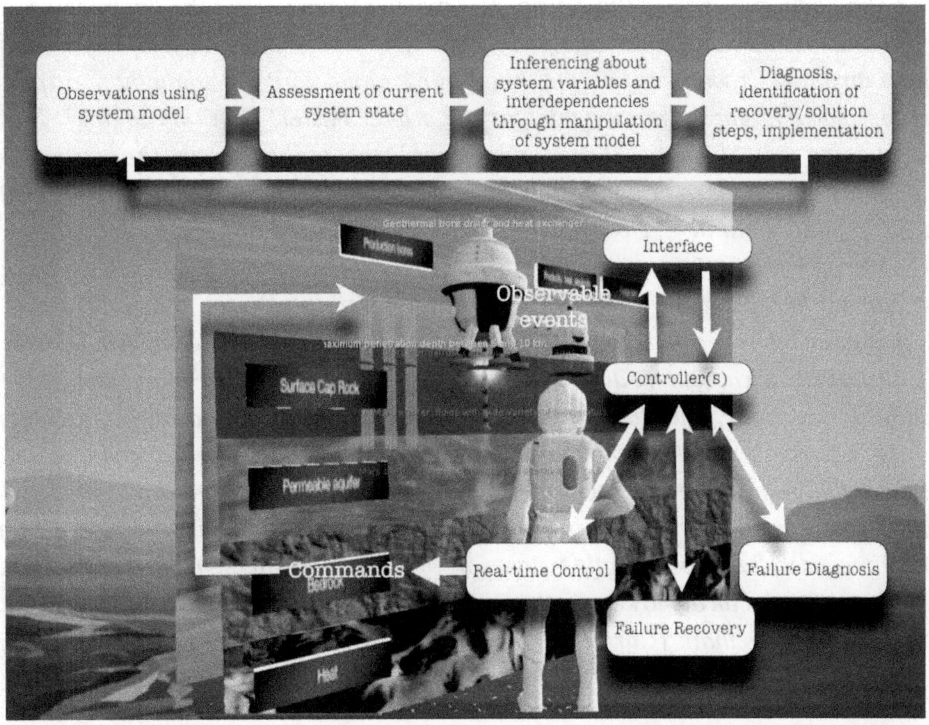

Participants are also instructed on how to use the 3D-viewer interface for moving their avatar, selecting and interacting with 3D models, adjusting camera distance and angle, communicating with other participants via voice or text, and how to pause and resume gameplay.

After the orientation, participants start gameplay with being introduced to the first Red Queen interaction kiosk before liftoff in a rocket to an orbiting space station for transfer to an interplanetary craft for transportation to Mars. Once in Mars orbit, the participant takes an orbiter lander to a Mars station containing above ground energy generation and storage devices and underground facilities supporting a laboratory, medical bay, power generators, crew quarters, and other life-sustaining resources. Along the journey to Mars, starting with the launch facility, there are challenges and tasks presented to participants for engaging them in learning about and practicing the use of patterns of thought (contemplative mindsets) for addressing complicated and complex challenges.

The simulation supports developmental instruction on the mindsets via the assistance provided by the AI-augmented tutoring aid which introduces relevant cues for helping to perceive a situation as presenting a complex or complicated context. The AI-augmented tutoring aid is named in the simulation after the "Red Queen" from *Through the Looking Glass* (Carroll, 1872) as a metaphor to express its role in gameplay for helping participants with improving contemplative practices in the face of complexity. In Carroll's story, Alice has a dream about the looking glass house, wherein she first finds that things appear left-to-right, as if shown in a mirror. The Red Queen then leads Alice directly to the top of the hill. Along the way, the Red Queen explains that hills can become valleys, which confuses Alice. Already, in this world, straight can become curvy, and progress can be made only by going the opposite direction:

Alice never could quite make out, in thinking it over afterwards, how it was that they began: all she remembers is, that they were running hand in hand, and the Queen went so fast that it was all she could do to keep up with her: and still the Queen kept crying 'Faster! Faster!' but Alice felt she could not go faster, though she had not breath left to say so. The most curious part of the thing was, that the trees and the other things round them never changed their places at all: however fast they went, they never seemed to pass anything. 'I wonder if all the things move along with us?' thought poor puzzled Alice. And the Queen seemed to guess her thoughts, for she cried, 'Faster! Don't try to talk!' Not that Alice had any idea of doing that. She felt as if she would never be able to talk again, she was getting so much out of breath: and still the Queen cried 'Faster! Faster!' and dragged her along. 'Are we nearly there?' Alice managed to pant out at last. 'Nearly there!' the Queen repeated. 'Why, we passed it ten minutes ago! Faster!' And they ran on for a time in silence, with the wind whistling in Alice's ears, and almost blowing her hair off her head, she fancied. 'Now! Now!' cried the Queen. 'Faster! Faster!' And they went so fast that at last they seemed to skim through the air, hardly touching the ground with their feet, till suddenly, just as Alice was getting quite exhausted, they stopped, and she found herself sitting on the ground, breathless and giddy. The Queen propped her up against a tree, and said kindly, 'You may rest a little now.' Alice looked round her in great surprise. 'Why, I do believe we've been under this tree the whole time! Everything's just as it was!' 'Of course it is,' said the Queen, 'what would you have it?' 'Well, in our country,' said Alice, still panting a little, 'you'd generally get to somewhere else—if you ran very fast for a long time, as we've been doing.' 'A slow sort of country!' said the Queen. 'Now, here, you see, it takes all the running you can do, to keep in the same place. If you want to get somewhere else, you must run at least twice as fast as that!' (Carroll, 1872, Chapter II. The Garden of Live Flowers, pp. 19-20)

The above snippet from *Through the Looking Glass* depicts a situation presenting Alice with the challenge to make sense of a confusing situation. As the story unfolds Alice improves upon her awareness and means to make sense of chaotic or complex challenges she encounters with unfolding circumstances. As mentioned above, Dietrich Dörner refers to this form of self-awareness as *operative intelligence*. A Contemplative Mindsets and Switching Model (CMSM) was created for usage by the Red Queen to help participants with their operative intelligence by tutoring and coaching on the use of appropriate contemplative mindsets with consideration given to question responses as indicators of developmental needs (see Figure 5). CMSM is used to support developmental instruction for simulation participants on the contemplative patterns of thought flows, and switching reflection meta-skills, associated with selection and usage of the mindsets. As depicted in Figure 5, reflection meta-skills are coached to participants for engaging in forms of reflection regarding possible courses of action using cognitive and moral reasoning mental simulations. Coaching by the Red Queen on mental simulations follow the insights on reflection-in-action offered by Argyris and Schön (1974):

Figure 5. Contemplative mindsets and switching model used by AI-augmented tutoring aid

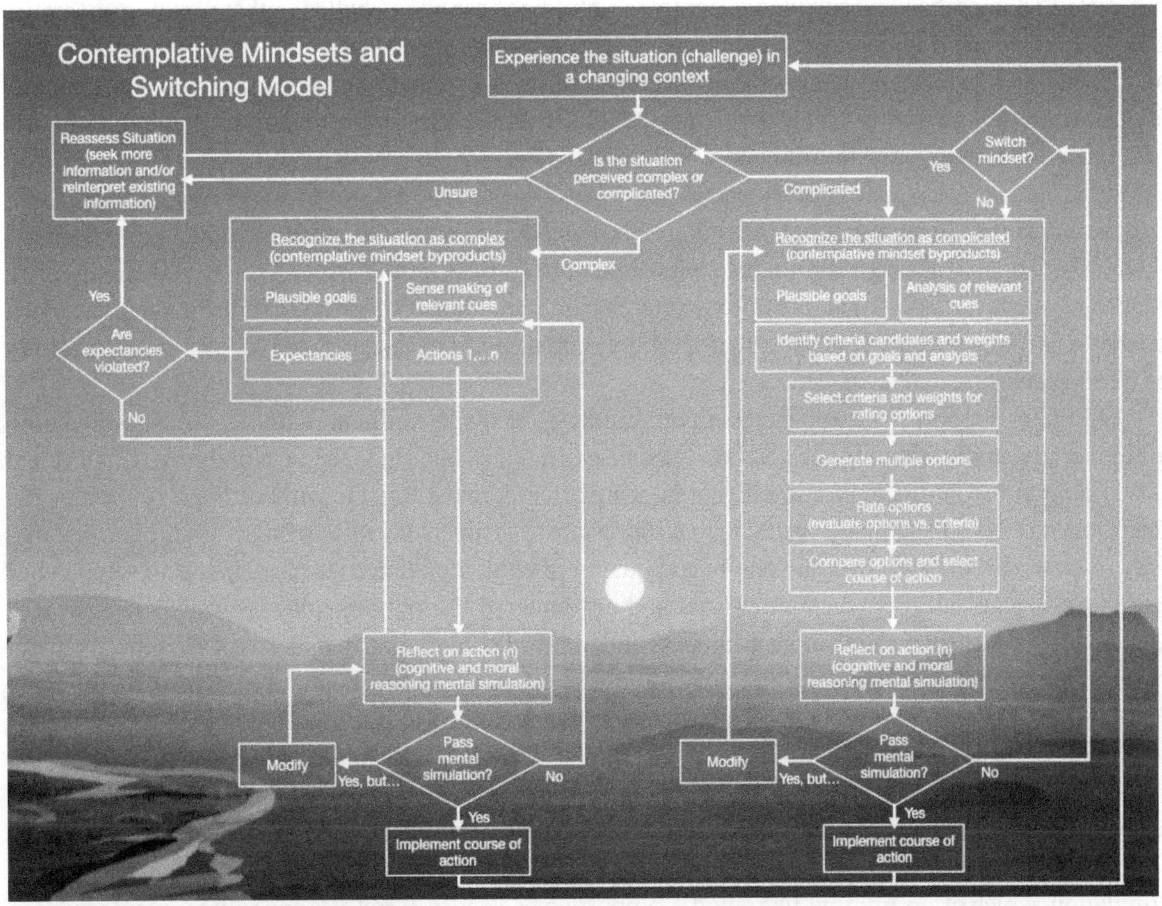

When a practitioner reflects in and on his practice, the possible objects of his reflection are as varied as the kinds of phenomena before him and the systems of knowing-in-practice which he brings to them. He may reflect on the tacit norms and appreciations which underlie a judgment, or on the strategies and theories implicit in a pattern of behavior. He may reflect on the feeling for a situation which has led him to adopt a particular course of action, on the way in which he has framed the problem he is trying to solve, or on the role he has constructed for himself within a larger institutional context. Reflections-in-action, in these several modes, is central to the art through which practitioners sometimes cope with the troublesome 'divergent' situations of practice. When the phenomenon at hand eludes the ordinary categories of knowledge-in-practice, presenting itself as unique or unstable, the practitioner may surface and criticize his initial understanding of the phenomenon, construct a new description of it, and test the new description by an on-the-spot experiment. (p. 62)

Coaching offered on mental simulations promotes what Argyris and Schön (1974) refer to as *double-loop learning* entailing willingness to examine one's current theory of action and on the basis of diverse feedback and follow-on discernments make appropriate adjustments (p. 19). Overall, developmental instruction, offered in the simulation helps a person to improve upon their use of contemplative mindsets to comprehend, shape, and adapt to an unfolding, evolving challenge that remains uncertain, ever-changing, and unpredictable. This level of strategic thinking, and use of strategy, is fundamental to survival and growth and is directly connected with means to address the uncertain, ever-changing, and unpredictable world (Osinga, 2007, pp. 227-233). Responses are semantically examined by the Red Queen (AI-augmented tutoring aid), using a Web Ontology Language (OWL) structure, for giving feedback and contemplative recommendations to participants (see Figure 6). OWL is a semantic web language designed to represent rich and complex knowledge about things, groups, and relations between them. The language is derived from the Defense Advanced Research Projects Agency (DARPA) Agent Markup Language (DAML) and Ontology Interchange Language (OIL). OWL helps to guide feedback on the basis of the relevant concepts of an ontology addressing Mars research and science across a variety of STEM topics related to space.

Additional support for extending the core ontology is made available with a backend simulation administrative tool for tuning the level of assistance offered by the Red Queen. Combined, CMSM and OWL support model-tracing for intelligent tutoring offered by the Red Queen. Feedback offered by the Red Queen is stored and made available to participants as artifacts for reflection across levels of gameplay to better discern the changing nature and quality of contemplations. As participants develop better understandings of all the issues introduced and encountered during gameplay their responses to Red Queen questions display much more awareness and usage of contemplative patterns of thought. Example of participant feedback is provided in Figure 7. Feedback includes a breakout of key constructs provided from the examination of a participant's response to a task, linked to relevant topics with a rated score, web links for further exploration, and a brief contemplative mindset reflection provided to the participant.

Since the Mars Expedition Strategy Challenge is designed to also be a participatory simulation there are tasks supporting interactivity and exchange of information among peers to include teams with teams. For example, one pathway of gameplay involves the use of an Unity3D application, designed for the simulation, which offers Enigma-like devices supporting backstory narratives and sources of information wherein encrypted networks, ciphered clues, and decryption tools help team play. Team learning can take place with the development of practices and abilities to negotiate meaning with others in contexts of unfolding, multidimensional complexity (Stricker, et.al., 2018). The Unity3D-based interface tool,

Figure 6. Web Ontology Language (OWL) structure used by AI-augmented tutoring aid

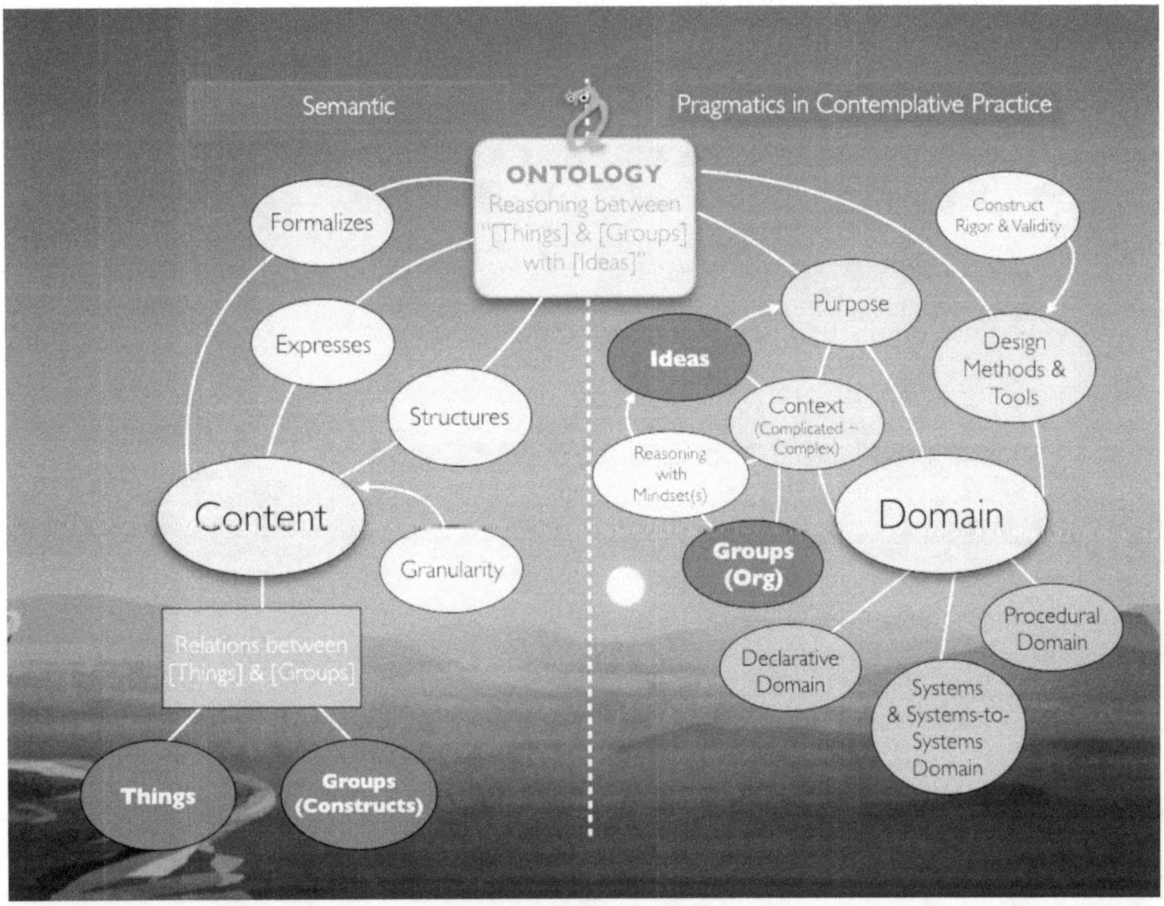

interconnected with the simulation throughout gameplay, offers a way for teams of players to obtain, interpret, and align clues and narratives revealed by simulated messages between scientists on Earth and Mars, news releases, scientific reports, obtainable from across simulation networks (see Figure 8).

The backstory narratives, spanning the diverse sources of information from across the simulation networks, help to engage participants in a hero's journey as they grapple with difficult situations requiring decisions involving incomplete, uncertain levels of accuracy, missing information, and making sense of moral incongruities presented along the way towards higher levels of intellectual and moral reasoning.

SIMULATION GAMEPLAY AND INSIGHTS

Participants are encouraged to formulate an intended strategy at onset of gameplay, at Level 1, when knowns about the introductory challenge are presented at the start of the simulation journey (see Figure 9). By Levels 2 and 3 of gameplay, participants are encouraged to adjust their intended strategy more deliberatively to account for new information. Gradually, as the journey unfolds through gameplay Levels 4 to 5, more and more unknowns are introduced and participants gain insights about the role of adap-

Figure 7. Example of AI-augmented tutoring aid processing results and feedback

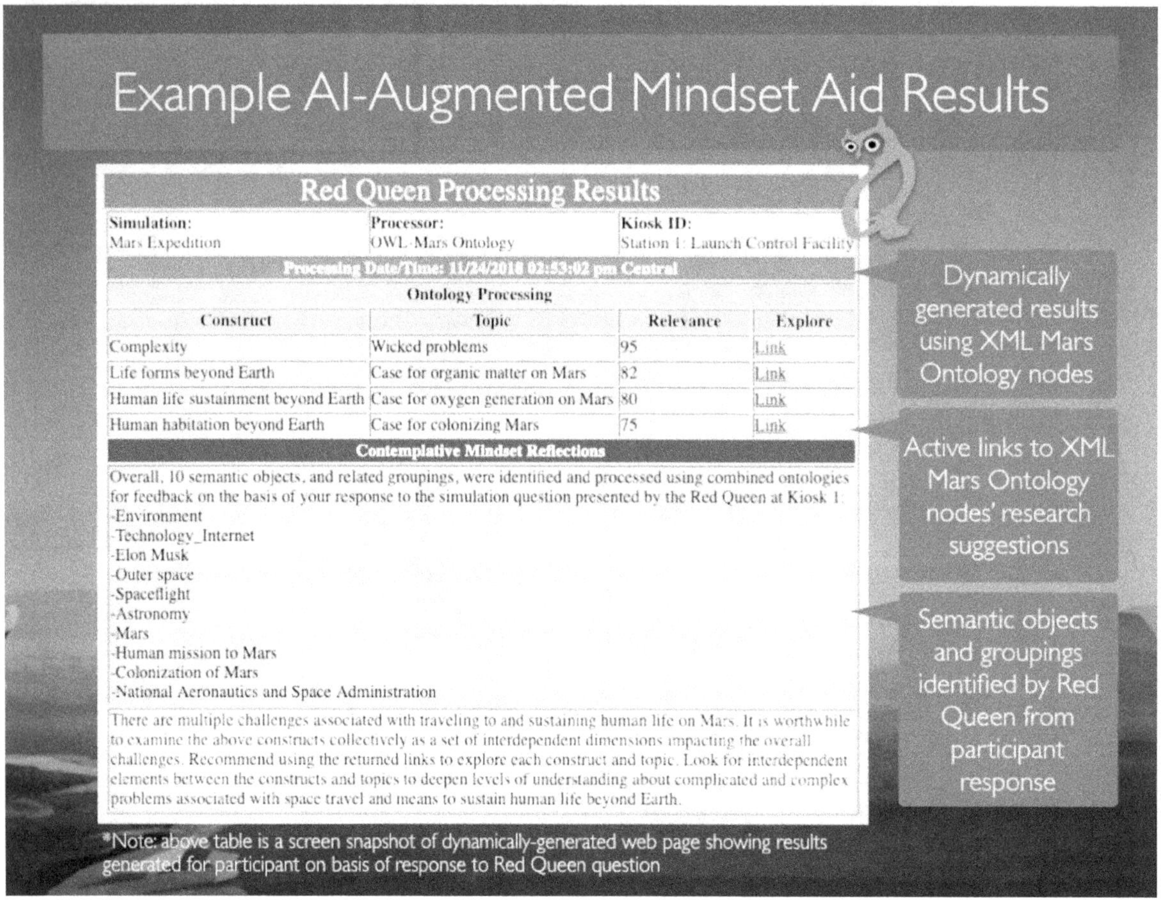

tive nature and usage of emergent strategy in the face of complexity ultimately leading towards realized strategy as gameplay wraps up at Level 5.

Levels 6 and 7 are optional gameplay levels where fictional themes are introduced to illustrate and enhance a participants' insights regarding the role played by science fiction with ideas and inspiration for theoretical speculation in science. Several themes from science fiction, regarding Mars and human space exploration, are highlighted; for instance: ancient artifacts, interplanetary travel, terraforming, space-time passages. For example, at Level 6, participants can learn about the ways science fiction addressing interplanetary travel can inspire theoretical speculation such as the Alcubierre drive and Krasnikov tube (Everett & Roman, 1997). A digital bibliography is also made available for participants to further learn about how Mars is represented in science and fiction across a variety of literary forms.

Author Ursula K. Le Guin has called speculative fiction – fantasy, science fiction, and their uncountable variations and sub-genres – "modern day myths." They are our more-then-human-sized stories of heroism and villainy, encounters with the unheard of and incredible, and our way of measuring ourselves against the known and the unknown. Science fiction and techno-fantasy fill the place of myths in our modern world by using the sure-bet elements of timeless stories. That these elements are striking and deeply memorable makes them ideal for learning. The stories stay with us because they developed within

Figure 8. ENIGMA console

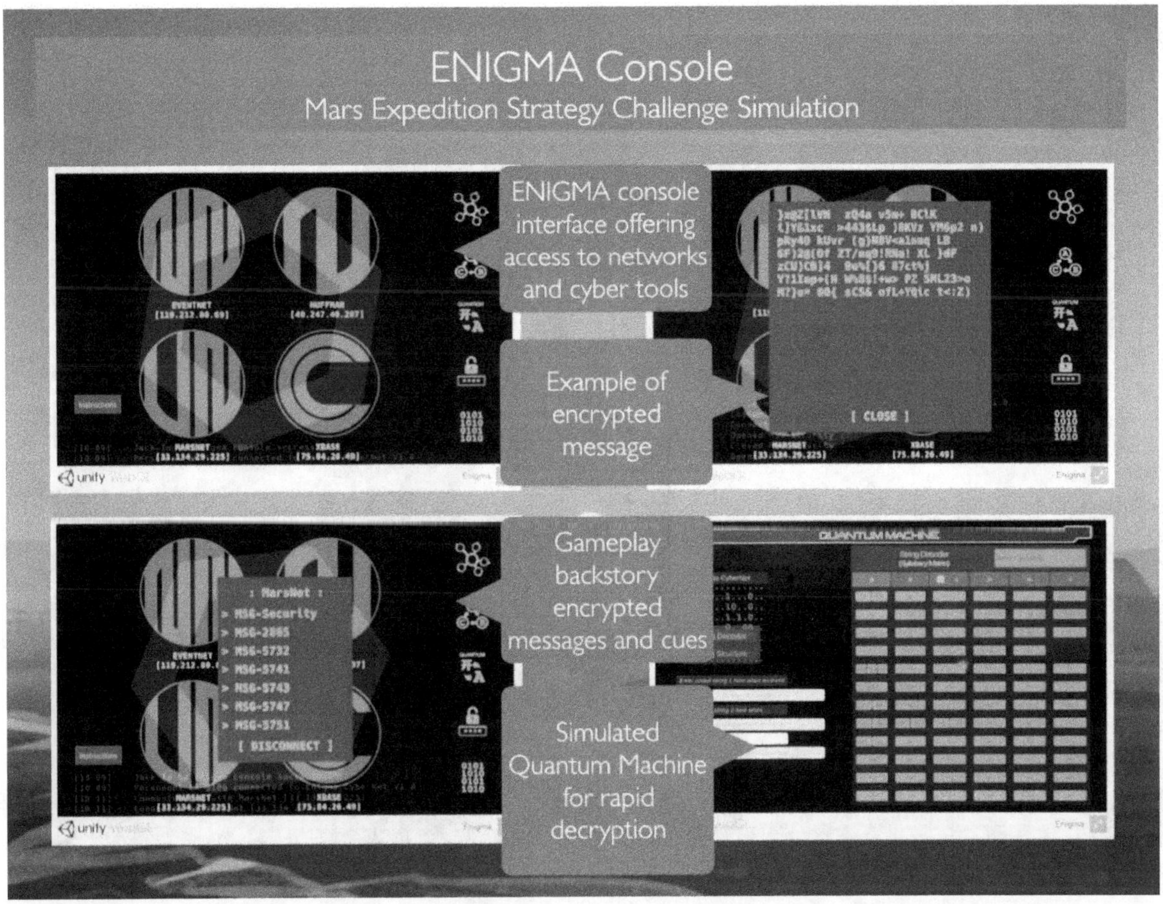

a specialized and highly robust apparatus of personal and cultural memory - which means they have a culturally determined resonance inside mental and emotional selves.

At the same time, science fiction has often been a deliberate challenger of norms, re-imagining or imaginatively recasting patterns and social expectations that have become invisible through being taken for granted as The Way Things Just Are. *Stranger in a Strange Land (1961)*, the most sophisticated of Robert Heinlein's six Mars novels, subverts long-held ideas of identity as something based in genetics. Instead of the time-tested Martian "them" and Terran "us", in Michael Valentine Smith we have a crucial figure who is both and neither, and whose identity is therefore on the boundary, or crosses and confuses the crenelated certainties about who is an Earthling, and who is a Martian. Smith, the only Martian we meet in the story, is a sort of a boundary object here - something that exists where two categories meet, and by fitting into both, queries both, and queries both what divides and what unites them. In this role, he forces us to abandon both genetics and nominal homeland as authoritative sources of identity.

The immersive virtual environment for each game play level was crafted with the guiding principles outlined in Chapter 1. The principles were kept in mind for helping to promote mindfulness and rendering favorable impressions by participants for developmental instruction via simulation gameplay. Each level offers creative interfaces and expansive exploratory virtual landscapes. Participants are offered virtual

Figure 9. Simulation gameplay levels

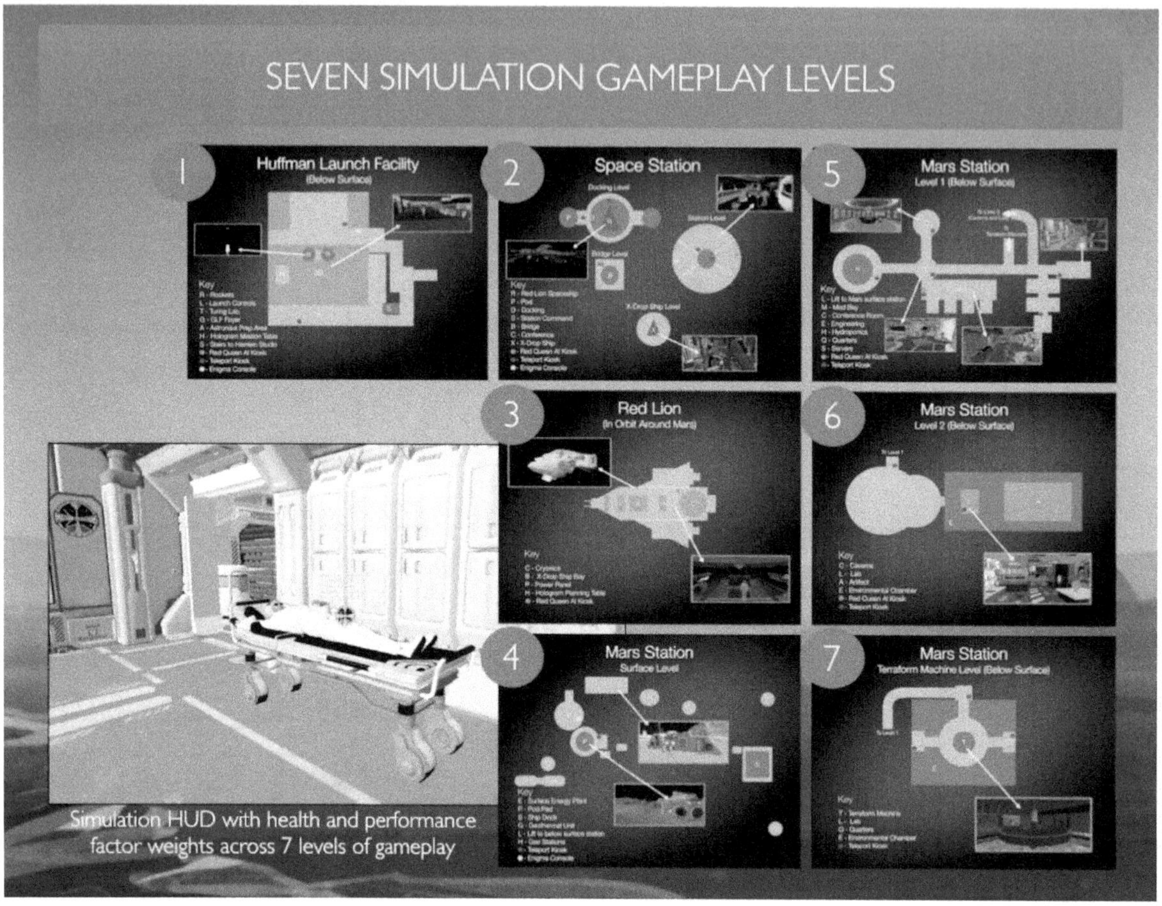

inhabitable spaces during prolong gameplay to strengthen a sense of in-situ presence, interaction, and socialization with instructor facilitators and peers. Spaces at each level were also created to support an element of mystery and intrigue by offering less than obvious sources of interactivity with 3D objects containing additional clues and information (e.g., manipulation of scientific equipment, lab notebooks, virtual computers connected to external knowledge banks and data sources, virtual machines that turn on or control other virtual machines that reveal aspects of operations not otherwise apparent when offline or disconnected from the core simulation).

Gradually, by exploring the environments while working on the scientific dilemmas presented during the simulation, participants are better able to jigsaw together the clues and information (involving real-life content brought into gameplay), and reformulate strategy on the basis of building a more holistic view using their discoveries, insights, and feedback. And, when the simulation is played by teams there are greater opportunities for collaborative sharing of clues, group processing involving sense-making, reflection, and strategizing in situ. Overall, gameplay levels were designed to support rich authentic learning experiences.

CONCLUSION

Complex challenges cannot be solved in a linear fashion. Facing complexity requires deep understanding of systems and processes. Contemplative patterns of thought, associated with mindsets for addressing complicated and complex challenges, are necessary for developing deep understanding and means to be effective with skills involving combinations of deductive and inductive reasoning, making inferences, sense-making of conflicting and confusing data, and determining and adjusting courses of action. Several years ago the National Research Council (1999) identified critical skills for which people should be prepared for a modern world:

- Means to engage in sustained reasoning
- Capability to address complexity
- Self-knowledge of how to test solutions and manage issues when solutions are faulty
- Navigate information structures and evaluate ways to understand information
- Ability to collaborate

The above skills are not only still relevant but decidedly more so as systems and people increasingly interconnect and get networked together worldwide. The discussion and research offered in this chapter outlined the value, design, and use of AI-augmented developmental instruction for helping to prepare people for the modern world. Preparation takes the form of improved self-awareness and usage of critical skills with wisdom, involving cognitive and moral reasoning, to "*think of, and then do, the right things at the right times and in the right way*" in the face of complexity.

Indeed, sustained reasoning in wise practices is inherently moral. The science fiction of Cixin Liu offers poignant reminders of where thinking and science has taken humanity up to the second half of the twentieth century and the importance of being better prepared in this millennial to face a more complex, vague, and uncertain future with wisdom in service for the common good.

The ultimate fate of all intelligent beings has always been to become as grand as their thoughts. (Death's End, Cixin Liu, 2016, p. 597)

SUGGESTIONS FOR FUTURE SCHOLARSHIP AND RESEARCH

The rapid pace of design and use of immersive 3D environments, for supporting developmental instruction via embedded AI-augmented simulations, involves a plethora of innovative ways to mix, blend, and integrate advances in technology with improved insights from learning and assessment sciences. And, while learning generally improves by deepening levels of engagement, interactivity, and meaningfulness there is much more to be understood for how best to offer greater precision for helping specific growth needs of each person with the use of personalized ZPD approaches supported by AI. Additional interdisciplinary research is needed too for informing the psychology of human interdependence with AI. Future AI-augmented developmental instruction will benefit considerably from improved insights on how the mind perceives, interprets, and associates current views of selfhood in relation to interaction, socialization, and interdependence with AI systems. The same holds true for improving insights for how best to support team learning and performance with AI-augmented developmental instruction.

The use of networked immersive 3D environments, for developmental instruction of people and teams, makes sense in a world where people are increasingly learning and working with others in virtual and networked ways across different time zones. In many cases, people and teams working together under such circumstances may never actually meet face-to-face. Considerable research remains for informing how best to develop people with the skills and literacies discussed in this chapter, via AI-augmented developmental instruction, wherein multicultural differences are very likely when it comes to environment and technological considerations, social organization, and temporal conception.

DISCLAIMER

The views and opinions expressed in this chapter do not necessarily reflect the views and opinions held by the U.S. Department of Defense, The United States Air Force, or The Air University. This chapter is cleared for public release; case number: AETC-2019-0100.

REFERENCES

Argyris, C., & Schön, D. A. (1974). *Theory in practice: Increasing professional effectiveness*. San Francisco, CA: Jossey-Bass.

Bransford, J. D., Brown, A., & Cocking, R. (1999). *How people learn: Brain, mind, experience, and school*. Washington, DC: National Academies Press.

Bransford, J. D., & Schwartz, D. (1999). Rethinking transfer: A simple proposal with multiple implications. In A. Iran-Nejad & P. D. Pearson (Eds.), *Review of Research in Education* (Vol. 24, pp. 61–100). Washington, DC: American Educational Research Association.

Bransford, J. D., Sherwood, R., Vye, N., & Rieser, J. (1986). Teaching thinking and problem solving. *The American Psychologist*, *41*, 1078–1089.

Brown, J. A., Collins, A., & Duguid, S. (1989). Situated cognition and the culture of learning. *Educational Researcher*, *18*(1), 32–42.

Carroll, L. (1872). Through the looking-glass. New York, NY: Dover Publications.

Checkland, P. (1981). *Systems thinking, systems practice*. New York, NY: John Wiley & Sons.

Churchman, C. W. (1971). *The design of inquiring systems*. New York, NY: Basic Books.

Cixin, L. (2014). *The three-body problem* (K. Liu, Trans.). New York, NY: Tor Books.

Cixin, L. (2016). *Death's end* (K. Liu, Trans.). New York, NY: Tor Books.

Craik, K. (1943). *The nature of explanation*. Cambridge, UK: Cambridge University Press.

Csikszentmihalyi, M. (1990). *Flow*. New York, NY: Harper & Row.

Csikszentmihalyi, M. (1996). *Creativity. Flow and the psychology of discovery and invention*. New York, NY: Harper Perennial.

De Kleer, J., & Brown, J. S. (1983). Assumptions and ambiguities in mechanistic mental models. In D. Gentner & A. Stevens (Eds.), *Mental models* (pp. 155–190). Hillsdale, NJ: Lawrence Erlbaum.

Dörner, D. (1989). *The logic of failure: Recognizing and avoiding error in complex situations*. New York, NY: Basic Books, Perseus Books Group.

Engelbart, D. C. (1962). *Augmenting human intellect: A conceptual framework. AFOSR-3223 Summary Report. Director of Information Sciences, AFOSR*. Washington, DC: Air Force Office of Scientific Research.

Everett, A., & Roman, T. (1997). A Superluminal subway: The Krasnikov tube. *Physical Review D: Particles and Fields*, *56*. doi:10.1103/PhysRevD.56.2100

Ferguson, N. (2017). *The square and the tower: Networks and power, from the Freemasons to Facebook*. New York, NY: Penguin Press.

Flavell, J. H. (1978). Metacognitive development. In J. M. Scandura & C. J. Brainerd (Eds.), *Structural/process theories of complex human behavior*. Sijthoff & Noordoff.

Flavell, J. H. (1979). Metacognition and cognitive monitoring: A new area of psychological inquiry. *The American Psychologist*, *34*, 906–911.

Flood, R. L., & Carson, E. R. (1993). *Dealing with complexity: An introduction to the theory and application of systems science* (2nd ed.). New York, NY: Plenum Press.

Fogg, M. J. (1997). The utility of geothermal energy on Mars. The *Smithsonian/NASA Astrophysics Data System (ADS)*. Smithsonian Astrophysical Observatory.

Gentner, D., & Gentner, D. R. (1983). Flowing waters or teaming crowds: mental models of electricity. In D. Gentner & A. Stevens (Eds.), *Mental models* (pp. 99–130). Hillsdale, NJ: Lawrence Erlbaum.

Gentner, D., & Stevens, A. L. (1983). *Mental models*. Hillsdale, NJ: Lawrence Erlbaum.

Gleick, J. (1988). *Chaos: Making a new science*. New York, NY: Penguin Books.

Glenberg, A. M. (1997). Mental models, space, and embodied cognition. In T. Ward, S. M. Smith, & J. Vaid (Eds.), *Creative thought: An investigation of conceptual structures and processes* (pp. 495–522). Washington, DC: American Psychological Association.

Heinlein, R. A. (1961). *A stranger in a strange land*. New York, NY: Penguin Random House.

Johnson-Laird, P. N. (1983). *Mental models*. Cambridge, MA: Harvard University Press.

Klein, G. (2009). *Streetlights and shadows: The keys to adaptive decision making*. Cambridge, MA: MIT Press.

Klopfer, E. (2008). *Augmented learning*. Cambridge, MA: MIT Press.

Kobus, D.A., Brown, C.M., Morrison, J.G., Kollmorgen, G., Cornwall, R. (2005). *DARPA improving warfighter information intake under stress–augmented cognition phase II: The concept validation experiment (CVE)*. DARPA/IPTO technical report submitted to CDR Dylan Schmorrow.

Lave, J., & Wenger, E. (1991). *Situated learning: Legitimate peripheral participation*. Cambridge, UK: Cambridge University Press.

Mitchell, M. (2009). *Complexity: A guided tour*. New York, NY: Oxford University Press.

Morgan, P. (2009). Geothermal energy on Mars. In V. Badescu (Ed.), *Mars: Prospective energy and material resources* (pp. 331–349). Berlin, Germany: Springer-Verlag.

National Research Council. (1999). *Being fluent with information technology*. Washington, DC: National Academies Press.

Nersessian, N. J. (1999). Model-based reasoning in conceptual change. In L. Magnani, N. J. Nersessian, & P. Thagard (Eds.), *Model-Based Reasoning in Scientific Discovery*. Kluwer Academic/Plenum Publishers.

Nersessian, N. J. (2002). The cognitive basis of model-based reasoning in science. In P. Carruthers, S. Stich, & M. Siegal (Eds.), The cognitive basis of science (pp. 133-153). Cambridge, UK: Cambridge University Press.

Nersessian, N. J. (2007). Mental modeling in conceptual change. In S. Vosniadou (Ed.), *Handbook of Conceptual Change*. Mahwah, NJ: Erlbaum.

Osinga, F. (2007). *Science, strategy, and war: The strategic theory of John Boyd*. New York, NY: Routledge.

Perrig, W., & Kintsch, W. (1985). Propositional and situational representations of text. *Journal of Memory and Language*, (24): 503–518.

Perry, W. G. (1999). *Forms of ethical and intellectual development in the college years: A scheme*. San Francisco, CA: Jossey-Bass, Inc.

Rambusch, J., & Ziemke, T. (2005). The role of embodiment in situated learning. In *Proceedings of the 27th annual conference of the Cognitive Science Society* (pp. 1803-1808). Mahwah, NJ: Erlbaum.

Reeves, L. M., Schmorrow, D. D., & Stanney, K. M. (2007). Augmented cognition and cognitive state assessment technology – near-term, mid-term, and long-term research objectives. In D. D. Schmorrow & L. M. Reeves (Eds.), Lecture Notes in Computer Science: Vol. 4565. *Foundations of Augmented Cognition. FAC 2007*. Berlin: Springer.

Shaffer, D., & Resnick, M. (1999). Thick authenticity: New media and authentic learning. *Journal of Interactive Learning Research, 10*(2), 195–215.

Slaughter, A. (2017). *The chessboard and the web: Strategies of connection in a networked world*. New Haven, CT: Yale University Press.

Sternberg, R. J. (1983). Components of human intelligence. *Cognition, 15*, 1–48. PMID:6686504

Sternberg, R. J. (1985). Instrumental and componential approaches to the nature and training of intelligence. In S. F. Chipman, J. W. Segal, & R. Glaser (Eds.), Thinking and learning skills: Vol. 2. Research and open questions. Hillsdale, NJ: Erlbaum.

Sternberg, R. J. (1986). Toward a unified theory of human reasoning. *Intelligence, 10*, 281–314.

Sternberg, R. J. (1994). Intelligence. In R. J. Sternberg (Ed.), *Thinking and problem solving: Handbook of perception and cognition* (2nd ed.). New York, NY: Academic Press.

Stricker, A. G., McCrocklin, M., Calongne, C. A., & Holm, J. (2011). *Situating community construction of learning ecosystems and innovations in a 3D world. International Journal of Learning and Media, 3(1).*

Stricker, A. G., Westhauser, T., Sheets, T., Hawkins-Scribner, T., & Calongne, C. (2018). Values-based network leadership in an interconnected world. *The Journal of Values Based Leadership, 11*(1), 1–21.

Turban, E., Aronson, J. E., & Liang, T. (2005). *Decision support systems and intelligent systems* (7th ed.). New York, NY: Pearson.

Vygotsky, L. (1978). *Mind in society. The development of higher psychological processes* (M. Cole, S. S. Vera John-Steiner, & E. Souberman, Eds.). Cambridge, MA: Harvard University Press.

KEY TERMS AND DEFINITIONS

Artificial Intelligence: There are multiple definitions for artificial intelligence. A common definition associates artificial intelligence to the means of a machine or software to imitate how humans reason, discover meaning, generalize, learn from past experiences, and behave. Some AI experts predict, however, the continued evolution of AI neural networks will introduce processing of information and adaptive neural networks that are very likely to become less like an imitation of human intelligence to the point of distinct forms of machine intelligence.

Augmented Cognition: Augmented cognition is an interdisciplinary field of scholarship addressing how cognitive processes can be supported directly with computer assistance or is influenced by human-computer interactions (to include robot assistance and interaction). Generally, with the application of AI, human cognition can be enhanced or augmented for improving metacognitive skills, reasoning, problem solving, and decision making. Applications offering augmented cognition have seen the most progress when applied using intelligent systems in domain-specific contexts and applications supporting interaction between machines and humans to improve performance of cognitively demanding tasks.

Complexity: Complexity is an evolving scientific theory addressing properties and behavioral phenomena of systems not well understood, explained, or predictable by means of conventional analysis of its' parts or subsystems. Complex systems involve many components that are dynamically interacting across size and time scales. The components are self-organizing and form hierarchies and over time reveal emergent properties and or features that cannot be simply inferred from the behavior of the components making up the complex system.

Contemplative Practices: The discernment of a situation or challenge for appropriate action makes use of contemplative practices involving holistic and deep patterns of thought (mindsets) associated with sense making and determining courses of action. Contemplative practices are supported by internal mental processes involved with metacognition associated with thought processes and awareness of one's own cognitive strengths and weaknesses, knowledge about how to interpret the nature or type of challenge encountered, sense-making of new information, employment and switching of mindsets suitable to a challenge, with means to ultimately judge performance.

Developmental Instruction: With developmental instruction, consideration is given toward offering instructional practices for helping a person transition to higher levels of cognitive and moral reasoning in alignment with expected developmental growth and demonstrated capabilities. Developmental growth to higher levels can be facilitated by instructional practices to introduce calculated incongruities encountered with the use of existing levels of cognitive and moral reasoning for facing challenges requiring higher levels of reasoning. Awareness of incongruities can help a person to perceive the need for growth and consequently be more likely to engage with developmental effort.

Immersive 3D-World Simulation: Immersive 3D worlds provide a way to experience a physics-based virtual reality (VR) modeled to support land, sea, air, and space environments as might be found in physical reality. Viewing applications are used to access an immersive 3D world and provide the means to establish a sense of presence over time and support interaction with 3D models and with other people, represented in the form avatars, in context of the environment. Interaction can take the form of text, voice, sharing content, and manipulation of models generating effects and responses. An immersive 3D-world can also allow users to create and place content in the environment. The environment size of an immersive 3D world can vary considerably from a few virtual acres to thousands of explorable acres. And, 3D worlds can be linked together across computer servers on a scale spanning the globe. Visits to 3D worlds can also be supported using hyper grid technology whereby a person's avatar can travel easily from one 3D world to another. Increasingly, educators are making use of immersive 3D worlds to offer the means to embed simulations in context of VR real-world representations of problems and challenges to strengthen engagement, interaction, and meaningfulness of learning activities making use of model-based reasoning (MBR) and AI-augmented tutoring assistance.

Model-Based Reasoning: The history of model-based reasoning (MBR) started with the creation of inferences in artificial intelligence (AI) to represent and model systems and their expected behavior in the physical world. Reasoning processes, making use of the inferences, involved comparison of the model system with observed data to gauge the degree of efficacy and accuracy of employed AI tools offered in intelligent decision- and performance-support systems. Over the years, MBR techniques employed in AI tools have been expanded for use in learning simulations to model a physical system, represent expertise usage of the system, with means to employ tutoring assistance for reasoning activities by learners to acquire or deepen understanding of the system and usage on the basis of how well the fit is between the learner and expert understanding levels and usage of the system. MBR, employed within immersive 3D simulations, can be designed to support usage of zone-of-proximal development (ZPD) to help guide the level and timing of tutoring offered to a learner on the basis of gaps revealed regarding system-model understanding and usage in context of a challenge.

APPENDIX

Simulation Administrative Dashboard

Gameplay data flows into multiple databases, is stored, and exchanged on demand with related simulation datasets. User gameplay data and configuration settings are also retrieved on demand by the interconnected platforms (OpenSim and Unity3D) supporting the simulation. Access to the dashboard is controlled by role and permissions and requires secured access and authentication. When the simulation is used to support human subject research, an Institutional Review Board (IRB) application is completed and must be approved by the sponsoring university. The dashboard supports the use of subject IDs, confidentiality safeguards, and data protection in accordance with IRB standards for human subject research. Over the years, the simulation has supported multiple doctoral and masters' level research from across a variety of disciplines.

Figure 10. Mars expedition strategy challenge simulation administrative dashboard

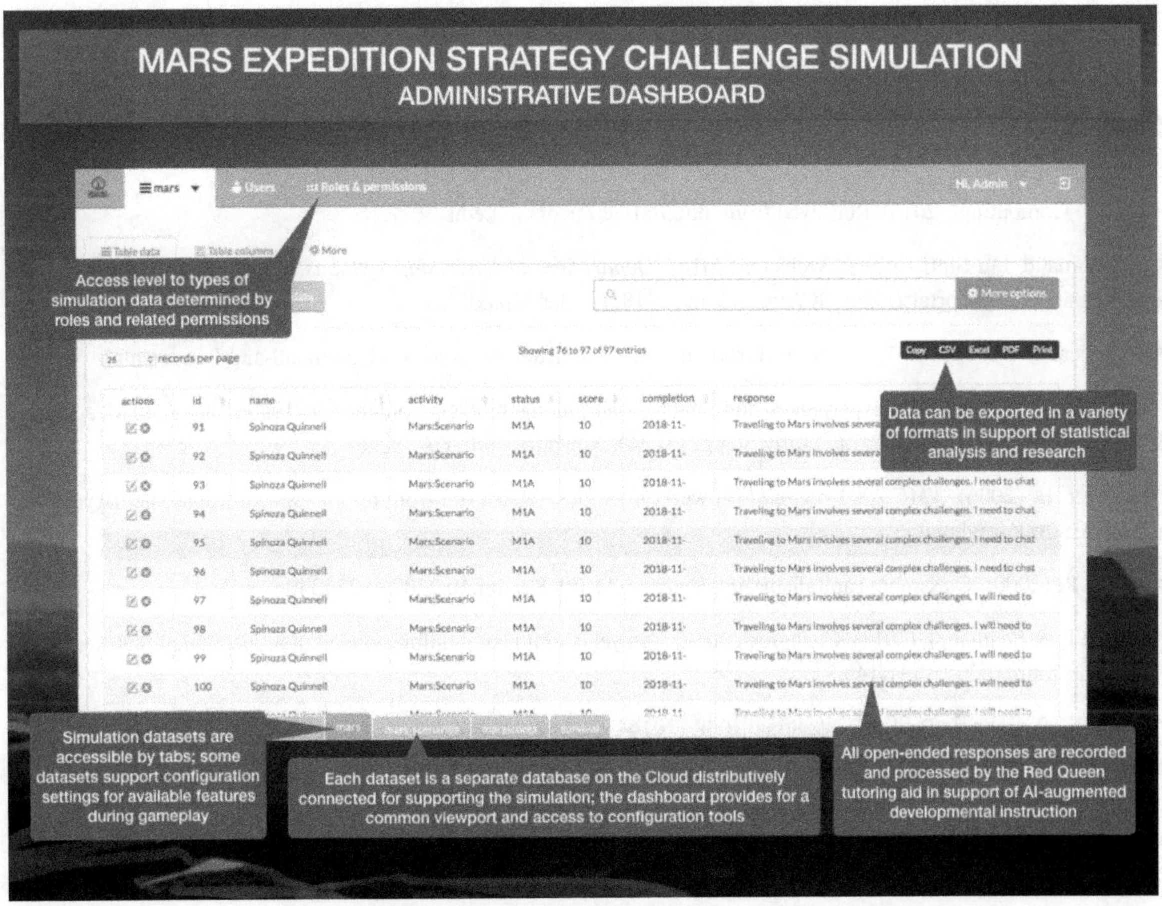

Compilation of References

5G. launch: The Top Countries Most Likely to Launch 5G First – SDXCentral. (2018). Retrieved from https://www.sdxcentral.com/5g/definitions/5g-network-countries/

Abbey, R. (2004). Charles Taylor (R. Abbey, Ed.). Cambridge, UK: Cambridge University Press. doi:10.1017/CBO9780511610837

Abowd, G. D., Mynatt, E. D., & Rodden, T. (2002, January - March). The human experience. *Pervasive Computing.*

Ackermann, E. (2001). Piaget's constructivism, Papert's constructionism: What's the difference. *Future of Learning Group Publication, 5*(3), 438.

Adams, K., Hean, S., Sturgis, P., & Clark, J. M. (2006). Investigating the factors influencing professional identity of first-year health and social care students. *Learning in Health and Social Care, 5*(2), 55–68. doi:10.1111/j.1473-6861.2006.00119.x

Advanced Distributed Learning Initiative. (2019). Retrieved from https://adlnet.gov

AdvertisingAge. (2007, September 10). Second Life has some firms second guessing [Weblog post]. Retrieved from http://adage.com/article/btob/life-firms-guessing/268564/

Affective Computing. (2016). Retrieved from: http://affect.media.mit.edu

Air Command and Staff College Website. (2018). *Department of leadership syllabus.* Retrieved from https://www.airuniversity.af.edu/Portals/10/ACSC/curriculum/AY18_Leadership.pdf

Air University Website. (2018). Retrieved from https://www.airuniversity.af.edu/Command-and-Leadership/

Albert, R. S. (1990). Identity, experiences, and career choice among the exceptionally gifted and eminent. In M. A. Runco & R. S. Albert (Eds.), *Theories of creativity* (pp. 13–34). Newbury Park, CA: Sage.

Alexander, B. (2006). *NMC 2006 regional* [PowerPoint slides]. Retrieved from http://www.slideshare.net/BryanAlexander/nmc-2006-regional

Alger, J. R. (2000). Classroom capitalism. *Academe, 86*(1), 79–80. doi:10.2307/40252348

Allen, E. I., & Seaman, J. (2014). Changing course: Ten years of tracking online education in the United States. Atlantic Marketing Journal, 3(2), 131-149.

Allen, I. E., Seaman, J., Poulin, R., & Straut, T. T. (2016). *Online Report Card: Tracking Online Education in the United States.* Retrieved from: http://onlinelearningsurvey.com/reports/onlinereportcard.pdf

Alston, A. L., & Schatz, S. (2013, December). *Beyond scenarios: Designing holistic experiences for simulation-based training.* Interservice/Industry Training, Simulation, and Education Conference.

American Association of School Librarians. (2007). *Standards for the 21st century learner*. Chicago: American Association of School Librarians. Retrieved March 1, 2017 from http://www.ala.org/ala/mgrps/divs/aasl/guidelinesandstandards/learningstandards/standards.cfm

American Association of School Librarians. (2018). *AASL Standards framework for learners*. Retrieved February 17, 2019 from https://standards.aasl.org/wp-content/uploads/2017/11/AASL-Standards-Framework-for-Learners-pamphlet.pdf

Anarbaeva, S. (2016). Youtubing difference: Performing identity in video communities. *Journal of Virtual Worlds Research*, *9*(2). doi:10.4101/jvwr.v9i2.7193

Anderson, H. H. (1959). *Creativity as personality development. Creativity and its cultivations*. Academic Press.

Anderson, C. A., & Bushman, B. (2001). Effects of violent video games on aggressive behavior, aggressive cognition, aggressive affect, physiological arousal, and prosocial behavior: A meta-analytic review of the scientific literature. *Psychological Science*, *12*(5), 353–359. doi:10.1111/1467-9280.00366 PMID:11554666

Appelboom, G., Camacho, E., Abraham, M. E., Bruce, S. S., Dumont, E. L., Zacharia, B. E., ... Connolly, E. S. (2014). Smart wearable body sensors for patient self-assessment and monitoring. *Archives of Public Health*, *72*(1), 28. doi:10.1186/2049-3258-72-28 PMID:25232478

Arenas, F.J. (2018). *North star leadership course*. Air Command and Staff College, Air University.

Argyris, C., & Schön, D. (1974). *Theory in practice: Increasing professional effectiveness*. San Francisco, CA: Jossey-Bass Publishers.

Aristotle. (1999). Nicomachean ethics (T. Irwin, Trans.). Indianapolis, IN: Hackett Publishing Company, Inc.

Armitage, C. J., & Conner, M. (2000). Social cognition models and health behaviour: A structured review. *Psychology & Health*, *15*(2), 173–189. doi:10.1080/08870440008400299

Armstrong, S. (2014). *Smarter Than Us: The Rise of Machine Intelligence*. Berkeley, CA: Machine Intelligence Research Institute (MIRI).

Army Regulation 350-53. (2014). *Comprehensive soldier and family fitness*. Washington, DC: Headquarters, Department of the Army.

Arndt, K. (1965). *George Rapp's Harmony Society 1785-1847* (Revised Edition). Cranbury, NJ: Associated University Presses, Inc.

Arndt, K. (1978). *A documentary history of the Indiana decade of the Harmony Society 1814-1824* (Vol. 2). Indianapolis, IN: Indiana Historical Society.

Arteaga, S. M., Kudeki, M., Woodworth, A., & Kurniawan, S. (2010). Mobile system to motivate teenagers' physical activity. *Proceedings of the 9th International Conference on Interaction Design and Children*, 1-10. doi: 10.1145/1810543.1810545

ASCD Website. (2016). *ASCD announces partnership with Mursion to develop leadership institutes that leverage simulations in virtual reality*. Retrieved from http://www.ascd.org/news-media/Press-Room/News-Releases/ASCD-Announces-Partnership-with-Mursion.aspx

Association of College & Research Libraries. (2000). *Information literacy competency standards for higher education*. Retrieved March 1, 2017, from http://www.ala.org/acrl/standards/informationliteracycompetency

Association of College & Research Libraries. (2016). *Framework for information literacy for higher education*. Retrieved February 4, 2019 from http://www.ala.org/acrl/standards/ilframework

Attie, I., & Brooks-Gunn, J. (1989). Development of eating problems in adolescent girls: A longitudinal study. *Developmental Psychology*, *25*(1), 70–79. doi:10.1037/0012-1649.25.1.70

Augustine. (412). *City of God* (H. Bettenson, Trans.). New York, NY: Penguin Books.

Avacon Grid. (2018). Retrieved from http://www.avacon.org

Avolio, B. J., Sosik, J. J., Kahai, S. S., & Baker, B. (2013). E-leadership: Re-examining transformations in leadership source and transmission. *The Leadership Quarterly*, *25*(1), 105–131. doi:10.1016/j.leaqua.2013.11.003

Avolio, B., & Hannah, S. (2008). Developmental readiness: Accelerating leader development. *Consulting Psychology Journal: Practice and Research*, *60*(4), 331–347. doi:10.1037/1065-9293.60.4.331

Babic, S., Kresic, M., & Kucel, K. (2014, May). E-Education 2.0: Students' digital identity and online learning activities. In *Information and Communication Technology, Electronics and Microelectronics (MIPRO), 2014 37th International Convention on* (pp. 756-761). IEEE.

Babson Survey Research Group. (2018). *Freeing the Textbook: Educational Resources in U.S. Higher Education.* Released under a Creative Commons Attribution-ShareAlike 4.0 International license. Report available at: www.onlinelearningsurvey.com/oer.html

Bachelard, G. (1964). *The poetics of space*. New York: Orion Press.

Bailenson, J. (2018). *Experience on demand: What virtual reality is, how it works, and what it can do*. New York, NY: W. W. Norton & Company.

Bai, X., Duncan, R., Horowitz, D., Graffeo, J., Glodstein, S., & Lavin, J. (2012). The added value of 3D simulations in healthcare education. *International Journal of Nursing Education*, *4*(2), 67–72.

Baker, D. P., Day, R., & Salas, E. (2006). Teamwork as an essential component of high-reliability organizations. *Health Services Research, 41*(4p2), 1576-1598.

Bandara, I., Ioras, F., & Maher, K. (2014, November). Cybersecurity concerns in e-learning education. *Proceedings of ICERI2014 Conference*.

Bandura, A. (1986). *Social foundations of thought and action: A social cognitive theory*. Englewood Cliffs, NJ: Prentice-Hall.

Bandura, A. (1998). Health promotion from the perspective of social cognitive theory. *Psychology & Health*, *13*(4), 623–649. doi:10.1080/08870449808407422

Bandura, A. (2001). Social cognitive theory of mass communication. *Media Psychology*, *3*(3), 265–299. doi:10.1207/S1532785XMEP0303_03

Bandura, A. (2004). Health promotion by social cognitive means. *Health Education & Behavior*, *31*(2), 143–164. doi:10.1177/1090198104263660 PMID:15090118

Bandura, A., & Menlove, F. L. (1968). Factors determining vicarious extinction of avoidance behavior through symbolic modeling. *Journal of Personality and Social Psychology*, *8*(2, Pt. 1), 99–108. doi:10.1037/h0025260 PMID:5644484

Banfield, E. C., Liu, Y., Davis, J. S., Chang, S., & Frazier-Wood, A. C. (2016). Poor adherence to US dietary guidelines for children and adolescents in the national health and nutrition examination survey population. *Journal of the Academy of Nutrition and Dietetics*, *116*(1), 21–27. doi:10.1016/j.jand.2015.08.010 PMID:26391469

Barlow, A., & Leston, R. (2012). *Beyond the Blogosphere: Information and Its Children.* Santa Barbara, CA: ABC-CLIO, LLC.

Barrows, H., & Bennett, K. (1972). The diagnostic (problem-solving) skill of the neurologist: experimental studies and implications for neurology training. *Archives of Neurology,* 26, 273-277. Retrieved from http://archneur.jamanetwork.com/article.aspx?articleid=571194

Barrows, H., & Tamblyn, R. (1980). *Problem-Based Learning: An Approach to Medical Education.* New York, NY: Springer.

Bartle, R. (2012). Early MUD history. In I. Duncan, A. Miller, & S. Jiang. A taxonomy of virtual worlds usage in education. *British Journal of Educational Technology, 43*(6), 949–964.

Bass, B. M. (2008). *The Bass Handbook of Leadership: Theory, Research & Managerial Applications.* New York: Free Press.

Bass, B. M., & Riggio, R. E. (2006). *Transformational Leadership.* Mahwah, NJ: Lawrence Erlbaum Associates, Inc.

Baudrillard, J. (1990). *Seduction.* Montreal: New World Perspectives. doi:10.1007/978-1-349-20638-4

Baudrillard, J. (1994). *Simulacra and simulation.* Ann Arbor, MA: University of Michigan Press.

Baylor, A. L. (2009). Promoting motivation with virtual agents and avatars: Role of visual presence and appearance. *Philosophical Transactions of the Royal Society of London. Series B, Biological Sciences, 364*(1535), 3559–3565. doi:10.1098/rstb.2009.0148 PMID:19884150

Bearman, S. K., Presnell, K., Martinez, E., & Stice, E. (2006). The skinny on body dissatisfaction: A longitudinal study of adolescent girls and boys. *Journal of Youth and Adolescence, 35*(2), 217–229. doi:10.100710964-005-9010-9 PMID:16912810

Begg, A. (2000). *Enactivism: a personal interpretation.* Unpublished manuscript. Retrieved July 20th, 2009 from http://www.emr.vic.edu.au/Downloads/enactivism_andybegg.doc

Behm Morawitz, E. (2013). Mirrored Selves: The influence of self-presence in a virtual world on health, appearance, and well-being. *Computers in Human Behavior, 29*(1), 119–128. doi:10.1016/j.chb.2012.07.023

Benjamin, E. J., Blaha, M. J., Chiuve, S. E., Cushman, M., Das, S. R., Deo, R., ... Muntner, P. (2017). Heart disease and stroke statistics—2017 update: A report from the American Heart Association. *Circulation, 135*(10), e146–e603. doi:10.1161/CIR.0000000000000485 PMID:28122885

Bennett, K. S. (1981). *A construction of a diagnosis: a study of a physician's mental strategies for fitting a patient's symptoms and signs to a disease category* (Doctoral Dissertation). UCLA. Retrieved from 2018 http://search.proquest.com/docview/303106298/abstract

Bennett, K. (2000). Perceptions of Lyme Borreliosis. *Journal of Spirochetal and Tick-borne Diseases, 7,* 42–51. Retrieved from https://www.academia.edu/12300945/Perceptions_of_Lyme_Borreliosis_Kara_Bennett

Bennett, K., & Barrows, H. (1972). An investigation of the diagnostic problem-solving methods used by resident neurologists. *Mathematical Biosciences, 15*(1-2), 63–181. doi:10.1016/0025-5564(72)90071-5

Bennett, K., & Patrice, S. (2013). Exploring the Virtual World of Second Life to help bring Human Rights to Health Care. In D. Baldwin & J. Achterberg (Eds.), *Women and Second Life.* London: McFarland and Co. Inc.

Benthall, S., Gürses, S., & Nissenbaum, H. (2017). *Contextual integrity through the lens of computer science.* Now Publishers Incorporated. doi:10.1561/3300000016

BerrettL. (2018). Retrieved from https://agelessmindproject.org https:VirtualInspirationIsland.org

Berube, P. (2018, Dec 28). *Air university's new leader development course helps squadron commanders 'thrive."* Air University Website news article. Retrieved from https://www.af.mil/News/Article-Display/Article/1721978/air-universitys-new-leader-development-course-helps-squadron-commanders-thrive/

Blakely, G., Skirton, H., Cooper, S., Allum, P., & Nelmes, P. (2009). Educational gaming in the health sciences: Systematic review. *Journal of Advanced Nursing*, *65*(2), 259–269. doi:10.1111/j.1365-2648.2008.04843.x PMID:19032512

Blascovich, J., & Bailenson, J. (2011). *Infinite reality - Avatars, eternal life, new worlds, and the dawn of the virtual revolution*. New York, NY: HarperCollins Publishers.

Blascovich, J., & Bailenson, J. (2011). *Infinite reality: Avatars, eternal life, new worlds, and the dawn of the virtual revolution*. New York: Harper Collins.

Blascovich, J., & Bailenson, J. (2011). *Infinite Reality: Avatars, Eternal Life, New Worlds, and the Dawn of the Virtual Revolution*. New York: HarperCollins Publishers.

Blascovich, J., & Bailenson, J. (2011). *Infinite reality: The hidden blueprint of our virtual lives*. New York, NY: HarperCollins Publishers.

Blizzard Entertainment. (2004). *The World of Warcraft* [Computer software]. Austin, TX: Blizzard Entertainment.

Bobro, M. (2018). Collective identity in the age of globalisation. *The Person and the Challenges*, *8*(1), 121–133.

Bolkan, J. (2014). Resources to help you teach digital citizenship. *T.H.E. Journal*, *41*(12), 21–23.

Bonk, C. J. (2010). For openers: How technology is changing school. In R. Dufour & C. Reason (Eds.), *Professional Learning Communities at Work and Virtual Collaboration* (p. 3). Bloomington, IN: Solution Tree Press.

Botta, R. A. (2003). For your health? The relationship between magazine reading and adolescents' body image and eating disturbances. *Sex Roles*, *48*(9-10), 389–399. doi:10.1023/A:1023570326812

Bourke, M., Whittaker, P. J., & Verma, A. (2014). Are dietary interventions effective at increasing fruit and vegetable consumption among overweight children? A systematic review. *Journal of Epidemiology and Community Health*, *68*(5), 485–490. doi:10.1136/jech-2013-203238 PMID:24436339

Bower, J. M., & Richmond, J. R. (2016). *Learning competencies used in the U.S. Navy's Virtual Schoolhouse learning environment*. Naval Postgraduate School Monterey United States. Retrieved from: https://apps.dtic.mil/dtic/tr/fulltext/u2/1030717.pdf

Boyd, D. (2006, October 21). Announcing the Macarthur Foundation's digital media and learning initiative [Weblog post]. Retrieved from http://www.zephoria.org/thoughts/archives/2006/10/21/announcing_the.html

Bransford, J. D., Brown, A., & Cocking, R. (1999). *How people learn: Brain, mind, experience, and school*. Washington, DC: National Academies Press.

Bransford, J. D., & Schwartz, D. (1999). Rethinking transfer: A simple proposal with multiple implications. In A. Iran-Nejad & P. D. Pearson (Eds.), *Review of Research in Education* (Vol. 24, pp. 61–100). Washington, DC: American Educational Research Association.

Bransford, J. D., Sherwood, R., Vye, N., & Rieser, J. (1986). Teaching thinking and problem solving. *The American Psychologist*, *41*, 1078–1089.

Brewer, M. B., & Gardner, W. (1996). Who is this we? Levels of collective identity and self representations. *Journal of Personality and Social Psychology*, *71*(1), 83–93. doi:10.1037/0022-3514.71.1.83

Brown, T. (2008). Design thinking. *Harvard Business Review*. Retrieved from https://hbr.org/2008/06/design-thinking

Brown, J. A., Collins, A., & Duguid, S. (1989). Situated cognition and the culture of learning. *Educational Researcher*, *18*(1), 32–42.

Bryant, M. (2015, December). *Think Second Life died? It has a higher GDP than some countries*. Retrieved from http://thenextweb.com/insider/2015/11/07/think-second-life-died-it-has-a-higher-gdp-than-some-countries/

Buber, M. (1947). *Between man and man* (R. Gregor-Smith, Trans.). New York, NY: Routledge & Kegan Paul.

Buber, M. (1958). *I and thou*. New York, NY: Collier Books, Macmillan Publishing Company.

Bulu, S. T. (2012). Place presence, social Presence, and satisfaction in virtual worlds. *Computers & Education*, *58*(1), 154–161. doi:10.1016/j.compedu.2011.08.024

Buring, S. M., Bhushan, A., Broeseker, A., Conway, S., Duncan-Hewitt, W., Hansen, L., & Westberg, S. (2009). Interprofessional education: Definitions, student competencies, and guidelines for implementation. *American Journal of Pharmaceutical Education*, *73*(4), 59. doi:10.5688/aj730459 PMID:19657492

Burke, P. J., & Stets, J. E. (2009). *Identity theory*. New York, NY: Oxford University Press. doi:10.1093/acprof:oso/9780195388275.001.0001

Burstein, D. D. (2013). Fast future: How the millennial generation is shaping our world. In R. Dufour & C. Reason (Eds.), *Professional Learning Communities at Work and Virtual Collaboration* (p. 4). Bloomington, IN: Solution Tree Press.

Busciglio, D. F. (2015). *Not Covering but Discovering: Agency and Shared Autonomy in Deep Project-Based Language Learning* (Doctoral dissertation). The University of Wisconsin-Madison.

Caire, P. (2008). Designing convivial digital cities. *Proc. of 7th Int. Conf. on Autonomous Agents and Multi-agent Systems (AAMAS 2008)*, 1727-1729.

Caire, P. (2009). How to import the concept of conviviality to web communities. *International Journal of Web Based Communities*, *6*(1), 99–113. doi:10.1504/IJWBC.2010.030019

Calandra, B., & Puvirajah, A. (2014). Teacher practice in multi user virtual environments: A fourth space. *TechTrends*, *58*(6), 29–35. doi:10.100711528-014-0800-3

Calongne, C. (2009). Virtual worlds: Explorations and implications [PowerPoint slides]. *Association for Information Technology Professionals*. Retrieved from http://www.slideshare.net/lyrlobo/aitp-keynote-on-virtual-worlds

Calongne, C. (2012, August 21). *Highlights from 33 classes with Lyr Lobo* [Video recording]. Retrieved from http://ctusoftware.blogspot.com/2012/08/highlights-from-33-classes-with-lyr.html

Calongne, C. (2016, June). *Future of games in education*. Keynote address at the International Society for Technology in Education Conference Games & Simulations Network Playground, Denver, CO. Retrieved from https://www.slideshare.net/lyrlobo/future-of-games-iste-ven-gsn-calongne-keynote

Calongne, C., Sheehy, P., & Stricker, A. (2013). Gemeinschaft identity in a gesellschaft metaverse. In R. Teigland & D. Power (Eds.), The Immersive Internet: Reflections on the entangling of the virtual with society, politics and the economy (pp. 180-191). Basingstoke, UK: Palgrave Macmillan.

Calongne, C. (2008). Educational frontiers: Learning in a virtual world. *EDUCAUSE Review*, *43*(5), 36–48.

Calongne, C., & Hiles, J. (2007). Blended realities: A virtual tour of education in Second Life. *Proceedings of the 12th Annual Technology, Colleges & Community (TCC) Worldwide Conference*.

Calvert, S. L., Jordan, A. B., & Cocking, R. R. (2002). *Children in the digital age: influences of electronic media on development*. Westport, CT: Praeger.

Campbell, J. (1949). *The hero with a thousand faces*. New York, NY: Pantheon Books.

CanLyme. (2018). Retrieved from https://canlyme.com/2018/06/14/corruption-and-human-rights-violations-against-lyme-doctors-scientists-and-parents-now-on-united-nations-record/

Carmichael, P. M., & Tscholl, M. (2013). Cases, simulacra, and semantic web technologies. *Journal of Computer Assisted Learning*, *29*(1), 31–42. doi:10.1111/j.1365-2729.2011.00459.x

Carr, N. (2010). *The shallows: What the internet is doing to our brains*. New York: W.W. Norton & Co.

Carroll, L. (1872). Through the looking-glass. New York, NY: Dover Publications.

Castronova, E. (2010). *Synthetic worlds – The business and culture of online games*. Chicago University Press.

Caza, B. B., & Creary, S. J. (2016). *The construction of professional identity*. Retrieved from Cornell University, SHA School site: http://scholarship.sha.cornell.edu/articles/878

CES. (2019, January). *Consumer Electronics Show Las Vegas Jan 8 – Jan 11*. Retrieved from https://www.ces.tech/About-CES.aspx

Chaiton, M., Sabiston, C., O'loughlin, J., McGrath, J. J., Maximova, K., & Lambert, M. (2009). A structural equation model relating adiposity, psychosocial indicators of body image and depressive symptoms among adolescents. *International Journal of Obesity*, *33*(5), 588–596. doi:10.1038/ijo.2009.43 PMID:19274053

Checkland, P. (1981). *Systems thinking, systems practice*. New York, NY: John Wiley & Sons.

Chen, G., Xu, B., Lu, M., & Chen, N. S. (2018). Exploring blockchain technology and its potential applications for education. *Smart Learning Environments*, *5*(1), 1. doi:10.118640561-017-0050-x

Choi, B. C., & Pak, A. W. (2006). Multidisciplinarity, interdisciplinarity and transdisciplinarity in health research, services, education and policy: 1. Definitions, objectives, and evidence of effectiveness. *Clinical and Investigative Medicine, 29*(6), 351.

Cho, J. H., Han, S. N., Kim, J. H., & Lee, H. M. (2012). Body image distortion in fifth and sixth grade students may lead to stress, depression, and undesirable dieting behavior. *Nutrition Research and Practice*, *6*(2), 175–181. doi:10.4162/nrp.2012.6.2.175 PMID:22586508

Chreim, S., Williams, B. B., & Hinings, C. B. (2007). Interlevel influences on the reconstruction of professional role identity. *Academy of Management Journal*, *50*(6), 1515–1539. doi:10.5465/amj.2007.28226248

Churchman, C. W. (1971). *The design of inquiring systems*. New York, NY: Basic Books.

Cixin, L. (2014). *The three-body problem* (K. Liu, Trans.). New York, NY: Tor Books.

Cixin, L. (2016). *Death's end* (K. Liu, Trans.). New York, NY: Tor Books.

Clark, R. (2008). *GEL, Adaptable Expertise and Transfer of Training*. U.S.C Center for Cognitive Technology.

Clark, A. (2007). Re-Inventing Ourselves: The Plasticity of Embodiment, Sensing, and Mind. *The Journal of Medicine and Philosophy*, *32*(3), 262–281. doi:10.1080/03605310701397024 PMID:17613705

Clausewitz, C. V. (1984). On war (M. Howard & P. Paret, Trans.). Princeton, NJ: Princeton University Press. (Originally published 1832)

CNN Heroes Solar Light. (2018). Retrieved from http://www.cnn.com/2010/LIVING/02/11/cnnheroes.wadongo/index.html

CNN. (2015). *28 Internet acronyms every parent should know*. Retrieved February 1, 2019, from http://www.cnn.com/2014/12/08/living/internet-acronyms-every-parent-should-know/

Cohen, G. L., & Sherman, D. K. (2014). The psychology of change: Self-affirmation and social psychological intervention. *Annual Review of Psychology*, *65*(1), 333–371. doi:10.1146/annurev-psych-010213-115137 PMID:24405362

Cohen, S. (2004). Social Relationships and Health. *The American Psychologist*, *59*(8), 676–684. doi:10.1037/0003-066X.59.8.676 PMID:15554821

Cohen, S. E., & Syme, S. (1985). *Social support and health*. San Diego, CA: Academic Press.

Cohen, S., & Willis, T. A. (1985). Stress, social support, and the buffering hypothesis. *Psychological Bulletin*, *98*(2), 310–357. doi:10.1037/0033-2909.98.2.310 PMID:3901065

Cohen, W. M., & Levinthal, D. A. (2010). Absorptive capacity: A new perspective on learning and innovation. *Administrative Science Quarterly, 35*, 554-568.

Coles, C. D., Strickland, D. C., Padgett, L., & Bellmoff, L. (2007). Games that "work": Using computer games to teach alcohol-affected children about fire and street safety. *Research in Developmental Disabilities*, *28*(5), 518–530. doi:10.1016/j.ridd.2006.07.001 PMID:16965894

College of Education Virtual Avatar Laboratory Website. (2018). Retrieved from http://www.education.aum.edu/VAL

Collins, J., & Selina, H. (1998). *Introducing Heidegger*. New York, NY: Totem Books.

Common Sense Media. (2018). Retrieved from https://www.commonsense.org/education/digital-citizenship

Common Sense Media. (2019). *Common sense digital citizenship*. Retrieved February 20, 2019, from https://www.commonsensemedia.org/educators/digital-citizenship

Community Virtual Library. (2019). *Digital citizenship museum*. Retrieved February 18, 2019 from https://community-virtuallibrary.org/digital-citizenship-museum/

Community Virtual Library. (2019). *Real librarianship in virtual worlds*. Retrieved from https://communityvirtuallibrary.org/

Cooke, L. (2007). The importance of exposure for healthy eating in childhood: A review. *Journal of Human Nutrition and Dietetics*, *20*(4), 294–301. doi:10.1111/j.1365-277X.2007.00804.x PMID:17635306

Cooke, N. J., & Hilton, M. L. (Eds.). (2015). *Enhancing the Effectiveness of Team Science*. National Academies Press.

Cook, N. S. D., & Brown, J. S. (2010). Bridging epistemologies – the generative dance between organizational knowledge and organizational knowing. *Organization Science, 10*, 381-400.

Counts, G. (1932). *Dare the school build a new social order?* New York, NY: The John Day Company.

Covey, S. R. (2006). *The eighth habit*. Simon and Schuster.

Cowdery, J., Kindred, J., Michalakis, A., & Suggs, L. S. (2011). Promoting health in a virtual world: Impressions of health communication messages delivered in Second Life. *First Monday*, *16*(9). doi:10.5210/fm.v16i9.2857

Craik, F. I. M., & Lockhart, R. S. (1972). Levels of processing: A framework for memory research. *Journal of Verbal Learning and Verbal Behavior*, *11*(6), 671–684. doi:10.1016/S0022-5371(72)80001-X

Craik, K. (1943). *The nature of explanation*. Cambridge, UK: Cambridge University Press.

Cruz, G., Costa, A., Martins, P., Goncalves, R., & Barroso, J. (2013, September). Federation Technology and Virtual Worlds for Learning: Research Trends and Opportunities Towards Identity Federation. In *Games and Virtual Worlds for Serious Applications (VS-GAMES), 2013 5th International Conference on* (pp. 1-4). IEEE.

Cruz, G., Costa, A., Martins, P., Gonçalves, R., & Barroso, J. (2015). Toward educational virtual worlds: Should identity federation be a concern? *Journal of Educational Technology & Society, 18*(1), 27–36.

Csíkszentmihályi, M. (1997). *Creativity: flow and the psychology of discovery and invention.* Harper Perennial.

Csíkszentmihályi, M. (2008). Flow: The psychology of optimal experience. New York, NY: Harper Collins.

Csikszentmihalyi, M. (1990). *Flow.* New York, NY: Harper & Row.

Csikszentmihalyi, M. (1990). *Flow: The Psychology of Optimal Experience.* New York, NY: Harper and Row.

Csikszentmihalyi, M. (1992). *Flow: The psychology of happiness.* London: Rider.

Csikszentmihalyi, M. (1996). *Creativity. Flow and the psychology of discovery and invention.* New York, NY: Harper Perennial.

Csikszentmihalyi, M. (1999). Implications of a systems perspective for the study of creativity. In R. J. Sternberg (Ed.), *Handbook of Creativity.* Cambridge University Press.

Csikszentmihalyi, M. (2000). *Beyond boredom and anxiety.* San Francisco: Jossey-Bass.

Cuban, L., & Shipps, D. (2000). *Reconstructing the common good in education: Coping with intractable American dilemmas.* Stanford, CA: Stanford University Press.

Cybersecurity, G. (2014). *The Global Cybersecurity Market 2014-2024.* Retrieved from https://www.globaldata.com/store/report/gd-df0053sr--the-global-cybersecurity-market-2014-2024/

D'Onfro, J. (2015, April 17). The truth about Google's famous '20% time' policy. *Business Insider, Tech.* Retrieved from www.businessinsider.com

Da Silva, M. (2015, February 17). The meaning of social objects [Weblog post]. Retrieved from http://abcofinternet-marketing.co.za/blogging/social-media/meaning-social-objects/

Dalgarno, B., & Lee, M. J. (2010). What are the learning affordances of 3-D virtual environments? *British Journal of Educational Technology, 41*(1), 10–32. doi:10.1111/j.1467-8535.2009.01038.x

Damasio, A. (2012). *Self comes to mind: constructing the conscious brain.* Random House Digital, Inc.

Damon, F., & Coetzee, M. (2018, August). Evaluation of Identity and Access Assurance Component Model Dimensions. In *The 2018 International Conference on Advances in Big Data, Computing and Data Communication Systems (icABCD)* (pp. 1-6). IEEE. 10.1109/ICABCD.2018.8465126

Daneshi, T. (2016). *Cyber Ethics: A Global Conversation.* Retrieved from DeVry University blog website: http://www.devry.edu/blog/2014/02/cyber-ethics-a-global conversation.html

Davenport, T. H., & Prusak, L. (2010). *Working Knowledge – How organizations manage what they know.* Harvard Business School Press.

Davis, D., & Boellstorff, T. (2018). *Virtual worlds, disability, and new cultures of the embodied self.* Retrieved from http://www.ourdigitalselves.com/

Davison, K. K., Markey, C. N., & Birch, L. L. (2003). A longitudinal examination of patterns in girls' weight concerns and body dissatisfaction from ages 5 to 9 years. *International Journal of Eating Disorders*, *33*(3), 320–332. doi:10.1002/eat.10142 PMID:12655629

De Freitas, S. (2010). *Serious virtual worlds: A scoping study*. Academic Press.

De Freitas, S., Rebolledo-Mendez, G., Liarokapis, F., Magoulas, G., & Poulovassilis, A. (2010). Learning as immersive experiences: Using the four-dimensional framework for designing and evaluating immersive learning experiences in a virtual world. *British Journal of Educational Technology*, *41*(1), 69–85. doi:10.1111/j.1467-8535.2009.01024.x

De Kleer, J., & Brown, J. S. (1983). Assumptions and ambiguities in mechanistic mental models. In D. Gentner & A. Stevens (Eds.), *Mental models* (pp. 155–190). Hillsdale, NJ: Lawrence Erlbaum.

de la Guía, E., López, V., Olivares, T., Lozano, M. D., Penichet, V., & Orozco, L. (2015, October). Easy Smart-Home Environment to Assist Patients with Mobility Impairment. In *Proceedings of the 3rd 2015 Workshop on ICTs for improving Patients Rehabilitation Research Techniques* (pp. 122-125). ACM. 10.1145/2838944.2838974

De Leon, L., & Bennett, K. (2015). *The Magic in the Drums: Using Imagination and Think Aloud Processes to Develop Humanitarian Identities*. Presentation, The Science Circle Second Life.

De Leon, L., & Bennett, K. (in press). Human Rights, Think Aloud Protocols and Magic Drums: Revealing Character in Pre-Service Teachers. *Journal of Interactive Learning Research*.

De Zwart, M., & Lindsay, D. (2012). My self, my avatar, my rights? Avatar identity in social virtual worlds. *At the Interface / Probing the Boundaries, 85*, 81-100.

Deci, E. L., & Ryan, R. M. (2000). The" what" and" why" of goal pursuits: Human needs and the self-determination of behavior. *Psychological Inquiry*, *11*(4), 227–268. doi:10.1207/S15327965PLI1104_01

Deci, E. L., & Ryan, R. M. (2008). Self-determination theory: A macrotheory of human motivation, development, and health. *Canadian Psychology*, *49*(3), 182–185. doi:10.1037/a0012801

Dede, C. (2003). Multi-user virtual environments. *EDUCAUSE Review*, *38*(3), 60–61.

Dede, C., & Ketelhut, D. J. (2003). Designing for motivation and usability in a museum-based multi-user virtual environment. *American Educational Research Association Conference*, Chicago, IL.

Dede, C., Nelson, B., Ketelhut, D. J., Clarke, J., & Bowman, C. (2004). *Design-based research strategies for studying situated learning in a multi-user virtual environment*. Academic Press.

Delfabbro, P. H., Winefield, A. H., Anderson, S., Hammarström, A., & Winefield, H. (2011). Body image and psychological well-being in adolescents: The relationship between gender and school type. *The Journal of Genetic Psychology*, *172*(1), 67–83. doi:10.1080/00221325.2010.517812 PMID:21452753

Deneen, P. (2011). The science of politics and the conquest of nature. *New Atlantis (Washington, D.C.)*, *32*(3), 90–102.

Dennett, D. C. (1991). Consciousness explained. Boston: Little, Brown and Co.

Dennett, D. C. (1992). The self as a center of narrative gravity. In F. S. Kessel, P. M. Cole, & D. L. Johnson (Eds.), Self and consciousness: Multiple perspectives. Hillsdale, NJ: Lawrence Erlbaum Associates.

Deodato, J. (2014). The patron as producer: Libraries, web 2.0, and participatory culture. *The Journal of Documentation*, *70*(5), 734–758. doi:10.1108/JD-10-2012-0127

Derrida, J. (1967/1997). *Of grammatology* (G. Spivak, Trans.). Baltimore, MD: Johns Hopkins University Press.

Devices, C. (2016). *Popular Internet of Things Forecast of 50 Billion Devices by 2020 Is Outdated.* Retrieved from https://spectrum.ieee.org/tech-talk/telecom/internet/popular-internet-of-things-forecast-of-50-billion-devices-by-2020-is-outdated

Dewey, J. (1938). *Experience and education.* New York, NY: Macmillan.

Dickey, M. D. (2005). Three-dimensional virtual worlds and distance learning: Two case studies of active worlds as a medium for distance education. *British Journal of Educational Technology, 36*(3), 439–451. doi:10.1111/j.1467-8535.2005.00477.x

Diehl, W. C., & Prins, E. (2008). Unintended outcomes in Second Life: Intercultural literacy and cultural identity in a virtual world. Language. *Intercultural Communication Language and Intercultural Communication, 8*(2), 101–118. doi:10.1080/14708470802139619

Domingo, M. C. (2012). An overview of the Internet of Things for people with disabilities. *Journal of Network and Computer Applications, 35*(2), 584–596. doi:10.1016/j.jnca.2011.10.015

Dörner, D. (1989). *The logic of failure: Recognizing and avoiding error in complex situations.* New York, NY: Basic Books.

Downes, S. (2016). *Personal and Personalized Learning.* Retrieved from: http://www.downes.ca/post/65065

DQ Institute. (2019). *What is DQ?* Retrieved January 25, 2019 from https://www.dqinstitute.org/what-is-dq/

Drax, B. [Draxtor Despres]. (2018, May 17). *Our digital selves: My avatar is me* [Video file]. Retrieved from https://youtu.be/GQw02-me0W4

Drewnowski, A. (2004). Obesity and the food environment: Dietary energy density and diet costs. *American Journal of Preventive Medicine, 27*(3), 154–162. doi:10.1016/j.amepre.2004.06.011 PMID:15450626

Dufour, R., & Reason, C. (2016). *Professional Learning Communities at Work and Virtual Collaboration.* Bloomington, IN: Solution Tree Press.

Duncan, I., Miller, A., & Jiang, S. (2012). *A taxonomy of virtual worlds usage in education.* Academic Press.

Duncan, I., Miller, A., & Jiang, S. (2012). A taxonomy of virtual worlds usage in education. *British Journal of Educational Technology, 43*(6), 949–964. doi:10.1111/j.1467-8535.2011.01263.x

Dunphy, P., & Petitcolas, F. A. (2018). *A first look at identity management schemes on the blockchain.* arXiv preprint arXiv:1801.03294

Dweck, C. (2016). *Mindset: The new psychology of success.* New York, NY: Penguin Random House.

EDUCAUSE. (2019). *7 Things You Need to Know about Learning Engineering.* Retrieved from: https://library.educause.edu/resources/2018/9/7-things-you-should-know-about-learning-engineering

Eisenberg, E. M. (2008). The social construction of healthcare teams. *Improving Healthcare Team Communication*, 9-20.

Elder Voices, Inc. (2018). Retrieved from www.eldervoices.net

Ellis, S. R. (1996). Virtual environments and environmental instruments. In Simulated and Virtual Realities (pp. 11-51). London, UK: Taylor Francis.

Ellis, L. (2012). *Leading with honor: Leadership lessons from the Hanoi Hilton.* Atlanta, GA: Freedom Star Media.

Elstein, A. S., Shulman, L. S., & Sprafka, S. A. (1978). *Medical problem solving: an analysis of clinical reasoning.* Cambridge, MA: Harvard University Press. doi:10.4159/harvard.9780674189089

Ember, T. (2011, October 19). HG safari [Weblog post]. Retrieved from https://hgsafari.blogspot.com/2011/

Engelbart, D. C. (1962). *Augmenting human intellect: A conceptual framework. AFOSR-3223 Summary Report. Director of Information Sciences, AFOSR.* Washington, DC: Air Force Office of Scientific Research.

Engeström, J. (2005, April 13). Why some social network services work and others don't -- Or: the case for object-centered sociality [Weblog post]. Retrieved from http://www.zengestrom.com/blog/2005/04/why-some-social-network-services-work-and-others-dont-or-the-case-for-object-centered-sociality.html

Erickson, E. (1956). The problem of ego identity. *Journal of the American Psychoanalytic Association*, *4*(1), 56–121. doi:10.1177/000306515600400104 PMID:13286157

Erickson, E. (1959). *Identity and the life cycle*. New York, NY: International Universities Press, Inc.

Erickson, R. J. (1995). The importance of authenticity for self and society. *Symbolic Interaction*, *18*(2), 121–144. doi:10.1525i.1995.18.2.121

Ericsson, K. A., & Simon, H. A. (1993). *Protocol analysis: verbal reports as data*. Cambridge, MA: MIT Press.

Erikson, E. H. (1968). *Identity*. Norton.

Errasti, J., Amigo, I., & Villadangos, M. (2017). Emotional uses of Facebook and Twitter: Its relation with empathy, narcissism, and self-esteem on adolescence. *Psychological Reports*, *120*(6), 997–1018. doi:10.1177/0033294117713496

Ershow, A. G., Peterson, C. M., Riley, W. T., Rizzo, A. S., & Wansink, B. (2011). Virtual reality technologies for research and education in obesity and diabetes: Research needs and opportunities. *Journal of Diabetes Science and Technology*, *5*(2), 212–224. doi:10.1177/193229681100500202 PMID:21527084

Everett, A., & Roman, T. (1997). A Superluminal subway: The Krasnikov tube. *Physical Review D: Particles and Fields*, *56*. doi:10.1103/PhysRevD.56.2100

Facebook. (2014). Statistics. In A. Kellerman. The satisfaction of human needs in physical and virtual spaces. *The Professional Geographer*, *66*(4), 538-546.

Feingold, A., & Mazzella, R. (1998). Gender differences in body image are increasing. *Psychological Science*, *9*(3), 190–195. doi:10.1111/1467-9280.00036

Ferguson, N. (2017). *The square and the tower: Networks and power, from the Freemasons to Facebook*. New York, NY: Penguin Press.

Flavell, J. H. (1978). Metacognitive development. In J. M. Scandura & C. J. Brainerd (Eds.), *Structural/process theories of complex human behavior*. Sijthoff & Noordoff.

Flavell, J. H. (1979). Metacognition and cognitive monitoring: A new area of psychological inquiry. *The American Psychologist*, *34*, 906–911.

Flood, R. L., & Carson, E. R. (1993). *Dealing with complexity: An introduction to the theory and application of systems science* (2nd ed.). New York, NY: Plenum Press.

Fogg, M. J. (1997). The utility of geothermal energy on Mars. The *Smithsonian/NASA Astrophysics Data System (ADS)*. Smithsonian Astrophysical Observatory.

Fogg, B. (2003). *Persuasive Technology: Using Computers to Change What We Think and Do*. San Francisco, CA: Morgan Kaufmann Publisher. doi:10.1016/B978-155860643-2/50011-1

Folsom-Kovarik, J. T., & Raybourn, E. M. (2016, November). Total Learning Architecture (TLA) Enables Next-generation Learning via Meta-adaptation. *Interservice/Industry Training, Simulation, and Education Conference Proceedings.* Retrieved from: https://www.adlnet.gov/public/uploads/Total-Learning-Architecture-TLA-Enables-Next-generation-Learning-via-Meta-adaptation.pdf

Foss, B., & Haraldseid, C. (2014). Improvement of Health Education: The Opportunities of Technology and Digital Learning Tools. *Journal of Biosafety and Health Education*, *2*(1), e114. doi:10.4172/2332-0893.1000e114

Fowler, M. (2005, December 13). *The new methodology.* Retrieved from http://www.martinfowler.com/articles/new-Methodology.html

Fox, J., Arena, D., & Bailenson, J. N. (2009). Virtual reality - A survival guide for the social scientist. *Journal of Media Psychology*, *21*(3), 95–113. doi:10.1027/1864-1105.21.3.95

Fox, J., & Bailenson, J. N. (2009). Virtual self-modeling: The effects of vicarious reinforcement and identification on exercise behaviors. *Media Psychology*, *12*(1), 1–25. doi:10.1080/15213260802669474

Fox, J., Bailenson, J. N., & Binney, J. (2009). Virtual experiences, physical behaviors: The effect of presence on imitation of an eating avatar. *Presence (Cambridge, Mass.)*, *18*(4), 294–303. doi:10.1162/pres.18.4.294

Fox, J., Bailenson, J. N., & Tricase, L. (2013). The embodiment of sexualized virtual selves: The Proteus effect and experiences of self-objectification via avatars. *Computers in Human Behavior*, *29*(3), 930–938. doi:10.1016/j.chb.2012.12.027

Fredrickson, B. L. (2013). *Love 2.0: Finding happiness and health in moments of connection.* Penguin.

Friedrich, M. J. (2017). Global Obesity Epidemic Worsening. *Journal of the American Medical Association*, *318*(7), 603. doi:10.1001/jama.2017.10693 PMID:28810033

Gaba, D. (2004). The future vision of simulation in health care. *Quality & Safety in Health Care*, *13*(suppl_1), 2–10. doi:10.1136/qshc.2004.009878 PMID:15465951

Gamalielsson, J., & Lundell, B. (2014). Sustainability of open source software communities beyond a fork: How and why has the libreoffice project evolved? *Journal of Systems and Software*, *89*, 128–145.

Gao, Y., Li, X., Li, J., Gao, Y., & Philip, S. Y. (2019). Info-Trust: A Multi-Criteria and Adaptive Trustworthiness Calculation Mechanism for Information Sources. *IEEE Access: Practical Innovations, Open Solutions.*

Gardner, W. L., Cogliser, C. C., Davis, K. M., & Dickens, M. P. (2011). Authentic leadership: A review of the literature and research agenda. *The Leadership Quarterly*, *22*(6), 1120–1145. doi:10.1016/j.leaqua.2011.09.007

Gartner. (2007). *Gartner says 80 percent of active internet users will have a "Second Life" in the virtual world by the end of 2011.* Retrieved from http://www.gartner.com/newsroom/id/503861

Gartner. (2016). *Gartner's 2016 hype cycle for emerging technologies identifies three key trends that organizations must track to gain competitive advantage.* Retrieved from http://www.gartner.com/newsroom/id/3412017

Gazzard, A. (2009). *The avatar and the player: Understanding the relationship beyond the screen. In Proceedings from VS-GAMES'09, Coventry, 2009.* Washington, DC: IEEE. doi:10.1109/VS-GAMES.2009.11

Gentner, D., & Gentner, D. R. (1983). Flowing waters or teaming crowds: mental models of electricity. In D. Gentner & A. Stevens (Eds.), *Mental models* (pp. 99–130). Hillsdale, NJ: Lawrence Erlbaum.

Gentner, D., & Stevens, A. L. (1983). *Mental models.* Hillsdale, NJ: Lawrence Erlbaum.

George, B. (2007). *True North.* San Francisco, CA: Jossey-Bass.

Ghormley, Y. (2015). Medical Errors In US Healthcare Organizations: Have We Made Any Progress? *American Journal of Health Sciences*, *6*(1), 45–52. doi:10.19030/ajhs.v6i1.9269

Gibson, W. (1984). *Neuromancer*. New York, NY: The Berkley Publishing Group.

Gieryn, T. F. (2000). A space for place in sociology. *Annual Review of Sociology*, *26*(1), 463–496. doi:10.1146/annurev.soc.26.1.463

Gilbert, D. T. (1991). How mental systems believe. *The American Psychologist*, *46*(2), 107–119. doi:10.1037/0003-066X.46.2.107

Gillespie, T. (2010). The politics of 'platforms.'. *New Media & Society*, *12*(2), 347–364. doi:10.1177/1461444809342738

Girvan, C. (2018). What is a virtual world? Definition and classification. *Educational Technology Research and Development*, *66*(5), 1087–1100. doi:10.100711423-018-9577-y

Gladwell, C., & Currie, J. (2011). Online gaming: Child's play or obsession? In K. M. Yust, B. Hyde, & C. Ota. *International Journal of Children's Spirituality*, *16*(1), 1–3.

Gleick, J. (1988). *Chaos: Making a new science*. New York, NY: Penguin Books.

Glenberg, A. M. (1997). Mental models, space, and embodied cognition. In T. Ward, S. M. Smith, & J. Vaid (Eds.), *Creative thought: An investigation of conceptual structures and processes* (pp. 495–522). Washington, DC: American Psychological Association.

Glick, J. (1997). Discourse and development: Notes from the field. In L. B. Resnick, R. Säljö, C. Pontecorvo, & B. Burge (Eds.), *Discourse, Tools, and Reasoning: Essays on Situated Cognition*. Berlin: Springer. doi:10.1007/978-3-662-03362-3_11

Global IoT Education. (2019). *Global IoT in Education Markets, 2018-2023*. Retrieved from https://globenewswire.com/news-release/2019/01/23/1704060/0/en/Global-IoT-in-Education-Markets-2018-2023-Potential-Growth-Opportunities-for-System-Integrators-Declining-Cost-of-Connectivity-and-Connected-Devices.html

GluckJ. (2018). Retrieved from http;//AIinHealthCare.net https://healthitanalytics.com/features/artificial-intelligence-promises-a-new-paradigm-for-healthcare

Goertzel, B. (2014). *Between Ape and Artilect: Conversations with Pioneers of Artificial General Intelligence and Other Transformative Technologies*. Create Space Independent Publishing Platform.

Goh, J., Truman, B., & Barber, D. (2018). Exploring individual differences as factors to maximize interactive learning environments for future learning. *Interactive Learning Environments*, 1–11.

Goldman Sachs. (2014). *IoT Primer The Internet of Things: Making sense of the next mega-trend. Equity research*. Author.

Goleman, D. (2013). Focus: the Hidden Driver of Excellence. In *Talks at Google* [Video file]. Retrieved from: http://bit.ly/264GIvu

Goleman, D. (2007). *Social intelligence: The new science of human relationships*. New York, NY: Random House, Inc.

Goleman, D., & Senge, P. (2014). The Triple Focus. *Reflections: The SoL Journal*, *14*(1).

Goodyear, P., & Retalis, S. (2012). *Technology-enhanced learning: Design patterns and pattern languages*. Academic Press. doi:10.17705/1jais.00309

Gottesdiener, E. (2001). Decide how to decide: A collaboration pattern. Software Development Magazine, *9*(1).

Gottfried, A. E. (1990). Academic intrinsic motivation in young elementary school children. *Journal of Educational Psychology*, *82*(3), 525–538. doi:10.1037/0022-0663.82.3.525

Grabe, S., Ward, L. M., & Hyde, J. S. (2008). The role of the media in body image concerns among women: A meta-analysis of experimental and correlational studies. *Psychological Bulletin*, *134*(3), 460–476. doi:10.1037/0033-2909.134.3.460 PMID:18444705

Grajek, S. (2016). *Higher Education's Top 10 Strategic Technologies for 2016*. Research report. Louisville, CO: ECAR. Available from http://www.educause.edu/ecar

Grajek, S., & Grama, J. L. (2018). *Higher Education's 2018 Trend Watch and Top 10 Strategic Technologies*. Research report. Louisville, CO: ECAR. Available from http://www.educause.edu/ecar

Grant, R.M. (n.d.). Toward a knowledge-based theory of the firm. *Strategic Management Journal, 17*, 109-122.

Greenfield, D., Nugus, P., Travaglia, J., & Braithwaite, J. (2010). Auditing an organization's interprofessional learning and interprofessional practice: The interprofessional praxis audit framework (IPAF). *Journal of Interprofessional Care*, *24*(4), 436–449. doi:10.3109/13561820903163801 PMID:20377396

Gregory, S., Lee, M. J., Dalgarno, B., & Tynan, B. (Eds.). (2016). *Learning in Virtual Worlds: Research and Applications*. Athabasca University Press.

Gregory, S., Scutter, S., Jacka, L., McDonald, M., Farley, H., & Newman, C. (2015). Barriers and enablers to the use of virtual worlds in higher education: An exploration of educator perceptions, attitudes and experiences. *Journal of Educational Technology & Society*, *18*(1), 3–12.

Gregory, S., Scutter, S., Jacka, L., McDonald, M., Farley, H., & Newman, C. (2015). Barriers and Enablers to the Use of Virtual Worlds in Higher Education: An Exploration of Educator Perceptions, Attitudes and Experiences. *Journal of Educational Technology & Society*, *18*(1), 3–12.

Griffin, P. H. (2015). *Security for Ambient Assisted Living: Multi-factor Authentication in the Internet of Things*. Paper presented at the IoTAAL Ambient Assisted Living Workshop (IoTAAL), IEEE Globecom 2015 Conference, San Diego, CA.

Groom, D. (2009). *To quote, unquote, and requote- 21st century illiteracy?* Retrieved January 15, 2019, from https://deangroom.wordpress.com/2009/12/21/to-quote-unquote-and-requote-21st-century-illiteracy/

Groth, O., & Nitzberg, M. (2018). *Solomon's Codes: Humanity in a World of Thinking Machines*. New York, NY: Pegasus Books.

Guthrie, K. L., Phelps, K., & Downey, S. (2011). Virtual worlds: A developmental tool or leadership education. *The Journal of Leadership Studies*, *5*(2), 6–13. doi:10.1002/jls.20214

Guyette, R. W., King, C. G., & Piotrowski, C. (2008). Business faculty views of online course cheating: Evidence for a cohort effect. *Organization Development Journal*, *26*(4), 25–31.

Hackett, J. W. (1962). *The profession of arms. The 1962 Lees Knowles lectures given at Trinity College*. Cambridge. Washington, DC: Center of Military History.

Hagobian, T. A., & Phelan, S. (2013). Lifestyle interventions to reduce obesity and diabetes. *American Journal of Lifestyle Medicine*, *7*(2), 84–98. doi:10.1177/1559827612449600

Hale, K. S., & Stanney, K. M. (2015). *Handbook of Virtual Environments: Design, Implementation, and Applications*. Boca Raton, FL: CRC Press.

Hall, K. L., Vogel, A. L., Stipelman, B. A., Stokols, D., Morgan, G., & Gehlert, S. (2012). A four-phase model of transdisciplinary team-based research: Goals, team processes, and strategies. *Translational Behavioral Medicine*, *2*(4), 415–430. doi:10.100713142-012-0167-y PMID:23483588

Hamari, J. (2013). Transforming homo economicus into homo ludens: A field experiment on gamification in a utilitarian peer-to-peer trading service. *Electronic Commerce Research and Applications*, *12*(4), 236–245. doi:10.1016/j.elerap.2013.01.004

Hamilton, B. J. (2011). Creating conversations for learning: School libraries as sites of participatory culture. *School Library Monthly*, *27*(8), 41–43.

Hamilton, E., & Cairns, H. (1961). *Plato*. Princeton University Press.

Han, V. (2017). Are chatbots the future of training? *TD: Talent Development, Learning Technologies*, *71*(9), 42–46.

Harari, Y. N. (2015, July 24). Why humans run the world. *Ted Talks - London*. Retrieved from https://www.youtube.com/watch?v=nzj7Wg4DAbs

Hart, M. (1990). *Drumming on the edge of magic*. San Francisco, CA: Harper.

Haslam, D. W., & James, W. P. T. (2005). Obesity. *Lancet*, *366*(9492), 1197–1209. doi:10.1016/S0140-6736(05)67483-1 PMID:16198769

Hattie, J. (2012). Visible learning for teachers: Maximizing impact on learning. In R. Dufour & C. Reason (Eds.), *Professional Learning Communities at Work and Virtual Collaboration* (p. 3). Bloomington, IN: Solution Tree Press. doi:10.4324/9780203181522

Hayles, N. K. (1999). How we became posthuman: Virtual bodies in cybernetics, literature, and informatics. Chicago: University of Chicago Press.

Heidegger, M. (1964). Basic writings: from Being and Time and The Task of Thinking (D. F. Krell, Trans.). San Francisco, CA: Harper. (Originally published 1927)

Heidegger, M. (1957/2002). *Identity and difference* (J. Stambaugh, Trans.). Chicago, IL: University of Chicago Press.

Heilmann, M., & Maxwell, D. (2016). Securing the Hypergrid. *Hypergrid Business*. Retrieved from: http://www.hypergridbusiness.com/wp-content/uploads/2016/09/Securing-the-Hypergrid-Michael-Heilmann-and-Douglas-Maxwell.pdf

Heim, M. (2005). Heidegger and McLuhan: The computer as component. In G. Genosko (Ed.), *Marshall McLuhan: Critical Evaluations in Cultural Theory* (Vol. 2, pp. 349–361). Routledge.

Heinlein, R. A. (1961). *A stranger in a strange land*. New York, NY: Penguin Random House.

Heinrichs, W. L., Youngblood, P., Harter, P. M., & Dev, P. (2008). Simulation for team training and assessment: Case studies of online training with virtual worlds. *World Journal of Surgery*, *32*(2), 161–170. doi:10.100700268-007-9354-2 PMID:18188640

Heiphetz, A., & Woodill, G. (2010). *Training and Collaboration with Virtual Worlds: How to Create Cost-Saving, Efficient, and Engaging Programs*. New York: McGraw-Hill.

Herlig, K., Taylor-Nelms, L., Bliton, D., & Reyher, T. (2011). *Recommendations for Designing Effective Learning Events in 3D Virtual Worlds*. Paper presented at the Inter-Industry Training Simulation and Training Conference, Orlando, FL.

Hew, K. F., & Cheung, W. S. (2010). *Use of three- dimensional (3-D) immersive virtual worlds in K-12 and higher education settings: A review of the research*. Academic Press.

Heylighen, F. (1994). *Cyberspace.* Retrieved from Principia Cybernetica Web: http://pespmc1.vub.ac.be/cybspace.html

Hill, V. (2013). *Math in 3D a library exhibit and tour.* Retrieved February 19, 2019, from https://youtu.be/DQ6783hYF8E

Hill, V. (2017). *CVL Dickens research project 2017.* Retrieved December 27, 2018, from https://youtu.be/xT-vgR7eXU4

Hill, J. P., & Lynch, M. E. (1983). The intensification of gender-related role expectations during early adolescence. In J. Brooks-Gunn & A. C. Petersen (Eds.), *Girls at puberty* (pp. 201–228). Boston, MA: Springer. doi:10.1007/978-1-4899-0354-9_10

Hill, V. (2015). Digital citizenship through game design in Minecraft. *New Library World, 116*(7/8), 369–382. doi:10.1108/NLW-09-2014-0112

Hill, V. J. (2017). Digital Citizenship in Participatory Culture. In A. Stricker, C. Calongne, B. Truman, & F. Arenas (Eds.), *Integrating an Awareness of Selfhood and Society into Virtual Learning* (pp. 60–73). Hershey, PA: IGI Global. doi:10.4018/978-1-5225-2182-2.ch005

Hill, V. J., & Knutzen, K. B. (2017). Virtual world global collaboration: An educational quest. *Information and Learning Science, 118*(9/10), 547–565. doi:10.1108/ILS-02-2017-0010

Hinduja, S., & Patchin, J. (2009). Bullying beyond the schoolyard. Thousand Oaks, CA: Corwin.

Hodge, D. (2010). Role-playing: Toward a theology of gamers. In C. Detweiler (Ed.), *Halos and avatars: Playing video games with God.* Louisville, KY: Westminster John Knox.

Hoffman, D., & Novak, T. (2009). Flow online: Lessons learned and future prospects. *Journal of Interactive Marketing, 23*(1), 23–34. doi:10.1016/j.intmar.2008.10.003

Hofkirchner, W. (2004). Unity through diversity: dialectics - systems thinking - semiotics. *Trans, Internet Journal for Cultural Sciences, 1*(15), 1728.

Holton, D. L. (2010). *Constructivism + Embodied Cognition = Enactivism: Theoretical and Practical Implications for Conceptual Change.* Paper presented at the American Educational Research Association, Denver, CO. Retrieved from: http://usu.academia.edu/edtechdev/Papers/168218/Constructivism_Embodied_Cognition_Enactivism_Theoretical_and_Practical_Implications_for_Conceptual_Change

Hopkins, J., & Turner, J. (2012). Go mobile: Location-based marketing, apps, mobile optimized, and campaigns, 2D codes, and other mobile strategies to grow your business. In R. Dufour & C. Reason (Eds.), *Professional Learning Communities at Work and Virtual Collaboration* (p. 3). Bloomington, IN: Solution Tree Press.

House, R. J., & Howell, J. A. (1992). Personality and charismatic leadership. *The Leadership Quarterly, 3*(2), 81–108. doi:10.1016/1048-9843(92)90028-E

Hughes, A. M., Gregory, M. E., Joseph, D. L., Sonesh, S. C., Marlow, S. L., Lacerenza, C. N., ... Salas, E. (2016). Saving lives: A meta-analysis of team training in healthcare. *The Journal of Applied Psychology, 101*(9), 1266–1304. doi:10.1037/apl0000120 PMID:27599089

Huizinga, J. (1955). *Homo ludens: A study in the play element in culture.* Boston, MA: Beacon Press.

Hu, Y. (2015). Health communication research in digital age: A systematic review. *Journal of Communication in Healthcare, 8*(4), 260–288. doi:10.1080/17538068.2015.1107308

Ibarra, H. (1999). *Provisional selves: Experimenting with image and identity in professional adaptation.* Boston, MA: Harvard University.

IEEE. (2019). *ICICLE Extended Reality (XR) Working Group*. Retrieved from https://www.ieeeicicle.org/xreality-sig/

Illeris, K. (2014). Transformative Learning re-defined: As changes in elements of the identity. *International Journal of Lifelong Education, 33*(5), 573–586. doi:10.1080/02601370.2014.917128

Illich, I. (1973). *Tools for Conviviality*. London: Marion Boyars.

IMS Global Learning Consortium. (2019). Retrieved from https://www.imsglobal.org/activity/accessibility

Ireland, J. L. (1999). *Provictim attitudes and empathy in relation to bullying behaviour among prisoners*. Academic Press.

ISACA. (2015). *Internet of Things: Risk and Value Considerations (registration required)*. Retrieved from: http://www.isaca.org/knowledge-center/research/researchdeliverables/pages/internet-of-things-risk-and-value-considerations.aspx

Izgiç, F., Akyüz, G., Doğan, O., & Kuğu, N. (2004). Social phobia among university students and its relation to self-esteem and body image. *Canadian Journal of Psychiatry, 49*(9), 630–634. doi:10.1177/070674370404900910 PMID:15503736

Jenkins, M., Browne, T., & Walker, R. (2012). *VLE surveys: A longitudinal perspective between March 2001, March 2003, and March 2005 for higher education in the United Kingdom*. Academic Press.

John Hopkins Medicine Simulation Center. (n.d.). Retrieved from: https://www.hopkinsmedicine.org/simulation_center/training/mannequin_based_simulations/index.html

Johnsen, K., Ahn, S. J., Moore, J., Brown, S., Robertson, T. P., Marable, A., & Basu, A. (2014). Mixed reality virtual pets to reduce childhood obesity. *IEEE Transactions on Visualization and Computer Graphics, 20*(4), 523–530. doi:10.1109/TVCG.2014.33 PMID:24650979

Johnson, L. F., & Levine, A. H. (2008). Virtual worlds: Inherently immersive, highly social learning places. *Theory into Practice, 47*(2), 161–170. doi:10.1080/00405840801992397

Johnson, M. (1989). Personal practical knowledge series: Embodied knowledge. *Curriculum Inquiry, 19*(4), 361–377. doi:10.1080/03626784.1989.11075338

Johnson, M., Cowin, L. S., Wilson, I., & Young, H. (2012). Professional identity and nursing: Contemporary theoretical developments and future research challenges. *International Nursing Review, 59*(4), 562–569. doi:10.1111/j.1466-7657.2012.01013.x PMID:23134142

Johnston, J. D., Massey, A. P., & DeVaneaux, C. A. (2012). Innovation in weight loss programs: A 3-dimensional virtual-world approach. *Journal of Medical Internet Research, 14*(5), e120. doi:10.2196/jmir.2254 PMID:22995535

Joint Chiefs of Staff. (2016). Retrieved from http://www.jcs.mil/Portals/36/Documents/Publications/aprofessionofarms.pdf

Jones, I., Blankenship, D., & Hollier, G. (2014). Am I cheating? An analysis of online student perceptions of their behaviors and attitudes. *Proceedings of ASBBS, 20*(1).

Kanter, B. (2006, October 19). The birth of a field: Digital media and learning [Weblog post]. Retrieved from https://beth.typepad.com/beths_blog/2006/10/the_birth_of_a_.html

Karwowski, W., Ahram, T., & Amaba, B. (2013). A system-of-systems engineering approach to leadership and innovation: Sustainable STEM education and workforce development through the Smart Cities initiative. In *QScience Proceedings (World Congress on Engineering Education 2013)* (p. 12). Academic Press.

Katsikogiannis, G., Mitropoulos, S., & Douligeris, C. (2016, December). An Identity and Access Management approach for SOA. In *Signal Processing and Information Technology (ISSPIT), 2016 IEEE International Symposium on* (pp. 126-131). IEEE. 10.1109/ISSPIT.2016.7886021

Kellerman, A. (2014). The satisfaction of human needs in physical and virtual spaces. *The Professional Geographer*, *66*(4), 538–546. doi:10.1080/00330124.2013.848760

Kelly, R. (2016). 9 Ed Tech Trends to Watch in 2016. *Campus Technology*. Retrieved from: https://campustechnology.com/Articles/2016/01/13/9-Ed-Tech-Trends-to-Watch-in-2016.aspx?p=1

Kiehl, E. M. (2008). Using an ethical decision-making model to determine consequences for student plagiarism. *Journal of Nursing Education, 45*, 199-203.

Killen, J. D., Taylor, C. B., Hayward, C., Haydel, K. F., Wilson, D. M., Hammer, L., ... Strachowski, D. (1996). Weight concerns influence the development of eating disorders: A 4-year prospective study. *Journal of Consulting and Clinical Psychology*, *64*(5), 936–940. doi:10.1037/0022-006X.64.5.936 PMID:8916622

Kim, D. S., & Kim, H. S. (2009). Body-image dissatisfaction as a predictor of suicidal ideation among Korean boys and girls in different stages of adolescence: A two-year longitudinal study. *The Journal of Adolescent Health*, *45*(1), 47–54. doi:10.1016/j.jadohealth.2008.11.017 PMID:19541249

Kimm, S. Y., Glynn, N. W., Kriska, A. M., Barton, B. A., Kronsberg, S. S., Daniels, S. R., ... Liu, K. (2002). Decline in physical activity in black girls and white girls during adolescence. *The New England Journal of Medicine*, *347*(10), 709–715. doi:10.1056/NEJMoa003277 PMID:12213941

Kim, Y., & Baylor, A. L. (2006). A social-cognitive framework for pedagogical agents as learning companions. *Educational Technology Research and Development*, *54*(6), 569–596. doi:10.100711423-006-0637-3

Kitchenham, A. (2011). *Blended learning across disciplines: Models for implementation*. Hershey, PA: Information Science Reference.

Klein, G. (2009). *Streetlights and shadows: The keys to adaptive decision making*. Cambridge, MA: MIT Press. doi:10.7551/mitpress/8369.001.0001

Klein, J. T. (2008). Evaluation of interdisciplinary and transdisciplinary research: A literature review. *American Journal of Preventive Medicine*, *35*(2Supplement), S116–S123. doi:10.1016/j.amepre.2008.05.010 PMID:18619391

Klopfer, E. (2008). *Augmented learning*. Cambridge, MA: MIT Press.

Knefelkamp, L. L. (1990). *The development of the multi-cultural self: Integrating theories of intellectual, intercultural and identity development*. Portland, OR: Summer Institute for Intercultural Communication.

Knowles, M. S., Holton, E. F. III, & Swanson, R. A. (2012). *The adult learner*. Routledge. doi:10.4324/9780080964249

Knutzen, K. B., & Kennedy, D. M. (2012). Designing the self: The transformation of the relational self-concept through social encounters in a virtual immersive environment. *Interactive Learning Environments*, *20*(3), 271–292. doi:10.1080/10494820.2011.641680

Kobus, D.A., Brown, C.M., Morrison, J.G., Kollmorgen, G., Cornwall, R. (2005). *DARPA improving warfighter information intake under stress–augmented cognition phase II: The concept validation experiment (CVE)*. DARPA/IPTO technical report submitted to CDR Dylan Schmorrow.

Kohlberg, L. (1976). Moral stages and moralization: The cognitive-developmental approach. In T. Lickona (Ed.), *Moral Development and Behavior: Theory, Research and Social Issues*. Holt, Rinehart and Winston.

Kohlberg, L. (1981). Essays on moral development: Vol. I. *The philosophy of moral development*. San Francisco, CA: Harper & Row.

Kohler, T., Matzler, K., & Fuller, J. (2009). Avatar-based innovation: Using virtual worlds for real-world innovation. *Technovation, 29*, 395-407.

Korolov, M. (2016). *November a solid month for opensim growth.* Retrieved from http://www.hypergridbusiness.com/2016/11/november-a-solid-month-for-opensim-growth/

Kroger, J. (2002). Identity processes and contents through the years of late adulthood. *Identity, 2*(1), 81–99. doi:10.1207/S1532706XID0201_05

Kücklich, J. (2018). Precarious playbour: Modders and the digital games industry. *Fibreculture Journal.* Retrieved February 17, 2019 from http://journal.fibreculture.org/issue5/kucklich_print.html

Kurtzberg, T. R. (2014). *Virtual Teams: Mastering Communication and Collaboration in the Digital Age.* Santa Barbara, CA: ABC-CLIO, LLC.

KyotoPrize. (2012). *Dr. Charles Margrave Taylor* [Video file]. Retrieved from: https://youtu.be/ayi8nlZQkDo

Kyoung Joo, Y., & Kim, K. (2017). When You Exercise Your Avatar in a Virtual Game: The Role of Avatars' Body Shape and Behavior in Users' Health Behavior. *Interacting with Computers, 29*(3), 455–466. doi:10.1093/iwc/iwx003

Lacerenza, C. N., Zajac, S., Savage, N., & Salas, E. (2015). Team training for global virtual teams: Strategies for success. In *Leading Global Teams* (pp. 91–121). Springer New York. doi:10.1007/978-1-4939-2050-1_5

Ladkin, D., & Taylor, S. S. (2010). Enacting the 'true self': Towards a theory of embodied authentic leadership. *The Leadership Quarterly, 21*(1), 64–74. doi:10.1016/j.leaqua.2009.10.005

Langer, A. (2005). Responsive organizational dynamism: Managing technology using reflective practice. *Reflective Practice*, 2.

Lankau, M. J., & Scandura, T. A. (2002). An investigation of personal learning in mentoring relationships: Content, antecedents, and consequences. *Academy of Management Journal, 45*(4), 779–790.

Latour, B. (1992). Where are the missing masses: The sociology of a few mundane artifacts. In W. E. Bijker & J. Law (Eds.), *Shaping technology/building society: Studies in Sociotechnical Change* (pp. 225–258). Cambridge, MA: MIT Press.

Lave, J., & Wenger, E. (1991). *Situated learning: Legitimate peripheral participation.* New York, NY: Cambridge University Press. doi:10.1017/CBO9780511815355

Lemheney, A., Bond, W., Padon, J., LeClair, M., Miller, J., & Susko, M. (2016). Developing virtual reality simulations for office-based medical emergencies. *Journal of Virtual Worlds Research, 9*(1), 1–18.

Lencioni, P. (2000). *The four obsessions of an extraordinary executive.* San Francisco, CA: Jossey-Bass.

Leonard, M., Graham, S., & Bonacum, D. (2004). The human factor: The critical importance of effective teamwork and communication in providing safe care. *Quality & Safety in Health Care, 13*(suppl 1), i85–i90. doi:10.1136/qshc.2004.010033 PMID:15465961

LeRouge, C., Dickhut, K., Lisetti, C., Sangameswaran, S., & Malasanos, T. (2015). Engaging adolescents in a computer-based weight management program: Avatars and virtual coaches could help. *Journal of the American Medical Informatics Association, 23*(1), 19–28. doi:10.1093/jamia/ocv078 PMID:26159466

Lester, J. (2014, July 29). Hypergrid safari -- The evolution of exploration across the interconnected Metaverse [Weblog post]. Retrieved from https://becunningandfulloftricks.com/2014/07/29/hypergrid-safari-the-evolution-of-exploration-across-the-interconnected-metaverse/

Levine, A. (2008). The NMC campus. *EDUCAUSE Review*, *43*(5).

Lewis, C. (2002). *On stories: And other essays on literature*. San Diego, CA: Harvest Books.

Lewis, R. (2015). Virtual reality: Soon to become mainstream in libraries? (cover story). *Information Today*, *32*(4), 1–29.

Lin, C., He, D., Huang, X., Khan, M. K., & Choo, K. K. R. (2018). A New Transitively Closed Undirected Graph Authentication Scheme for Blockchain-Based Identity Management Systems. *IEEE Access: Practical Innovations, Open Solutions*, *6*, 28203–28212. doi:10.1109/ACCESS.2018.2837650

Linden Lab. (2017). Retrieved from https://www.lindenlab.com

Li, Q. B. I., Clark, B., & Winchester, I. (2010). Instructional design and technology grounded in enactivism: A paradigm shift? *British Journal of Educational Technology*, *41*(3), 403–419. doi:10.1111/j.1467-8535.2009.00954.x

Lofton, J. (2015). Blogging with students: A vehicle for writing, digital citizenship, and more. *School Librarian's Workshop*, *35*(5), 13-15.

Loke, S. (2015). How do virtual world experiences bring about learning? A critical review of theories. *Australasian Journal of Educational Technology*, *31*(1), 112–122. doi:10.14742/ajet.2532

Lombard, M., & Ditton, T. (1997). At the heart of it all: The concept of presence. *Journal of Computer-Mediated Communication*, *3*. doi:10.1111/j.1083-6101.1997.tb00072.x

Lopez, S. J. (2013). *Making hope happen: Create the future you want for yourself and others*. Simon and Schuster.

Los Angeles Gang Intervention. (1985). Retrieved from www.edutopia.org/no-gangs-here- stage

Lotrean, L. M., Mocean, F., Laza, V., & Poledna, S. (2009). The Role of Information Technology in Health Education: Strengths and Weaknesses. In S. Vlad, R. V. Ciupa, & A. I. Nicu (Eds.), *International Conference on Advancements of Medicine and Health Care through Technology* (*Vol. 26*, pp. 73–76). Berlin: Springer Berlin Heidelberg. 10.1007/978-3-642-04292-8_16

Lotrecchiano, G. R. (2011). Complexity leadership in transdisciplinary (TD) learning environments: A knowledge feedback loop. *FormaMente: Rivista internazionale di ricerca sul futuro digitale*, (1), 103.

Lou, D. (2014). *Sedentary Behaviors and Youth: Current Trends and the Impact on Health*. San Diego, CA: Active Living Research. doi:10.13140/RG.2.1.4294.8884

Lubans, D. R., Morgan, P. J., Dewar, D., Collins, C. E., Plotnikoff, R. C., Okely, A. D., ... Callister, R. (2010). The Nutrition and Enjoyable Activity for Teen Girls (NEAT girls) randomized controlled trial for adolescent girls from disadvantaged secondary schools: Rationale, study protocol, and baseline results. *BMC Public Health*, *10*(1), 652. doi:10.1186/1471-2458-10-652 PMID:21029467

Mackey, T., & Jacobson, T. (2011). Reframing Information Literacy as a Metaliteracy. *C&RL*, *72*(1), 62–78. doi:10.5860/crl-76r1

Madsen, P. (2005). *Liberty Alliance Project White Paper: Liberty ID-WSF People Service- federated social identity*. Retrieved December 27, 2018, from http://www.projectliberty.org/liberty/content/download/387/2720/file/Liberty_Federated_Social_Identity.pdf

Maguire, M. B. R., Bremner, M. N., Bennett, D. N., & VanBrackle, L. (2015). Evaluation of TeamSTEPPS integration across a curriculum regarding team attitudes: A longitudinal study. *Journal of Nursing Education and Practice*, *5*(7), 131–138. doi:10.5430/jnep.v5n7p131

Mahajan, A. (2009). *Comparing self and others' perceptions of adolescent girls' body size using figural stimuli and 3d body scans*. Retrieved from WorldCat.

Maher, C. A., Mire, E., Harrington, D. M., Staiano, A. E., & Katzmarzyk, P. T. (2013). The independent and combined associations of physical activity and sedentary behavior with obesity in adults: NHANES 2003-06. *Obesity (Silver Spring, Md.)*, *21*(12), E730–E737. doi:10.1002/oby.20430 PMID:23512825

Mälkki, K. (2010). Building on Mezirows theory of transformative learning: Theorizing the challenges to reflection. *Journal of Transformative Education*, *8*(1), 42–62. doi:10.1177/1541344611403315

Malle, B. (2014). *Can robots be trusted to know right from wrong? Tufts University, Brown University, and Rensselaer Polytechnic Institute, and the U.S. Navy explore technology that would help develop robots capable of making moral decisions*. Retrieved from www.kurtzweilai.net

Mallow, P. J., Pandya, B., Horblyuk, R., & Kaplan, H. S. (2013). Prevalence and cost of hospital medical errors in the general and elderly United States populations. *Journal of Medical Economics*, *16*(12), 1367–1378. doi:10.3111/13696998.2013.848210 PMID:24063367

Maraj, C., Lackey, S., Badillo-Urquiola, K., Ogreten, S., & Maxwell, D. (2015). Empirically derived recommendations for training novices using virtual worlds. In *Interservice*. Orlando, FL: Industry Training, Simulation, and Education Conference.

Marcia, J. E. (1966). Development and validation of ego-identity status. *Journal of Personality and Social Psychology*, *3*(5), 551–558. doi:10.1037/h0023281 PMID:5939604

Mark, C. L. (2014). *Growth and decline of Second Life as an educational platform* (Doctoral dissertation). Available from ProQuest Dissertations & Theses Global. (Order No. 3584527)

Markham, A. N. (1998). *Life online: Researching real experience in virtual space* (Vol. 6). Rowman Altamira.

Markoff, J. (2015). *Machines of Loving Grace: The Quest for Common Ground Between Humans and Robots*. New York: Ecco/HarperCollins Publishers. Retrieved 2018 from http://www-robotics.usc.edu/~maja/

Maslow, A. H. (1943). A Theory of Human Motivation. *Psychological Review*, *50*(4), 370–396. doi:10.1037/h0054346

Mason, H. (2007). *Script Me!* Retrieved from http://3greeneggs.com/autoscript/

Mattis, P. (2010). Interactive immersive learning in higher education. *Creative Nursing*, *16*(3), 106–109. doi:10.1891/1078-4535.16.3.106 PMID:20879617

Maxwell, D. B. (2015). *Gauging Training Effectiveness of Virtual Environment Simulation Based Applications for an Infantry Soldier Training Task* (Doctoral dissertation). University of Central Florida, Orlando, FL.

Maxwell, D., & McLennan, K. (2012). Case study: leveraging government and academic partnerships in MOSES (Military Open Simulator [Virtual World] Enterprise Strategy). In *Proceedings of World Conference on Educational Multimedia, Hypermedia and Telecommunications* (pp. 1604-1616). Academic Press.

Maxwell, D. B. (2016). Application of Virtual Environments for Infantry Soldier Skills Training: We are Doing it Wrong. In *International Conference on Virtual, Augmented and Mixed Reality* (pp. 424-432). Springer International Publishing.

Mazzone, L. A. L., & Aguiar, S. (2017, December 30). *U.S. Navy Virtual World Schoolhouse Case Study*. Paper presented at the Interservice Industry Training Simulation and Education Conference, Orlando, FL.

Mazzone, L. A. L., & Aguiar, S. (2017a, December 30). *Rapid Prototyping Innovative Virtual Worlds that Include the WOW Factor*. Paper presented at the Interservice Industry Training Simulation and Education Conference, Orlando, FL.

McAuley, E., & Blissmer, B. (2000). Self-efficacy determinants and consequences of physical activity. *Exercise Sports Science Review, 28*(2), 85-88. Retrieved from: https://journals.lww.com/acsm-essr/pages/default.aspx

McChrystal, S. (2015). *Team of teams: New rules of engagement for a complex world.* New York, NY: Penguin Random House.

McClamrock, R. (1995). *Existential cognition: Computational minds in the world.* Chicago: The University of Chicago Press.

McGonigal, J. (2011). *Reality is broken: Why games make us better and how they can change the world.* London: Penguin Books.

McGregor, S. L. T. (2017). Transdisciplinary pedagogy in higher education: Transdisciplinary learning, learning cycles, and habits of mind. In *Transdisciplinary Higher Education: A Theoretical Basis Revealed in Practice* (pp. 3–14). London, UK: Springer. doi:10.1007/978-3-319-56185-1_1

McInerny, D. (2004). *Being logical: A guide to good thinking.* Random House.

McLeod, S. A. (2016). *Maslow's hierarchy of needs.* Retrieved from www.simplypsychology.org/maslow.html

McLuhan, M. (1964). *Understanding media: The extensions of man.* Cambridge, MA: MIT Press.

Mead, G. H. (1934). *Mind, self, and society.* Chicago, IL: Chicago University Press.

Mehling, W. E., Gopisetty, V., Daubenmier, J., Price, C. J., Hecht, F. M., & Stewart, A. (2009). Body awareness: Construct and self-report measures. *PLoS One, 4*(5), e5614. doi:10.1371/journal.pone.0005614 PMID:19440300

Méndez, F. (2015). Transdiscipline and research in health: Science, society and decision making. *Colombia Médica (Cali, Colombia), 46*(3), 128–134. Retrieved from http://www.scielo.org.co/pdf/cm/v46n3/v46n3a07.pdf PMID:26600628

Merleau-Ponty, M. (1962). *Phenomenology of perception.* London: Routledge and Kegan Paul.

Merrill, T. (2008). Masters and possessors of nature. *New Atlantis (Washington, D.C.), 19*(1), 91–107.

Metz, C. (1999). AAA protocols: Authentication, authorization, and accounting for the Internet. *IEEE Internet Computing, 3*(6), 75–79. doi:10.1109/4236.807015

Meyer, J. (2000). Reflections on education as transcendence. In *Reconstructing the common good in education: Coping with intractable American dilemmas.* Stanford, CA: Stanford University Press.

Mezirow, J. (1991). *Transformative dimensions of adult learning.* ERIC.

Mezirow, J. (1997). Transformative learning: Theory to practice. *New Directions for Adult and Continuing Education, 1997*(74), 5–12. doi:10.1002/ace.7401

Mihai, I. C., & Giurea, L. (2016). Management of eLearning platforms security. In *The International Scientific Conference eLearning and Software for Education* (*Vol. 1*, p. 422). "Carol I" National Defence University.

Mikula, T., & Jacobsen, R. H. (2018, August). Identity and Access Management with Blockchain in Electronic Healthcare Records. In *2018 21st Euromicro Conference on Digital System Design (DSD)* (pp. 699-706). IEEE. 10.1109/DSD.2018.00008

Miller, A., & Young-Jones, A. D. (2012). *Academic integrity: Online classes compared to face-to-face classes.* Paper presented at the meeting of the Southwestern Psychological Association, Oklahoma City, OK.

Miller, C. Z. (2016). Towards Transdisciplinarity: Liminality and the Transitions Inherent in Pluridisciplinary Collaborative Work. *Journal of Business Anthropology*, *1*(1), 35–57. doi:10.22439/jba.v1i1.4959

Mintzberg, H. (1994). *The rise and fall of strategic planning*. New York, NY: Simon and Schuster.

Mitchell, J. A., Pate, R. R., Beets, M. W., & Nader, P. R. (2013). Time spent in sedentary behavior and changes in childhood BMI: A longitudinal study from ages 9 to 15 years. *International Journal of Obesity*, *37*(1), 54–60. doi:10.1038/ijo.2012.41 PMID:22430304

Mitchell, M. (2009). *Complexity: A guided tour*. New York, NY: Oxford University Press.

Moghaddam, F. F., Wieder, P., & Yahyapour, R. (2017, November). A policy-based identity management schema for managing accesses in clouds. In *Network of the Future (NOF), 2017 8th International Conference on the* (pp. 91-98). IEEE. 10.1109/NOF.2017.8251226

Montuori, A. (2013). Complexity and Transdisciplinarity: Reflections on Theory and Practice. *World Futures*, *69*(4-6), 200–230. doi:10.1080/02604027.2013.803349

Moore, S. (1974). *The Stanislavski System*. New York: The Viking Press.

Moor, J. (2006). If Aristotle were a computing professional. In R. Baird, R. Ramsower, & S. Rosenbaum (Eds.), *Cyberethics: Social and Moral Issues in the Computing Age*. New York, NY: Prometheus Books.

Moreillion, J. (2015). #schoollibrarians Tweet for Professional Development: A Netnographic Case Study of #txlchat. *School Libraries Worldwide*, *21*(2), 127–137.

Moreillion, J. (2016). Building your personal learning network (PLN): 21st century school librarians seek self-regulatory professional development online. *Knowledge Quest*, *44*(3), 64–69.

Morgado, L., Paredes, H., Fonseca, B., Martins, P., Antunes, R., Moreira, L., . . . Santos, A. (2016). Requirements for the use of virtual worlds in corporate training: perspectives from the post-mortem of a corporate e-learning provider approach of Second Life and OpenSimulator. In *iLRN 2016: Immersive Learning Research Network Conference. Workshop, Short Paper and Poster Proceedings from the Second Immersive Learning Research Network Conference* (pp. 18-29). Technischen Universität Graz.

Morgan, P. (2009). Geothermal energy on Mars. In V. Badescu (Ed.), *Mars: Prospective energy and material resources* (pp. 331–349). Berlin, Germany: Springer-Verlag.

Morie, J. F., & Chance, E. (2011). Extending the reach of health care for obesity and diabetes using virtual worlds. *Journal of Diabetes Science and Technology*, *5*(2), 272–276. doi:10.1177/193229681100500211 PMID:21527093

Mueller, J., Hutter, K., Fueller, J., & Matzler, K. (2010). Virtual worlds as knowledge management platform – a practice-perspective. *Information Systems Journal*, *21*(6), 479–501. doi:10.1111/j.1365-2575.2010.00366.x

MWC19: Mobile World Congress. (2019, February). Retrieved from https://www.mwcbarcelona.com/

Naik, N., & Jenkins, P. (2016, March). A secure mobile cloud identity: Criteria for effective identity and access management standards. In *Mobile Cloud Computing, Services, and Engineering (MobileCloud), 2016 4th IEEE International Conference on* (pp. 89-90). IEEE.

Naik, N., & Jenkins, P. (2017, May). Securing digital identities in the cloud by selecting apposite federated identity management from saml, oauth and openid connect. In *Research Challenges in Information Science (RCIS), 2017 11th International Conference on* (pp. 163-174). IEEE. 10.1109/RCIS.2017.7956534

Napolitano, M. A., Hayes, S., Russo, G., Muresu, D., Giordano, A., & Foster, G. D. (2013). Using avatars to model weight loss behaviors: Participant attitudes and technology development. *Journal of Diabetes Science and Technology*, *7*(4), 1057–1065. doi:10.1177/193229681300700430 PMID:23911189

National Research Council. (1999). *Being fluent with information technology*. Washington, DC: National Academies Press.

Nelson, B. C., & Ketelhut, D. J. (2007). *Scientific inquiry in educational multi- user virtual environments*. Academic Press.

Nersessian, N. J. (2002). The cognitive basis of model-based reasoning in science. In P. Carruthers, S. Stich, & M. Siegal (Eds.), The cognitive basis of science (pp. 133-153). Cambridge, UK: Cambridge University Press.

Nersessian, N. J. (1999). Model-based reasoning in conceptual change. In L. Magnani, N. J. Nersessian, & P. Thagard (Eds.), *Model-Based Reasoning in Scientific Discovery*. Kluwer Academic/Plenum Publishers.

Nersessian, N. J. (2007). Mental modeling in conceptual change. In S. Vosniadou (Ed.), *Handbook of Conceptual Change*. Mahwah, NJ: Erlbaum.

Neumark-Sztainer, D. (2005). Preventing the broad spectrum of weight-related problems: Working with parents to help teens achieve a healthy weight and a positive body image. *Journal of Nutrition Education and Behavior*, *37*, S133–S139. doi:10.1016/S1499-4046(06)60214-5 PMID:16246282

Neumark-Sztainer, D., Story, M., Hannan, P. J., & Rex, J. (2003). New Moves: A school based obesity prevention program for adolescent girls. *Preventive Medicine*, *37*(1), 41–51. doi:10.1016/S0091-7435(03)00057-4 PMID:12799128

Newell, A., & Simon, H. A. (1963). GPS a program that simulates human thought. In E. Feigenbaum & J. Feldman (Eds.), *Computers and thought* (pp. 279–297). New York: McGraw Hill.

Newell, A., & Simon, H. A. (1972). *Human problem solving*. Englewood Cliffs, NJ: Prentice-Hall.

Nicolescu, B. (1997). *The Transdisciplinary Evolution of the University Condition for Sustainable Development. Presentation to the International Congress "Universities' Responsibilities to Society*. Bangkok, Thailand: International Association of Universities, Chulalongkorn University. Retrieved from http://ciret-transdisciplinarity.org/bulletin/b12c8.php

Nicolescu, B. (2002). *Manifesto of transdisciplinarity*. State University of New York Press.

Nicolescu, B. (2014). *From Modernity to Cosmodernity: Science, Culture, and Spirituality*. SUNY Press.

Nicolescu, B. (Ed.). (2008). *Transdisciplinarity: Theory and practice*. Cresskill, NJ: Hampton Press.

Niemi, P. (1997). Medical students professional identity: Self-reflection during the preclinical years. *Medical Education*, *31*(6), 408–415. doi:10.1046/j.1365-2923.1997.00697.x PMID:9463642

NMC. (2005, December). Symposium on Games in Education. *Learning Times*.

NMC. (2006). *Symposium on digital media and learning*. MacArthur Foundation.

Nonprofit Commons in Second Life. (2019). Retrieved from http://www.nonprofitcommons.org/

Nonprofit Commons. (2007, January 30). Welcome to the NPSL blog! [Weblog post]. Retrieved from http://nonprofitcommons.org/node?page=97

O'Connor, F. (1970). *Mystery and manners: Occasional prose*. Farrar, Straus and Giroux.

Oelofsen, N. (2012). Developing practical reflective skills (1/2): Personal learning. *British Journal of Healthcare Assistants*, *6*(6), 294–297. doi:10.12968/bjha.2012.6.6.294

Ogden, C. L., Carroll, M. D., Kit, B. K., & Flegal, K. M. (2014). Prevalence of childhood and adult obesity in the United States, 2011-2012. *Journal of the American Medical Association, 311*(8), 806–814. doi:10.1001/jama.2014.732 PMID:24570244

Oh, C. S., Bailenson, J. N., & Welch, G. F. (2018). A systematic review of social presence: Definition, antecedents, and implications. *Frontiers in Robotics and AI, 5*(114), 1–25.

Ohler, J. (2012). Digital Citizenship Means Character Education for the Digital Age. *Education Digest Readings Condensed for Quick Review, 77*(8), 14–17.

Oldenburg, R. (2002). *Celebrating the third place: Inspiring stories about the "great good places" at the heart of our communities.* New York: Marlow & Company.

Olvera, N., Kellam, S. F., Menefee, K., Lee, J., & Smith, D. W. (2010). Physical activity in Latino children: Research and its implications. *Journal of Applied Research on Children: Informing Policy for Children at Risk, 1*(1), 3. Retrieved from https://digitalcommons.library.tmc.edu/childrenatrisk/

Omohundro, S. (2014). Autonomous technology and the greater human good. *Journal of Experimental & Theoretical Artificial Intelligence, 26*(3), 303–315. doi:10.1080/0952813X.2014.895111

Open Eye Pictures. (2008). *Under Our Skin Trailer.* Retrieved 2018 from https://www.youtube.com/watch?v=sxWgS0XLVqw

OpenSimulator. (2016, October 27). *OpenSimulator* [Software]. Retrieved from http://opensimulator.org/

OpenSimulator. (2017). Retrieved from http://opensimulator.org

Osinga, F. (2007). *Science, strategy, and war: The strategic theory of John Boyd.* New York, NY: Routledge.

Othman, A., & Callahan, J. (2018, July). The Horcrux protocol: a method for decentralized biometric-based self-sovereign identity. In *2018 International Joint Conference on Neural Networks (IJCNN)* (pp. 1-7). IEEE. 10.1109/IJCNN.2018.8489316

Oyserman, D., Elmore, K., & Smith, G. (2012). Self, Self-Concept, and Identity. In M. R. Leary & J. P. Tangney (Eds.), *Handbook of Self and Identity* (pp. 69–104). New York, NY: The Guilford Press.

Page, R. L. (2000). Brief history of flight simulation. *SimTecT 2000 Proceedings*, 11-17.

Parker, B., & Myrick, F. (2010). Transformative learning as a context for human patient simulation. *The Journal of Nursing Education, 49*(6), 326–332. doi:10.3928/01484834-20100224-02 PMID:20210271

Park, H., & Seo, S. (2013). Effects of collaborative activities on group identity in virtual world. *Interactive Learning Environments, 21*(6), 516–527. doi:10.1080/10494820.2011.604037

Pate, R. R., O'Neill, J. R., & Lobelo, F. (2008). The evolving definition of "sedentary.". *Exercise and Sport Sciences Reviews, 36*(4), 173–178. doi:10.1097/JES.0b013e3181877d1a PMID:18815485

Patri, K. (2008). Deviances in the virtual reality or the character-altering power of virtual communities. *European Journal of Crime Criminal Law and Criminal Justice, 16*(3), 325–343. doi:10.1163/157181708X333373

Peachey, A., & Childs, M. (2011). Virtual worlds and identity. In *Reinventing Ourselves: Contemporary Concepts of Identity in Virtual Worlds* (pp. 1–12). London, UK: Springer-Verlag. doi:10.1007/978-0-85729-361-9_1

Pellicer, S., Santa, G., Bleda, A. L., Maestre, R., Jara, A. J., & Gomez Skarmeta, A. (2013, July). A global perspective of smart cities: a survey. In *Innovative Mobile and Internet Services in Ubiquitous Computing (IMIS), 2013 Seventh International Conference on* (pp. 439-444). IEEE. 10.1109/IMIS.2013.79

Peraković, D., Periša, M., & Prcić, A. B. (2015). Possibilities of Applying ICT to Improve Safe Movement of Blind and Visually Impaired Persons. In *Cutting Edge Research in Technologies*. Intech. doi:10.5772/61080

Peris, R., Gimeno, M. A., Ortet, G., Carrero, V., Sanchiz, M., & Ibanez, I. (2002). Online chat rooms: Virtual spaces of interaction for socially oriented people. *Cyberpsychology & Behavior*, *5*(1), 43–51. doi:10.1089/109493102753685872 PMID:11990974

Perlstein, D. (2000). There is no escape…from the ogre of indoctrination: George Counts and the civic dilemmas of democratic educators. In *Reconstructing the common good in education: Coping with intractable American dilemmas*. Stanford, CA: Stanford University Press.

Perrig, W., & Kintsch, W. (1985). Propositional and situational representations of text. *Journal of Memory and Language*, (24): 503–518.

Perry, W. G. (1999). *Forms of ethical and intellectual development in the college years: A scheme*. San Francisco, CA: Jossey-Bass, Inc.

Peterson, C., & Seligman, M. E. P. (2004). *Character strengths and virtues: A handbook and classification.* Washington, DC: American Psychological Association.

Peterson, C., & Seligman, M. E. P. (2004). *Character Strengths and Virtues:Handbook and Classification.* New York: Oxford University Press.

Pfeffer, J. (2015). *Leadership BS: Fixing workplaces and careers one truth at a time*. New York: Harper Business.

Piaget, J. (1950). *The psychology of intelligence*. New York, NY: Routledge and Kegan Paul.

Pineau, J. (2018). *The Reproducibility Problem: AI Agents should be trained in more realistic environments.* Retrieved from https://futureoflife.org/2018/12/05/neurips-2018/

Plemmons, A. (2014). *Expect the Miraculous*. Retrieved March 6, 2016, from http://expectmiraculous.com/2014/05/08/4th-grade-created-an-augmented-reality-wax-museum-using-layar-and-multiple-digital-tools/

Pohl, C., & Hadorn, G. H. (2008). Methodological challenges of transdisciplinary research. *Nature Sciences Sociétés*, *16*(2), 111–121. doi:10.1051/nss:2008035

Poirier, P., & Eckel, R. H. (2002). Obesity and cardiovascular disease. *Current Atherosclerosis Report, 4*(6), 448–453. Retrieved from https://link.springer.com/journal/11883

Poletti, A., & Rak, J. (2014). *Identity technologies: Constructing the self online*. University of Wisconsin Press.

Pratt, M. G., Rockmann, K. W., & Kaufmann, J. B. (2006). Constructing professional identity: The role of work and identity learning cycles in the customization of identity among medical residents. *Academy of Management Journal*, *49*(2), 235–262. doi:10.5465/amj.2006.20786060

Prensky, M. (2001). Digital natives, digital immigrants part 1. *On the Horizon*, *9*(5), 1–6. doi:10.1108/10748120110424816

Privacy Technical Assistance Center (PTAC). (2014). *Protecting Student Privacy While Using Online Educational Services: Requirements and Best Practices*. Retrieved from https://nces.ed.gov/programs/PTAC/

Proulx, M. J., Todorov, O. S., Aiken, A. T., & de Sousa, A. A. (2016). Where am I? Who am I? The relation between spatial cognition, social cognition and individual differences in the built environment. *Frontiers in Psychology*, *7*. Retrieved from http://www.ncbi.nlm.nih.gov/pmc/articles/PMC4749931/

Puentedura, R. R. (2006). *Game theory revisited: Third places and the new web* [Podcast]. Retrieved from http://hippasus.com/resources/thirdplace/

Pulgarón, E. R. (2013). Childhood obesity: A review of increased risk for physical and psychological comorbidities. *Clinical Therapeutics*, *35*(1), A18–A32. doi:10.1016/j.clinthera.2012.12.014 PMID:23328273

Quero, J. M., Perdigones, F., & Aracil, C. (2018). Microfabrication technologies used for creating smart devices for industrial applications. In Smart Sensors and MEMs (2nd ed.; pp. 291-311). Academic Press. doi:10.1016/B978-0-08-102055-5.00011-5

Raju, S., Boddepalli, S., Gampa, S., Yan, Q., & Deogun, J. S. (2017, May). Identity management using blockchain for cognitive cellular networks. In *Communications (ICC), 2017 IEEE International Conference on* (pp. 1-6). IEEE. 10.1109/ICC.2017.7996830

Rambusch, J., & Ziemke, T. (2005). The role of embodiment in situated learning. In *Proceedings of the 27th annual conference of the Cognitive Science Society* (pp. 1803-1808). Mahwah, NJ: Erlbaum.

Randhavane, T., Bera, A., & Manocha, D. (2017). F2F crowds: Planning agent movements to enable face-to-face interactions. *Presence (Cambridge, Mass.)*, *26*(2), 228–246. doi:10.1162/PRES_a_00294

Ratan, R. A. (2011). *Self-presence: Body, emotion, and identity extension into the virtual self* (Ph.D. 3477991). University of Southern California. Retrieved from https://login.ctu.idm/oclc.org/?url=http://search.proquest.com/docview/901452620?accountid=26967

Raybourn, E. M. (2018). Harnessing Transmedia Learning: How to Optimize Your Productivity with Learning Science, Media, and Technology. *Interservice/Industry Training, Simulation and Education Conference Proceedings*. doi: 10.6084/m9.figshare.7149383

Raybourn, E. M. (2014). A new paradigm for serious games: Transmedia learning for more effective training and education. *Journal of Computational Science*, *5*(3), 471–481. doi:10.1016/j.jocs.2013.08.005

Reeves, L. M., Schmorrow, D. D., & Stanney, K. M. (2007). Augmented cognition and cognitive state assessment technology – near-term, mid-term, and long-term research objectives. In D. D. Schmorrow & L. M. Reeves (Eds.), Lecture Notes in Computer Science: Vol. 4565. *Foundations of Augmented Cognition. FAC 2007*. Berlin: Springer.

Reeves, S., Zwarenstein, M., Goldman, J., Barr, H., Freeth, D., Hammick, M., & Koppel, I. (2008). Interprofessional education: Effects on professional practice and health care outcomes. *Cochrane Database of Systematic Reviews*, *1*(1). doi:10.1002/14651858.CD002213.pub2 PMID:18254002

Reid, D. (1995). *Enactivism*. Retrieved November 20, 2006, from http://plato.acadiau.ca/ courses/educ/reid/enactivism/EnactivismDef.html

Reigeluth, C. M., Aslan, S., Chen, Z., Dutta, P., Huh, Y., Lee, D., ... Watson, S. L. (2015). Personalized integrated educational system: Technology functions for the Learner-centered paradigm of education. *Journal of Educational Computing Research*, *53*(3), 459–496. doi:10.1177/0735633115603998

Reiners, T., Gregory, S., & Knox, V. (2016). Virtual Bots as seen in Gregory, S., Lee, M. J., Dalgarno, B., & Tynan, B. (Eds.). (2016). Learning in Virtual Worlds: Research and Applications. Athabasca University Press.

Resnick, M. (1996, July). Distributed constructionism. In *Proceedings of the International Conference on the Learning Sciences Association for the Advancement of Computing in Education*. Northwestern University.

Ribble, M. (2016). *Digital Citizenship: Using Technology Appropriately*. Retrieved February 21, 2016, from http://www.digitalcitizenship.net/

Rise, J., Sheeran, P., & Hukkelberg, S. (2010). The Role of Self-Identity in the Theory of Planned Behavior: A Meta-Analysis. *Journal of Applied Social Psychology*, *40*(5), 1085–1105. doi:10.1111/j.1559-1816.2010.00611.x

Robb, A., White, C., Cordar, A., Wendling, A., Lampotang, S., & Lok, B. (2015). A comparison of speaking up behavior during conflict with real and virtual humans. *Computers in Human Behavior*, *52*(C), 12–21. doi:10.1016/j.chb.2015.05.043

Roberts, M. (2018). *Google's day of reckoning is finally at hand.* Retrieved December 27, 2018, from https://www.washingtonpost.com/opinions/googles-day-of-reckoning-is-finally-at-hand/2018/09/14/782c6e26-b84c-11e8-a7b5-adaaa5b2a57f_story.html?utm_term=.bf524c108086

Roddenberry, G., Hurley, M., Baron, M., Barry, P., Beimler, H., Black, J. D. F., . . . Paramount Pictures Corporation. (2007). *Star trek, the next generation: Season 1*. Paramount Pictures.

Roddenberry, G., Hurley, M., Baron, M., Barry, P., Beimler, H., & Black, J. D. F.Paramount Pictures Corporation. (2007). *Star trek, the next generation: Season 1* [Television series]. Hollywood, CA: Paramount Pictures Corporation.

Rogers, C. (1961). *On becoming a person. A therapist's view of psychotherapy*. Boston, MA: Houghton Mifflin Company.

Roosevelt, E. (1958). *In Your Hands: A Guide for Community Action for the Tenth Anniversary of the Universal Declaration of Human Rights.* Retrieved from http://www.udhr.org/history/inyour.htm

Rosal, M. C., Heyden, R., Mejilla, R., Capelson, R., Chalmers, K. A., DePaoli, M. R., ... Wiecha, J. M. (2014). A virtual world versus face-to-face intervention format to promote diabetes self-management among African American women: A pilot randomized clinical trial. *JMIR Research Protocols*, *3*(4), e54. doi:10.2196/resprot.3412 PMID:25344620

Rosedale, P. (2015, January 13). OSCC14 - Philip Rosedale keynote: What is the metaverse? *Second Annual OpenSimulator Community Conference*. Retrieved from https://youtu.be/iR3uUVPyjhU

Rosenstock, I. M., Strecher, V. J., & Becker, M. H. (1988). Social learning theory and the health belief model. *Health Education & Behavior*, *15*(2), 175–183. doi:10.1177/109019818801500203 PMID:3378902

Roser, M., & Gazzaniga, M. S. (2004). Automatic brains—Interpretive minds. *Current Directions in Psychological Science*, *13*(2), 56–59. doi:10.1111/j.0963-7214.2004.00274.x

Rosi, A., Dall'Asta, M., Brighenti, F., Del Rio, D., Volta, E., Baroni, I., ... Scazzina, F. (2016). The use of new technologies for nutritional education in primary schools: A pilot study. *Public Health*, *140*(1), 50–55. doi:10.1016/j.puhe.2016.08.021 PMID:27756495

Ruggiero, L., Moadsiri, A., Quinn, L. T., Riley, B. B., Danielson, K. K., Monahan, C., ... Gerber, B. S. (2014). Diabetes island: Preliminary impact of a virtual world self-care educational intervention for African Americans with type 2 diabetes. *JMIR Serious Games*, *2*(2), e10. doi:10.2196/games.3260 PMID:25584346

Rumbaugh, J., Jacobson, I., & Booch, G. (1999). *The unified modeling language reference manual*. Reading, MA: Addison-Wesley.

Rybas, N. (2012). Producing the self at the digital interface. *New media and intercultural communication: Identity, community and politics*, 93-107.

Sabillon, R., Cano, J., Cavaller, V., & Serra, J. (2016). Cybercrime and cybercriminals: a comprehensive study. *International Journal of Computer Networks and Communications Security, 4*(6), 165.

Sacks, O. (1990). Chaos and awakenings. In Awakenings. New York: Harper Perennial.

Sadek, M. D., Bretier, P., & Panaget, E. (1997). ARTIMIS: Natural dialogue meets rational agency. *International Joint Conferences on Artificial Intelligence,* (2), 1030–1035.

Sanchez-Vives, M. V., & Slater, M. (2005). From presence to consciousness through virtual reality. *Nature Reviews. Neuroscience*, *6*(4), 332–339. doi:10.1038/nrn1651 PMID:15803164

Schanzenbach, M., Bramm, G., & Schütte, J. (2018). *reclaimID: Secure, Self-Sovereign Identities using Name Systems and Attribute-Based Encryption*. arXiv preprint arXiv:1805.06253

Scharmer, C. O. (2000). *Presencing: Learning from the future as it emerges*. Presentation at the Conference on Knowledge and Innovation, Helsinki School of Economics, Finland. Retrieved from http://www.ottoscharmer.com/docs/articles/2000_Presencing.pdf

Scharmer, O. (2011, October 24). *Entering the field of the future*. Presentation made at the First Presencing Global Forum, Boston, MA. Retrieved from: http://www.presencing.com/sites/default/files/page-files/2011_ForumOpening_0.pdf

Schein, E. (1978). *Career dynamics: Matching individual and organizational needs*. Reading, MA: Addison-Wesley.

Schleiner, A. M. (2001). Does Lara Croft wear fake polygons? Gender and gender-role subversion in computer adventure games. *Leonardo*, *34*(3), 221–226. doi:10.1162/002409401750286976

Schlosser, L., & Simonson, M. (2010). *Distance education: Definition and glossary of terms*. Charlotte, NC: Information Age Publishing.

Schön, D. A. (1983). *The reflective practitioner: How professionals think in action*. London: Temple Smith.

Schouten, A. P., van den Hooff, B., & Feldberg, F. (2016). Virtual team work group decision making in 3dvirtual environments. *Communication Research*, *43*(2), 180–210. doi:10.1177/0093650213509667

Schroeder, R. (2011). *Being there together: social interaction in virtual environments*. New York, NY: Oxford University Press.

Schroeder, R., & Axelsson, A. S. (2010). *Avatars at work and play: Collaboration and interaction in shared virtual environments*. Springer.

Schwartz, M., Oppold, P., & Hancock, P. A. (2019). Wearables and Workload. In H. Lum (Ed.), *Critical Issues Impacting Science, Technology, Society (STS), and Our Future* (pp. 145–170). Hershey, PA: IGI Global. doi:10.4018/978-1-5225-7949-6.ch007

Schwarzer, R. (2008). Modeling health behavior change: How to predict and modify the adoption and maintenance of health behaviors. *Applied Psychology*, *57*(1), 1–29. doi:10.1111/j.1464-0597.2007.00325.x

Science Circle. (2019). *Lectures, debates, excursions and symposia*. Retrieved from https://www.sciencecircle.org/lectures-debates-excursions-and-symposia/

Seaman, J. E., Allen, I. E., & Seaman, J. (2018). *Grade Increase: Tracking Distance Education in the United States, Babson Survey Research Group*. Released under a Creative Commons Attribution-ShareAlike 4.0 International license. Report available at: http://www.onlinelearningsurvey.com/highered.html

Seanchai Library. (2018). *The Dickens Project*. Retrieved December 27, 2018, from http://irelandslstory.blogspot.com/p/the-dickens-project-sl.html

Second Life History. (2017, December 29). Retrieved February 20, 2019 from the Second Life Wiki: http://wiki.secondlife.com/wiki/History_of_Second_Life

Second Life Virtual World. (2018). Retrieved from www.secondlife.com

Seligman, M. E. P., & Csikszentmihalyi, M. (2000). Positive psychology: An introduction. *The American Psychologist, 55*(1), 5–14. doi:10.1037/0003-066X.55.1.5 PMID:11392865

Senge, P. M. (1991). The fifth discipline, the art and practice of the learning organization. *Performance+ Instruction, 30*(5), 37-37.

Senge, P. M., Scharmer, C. O., Jaworski, J., & Flowers, B. S. (2005). *Presence: An Exploration of Profound Change in People social, Organizations, and Society*. Crown Publishing Group.

Senge, P. M. (2006). *The fifth discipline: The art and practice of the learning organization*. Broadway Business.

Shaffer, D., & Resnick, M. (1999). Thick authenticity: New media and authentic learning. *Journal of Interactive Learning Research, 10*(2), 195–215.

Siewiorek, A., Gegenfurtner, A., Lainema, T., Saarinen, E., & Lehtinen, E. (2013). The effects of computer-simulation game training on participants' opinions on leadership styles. *British Journal of Educational Technology, 44*(6), 1012–1035. doi:10.1111/bjet.12084

Simon, H. A. (1969). *The sciences of the artificial*. Cambridge, MA: M.I.T. Press.

Simon, H. A. (1979). *Models of thought*. New Haven, CT: Yale University Press.

Simonson, M. (1999). Equivalency theory and distance education. *TechTrends, 43*(5), 5–8. doi:10.1007/BF02818157

Simonton, D. K. (2010). Creativity in highly eminent individuals. In J. C. Kaufman & R. J. Sternberg (Eds.), *The Cambridge Handbook of Creativity* (pp. 174–188). Cambridge University Press. doi:10.1017/CBO9780511763205.012

Singer, P. (1983). *Hegel: A very short introduction*. Oxford, UK: Oxford University Press.

Sivunen, A., & Nordbäck, E. (2015). Social presence as a multidimensional group construct in 3D virtual environments. *Journal of Computer-Mediated Communication, 20*(1), 19–36. doi:10.1111/jcc4.12090

Six Million Dollar Man (SMDM): NBC Episodes. (1973). Retrieved from https://www.nbc.com/the-six-million-dollar-man

Slater, A., & Tiggemann, M. (2011). Gender differences in adolescent sport participation, teasing, self-objectification and body image concerns. *Journal of Adolescence, 34*(3), 455–463. doi:10.1016/j.adolescence.2010.06.007 PMID:20643477

Slaughter, A. (2017). *The chessboard and the web: Strategies of connection in a networked world*. New Haven, CT: Yale University Press.

Slay, H., & Smith, D. (2010). Professional identity construction using narrative to understand the negotiation of professional and stigmatized cultural identities. *Human Relations, 64*(1), 85–107. doi:10.1177/0018726710384290

Slear, J., Slear, S., Connelly, D., Reames, E., & Maggard, P. (2016). A Qualitative Method to Promote Equivalent Learning Outcomes. *Quarterly Review of Distance Education, 17*(2), 1–14.

Smith, A., & Anderson, M. (2018). *Social media use in 2018*. PEW Research Center. Retrieved from http://www.pewinternet.org/2018/03/01/social-media-use-in-2018/

Smith, S. M. (1995). Fixation, incubation, and insight in memory and creative thinking. In S. M. Smith, T. B. Ward, & R. A. Finke (Eds.), The creative cognition approach (pp. 135-156). Cambridge, MA: MIT Press.

Smith, K., & Klumper, D. (2018). Virtually in the classroom: Virtual reality platforms can give preservice teachers opportunities to develop real classroom management skills. *Educational Leadership, 76*(1), 60–65.

Smith, M. A., & Kollock, P. (1999). *Communities in Cyberspace*. New York, NY: Routledge Taylor & Francis Group. doi:10.5117/9789056290818

Soares, N. (2015). The Value Learning Problem. Berkeley, CA: Machine Intelligence Research Institute.

Sonnenwald, D. H. (2006). Collaborative virtual environments for scientific collaboration: Technical and organizational design frameworks. In R. Schroeder & A. Axelsson (Eds.), *Avatars at Work and Play* (pp. 63–96). Springer. doi:10.1007/1-4020-3898-4_4

Sosik, J. J. (2015). *Leading with Character: Stories of Valor and Virtue and the Principles they Teach*. Charlotte, NC: Information Age Publishing, Inc.

Southard, D. R., & Southard, B. H. (2006). Promoting Physical Activity in Children with MetaKenkoh. *Clinical and Investigative Medicine. Medecine Clinique et Experimentale*, *29*(5), 293–297. doi:10.1037/bar0000029 PMID:17144438

Sparrowe, R. T. (2005). Authentic leadership and the narrative self. *The Leadership Quarterly*, *16*(3), 419–439. doi:10.1016/j.leaqua.2005.03.004

Spruijt-Metz, D. (1995). Personal incentives as determinants of adolescent health behavior: The meaning of behavior. *Health Education Research*, *10*(3), 355–364. doi:10.1093/her/10.3.355 PMID:10158028

Steinbeck, J. (1937). *Of mice and men*. New York: Covici-Friede.

Stephenson, N. (1993). *Snow crash*. New York: Bantam Books.

Sternberg, R. J. (1985). Instrumental and componential approaches to the nature and training of intelligence. In S. F. Chipman, J. W. Segal, & R. Glaser (Eds.), Thinking and learning skills: Vol. 2. Research and open questions. Hillsdale, NJ: Erlbaum.

Sternberg, E. M. (2001). *The balance within: The science connecting health and emotions*. Macmillan.

Sternberg, R. J. (1983). Components of human intelligence. *Cognition*, *15*, 1–48. PMID:6686504

Sternberg, R. J. (1986). Toward a unified theory of human reasoning. *Intelligence*, *10*, 281–314.

Sternberg, R. J. (1994). Intelligence. In R. J. Sternberg (Ed.), *Thinking and problem solving: Handbook of perception and cognition* (2nd ed.). New York, NY: Academic Press.

Sternberg, R. J., & Lubart, T. I. (1999). The concept of creativity: Prospects and paradigms. In R. J. Sternberg (Ed.), *Handbook of Creativity*. New York, NY: Cambridge University Press.

Stokols, D. (2006). Toward a Science of Transdisciplinary Action Research. *American Journal of Community Psychology*, *38*(1), 63–77. doi:10.100710464-006-9060-5 PMID:16791514

Strachan, S. M., & Brawley, L. R. (2009). Healthy-eater identity and self-efficacy predict healthy eating behavior. *Journal of Health Psychology*, *14*(5), 684–695. doi:10.1177/1359105309104915 PMID:19515684

Strachan, S. M., Woodgate, J., Brawley, L. R., & Tse, A. (2005). The relationship of self-efficacy and self-identity to long-term maintenance of vigorous physical activity. *Journal of Applied Biobehavioral Research*, *10*(2), 98–112. doi:10.1111/j.1751-9861.2005.tb00006.x

Strauss, B. (2002). Social facilitation in motor tasks: A review of research and theory. *Psychology of Sport and Exercise*, *3*(3), 237–256. doi:10.1016/S1469-0292(01)00019-X

Streck, D. R. (2017). *What Can Action Research and Transdisciplinarity Learn from Each Other? Integration and Implementation Insights*. Retrieved from: https://i2insights.org/2017/08/29/action-research-and-transdisciplinarity/

Stricker, A., McCrocklin, M., Calongne, C., Scribner, T., & Holm, J. (2010). *The rise of avatars in positive psychology: Enabling military cultures in a 3D world for strengths of character development*. DTIC Document. Retrieved from http://www.dtic.mil/cgi-bin/GetTRDoc?AD=ADA516864

Stricker, A. G., McCrocklin, M., Calongne, C. A., & Holm, J. (2011). *Situating community construction of learning ecosystems and innovations in a 3D world. International Journal of Learning and Media, 3(1).*

Stricker, A. G., Westhauser, T. C., Sheets, T., Hawkins-Scribner, T., Calongne, C., & Truman, B. (2017). Values-Based Network Leadership in an Interconnected World. *The Journal of Values Based Leadership.*

Stricker, A., Arenas, F., Westhauser, T., & Hawkins-Scribner, T. (2016). Positive education of stoic warriors as reflective practitioners in the profession of arms. *Reflective Practice*, *18*(1), 133–146. doi:10.1080/14623943.2016.1251415

Stricker, A., & Calongne, C. (2015). Remapping mental models of collaboration using immersive 3D design thinking studios. In A. Kok & H. Lee (Eds.), *Cultural, behavioral, and social considerations in electronic collaboration*. Hershey, PA: IGI Global.

Stricker, A., Holm, J., Calongne, C. M., & McCrocklin, M. (2011). Collaborative Prototyping of Learning Innovations Across Loosely Coupled Educational Communities. *International Journal of Learning and Media*, *3*(1). doi:10.1162/ijlm_a_00064

Stricker, A., & Lyle, D. (submitted). The mind, personality, and networks of Henry H. "Hap" Arnold. *The Journal of Military History.*

Stricker, A., Westhauser, T., Sheets, T., Hawkins-Scribner, T., & Calongne, C. (2018). Values-based network leadership in an interconnected world. *The Journal of Values Based Leadership*, *11*(1), 1–21. doi:10.22543/0733.111.1210

Striker, A., Calogne, C., Truman, B., & Arenas, F. (2017). *Integrating an awareness of selfhood and society into virtual learning*. Hershey, PA: IGI Global. doi:10.4018/978-1-5225-2182-2

Stryker, S. (1980). *Symbolic interactionism: A social structural version*. Menlo Park, CA: Benjamin/Cummings Publishing Company.

Student Privacy. (2019). *Protecting Student Privacy*. Retrieved from https://studentprivacy.ed.gov/about-us

Studies, H. (2019). *WPI Center for Holographic Studies & Laser micro-mechatronics*. Retrieved from http://chslt.wpi.edu/

Suedfeld, P. (1997). Reactions to societal trauma: Distress and/or eustress. *Political Psychology*, *18*(4), 849–861. doi:10.1111/0162-895X.00082

Suguna, M., Anusia, R., Shalinie, S. M., & Deepti, S. (2017, March). Secure identity management in mobile cloud computing. In *Nextgen Electronic Technologies: Silicon to Software (ICNETS2), 2017 International Conference on* (pp. 42-45). IEEE. 10.1109/ICNETS2.2017.8067894

Sullivan, D. K., Goetz, J. R., Gibson, C. A., Washburn, R. A., Smith, B. K., Lee, J., ... Donnelly, J. E. (2013). Improving weight maintenance using virtual reality (Second Life). *Journal of Nutrition Education and Behavior*, *45*(3), 264–268. doi:10.1016/j.jneb.2012.10.007 PMID:23622351

Sung, D. (2015, November 13). *Virtual reality realism: Why 2016 might not be VR's big year. Three experts fail to agree on whether 2016 will be the year VR breaks through.* Retrieved from http://www.wareable.com/vr/is-2016-the-year-vr-goes-mainstream

Swan, M. (2012). Sensor mania! The internet of things, wearable computing, objective metrics, and the quantified self 2.0. *Journal of Sensor and Actuator Networks*, *1*(3), 217–253. doi:10.3390/jsan1030217

Sweigart, L. I., Umoren, R. A., Scott, P. J., Carlton, K. H., Jones, J. A., Truman, B., & Gossett, E. J. (2016). Virtual TeamSTEPPS Simulations Produce Teamwork Attitude Changes Among Health Professions Students. *The Journal of Nursing Education*, *55*(1), 31–35. doi:10.3928/01484834-20151214-08 PMID:26812380

Sweigart, L., & Hodson-Carlton, K. (2013). Improving student interview skills: The virtual avatar as client. *Nurse Educator*, *38*(1), 11–15. doi:10.1097/NNE.0b013e318276df2d PMID:23222623

Tagliaventi, M. R., & Mattarelli, E. (2010). The role of networks of practice, value sharing, and operational proximity in knowledge flows between professional groups. *Human Relations, 59*, 291-319.

Taylor, C. (2011). Charles Taylor: Solidarity and Diversity in a Secular Age. *SweatmanMedia*. Retrieved from: https://youtu.be/96u-ijmn_uI

Taylor, M. (2004). Oh no it isn't: Audience participation and community identity. *Trans, Internet Journal for Cultural Sciences*, *1*(15).

Taylor, E. W. (2007). An update of transformative learning theory: A critical review of the empirical research (1999–2005). *International Journal of Lifelong Education*, *26*(2), 173–191. doi:10.1080/02601370701219475

Thakur, M. A., & Gaikwad, R. (2015, January). User identity and Access Management trends in IT infrastructure-an overview. In *Pervasive Computing (ICPC), 2015 International Conference on* (pp. 1-4). IEEE. 10.1109/PERVASIVE.2015.7086972

The Air University. (2017). *Squadron Learning Experience*. Prototyping Effort Status Report. Unpublished report.

The Arnold Project. (1961). *Oral transcripts. Oral History Research Office, Columbia University*. New York, NY: Columbia University Libraries Rare Books and Manuscripts.

The Magic Drums. (2018). Retrieved from http://maps.secondlife.com/secondlife/Aloft%20Nonprofit%20Commons/240/126/23

The Quest for the Galaxy Language. (2018). Retrieved from http://conference.opensimulator.org/2018/program/learning-lab/

The Random House College Dictionary. (1982). New York: Random House, Inc.

The Tech Virtual Museum Exhibit. (2008-2015). Retrieved from http://legacy.www.thetech.org/about-us/media-room/tech-museum-innovation-announces-winners-ucantu-virtual-exhibit-creation-contest

Thompson, D. R., Obarzanek, E., Franko, D. L., Barton, B. A., Morrison, J., Biro, F. M., ... Striegel-Moore, R. H. (2007). Childhood overweight and cardiovascular disease risk factors: The National Heart, Lung, and Blood Institute Growth and Health Study. *The Journal of Pediatrics*, *150*(1), 18–25. doi:10.1016/j.jpeds.2006.09.039 PMID:17188606

Toapanta, S. M. T., Gallegos, L. E. M., & Trejo, J. A. O. (2016, September). Analysis to define management of identities access control of security processes for the registration civil from Ecuador. In *Smart Cities Conference (ISC2), 2016 IEEE International* (pp. 1-4). IEEE. 10.1109/ISC2.2016.7580753

Tobin, D. L., Reynolds, R. V., Holroyd, K. A., & Creer, T. L. (1986). Self-management and social learning theory. In K.A. Holroyd & T.L. Creer (Eds.), Self-Management of Chronic Disease (pp. 29-55). Orlando, FL: Academic Press. doi:10.1016/j.outlook.2008.10.004

Toffler, A. (1980). *The third wave*. New York: Morrow.

Tonnies, F. (1887). *Community and society* (C. P. Loomis & N. York, Trans.). Dover Publications, Inc.

Tremblay, M. S., LeBlanc, A. G., Kho, M. E., Saunders, T. J., Larouche, R., Colley, R. C., & Gorber, S. C. (2011). Systematic review of sedentary behaviour and health indicators in school-aged children and youth. *The International Journal of Behavioral Nutrition and Physical Activity*, *8*(1), 98. doi:10.1186/1479-5868-8-98 PMID:21936895

Troll, L. E., & Skaff, M. M. (1997). Perceived continuity of self in very old age. *Psychology and Aging*, *12*(1), 162–169. doi:10.1037/0882-7974.12.1.162 PMID:9100277

Trotter, R. (1985, September). Profile: Muzafer Sherif, a life of conflict and goals. *Psychology Today*, 55–59.

Truman, B. (2013). *Transformative interactions using embodied avatars in collaborative virtual environments: Towards transdisciplinarity* (Doctoral dissertation). Available from ProQuest Dissertations & Theses Global. (Order No. 3628698)

Truman, B. (2017). *Computer-Based Simulation Spectrum.* Retrieved from: http://barbaratruman.com/cbs-spectrum

Truman, B. E. (2014). *Transformative interactions using embodied avatars in collaborative virtual environments: Towards transdisciplinarity* (Doctoral dissertation). Colorado Technical University.

Truman, B., & Metcalf, D. (2015). Advancing Interagency Collaboration through Constructive Simulation: Results from the 2015 Federal Consortium of Virtual Worlds Workshop. In *Proceedings of the HCI International 2015 Conference.* Springer.

Truman, J. (2015). *Case Study on Church Ethics and exemption from ADA Law* (Unpublished report). Asbury Theological Seminary.

Truman, J. (2019). *Intersectional Deaf Spirituality in America: Imagining a Next Generation Intercultural Deaf Community Center* (Unpublished doctoral dissertation). Columbia International University, Columbia, SC.

Truman, B. E. (2004). UCF's Exemplary Faculty Support: An institutionalized ecosystem. *Journal of Asynchronous Learning Networks*, *8*(3), 89–96.

Tuan, Y.-F. (1977). *Space and place: The perspective of experience.* Minneapolis, MN: The University of Minnesota Press.

Turban, E., Aronson, J. E., & Liang, T. (2005). *Decision support systems and intelligent systems* (7th ed.). New York, NY: Pearson.

Turkle, S. (2015). *Reclaiming Conversation: The Power of Talk in a Digital Age.* New York: Penguin Press.

Turner, M. (1996). The literary mind: The origins of thought and language. Oxford University Press.

Turner, J. C., Hogg, M., Oakes, P., Reicher, S., & Wetherell, M. (1987). *Rediscovering the Social Group: A Self-categorization theory.* Oxford, UK: Basil Blackwell.

Tyack, D. (1966). Forming of the national character: Paradox in the educational thought of the revolutionary generation. *Harvard Educational Review*, *36*(1), 29–41. doi:10.17763/haer.36.1.213504687324p76g

Tyack, D., & Hansot, E. (1982). *Managers of virtue: Public school leadership in America, 1820-1980.* New York, NY: Basic Books.

U.S. Dept. of Ed. (n.d.). *Family educational rights and privacy act (FERPA).* U.S. Department of Education. Retrieved from http://www2.ed.gov/policy/gen/guid/fpco/ferpa/index.html

UCF Center for Distributed Learning. (2017). *Distributed Learning Impact Evaluation.* Retrieved from https://online.ucf.edu/research/dl-impact-evaluation

UCF Today. (2019). *UCF's Partnership IV Building to be New Home for Army's Synthetic Training Environment.* Retrieved from: https://today.ucf.edu/ucfs-partnership-iv-building-new-home-armys-simulation-training-environment/

Udroiu, M. (2017). The cybersecurity of e-learning platforms. In *The International Scientific Conference eLearning and Software for Education* (*Vol. 3*, p. 374). "Carol I" National Defence University.

Umberson, D., Crosnoe, R., & Reczek, C. (2010). Social relationships and health behavior across life course. *Annual Review of Sociology*, *36*(1), 139–157. doi:10.1146/annurev-soc-070308-120011 PMID:21921974

Umoren, R., Stadler, D. J., Gasior, S. L., Al-Sheikhly, D., Truman, B., & Lowe, C. (2014). Global collaboration and team-building through 3D virtual environments. *Innovations in Global Medical and Health Education, 1*. Retrieved from: http://www.qscience.com/doi/full/10.5339/igmhe.2014.1

Umoren, R. A., Poore, J. A., Sweigart, L., Rybas, N., Gossett, E., Johnson, M., ... Das, R. (2017). TeamSTEPPS Virtual Teams: Interactive Virtual Team Training and Practice for Health Professional Learners. *Creative Nursing*, *23*(3), 184–191. doi:10.1891/1078-4535.23.3.184 PMID:28789739

Umoren, R. A., Scott, P. J., Sweigart, L., Gossett, E., Hodson-Carlton, K., Johnson, M., ... Das, R. (2018). A comparison of teamwork attitude changes with virtual TeamSTEPPS® simulations in health professional students. *Journal of Interprofessional Education & Practice*, *10*, 51–55. doi:10.1016/j.xjep.2017.12.001

Umoren, R., & Rybas, N. (2017). Who am I as a Healthcare Provider?: Identity and Transformative Learning in Virtual Environments. In A. Stricker, C. Calongne, B. Truman, & F. Arenas (Eds.), *Integrating an Awareness of Selfhood and Society into Virtual Learning* (pp. 148–163). Hershey, PA: IGI Global; doi:10.4018/978-1-5225-2182-2.ch011

Unity Technologies. (2017). Retrieved from https://unity3d.com

Universal Declaration of Human Rights. (1948). Retrieved from http://www.ohchr.org/EN/UDHR/Pages/SearchByLang.aspx

Valadares, A., Gabrielova, E., & Lopes, C. V. (2016). On designing and testing distributed virtual environments. *Concurrency and Computation.*

Van Camp, J. C. (2014). *Ethics*. Boston, MA: Wadsworth.

Van Den Bos, J., Rustagi, K., Gray, T., Halford, M., Ziemkiewicz, E., & Shreve, J. (2011). The $17.1 billion problem: The annual cost of measurable medical errors. *Health Affairs*, *30*(4), 596–603. doi:10.1377/hlthaff.2011.0084 PMID:21471478

Van der Horst, K., Paw, M., Twisk, J., & Van Mechelen, W. (2007). A brief review on correlates of physical activity and sedentariness in youth. *Medicine and Science in Sports and Exercise*, *39*(8), 1241–1250. doi:10.1249/mss.0b013e318059bf35 PMID:17762356

Vander Wal, J. S., & Thelen, M. H. (2000). Eating and body image concerns among obese and average-weight children. *Addictive Behaviors*, *25*(5), 775–778. doi:10.1016/S0306-4603(00)00061-7 PMID:11023018

Vans, M., Hill, V., & Dunavant-Jones, A. (2018). Improving Digital Literacy: A Solvable Challenge Using Virtual Worlds. *Journal of Virtual Studies*, *9*(2), 14–24.

Varble, D. L. (2014). Reducing cheating opportunities on online tests. *Atlantic Marketing Journal*, *3*(2), 131–149.

Virtual Ability. (2019a). *Virtual Ability, Inc.* Retrieved from https://virtualability.org/

Virtual Ability. (2019b). *International disability rights affirmation conference (IDRAC) 2012-2018.* Retrieved from https://virtualability.org/idrac/

Virtual Ability. (2019c). *Mental health symposia 2012-2018.* Retrieved from https://virtualability.org/mental-health-symposia/

Virtual Avatar Laboratory Website. (2019). Retrieved from http://www.education.aum.edu/VAL

Vo, T. H., Fuhrmann, W., & Fischer-Hellmann, K. P. (2018, February). Privacy-preserving user identity in Identity-as-a-Service. In *2018 21st Conference on Innovation in Clouds, Internet and Networks and Workshops (ICIN)* (pp. 1-8). IEEE. 10.1109/ICIN.2018.8401613

Voulgari, I., Komis, V., & Sampson, D. (2014). Learning outcomes and processes in massively multiplayer online games: Exploring the perceptions of players. *Educational Technology Research and Development*, *62*(2), 245–270. doi:10.100711423-013-9312-7

VWBPE. (2016). *Virtual Worlds Best Practices in Education Conference*. Retrieved March 6, 2016, from http://vwbpe.org/

Vygotsky, L. (1978). Mind in society: The development of higher psychological processes (M. Cole, V. John-Steiner, S. Scribner & E. Souberman., Eds.; A. R. Luria, M. Lopez-Morillas & M. Cole, Trans.). Cambridge, MA: Harvard University Press. (Original manuscripts published 1930-1934)

Vygotsky, L. (1978). *Mind in society. The development of higher psychological processes* (M. Cole, S. S. Vera John-Steiner, & E. Souberman, Eds.). Cambridge, MA: Harvard University Press.

Vygotsky, L. S. (1978). *Mind in society*. Cambridge, MA: Harvard University Press.

Vygotsky, L. S. (1986). *Thought and language* (A. Kozulin, Trans.). Cambridge, MA: MIT Press.

Waggoner, Z. (2009). *My avatar, my self: Identity in video role-playing games*. McFarland.

Wallace, L. S., Buckworth, J., Kirby, T. E., & Sherman, W. M. (2000). Characteristics of exercise behavior among college students: Application of social cognitive theory to predicting stage of change. *Preventive Medicine*, *31*(5), 494–505. doi:10.1006/pmed.2000.0736 PMID:11071829

Wang, Y., & Lim, H. (2012). The global childhood obesity epidemic and the association between socio-economic status and childhood obesity. *International Review of Psychiatry (Abingdon, England)*, *24*(3), 176–188. doi:10.3109/09540261.2012.688195 PMID:22724639

Ward, T. B., Smith, S. M., & Finke, R. A. (1999). Creative cognition. In R.J. Sternberg (Ed.), The handbook of creativity (pp. 189-212). Cambridge, MA: MIT Press.

Ward, Z. J., Long, M. W., Resch, S. C., Giles, C. M., Cradock, A. L., & Gortmaker, S. L. (2017). Simulation of growth trajectories of childhood obesity into adulthood. *The New England Journal of Medicine*, *377*(22), 2145–2153. doi:10.1056/NEJMoa1703860 PMID:29171811

Ware, W. H. (1970). *Security controls for computer systems. Report of defense science task force on computer security (No. RAND/R-609-1)*. Rand Corp.

Wark, M. (2006). Hackers. *Theory, Culture & Society*, *23*(2-3), 320–322. doi:10.1177/026327640602300242

Wasko, M. M., & Faraj, S. (2010). It is what one does: Why people participate and help others in electronic communities of practice. *Journal of Strategic Information Systems, 9*, 155-173.

Wellman, B., Salaff, J., Dimitrova, D., Garton, L., Gulia, M., & Haythornthwaite, C. (1996). Computer networks as social networks. *Annual Review of Sociology*, *22*(1), 211–238. doi:10.1146/annurev.soc.22.1.213

Wenden, A. (2004). Value-based perspective development. In A. L. Wenden (Ed.), *Educating for a Culture of Social and Ecological Peace*. Albany, NY: State University of New York Press.

Wenger, E. (1998). *Communities of practice: Learning, meaning, and identity*. Cambridge, UK: Cambridge University Press. doi:10.1017/CBO9780511803932

Wenger, E., McDermott, R., & Snyder, W. (2002). *Cultivating communities of practice*. Boston, MA: Harvard Business School Press.

West, C. P., & Shanafelt, T. D. (2007). The influence of personal and environmental factors on professionalism in medical education. *BMC Medical Education*, *7*(1), 29. doi:10.1186/1472-6920-7-29 PMID:17760986

West, C., Graham, L., Palmer, R. T., Miller, M. F., Thayer, E. K., Stuber, M. L., ... Joo, P. A. (2016). Implementation of interprofessional education (IPE) in 16 US medical schools: Common practices, barriers and facilitators. *Journal of Interprofessional Education & Practice*, *4*, 41–49. doi:10.1016/j.xjep.2016.05.002 PMID:28184380

Whitbourne, S. K. (2002). *The aging individual: Physical and psychological perspectives* (2nd ed.). New York, NY: Springer Publishing Company, Inc.

Whittier, D. B. (2006). Cyberethics in the Googling age. *Journal of Education*, *187*(2), 1–86. doi:10.1177/002205740718700202

Whittier, D. B. (2013). Cyberethics: Envisioning character education in cyberspace. *Peabody Journal of Education*, *88*(2), 225–242. doi:10.1080/0161956X.2013.775882

Wielsch, D. (2010). Governance of Massive Multiauthor Collaboration – Linux, Wikipedia, and Other Networks: Governed by Bilateral Contracts, Partnerships, or Something in Between? JIPITEC, 1.

Wikipedia. (2019). *Participatory Culture*. Retrieved February 17, 2019, from https://en.wikipedia.org/wiki/Participatory_culture

Willard, N. (2005). *Educator's guide to cyberbullying and cyberthreats*. Retrieved from http://csriu.org, http://cyberbully.org

Williams, E. P., Mesidor, M., Winters, K., Dubbert, P. M., & Wyatt, S. B. (2015). Overweight and obesity: Prevalence, consequences, and causes of a growing public health problem. *Current Obesity Reports*, *4*(3), 363–370. doi:10.100713679-015-0169-4 PMID:26627494

Winkelmann, K., Keeney-Kennicutt, W., Fowler, D., & Macik, M. (2017). Development, implementation, and assessment of General Chemistry Lab experiments performed in the virtual world of Second Life. *Journal of Chemical Education*, *94*(7), 849–858.

Wired. (2018). *The Facebook Effect Hits Oculus: In VR Other People are Everything*. Retrieved from https://www.wired.com/story/facebook-oculus-connect-social/

Wiseman, C. V., Gray, J. J., Mosimann, J. E., & Ahrens, A. H. (1992). Cultural expectations of thinness in women: An update. *International Journal of Eating Disorders*, *11*(1), 85–89. doi:10.1002/1098-108X(199201)11:1<85::AID-EAT2260110112>3.0.CO;2-T

Witness Organization. (2018). Retrieved from http://hub.witness.org

Wong, J., Nguyen, A., & Ogren, L. (2012). *Serious Game and Virtual World Training: Instrumentation and Assessment*. Newport, RI: Naval Undersea Warfare Center. doi:10.21236/ADA582033

Wright, R. (2006). *Better life* [Video file]. Retrieved from https://youtu.be/8_4dW1rZBhI

Xu, X., Li, D., Sun, M., Yang, S., Yu, S. J., Manogaran, G., ... Mavromoustakis, C. X. (2019). Research on Key Technologies of Smart Campus Teaching Platform Based on 5G Network. *IEEE Access*.

Yang, Y., Chen, X., Wang, G., & Cao, L. (2014, December). An Identity and Access Management Architecture in Cloud. In *Computational Intelligence and Design (ISCID), 2014 Seventh International Symposium on* (Vol. 2, pp. 200-203). IEEE. 10.1109/ISCID.2014.221

Yang, G. Z. (Ed.). (2018). *Implantable Sensors and Systems: From Theory to Practice*. Springer. doi:10.1007/978-3-319-69748-2

Yee, N., & Bailenson, J. N. (2009). The difference between being and seeing: The relative contribution of self-perception and priming to behavioral changes via digital self-representation. *Media Psychology*, *12*(2), 195–209. doi:10.1080/15213260902849943

Yee, N., Bailenson, J. N., & Ducheneaut, N. (2009). The Proteus effect. Implications of transformed digital self-representation on online and offline behavior. *Communication Research*, *36*(2), 285–312. doi:10.1177/0093650208330254

Yildirim, A. (1997). Gender role influences on Turkish adolescents' self-identity. *Adolescence*, *32*(125), 217–231. PMID:9105502

Young, J. R. (2010, October 14). Academics discuss mass migration from Second Life, The Chronicle of Higher Education [Weblog post]. Retrieved from http://www.chronicle.com/blogs/wiredcampus/academics-discuss-mass-migration-from-second-life/27672

Young, G., & Whitty, M. (2011). Progressive embodiment within cyberspace: Considering the psychological impact of the supermorphic persona. *Philosophical Psychology*, *24*(4), 537–560. doi:10.1080/09515089.2011.556606

Young, M. D., Plotnikoff, R. C., Collins, C. E., Callister, R., & Morgan, P. J. (2014). Social cognitive theory and physical activity: A systematic review and meta-analysis. *Obesity Reviews*, *15*(12), 983–995. doi:10.1111/obr.12225 PMID:25428600

Yu, L. (2013). The market-driven software ecosystem. *IT Professional*, *15*(5), 46–50.

Yust, K. M., Hyde, B., & Ota, C. (2011). Cyber spirituality II: Virtual reality and spiritual exploration. *International Journal of Children's Spirituality*, *16*(1), 1–3. doi:10.1080/1364436X.2011.564846

Zahneis, M. (2018). Some Colleges and Scholars Cautiously Embrace Wikipedia. *The Chronicle of Higher Education*, *64*(39), A25.

Zeide, E., & Nissenbaum, H. (2018). Learner Privacy in MOOCs and Virtual Education. *Theory and Research in Education*, *16*(3), 280–307. doi:10.1177/1477878518815340

About the Contributors

Andrew Stricker serves Air University as a distributed learning architect. In this role he helps to apply advances in learning and assessment sciences into U.S. Air Force educational and professional military education programs. Prior to his arrival to Air University Andrew served Vanderbilt University as Associate Provost for Innovation Through Technology. He was responsible for working with academic, technology and administrative leaders for improving learning, teaching and research. Dr. Stricker also spent four years at Texas A&M University, College Station, Texas, creating and then serving as Director of the Cognition and Instructional Technologies Laboratory, and Director of the Knowledge Engineering Complex with the Texas Engineering Extension Service. His graduate work was conducted at Texas A&M University, College Station, Texas and Yale University, New Haven, Connecticut. He is a member of the American Psychological Association. His current research addresses developmental growth in reflective mindsets and contemplative practices and augmented reality simulations for helping to improve complex problem-solving among teams.

Cynthia Calongne joined the computer science faculty at Colorado Technical University in 1996. Today, she teaches in the CTU Doctoral department. Prior to teaching, she worked as a software engineer and systems programmer with a defense contractor supporting Air Force Space Command and as a business manager for an environmental organization in Washington, D.C. Her team won the $25,000 grand prize for the Mars Expedition Strategy Challenge in 2010. She supported Will Wright's community-developed TV Show called Bar Karma and appeared in the closing credits of Episode One as Myxen. Using her avatar name, Lyr Lobo, she conducts research in virtual world simulation, game design and writes fiction.

Barbara Truman is a research scientist and graduate faculty member in the Institute for Simulation & Training (IST) for the Mixed Emerging Technology Integration Lab (METIL) at the University of Central Florida (UCF). Barbara founded an award-winning department at UCF responsible for creating online programs and online campus services that helped the campus grow with quality. Barbara's background is in Instructional Systems Design, Human Performance Technology, and Computer Science, Emerging Media. She actively participates in activities to discover, extend, and translate effective learning practices across education, government, industry, and military research projects. Barbara serves as an advisor for the US Air Force's immersive learning research activities and was the Community Manager for the US Army's Military Open Simulation Enterprise Strategy.

Fil Arenas is an Associate Professor of Organizational Leadership Studies at the USAF Squadron Officer College, Maxwell AFB, Alabama. Reporting in August 2007, he is also the Course Director for three USAF distance learning programs to include the Squadron Officer School DL Course which currently hosts nearly 7,000 active students worldwide, developing advanced leadership skills in their professional military education. He received his doctorate degree from The George Washington University in Higher Education Administration. His current areas of research study focus on: virtual immersive learning, emotional intelligence, and transformational leadership. Dr. Arenas retired from the military after 28 years of faithful service (14 USAF & 14 USN) in 2005.

* * *

Marissa D. Alert is currently a postdoctoral fellow at the Johns Hopkins University School of Medicine, and received her PhD in clinical psychology from the University of Miami. Her research centers on improving obesity prevention efforts among disadvantaged groups and understanding the determinants and trajectory of sedentary behavior. Her work has also explored the correlates of physical activity among Hispanic adolescents and the manifestation of sleep disorders among African American and Hispanic veterans. Marissa's interest in health promotion and prevention grew during her undergraduate years at Dartmouth College, where she received a Bachelor of Arts in Psychology. She is a Certified Lifestyle Coach for the Diabetes Prevention Program in East Baltimore and has been involved in various health promotion initiatives to teach children and families about ways to improve poor dietary and physical activity habits.

Kara Bennett, PhD, is a psychologist for Elder Voices Inc. a nonprofit organization founded by health professionals to explore ways of bringing human rights to health care with education, prevention, and intervention. Co-founded by Kara Bennett, PhD and Susan Patrice Weiner, MD, MPH in 2006 as a 501(c)(3) charity, we support the World Health Organization concept of health as "a state of complete physical, mental, and social well-being, not merely the absence of disease or infirmity." The author's research in cognitive psychology began in 1967 with the National Institute of Mental Health in Washington, D. C. studying concept formation with children. Her work continued with a PhD from the University of California, Los Angeles in 1981 and psychologist license in California in 1987. She also has a background in the dramatic arts and combines psychology and community theater to offer education about human rights in virtual world environments.

Renee Carrillo is Assistant Director of the Online Education Department at Parker University.

Daniella Carucci is a graduate student at the University of Miami where she researches the psychosocial determinants of health behavior change.

Shannon Chiles is the co-founder of SEC Prestige Consulting.

Andrew Clayton serves an Assistant Professor in the Department of Leadership at Air Command and Staff College, Maxwell Air Force Base, Alabama. He is a 1999 graduate of Purdue University and earned his commission through the Reserve Officer Training Corps. Additionally, Dr. Clayton holds a Masters degree in Adult Education and Training from the University of Phoenix, is certified as a master level instructor, and distance learning instructor. Further, he holds a Doctorate degree in Organizational Leadership with an emphasis in Higher Education from Grand Canyon University.

Mary Kate Clennan, a Clinical Psychology graduate student at the University of Miami, studies the factors that promote health in youth, particularly those from disadvantaged backgrounds. She is mainly interested in the social-cognitive predictors of healthy weight behaviors in children. By examining these predictors, her overarching research goal is to identify effective health promotion methods.

Twana Cochran is Director for the General Education Program at Parker University.

Daniel Connelly is an Assistant Professor of the Leadership Department at the Air Command & Staff College, Maxwell AFB, Alabama. He is a retired US Air Force officer teaching courses in: international security, leadership studies, air power theory, the Just War tradition, and Russian studies. He holds a PhD in educational psychology from Auburn University and master's degrees in strategic intelligence and Russian culture.

Festus Elleh is part of the Faculty team for the Computer Information Systems Program at Parker University.

Erin N. Etzel is currently a licensed clinical psychologist at the VA Maryland Health Care System in Baltimore, MD. In 2015, she completed her graduate training at the University of Miami and predoctoral internship at the Bruce W. Carter VA Medical Center in Miami, FL, specializing in integrated clinical health psychology. She also completed a postdoctoral residency in pain psychology and behavioral sleep medicine at the New Mexico VA Health Care System in Albuquerque, NM.

Valerie Hill received her MLS in Library and Information Science from Texas Woman's University in 2007 and a PhD in Library and Information Science in 2012. Dr. Hill is a National Writing Project trainer, served as a school librarian for twenty years and taught language arts and information literacy at all grade levels from kindergarten through college. She is currently an information literacy consultant with a research focus on the intersection of information literacy and libraries with virtual worlds and digital culture. Her dissertation was "Factors Contributing to the Adoption of Virtual Worlds by Librarians". She earned a Certificate in Virtual Worlds from the University of Washington.

JJ Jacobson is a librarian with longstanding interests in narrative, the history of everyday life, interdisciplinarity, and intentional community. JJ holds a MSI from the University of Michigan School of Information, and has taught, spoken, and published on librarianship in Virtual Spaces, curating Culinary History, curating Speculative Fiction, and Interactive/Improvisatory/Immersive Narrative. Her current research involves Interactive/Immersive/Improvisatory Narrative in Virtual Environments.

Roxanne Kemp serves as the Dean of Online & General Education Programs at Parker University. Since embarking on a career in education in 2008, Mrs. Kemp has served as an academic coordinator, campus director, director of supplemental education programs, instructional design consultant, general education Program Director, director of online education, dean of online and general education programs, K-12 teacher, and college professor. Before entering the field of education, Mrs. Kemp worked as a sales executive and marketing consultant for various organizations including: Dell Computers, Hewlett Packard, Microsoft, Trend Micro, Lexmark, Cave & Cheney, and Data Base Marketing Group. Previously, Mrs. Kemp served in the United States Army Signal Corps and as a direct report to several battalion and brigade sr. leaders in 3rd Signal Brigade, III Corps in Fort Hood, TX. Mrs. Kemp received her B.S. (magna cum laude) and MS degrees from Tarleton State University, completed an 18hr graduate Educational Leadership program for K-12 Principal preparation at Stephen F. Austin University, and is currently a doctoral student at University of Incarnate Word in San Antonio, TX. Mrs. Kemp is also a certified Blackboard Learn administrator and has recently completed an accessibility certification program through the Texas Distance Learning Association (TXDLA).

Maria Isabel Leeder, born in Havana Cuba, is an educator with over twenty years' experience working with learners in both formal and informal settings. A majority of her work has focused on equity projects, including those that inform the field through research studies that have shed light on how children learn and teachers become more skilled in their field of practice. Mrs. Leeder, earned a Bachelors in Science in Biology from Florida International University, and a Master's in Education with a Specialization in Technology at Nova Southeastern University.

Frankie Lloyd is part of the Faculty team for the Computer Information Systems Program at Parker University. He is a Principal Industrial Security Specialist at one of the largest defense contractors in the world, Raytheon. He has over 9 years' experience in designing and deploying Computer Based Training (CBT) modules for various security education projects to include interfaces from CBT modules into online training databases. He also develops and implements electronic workflow for various security processes to incorporate. Frankie is currently an Adjunct Instructor in Computer Science & College Algebra at various college and universities. He is a highly organized, detail oriented Computer Scientist. Known for strong communication and analytical skills. Additional areas of experience and expertise include being a highly motivated team player with excellent interpersonal skills. He has a Bachelor of Science in Computer Science from Jackson State University and a Master of Science Management Information System Security from Colorado Technical University.

C. Christian Lowry is an Air Force Officer and former Marine Infantryman with over 20 years in the military and extensive combat experience both in the air and on the ground. In 1997 he enlisted in the U.S. Marine Corps Reserves while attending Auburn University where he studied history and philosophy. In 2003 he was part of the U.S. invasion of Iraq. Christian commissioned in the U.S. Air Force in 2004 and was selected for Air Force Special Operations as an AC-130U navigator and U-28A combat systems officer, and has over 1,300 combat hours. His love of history and philosophy informs a deeply held belief that ethical growth and creativity are vital for leaders in any profession and should be deliberately taught at all levels of education. In 2015 Christian was selected as one of eight Air University Fellows to teach Air Force Captains leadership at Squadron Officers School. He holds a Masters of Diplomacy from Norwich University and a Masters in Military Operational Art and Science from Air University. He is married to the former Korie Lynn Kohn of Prattville, Alabama and they have two wonderful boys, Carson and Max.

David J. Lyle (BS in Humanities, USAFA; MBA, Louisiana Tech; MMAS, US Army Command and General Staff College; MAAS, School of Advanced Air and Space Studies) is an Air Education and Training Command (AETC) and Air University liaison in the National Capital Region, currently stationed in the Pentagon. He has served in various strategy and operational planning assignments, including as the Director for the Combined Personnel Recovery Center for Afghanistan, Deputy Director of Strategy & Concepts/Warfighting Education at Air University, the A-5 (Strategic Plans) of the 9th Air and Space Expeditionary Task Force–Afghanistan in Kabul; director of staff for the 505th Command and Control Wing, Hurlburt Field, Florida, and has served on numerous joint air component coordination element (JACCE) assignments. Lt Col Lyle is an Air Operations Center initial qualification honor graduate and Command and Control Warrior Advanced Course graduate, holding US Army qualifications as a joint planner and distinguished master strategist. A master navigator with more than 2,400 flying hours in the B-52H, Lieutenant Colonel Lyle flew 43 combat missions over Kosovo and Afghanistan.

Coleman McKoy is part of the Faculty team for the Computer Information Systems Program at Parker University.

Themba M. Ngwenya is Director for the Computer Informations Systems Program and Co-Director for the Cyber Defense Center at Parker University.

Mayra Quezada is e-Learning Bilingual Program Assistant for the Online Education Department at Parker University.

Natalia Rybas, Associate Professor at Indiana University East, teaches courses in New Media and Cross-Cultural Communication. Her research focuses on examining identities and cultural practices in mediated contexts. She is passionate about studying interactions of teaching and learning online. Her research appeared in edited collections, such as "Mediating Cultures: Parent Communication in Intercultural Contexts," "Communication in the Classroom," and academic journals, such as "Kairos," and "Forum: Qualitative Social Research."

Patrice G. Saab, Ph.D., is a Professor in the Department of Psychology at the University of Miami. She has expertise in both basic cardiovascular research and in applied research designing and conducting randomized controlled trials for children, adolescents, and adults. Her current research program incorporates health promotion to reduce cardiometabolic risk. Dr. Saab's prevention work is aimed at improving physical activity, nutrition, stress management, and promoting and maintaining a healthy lifestyle.

Travis H. Sheets is an Operations Officer assigned to Deputy Director for Special Operations and Counterterrorism on the Joint Staff. He advises the Chairman of the Joint Chiefs of Staff on employing Special Operations Forces, counterterrorism and detainee affairs. He conducts staffing of Combatant Commander-approved concepts and preparation of briefings and position papers for the CJCS and Secretary of Defense. Maj Sheets received his commission from Virginia Tech ROTC Detachment in 2005. He is a command special operations pilot with deployments to Europe, Middle East, Southeast Asia, and Africa. Prior to his current position, the Major was an Air University Fellow, Maxwell AFB, Ala.

Kate D. Simmons is a Professor of Special Education with an appointment in the Department of Counselor, Leadership, and Special Education in the College of Education at Auburn University at Montgomery. She was appointed to the faculty following five years of teaching in the public school system. She is also the director of Virtual Avatar Laboratory. Dr. Simmons teaches a variety of undergraduate, graduate, and Ed.S. level courses. In May 2013, she received the Donna M. Wolfinger Distinguished Teaching Award and the Emerging Professor Award within the College of Education.

Jaclyn M. Truman holds a Master's degree in Theological Studies from Asbury Theological Seminary. She is finalizing her PhD. (May 2019) in Intercultural Studies at Columbia International University. Her research interests include Deaf Studies, Gender studies, LGBT studies, Intersectionality in the Social Sciences, Semiotics, Spirituality, and Comparative Religions. She practices creating works of stained glass art at the intersections of cultural and spiritual symbolism.

Rachel Umoren is an Assistant Professor of Pediatrics and Director of the Neonatal Education & Simulation-based Training (NEST) Program at the University of Washington. Her research focuses on improving neonatal outcomes and enhancing global-public health partnerships through team science and simulation education. She has published and presented internationally on virtual simulations for health professional education.

Todd C. Westhauser is the Director of Strategy and Concepts, Curtis E. LeMay Center for Doctrine Development and Education, Air University, Maxwell Air Force Base, Alabama. A distinguished graduate of the U.S. Air Force Academy in 1986, he was a command pilot with more than 3,200 flying hours. He served as a B-52 group commander, a B-1 squadron commander, a Joint/Air Staff planner, and an Air War College faculty member. In 2014, he retired as a Colonel with 28 years of service.

Francisca Yonekura is Associate Department Head at the Center for Distributed Learning (CDL). Her responsibilities include the areas of course, media, and application development, learning systems integrations, and the R&D of emerging technologies to support online learning. She brings twenty years of experience in instructional technology in higher education, military, and hospitality industry. Her research interests are immersive learning environments, game based learning, and emerging technologies for learning and innovation. Francisca holds a Ph.D. in Curriculum and Instruction and an M.A.in Instructional Systems and Technology. She has facilitated the procurement of patents, trademarks, and service marks for instructional web applications. Her very talented team of web developers, faculty, and staff have received several state and national recognitions for their contributions. As a strong believer of service to the profession and society, Francisca has served on a variety of peer review, advisory, and special project committees.

Index

D

E

F

G

H

I

K

L

M

www.ingramcontent.com/pod-product-compliance
Lightning Source LLC
LaVergne TN
LVHW081250011026
849162LV00006BA/1306